Fundamentals of United States Intellectual Property Law

Fundamentals of United States Intellectual Property Law

Copyright, Patent, and Trademark

Eighth Edition

Amanda Reid
S. Sean Tu
Jessica M. Kiser

Wolters Kluwer

Published by:
Kluwer Law International B.V.
PO Box 316
2400 AH Alphen aan den Rijn
The Netherlands
E-mail: international-sales@wolterskluwer.com
Website: www.wolterskluwer.com/en/solutions/kluwerlawinternational

Sold and distributed by:
Wolters Kluwer Legal & Regulatory U.S.
7201 McKinney Circle
Frederick, MD 21704
United States of America
E-mail: customer.service@wolterskluwer.com

Printed on acid-free paper.

ISBN 978-94-035-1938-8

e-Book: ISBN 978-94-035-1948-7
web-PDF: ISBN 978-94-035-1958-6

About the Authors

Amanda Reid is an Associate Professor in the Hussman School of Journalism and Media at the University of North Carolina at Chapel Hill, where she teaches media law courses. She also holds secondary appointments at both the UNC School of Law and the UNC School of Information and Library Science. She serves as faculty co-director of the UNC Center for Media Law and Policy. Prior to entering academia, she served as a commercial litigation associate with Holland & Knight, LLP. She also served as a one-year judicial law clerk for the Honorable Susan H. Black of the Eleventh Circuit Court of Appeals, and as a two-year judicial law clerk for the Honorable Harvey E. Schlesinger of the Middle District of Florida. She graduated with high honors from the University of Florida Levin College of Law, and she holds a Ph.D. from the University of Florida College of Journalism and Communications. She is a scholar and teacher whose work focuses on the intersection of law, technology, and society, with particular emphasis on the First Amendment, copyright, and privacy.

S. Sean Tu is a Professor of Law at the West Virginia University College of Law. Prior to joining WVU's faculty in 2011, he was with Foley & Lardner LLP and was a member of the firm's chemical, biotechnology and pharmaceutical practice. Dr. Tu holds a Ph.D. in Pharmacology from Cornell University, New York, and is a graduate of the University of Chicago's Law School, where he was a research assistant to Judge Richard Posner. At WVU, he teaches Patent Law, Patent Prosecution, Copyright Law, Trademark Law, and Property Law.

Jessica M. Kiser is an Associate Professor at Gonzaga University School of Law and Director of the Gonzaga University Wine Institute. Prior to joining the faculty at Gonzaga, she was a Westerfield Fellow at Loyola New Orleans College of Law and was an Associate in the Transactional Intellectual Property group in the New York office of Kirkland & Ellis LLP. She graduated from Columbia Law School, where she was a Harlan Fiske Stone Scholar and Senior Editor of the *Columbia Journal of Law & the Arts*. At Gonzaga, she teaches various courses, including Intellectual Property Law, Advanced Trademark and Unfair Competition Law, International and Comparative Intellectual Property Law, Property Law, and advanced courses related to business law. Her scholarship is primarily concerned with the evolution of trademark law and the creation and development of brands. One of her articles on brands won the Ladas Memorial Award from the International Trademark Association in 2018.

The authors above would like to thank the following individuals for their valuable contributions as authors of prior editions of this book.

Sheldon W. Halpern (1935–2016)
Kenneth L. Port (1960–2019)
Craig Allen Nard
Sean B. Seymore

Summary of Contents

Table of Contents

List of Abbreviations

ACPA	Anticybersquatting Consumer Protection Act
ACTA	Anti-Counterfeiting Trade Agreement
AIA	America Invents Act
AIPA	American Inventors Protection Act
AMDC	Analog Motor Drive Circuit
ANDA	Abbreviated New Drug Application
API	Application Programming Interface
APJ	Administrative Patent Judge
ASCAP	American Society of Composers, Authors and Publishers
BMI	Broadcast Music, Inc.
C.F.R.	Code of Federal Regulations
CASE Act	Copyright Alternative in Small-Claims Enforcement Act
CBM	Covered Business Method
Cir.	Federal Court of Appeal, by Federal Circuit
CONTU	Commission on New Technological Uses of Copyrighted Works
D.C.	Federal District Court
DMCA	Digital Millennium Copyright Act
DOE	Doctrine of Equivalents
F.	Federal Reporter
F. Supp.	Federal Supplement
F. Supp. 2d	Federal Supplement, Second Series
F. Supp. 3d	Federal Supplement, Third Series
F.2d	Federal Reporter, Second Series
F.3d	Federal Reporter, Third Series

F.4th	Federal Reporter, Fourth Series
FDA	Food and Drug Administration
FDCA	Food, Drug, and Cosmetic Act
FTDA	Federal Trademark Dilution Act
GATT	General Agreement on Tariffs and Trade
ICANN	Internet Corporation for Assigned Names and Numbers
IP	Internet Protocol
IPR	*Inter Partes* Review
ISP	Internet Service Provider
ITC	International Trade Commission
ITU	Intent-to-Use
MCL	Mechanical Licensing Collective
MMA	Music Modernization Act
MPEP	Manual of Patent Examining Procedure
NAFTA	North American Free Trade Agreement
PCT	Patent Cooperation Treaty
PGR	Post-Grant Review
PRO	Performing Rights Organization
PTAB	Patent Trial and Appeal Board
PTO	Patent and Trademark Office
RCE	Request for Continued Examination
RTP	Reduction to Practice
S. Ct.	Supreme Court Reporter
SCRTP	Simultaneous Conception and Reduction to Practice
T.T.A.B.	Trademark Trial and Appeals Board
TDRA	Trademark Dilution Revision Act
TLT	Trademark Law Treaty
TMA	Trademark Modernization Act
TRCA	Trademark Remedy Clarification Act
TRIPS	Trade-Related Aspects of Intellectual Property Rights
TSM	Teach, Suggest, or Motivate
U.S. (in citations)	United States (Supreme Court) Reporter
U.S.C.	United States Code
U.S.P.Q.	United States Patent Quarterly
U.S.P.Q.2d	United States Patent Quarterly, Second Series
UDRP	Uniform Dispute Resolution Policy

UL	Underwriters Laboratory
USPTO	United States Patent and Trademark Office
VARA	Visual Artists Rights Act
WIPO	World Intellectual Property Organization
WTO	World Trade Organization

General Introduction

CHAPTER 1
General Background

§1 GEOGRAPHY

The United States (US) covers more than 9.8 million square kilometers (3.8 million square miles).[1] The center of the country is a vast plain, with hills and low mountains along the Atlantic seaboard and high mountains, interspersed with higher plains and valleys, covering the western third of the country to the Pacific coast. The climate of most of the country is temperate, with cold to cool winters and hot to warm summers. Across the country, however, climates span the entire range from Arctic conditions in Northern Alaska to tropical conditions in Southern Florida and Hawaii.

§2 CULTURAL COMPOSITION

Most residents of the US trace their ancestry to persons who migrated from Europe over the past four centuries, with Germany, England, and Ireland being the most common countries of ancestral origin. The US census data indicates that 60.9% of the population identify as white, 12.2% of the population identify as Black or African American, and 12.5% of respondents identify as two or more races. In recent decades, the majority of immigrants have come from Asia and Latin America. Most Americans speak English, though Spanish is spoken in 13.3% of households, and small pockets of persons who speak other languages can be found in large cities. Nearly 70% of Americans claim a religious preference, with about 40% identifying as Protestant, 20% as Catholic, and 9% as other faiths.[2] While nearly half of such individuals are members of a church or synagogue, fewer attend regularly. Religion plays an ambiguous role in American life. The US Constitution officially embraces separation of church and State, guaranteeing

1. *See* U.S. DEP'T OF COM., BUREAU OF THE CENSUS, https://data.census.gov/.
2. Pew Research Center, *National Public Opinion Reference Survey*, Oct. 3, 2023, https://www.pewresearch.org/methods/fact-sheet/national-public-opinion-reference-survey-npors/.

freedom of religious expression and forbidding governmental support for religion or religious requirements. Nevertheless, most Americans identify with a Judeo-Christian heritage, and politicians regularly call for greater involvement of religion and religious values in public life.

Most Americans (80%) live in urban areas, with 13% living in cities with a population of at least 1 million. Most Americans over the age of 25 (90%) have had at least twelve years of primary and secondary education, and 36% have had at least four years of higher education. Nearly 70% of all men and 60% of all women over the age of 16 are in the labor force. The most common categories of employment are education and health services (18.6%), professional and business services (11.9%), and retail (12.2%).

§3 POLITICAL SYSTEM

The United States of America, as its name implies, is a federation of 50 states that retain sovereignty over all matters that do not fall within the purview of the federal government.[3] As discussed below, a federal copyright and patent structure was envisioned in the Constitution and copyright and patent are peculiarly within the province of the federal government.[4] Essentially, copyright and patent questions are governed by the federal law as interpreted by the federal courts.[5] The state courts and state law play only a limited role. As discussed below, however, the law of trademark has both state and federal sources and implications.

A fundamental principle evidenced by the federal Constitution is the limitation of governmental power. To this end, the federal government is divided into three branches: the executive branch, headed by a popularly elected President; a bicameral legislature; and an independent, life-tenured, judiciary.[6] The legislature must initiate all legislation (including tax legislation),[7] but the President may veto legislation of which he or she disapproves (subject to a legislative override if a two-thirds majority can be mustered).[8] The judiciary may declare legislation invalid as in conflict with the Constitution and retains substantial authority to interpret legislation. Further, both houses of the legislature must adopt legislation before it is sent on to the President. A constitutional Bill of Rights further limits the government's power, prohibiting interference with expression of opinion or religious beliefs; affording protection from arbitrary searches and the right to be tried by a jury on criminal and important civil matters; providing procedural protections for property and liberty interests; and

3. *See*, e.g., James Q. Wilson et al., American Government Institutions & Policies (15th ed. 2015); James MacGregor Burns et al., Government by the People (16th ed. 1995).
4. U.S. Const. Art. I, § 8, cl. 8.
5. *See* 28 U.S.C. § 1338.
6. U.S. Const. Art. II, Art. I & Art. III.
7. U.S. Const. Art. I, § 8, cl. 1.
8. U.S. Const. Art. I, § 7, cl. 2.

guaranteeing equal protection of the law to minority groups.[9] Constitutional protections are limited, however, to negative protections against abuses of government power.

The governmental structures of most of the states resemble the federal government in that most have three branches with a balance of power among the branches.[10] States are further subdivided into smaller units, usually called counties, which are responsible for provision of many governmental services and for regulation and law enforcement at the local level. Finally, a host of municipal governments—variously called cities, towns, villages, townships, and other names—provide local services, regulation, and law enforcement within their corporate boundaries. In some states, these municipalities have only the power delegated to them by state legislation. In others, larger municipalities possess powers independently granted to them by the state constitution. All levels of government have independent power to tax and to pass laws within their jurisdiction. State and local government officials are in most instances directly elected rather than centrally appointed.

The federal/state division is mirrored in the court system. Each state has its own judicial structure, usually involving numerous "lower" courts of general jurisdiction in which litigation is commenced, a smaller number of intermediate appellate courts, and a "supreme" or final appellate court.[11] In a parallel structure, in each state, there are one or more federal district courts.[12] At the next level, the nation is divided into "circuits," each usually embracing several states, for each of which there is designated a Court of Appeals with appellate jurisdiction over all of the district courts within the states embraced by the circuit.[13] The Court of Appeals in a given circuit may have 12 or more designated judges. Panels of three judges hear appeals, although their decisions may be reheard en banc by the full court. The US Supreme Court, with nine justices, is the final appellate court.[14]

The US has two major political parties, the Democrats and the Republicans. Elections are almost always winner-take-all. Proportional representation is rare. The Democrats tend to be left-leaning, and the Republicans tend to the right. The federal President often belongs to one party and the majority of one or more houses of the legislature to the other. Political parties have relatively little control over elected officials, who are largely responsible for raising their own campaign funds and are thus often more responsive to parochial interest groups than to national party leaders. More than a third of Americans self-identify as political independents, and nearly half of voting-age Americans do not vote.

9. U.S. CONST. amend. I-X.
10. *See*, e.g., DAVID BRUNORI, STATE TAX POLICY: A PRIMER (4th ed. 2016); DAVID R. BERMAN, STATE AND LOCAL POLITICS (9th ed. 2015); RUSSELL DUNCAN & JOSEPH GODDARD, CONTEMPORARY AMERICA (4th ed. 2013).
11. *See* CHRISTOPHER P. BANKS & DAVID M. O'BRIEN, THE JUDICIAL PROCESS: LAW, COURTS, AND JUDICIAL POLITICS 62–64 (2016).
12. *See*, e.g., RONALD A. CARP & RONALD STIDHAM, THE FEDERAL COURTS (4th ed. 2001).
13. There are 11 multistate circuits plus the District of Columbia and Federal Circuit.
14. *See* U.S. CONST. Art. III, § 2, cl. 2.

§4 POPULATION AND VITAL STATISTICS

The population of the US is nearly 340,000,000. The median age is 39.04 years, with 21.79 % of the population under the age of 18, and 17.3 % of the population over the age of 65. Females make up 50.4 % of the population and males make up 49.6 %.

Life expectancy at birth is 73.5 years for men and 79.3 for women. Life expectancy at the age of 65 is 18.1 years for men and 20.7 years for women. The infant mortality rate was 5.44 per 1,000. The infant mortality rate for African-Americans, however, was 10.7 per 1,000. The life expectancy rate for African-Americans was also lower than whites: 71.3 years for men and 78.0 years for women. The birth rate was 11.4 per 1,000 total population, and the fertility rate was 58.3 live births per 1,000 women aged 15–44. The death rate was 1,043.8 per 100,000. The most common cause of death was diseases of the heart, which caused 695,213 deaths, followed by cancer, which caused 605,213 deaths.

§5 SOCIAL AND CULTURAL VALUES

Describing the social and cultural values of a country as large and diverse as the US with any precision is, of course, impossible. Nevertheless, a few generalizations can be made concerning these values that might help in an understanding of the shape of intellectual property law and policy.

Property and property values are strong concepts in American law and society. The laws relating to intellectual property are looked upon essentially as directed to the economic interest in an author's creation. The property interest is seen essentially as superior to the interest in creativity, so that the ultimate owner of that interest may be removed from the creative process. The result is a rich body of law and practice relating to issues of ownership and transfer of intellectual property interests underlying a comparatively new and only lightly adumbrated concept of personality interest and moral right.

Related values are a distrust in government and a belief in the market as the superior means of allocating goods and services. Most Americans believe that government is generally less efficient at providing services than the private sector and resist government involvement where there is clear lack of evidence of the inability of the market to provide a service. There is a corresponding resistance to taxation, causing the US to have lower rates of taxation than most European countries. The one exception where Americans have consistently entrusted the delivery of social services to government is education, which the US has historically provided through state and local government.

History and tradition are less often relied upon as justifications for public policy in the US than in European countries. Moreover, Americans conceive of themselves as independent and not connected to other legal systems, with the result that, until quite recently, intellectual property movements and developments in the Civil Law countries have had little influence on the American law.

PART I Copyright and Neighboring Rights

CHAPTER 1
Copyright

§1 CONGRESSIONAL POWER

I Constitutional Grant of Power

The US Congress alone has the power to regulate copyright.[15] The power derives from Article I, section 8 of the US Constitution:

> The Congress shall have power … To promote the Progress of Science and useful Arts, by securing for limited Times to Authors and Inventors the exclusive Right to their respective Writings and Discoveries.

This language provides the basis for congressional action to grant, define, and limit copyright and patent. Congressional action has come in the form of legislation, and the first Copyright Act was enacted in 1790.

The constitutional language also sets the conceptual basis for copyright: to promote the public interest, the "author" of an appropriate "writing" will be given a limited monopoly. Implementing congressional action adumbrates the fundamental compromise of harmonizing the desire to encourage intellectual creativity with the need to keep intellectual products flowing freely in society. Since the source of congressional power is the constitutional language, much of the development of the law of copyright with respect to the permissible scope of protection has been concerned with judicial determination of who are "authors" and what are "writings," as those terms are used in the Constitution.[16]

With respect to the constitutional linkage of congressional power to a "purpose"—namely, "to promote the progress of science and useful arts"—there has been some uncertainty over whether this language is an aspirational justification for the general grant of power or a condition, limiting specific exercise of the power. The

15. *See infra* §1.II (for discussion of federal preemption).
16. *See infra* §3.II.A.

Supreme Court has now made it clear that although the relevant language ("progress of science") refers broadly to "the creation and spread of knowledge and learning,"[17] the clause is to be seen as a measure not of any specific congressional action, but of the entirety of the overall congressional copyright scheme:

> [T]he Copyright Clause does not demand that each copyright provision, examined discretely, operate to induce new works. Rather, ... the Clause "empowers Congress to determine the intellectual property regimes that, overall, in that body's judgment, will serve the ends of the Clause." ... And those permissible ends, we held, extended beyond the creation of new works.[18]

Finally, there remains an open question as to the preclusive effect of the constitutional language. In other words, it is unclear the extent to which Congress may use its overall power with respect to matters affecting interstate commerce to create copyright-like rights and remedies not otherwise within the scope of the constitutional grant of power.[19]

II The Copyright Act

Congress has, from time to time, implemented its constitutional power through the enactment of comprehensive copyright legislation, beginning with the first copyright statute in 1790, to the present statutory structure embodied in the Copyright Act of 1976.[20]

The Copyright Act, which aims to be comprehensive, continues to evolve. The common law tradition of judicial interpretation, as well as the language of the Act, has made it subject to extensive judicial interpretation by the federal courts. These courts include the various US District Courts, the US Courts of Appeal, and the US Supreme Court. The 1976 Act, which was the first major copyright revision in more than seventy years, was the product of more than two decades of congressional investigation and hearings, culminating in voluminous reports. This legislative history is significant in interpreting the Act.

Today there is no federal nonstatutory, "common law" of copyright.[21] The 1976 Copyright Act, as amended from time to time, is the sole reference point for granting and regulating copyrights. The various states and state courts play no significant role. General principles of federal preemption preclude enforcement of state copyright laws relating to published works,[22] at least with respect to areas in which Congress has acted,[23] prior to January 1, 1978, the effective date of the 1976 Copyright Act.

17. *Golan v. Holder*, 565 U.S 302, 326 (2012).
18. *Id.* (quoting *Eldred v. Ashcroft*, 537 U.S. 186, 205–06 (2003)).
19. *See, e.g., infra* §3.I.A.
20. Copyright Act of 1976, Pub. L. No. 94-553, 90 Stat. 2541 (codified as amended at 17 U.S.C. §§ 101–810, §§ 1001–1101).
21. *See Wheaton v. Peters*, 33 U.S. (8 Pet.) 591, 658 (1834) (denying existence of common law copyright in a published work).
22. *See Sears, Roebuck & Co. v. Stiffel Co.*, 376 U.S. 225 (1964); *Compco Corp. v. Day-Brite Lighting, Inc.*, 376 U.S. 234 (1964).
23. *See Goldstein v. California*, 412 U.S. 546 (1973).

Nevertheless, a so-called common law or state law copyright has been recognized, and enforced by the states, with respect to unpublished works.[24]

The 1976 Act, the culmination of decades of effort, superseded the basic law that had been in effect since 1909. The 1976 Act replaced the then-existing dual federal/state scheme with a unitary and virtually completely federal structure. The 1976 Act completely preempts any state-created rights that are equivalent to any of the exclusive rights of a copyright owner provided by the Act "in works of authorship that are fixed in a tangible medium of expression and come within the subject matter of copyright."[25] In other words, the 1976 Act preempts state law claims when: (1) the claims fall within the subject matter of copyright and (2) the claims seek to protect rights that are equivalent to any of the exclusive rights within the scope of federal copyright. Therefore, federal copyright preempts more than it protects.[26] Federal copyright can preempt state law claims even if the subject matter falls within one of the statute's exclusions in section 102(b).[27]

The Act specifically does not preempt a state action as to "subject matter that does not come within the subject matter of copyright as specified by sections 102 and 103, including works ... not fixed in any tangible medium of expression [or] activities violating legal or equitable rights that are not equivalent to any of the exclusive rights ... as specified by section 106."[28] There is an increasingly complicated body of federal case law dealing with the questions of what rights are "equivalent" to the exclusive rights of a copyright owner under the Act and of what comes "within the subject matter of copyright" for the purposes of determining whether a state law claim has been preempted.[29] It is clear that federal preemption is not predicated on a determination that the state law claim is one that could succeed as a federal copyright claim.[30] It is sufficient for preemption that the matter involved in the state law claim, however it

---

24. *See Estate of Hemingway v. Random House*, 244 N.E.2d 250 (N.Y. 1968).
25. 17 U.S.C. § 301(a).
26. *Motion Med. Techs., L.L.C. v. Thermotek, Inc.*, 875 F.3d 765, 773 (5th Cir. 2017); *see also* United States ex rel. *Berge v. Bd. of Trustees of the Univ. of Ala.*, 104 F.3d 1453, 1463 (4th Cir. 1997) ("[S]cope and protection are not synonyms .... [T]he shadow actually cast by the Act's preemption is notably broader than the wing of its protection").
27. *Ultraflo Corp. v. Pelican Tank Parts, Inc.*, 845 F.3d 652, 655 (5th Cir. 2017).
28. 17 U.S.C. § 301(b).
29. *ProCD, Inc. v. Zeidenberg*, 86 F.3d 1447, 1454 (7th Cir. 1996) ("Rights 'equivalent to any of the exclusive rights within the general scope of copyright' are rights established *by law*—rights that restrict the options of persons who are strangers to the author. Copyright law forbids duplication, public performance, and so on, unless the person wishing to copy or perform the work gets permission; silence means a ban on copying. A copyright is a right against the world").
30. *See*, e.g., *National Basketball Ass'n v. Motorola*, 105 F.3d 841, 849 (2d Cir. 1997) ("Section 301 preemption bars state law misappropriation claims with respect to uncopyrightable as well as copyrightable elements"); *Barclay's Capital, Inc. v. Theflyonthewall.com*, 650 F.3d 876, 892 (2d Cir. 2011) ("In deciding whether a state-law claim is preempted by the Copyright Act, then, it is not determinative that the plaintiff seeks redress with respect to a defendant's alleged misappropriation of uncopyrightable material—e.g., facts—contained in a copyrightable work"); *ProCD, Inc. v. Zeidenberg*, 86 F.3d 1447, 1453 (7th Cir. 1996) ("subject matter of copyright" must include "all works of a type covered by sections 102 and 103, even if federal law does not afford protection to them"); *Wrench LLC v. Taco Bell Corp.*, 256 F.3d 446, 455 (6th Cir. 2001) ("We join our sister circuits in holding that the scope of the Copyright Act's subject matter is broader than the scope of the Act's protections").

might be resolved, is generally within the subject matter of copyright, even if the material itself is uncopyrightable. What is not nearly as clear is the determination of when a state law claim is "equivalent" to a copyright claim. As the Sixth Circuit has explained:

> Equivalency exists if the right defined by state law may be abridged by an act which in and of itself would infringe one of the exclusive rights. Conversely, if an extra element is required instead of or in addition to the acts of reproduction, performance, distribution or display in order to constitute a state-created cause of action, there is no preemption, provided that the extra element changes the nature of the action so that it is qualitatively different from a copyright infringement claim.[31]

Although it is generally agreed that a state claim will be preempted if it contains no essential elements in addition to those necessary for a copyright claim, there is no unanimity as to how one determines those elements.[32] The matter has been particularly troublesome in its application to contract claims, and especially so with respect to "shrink-wrap" contracts.[33] Courts have also taken pains to parse state law right of publicity claims to render them consistent with preemption doctrine.[34]

III Treaties and International Agreements

The US is party to several international treaties and agreements, including the Berne Convention, the Universal Copyright Convention, the Geneva Convention for the Protection of Phonograms, and the World Trade Organization (WTO) Agreement. Among other things, these agreements provide for reciprocal "national treatment" of foreign authors suing in the courts of Member States for local infringement of their works.[35] The US is bound by the Agreement on Trade-Related Aspects of Intellectual Property Rights (TRIPS), which grew out of the General Agreement on Tariffs and Trade (GATT). As part of these obligations, the US has signed, and to a limited extent implemented,[36] the World Intellectual Property Organization (WIPO) Copyright Treaty and the WIPO Performances and Phonograms Treaty.[37] There remains a degree of

31. *Wrench LLC v. Taco Bell Corp.*, 256 F.3d 446, 456 (6th Cir. 2001) (citations omitted). *See also Utopia Provider Sys., Inc. v. Pro-Med Clinical Sys., L.L.C.*, 596 F.3d 1313, 1325 (11th Cir. 2010) ("Preemption occurs if the rights at issue (1) fall within the subject matter of copyright set forth in sections 102 and 103 and (2) are equivalent to the exclusive rights of section 106.") (citations omitted).
32. *Compare ProCD, Inc. v. Zeidenberg*, 86 F.3d 1447 (7th Cir. 1996), *and Nat'l Car Rental Sys., Inc. v. Computer Assocs., Int'l*, 991 F.2d 426 (8th Cir. 1993) (finding no preemption in either case), *with Vault Corp. v. Quaid Software, Ltd.*, 847 F.2d 255 (5th Cir. 1988), *and Rano v. Sipa Press, Inc.*, 987 F.2d 580 (9th Cir. 1993) (finding preemption in both cases). *See also Baltimore Orioles v. Major League Baseball Players*, 805 F.2d 663 (7th Cir. 1986).
33. *See Bowers v. Baystate Techs, Inc.*, 320 F.3d 1317 (Fed. Cir. 2003).
34. *Compare Baltimore Orioles v. Major League Baseball Players*, 805 F.2d 663 (7th Cir. 1986), *and Brown v. Ames*, 201 F.3d 654 (5th Cir. 2000), *and Toney v. L'Oreal USA, Inc.*, 406 F.3d 905 (7th Cir. 2005).
35. *See infra* §2.II.
36. *See infra* §11.
37. *See generally Golan v. Holder*, 565 U.S. 302 (2012) (discussing these various treaty obligations).

uncertainty as to the extent to which the power of the President to enter into treaties and the concomitant congressional power of implementation might override the Copyright Clause limitations on congressional power.[38]

§2 SUBJECT MATTER OF PROTECTION

I Categories of Protected Works

Works of authorship within the subject matter of copyright include:

(1) literary works;
(2) musical works, including any accompanying words;
(3) dramatic works, including any accompanying music;
(4) pantomimes and choreographic works;
(5) pictorial, graphic, and sculptural works;
(6) motion picture and other audiovisual works;
(7) sound recordings; and
(8) architectural works.[39]

These categories are not meant to be exclusive. Rather, they function as administrative categories employed in registering copyrighted works. Thus, for example, as discussed below, computer software will come within the subject matter of copyright as a "literary work." The fundamental concept is that, except as specifically excluded, all original creative expression fixed in a tangible medium of expression is eligible for copyright protection.

II National Origin

Unpublished works are subject to protection without regard to the nationality or domicile of the author.[40] Published works are subject to protection if:

(1) on the date of first publication, one or more of the authors is a national or domiciliary of the US, or is a national, domiciliary, or sovereign authority of a treaty party, or is a stateless person, wherever that person may be domiciled; or
(2) the work is first published in the US or in a foreign nation that, on the date of first publication, is a treaty party; or
(3) the work is a sound recording that was first fixed in a treaty party; or

38. *See generally* SHELDON W. HALPERN & PHILLIP JOHNSON, HARMONISING COPYRIGHT LAW AND DEALING WITH DISSONANCE: A FRAMEWORK FOR CONVERGENCE OF US AND EU LAW (2014).
39. 17 U.S.C. § 102(a).
40. 17 U.S.C. § 104(a).

(4) the work is a pictorial, graphic, or sculptural work that is incorporated in a building or other structure, or an architectural work that is embodied in a building and the building or structure is located in the US or a treaty party; or
(5) the work is first published by the United Nations or any of its specialized agencies, or by the Organization of American States; or
(6) the work comes within the scope of a Presidential proclamation.[41]

A "treaty party" is a country or intergovernmental organization other than the US that is a party to the Universal Copyright Convention, the Geneva Phonograms Convention, the Berne Convention, the WTO Agreement, the WIPO Copyright Treaty, and Performances and Phonograms Treaty, or any other copyright treaty to which the US is a party.[42]

When action is brought for infringement in the US of a work of foreign authorship published in a nation that is a "treaty party," the choice of applicable law may differ as between issues of infringement and issues of ownership of the work.[43] As the Second Circuit has noted, "though the issues are related, the nature of a copyright interest is an issue distinct from the issue of whether the copyright has been infringed."[44] The principle of "national treatment" underlying the Berne Convention applies to assure that the substantive law of copyright protection of the country of infringement "will be applied uniformly to foreign and domestic authors."[45] However, issues of initial ownership of the work and the rights attendant thereto are to be governed by the laws of the country of origin.[46]

III Excluded Works

A *Intangible Expression: Unfixed Works*

The Copyright Act prescription that copyright protection subsists "in original works of authorship fixed in any tangible medium of expression"[47] also serves as a proscription: this language, together with the constitutional limitation of congressional power to "writings," excludes from protection any works not fixed in a tangible medium of expression. Thus, intangible expression—such as unfixed speeches, lectures, or dance—is outside the scope of protection unless and until reduced to some tangible

41. 17 U.S.C. § 104(b). "For purposes of paragraph (2), a work that is published in the United States or a treaty party within 30 days after publication in a foreign nation that is not a treaty party shall be considered to be first published in the United States or such treaty party, as the case may be." *Id.*
42. 17 U.S.C. § 101 (defining "treaty party" and "international agreement"). Adherence of the US to the Geneva Phonograms Convention or the WIPO Performances and Phonograms Treaty will not of itself be the basis for protection of any works other than sound recordings. *Id.* § 104(d).
43. *Itar-Tass Russian News Agency v. Russian Kurier, Inc.*, 153 F.3d 82 (2d Cir. 1998).
44. *Id.*, at 91.
45. *Id.*, at 89.
46. *Id.*, at 90–91.
47. 17 U.S.C. § 102(a) (emphasis added).

form.[48] Since such intangible works are outside of the scope of protection of the federal scheme, they could form the subject matter of state law protection without conflicting with the preemption provisions of the 1976 Act.

B *Government Works*

The Copyright Act also specifically excludes from protection "any work of the United States Government."[49] The Act defines a work of the US government as "a work prepared by an officer or employee of the United States Government as part of that person's official duties."[50] There are two exceptions to this exclusion.[51] First, the Act allows civilian members of faculties at 12 specified military educational institutions to receive copyright protection for literary works that are produced in the course of faculty members' employment for publication in a scholarly press or journal.[52] Second, the US government may claim copyright in "standard reference data" complied and evaluated by the National Institute of Standards and Technology.[53] Despite the general exclusion on protection for governmental works, the federal government may, nevertheless, enforce rights with respect to copyrighted works transferred to it by assignment or bequest.[54]

The Act does not, however, exclude copyright protection for works of state or local governments.[55] Lower courts are split on whether privately authored codes can maintain copyright protection once the codes are adopted and incorporated into law.[56]

48. *See infra* §3.I.A. Note the discussion there of the special treatment of "bootleg" unauthorized recordings of live performances and the definition of "fixed" in the Copyright Act, which treats the live television broadcast of an athletic event as "fixed" if a simultaneous recording of that broadcast is made.
49. 17 U.S.C. § 105.
50. 17 U.S.C. § 101.
51. *See* 17 U.S.C. § 105(b) and 15 U.S.C. § 290e(a).
52. 17 U.S.C. § 105. The specified institutions are as follows: National Defense University; United States Military Academy; Army War College; United States Army Command and General Staff College; United States Naval Academy; Naval War College; Naval Post Graduate School; Marine Corps University; United States Air Force Academy; Air University; Defense Language Institute; and United States Coast Guard Academy.
53. 15 U.S.C. § 290e(a).
54. Questions about: (1) what is a "work of the United States Government" and (2) what kind of assignment would properly vest rights in the government can become quite complex. *See*, e.g., *Schnapper v. Foley*, 667 F.2d 102 (D.C. Cir. 1981).
55. States are divided on the extent to which works created by state or local agencies may claim copyright. *Compare Microdecisions, Inc. v. Skinner*, 889 So. 2d 871, 876 (Fla. Dist. Ct. App. 2004) ("Florida's Constitution and its statutes do not permit public records to be copyrighted unless the legislature specifically states they can be."), *with Seago v. Horry Cty.*, 663 S.E.2d 38, 43 n.6 (S.C. 2008) ("Unlike the case in *Microdecisions*, while our [South Carolina] Legislature and state constitution do not specifically allow counties to copyright, they do not specifically prohibit it, either.").
56. *Compare Veeck v. S. Bldg. Code Cong. Int'l, Inc.*, 293 F.3d 791 (5th Cir. 2002) (en banc) (holding that privately authored model codes, once adopted by a legislative body, become "the law" and cannot be copyrighted), *with Am. Soc'y for Testing & Materials v. Public.Resource.Org, Inc.* 896 F.3d 437 (D.C. Cir. 2018) (rejecting a bright-line rule on copyright protection of privately authored technical standards that were incorporated by reference into law, and remanding for fair use analysis the defendant's distribution of the standards on the internet).

The Supreme Court recently considered whether the *Official Code of Georgia Annotated*—published under the authority of the state and yet containing nonbinding annotations on and summaries of Georgia law—was eligible for copyright protection.[57] It has long been established that judicial opinions—from state and federal judges—are not eligible for copyright protection.[58] Under the government edicts doctrine, the Supreme Court clarified that "copyright does not vest in works that are (1) created by judges and legislators (2) in the course of their judicial and legislative duties."[59]

C *The Idea/Original Expression Continuum*

1 *Generally*

It is fundamental that copyright protection extends only to the original "expression" of an idea and not to the "idea" itself. Section 102(b), which was intended to codify Supreme Court precedent,[60] provides: "In no case does copyright protection for an original work of authorship extend to any idea, procedure, process, system, method of operation, concept, principle, or discovery, regardless of the form in which it is described, explained, illustrated, or embodied in such work."[61]

In *Baker v. Selden*, Selden developed a "peculiar system of book-keeping," which employed "certain forms," and the Court held that these forms were excluded from copyright protection.[62] Selden held a copyright in a book that explained a system of accounting and included forms that could be used to implement the system.[63] But the copyright in the book itself did not prevent others from using substantially similar forms to practice the accounting method described in the book.[64] Copyright thus extends to the explanation of a method, but not to its use and application.

---

57. *Georgia v. Public.Resource.Org, Inc.* 140 S. Ct. 1498 (2020).
58. *Wheaton v. Peters*, 33 U.S. (8 Pet.) 591, 668 (1834) (holding, unanimously, that "no reporter has or can have any copyright in the written opinions delivered by this Court; and that the judges thereof cannot confer on any reporter any such right"); *Banks v. Manchester*, 128 U.S. 244, 253 (1888) (state court judges may not assert copyright in "whatever work they perform in their capacity as judges"—be it "the opinion or decision, the statement of the case and the syllabus or the head note"); *Callaghan v. Myers*, 128 U.S. 617 (1888) (holding that an official reporter cannot hold a copyright interest in opinions created by judges); *see also John G. Danielson, Inc. v. Wincheswter-Conant*, 322 F.3d 26 (1st Cir. 2003) ("it is well-established that judicial decisions and statutes are in the public domain").
59. *Georgia v. Public.Resource.Org, Inc.*, 140 S. Ct. 1498, 1508 (2020).
60. *Baker v. Selden*, 101 U.S. 99, 107 (1879) ("The conclusion to which we have come is, that blank account-books are not the subject of copyright; and that the mere copyright of Selden's book did not confer upon him the exclusive right to make and use account-books, ruled and arranged as designated by him and described and illustrated in said book.").
61. 17 U.S.C. § 102(b).
62. *Baker v. Selden*, 101 U.S. 99, 103, 107 (1879).
63. *Id.*, at 104 ("Now, whilst no one has a right to print or publish his book, or any material part thereof, as a book intended to convey instruction in the art, any person may practise and use the art itself which he has described and illustrated therein. The use of the art is a totally different thing from a publication of the book explaining it.").
64. *Id.*, at 104–05 ("The copyright of a book on book-keeping cannot secure the exclusive right to make, sell, and use account-books prepared upon the plan set forth in such book .... The

To amplify this principle—and the statutory language—the Copyright Office Regulations provide examples of excluded material.[65] Such matter may indeed be "expressive," but it does not rise to the level of protectable works:

> § 202.1 Material not subject to copyright.
>
> The following are examples of works not subject to copyright and applications for registration of such works cannot be entertained:
>
> a. Words and short phrases such as names, titles, and slogans; familiar symbols or designs; mere variations of typographic ornamentation, lettering or coloring; mere listing of ingredients or contents.
> b. Ideas, plans, methods, systems, or devices, as distinguished from the particular manner in which they are expressed or described in a writing.
> c. Blank forms, such as time cards, graph paper, account books, diaries, bank checks, scorecards, address books, report forms, order forms and the like, which are designed for recording information and do not in themselves convey information.
> d. Works consisting entirely of information that is common property containing no original authorship, such as, for example: Standard calendars, height and weight charts, tape measures and rulers, schedules of sporting events, and lists or tables taken from public documents or other common sources.
> e. Typeface as typeface.

While it is clear that "blank forms" are uncopyrightable, forms that explain an underlying method or system can be copyrightable. Forms that are primarily designed for recording information, and that do not themselves convey information, are not copyrightable.[66] Such forms often lack the modicum of originality needed to justify copyrightability.[67] On the other hand, forms that display minimal creativity in the selection and arrangement of information can be copyrightable.[68]

---

description of the art in a book, though entitled to the benefit of copyright, lays no foundation for an exclusive claim to the art itself.").

65. 37 C.F.R. § 202.1.
66. *See*, e.g., *John H. Harland Co. v. Clarke Checks, Inc.*, 711 F.2d 966, 971 (11th Cir. 1983) ("It is well-established that blank forms which do not convey information or contain original pictorial expression are not copyrightable."); M.M. Bus. *Forms Corp. v. Uarco, Inc.*, 472 F.2d 1137 (6th Cir. 1973) (holding that blank forms for electrical appliance service dealers to use were not copyrightable); *Portionpac Chemical Corp. v. Sanitech Systems, Inc.*, 217 F. Supp. 2d 1238 (M.D. Fla. 2002) (holding that kitchen cleaning checklists were not copyrightable); *Advanz Behavioral Mgmt. Res., Inc. v. Miraflor*, 21 F. Supp. 2d 1179 (C.D. Cal. 1998) (holding that blank forms used for home health-care management services were not copyrightable).
67. *See*, e.g., *Donald v. Uarco Business Forms*, 478 F.2d 764, 766 (8th Cir. 1973) (concluding "minimum degree of creativity and originality necessary to support a valid copyright" absent when plaintiff's form was no more than "a trivial variation from that already in the public domain"); *Donald v. Zack Meyer's T.V. Sales & Serv.*, 426 F.2d 1027, 1031 (5th Cir. 1970) (holding plaintiff's copyright "invalid for lack of originality" when the blank form was "nothing more than a mosaic of the existing forms, with no original piece added"). *Cf. Phoenix Renovation Corp. v. Rodriguez*, 439 F. Supp. 2d 510, 515 (E.D. Va. 2006) ("Legal forms, if original, may properly be the subject of copyright protection.").
68. *Kregos v. Associated Press*, 937 F.2d 700, 709 (2d Cir. 1991) (concluding that a blank form, which displays an author's minimal creativity, can be eligible for copyright protection); *accord Utopia Provider Sys., Inc. v. Pro-Med Clinical Sys., L.L.C.*, 596 F.3d 1313, 1322 (11th Cir. 2010) (examining whether terms on blank medical forms "actually convey information to the treating

The Copyright Regulations' exclusion of simple words and phrases reflects that copyrightability is predicated on original expression.[69] The bedrock proposition is that copyright protection extends only to the expression of ideas and not to the ideas themselves; however, copyright law requires a set of standards for separating protected "expression" from unprotected "idea." Except for the general language of section 102(b), the Copyright Act provides no further guidance. The judicially created separation process has become quite complex and defies broad generalization. Complexity arises from the proposition that copyright protection extends beyond the taking of literal expression; nonliteral, structural elements of a copyrighted work may be protected if they are detailed and concrete enough.[70] Accordingly, under appropriate circumstances, the details of the plot of a literary work, the detailed structure of a play or motion picture, the harmonic and rhythmic structure of a musical work, and the arrangement of a set of algorithms in a computer program may all come within the ambit of copyright protection. In such cases, the use of these nonliteral, structural elements could constitute infringement of the copyrighted works to which they relate.

With such an expansive view of "expression," it necessarily follows that with respect to the elements of any given work, there is a spectrum. The spectrum of protection ranges from the clearly unprotected abstract idea underlying the work to the literal expression constituting the work as a whole. In a given case, where the defendant is alleged to have infringed the plaintiff's work, it is frequently necessary to determine where, on that spectrum, the material allegedly taken lies.[71] Thus, for example, as discussed below, courts have diverged in their attempts to separate protected expression from unprotected "ideas" or "processes" involved in computer software.[72] As one court observed, "[t]he first axiom of copyright is that copyright protection covers only the expression of ideas and not ideas themselves. The second axiom of copyright is that the first axiom is more of an amorphous characterization that it is a principled guidepost."[73] Nevertheless, while the process of differentiation becomes, in practice, essentially ad hoc, the courts have articulated helpful analytic concepts, such as the doctrine of merger and the unprotectability of scenes à faire.

---

physician" and concluding that "the selection and arrangement of the terms does not convey information and is not sufficiently original"); *Whelan Assocs., Inc. v. Jaslow Dental Lab., Inc.*, 797 F.2d 1222, 1243 (3d Cir. 1986) ("[B]lank forms may be copyrighted if they are sufficiently innovative that their arrangement of information is itself informative."). *But see Bibbero Sys., Inc. v. Colwell Sys., Inc.*, 893 F.2d 1104 (9th Cir. 1990) (evincing a "bright-line" approach to noncopyrightability of blank forms).

69. *See, e.g., Mattel, Inc. v. Goldberger Doll Mfg. Co.*, 365 F.3d 133, 135–36 (2d Cir. 2004) ("[C]opyright does not protect ideas; it protects only the author's particularized expression of the idea."); *see also CMM Cable Rep, Inc. v. Ocean Coast Pros., Inc.*, 97 F.3d 1504 (1st Cir. 1996); *Narell v. Freeman*, 872 F.2d 907 (9th Cir. 1989).
70. *Nichols v. Universal Pictures Corp.*, 45 F.2d 119 (2d Cir. 1930); *Sheldon v. Metro-Goldwyn Pictures Corp.*, 81 F.2d 49 (2d Cir. 1936).
71. *See infra* §9.III.
72. *See infra* §2.IV.A.
73. *Chuck Blore & Don Richman Inc. v. 20/20 Advertising Inc.*, 674 F. Supp. 671, 676 (D. Minn. 1987).

2 Merger

To avoid the impermissible protection of an idea, courts may withhold protection of matter that is clearly expressive when that expression is one of only a very limited number of ways of expressing that idea. Such expression is said to have merged into the idea, so that protection for the expression would, in effect, improperly grant a monopoly on the idea. The doctrine was first articulated in a 1967 First Circuit opinion[74] and has been restated with approval (albeit frequently in dicta) by most of the circuits which have dealt with the question.[75] The Eighth Circuit summarized it well:

> Under the copyright law doctrine of merger, a close cousin to the idea/expression dichotomy, copyright protection will be denied to even some expressions of ideas if the idea behind the expression is such that it can be expressed only in a very limited number of ways. The doctrine is designed to prevent an author from monopolizing an idea merely by copyrighting a few expressions of it.[76]

However, conflict has emerged between the "copyrightability" and the "infringement" analytic models of the merger doctrine.[77] Some courts expressly follow the classic statement of the merger doctrine denying copyrightability (and, therefore, any protection) to expression essentially dictated by the idea.[78] On the other hand, some courts seem to reject the "noncopyrightability" approach to merger,[79] and instead hold that the issue is one of infringement.[80] Under this latter view, where the expression is one of only a limited number of ways of expressing the idea, liability for infringement might be found if, and only if, there is a literal, verbatim taking of that expression.

Application of the merger doctrine, finding that a given expression is so closely related to the idea expressed as to give rise to merger, requires a determination of

74. *Morissey v. Procter & Gamble Co.*, 379 F.2d 675 (1st Cir. 1967).
75. *See, e.g.*, *BUC Int'l Corp. v. International Yacht Council Ltd.*, 489 F.3d 1129 (11th Cir. 2007); *Lexmark Int'l, Inc. v. Static Control Components*, 387 F.3d 522 (6th Cir. 2004); *John G. Danielson, Inc. v. Winchester-Conant*, 322 F.3d 26 (1st Cir. 2003); *Veeck v. Southern Bldg. Code Cong., Int'l*, 293 F.3d 791 (5th Cir. 2002); *Warren Publ'g Inc. v. Microdos Data Corp.*, 115 F.3d 1509 (11th Cir. 1997); *Allen v. Academic Games League of Am.*, 89 F.3d 614 (9th Cir. 1996); *Gates Rubber Co. v. Bando Chem. Indus., Ltd.*, 9 F.3d 823 (10th Cir. 1993); *Concrete Mach. Co. v. Classic Lawn Ornaments, Inc.*, 843 F.2d 600 (1st Cir. 1988); *Toro Co. v. R&R Prods.*, 787 F.2d 1208 (8th Cir. 1986); *Educ. Testing Servs. v. Katzman*, 793 F.2d 533 (3d Cir. 1986).
76. *Toro Co. v. R&R Prods.*, 787 F.2d 1208, 1212 (8th Cir. 1986).
77. *Ets-Hokin v. Skyy Spirits, Inc.* 225 F.3d 1068, 1082 (9th Cir. 2000) (acknowledging "some disagreement among courts as to whether these two doctrines [merger and scènes à faire] figure into the issue of copyrightability or are more properly defenses to infringement").
78. *See, e.g.*, *N. Y. Mercantile Exch., Inc. v. Intercontinental Exch., Inc*, 497 F.3d 109 (2d Cir. 2007); *Mywebgrocer, LLC v. Hometown Info., Inc.*, 375 F.3d 190 (2d Cir. 2004); *Computer Assocs., Int'l, Inc. v. Altai, Inc.*, 982 F.2d 693 (2d Cir. 1992) ("In order not to confer a monopoly of the idea upon the copyright owner, such expression should not be protected").
79. *See, e.g.*, *CCC Info. Servs., Inc. v. Maclean Hunter Mkt. Reports, Inc.*, 44 F.3d 61 (2d Cir. 1994); *Kregos v. Associated Press*, 937 F.2d 700 (2d Cir. 1991); *Continental Casualty Co. v. Beardsley*, 253 F.2d 702 (2d Cir. 1958).
80. *Satava v. Lowry*, 323 F.3d 805, 812 n.5 (9th Cir. 2003) ("Under the merger doctrine, courts will not protect a copyrighted work from infringement if the idea underlying the copyrighted work can be expressed in only one way, lest there be a monopoly on the underlying idea.").

precisely what is the underlying "idea." This task can often engender judicial disagreement, even in the same case.[81] For these purposes of separating ideas and expression, a distinction can be made between "hard" and "soft" ideas. Hard ideas are "those ideas that undertake to advance the understanding of phenomena or the solution of problems," whereas "soft" ideas are those that "are infused with the author's taste or opinion."[82] As to the latter, the court may well exercise its discretion to "withhold" application of the merger doctrine.[83]

3 *Scenes à Faire*

Similar to the concept of merger is the proposition that copyright protection will not extend to scenes à faire, which are thematic concepts or events that necessarily must follow from certain plot situations.[84] These stock elements, or must-do scenes, are not protectable under copyright law.[85] The scenes à faire exclusion is not limited to literary or dramatic works.[86] It has been extended to the analysis of claims involving computer software[87] and musical works.[88]

Like with merger, "the rationale is that there should be no monopoly on the underlying unprotectable idea."[89] But "ideas," as such, are not within the subject matter of copyright, state laws purporting to protect ideas may be enforceable, and will not be subject to preemption. The states vary considerably in their approach to the protection of ideas.[90]

---

81. *See cf. Kregos v. Associated Press*, 937 F.2d 700, 716 (2d Cir. 1991) (Sweet, J., dissenting) ("Therefore, because I believe that the district court was correct in holding that Kregos' form is uncopyrightable because his idea has merged with his expression of that idea, I respectfully dissent").
82. *CCC Info. Servs., Inc. v. Maclean Hunter Mkt. Reports, Inc.*, 44 F.3d 61, 71 (2d Cir. 1994).
83. *Id.*, at 72 ("Unbridled application of the merger doctrine would undo the protection the copyright law intends to accord to compilations. Complete failure to apply it, however, would result in granting protection to useful ideas .... [Thus] [i]n cases of wholesale takings of compilations, a selective application of the merger doctrine, withholding its application as to soft ideas infused with taste and opinion, will carry out the statutory policy to protect innovative compilations without impairing the policy that requires public access to ideas of a more important and useful kind").
84. *Murray Hill Publ'ns, Inc. v. Twentieth Century Fox*, 361 F.3d 312 (6th Cir. 2004); *Reyher v. Children's Television Workshop*, 533 F.2d 87 (2d Cir. 1976); *Hartman v. Hallmark Cards, Inc.*, 833 F.2d 117 (8th Cir. 1987) (copyrights do not protect thematic concepts or *scenes à faire*).
85. *Satava v. Lowry*, 323 F.3d 805, 810, n.3 (9th Cir. 2003).
86. For example, *Corbello v. Valli*, 974 F.3d 965, 975 (9th Cir. 2020) ("Non-protectable elements include ideas; historical facts; common phrases; *scenes-a-faire* (that is, situations and incidents that flow necessarily or naturally from a basic plot premise or generic plot line) and familiar stock scenes and themes that are staples of literature.") (internal quotation and citation omitted).
87. *Dun & Bradstreet Software v. Grace Consulting*, 307 F.3d 197 (3d Cir. 2002); *Mitel, Inc. v. Iqtel, Inc.*, 124 F.3d 1366 (10th Cir. 1997) (extending *scenes à faire* analysis "to exclude from protection against infringement those elements of a work that necessarily result from external factors inherent in the subject matter of the work"); *Computer Assocs., Int'l, Inc. v. Altai, Inc.*, 982 F.2d 693 (2d Cir. 1992); *Apple Computer, Inc. v. Microsoft Corp.*, 35 F.3d 1435 (9th Cir. 1994).
88. *Swirsky v. Carey*, 376 F.3d 841 (9th Cir. 2004); *Smith v. Jackson*, 84 F.3d 1213 (9th Cir. 1996).
89. *Ets-Hokin v. Skyy Spirits*, Inc., 225 F.3d 1068, 1082 (9th Cir. 2000).
90. *See*, e.g., *Murray v. Nat'l Broad. Co.*, Inc., 844 F.2d 988 (2d Cir. 1988).

IV Special Categories of Works

While the Copyright Act does not create special categories of works, with separate schema for protection (except for semiconductor chips), the combination of certain specific provisions of the Act and judicial development has resulted in different, if not special, treatment for computer software, compilations and databases, historical and factual material, utilitarian works, architectural works, sound recordings, and fictional characters.

A *Computer Software*

1 *Software as a "Literary Work"*

In connection with the passage of the 1976 Act, Congress created the National Commission on New Technological Uses of Copyrighted Works (CONTU), whose task was to determine what, if any, special legislation was needed to deal with computer software. Ultimately, CONTU's deliberations resulted in minimal recommendations: the inclusion in the Act of a definition of a computer program and special provisions relating to permissible copying. In short, it was determined that broad, separate provisions dealing exclusively with computer software were not necessary.

Consistent with the CONTU recommendation, the Copyright Act defines a computer program as "a set of statements or instructions to be used directly or indirectly in a computer in order to bring about a certain result."[91] While so defining software, the Act does not address software specifically in its exemplary listing of "works of authorship" within the subject matter of copyright. Rather, such a "set of statements or instructions," if sufficiently original, would qualify for protection as a "literary work." In short, with certain highly specific exceptions, computer programs are not treated by the Copyright Act, or other legislation, as a special category of intellectual property, subject to idiosyncratic rules. The conceptual problem that results is whether computer programs, as literary works, are to be analyzed, and their protection determined and limited by the same standards applicable to traditional literary works.

2 *Protection of the Code Itself*

With respect to the literal work constituting the program—the "code" in which the literary work is written—certain propositions have been clearly enunciated by the courts. First, so long as it meets the minimal requirements of originality, the code is a "work of authorship" subject to copyright.[92] This protection applies irrespective of whether it is "source code" or "object code." It does not matter if it is written in a

91. 17 U.S.C. § 101.
92. *Williams Elecs., Inc. v. Artic Int'l, Inc.*, 685 F.2d 870 (3d Cir. 1982).

directly perceptible high-level programming language, or in machine language comprehensible only to the computer. Second, the form in which it is "fixed" is irrelevant so long as it is "fixed" in some form.[93] In other words, it may be fixed as writing on paper, in magnetic form on disc or tape, or even embedded in a ROM chip. And third, the function of the program, including whether it is an application used by the human user of the system or an internal control program, such as an operating system, that is addressed to the machine rather than to a person, is irrelevant.[94] Protection exists independent of the nature of the program.

3 *Protection of Structure and "Look and Feel"*

The significant problems and controversial issues relating to computer programs concern the protectability of the nonliteral, structural elements of a program and the program's "look and feel."[95] Although the overall structure of a program is not protectable, other nonliteral elements may be sufficiently concrete to constitute protected "expression," just as copyright protection will extend to sufficiently detailed, concrete nonliteral elements of any other "literary work" to the extent those elements are sufficiently original and creative. The problem for the courts has been the development of standards to determine when and how to protect the detailed structure. The opposing lines were drawn in conflicting opinions from the Third and Second Circuits: *Whelan Associates, Inc. v. Jaslow Dental Laboratory, Inc.*[96] and *Computer Associates, International, Inc. v. Altai, Inc.*,[97] respectively.

In Whelan, the Third Circuit, in finding protection for the set of algorithms constituting the structure of a program, started with the proposition, now universally accepted, that "[b]y analogy to other literary works" copyright of a computer program "can be infringed even absent copying of the literal elements of the program."[98] The court found that the structure of the program was analogous to a compilation of routines and algorithms. The court concluded that it could protect "the sequence and order" of that compilation, so long as it contained the requisite originality and creativity and was not subject to application of the doctrine of merger.[99] The court's approach was expansive, particularly in the way it distinguished between idea and original expression in the compilation.

93. *Id.*
94. *Apple Computer, Inc. v. Franklin Computer Corp.*, 714 F.2d 1240 (3d Cir. 1983). *See also Lexmark Int'l, Inc. v. Static Control Components*, 387 F.3d 522 (6th Cir. 2004).
95. *See*, e.g., *GlobeRanger Corp. v. Software AG*, 691 F.3d 702, 707 (5th Cir. 2012) ("[A]s one moves away from the literal code to more general levels of a program, it becomes more difficult to distinguish between unprotectable ideas, processes, methods or functions, on one hand, and copyrightable expression on the other. This difficulty has led us to conclude that some nonliteral aspect of computer programs are within the scope of copyright.") (internal quotation and citation omitted).
96. *Whelan Assocs. v. Jaslow Dental Lab, Inc.*, 797 F.2d 1222 (3d Cir. 1986).
97. *Computer Assocs. Int'l v. Altai*, 982 F.2d 693 (2d Cir. 1992).
98. *Whelan Assocs. v. Jaslow Dental Lab, Inc.*, 797 F.2d 1222, 1234 (3d Cir. 1986).
99. *Id.*, at 1239.

On the other hand, the Second Circuit's 1992 Computer Associates opinion took a far more restrictive approach to protecting nonliteral elements of computer programs. Expressly criticizing the then five-year-old Whelan for "the opinion's somewhat outdated appreciation of computer science," the court proposed "abstraction, filtration, comparison" tests to determine copyrightability and infringement of nonliteral elements.[100] Specifically, the court proposed a three-part test when looking at claims for protecting structure. First, one must place that structure on a continuum from the literal code to the ultimate function of the program, eliminating that which is found to be too abstract, and thus in the realm of idea. Second, sift out nonprotectable matter. And third, compare what remains to the allegedly infringing program. In the process of "sifting," it is necessary to separate out: (i) expression that merges into the relevant ideas; (ii) elements of a program necessarily incidental to its function; (iii) scenes à faire; (iv) matter in the public domain; and (v) matter necessary for "efficiency." Anything of the structure that is left may be protected if found to have been taken. The court acknowledged the restrictive nature of its approach[101] and its rather grudging acceptance of computer programs as "literary works."[102]

The question of protecting a program's "look and feel"—where the taking involves neither the actual code nor the structure of a program, but rather the recreation of its appearance and manner of operation—remains unsettled.[103] In one early leading case, *Lotus Development Corp. v. Borland International, Inc.*,[104] the First Circuit found that the command menu structure of a spreadsheet program was an unprotectable "process," analogous to the functional controls of a VCR. The court compared Lotus' command menu hierarchy to the buttons used to control a VCR, noting that choosing the "print" command, or typing the letter "P," was akin to

100. *Computer Assocs. Int'l v. Altai*, 982 F.2d 693, 706 (2d Cir. 1992).
101. *Id.*, at 711 ("[Plaintiff] and some amici argue against the type of approach that we have set forth on the grounds that it will be a disincentive for future computer program research and development .... The interest of the copyright law is not in simply conferring a monopoly on industrious persons, but in advancing the public welfare through rewarding artistic creativity, in a manner that permits the free use and development of non-protectable ideas and processes.").
102. *Id.*, at 712 ("In the meantime, Congress has made clear that computer programs are literary works entitled to copyright protection. Of course, we shall abide by these instructions, but in so doing we must not impair the overall integrity of copyright law .... If the test we have outlined results in narrowing the scope of protection, as we expect it will, that result flows from applying, in accordance with Congressional intent, long-standing principles of copyright law to computer programs. Of course, our decision is also informed by our concern that these fundamental principles remain undistorted.").
103. The Ninth Circuit, in *Apple Computer, Inc. v. Microsoft Corp.*, 35 F.3d 1435, 1439 (9th Cir. 1994), dealt "for the first time, with a claim of copying a computer program's artistic look as an audiovisual work instead of program codes registered as a literary work." In a context limited by the parties' license agreement, the court upheld the use of "the limiting doctrines of originality, functionality, standardization, *scenes à faire* and merger to find no copying of protectable elements" with respect to Apple's graphical user interface. *Id.*, at 1438. *See also Lotus Dev. Corp. v. Borland Int'l, Inc.*, 49 F.3d 807, 820 (1st Cir. 1995) (Boudin, J., concurring) ("Applying copyright law to computer programs is like assembling a jigsaw puzzle whose pieces do not quite fit.").
104. *Lotus Dev. Corp. v. Borland Int'l*, 49 F.3d 807 (1st Cir. 1995), *aff'd by an equally divided Court*, 516 U.S. 233 (1996).

pressing the "play" button on a VCR.[105] The menu commands were an uncopyrightable "method of operation" equivalent to unprotectable VCR buttons because "[w]ithout the menu commands, there would be no way to 'push' the Lotus buttons, as one could push unlabeled VCR buttons."[106]

In *Google LLC v. Oracle America, Inc.*,[107] the Supreme Court resolved a decade-long dispute between software giants Google and Oracle, finding Google engaged in a fair use. In 2010, Oracle purchased Sun Microsystems, the developer of the Java programming language. When Google created its Android platform for mobile smartphone devices, it used many of the names of methods that were part of the Java SE (Standard Edition) Application Programming Interface (API), as well as the structure of the classes and the packages in which those methods were organized. Oracle sued Google for copyright infringement. On de novo review, the Supreme Court held that it was a fair use when Google copied 11,500 lines of code from the Java API in creating the Android operating system. These method calls, according to the Court, were "similar to a gas pedal in a car that tells the car to move faster or the QWERTY keyboard on a typewriter that calls up a certain letter when you press a particular key."[108] Notably, the Court declined to answer whether copyright protection extends to software interface specifications: "[W]e assume, for argument's sake, that the material [copied] was copyrightable."[109] Sidestepping the software copyrightability question, the majority held Google's use of the Java declaring code, defining the names of the methods and their organization into packages, classes, and methods, was fair: "[W]here Google reimplemented a user interface, taking only what was needed to allow users to put their accrued talents to work in a new and transformative program,

105. *Lotus Dev. Corp.*, 49 F.3d at 817.
106. *Id.*, at 815, 817. While the *Lotus* court found the nonliteral elements unprotectable, other courts have protected both literal and nonliteral elements of a computer program. *See, e.g.*, *General Universal Systems, Inc. v. Lee*, 379 F.3d 131 (5th Cir. 2004) (finding literal and nonliteral elements of computer software protectable); *Autoskill, Inc. v. Nat'l Educ. Support Sys., Inc.*, 994 F.2d 1476 (10th Cir. 1993) (finding nonliteral elements of computer programs protectable). Nonliteral elements of a computer program, like a program's sequence, structure, organization, and user interface, may be protected by copyright when they constitute an expression of an idea, rather than an idea itself.
107. *Google LLC v. Oracle Am., Inc.*, 141 S. Ct. 1183 (2021), *rev'g*, *Oracle Am., Inc. v. Google LLC*, 886 F.3d 1179 (Fed. Cir. 2018) (concluding that Google's use of the 37 Java API packages was not fair as a matter of law). The appeal to the Federal Circuit was from a decision of a federal district court in California (in the Ninth Circuit) because of the existence of patent infringement claims. The patent claims were ultimately rejected; however, the Federal Circuit's jurisdiction is exclusive, so the copyright claims were reviewed by the Federal Circuit—under Ninth Circuit law. *Oracle Am., Inc. v. Google LLC*, 886 F.3d 1179, 1190 (Fed. Cir. 2018) ("This court has exclusive jurisdiction over all appeals in actions involving patent claims, including where, as here, an appeal raises only non-patent issues. 28 U.S.C. § 1295(a)(1). Because copyright law is not within this court's exclusive jurisdiction, we apply the law of the regional circuit in which the district court sits; here, the Ninth Circuit."), *rev'd*, 141 S. Ct. 1183 (2021). For commentary on this jurisdictional quirk, *see* Peter Menell, *API Copyrightability Bleak House: Unraveling and Repairing the Oracle v. Google Jurisdictional Mess*, 31 Berkeley Tech. L.J. 1515 (2016).
108. *Google LLC v. Oracle Am., Inc.*, 141 S. Ct. 1183, 1192 (2021).
109. *Id.*, at 1190.

Google's copying of the Sun Java API was a fair use of that material as a matter of law."[110]

Computer software remains in a peculiar, hybrid position.[111] While it is recognized that computer software does not fit exactly within the patent or copyright constructs, it nevertheless can find protection, to a greater or lesser extent, as a species of "literary works" under the Copyright Act. The courts have had to apply traditional copyright concepts to this quite untraditional form of intellectual property. The judicial discomfort has been clearly expressed:

> To be frank, the exact contours of copyright protection for nonliteral program structure are not completely clear .... Indeed, it may well be that the Copyright Act serves as a relatively weak barrier against public access to the theoretical interstices behind a program's source and object codes. This results from the hybrid nature of a computer program, which, while it is literary expression, is also a highly functional, utilitarian component in the larger process of computing.
>
> Generally, we think that copyright registration—with its indiscriminating availability—is not ideally suited to deal with the highly dynamic technology of computer science. Thus far, many of the decisions in this area reflect the courts' attempt to fit the proverbial square peg in a round hole .... [N]ow that more than 12 years have passed since CONTU issued its final report, the resolution of this specific issue could benefit from further legislative investigation—perhaps a CONTU II.[112]

B *Compilations and Databases*

As the Second Circuit has noted, "Copyright law and compilations are uneasy bed fellows."[113] The Copyright Act expressly provides that the subject matter of copyright "includes compilations."[114] The Act defines a "compilation" as "a work formed by the collection and assembling of preexisting materials or of data that are selected, coordinated, or arranged in such a way that the resulting work as a whole constitutes an original work of authorship."[115] In protecting an original compilation, the Act distinguishes between the compilation—the arrangement or selection of the material—and the material itself. As one court has observed, "the law of copyright defies the laws of logic ... since it affords to the summation of one hundred ...

110. *Id.*, at 1209.
111. The extent to which copyright should protect more abstract features of computer software was thrown into doubt by the Federal Circuit in 2014: "Section 102(b) does not ... automatically deny copyright protection to elements of a computer program that are functional." *Oracle America, Inc. v. Google Inc.*, 750 F.3d 1339, 1367 (Fed. Cir. 2014). This doubt was not resolved by the Supreme Court's 2021 decision: "Given the rapidly changing technological, economic, and business-related circumstances, we believe we should not answer more than is necessary to resolve the parties' dispute. We shall assume, but purely for argument's sake, that the entire Sun Java API falls within the definition of that which can be copyrighted." *Google LLC v. Oracle America, Inc.*, 141 S. Ct. 1183, 1197 (2021).
112. *Computer Assocs. Int'l v. Altai*, 982 F.2d 693, 712 (2d Cir. 1992).
113. *Eckes v. Card Prices Update*, 736 F.2d 859, 862 (2d Cir. 1984).
114. 17 U.S.C. § 103.
115. 17 U.S.C. § 101.

individual facts and their unadorned expression a significant measure of protection while affording none to the facts themselves. The whole of a compilation thus is greater than the sum of its parts."[116]

Irrespective of the material constituting the compilation, it is the originality of the compilation itself that determines the nature and extent of copyright protection. In *Feist Publications, Inc. v. Rural Telephone Service Co., Inc.*,[117] the US Supreme Court resolved some conflict in the Courts of Appeal over the role of effort, as opposed to originality, in establishing copyrightability for compilations. The Court firmly put to rest the notion that effort alone can render copyrightable a compilation that is otherwise lacking in originality. The Court addressed the extent to which "sweat of the brow," like that involved in creation of an alphabetical listing of names and telephone numbers in a telephone directory, is protectable. Speaking for the majority, Justice Sandra Day O'Connor's language is unequivocal:

> It may seem unfair that much of the fruit of the compiler's labor may be used by others without compensation. [T]his is not "some unforeseen byproduct of a statutory scheme." ... It is, rather, "the essence of copyright," ... and a constitutional requirement. The primary objective of copyright is not to reward the labor of authors, but "to promote the Progress of Science and useful Arts." Art. I, § 8, cl. 8 .... To this end, copyright assures authors the right to their original expression, but encourages others to build freely upon the ideas and information conveyed by a work.[118]

For compilations, just as for any other work for which copyright protection is sought, "the sine qua non of copyright is originality."[119] Again, the language in Feist is instructive: "the 1976 revisions to the Copyright Act leave no doubt that originality, not 'sweat of the brow,' is the touchstone of copyright protection in directories and other fact-based works."[120]

The originality threshold, however, is not very high. While a mechanical arrangement, or one dictated by the material itself, not involving any creative effort, will not be protected,[121] where originality can be found in the arrangement or selection of the material, the compilation will be copyrightable.[122] Even when the compilation is

116. *Financial Info., Inc. v. Moody's Investors Servs., Inc.*, 751 F.2d 501, 505 (2d Cir. 1984) (internal quotation and citation omitted).
117. *Feist Publ'ns, Inc. v. Rural Tel. Serv. Co.*, 499 U.S. 340 (1991).
118. *Id.*, at 349–51 (quoting *Harper & Row Publishers, Inc. v. Nation Enters.*, 471 U.S. 539, 589 (1985) (Brennan, J., dissenting)).
119. *Id.*, at 345. *See also infra* §3.II.B.
120. *Feist Publ'ns, Inc. v. Rural Tel. Serv. Co.*, 499 U.S. 340, 359–60 (1991).
121. *Id.*, at 349–50. *See also Financial Info., Inc. v. Moody's Investors Servs., Inc.*, 808 F.2d 204 (2d Cir. 1986); *Mid Am. Title Co. v. Kirk*, 59 F.3d 719, 722 (7th Cir. 1995) (refusing to protect a selection that is "too rote and mechanical a task to constitute an original element of the work"); *Warren Publ'g Inc. v. Microdos Data Corp.*, 115 F.3d 1509 (11th Cir. 1997) (concluding that alphabetical listing of communities served by cable systems lacks sufficient originality in selection to warrant protection for the compilation).
122. *See*, e.g., *BUC Int'l Corp. v. International Yacht Council Ltd.*, 489 F.3d 1129 (11th Cir. 2007) (discussing yatch prices); *Lipton v. Nature Co.*, 71 F.3d 464 (2d Cir. 1995) (protecting a compilation of "terms of venery"—sets of collective nouns, ranging from "a pride of lions" to "a bench of judges"—which plaintiff had selected and compiled from a variety of texts and

sufficiently original to be protected, that protection may be quite "thin." Protection extends only to that which is original in the compilation, leaving much of the work itself available to others.[123]

The problem of copyrightability of compilations is closely related to the question of protection of data and databases. Data as such, either in the form of individual datum or in the aggregate in a database, does not come within the subject matter of copyright. Facts, as ideas, have not been protectable individually or in the aggregate.[124] As the Supreme Court made clear in Feist: "That there can be no valid copyright in facts is universally understood. The most fundamental axiom of copyright law is that 'no author may copyright his ideas or the facts he narrates'."[125] Justice O'Connor explained:

> This is because facts do not owe their origin to an act of authorship. The distinction is one between creation and discovery: The first person to find and report a particular fact has not created the fact; he or she has merely discovered its existence .... The same is true of all facts—scientific, historical, biographical, and news of the day. They may not be copyrighted and are part of the public domain available to every person.[126]

Notwithstanding the effort that may be involved in individual instances of fact gathering and database creation, copyright protection, if any, can be found only in the way in which the data is selected and/or arranged. The result has been a sophisticated focus on the originality involved in data selection (rather than arrangement) in the more recent cases involving compiled databases.[127] Concomitantly, there has been increased interest in, and serious debate over, sui generis database protection, similar to that adopted by the European Union.[128]

C *Historical and Factual Material*

A corollary of the proposition that facts, as such, are outside the scope of copyright is the more limited copyright protection accorded to historical, biographical, and other

manuscripts); *CCC Info. Servs., Inc. v. Maclean Hunter Mkt. Reports, Inc.*, 44 F.3d 61, 65 n.4 (2d Cir. 1994) (protecting a compilation of selected used car valuations; "so long as [these choices as to selection and arrangement] are made independently by the compiler and entail a minimal degree of creativity, are sufficiently original that Congress may protect such compilations through the copyright laws").

123. *See, e.g.*, *Kregos v. Associated Press*, 937 F.2d 700 (2d Cir. 1991) (finding compilation of baseball pitcher statistics not copyrightable); *Kregos v. Associated Press*, 3 F.3d 656 (2d Cir. 1993) (same).
124. *See, e.g.*, *Assessment Techs. of Wisconsin, LLC. v. WIREdata, Inc.*, 350 F.3d 640 (7th Cir. 2003).
125. *Feist Publ'ns, Inc. v. Rural Tel. Serv. Co.*, 499 U.S. 340, 344–45 (1991) (quoting *Harper & Row, Publishers, Inc. v. Nation Enters.*, 471 U.S. 539, 556 (1985)).
126. *Id.*, at 347–48 (internal quotation and citations omitted).
127. *See, e.g.*, *Lipton v. Nature Co.*, 71 F.3d 464 (2d Cir. 1995); *CCC Info. Servs., Inc. v. Maclean Hunter Mkt. Reports, Inc.*, 44 F.3d 61 (2d Cir. 1994).
128. Such legislation has been introduced in Congress over the years; however, it has not yet been adopted. *See* Dov S. Greenbaum, *The Database Debate: In Support of an Inequitable Solution*, 13 ALB. L.J. SCI. & TECH. 431 (2003); Paul Durdick, *Ancient Debate, New Technology: The European Community Moves to Protect Computer Databases*, 12 B.U. INT'L L.J. 153 (1994).

factual works. Neither historical facts nor interpretive theories are protectable, and the labor of research will not form the basis for copyright protection. As the Second Circuit noted: "To avoid a chilling effect on authors who contemplate tackling an historical issue or event, broad latitude must be granted to subsequent authors who make use of historical subject matter, including theories or plots."[129]

Courts look closely at claims of infringement of factual or historical works to distill the protected expression from the unprotected idea. Again, Justice O'Connor in Feist is informative: "This court has long recognized that the fact/expression dichotomy limits severely the scope of protection in fact-based works."[130] Although copyright protection certainly is available for such types of literary work, the scope of that protection is more limited than it is for fictional or other purportedly more creative material. Thus, for example, while cookbooks may well be protectable as compilations of recipes, assuming a modicum of creativity in the arrangement, the individual recipes will normally not be protected.[131] In essence, to avoid protecting the facts comprising the work, the courts will protect such works against only wholesale, literal appropriation.[132] As the Ninth Circuit has observed:

> Because authors who wish to express ideas in factual works are usually confined to a "narrow range of expression ..., similarity of expression may have to amount to verbatim reproduction or very close paraphrasing before a factual work will be deemed infringed."[133]

Of course, bodily appropriation of an entire factual work may well be infringing.[134]

Generally, the courts will not speculate as to whether a given work is "factual" or "historical" as opposed to "fictional." Rather, for the purposes of defining the scope of protection, the author's own characterization of the work can be determinative. Thus, a work that purports to be "historical fiction" will have a greater claim to protection than one that purports to be an accurate history.[135]

129. *Hoehling v. Universal City Studios, Inc.*, 618 F.2d 972 (2d Cir. 1980).
130. *Feist Publ'ns, Inc. v. Rural Tel. Serv. Co.*, 499 U.S. 340, 350 (1991).
131. *Publications Int'l Ltd. v. Meredith Corp.*, 88 F.3d 473 (7th Cir. 1996).
132. *Hoehling v. Universal City Studios*, 618 F.2d 972, 972 (2d Cir. 1980) ("In works devoted to historical subjects ... a second author may make significant use of prior work, so long as he does not bodily appropriate the expression of another."); *see also Nash v. CBS, Inc.*, 899 F.2d 1537 (7th Cir. 1990); *Narell v. Freeman*, 872 F.2d 907 (9th Cir. 1989).
133. *Worth v. Selchow & Righter*, 827 F.2d 569, 572 (9th Cir. 1987) (citing *Landsberg v. Scrabble Crossword Game Players, Inc.*, 736 F.2d 485, 488 (9th Cir. 1984)).
134. *See Applied Innovations, Inc. v. Regents of Univ. of Minnesota*, 876 F.2d 626 (8th Cir. 1989) (psychological inventory); *Educational Testing Servs. v. Katzman*, 793 F.2d 533 (3d Cir. 1986) (standardized test).
135. *See Nash v. CBS, Inc.*, 899 F.2d 1537 (7th Cir. 1990).

D Utilitarian Works and Industrial Design

1 "Useful Articles"

The Copyright Act does neither deal directly with "industrial design"[136] nor is there a separate body of law, outside of the law relating to design patent, to deal specifically with such utilitarian works. Rather, the Act distinguishes between copyrightable (broadly defined) "pictorial, graphic, and sculptural works" and uncopyrightable "useful articles." The Act defines the uncopyrightable articles as "having an intrinsic utilitarian function that is not merely to portray the appearance of the article or to convey information."[137]

The definitional questions, of course, can be of crucial importance.[138] The fact that a work is "useful"—in that it performs, or can be employed to perform some function—will not necessarily result in it being defined as a "useful article." Thus, toy models or toy objects can be protected as "sculptural works" without reference to their utility as toys.[139] Similarly, masks designed to resemble the noses of a pig, an elephant, and a parrot have been held to be copyrightable "sculptural works," and not "useful articles."[140] Forms in the shape of animals, used by taxidermists to hold animal skins, are considered sculptural works as "any utilitarian aspect of the mannequin exists 'merely to portray the appearance' of the animal,"[141] but mannequins in the form of a human torso, designed to display clothing, have been held to be "useful articles."[142]

A model or photograph of an article may itself be copyrightable as a pictorial or sculptural work, yet such copyright does not extend to the manufacture of the useful article depicted.[143] Similarly, the copyright owner of a work, which is lawfully reproduced in useful articles that "have been offered for sale or other distribution to the public," may not prevent "the making, distribution, or display of pictures or photographs of such articles in connection with advertisements or commentaries related to the distribution or display of such articles, or in connection with news reports."[144]

---

136. Except for the limited purposes of Ch. 13 with respect to "vessel hulls." 17 U.S.C. §§ 1301 et seq.; *see infra* §2.IV.D.4.
137. 17 U.S.C. § 101.
138. *See*, e.g., *Poe v. Missing Persons*, 745 F.2d 1238, 1243 (9th Cir. 1984) (concluding that a genuine issue of fact existed as to whether plaintiff designed a functional swimsuit or a work of art).
139. *See*, e.g., *Gay Toys, Inc. v. Buddy L Corp.*, 703 F.2d 970, 973 (6th Cir. 1983) ("To be sure, a toy airplane is to be played with and enjoyed, but a painting of an airplane, which is copyrightable, is to be looked at and enjoyed. Other than the portrayal of a real airplane, a toy airplane, like a painting, has no intrinsic utilitarian function."); *accord Masquerade Novelty, Inc. v. Unique Indus., Inc.*, 912 F.2d 663 (3d Cir. 1990).
140. *Masquerade Novelty, Inc. v. Unique Indus., Inc.*, 912 F.2d 663, 671 (3d Cir. 1990) ("That nose masks are meant to be worn by humans to evoke laughter does not distinguish them from clearly copyrightable works of art like paintings .... The utilitarian nature of an animal nose mask ... inheres solely in its appearance ....").
141. *Superior Form Builders, Inc. v. Dan Chase Taxidermy Supply Co.*, 74 F.3d 488, 494 (4th Cir. 1996); *see also Hart v. Dan Chase Taxidermy Supply Co.*, 86 F.3d 320 (2d Cir. 1996).
142. *Carol Barnhart Inc. v. Economy Cover Corp.*, 773 F.2d 411 (2d Cir. 1985).
143. 17 U.S.C. § 113(b).
144. 17 U.S.C. § 113(c).

2 *Separability of Form and Function*

Although a useful article, as such, is not copyrightable, its design may, under certain circumstances, be protected as a pictorial, graphic, or sculptural work. The operative question is whether the formal, esthetic elements of the article's design are separable from the functional, utilitarian elements. In the language of the Act, copyrightable pictorial, graphic, and sculptural works include "works of artistic craftsmanship insofar as their form but not their mechanical or utilitarian aspects are concerned."[145] The design of a useful article is considered a pictorial, graphic, or sculptural work "only if, and only to the extent that, such design incorporates pictorial, graphic, or sculptural features that can be identified separately from, and are capable of existing independently of, the utilitarian aspects of the article."[146]

The statutory language is an attempt[147] to codify the US Supreme Court opinion in *Mazer v. Stein*.[148] The Mazer Court held that a statuette incorporated into the design of a lamp was copyrightable as a sculptural work, even if it might also be the subject of a design patent. In so doing, the Court restated the "nondiscrimination" doctrine to the effect that copyright is not limited to the fine arts.[149] The Court also made clear that an otherwise copyrightable work (e.g., a sculpture) does not lose its copyrightability by virtue of being incorporated into a commercial, useful article.[150] The crucial issue concerned the separability of the aesthetic from the functional.

In Mazer, it was quite easy to separate the "sculpture" from the rest of the lamp; it was obviously physically separable. Physical separability, however, is not the only factor to be considered. The House Committee Report relating to the 1976 Act, in commenting on the language of "separability" in the definition of "pictorial, graphic, and sculptural works" and a "useful article," referred to elements that, "physically or conceptually, can be identified as separable from the utilitarian aspects of that article."[151] In a series of not entirely consistent opinions, the courts have attempted to refine and apply the idea of conceptual separability for determining copyrightability of the design of a useful article. Thus, divided panels held that the aesthetic elements were not conceptually separable from the utilitarian in mannequins in the form of human torsos used to display clothing[152] and in a bicycle rack,[153] while mannequins for

145. 17 U.S.C. § 101.
146. *Id.*
147. The attempt is reflected in § 101 (definitions) and § 113 (scope of exclusive rights in pictorial, graphic, and sculptural works).
148. *Mazer v. Stein*, 347 U.S. 201 (1954).
149. *Id.*, at 214; ("Individual perception of the beautiful is too varied a power to permit a narrow or rigid concept of art"). *Cf. Bleistein v. Donaldson Lithographing Co.*, 188 U.S. 239, 251–52 (1903) (Holmes, J.) ("It would be a dangerous undertaking for persons trained only to the law to constitute themselves final judges of the worth of pictorial illustrations, outside of the narrowest and most obvious limits").
150. 17 U.S.C. § 113 incorporates *Mazer* by providing "the exclusive rights to reproduce a copyrighted pictorial, graphic, or sculptural work in copies ... includes the right to reproduce the work in or on any kind of article, whether useful or otherwise." 17 U.S.C. § 113(a).
151. H.R. Rep. No. 94-1476, at 55 (1976), *as reprinted in* 1976 U.S.C.C.A.N. 5659, 5668 (emphasis added).
152. *Carol Barnhart Inc. v. Economy Cover Corp.*, 773 F.2d 411 (2d Cir. 1985).

applying makeup and forms for mounting animal skins were found both to be not useful articles and to demonstrate conceptual separability of form and function.[154] While the courts recognize that "conceptual separability" is alive and well, the problem is determining "exactly what it is and how it is to be applied."[155]

In *Star Athletica v. Varsity Brands*, the Supreme Court addressed the separability issue and held that two-dimensional designs appearing on the surface of cheerleading uniforms were entitled to copyright protection.[156] The ultimate separability question is "whether the feature for which copyright protection is claimed would have been eligible for copyright protection as a pictorial, graphic, or sculptural work had it originally been fixed in some tangible medium other than a useful article before being applied to a useful article."[157] Copyright protects features that can be separately identified from, and exist independently of, the utilitarian aspects of a useful article.[158] Imaginatively separating the surface decorations from the uniforms, and applying them to some other medium, would not replicate the functional uniform itself; thus, the

153. *Brandir Int'l, Inc. v. Cascade Pacific Lumber Co.*, 834 F.2d 1142 (2d Cir. 1987).
154. *Pivot Point Int'l, Inc. v. Charlene Prods.*, 372 F.3d 913 (7th Cir. 2004); *Superior Form Builders, Inc. v. Dan Chase Taxidermy Supply Co.*, 74 F.3d 488 (4th Cir. 1996); *Hart v. Dan Chase Taxidermy Supply Co.*, 86 F.3d 320 (2d Cir. 1996).
155. *Brandir Int'l, Inc. v. Cascade Pacific Lumber Co.*, 834 F.2d 1142, 1144 (2d Cir. 1987). *See also Pivot Point Int'l, Inc. v. Charlene Prods.*, 372 F.3d 913 (7th Cir. 2004) (reviewing the various analytic models); *Galiano v. Harrah's Operating Co., Inc.*, 416 F.3d 411 (5th Cir. 2005) (proposing a sui generis approach to clothing and costume design). The problem is perhaps best exemplified by the language of the Second Circuit in denying copyright protection for the design of a bicycle rack:

> Form and function are inextricably intertwined in the rack, its ultimate design being as much the result of utilitarian pressures as aesthetic choices. [The designer] has achieved ... the highest goal of modern industrial design, that is, the harmonious fusion of function and aesthetics. Thus there remains no artistic element ... that can be identified as separate and "capable of existing independently of, the utilitarian aspects of the article."

Brandir Int'l, Inc., 834 F.2d at 1147–48 (quoting 17 U.S.C. § 101). *See also Inhale, Inc. v. Starbuzz Tobacco, Inc.*, 755 F.3d 1038, 1042 (9th Cir. 2014) (analyzing the shape of a hookah and determining that it is essentially a container and "that any part of a container that merely accomplishes the containing is not copyrightable").

156. *Star Athletica, L.L.C. v. Varsity Brands, Inc.*, 137 S. Ct. 1002 (2017).
157. *Id.*, at 1011. An artistic feature of a useful article's design is eligible for copyright protection only if it satisfies: (1) the separate identification requirement and (2) the independent-existence requirement. The feature must be perceived as a two- or three-dimensional work of art separate from the useful article, and the feature must qualify as a protectable pictorial, graphic, or sculptural work—either on its own or fixed in some other tangible medium of expression—if it were imagined separately from the useful article into which it is incorporated. The Court thus abandoned the distinction between physical and conceptual separability that some courts had used. *Compare Star Athletica, L.L.C. v. Varsity Brands, Inc.*, 137 S. Ct. 1002, 1014 (2017) ("Because we reject the view that a useful article must remain after the artistic feature has been imaginatively separated from the article, we necessarily abandon the distinction between 'physical' and 'conceptual' separability, which some courts and commentators have adopted based on the Copyright Act's legislative history."), *with Chosun International, Inc. v. Chrisha Creations, Ltd.*, 413 F.3d 324 (2d Cir. 2005); *Whimsicality, Inc. v. Rubie's Costume Co.*, 891 F.2d 452 (2d Cir. 1989).
158. *Star Athletica, LLC v. Varsity Brands, Inc.*, 137 S. Ct. 1002, 1010 (2017) (quoting 17 U.S.C. § 101).

Court concluded that the arrangement of lines, chevrons, and colored shapes would qualify as two-dimensional works of art.[159]

3 *Sui Generis Protection for Mask Works: The Semiconductor Chip Protection Act*

a Generally

The nature of semiconductor chips is such that, in the normal course, they would not meet the stringent requirements for patent protection, nor, as inherently "useful articles," could they qualify for copyright protection.[160] The circuit designs or technical drawings from which the chip is produced could possibly be protected as pictorial works, but neither the "mask" used to produce the embedded patterns in the chip, nor the patterns, nor the chip itself would receive protection.

Recognizing that the Copyright Act was not an effective instrument for protecting against the unauthorized copying of "mask works"[161] embodied in semiconductor chips, Congress enacted special protections. Congress was quite clear in stating that this legislation, although technically incorporated into the Copyright Act, is not a part of the Copyright Act's general provisions, but is "a sui generis form of intellectual property right, similar in many respects to existing copyright law but differing from copyright law in various ways."[162] Avoiding the somewhat murky issue of whether semiconductor chip protection is a proper exercise of Congress' power with respect to

---

159. *Id.*, at 1013 (2017) ("To be clear, the only feature of the cheerleading uniform eligible for a copyright in this case is the two-dimensional work of art fixed in the tangible medium of the uniform fabric .... [R]espondents have no right to prohibit any person from manufacturing a cheerleading uniform of identical shape, cut, and dimensions to the ones on which the decorations in this case appear."). *Compare Silvertop Assoc., Inc. v. Kangaroo Mfg. Inc.*, 931 F.3d 215 (3d Cir. 2019) (finding that banana costume's artistic features, including colors, lines, shape, and length, were "separable" from its utilitarian aspects and thus protectable as a copyrighted work), *with Lanard Toys Ltd. v. Dolgencorp LLC*, 958 F.3d 1337 (Fed. Cir. 2020) (rejecting copyright protection for an exaggerated, cartoonish chalk holder because plaintiff sought protection for the overall design of the entire object (i.e., for the "dimensions and shape of the useful article itself"), and not for some separable aspect (e.g., the chevrons on the uniforms in Star Athletica)).

160. For a more detailed discussion of this material, *see* Richard H. Stern, Semiconductor Chip Protection (1986); Paul Goldstein, Goldstein on Copyright §§ 17.26 et seq. (3d ed. 2005).

161. A "mask work" is a series of related images, however fixed or encoded:

    (a) having or representing the predetermined, three-dimensional pattern of metallic, insulating, or semiconductor material present or removed from the layers of a semiconductor chip product; and

    (b) in which series the relation of the images to one another is that each image has the pattern of the surface of one form of the semiconductor chip product.

    17 U.S.C. § 901(a)(2). The House Report with respect to the Semiconductor Chip Protection Act describes the mask work as "the layout determination and the sum total of the individual masks, set upon each other, used to fabricate the entire chip." H.R. Rep. No. 98-781, at 14 (1984), *as reprinted in* 1984 U.S.C.C.A.N. 5750, 5762–63.

162. H.R. Rep. No. 98-781, at 16 (1984), *as reprinted in* 1984 U.S.C.C.A.N. 5750, 5765. Implementing that idea, § 912(b) specifically states that, with a minor exception, the other provisions of the Copyright Act are not applicable to Ch. 9.

"writings" under Article I, section 8 of the Constitution,[163] as opposed to the general congressional power with respect to interstate commerce, chip protection is limited to remedies for acts of infringement "by conduct in or affecting commerce."[164]

The legislation is designed to provide the exclusive source for protection of mask works, as its provisions expressly "preempt the laws of any State to the extent those laws provide any rights or remedies with respect to a mask work which are equivalent to those rights or remedies provided by [Chapter Nine]."[165] However, it expressly does not preempt any federal copyright or patent claims which might be applicable to a semiconductor chip.[166] Such claims could include copyright claims with respect to computer programs embedded in a chip, or patent claims if a chip design can pass the stringent tests of patentability.

Protection under the Chip Protection Act extends only to "a mask work fixed in a semiconductor chip product, by or under the authority of the owner of the mask work."[167] It is the "mask work" used as the template for etching the circuitry into the chip, not the chip itself, that is protected. Since protection is limited to mask works fixed in semiconductor chips, other technologies, accomplishing similar results but without the use of semiconductors or masks in the manufacturing process, would not come within the ambit of protection. The Act is not limited to any particular kind of semiconductor material.

Protection for a qualifying mask work commences on the earlier of the date on which the work is registered or the date on which the work is first commercially exploited anywhere in the world and endures for a period of ten years thereafter.[168] However, if protection commences by virtue of commercial exploitation, the protection will terminate (prospectively) if application for registration is not made within two years after such commencement date.[169]

Mirroring the Copyright Act,[170] the Chip Protection Act excludes from protection mask works "prepared by an officer or employee of the US Government as part of that person's official duties," while recognizing the right of the US government to hold and enforce rights it receives as a transferee from one not an officer or employee.[171]

163. Cf. *supra*, §1.
164. 17 U.S.C. § 910(a).
165. 17 U.S.C. § 912(c).
166. 17 U.S.C. § 912(a).
167. 17 U.S.C. § 902(a)(1). A "semiconductor chip product" is the final or intermediate form of any product:
    (a) having two or more layers of metallic, insulating, or semiconductor material, deposited or otherwise placed on, or etched away or otherwise removed from, a piece of semiconductor material in accordance with a predetermined pattern; and
    (b) intended to perform electronic circuitry functions. 17 U.S.C. § 901(a)(1).
168. 17 U.S.C. § 904. For these purposes, terms of protection run to the end of the calendar year in which they would otherwise expire.
169. 17 U.S.C. § 908(a).
170. *See supra* §2.III.B.
171. 17 U.S.C. § 903(d).

b Substantive Conditions of Protection

As with copyright, chip protection is limited to "original expression,"[172] which requires both independent origin and some minimal degree of creativity. It may be presumed that this standard will be applied to mask work protection in a manner similar to that in which it is applied to copyright.[173] Indeed, the Chip Protection Act is even more explicit than the overall copyright standard in denying protection to staple, commonplace, or familiar articles.[174]

Further, the Chip Protection Act follows the Copyright Act verbatim in limiting protection to "expression" rather than "idea."[175] Although there is a rich body of copyright law attempting to grapple with the problem of separating "idea" from "expression,"[176] given the nature of the work involved, it is not likely that the same degree of complexity will attach to this analysis with respect to mask works.

Protection is further limited to mask works whose owners are nationals or domiciliaries of the US at the time the work is registered or is first commercially exploited anywhere in the world, whichever occurs first (or whose owners are nationals or domiciliaries of foreign nations that are parties to a treaty, to which the US is also party, protecting mask works, or whose owners are stateless persons); or that are first commercially exploited in the US; or are the subject of a special Presidential proclamation.[177]

c Formal Conditions of Protection

The Chip Protection Act again follows the Copyright Act in conditioning protection for a mask work on "fixation." However, unlike the Copyright Act, fixation must be in a particular medium, namely "a semiconductor chip product."[178] In the words of the statute, "A mask work is 'fixed' in a semiconductor chip product when its embodiment in the product is sufficiently permanent or stable to permit the mask work to be perceived or reproduced from the product for a period of more than transitory duration."[179]

To "commercially exploit" a mask work "is to distribute to the public for commercial purposes a semiconductor chip product embodying the mask work."[180]

172. 17 U.S.C. § 902(b)(10).
173. *See supra* §2.III.C.; *infra* §3.II.B.
174. 17 U.S.C. § 902(b)(2).
175. 17 U.S.C. § 902(c): "In no case does protection … for a mask work extend to any idea, procedure, process, system, method of operation, concept, principle, or discovery, regardless of the form in which it is described, explained, illustrated, or embodied in such work."
176. *See generally infra* §3.II.B.
177. 17 U.S.C. § 902(a)(1). The President may extend protection to mask works whose owners are nationals or domiciliaries of a foreign nation, who would not otherwise come within the provisions of this section, upon finding that that nation extends equivalent protection to mask works of owners who are nationals or domiciliaries of the United States. 17 U.S.C. § 902(a)(2).
178. 17 U.S.C. § 902(a)(1).
179. 17 U.S.C. § 901(a)(3).
180. 17 U.S.C. § 901(a)(5).

The term also includes an offer to sell or transfer a semiconductor chip product "when the offer is in writing and occurs after the mask work is fixed in the semiconductor chip product."[181]

While protection is framed in the disjunctive (registration or commercial exploitation), registration in fact is essential to continuing protection. Any protection for a mask work will terminate "if application for registration ... is not made ... within two years after the date on which the mask work is first commercially exploited anywhere in the world." The Register of Copyrights examines a mask work application much the same way copyright applications are examined. If the application is in order, a certificate of registration will be issued and effective as of the date on which the application is received by the Copyright Office.[182] If registration is refused, the applicant may bring an action for judicial review in the US District Court within sixty days after the date of refusal.[183]

In much the same way as with copyrighted works,[184] the Chip Protection Act makes the certificate of registration prima facie evidence of the facts stated therein and of compliance with the registration requirements.[185] Note, however, that it does not mirror the Copyright Act's further presumption of validity. If registration has been refused and the applicant has not directly appealed the refusal, the applicant may nevertheless institute a civil action for infringement if notice thereof, together with a copy of the complaint, is served on the Register of Copyrights, who may then choose to become a party to the action.[186] Notice may be placed upon protected mask works and semiconductor chip products embodying protected mask works so as "to give reasonable notice of such protection."[187]

d Ownership and Transfer

The "owner" of a mask work is "the person who created the mask work, the legal representative of that person if that person is deceased or under a legal incapacity, or a party to whom all the rights ... of such person or representative are transferred."[188] Where a mask work has been made within the scope of a person's employment, "the owner is the employer for whom the person created the mask work or a party to whom all the rights ... of the employer are transferred."[189] Presumably, in determining whether a work has been made within the scope of a person's employment, the "work for hire" standards developed by the courts under the Copyright Act would be

181. *Id.*
182. 17 U.S.C. § 908(e).
183. 17 U.S.C. § 908(g).
184. *See infra* §3.I.D.3.
185. 17 U.S.C. § 908(f).
186. 17 U.S.C. § 910(b)(2) ("the failure of the Register to become a party to the action shall not deprive the court of jurisdiction to determine [eligibility for registration]").
187. 17 U.S.C. § 909. Notice is to be in the form of the words "mask work," the symbol "*M*," or the symbol "Ⓜ" ("M" in a circle) together with the name of the owner or owners of the work.
188. 17 U.S.C. § 901(a)(6).
189. *Id.*

applicable.[190] Unlike the Copyright Act's definitions, the Chip Protection Act does not contemplate an alternative employer for hire status for specially commissioned work not within an employee's scope of employment. Presumably, a mask work might be developed jointly and the Copyright Act's standards with respect to determining joint authorship should be helpful.[191]

The Chip Protection Act expressly recognizes the right of the owner of "the exclusive rights" in a mask work to "transfer all of those rights, or license all or less than all of those rights."[192] Such transfer or license, however, even for a nonexclusive license, may be made only by a written instrument signed by the "owner" or the owner's authorized agent.[193] Transfer or license may also be effected by operation of law, by will, and by the applicable state laws of intestate succession.[194]

Transfers and any other document "pertaining to a mask work" may be recorded in the Copyright Office if properly executed; recordation of any transfer or license "gives all persons constructive notice of the facts stated in the recorded document concerning the transfer or license."[195] Recording, and the concomitant constructive notice, will determine the resolution of conflicting transfers.[196]

e Nature of the Rights

The Chip Protection Act grants a broad reproduction right with respect to the mask work, covering any means of reproduction, an exclusive distribution and importation right, and a right against contributory infringement.[197] The Chip Protection Act, however, expressly exempts certain forms of reverse engineering from liability for

190. *See infra* §4.VI.A.
191. *See infra* §4.IV.
192. 17 U.S.C. § 903(b).
193. *Id.*
194. *Id.*
195. 17 U.S.C. § 903(c)(1).
196. 17 U.S.C. § 903(c)(2):

> In any case in which conflicting transfers of the exclusive rights in a mask work are made, the transfer first executed shall be void as against a subsequent transfer which is made for a valuable consideration and without notice of the first transfer, unless the first transfer is recorded ... within three months after the date on which it is executed, but in no case later than the day before the date of such subsequent transfer.

197. The exclusive rights of the owner of a mask work are limited to the rights to:

> (1) reproduce the mask work by optical, electronic, or any other means;
> (2) import or distribute a semiconductor chip product in which the mask work is embodied; and
> (3) induce or knowingly to cause another person to do any of the acts described in paras (1) and (2).

17 U.S.C. § 905. For these purposes, "the distribution or importation of a product incorporating a semiconductor chip product as a part thereof is a distribution or importation of that semiconductor chip product." 17 U.S.C. § 901(b).

infringement of the exclusive reproduction right.[198] The effect of this provision is to allow a competitor to use the results of a reverse engineering analysis to create a competing product that does not simply incorporate the protected mask work.[199] The Ninth Circuit has confirmed that reverse engineering provisions in the Act allow copying of entire mask work; it does not distinguish between protectable and nonprotectable elements as long as copying is for the purpose of teaching, evaluating, or analyzing chip.[200]

As a limitation upon the exclusive rights to import or distribute a semiconductor chip product in which the mask work is embodied, the Chip Protection Act follows the Copyright Act[201] in creating a "first sale" exemption.[202]

f Infringement and Remedies

Except to the extent specifically exempted, "any person who violates any of the exclusive rights of the owner of a mask work … by conduct in or affecting commerce, shall be liable as an infringer of such rights."[203] As opposed to actions for infringement of copyright, it is only the "owner" of a protected mask work, or "the exclusive licensee of all rights" to a protected mask work, who may institute a civil action for infringement with respect to the mask work.[204]

As discussed below in connection with copyright,[205] there are serious open questions as to the constitutionality of such abrogation of immunity. The Act authorizes injunctive relief (both temporary and permanent), the award of actual damages, as well as the nonduplicative profits of the infringer, the alternative of statutory damages (in an amount up to USD 250,000), as well as impoundment, seizure, and

198. Specifically, it is not an infringement of the exclusive rights of the owner of a mask work for:

> (1) a person to reproduce the mask work solely for the purpose of teaching, analyzing, or evaluating the concepts or techniques embodied in the mask work or circuitry, logic flow, or organization of components used in the mask work; or
> (2) a person who performs the analysis or evaluation described in para. (1) to incorporate the results of such conduct in an original mask work which is made to be distributed. 17 U.S.C. § 906(a).

199. *See Brooktree Corp. v. Advanced Micro Devices, Inc.*, 705 F. Supp. 491 (S.D. Cal. 1988).
200. *Altera Corp. v. Clear Logic, Inc.*, 424 F.3d 1079, 1088 (9th Cir. 2005) (holding that the district court's jury instruction that initially defined "legitimate reverse engineering" to allow copying and analyzing only "non-protectable concepts or techniques" was an incorrect statement of the law).
201. *See infra* §6.III.B.
202. 17 U.S.C. § 906(b):

> The owner of a particular semiconductor chip product made by the owner of the mask work, or by any person authorized by the owner of the mask work, may import, distribute, or otherwise dispose of or use, but not reproduce, that particular semiconductor chip product without the authority of the owner of the mask work.

203. 17 U.S.C. § 910(a).
204. 17 U.S.C. § 910(b)(1).
205. *See infra* §9.I.F.

disposition of infringing physical items.[206] For the most part, the language is identical to that in the Copyright Act, and presumably will be interpreted in much the same way. Given the similarity of statutory language, the US Supreme Court holding of a constitutional right to jury determination in claims involving statutory damages for copyright infringement,[207] and its determination that prevailing plaintiffs and prevailing defendants are to be treated alike in the exercise of the court's discretion in awarding attorney's fees,[208] would appear to be applicable to claims under the Chip Protection Act.

4 *Sui Generis Protection for Vessel Hulls*

In October 1998, Congress enacted similar sui generis protection for the design of vessel hulls. With the "Vessel Hull Design Protection Act," it added to the Copyright Act a new Chapter 13, "Protection of Original Designs,"[209] modeled substantially upon the Semiconductor Chip Protection Act. It provides, to the designer of an original design, limited protection for a ten-year term, with respect to the making, importing, selling, or distributing, of vessel hulls embodying that design.[210] Purely utilitarian designs providing no more than an appealing or distinctive design are ineligible for protection.[211] Provision is made for registration and a unique notice.[212] There are detailed provisions with respect to remedies, immunity for innocent infringement, ownership and transfer, and similar matters. Protection under these provisions terminates upon issuance of a design patent for a protected design.[213]

The legislation was clearly experimental and of an interim nature, as it originally contained a "sunset" provision, directing that Chapter 13 remain in effect only for two years following the date of enactment. In addition, there were to be two joint studies of the Vessel Hull Design Protection Act's effect, to be conducted by the Register of Copyrights and the Commissioner of Patents and Trademarks, culminating in reports to Congress, originally within two years. However, with the Intellectual Property and Communications Omnibus Reform Act of 1999, Congress repealed the "sunset" provision as well as the requirement for two reports. Instead, it required a single joint report by the Register and the Under Secretary of Commerce for Intellectual Property and Director of the United States Patent and Trademark Office (USPTO). That report, when issued, found only "scant and anecdotal" evidence that the Act was effective in suppressing infringement, but it concluded "that it is too soon to tell whether the

206. 17 U.S.C. § 911.
207. *See infra* §10.II.B.3.
208. *See infra* §10.III.
209. 17 U.S.C. §§ 1301 et seq.
210. 17 U.S.C. §§ 1301, 1305, 1308.
211. 17 U.S.C. § 1302(4).
212. 17 U.S.C. §§ 1306, 1310. Notice is to be in the form of the words "Protected Design," or "Prot'd Des.," the letter "D" with a circle, or the symbol "*D*," together with the name of the owner(s) of the design and the date on which protection commenced.
213. 17 U.S.C. § 1329.

[Vessel Hull Design Protection Act] has had significant overall effect on the boat building industry."[214]

E Architectural Works

Architectural works would appear to be quintessentially "useful articles" and subject to the same analytic model and constraints as other utilitarian works. For all architectural works constructed prior to December 1, 1990, the "useful articles" paradigm was indeed applicable to architectural works; that is, buildings and similar structures, as "useful articles," were not themselves copyrightable.[215] A distinction was drawn, however, between the structure and the plans or drawings upon which it was based. While the former was unprotectable as a useful article, the plans or drawings, as "pictorial or graphical works," could be protected. As the Fifth Circuit has noted, "One may construct a house which is identical to a house depicted in architectural plans, but one may not directly copy those plans and then use the infringing copy to construct the house."[216] Moreover, while protection was limited to the plans or drawings, the courts were quite expansive in determining damages when plans were copied. Thus, it was held that one who infringed the plans and built a building from those plans could be held responsible not merely for the direct value of the plans but also for losses to the plaintiff resulting from the infringer's use of the plans[217] or profits the infringer realized upon resale of the structure built from the plans.[218]

Prompted both by the US accession to the Berne Convention in 1989 and to sharp criticism of the existing state of the law, Congress passed the Architectural Works Copyright Protection Act, which became effective on, and covers works created after, December 1, 1990. That legislation defines "architectural works" as:

> the design of a building as embodied in any tangible medium of expression, including a building, architectural plans, or drawings. The work includes the overall form as well as the arrangement and composition of spaces and elements in the design, but does not include individual standard features.[219]

More significantly, it adds "architectural works" to the enumerated "works of authorship,"[220] thereby distinguishing such works from "pictorial, graphic, and sculptural works" and rendering them no longer subject to the "useful article" and separability standards.[221]

---

214. U.S. Copyright Office & U.S. Patent And Trademark Office, The Vessel Hull Design Protection Act: Overview And Analysis (November 2003), available at https://www.copyright.gov/reports/vhdpa-report.pdf.
215. *Imperial Homes Corp. v. Lamont*, 458 F.2d 895 (5th Cir. 1972).
216. *Id.; see also Robert R. Jones Assocs., Inc. v. Nino Homes*, 858 F.2d 274 (6th Cir. 1988).
217. *Robert R. Jones Assocs*, 858 F.2d at 274.
218. *Arthur Rutenberg v. Dawney*, 647 F. Supp. 1214 (M.D. Fla. 1986).
219. 17 U.S.C. § 101.
220. 17 U.S.C. § 102(8).
221. As the House Committee Report observed: "By creating a new category of protectable subject matter ... and, therefore, by deliberately not encompassing architectural works as pictorial, graphic, or sculptural works ... the copyrightability of architectural works shall not be

The House Committee Report accompanying the legislation contemplates a "two-step analysis":

> First, an architectural work should be examined to determine whether there are original design elements present, including overall shape and interior architecture. If such design elements are present, a second step is reached to examine whether the design elements are functionally required. If the design elements are not functionally required, the work is protectable without regard to physical or conceptual separability.[222]

The result is that, subject to the standards of originality applicable to all works, "the aesthetically pleasing overall shape of an architectural work" is protected.[223]

Protection for architectural works, however, is not quite as broad as that for other works. Thus, the architect retains no moral rights in the work and may not object to alteration or destruction of the structure.[224] Moreover, ownership of copyright in an architectural work embodied in a building "located in or ordinarily visible from a public place" does not prevent the making, distribution, or display of photographs or other pictorial representations of the work.[225]

F Sound Recordings

The Copyright Act recognizes "sound recordings" as a special class of works of authorship, distinct both from the works (musical or other sounds) of which the sound recordings are composed and from the physical form—"the phonorecords"—in which they are embodied. Sound recordings are defined as "works that result from the fixation of a series of musical, spoken, or other sounds [excluding the sounds accompanying audiovisual works] and regardless of the nature of the material objects ... in which they are embodied."[226]

The sound recording copyright is limited and highly specific: it is designed to protect a specific recorded performance of a work and provides a copyright in the performance of a work, independent of the copyright in the work being performed. Before 1972, federal copyright law did not protect sound recordings. Congress extended copyright protection to sound recordings in the Sound Recording Act of 1971,[227] and it did so only prospectively, thereby limiting the protection to sound recordings that were "fixed, published, and copyrighted" on or after February 15, 1972.[228] This

evaluated under the separability test applicable to pictorial, graphic, the sculptural works embodied in useful articles." H.R. Rep. No. 101-735 (1990), *as reprinted in* 1990 U.S.C.C.A.N. 6935, 6951.

222. H.R. Rep. No. 101-735 (1990), *as reprinted in* 1990 U.S.C.C.A.N. 6935, 6951.
223. *Id.*, at 6952. *See also Intervest Constr., Inc. v. Canterbury Estate Homes, Inc.*, 554 F.3d 914 (11th Cir. 2008).
224. 17 U.S.C. § 120(b).
225. 17 U.S.C. § 120(a).
226. 17 U.S.C. § 101.
227. Sound Recording Act of 1971, Pub. L. No. 92-140, 85 Stat. 391 (1971).
228. Until the Music Modernization Act in 2018, pre-1972 sound recordings were protected only under state law. For a discussion by the New York Court of Appeals of the history of the sound

legislation, directed at "record piracy"—the unauthorized commercial duplication of phonograph and other recordings—was incorporated into the 1976 Act with the recognition of "sound recordings" as works of authorship.[229] This legislation is consistent with the 1971 Geneva Convention for the Protection of Producers of Phonograms Against Unauthorized Duplication of Their Phonograms, which entered into force in the US in 1974. The owner of the sound recording copyright has the following exclusive rights: (1) to "duplicate the sound recording in the form of phonorecords or copies that directly or indirectly recapture the actual sounds fixed in the recording"; (2) to create derivative works "in which the actual sounds fixed in the sound recordings are rearranged, remixed, or otherwise altered in sequence or quality"; (3) to publicly distribute copies of the sound recording (for which purpose, internet uploading is considered a "distribution"); and (4) to publicly perform the sound recording "by means of a digital audio transmission."[230]

It has been suggested that "[t]he analysis that is appropriate for determining infringement of a musical composition copyright, is not the analysis that is to be applied to determine infringement of a sound recording."[231] This would mean that matters such as "substantial similarity"[232] and de minimis copying may not be appropriate to a sound recording infringement inquiry.

Inasmuch as a sound recording of a copyrighted musical work is a derivative work, the creator of such a sound recording who makes the recording without permission of the copyright owner of the musical work may not assert a copyright interest in that sound recording.[233] A sound recording copyright lacks a general public performance right. Except for the performance by "digital audio transmission," the sound recordings copyright does not give the rightsholder public performance rights with respect to the sound recordings.[234] In 1995, a limited performance right was created by the Digital Performance Right in Sound Recordings Act,[235] and then expanded in 1998 by the Digital Millennium Act. Digital audio transmissions are divided into three categories: (1) exempt transmissions made by FCC-licensed broadcast stations, (2) compulsory license transmissions made by noninteractive services,

recording copyright and "common law" copyright *see Capitol Records, Inc. v. Naxos of Am., Inc.*, 830 N.E.2d 250 (N.Y. 2005). To comply with US obligations under the Berne Convention, Congress, in 1994, provided retroactive federal copyright protection for pre-1972 sound recordings that were of foreign origin. 17 U.S.C. § 104A(h)(6)(ii).

229. 17 U.S.C. § 102(7).
230. 17 U.S.C. §§ 106, 114.
231. *Bridgeport Music, Inc. v. Dimension Films*, 410 F.3d 792, 798 (6th Cir. 2005).
232. *See infra* §9.III.A.
233. *Palladium Music, Inc. v. Eatsleepmusic, Inc.*, 398 F.3d 1193, 1200 (10th Cir. 2005) ("Palladium's sound recordings are derivative works, and its copyrights in the sound recordings are invalid and unenforceable because it has failed to obtain compulsory or consensual licenses from the copyright owners of the underlying musical compositions ....").
234. The exclusive right to perform a sound recording by means of a "digital audio transmission" granted by 17 U.S.C. § 106(6) is qualified by 17 U.S.C. § 114(d), which exempts certain types of digital audio transmissions and subjects others to a compulsory license.
235. Digital Performance Right in Sound Recordings Act of 1995, Pub. L. No. 104-39, 109 Stat. 336 (1995).

and (3) negotiated-license transmissions made by interactive services.[236] This legislation creating a limited performance right was essentially directed to those applications that could displace the market for the recordings, as opposed to those, such as over the air broadcast, which could enhance the market and promote sales of sound recordings. Terrestrial radio broadcasters have never paid sound recordings copyrights when they played them on the air, and these broadcasters continue to be exempt. The growth and proliferation of nonbroadcast radio and internet "streaming" services has expanded the importance of sound recordings' "limited" performance right.

With the rise of streaming services, stakeholders in the music industry pushed for copyright reform. In 2018, the Orrin G. Hatch-Bob Goodlatte Music Modernization Act (MMA) was signed into law.[237] The MMA consists of three separate Titles. Title I is the Musical Works Modernization Act,[238] which amends the licensing schema for "digital phonorecord delivery of a musical work, including in the form of a permanent download, limited download, or interactive stream."[239] With this new law, a blanket license is now available to digital music providers for the reproduction and distribution of songwriter's musical works. To administer this new compulsory license for digital downloads and reproductions of sound recordings that use songwriters' musical works, the Register of Copyrights may designate a "mechanical licensing collective" (MCL). This nonprofit collective will: (1) create and maintain a comprehensive database of musical works and their rightsholders; (2) collect royalties from digital music providers; and (3) then distribute those royalties to songwriters. Note that the law leaves intact the existing system for musical work performance licenses (e.g., American Society of Composers, Authors and Publishers (ASCAP), Broadcast Music, Inc. (BMI), and other performing rights organizations (PROs)). Under this law, interactive streaming services (e.g., Spotify) require mechanical licenses (to reproduce) and performance licenses (to publicly perform).[240] The MCL will offer a blanket license and ameliorate the transaction costs associated with obtaining mechanical licenses. However, interactive streaming services must still get a license to publicly perform the musical work (via a PRO) and negotiate a license to publicly perform the sound recording by means of digital audio transmission (under 17 U.S.C. § 114(d)(3)).

Title II is the Classics Protection and Access Act, which grants new federal rights in pre-1972 sound recordings.[241] Federal law now extends protection to sound recordings made prior to February 15, 1972 ("pre-1972 sound recordings") against their

236. 17 U.S.C. § 114(d).
237. The Orrin G. Hatch-Bob Goodlatte Music Modernization Act, Pub. L. No. 115-264 (2018).
238. Musical Works Modernization Act, Pub. L. No. 115-264, Title I, §§ 101–106, 132 Stat. 3676, 3676–28 (2018).
239. 17 U.S.C. §115(e)(7).
240. 17 U.S.C. § 115(e)(10). On the other hand, noninteractive services only require public performance licenses.
241. Classics Protection and Access Act, Pub. L. No. 115-264, Title II, §§ 201–202, 132 Stat. 3676, 3728–37 (2018). Protection for pre-1972 sound recordings is codified in a new Ch. 14 of the Copyright Act. As such, this law creates "quasi-copyright" or "neighboring rights" because the rights and remedies are parallel to—but are not identical to—other provisions in the Copyright Act. For example, criminal remedies are omitted from Ch. 14 and registration requirements

unauthorized public performance by means of digital audio transmissions.[242] This means platforms like SiriusXM and Pandora must now pay a sound recording performance license for pre-1972 sound recordings. Note that this new law does not implicate terrestrial radio broadcasts, which only needs a performance license for the musical composition (via a PRO).

Title III of the MMA is the Allocation for Music Producers Act, and it is directed to sound recording licensing. The law allocates a small portion (~ 2 %) of the proceeds from the compulsory license for digital public performance rights for sound recordings to producers, mixers, and sound engineers.[243]

G *Fictional Characters*

Fictional characters may be quite valuable. Merchandising rights, television production and advertising, and an array of commercial development may be based upon exploitation of fictional characters. Such exploitation may give rise to rights under the law of trademark or unfair competition. The position of fictional characters in the law of copyright, however, is not clear.

The Copyright Act does not expressly include "characters" within the umbrella of "works of authorship." Of course, the work in which a character appears will normally be within the subject matter of copyright. The problem arises when a "character" is used by one other than the copyright owner of that work in another work. One mode of analysis would be to ask whether such a taking of the character is an infringement of the work in which the character was first created.[244] The reality of the exploitation of characters, however, makes the question more difficult. It has, in short, become one of the protectability of the character as such apart from the setting in which it first appeared.

The issue is more academic than real when dealing with purely pictorial characters such as cartoons. Such works may easily be analyzed as "pictorial" works for determining copyrightability and infringement and their status as "characters" is not really significant.[245] However, with respect to literary characters and those taken from audiovisual works, the issue is not so easily resolved. The Second Circuit,

---

under §412 are modified. Important limitations and exceptions are included, like fair use (§107), library and archival use (§108), and the first sale doctrine (§109).

242. 17 U.S.C. § 1401. For sound recordings made between Jan. 1, 1923, and Feb. 15, 1972, performance rights are provided for a term of ninety-five years from the date of the recordings first publication. A sound recording is deemed first "published" when phonorecords of a work were first sold to the public.

243. 17 U.S.C. § 114(g).

244. David Nimmer, Nimmer on Copyright § 2.12[A][1] (2018) ("[T]he inquiry into the scope of copyright protection for a character from a work of fiction, along with the question whether infringement of that character has taken place, belong not to the current discussion of copyright's subject matter but, instead, to the inquiry into substantial similarity."). *See also* Leslie A. Kurtz, *The Independent Legal Lives of Fictional Characters*, 1986 Wis. L. Rev. 429 (1986); Elizabeth L. Rosenblatt, *The Adventure of the Shrinking Public Domain*, 86 U. Colo. L. Rev. 561 (2015).

245. *See*, e.g., *Walt Disney Prods. v. Air Pirates*, 581 F.2d 751 (9th Cir. 1978); *Detective Comics v. Bruns Publ'ns*, 111 F.2d 432 (2d Cir. 1940).

building on dicta of Judge Learned Hand,[246] has essentially assumed the copyrightability and protectability of characters as such to the extent that they are "developed."[247] The Ninth Circuit, however, began, in 1954, with the absolute position that characters as such are not copyrightable and will be protected only to the extent they "really constitute" the story of which they are a part.[248] Subsequent Ninth Circuit cases appeared to ameliorate the absolute rejection of independent copyrightability,[249] leaving the situation unclear,[250] but the more recent opinions of that court suggest that the gap between the circuits has been effectively bridged.[251]

With respect to continuing characters, when the work or works in which the character was created and developed fall into the public domain or otherwise lose copyright protection, use of the character in subsequent works will not be protected by copyright except to the extent that the newer use consists of more than trivial variations from the original character.[252] For example, modern authors, inspired by Arthur Conan Doyle's Sherlock Holmes character, are free to use material in Sherlock Holmes stories that are no longer under copyright, even though the author's ten last Sherlock Holmes stories remained under copyright protection.[253]

§3 CONDITIONS OF PROTECTION

I Formal Requirements

A *Fixation as the Point of Attachment of Copyright*

The 1976 Act effectively eliminated the earlier formal requirements for attachment of copyright, focusing instead on fixation of the work. Prior to January 1, 1978 (the effective date of the Copyright Act of 1976), the essential formal element for the attachment of copyright and invocation of the federal copyright scheme was "publication" of the work, with appropriate notice of copyright. Until publication, a work was protected by state law, the so-called common law copyright, and the act of publication terminated that protection. Upon such publication, a work would become protected by the federal scheme if publication was accompanied with appropriate notice; if not so accompanied, all protection would be lost, and the work would fall into the public

246. *Nichols v. Universal Pictures Corp.*, 45 F.2d 119 (2d Cir. 1930) ("[T]he less developed the characters, the less they can be copyrighted.").
247. *Silverman v. CBS Inc.*, 870 F.2d 40 (2d Cir. 1989).
248. *Warner Bros. Pictures v. Columbia Broad. Sys.*, 216 F.2d 945 (9th Cir. 1954).
249. *Olson v. National Broad. Co.*, 855 F.2d 1446 (9th Cir. 1988); *Walt Disney Prods. v. Air Pirates*, 581 F.2d 751 (9th Cir. 1978).
250. *See Rice v. Fox Broad. Co.*, 330 F.3d 1170 (9th Cir. 2003); *Anderson v. Stallone*, 11 U.S.P.Q.2d 1161 (C.D. Cal. 1989).
251. *See Halicki Films LLC v. Sanderson Sales & Mkt.*, 547 F.3d 1213 (9th Cir. 2008). In *Gaiman v. McFarlane*, 360 F.3d 644, 660 (7th Cir. 2004), Judge Richard Posner suggested that the Ninth Circuit "has killed" its 1954 decision.
252. *Klinger v. Conan Doyle Estate*, 755 F.3d 496 (7th Cir. 2014); *Silverman v. CBS Inc.*, 870 F.2d 40 (2d Cir. 1989).
253. *Klinger*, 755 F.3d at 496.

domain. This formal requirement of publication with proper notice produced a substantial judicial gloss on the definition of "publication"[254] and "notice."

One of the most significant changes effected by the 1976 revision was the elimination of common law copyright, with its distinction between published and unpublished works, and the concomitant formalities attendant to the attachment of copyright. Instead, copyright attaches, and protection begins, once an "original work of authorship" has been "fixed in any tangible medium of expression"[255] by or under the authority of the author. The nature of that medium is immaterial, so long as it is such that the work "can be perceived, reproduced, or otherwise communicated, either directly or with the aid of a machine or device"[256] and "is sufficiently permanent or stable to permit it to be perceived, reproduced, or otherwise communicated for a period of more than transitory duration."[257] Thus, assuming it meets the test of originality, and the fixation is done by or on behalf of the author, a work is "fixed" and copyright protection attaches, whether that fixation takes the form of a writing on paper, magnetic impulses on media such as audio or video tape, or a computer hard drive, or a floppy disk, or etching embedded in a silicon chip. With the constitutional grant of power to deal with copyright predicated upon the "writings" of "authors," the requirement of "fixation" in a tangible medium of expression would appear to be constitutionally mandated.[258] So, the requirement that the fixation be of "more than transitory duration" is a predicate to copyrightability.[259]

Unrecorded speech or live musical performances, or other ephemera, would not be considered fixed and therefore not subject to copyright protection. To deal with the problem of "bootleg" unauthorized recordings of live performances (performances, even of newly created work, which would not be considered "fixed" and would therefore involve works not protected by copyright), Congress enacted the Uruguay Round Agreements Act, signed in December 1994, implementing the GATT, which added a new section 1101, "Unauthorized Fixation and Trafficking in Sound Recordings and Music Videos." Section 1101 specifically protects against the unauthorized making and distribution of recordings of live performances.[260] Recognizing the difficulty this legislation poses as a proper exercise of Congress' constitutional power under

254. *See La Cienega Music Co. v. ZZ Top*, 53 F.3d 950 (9th Cir. 1995); *Rosette v. Rainbow Record Mfg. Corp.*, 546 F.2d 461 (2d Cir. 1976). The *La Cienega* decision, which held that public distribution of a recording was "publication" under the 1909 Act, was overruled by legislation in 1997 (17 U.S.C. § 303(b)), which now provides that "the distribution before Jan. 1, 1978, of a phonorecord shall not for any purpose constitute a publication of the musical work embodied therein." *Cf. Society Civile Succession Guino v. Renoir*, 549 F.3d 1182 (9th Cir. 2008) (holding that a pre-1976 Act publication without notice of a work *outside* of the United States would not place the work in the public domain in the United States) (reaffirming *Twin Books v. Walt Disney Co.*, 83 F.3d 1162 (9th Cir. 1996)).
255. "Copyright protection subsists ... in original works of authorship fixed in any tangible medium of expression." 17 U.S.C. § 102.
256. *Id.*
257. 17 U.S.C. § 101.
258. *See United States v. Moghadam*, 175 F.3d 1269, 1273–74 (11th Cir. 1999).
259. *See Cartoon Network LP, LLLP v. CSC Holdings, Inc.*, 536 F.3d 121 (2d Cir. 2008).
260. 17 U.S.C. § 1101. Section 1101(a) provides:

Article I, section 8 of the Constitution, which deals with "writings," the Eleventh Circuit upheld the statute as a proper exercise of the general congressional power to deal with matters affecting interstate commerce.[261] Although the Second Circuit came to the same ultimate conclusion, it left open questions relating to the proper exercise of congressional power.[262]

Similar protective legislation, largely for the benefit of organized sports, is contained in the definition of "fixed" in the Copyright Act, which treats as "fixed" for the purpose of attachment of copyright, works "consisting of sounds, images, or both, that are being transmitted ... if a fixation of the work is being made simultaneously with its transmission."[263] Thus, the live television broadcast of an athletic event would be subject to copyright protection as "fixed" if a simultaneous recording of that broadcast were made.[264]

B *Publication*

With the 1976 Act abolition of common law copyright, the defining role of "publication" also came to an end. Publication of a work is no longer required for copyright protection to attach. Of course, for works published before January 1, 1978, the rich judicial development elaborating upon what constitutes "publication" for the purpose of divesting copyright remains applicable. Moreover, publication may still have serious consequences under the Act. It can, for example, affect the duration of copyright and right of termination, as well as rights under the Berne Convention and Universal Copyright Convention. "Publication" is defined as:

> the distribution of copies or phonorecords of a work to the public by sale or other transfer of ownership, or by rental, lease, or lending. The offering to distribute copies or phonorecords to a group of persons for purposes of further distribution,

---

> Anyone who, without the consent of the performer or performers involved—(1) fixes the sounds or sounds and images of a live musical performance in a copy or phonorecord, or reproduces copies or phonorecords of such a performance from an unauthorized fixation, (2) transmits or otherwise communicates to the public the sounds or sounds and images of a live musical performance, or (3) distributes or offers to distribute, sells or offers to sell, rents or offers to rent, or traffics in any copy or phonorecord fixed as described in paragraph (1), regardless of whether the fixations occurred in the United States, shall be subject to the remedies provided in Sections 502 through 505, to the same extent as an infringer of copyright.

The legislation expressly does *not* preempt state law. 17 U.S.C. § 1101(d).

261. *United States v. Moghadam*, 175 F.3d 1269 (11th Cir. 1999).
262. *United States v. Martignon*, 492 F.3d 140 (2d Cir. 2007). For a discussion of the use of the "commerce clause" power where action would appear to be prohibited under the "copyright clause," *see* SHELDON W. HALPERN & PHILLIP JOHNSON, HARMONISING COPYRIGHT LAW AND DEALING WITH DISSONANCE: A FRAMEWORK FOR CONVERGENCE OF US AND EU LAW (2014).
263. 17 U.S.C. § 101.
264. *See, e.g., Nat'l Football League v. McBee & Bruno's, Inc.*, 792 F.2d 726 (8th Cir. 1986); *Baltimore Orioles, Inc. v. Major League Baseball Players Ass'n*, 805 F.2d 663 (7th Cir. 1986).

public performance, or public display, constitutes publication. A public performance or display of a work does not of itself constitute publication.[265]

Generally, the owner of copyright in a published work must, within three months after publication, deposit with the Library of Congress two copies of the "best edition" of the work.[266]

C Notice

While the Copyright Act contains numerous provisions concerning notice,[267] the shift from "publication" to "fixation" as the point of copyright attachment has minimized the formerly central importance of notice. The Act provides that notice of copyright "may" (rather than "shall") be placed on publicly distributed copies of a work.[268] Appropriate notice of copyright is still advisable and the better practice, but that formality no longer is determinative of the vesting of rights. Where there is proper notice, a claim of innocent infringement would generally not serve to mitigate damages.[269] The Act prescribes the form of notice: generally, the word "Copyright," or the abbreviation "Copr.," or the symbol "©"; the year of first publication; and designation of the copyright owner.[270]

Under the Act, defects in notice, or even omission of notice, no longer have the fatal impact they had under the prior law. Moreover, the Berne Convention Implementation Act of 1988 (effective March 1, 1989) substantially reduces, if not entirely eliminates, the consequences of failure to affix notice to a copyrighted work. Nevertheless, notice, or its omission, can be significant, particularly for certain works of US origin. Omission of notice can serve to insulate an innocent infringer, at least with respect to works publicly distributed prior to March 1, 1989. Such omission, from works distributed prior to March 1, 1989, if authorized by the copyright owner, can serve to forfeit copyright if the works were distributed in substantial copies and if no registration of copyright was made within five years of publication.[271]

Consistent with Berne Convention implementation, the Uruguay Round Agreements Act provides for restoration of copyright in certain foreign works which had become unprotected in the US (while remaining protected in their country of origin) because of failure to comply with formalities such as notice.[272] These provisions are quite elaborate, as they seek to protect the rights of innocent parties ("reliance parties") who had relied on the earlier public domain status of such works. The constitutionality of section 104A has been challenged, and while the D.C. Circuit simply upheld the

265. 17 U.S.C. § 101.
266. 17 U.S.C. § 407.
267. 17 U.S.C. §§ 401–12.
268. 17 U.S.C. § 401(a).
269. 17 U.S.C. § 401(d).
270. 17 U.S.C. § 401(b).
271. 17 U.S.C. § 405(a).
272. 17 U.S.C. § 104A.

constitutionality of the restoration provisions,[273] the Tenth Circuit initially held that, although section 104A is not inconsistent with the constitutional limitations on congressional power, by removing material from the public domain it "has altered the traditional contours of copyright protection and requires First Amendment scrutiny."[274] The Tenth Circuit, reversing a district court determination on remand that the statute was not "narrowly tailored,"[275] upheld the statute's constitutionality.[276] The US Supreme Court ultimately affirmed the Tenth Circuit determination that the provision is constitutionally permissible.[277]

D *Registration and Deposit*

1 *Registration*

Under the Act, the Copyright Office, a division of the Library of Congress, administers the copyright registration and deposit system. Registration of copyright in a work, accompanied by deposit of copies of the work, provides a central place for the recording, and constructive notice of the copyright interest in the work. It also ensures that copies of the work will be publicly accessible. Except with respect to renewal of copyright term for certain pre-1976 Act works,[278] registration is permissive and does not affect the existence or vesting of copyright.[279] Nonetheless, registration remains an important procedure, with important consequences for the copyright owner.

What is the requisite level of knowledge to invalidate a copyright registration? In *Unicolors, Inc. v. H&M Hennes & Mauritz, L.P.*, the Supreme Court held that lack of either factual or legal knowledge can excuse an inaccuracy in a copyright registration under the Act's safe harbor provision.[280] Unicolors filed a single application to register thirty-one separate works for various fabric designs; however, a single application may cover multiple works only if the works were included in the same unit of publication. Unicolors sued H&M for infringement based on its copyright registration, yet its application failed to satisfy the "single unit of publication" requirement. The question was whether the safe harbor provision excuses only good faith mistakes of facts, but not law. The Copyright Act's safe harbor[281] says a certificate of registration is valid regardless of whether it contains inaccurate information, unless the inaccurate information was included "with knowledge that it was inaccurate." The statutory language makes no distinction between lack of legal knowledge or lack of factual knowledge.

273. *Luck's Music Library v. Gonzalez*, 407 F.3d 1262 (D.C. Cir. 2005).
274. *Golan v. Gonzalez*, 501 F.3d 1179 (10th Cir. 2007).
275. *Golan v. Holder*, 611 F. Supp. 2d 1165 (D. Col. 2009).
276. *Golan v. Holder*, 609 F.3d 1076 (10th Cir. 2010).
277. *Golan v. Holder*, 565 U.S. 302 (2012).
278. *See infra* §8, for discussion of renewal for pre-1976 Act works.
279. 17 U.S.C. § 408(a). *See also Neri v. Monroe*, 726 F.3d 989, 991 (7th Cir. 2013) ("Registration is required for litigation but not for the existence of copyright. This implies that registration serves a record-keeping function.").
280. *Unicolors, Inc. v. H&M Hennes & Mauritz, L.P.*, 595 U.S. 178 (2022).
281. 17 U.S.C. § 411(b)(1)(A).

Thus, the Supreme Court determined lower court erred in holding that a copyright holder cannot benefit from the safe harbor if its lack of knowledge stems from a failure to understand the law.[282] Therefore, inadvertent mistakes on registration certificates—which may involve mistakes of law or of fact—neither invalidate copyright registrations nor disallow infringement actions.

2 *Registration Procedure*

Registration is accomplished by filing with the Copyright Office a completed official application form, together with payment of a rather modest fee and deposit of copies of the work.[283] Registration will be effective as of the date of receipt by the Copyright Office, irrespective of the length of time for processing the application. The completed application is examined, in a process much less extensive and time-consuming than in the case of a patent application, and a certificate of registration is issued by the Register of Copyright, unless registration is denied because of infirmity in the process or because the work does not properly come within the subject matter of copyright. The vast majority of registration applications are granted; under a "rule of doubt," registration will issue as long as there is at least a reasonable doubt in favor of copyrightability. Action by the Register of Copyright denying registration is appealable to the federal courts.

3 *Benefits*

Registration, while not mandatory for the attachment of copyright to a work, is a prerequisite to the institution of actions for infringement[284] of a "United States work."[285] The limitation to a "United States work" is designed to keep the US copyright

282. *Unicolors, Inc.*, 595 U.S. at 188-89.
283. 17 U.S.C. §§ 408–09. Deposit of copies with the Library of Congress pursuant to 17 U.S.C. § 407 will satisfy the registration deposit requirement.
284. Other than claims for violation of the attribution and integrity rights of works of visual art protected by § 106A. *See infra* §6.VII.B.
285. 17 U.S.C. § 411. For the purposes of § 411, a work is a "United States work" only if:

> 1. in the case of a published work, the work is first published—
>   a. in the United States;
>   b. simultaneously in the United States and another treaty party or parties, whose law grants a term of copyright protection that is the same as or longer than the term provided in the United States;
>   c. simultaneously in the United States and a foreign nation that is not a treaty party; or
>   d. in a foreign nation that is not a treaty party, and all of the authors of the work are nationals, domiciliaries, or habitual residents of, or in the case of an audiovisual work legal entities with headquarters in, the United States;
> 2. in the case of an unpublished work, all the authors of the work are nationals, domiciliaries, or habitual residents of the United States, or, in the case of an unpublished audiovisual work, all the authors are legal entities with headquarters in the United States; or
> 3. in the case of a pictorial, graphic, or sculptural work incorporated in a building or structure, the building or structure is located in the United States.

laws consistent with the Berne Convention and other treaty prohibitions on conditioning protection for foreign authors upon compliance with domestic formalities. Resolving the existing circuit split as to whether registration is a jurisdictional matter, affecting the ability of a court to entertain an action if any of the matters at issue concern works not registered, the US Supreme Court has held that the Copyright Act registration requirement is procedural, and not "jurisdictional."[286] The Supreme Court also clarified that registration occurs—for the purposes of commencing an infringement suit—when the Copyright Office registers a copyright, not merely when the claimant submits the application.[287] Resolving a circuit split, the Supreme Court unanimously held that section 411 requires a final action by the Copyright Office—either an issued registration or a formal denial—before an infringement suit may be filed.[288]

If proper application for registration has been made and refused, the applicant may nevertheless institute an action for infringement if notice of such action, together with a copy of the complaint, is served on the Register of Copyrights:[289]

> [S]ection 411(a) is explicit that an applicant refused registration may still sue for infringement ... But the applicant must notify the Register of Copyrights .... The notification requirement is undemanding: the complaint must merely be sent by registered or certified mail to the general counsel of the Copyright Office .... The requirement "merely provides that the Office must be accorded a second opportunity to express its views on the claim's validity after suit is filed if it has refused to recognize the claim before the suit is filed. Of course, the court is not bound by the views expressed by the Register in a case in which suit is filed despite his refusal to register the claim."[290]

Under the "effective registration" doctrine, "the registration of a derivative work satisfies the registration requirement for all aspects of the registered work, even the aspects copied from an unregistered preexisting work, so long as the owner of both

---

17 U.S.C. § 101. A "treaty party" is a country or intergovernmental organization other than the United States that is a party to the Universal Copyright Convention, the Geneva Phonograms Convention, the Berne Convention, the WTO Agreement, the WIPO Copyright Treaty, the WIPO Performances and Phonograms Treaty, and any other copyright treaty to which the United States is a party (definitions of "treaty party" and "international agreement"). *Id.*

286. *Reed Elsevier, Inc. v. Muchnick*, 559 U.S. 154 (2010), *rev'g*, *In re* Literary Works in Elec. Databases Copyright Litig., 509 F.3d 116 (2d Cir. 2007). *See Brooks-Ngwenya v. Indianapolis Public Sch.*, 564 F.3d 804 (7th Cir. 2009) ("Even though nonjurisdictional, the notification requirement is a prerequisite to suit. Congress wanted to ensure that the Copyright Office could intervene and defend its refusal to register a work."); *see also Perfect 10, Inc. v. Amazon.com, Inc.* 508 F.3d 1146 (9th Cir. 2007) ("Once a court has jurisdiction over an action for copyright infringement under section 411, the court may grant injunctive relief to restrain infringement of any copyright, whether registered or unregistered.").

287. *Fourth Estate Pub. Benefit Corp. v. Wall-Street.com, LLC*, 139 S. Ct. 881 (2019). Note that the registration requirement in § 411 applies only to a "United States work." Infringement suits for works that are not defined as a "United States work" do not have a registration prerequisite.

288. *Fourth Estate Pub. Benefit Corp. v. Wall-Street.com, LLC*, 139 S. Ct. 881 (2019). The Supreme Court also clarified that upon registration, a copyright owner may recover for infringement that occurred both before and after registration.

289. 17 U.S.C. § 411.

290. *Brooks-Ngwenya, v. Indianapolis Public Sch.*, 564 F.3d 804 (7th Cir. 2009).

copyrights is the same."[291] However, such "effective registration" cannot constructively register aspects of the underlying work that are not part of the registered derivative work.

Moreover, in an action for infringement, registration provides procedural and remedial advantages, unavailable for unregistered works, even works for which registration is not a prerequisite to suit. If the work was registered within five years after first publication, the certificate of registration is prima facie evidence of the validity of the copyright and of the facts stated in the certificate.[292] Further, registration can have a significant influence on damages in an infringement action. The successful plaintiff may recover statutory damages and attorneys' fees if registration preceded the acts of infringement. On the other hand: (1) if the infringement preceded registration of an unpublished work or (2) if the infringement began after first publication and before registration, a successful plaintiff may recover statutory damages and attorneys' fees if registration is made within three months after first publication.[293]

4 *Recordation and Registration*

Registration is also significant, and in fact essential, with respect to protecting rights of transferees or holders of security interests in a work. Thus, while the Act contains provisions for recording, in the Copyright Office, of documents relating to transfers of copyright ownership or the granting of any other interest in a copyrighted work, with recordation serving as constructive notice of the facts stated in the recorded document,[294] such recordation will be effective only if the work to which it relates has been registered.[295] Proper recordation in the Copyright Office of a security interest in a work is a necessary condition to the establishment of a priority for that interest, irrespective of any filings that may be made under state law.[296] Such recordation, and concomitant priority, however, is possible only if the underlying work has been registered. There is some uncertainty as to the determination of priorities of interests in unregistered works.

5 *Deposit*

As noted above, in the case of works published in the US, with notice of copyright, two copies or phonorecords of the work must be deposited for use by the Library of Congress and failure to make such deposit can invoke a series of fines. Proper deposit for the Library of Congress will satisfy the deposit requirements for registration (which, in fact, require only one copy). The requirement of section 408(b) that a "complete

291. *Oravec v. Sunny Isles Luxury Ventures, L.C.*, 527 F.3d 1218 (11th Cir. 2008).
292. 17 U.S.C. § 410(c).
293. 17 U.S.C. § 412.
294. 17 U.S.C. § 205(a)-(c).
295. 17 U.S.C. § 205(c)(2).
296. 17 U.S.C. § 205(d). *See Nat'l Peregrine, Inc. v. Capitol Fed. Sav. & Loan Ass'n of Denver*, 116 B.R. 194 (D.C. Cal. 1990).

copy" of the work be deposited as part of the registration process is not satisfied by the furnishing of a "reconstructed" version of the work; "reconstruction, created without first-hand access to the original, cannot constitute a 'copy' sufficient to satisfy the deposit copy requirement."[297] The effect of such ineffective deposit is to invalidate any resulting registration, with the consequent loss of subject matter jurisdiction, precluding maintenance of an infringement action.

E *Domestic Manufacture*

The 1976 Act carried forward, albeit with some modification, provisions of the earlier law requiring that English language books or periodicals, and foreign language books written by American authors, be manufactured in the US. The 1976 Act provisions, while less inclusive and less draconian, nevertheless prohibited, until July 1, 1986, importation and/or public distribution in the US "of copies of a work consisting primarily of nondramatic literary material that is in the English language ... unless the portions consisting of such material have been manufactured in the United States or Canada."[298] There are a number of exceptions to this requirement, and noncompliance did not result in forfeiture of copyright.[299] What is most significant, however, is the fact that, by its terms, this prohibition on importation and distribution expired on July 1, 1986.

II Substantive Requirements: "Writings" of "Authors" Consisting of "Original Expression"

A *"Authors" and Their "Writings"*

To be protected under the Copyright Act, a work must be a "writing" of an "author." The interpretation of these constitutionally required terms is crucial to the development of the law. Beginning with the 1884 US Supreme Court opinion in *Burrow-Giles Lithographic Co. v. Sarony*,[300] holding that a photographer may be an "author" whose photograph is a "writing," there has been a consistent expansive interpretation of these terms. With the Supreme Court's defining statement that "[a]n 'author' is one to whom anything owes its origin," it has readily been accepted that not only "authors" in the traditional sense but also artists, sculptors, composers, photographers, and other expressive creators are "authors," whose works, if appropriately fixed, are "writings" in the sense constitutionally required for protection. As the House Committee Report in connection with the 1976 Act notes: "The history of copyright law has been one of gradual expansion in the types of work accorded protection ...." Nevertheless,

297. *Torres-Negron v. J & N Records, LLC*, 504 F.3d 151 (1st Cir. 2007).
298. 17 U.S.C. § 601(a).
299. 17 U.S.C. § 601(b)–(d).
300. *Burrow-Giles Lithographic Co. v. Sarony*, 111 U.S. 53 (1884).

however broadly defined, there must be a "writing" as a predicate to protection; thus an arrangement of growing flowers, even if "original," cannot be a protected "writing":

> We fully accept that the artistic community might classify Kelley's garden as a work of postmodern conceptual art. We acknowledge as well that copyright's prerequisites of authorship and fixation are broadly defined. But the law must have some limits; not all conceptual art may be copyrighted. In the ordinary copyright case, authorship and fixation are not contested; most works presented for copyright are unambiguously authored and unambiguously fixed. But this is not an ordinary case. A living garden like Wildflower Works is neither "authored" nor "fixed" in the senses required for copyright ....
>
> Simply put, gardens are planted and cultivated, not authored. A garden's constituent elements are alive and inherently changeable, not fixed. Most of what we see and experience in a garden—the colors, shapes, textures, and scents of the plants—originates in nature, not in the mind of the gardener.[301]

This expansion has taken the form of both direct congressional action to include certain types of expression as works of authorship (e.g., photographs, motion pictures, choreography, architectural works, etc.) and judicial recognition that new forms of creative expression are simply extensions of already recognized copyrightable subject matter. Recognizing that "authors are continually finding new ways of expressing themselves, but it is impossible to foresee the forms that these new expressive methods will take," the House Report makes clear that the new Act was not intended "either to freeze the scope of copyrightable technology or to allow unlimited expansion into areas completely outside the present congressional intent."

Presumably, "author" infers the existence of a human creative force, rather than mechanical or other nonhuman generation of a work.[302] Referring to the question of "authorship" of computer-generated works, the CONTU Report noted: "the eligibility of any work for protection by copyright depends not upon the device or devices used in its creation, but rather upon the presence of at least minimal human creative effort at the time the work is produced."[303]

Generally, the author of a work is not simply the person who mechanically fixes it, but the intellectual creator of the subject matter.[304] There are situations, of course, such as the work-for-hire context, in which the "author" for copyright purposes is a corporate entity, but the generative force is still human.[305]

301. *Kelley v. Chicago Park Dist.*, 635 F.3d 290 (7th Cir. 2011).

302. *Id.*, at 304; ("[A]uthorship is an entirely human endeavor. Authors of copyrightable works must be human; works owing their form to the forces of nature cannot be copyrighted."); *cf. Urantia Found. v. Maaherra*, 114 F.3d 955, 957–59 (9th Cir. 1997) (concluding that while "[b]oth parties believe that the words in the [book at issue] were 'authored' by nonhuman spiritual beings," the work was nevertheless held copyrightable because the human intervention by the producers of the book in selecting and arranging these nonhuman revelations was not so "mechanical or routine" as to preclude the creativity threshold).

303. National Commission on New Technological Uses of Copyrighted Works, Final Report 45 (1979).

304. *See Andrien v. Southern Ocean Cnty., Chamber of Commerce*, 927 F.2d 132 (3d Cir. 1991).

305. *See Naruto v. Slater*, No. 15-cv-04324, 2016 WL 362231, at *1 (N.D. Cal. Jan. 28, 2016) (denying a macaque monkey authorship rights in a selfie photograph "[b]ecause the Copyright Act does not confer standing upon animals like Naruto"), *aff'd* 888 F.3d 418 (9th Cir. 2018).

B *Artificial Intelligence and Authorship*

The Copyright Office's Compendium clarifies that "the Office will not register works produced by a machine or mere mechanical process that operates randomly or automatically without any creative input or intervention from a human author."[306] Indeed, the Office rejected applications for two-dimensional artwork "autonomously created by a computer algorithm running on a machine."[307] While the Office is clear that human authorship is required, there still remain open questions around the use of generative AI.[308] To that end, the Office has undertaken a study of the law and policy implications raised by AI systems.[309] In particular, the Office has sought comment on the use of copyrighted works to train AI models, the appropriate levels of transparency and disclosure with respect to the use of copyrighted works, and the legal status of AI-generated outputs.[310]

C *Original Expression*

1 *Generally*

In *Feist Publications, Inc. v. Rural Telephone Service Co., Inc.*,[311] the US Supreme Court made clear that "the sine qua non of copyright is originality," and that originality is a constitutional prerequisite to copyrightability.[312] Such "originality" embodies both the concept of independent origin and a minimal level of creativity, some modest amount of intellectual labor. Justice Sandra Day O'Connor observed that original "means only that the work was independently created by the author (as opposed to copied from other works), and that it possesses at least some minimal degree of creativity."[313] The

306. Compendium of the U.S. Copyright Office Practices, § 313.2 (3d ed. 2021) ("The crucial question is whether the 'work' is basically one of human authorship, with the computer [or other device] merely being an assisting instrument, or whether the traditional elements of authorship in the work (literary, artistic, or musical expression or elements of selection, arrangement, etc.) were actually conceived and executed not by man but by a machine.").
307. Copyright Review Board, Re: Second Request for Reconsideration for Refusal to Register A Recent Entrance to Paradise (Correspondence ID 1-3ZPC6C3; SR # 1-7100387071) (Feb. 14, 2022), *available at* https://www.copyright.gov/rulings-filings/review-board/docs/a-recent-entrance-to-paradise.pdf; Copyright Review Board, Re: Second Request for Reconsideration for Refusal to Register SURYAST (SR # 1-11016599571; Correspondence ID: 1-5PR2XKJ) (Dec. 11, 2023), *available at*, https://copyright.gov/rulings-filings/review-board/docs/SURYAST.pdf. *See also Thaler v. Perlmutter*, No. CV 22-1564 (BAH), 2023 WL 5333236 (D.D.C. Aug. 18, 2023) (upholding decision to deny copyright application to register a piece of visual art generated by an artificial intelligence (AI) computer system).
308. Congressional Research Service, *Generative Artificial Intelligence and Copyright Law*, Sept. 29, 2023, https://crsreports.congress.gov/product/pdf/LSB/LSB10922.
309. U.S. Copyright Office, *Copyright and Artificial Intelligence*, https://www.copyright.gov/ai/.
310. A Notice by the Copyright Office, *Artificial Intelligence and Copyright*, https://www.federalregister.gov/documents/2023/08/30/2023-18624/artificial-intelligence-and-copyright.
311. *Feist Publ'ns, Inc. v. Rural Tel. Serv. Co.*, 499 U.S. 340, 348 (1991).
312. *Id.*, at 348.
313. *Id.*

constitutional requirement of originality, therefore, carries within it a further requirement of "creativity."[314] However, as Feist Court further noted, "the requisite level of creativity is extremely low; even a slight amount will suffice."[315]

On the other hand, the fact that a work as a whole meets the originality/creativity standard and is therefore subject to protection does not serve to extend copyright protection to everything contained in that work. Rather, copyright protection will extend only to those portions of the work which are considered original expression.[316]

Underlying the determination whether a work purporting to be original expression is copyrightable is the principle of nondiscrimination; that is, esthetic or artistic judgments as to the inherent worth or cultural value are to be avoided. A work that is original, creative expression, otherwise eligible for copyright protection, will not be denied such protection because it may have been created for commercial purposes, or as an advertisement, or may be considered pedestrian or lacking in esthetic value.[317] "Any original literary work may be copyrighted. The necessary degree of 'originality' is low, and the work need not be aesthetically pleasing to be 'literary'."[318]

The House Report to the 1976 Act expressed the congressional intention to follow the existing case law for the originality standard. Courts were clear that there were only minimal standards of originality and creativity, such that "[t]he least pretentious picture"[319] could meet it. As the House Report noted, "[t]he phrase 'original works of authorship,' which is purposely left undefined, is intended to incorporate without change the standard of originality established by the courts under the present [1909] copyright statute. This standard does not include requirements of novelty, ingenuity, or esthetic merit, and there is no intention to enlarge the standard of copyright protection to require them."[320] And since there is no requirement of "novelty," separate copyrights exist in independently created works, even if the works, on close examination, are identical.[321]

---

314. *See Baltimore Orioles, Inc. v. Major League Baseball Players Ass'n*, 805 F.2d 663, 668, n.6 (7th Cir. 1986) ("The requirement of originality actually subsumes two separate conditions, i.e., the work must possess an independent origin and a minimal amount of creativity .... A work is original if it is the independent creation of its author .... A work is creative if it embodies some modest amount of intellectual labor.").
315. *See Atari Games v. Oman*, 979 F.2d 242 (D.C. Cir. 1992) (reversing denial of registration of a simple geometric "paddle" video game). Judge (subsequently Justice) Ruth Bader Ginsburg emphasized how minimal the creativity standard is: "We are mindful ... of the teaching of *Feist* that '[t]he vast majority of works make the [copyright] grade quite easily'." *Id.*, at 247.
316. *See Boisson v. Banian, Ltd.*, 273 F.3d 262, 266 (2d Cir. 2001) ("Plaintiffs must also demonstrate 'substantial similarity' between defendants' [works] and the *protectable* elements of their own [works].") (emphasis in original).
317. *Bleistein v. Donaldson Lithographing Co.*, 188 U.S. 239, 251 (1903) (famously noting that "it would be a dangerous undertaking for persons trained only to the law to constitute themselves final judge of the worth of pictorial illustrations, outside of the narrowest and most obvious limits"); *see also Mazer v. Stein*, 347 U.S. 201 (1954).
318. *Am. Dental Ass'n v. Delta Dental Plans Ass'n*, 126 F.3d 977, 979 (7th Cir. 1997) (holding that a taxonomy of dental procedures was copyrightable). *But see ATC Distrib. Grp., Inc. v. Whatever it Takes Transmissions & Parts, Inc.*, 402 F.3d 700 (6th Cir. 2005) (holding that catalog of automobile parts was not copyrightable).
319. *Bleistein v. Donaldson Lithographing Co.*, 188 U.S. 239, 250 (1903).
320. H.R. Rep. No. 94-1476, at 51 (1976), *as reprinted in* 1976 U.S.C.C.A.N. 5659, 5664.
321. *Mag Jewelry Co., Inc. v. Cherokee, Inc.*, 496 F.3d 108 (1st Cir. 2007).

It is now generally accepted that virtually all but the most mechanical photographs contain sufficient originality and creativity for copyright protection.[322] So too, there is sufficient originality/creativity in the decisions as to camera placement, choice of shots, and the like in creating the television broadcast of an athletic event to make that broadcast copyrightable.[323]

It is clear, of course, that copyright in an image—a pictorial representation meeting standards of originality—does not confer any rights with respect to the subject as such. As Justice Oliver Wendell Holmes said in Bleistein, "Others are free to copy the original. They are not free to copy the copy. The copy is the personal reaction of the individual upon nature."[324] One may generally take a photograph of the same scene that is the subject of another's photograph, without infringing the rights of the first photographer. However, the deliberate recreation of a scene depicted by another, as opposed to portraying the same general subject matter, may constitute an infringing "copy" of the "copy."[325]

2 *Originality in Derivative Works*

The above words of Justice Holmes have proven troublesome, if not cryptic, in dealing with the issue of the originality standard for derivative works. That is, where one creates a derivative work, a work based upon a preexisting work, what quantum of originality is necessary for that derivative work itself to be protected? The issue arises usually where the derivative work is based upon a work in the public domain, or is one created with the consent of the copyright owner of the underlying work. As the Seventh Circuit explained, "The requirement of originality is significant chiefly in connection with derivative works, where if interpreted too liberally it would paradoxically inhibit rather than promote the creation of such works by giving the first creator considerable power to interfere with the creation of subsequent derivative works from the same underlying work."[326]

Consequently, more is required in the case of derivative works than other works to meet the low originality threshold;[327] there must be substantial difference or more than a trivial variation between the underlying work and the derivative work.[328] Effort

322. *See Burrow-Giles Lithographic Co. v. Sarony*, 111 U.S. 53 (1884); *Meshwerks, Inc. v. Toyota Motor Sales U.S.A., Inc.*, 528 F.3d 1258 (10th Cir. 2008); *Ets-Hokin v. Skyy Spirits, Inc.*, 225 F.3d 1068 (9th Cir. 2000); *Time, Inc. v. Bernard Geis Assocs.*, 293 F. Supp. 130 (S.D.N.Y. 1968).
323. *Baltimore Orioles, Inc. v. Major League Baseball Players Ass'n*, 805 F.2d 663 (7th Cir. 1986).
324. *Bleistein v. Donaldson Lithographing Co.*, 188 U.S. 239, 249–50 (1903).
325. *See Leibovitz v. Paramount Pictures Corp.*, 137 F.3d 109 (2d Cir. 1998); *Gross v. Seligman*, 212 F. 930 (2d Cir. 1914); *Kisch v. Ammirati & Puris Inc.*, 657 F. Supp. 380 (S.D.N.Y. 1987).
326. *Gracen v. Bradford Exch.*, 698 F.2d 300 (7th Cir. 1983).
327. *See, e.g.*, *Entm't Research Grp., Inc. v. Genesis Creative Grp., Inc.*, 122 F.3d 1211, 1218–19 (9th Cir. 1997) ("[T]the copyright protection afforded to derivative works is more limited than it is for original works of authorship.").
328. *Meshwerks, Inc. v. Toyota Motor Sales U.S.A., Inc.*, 528 F.3d 1258 (10th Cir. 2008); *Gracen v. Bradford Exch.*, 698 F.2d 300 (7th Cir. 1983); *L. Batlin & Son, Inc. v. Snyder*, 536 F.2d 486 (2d Cir. 1976); *Durham Indus., Inc. v. Tomy Corp.*, 630 F.2d 905 (2d Cir. 1980); *Hearn v. Meyer*, 664 F. Supp. 832 (S.D.N.Y. 1987). *See also U.S. Auto Parts Network, Inc. v. Parts Geek, LLC*, 692 F.3d

alone, however sophisticated or intensive, in reproducing an earlier work, appears no longer to be sufficient to create a copyrightable derivative work.[329] For a work based on preexisting works to be protected, it must contribute "a distinguishable variation from the older works [which] variation must be substantial and not merely trivial."[330] Further, the original aspects of a derivative work must reflect the degree to which it relies on preexisting material and must not in any way affect the scope of any copyright protection in that preexisting material.[331] Thus, the Copyright Office will allow registration as derivative works of "colorized" versions of black and white films if the colorization constitutes more than a trivial variation with respect to the underlying work. In contrast, a wooden version of the traditional paper doll has been held to be an unprotectable idea rather than a copyrightable derivative work,[332] and the extraordinarily exact digital reproduction of public domain art has been held to be unprotectable as a derivative work, notwithstanding its technological advance, because of its slavish "copying."[333]

As noted above, in connection with sound recordings, in general, one who creates a derivative work without the consent of the copyright owner of the underlying work is an infringer and may not assert rights in the derivative work, irrespective of how "creative" that work may be.[334]

§4 OWNERSHIP

I Ownership of Copyright Versus Ownership of the Material Object

Ownership of copyright in a work must be distinguished from ownership of the physical object in which the work is embodied. One who writes a poem in a letter mailed to another continues to own the copyright in the poem, while the recipient of the letter owns the physical object, the piece of paper on which the poem was written. Thus, mailing the letter neither divests the author of the copyright interest in the poem

1009, 1016 (9th Cir. 2012) ("We have adopted the Second Circuit's test for ascertaining whether a derivative work meets copyright law's fundamental requirement of originality.").

329. *See L. Batlin & Son, Inc. v. Snyder*, 536 F.2d 486 (2d Cir. 1976); *The Bridgeman Art Library, Ltd. v. Corel Corp.*, 36 F. Supp. 2d 191 (S.D.N.Y. 1999). The cases, beginning with *Batlin*, appear to have overruled earlier, less demanding cases such as *Alfred Bell & Co. v. Catalda Fine Arts*, 191 F.2d 99 (2d Cir. 1951).
330. *Norma Ribbon & Trimming, Inc. v. Little*, 51 F.3d 45, 47 (5th Cir. 1995); *accord Entm't Research Grp., Inc. v. Genesis Creative Grp., Inc.*, 122 F.3d 1211 (9th Cir. 1997).
331. *Durham Indus., Inc. v. Tomy Corp.*, 630 F.2d 905, 909 (2d Cir. 1980), cited with approval in *Entm't Research Grp., Inc. v. Genesis Creative Grp., Inc.*, 122 F.3d 1211, 1217 (9th Cir. 1997).
332. *Country Kids 'N City Slicks, Inc. v. Sheen*, 77 F.3d 1280 (10th Cir. 1996).
333. *Bridgeman Art Library, Ltd. v. Corel Corp.*, 36 F. Supp. 2d 191 (S.D.N.Y. 1999).
334. *See, e.g.*, *Mulcahy v. Cheetah Learning, LLC*, 386 F.3d 849 (8th Cir. 2004) ("because the owner of the original copyright has the exclusive right to prepare derivative works, the creator of an original derivative work is only entitled to a copyright if she had permission to use the underlying copyrighted work").

nor invests the recipient with such interest.[335] This principle of separation is codified in the 1976 Act:

> §202 Ownership of copyright as distinct from ownership of material object
>
> Ownership of a copyright, or of any of the exclusive rights under a copyright, is distinct from ownership of any material object in which the work is embodied. Transfer of ownership of any material object, including the copy or phonorecord in which the work is first fixed, does not of itself convey any rights in the copyrighted work embodied in the object; nor, in the absence of an agreement, does transfer of ownership of a copyright or of any exclusive rights under a copyright convey property rights in any material object.[336]

II Divisibility

The owner of copyright in a work possesses a right that is virtually infinitely divisible. That is, "copyright" should really be considered "copyrights," as the copyright interest really consists of an array, or bundle, of separate exclusive rights, each of which may be owned separately, transferred, and further subdivided. The divisibility of copyright interests is expressly recognized by the 1976 Act:

> Any of the exclusive rights comprising copyright, including any subdivision of any of the rights ..., may be transferred ... and owned separately. The owner of any particular exclusive right is entitled, to the extent of that right, to all of the protection and remedies accorded to the copyright owner.[337]

Thus, an assignee of the right to reproduce a work is the "owner" of the work to the extent of that right and may maintain an action for infringement of that right. For these purposes, an exclusive license (but not a nonexclusive license) is equivalent to an assignment.[338]

III Authorship

Copyright "vests initially in the author or authors of the work."[339] Authorship is the central concept for the creation of a copyright interest. However, while vesting initial rights in the "author" of a work, the Act itself does not define the term. Rather,

335. *See, e.g., Salinger v. Random House, Inc.*, 811 F.2d 90 (2d Cir. 1987). This principle was illustrated in the unexpected context of a tax case. In *Norwest Corp v. Commissioner*, 108 T.C. No. 18, 1997 WL 211303 (U.S. Tax Ct. 1997), a divided panel of the Tax Court held that computer software acquired by a company for use in its business is tangible personal property eligible for the investment tax credit, rather than intangible property, so long as the company acquired the software without acquiring any copyright or other intangible property rights in it.
336. 17 U.S.C. § 202.
337. 17 U.S.C. § 201(d)(2).
338. *See infra* §5.I, §9.I.D.
339. 17 U.S.C. § 201(a).

ownership issues begin with the proposition, as noted above, that an "author" is one to whom anything owes its origin.[340]

The author, as the one in whom copyright initially vests, is possessed of all the rights of a copyright owner, and therefore may license or transfer all or any of these rights (except for moral rights under the Visual Artists Rights Act (VARA), section 106A) and terminate such transfer or other grants.[341] Similarly, it is the nature of the author (e.g., identified individual, joint author, employer of an employee for hire, or anonymous creator) that will determine the duration of the copyright term, as well as rights of renewal in connection with pre-1976 Act works.[342]

IV Joint Works/Multiple Authorship

Joint authorship issues arise when a single work is purportedly created by more than one individual. The property interests in such a work are analogous to the interests in other jointly held property.[343] The first inquiry is definitional, determining if a given work is a "joint" work, as distinct from a work in which each participant has his or her own, severable copyright interest. The consequences of the appropriate definition are quite serious. For example, the term of copyright for a joint work is generally measured by the life of the last surviving joint author.[344] Of greater significance is the fact that the "authors of a joint work are co-owners of copyright in the work."[345] As such, each joint author, with an undivided interest in the whole, can deal with the work, or grant nonexclusive license rights to it or exploit it, without the consent of the other joint authors, subject to a duty to account for profits realized upon any such dealing or exploitation.[346] In short, and subject to a duty to account, each joint owner of a work may exercise all the rights of a copyright owner with respect to that work, except only the right to transfer, by assignment or exclusive license, all or any of the exclusive rights to the work. Importantly, one co-owner cannot grant an exclusive license to use a work without the consent of the other co-owners because one co-owner cannot limit the other co-owners' right to exploit the copyright.[347]

The 1976 Act defines a "joint work" as "a work prepared by two or more authors with the intention that their contributions be merged into inseparable or interdependent parts of a unitary whole."[348] The earlier copyright act did not expressly define joint

340. *Burrow-Giles Lithographic Co. v. Sarony*, 111 U.S. 53, 57–58 (1884).
341. *See infra* §5.
342. *See infra* §8.
343. *Davis v. Blige*, 505 F.3d 90 (2d Cir. 2007) (discussing the rights of coauthors with respect to transfer, licensing, and other dealings with the joint work).
344. *Id.*
345. 17 U.S.C. § 201.
346. *See*, e.g., *Shapiro Bernstein & Co. v. Jerry Vogel Music Co.*, 221 F.2d 569 (2d Cir. 1955). As the congressional Committee Report noted, "co-owners of copyright would be treated generally as tenants in common, with each co-owner having an independent right to use or license the use of a work, subject to a duty of accounting to the other co-owners for any profits." H.R. REP. NO. 94-1476, at 121 (1976), *as reprinted in* 1976 U.S.C.C.A.N. 5659, 5736.
347. *Tresona Multimedia, LLC v. Burbank High Sch. Vocal Music Ass'n*, 953 F.3d 638 (9th Cir. 2020).
348. 17 U.S.C. § 101.

works; the result was case-by-case determination that was not always consistent. The 1976 Act, departing from the earlier case law, created a definition predicated upon the contemporaneous intention of the parties. The House Committee Report is clear in expressing the importance of intention:

> The touchstone here is the intention, at the time the writing is done, that the parts be absorbed or combined into an integrated unit, although the parts themselves may be either "inseparable" (as in the case of a novel or painting) or "interdependent" (as in the case of a motion picture, opera, or the words and music of a song).[349]

The cases under the Act have underlined the primacy of contemporaneous intention of the parties for determining whether a given work is a "joint work." For a work to be a "joint work": (i) it must be contemplated by each of the parties (when each makes a contribution) that the contribution will be part of a unitary work to which another will make or already has made a contribution; and (ii) each purported joint author must intend to contribute to a joint work at the time his or her alleged contribution is made.[350] As the Second Circuit has observed:

> Examination of whether the putative co-authors ever shared an intent to be coauthors serves the valuable purpose of appropriately confining the bounds of joint authorship arising by operation of copyright law, while leaving those not in a true joint authorship relationship with an author free to bargain for an arrangement that will be recognized as a matter of both copyright and contract law. [Joint authorship] should be reserved for relationships in which all participants fully intend to be joint authors.[351]

Even the contribution of significant original material to a work will not itself make the contributor a joint author in the absence of evidence of coauthorship intention by the original author.[352]

It is not necessary that the participants actually work together or within the same time frame, or even that they know one another, so long as each participant created his or her contribution with the intention of integrating that contribution into a single unitary product. Joint authorship of a work, however, will not make one a joint author of a derivative work created by another joint author.[353]

There is some uncertainty as to the nature of the contribution of each purported joint author. It has been held that for a participant to be considered a joint author, even with such contemporaneous intention to merge that participant's contribution into a "unitary whole," his or her contribution itself must contain sufficient originality to be independently copyrightable.[354] Thus, providing ideas, direction or editorial guidance,

---

349. H.R. REP. NO. 94-1476, at 120 (1976), *as reprinted in* 1976 U.S.C.C.A.N. 5659, 5736.
350. *Weissmann v. Freeman*, 868 F.2d 1313 (2d Cir. 1989); *see also Childress v. Taylor*, 945 F.2d 500 (2d Cir. 1991); *Erickson v. Trinity Theatre, Inc.*, 13 F.3d 1061 (7th Cir. 1994).
351. *Childress v. Taylor*, 945 F.2d 500, 508–09 (2d Cir. 1991).
352. *Thomson v. Larson*, 147 F.3d 195 (2d Cir. 1998).
353. *Richlin v. Metro-Goldwyn-Mayer Pictures, Inc.*, 531 F.3d 962 (9th Cir. 2008).
354. *Gaylord v. United States*, 595 F.3d 1364 (Fed. Cir. 2010); *Childress v. Taylor*, 945 F.2d 500 (2d Cir. 1991); *Erickson v. Trinity Theatre, Inc.*, 13 F.3d 1061 (7th Cir. 1994).

however valuable, will not suffice to make one a joint author. However, this "requirement" has been questioned, at least in the Seventh Circuit.[355]

Under certain limited circumstances, the status of joint ownership—an undivided interest in the work—may result from acts apart from the process by which the work was created and rights initially vested. A subsequent transferee of a work from the copyright owner, by contract, or by the laws of inheritance or state property laws, may have a joint interest in the work. In such circumstances, the joint ownership rights are independent of issues of joint authorship.

V Collective Works

Contributions to collective works must be distinguished from joint works. A "collective work" "is a work, such as a periodical issue, anthology, or encyclopedia, in which a number of contributions, constituting separate and independent works in themselves, are assembled into a collective whole."[356] The creator of the individual contribution has, and retains, the sole copyright interest in that contribution, whereas the owner of copyright in the collective work itself, absent express transfer of rights, acquires only the right to reproduce and distribute that contribution as part of that particular collective work or any revision of that work.[357]

Section 201(c) of the 1976 Act significantly changed the law and balance of rights with respect to the individual contributions in a collective work in specifically keeping the copyright interest in the creator of that contribution. Thus, the Supreme Court has held that a freelance, independent author of a newspaper article may object to the reproduction of that article for use in an online database of the newspaper's material.[358] According to the Court in *New York Times Co., Inc. v. Tasini*, such digital reproduction is not a "revision" of the collective work, and the copyright owner of the collective work has no right so as to deal with that contribution. However, it has been held that a digital version of a complete issue of a collective work is such a "revision" and the individual contributor may not object.[359] As the Eleventh Circuit put it: "In sum, the teachings of Tasini are twofold. First, the concept of 'revision' necessarily includes some element of novelty or 'newness' as defined by the Court, and second, consideration of the context in which the contributions are presented is critical in determining whether that novelty is sufficient to defeat the publisher's § 201(c) privilege."[360]

355. *See Gaiman v. McFarlane*, 360 F.3d 644, 658–60 (7th Cir. 2004). In *Gaylord v. United States*, 595 F.3d 1364, 1377 n.4 (Fed. Cir. 2010), the Federal Circuit characterized the *Gaiman* opinion as "an 'exception' to this rule in a case where neither collaborator made independently copyrightable contributions, but the result of the collaboration produced a copyrightable work."
356. 17 U.S.C. § 101.
357. 17 U.S.C. § 201(c). *See also Jarvis v. K2 Inc.*, 486 F.3d 526 (9th Cir. 2007) (distinguishing "collective works"—and the protection afforded the copyright owner of the collective work in using another's material in a "revision,"—from "derivative works," as to which the owner of the collective work copyright has no rights).
358. *New York Times Co., Inc. v. Tasini*, 533 U.S. 483 (2001).
359. *Faulkner v. Mindscape, Inc.*, 409 F.3d 26 (2d Cir. 2005).
360. *Greenberg v. Nat'l Geographic Soc'y*, 533 F.3d 1244 (11th Cir. 2008).

VI Works Made for Hire

The 1976 Act continued the earlier law's recognition of a distinct status for works made for hire. It provides that, in the case of such works, "the employer or other person for whom the work was prepared is considered the author for purposes of [the Act], and, unless the parties have expressly agreed otherwise in a written instrument signed by them, owns all the rights comprised in the copyright."[361] The hiring party, while not the actual creator of the work, is the "author" entitled to all of the rights of an author (and the actual creator has none of those rights), except as those rights may be specifically limited.

Recognizing the different creative posture of an employer for hire "author," the Act provides for a fixed term (rather than one measured by the life of the author) for works for hire, and it excludes such works from the termination right and from the moral rights provisions of the VARA (section 106A).[362]

With fundamental ownership rights dependent upon the employer/employee status, determination of whether a given work is a "work for hire" is an important matter. The Act attempts to define "a work made hire" and in so doing creates two distinct ways in which that status can be created. The first, broad definition defines "a work made for hire" as "a work prepared by an employee within the scope of his or her employment," while the second, more limited definition refers to certain specially commissioned works.[363]

A *Work Prepared by an Employee Within the Scope of Employment*

A work prepared by an employee within the scope of his or her employment is considered a work for hire, and the employer is considered the "author" of the work, unless the parties have signed a writing expressly agreeing otherwise. Prior to the US Supreme Court opinion in *Community for Creative Non-Violence v. Reid,*[364] the Courts of Appeal had divided over the meaning of "employee" for the purposes of determining if a work was a work made for hire. Some courts construed the term broadly enough to include independent contractors under certain circumstances, depending upon the degree of control exerted by the hiring party. On the other hand, other courts construed it quite narrowly, limiting it to the traditional master-servant relationship, or even to a formal, salaried employee/employer relationship. Purporting to resolve the conflict, the Supreme Court held that the appropriate question is whether the creator of the work would be considered an "employee" under the master-servant definition of the "general common law of agency."

361. 17 U.S.C. § 201(b). "Where a work is 'made for hire,' copyright law deems the employer to be the 'author' for purposes of copyright ownership." *Marvel Characters Inc. v. Kirby,* 726 F.3d 119, 137 (2d Cir. 2013).
362. *See infra* §§6, 8.
363. 17 U.S.C. § 101.
364. *Cmty. for Creative Non-Violence v. Reid,* 490 U.S. 730 (1989).

While the Supreme Court thus appeared to eschew the "control" tests of some of the lower courts, in fact, the issue of control becomes one of the significant factors in determining whether one is an "employee" under the common law of agency. The Court relied upon section 220 of the Restatement (Second) of Agency, which itself enumerates 10 factors, including control over the details of the work. The result, therefore, is that while it would appear that a true "independent contractor" could not be considered an "employee for hire," the Court's less than explicit guidance for the lower courts has nevertheless created uncertainty.

In an attempt at clarifying the matter, the Second Circuit has suggested that, of these 10 factors, some "will often have little or no significance," while "there are some factors that will be significant in virtually every situation."[365] According to the court, these significant factors include: "(1) the hiring party's right to control the manner and means of creation; (2) the skill required; (3) the provision of employee benefits; (4) the tax treatment of the hired party; and (5) whether the hiring party has the right to assign additional projects to the hired party."

Determination of whether a work is a work made for hire is a legal conclusion based upon the underlying facts defining the relationship between the parties. Thus, it has been held that a work was created as part of an employment relationship and was therefore a work made for hire notwithstanding a coauthorship and co-ownership agreement between the parties.[366]

B *Specially Commissioned Works*

The Act alternatively provides that certain works, even if clearly created by an independent contractor and not by an "employee for hire," will be considered works made for hire. This category of work is limited to nine types of specially ordered or commissioned works. Specifically, the work must be:

> specially ordered or commissioned for use as a contribution to a collective work, as a part of a motion picture or other audiovisual work, as a translation, as a supplementary work, as a compilation, as an instructional text, as a test, as answer material for a test, or as an atlas ...[367]

365. *Aymes v. Bonelli*, 980 F.2d 857, 861 (2d Cir. 1992); *cf. Graham v. James*, 144 F.3d 229 (2d Cir. 1998) (applying *Aymes* and relying on the high level of skill involved and lack of benefits to find no employment for hire), *and Carter v. Helmsley-Spear, Inc.*, 71 F.3d 77 (2d Cir. 1995) (applying *Aymes* and relying heavily on the fifth factor to find an employment for hire).
366. *Saenger Org., Inc. v. Nationwide Ins. Licensing Assocs., Inc.*, 119 F.3d 55 (1st Cir. 1997).
367. 17 U.S.C. § 101. The "supplementary work" referred to in the definition is further defined as "a work prepared for publication as a secondary adjunct to a work by another author for the purpose of introducing, concluding, illustrating, explaining, revising, commenting upon, or assisting in the use of the other work, such as forewords, afterwords, pictorial illustrations, maps, charts, tables, editorial notes, musical arrangements, answer material for tests, bibliographies, appendixes, and indexes," and an "instructional text" "is a literary, pictorial, or graphic work prepared for publication and with the purpose of use in systematic instructional activities."

For works created prior to January 1, 1978 (the effective date of the 1976 Act), the earlier, case-based definition of a work for hire retains significance. For those works, the law created a presumption in favor of the hiring or commissioning party, and relevant factors were the right to supervise and control the work. With respect to commissioned works, it had been held "that an independent contractor is an 'employee' and a hiring party an 'employer' ... if the work is made at the hiring party's 'instance and expense', [i.e.,] when the 'motivating factor in producing the work was the employer who induced the creation'."[368]

Of course, even if a work is neither a joint work nor a work made for hire, other parties, whether participants, commissioning parties, or strangers, may succeed to rights by transfer or assignment of all or part of those rights. Such successors, however, are not "authors" for the purposes of the Act.

§5 TRANSFER OF COPYRIGHT INTERESTS

I Transfer Defined

As discussed above, copyright ownership is virtually infinitely divisible, so that all or part of all or any of the rights comprising a copyright owner's interest (except for the limited moral right created by section 106A) may be transferred or licensed to others. For the purposes of the Act, a "transfer of copyright ownership" is broadly defined as:

> an assignment, mortgage, exclusive license, or any other conveyance, alienation, or hypothecation of a copyright or of any of the exclusive rights comprised in a copyright whether or not it is limited in time or place of effect, but not including a nonexclusive license.[369]

Thus, if the author/copyright owner of a book grants to a motion picture producer the exclusive right to make a motion picture of that book, there has been a "transfer" of a subset of the author's exclusive right to prepare derivative works. For example, if the composer/copyright owner of a song grants to a singer the nonexclusive right to sing that song at a concert, there has been no "transfer" of any part of the composer's exclusive right publicly to perform the work.[370] On the other hand, a "transfer" will have occurred if the singer is given the exclusive right to sing that song at concerts—even if that grant is limited to one week or to a specific geographic area.

---

368. *Playboy Enters. v. Dumas, Inc.*, 53 F.3d 549 (2d Cir. 1995). As the Ninth Circuit put it: "It has been well established within this circuit that [1909 Act] works by independent contractors may qualify as works-for-hire so long as they were created at the instance and expense of the commissioning party." *20th Century Fox Film Corp. v. Entm't Distrib.*, 429 F.3d 869, 877 (9th Cir. 2005). The court expressly rejected the argument that the Supreme Court's *CCNV* decision alters this result with respect to 1909 Act works. *Id.*, at 878 ("No part of [that] decision rests on the meaning of the work-for-hire provision in the 1909 Act .... ").
369. 17 U.S.C. § 101.
370. *Johnson v. Jones*, 149 F.3d 494, 500 (6th Cir. 1998) ("It is ... well settled that a non-exclusive license is not a transfer of ownership.").

In short, there is no distinction between exclusive licenses and other kinds of transfers, assignments, or conveyances. On the other hand, there is a meaningful distinction between exclusive and nonexclusive licenses.

II Requirement of a Writing

Since the ownership of copyright in a work is distinct from ownership of the material object embodying that work,[371] prior to the effectiveness of the 1976 Act, there was dispute with respect to the extent to which unconditional transfer of such material object would carry, by implication, transfer of the copyright in the work. Resolution of the question of transfer involved determination of matters of intent and inconsistent presumptions. To buttress the separation between the intangible copyright interest and the interest in the tangible material object, and to put to rest dispute as to when transfer of ownership of an object might carry with it, by implication, transfer of the copyright interest in the work, the Act expressly requires a "writing" to effectuate a valid transfer of copyright ownership:

> A transfer of copyright ownership, other than by operation of law, is not valid unless an instrument of conveyance, or a note or memorandum of the transfer, is in writing and signed by the owner of the rights conveyed or such owner's duly authorized agent.[372]

The Act does not specify any particular form of writing to meet the statutory requirement. There has been some controversy among the Courts of Appeal over whether the transfer of copyright can be inferred from broad language of a writing.[373] Nevertheless, it is clear that there must be some writing in connection with the transfer and the writing requirement goes to the very validity of the transfer.

Section 204(a)'s requirement, while sometimes called the copyright statute of frauds, is in fact different from a statute of frauds. Rather than serving an evidentiary function and making otherwise valid agreements unenforceable, under section 204(a) "a transfer of copyright is simply 'not valid' without a writing."[374]

The writing requirement applies to conveyances of copyright interests, but does not apply to a nonexclusive license, which, as the statutory definition quoted above

371. *See supra* §4.I.
372. 17 U.S.C. § 204(a).
373. *Compare Playboy Enters., Inc. v. Dumas*, 53 F.3d 549 (2d Cir. 1995) (holding the legend on the back of checks did not satisfy writing requirement when checks were issued in payment for pictorial works endorsed by the author/payee that contained the legend "payee acknowledges payment in full for the assignment … of all right, title, and interest in and to"), *with Schiller & Schmidt, Inc. v. Nordisco Corp.*, 969 F.2d 410 (7th Cir. 1992) (holding writing requirement satisfied by an agreement that did not mention "copyright" expressly but where the circumstances surrounding the agreement showed that the parties intended to transfer copyright by the agreement). For issues of interpretation arising when agreements are silent as to new technology, not in existence at the time of the grant, *see Welles v. Turner Entm't Co.*, 503 F.3d 728 (9th Cir. 2007).
374. *Lyrick Studios, Inc. v. Big Idea Prods., Inc.*, 420 F.3d 388 (5th Cir. 2005) (citation omitted).

makes clear, is not considered a transfer, and therefore may be granted orally.[375] Indeed, an invalid oral exclusive license may, by virtue of the conduct of the parties, be treated as an implied and enforceable nonexclusive license.[376]

III Termination of Transfers and Grants

A *Nature of the Right*

As is discussed below in connection with duration of copyright,[377] the 1976 Act creates a single term of copyright commencing with the fixation of an original work of authorship in a tangible medium of expression and lasting generally for the life of the author plus fifty (now seventy) years. This scheme replaced the earlier dual-term structure which provided for an initial twenty-eight-year term, commencing with publication of the work with proper notice, and a renewal term of like duration commencing at the expiration of the initial term if proper registration for renewal were made. It was the apparent intention of Congress in creating that structure to give the author a recapture right with respect to the renewal term. In other words, authors were given the ability to undo licenses, transfers, and other grants made during the initial term. This renewal right was not inalienable,[378] and, therefore, an author was frequently pressured to assign the renewal right in connection with any grants. With the 1976 Act, Congress more effectively implemented the idea of giving the author a right to recapture rights, which had been the subject of grants, licenses, and other transfers, after a suitable period of time within which the transferee could exploit those rights.

The Act now grants to the author, or to specified statutory successors (the surviving spouse, children, or grandchildren of the author, or, if none survive, the author's estate), the right, during a five-year period, to terminate any and all grants and recapture the rights granted, provided that the notice and other statutory procedures are meticulously followed.[379] The termination right does not apply to grants made with respect to works made for hire.[380] The right is now inalienable.[381] The scope of the termination right has been held to be broad enough to make an oral license with an

375. *See*, e.g., *Johnson v. Jones*, 149 F.3d 494, 500 (6th Cir. 1999).
376. *Jacob Maxwell, Inc. v. Veeck*, 110 F.3d 749 (11th Cir. 1997). *See also MidlevelU, Inc. v. ACI Info. Grp.*, 989 F.3d 1205, 1216 (11th Cir. 2021) ("When an owner's conduct 'clearly' manifests a consent to use of copyrighted material, the owner impliedly grants a nonexclusive license."); *Unclaimed Property Recovery Serv., Inc. v. Kaplan*, 734 F.3d 142, 144 (2d Cir. 2013) (acknowledging an irrevocable implied license to use previously filed litigation documents).
377. *See infra* §8.
378. *Fred Fisher Music Co. v. M. Witmark & Sons*, 318 U.S. 643 (1943).
379. 17 U.S.C. §§ 203(a)(2), 304(c)(2). The author's estate was added as ultimate owner of the right by the 1998 Copyright Term Extension Act.
380. 17 U.S.C. §§ 203(a), 304(c).
381. 17 U.S.C. §§ 203(a)(5), 304(c)(5): "Termination of the grant may be effected notwithstanding any agreement to the contrary, including an agreement to make a will or to make any future grant."

indeterminate term terminable only after expiration of the statutory period, preempting state law making such a license terminable at will.[382]

The notice must state the effective date of termination, which must be within the permissible five-year termination period. The notice must be served at least two years, and not more than ten years, before that date; it must comply with regulations issued by the Register of Copyrights; and it must be recorded in the Copyright Office before the effective date of termination.[383] The notice provisions are quite stringent, and any failure to comply will forfeit the right to terminate.[384]

The termination right vests on the date that proper notice of termination is given. Accordingly, if an individual in whom the right vests dies prior to the actual reversion, the reverted rights will pass to that person's estate. So too, since the successors to the termination right of an author who dies prior to its exercise are fixed by statute, that succession cannot be changed by the author's will. As the Second Circuit noted, "the purpose of the [termination right] is to protect the rights of widows and children in copyrights [and] is not necessarily a provision for the effectuation of the author's 'intent'."[385] The statutory requirements are complex, and a history of grants and assignments can create complicated litigation issues.[386]

For the purposes of the termination right, the Act distinguishes between: (1) terminating grants made prior to January 1, 1978, and (2) terminating grants made after that date.

B *Grants Made Prior to January 1, 1978*

The 1976 Act essentially extends the renewal term for works in copyright at the effective date of the Act by thirty-nine (originally nineteen) years. Assignments, grants, or licenses, exclusive or nonexclusive, made prior to the effective date of the 1976 Act and during the renewal term of the copyright in the work subject to the grant, may be terminated during the five-year period beginning at the end of fifty-six years from the date copyright was originally secured in the work (or beginning January 1, 1978, if later).[387] In operation, the termination right here recaptures the extension of the renewal term. The right may be exercised by the "author" who executed the grant or, if the author does not survive to the time for effecting termination, the author's surviving spouse and children or grandchildren, or estate[388]—for grants executed by an

382. *Rano v. Sipa Press, Inc.*, 987 F.2d 580 (9th Cir. 1993). A contrary result—holding no preemption of state law for a license terminable at will—was reached by the *Seventh and Eleventh Circuits: Walthal v. Rusk*, 172 F.3d 481 (7th Cir. 1999); *Korman v. HBC Florida, Inc.*, 182 F.3d 1291 (11th Cir. 1999).
383. 17 U.S.C. §§ 203(a)(4), 304(c)(4).
384. 17 U.S.C. §§ 203(a)(4)(A)–(B), 304(c)(4)(A)–(B). *See Burroughs v. Metro-Goldwyn-Mayer, Inc.*, 683 F.2d 610 (2d Cir. 1982).
385. *Larry Spier, Inc. v. Bourne Co.*, 953 F.2d 774 (2d Cir. 1992).
386. *Compare Penguin Grp. (USA), Inc. v. Steinbeck*, 537 F.3d 193 (2d Cir. 2008), *with Classic Media, Inc. v. Newborn*, 532 F.3d 978 (9th Cir. 2008).
387. 17 U.S.C. § 304(c)(3).
388. Issues of survivorship and determination of who are qualifying spouses and children are governed by applicable state law.

author's statutory successor,[389] termination may be effected by the surviving person or persons who executed the grant.[390] These termination provisions do not relate to grants (made prior to January 1, 1978) during the initial term of then subsisting copyrights since the grantor, at least theoretically, has a limited "recapture" right in connection with the renewal term.

The 1998 amendments extending the duration of copyright by twenty years[391] also provide for a limited restoration of the termination right with respect to that twenty-year extension as to works in their renewal term as of the effective date of the amendments and for which the termination right, previously unexercised, had expired. The restored right may be exercised by notice given during the five-year period commencing seventy-five years after the date copyright was originally secured.[392]

C Grants Made from and after January 1, 1978

Grants, transfers, or other licenses made by the "author" and executed on or after January 1, 1978, may be terminated by the author (or the author's statutory survivors) at any time during the five-year period commencing at the expiration of thirty-five years from the date of execution of the grant, or, if the grant included a right of publication, the earlier of thirty-five years after publication or forty years after the date of execution of the grant.[393] For these purposes, it is immaterial when the copyright in the work began; the only consideration is the date of the grant.

D The Effect of Termination: Derivative Works

With proper notice, termination will be effective on the date specified in the notice, and on that date, the rights granted will revert to the author or to those holding the termination interest.[394] However, such termination cannot impair rights with respect to continued exploitation of derivative works "prepared under authority of the grant before its termination," and such works "may continue to be utilized under the terms of the grant," although such utilization "does not extend to the preparation after the termination of other derivative works based upon the copyrighted work covered by the terminated grant."[395] The question of exactly what is a derivative work "utilized under the terms of the grant" has been quite troublesome, particularly with respect to the rights of intermediate grantees.[396]

389. As defined in 17 U.S.C. § 304(a)(1)(C).
390. 17 U.S.C. § 304(c)(1), (2).
391. *See infra* §8.
392. 17 U.S.C. § 304(d).
393. 17 U.S.C. § 203(a).
394. 17 U.S.C. §§ 203(b), 304(c)(6).
395. 17 U.S.C. §§ 203(b)(1), 304(c)(6)(A).
396. This question gave rise to a divided US Supreme Court decision in *Mills Music, Inc. v. Snyder*, 469 U.S. 153 (1985). The effect of *Mills Music* appears to preserve, during the post-termination period, the panoply of contractual obligations that governed pretermination uses of derivative works by derivative work owners or their licensees. *Woods v. Bourne Co.*, 60 F.3d 978, 981 (2d

§6 SCOPE OF EXCLUSIVE RIGHTS

Section 106 enumerates the exclusive rights of the owner of copyright. Except for the limited moral rights accorded to certain authors of certain works of visual art under section 106A (discussed below), the enumeration is complete and exhaustive, and no other rights may be inferred. The owner of copyright has the exclusive rights to do and to authorize any of the following:

(1) reproduce the copyrighted work in copies or phonorecords;
(2) prepare derivative works based upon the copyrighted work;
(3) distribute copies or phonorecords of the copyrighted work to the public by sale or other transfer of ownership, or by rental, lease, or lending;
(4) in the case of literary, musical, dramatic, and choreographic works, pantomimes, and motion pictures and other audiovisual works, perform the copyrighted work publicly;
(5) in the case of literary, musical, dramatic, and choreographic works, pantomimes, and pictorial, graphic, or sculptural works, including the individual images of a motion picture or other audiovisual work, display the copyrighted work publicly; and
(6) in the case of sound recordings, perform the copyrighted work publicly by means of a digital audio transmission.[397]

The rights granted to the owner of copyright are subject to the highly specific limitations and exemptions of sections 108 through 121 of the Act and, as discussed below, the broad fair use limitation of section 107 of the Act.

I The Right to Reproduce the Work

A The Broadly Defined Right

The exclusive right to reproduce the copyrighted work is the most basic element in the bundle of rights constituting copyright. That right is infringed when one other than the copyright owner makes "copies" or "phonorecords" of the work. Those terms are broadly defined in the Act. "Copies" are material objects, other than phonorecords, in which a work is fixed by any method now known or later developed, and from which the work can be perceived, reproduced, or otherwise communicated, either directly or with the aid of a machine or device. The term "copies" includes the material object, other than phonorecords, in which the work is first fixed.[398] "Phonorecords" are

Cir. 1995) (holding that "when a musical arrangement is contained within an audiovisual work produced under license from a publisher prior to termination, the publisher is entitled to receive royalties from post-termination performances of the audiovisual work under the terms of pre-termination licenses governing performance rights").

397. 17 U.S.C. § 106.
398. 17 U.S.C. § 101.

material objects in which sounds, other than those accompanying a motion picture or other audiovisual work, are fixed by any method now known or later developed, and from which the sounds can be perceived, reproduced, or otherwise communicated, either directly or with the aid of a machine or device. The term "phonorecords" includes the material object in which the sounds are first fixed.[399]

The Act thus makes clear that questions as to the nature of the copying device, or the medium or the method used for copying, are all irrelevant to the determination of whether a "copy" has been made of a copyrighted work.[400] The concept of copying, thus, is as elastic as that of fixation and the definitional issues can create complex problems, including questions as to the authorship of the infringing conduct.[401]

In practice, certain types of reproduction, subsets of the reproduction right, receive specialized treatment and, in practice, are known by specific terms of art. For example, the "copying" involved in incorporating a sound recording into an audiovisual work, synchronizing the sound with the pictures, as is done with soundtracks for motion pictures, is, if done without consent, violative of the owner's exclusive "synchronization right" and industry practice has developed around procedures for license and exercise of that right. "Synchronization right" is an extra-statutory term of art for a special case of the exclusive reproduction right.[402]

Similarly, one speaks of the copyright owner's "mechanical right" in referring to the exclusive right to embody a copyrighted work in a phonorecord, and, as discussed below, a similar, specialized practice developed for dealing with the exercise of that right, based upon compulsory license provisions of the Act.

B Specific Statutory Limitations and Compulsory Licenses

Conditioning the broad reproduction right, a number of provisions of the Act exempt certain types of copying from infringement claims, while compulsory license provisions exempt certain activities upon compliance with the license terms. The compulsory license device, where it applies, is the product of a congressional determination that the principal value of a certain use is economic, and that the copyright owner should be satisfied with a fixed compensation for that use. With a compulsory license, the copyright owner, in exchange for a fee, relinquishes the right to determine who

399. *Id.*
400. *See*, e.g., *MAI Sys. Corp. v. Peak Computer, Inc.*, 991 F.2d 511 (9th Cir. 1993) (holding that copying an operating system into computer memory makes a "copy" of the program for the purposes of the Act).
401. *Cartoon Network LP, LLLP v. CSC Holdings, Inc.*, 536 F.3d. 121 (2d Cir. 2008), is particularly instructive, as the court held the fixation requirement of "more than temporary duration" part of the definition of "copy" and accordingly found that an ephemeral "copy" in a buffer was not a "copy" for the purposes of infringement in direct command to the system.
402. *See Agee v. Paramount Commc'ns, Inc.*, 59 F.3d 317 (2d Cir. 1995) (holding that the exclusive right to reproduce a sound recording is infringed by Paramount's unauthorized copying ("synchronization") of the recording onto the audio track of a video tape that was broadcast only once and was not distributed to the public for sale or rental); *see also ABKCO Music, Inc. v. Stellar Records, Inc.*, 96 F.3d 60 (2d Cir. 1996).

may exercise certain of the owner's rights. In connection with certain of the compulsory licensing and related provisions, the Librarian of Congress, in consultation with the Register of Copyright, is directed to "appoint 3 full-time Copyright Royalty Judges" who are empowered "to make determinations and adjustments of reasonable terms and rates of royalty payments as provided in Sections 112(e), 114, 115, 116, 118, 119 and 1004."[403]

1 *Library and Archival Copying*

Section 108 of the Act specifically exempts from infringement claims certain reproduction or distribution activities by libraries and archives. The exemption relates generally to noncommercial reproduction or distribution of not more than one copy or phonorecord of a work by libraries or archives that are open to the public or are available to persons, in addition to researchers affiliated with such libraries or archives, doing research in specialized fields.[404]

The exemption extends as well to: (i) reproduction and distribution of not more than three copies or phonorecords of an unpublished work in the collections of the library or archives "solely for purposes of preservation and security or for deposit for research use in another library or archives" if any such copy or phonorecord that is reproduced in digital format is not otherwise distributed in that format and is not made available to the public in that format outside the premises of the library or archives; and (ii) reproduction of not more than three copies of a published work "solely for the purpose of replacement of a copy or phonorecords that is damaged, deteriorating, lost, or stolen, or if the existing format in which the work is stored has become obsolete," if the library or archives have, after reasonable effort, determined that an unused replacement cannot be obtained at a fair price and any such copy or phonorecord that is reproduced in digital format is not made available to the public in that format outside the premises of the library or archives in lawful possession of such copy.[405]

Also exempt is reproduction and distribution "of no more than one article or other contribution to a copyrighted collection or periodical issue, or a copy or phonorecord of a small part of any other copyrighted work," at the request of a user or another library or archive, and reproduction and distribution of an entire work at the request of the user or another library if it has been determined, "on the basis of reasonable investigation, that a copy or phonorecord of the copyrighted work cannot be obtained at fair price." These exemptions are further conditioned on the absence of notice that the copy "would be used for any purpose other than private study,

403. 17 U.S.C. § 801. Sections 801–05, enacted in 2004, establish the Copyright Royalty Judges, amending and superseding the earlier "Copyright Arbitration Royalty Panels" created in Ch. 8.
404. 17 U.S.C. § 108(a).
405. 17 U.S.C. § 108(b)–(c). "[A] format shall be considered obsolete if the machine or device necessary to render perceptible a work stored in that format is no longer manufactured or is no longer reasonably available in the commercial marketplace." 17 U.S.C. § 108(c)(2).

scholarship, or research" and upon the library or archives prominently displaying appropriate notice of copyright and warning of infringement.[406]

The 1998 Copyright Term Extension Act, which effectively added twenty years to the duration of copyright,[407] provides a special exemption for library and archival copying. During the last twenty years of the copyright term of a published work, such institutions may reproduce, distribute, display, or perform a copy or phonorecord of the work for the purposes of preservation, scholarship, or research, unless "the work is subject to commercial exploitation," or a copy or phonorecord can be obtained at a reasonable price, or the copyright owner has provided notice of the existence of either of these conditions.[408] This exemption originally excluded musical works, pictorial, graphical and sculptural works, and most audiovisual works,[409] but that exclusion was removed in 2005.

2 *Ephemeral Recordings*

A broadcasting station, or other "transmitting organization" that is licensed or otherwise has the right to transmit to the public a performance or a display of a work, or a broadcast transmission of a performance of a sound recording in a digital format on a nonsubscription basis, may make a single copy or phonorecord of that transmission for its own use for archival preservation, or, if the copy or phonorecord is destroyed within six months from the date of first transmission, for the purposes of security or for transmission within its own service area.[410] If, for the purposes of making such permitted copy, it is necessary to circumvent technological measures, and the copyright owner does not make available the necessary means for making such copy, then such circumvention will not be a violation of the prohibition on circumvention of copyright protection systems contained in section 1201 of the Copyright Act.[411] Similarly, a transmitting organization with a statutory license or otherwise authorized under section 411 to transmit a performance of a sound recording[412] may, upon compliance with the further statutory conditions, make no more than one phonorecord of that recording.[413]

If the transmitting entity is a governmental body or other nonprofit organization, it may make up to thirty copies or phonorecords of a transmission, provided that all but one archival copy are destroyed within seven years from the date of first transmission. Moreover, if the work is a performance or sound recording of a nondramatic musical work of a religious nature, a governmental body or other nonprofit organization may make and distribute, without charge, one copy or phonorecord of a transmitted nondramatic musical religious work for use by broadcasters licensed to transmit the

406. 17 U.S.C. § 108(d)–(e).
407. *See infra* §8.
408. 17 U.S.C. § 108(h).
409. 17 U.S.C. § 108(i).
410. 17 U.S.C. § 112(a).
411. 17 U.S.C. § 112(a)(2). *See infra* §11.
412. *See infra* §6.VI.
413. 17 U.S.C. § 112(e).

work, provided that all copies, but one archival copy, are destroyed within one year of the date of first transmission. Further, a governmental body or other nonprofit organization entitled to transmit a performance of a work to certain handicapped recipients may make up to ten copies of such work for the purposes of such transmission or for archival preservation or security, so long as no charge is made for such use.[414]

3 *Certain Copies of Computer Programs*

In response to the CONTU Report,[415] Congress provided, in section 117 of the 1976 Act, that the reproduction right is not infringed when the owner of a copy of a computer program makes "another copy or adaptation of that computer program," if that copy or adaptation is used only "as an essential step in the utilization of the computer program in conjunction with a machine," or is made only for archival purposes.[416]

Under section 117, copying a program into a computer's random access memory in order to use it is not infringing, even if the "use" is not that for which the program was intended.[417] However, it has been held that that immunity will not extend to such copying by one who is not the "owner" of the copy of the program, but rather only a licensee.[418] To overrule that holding, Congress in 1998 amended section 117 to provide that copying of an authorized copy of a computer program that results solely from the activation of a machine by the owner or lessee of that machine is not an infringement if it is done only for the purposes of maintenance or repair of that machine.[419]

The safe harbor provisions of section 117(c) have been interpreted broadly. As the Federal Circuit explained, the "general policy underlying the enactment of section 117(c)" was to "ensure that independent service organizations do not inadvertently become liable for copyright infringement merely because they have turned on a machine in order to service its hardware components."[420] Congress was seeking to

---

414. 17 U.S.C. § 112(b)–(d).
415. *See supra* §2.IV.A.1.
416. 17 U.S.C. § 117(a).
417. *See Vault Corp. v. Quaid Software, Ltd.*, 847 F.2d 255 (5th Cir. 1988).
418. *MAI Sys. Corp. v. Peak Computer, Inc.*, 991 F.2d 511 (9th Cir. 1993) (concluding that loading by a computer servicing company of a licensed operating system into the licensee's computer RAM (an act incidental to turning on the computer) was "copying" not insulated by § 117). *See Krause v. Titleserve, Inc.*, 402 F.3d 119 (2d Cir. 2005) (noting that the exemption protects only "the owner of a copy of a computer program," the court emphasizes the distinction between owning the program and owning "a copy" of the program in an attempt to determine when "possession" becomes "ownership" of a copy). For these purposes, formal transfer of title is not essential: "Instead, courts should inquire into whether the party exercises sufficient incidents of ownership over a copy of the program to be sensibly considered the owner of the copy for purposes of § 117(a)." *Id.*, at 124. *See also Wall Data, Inc. v. Los Angeles Cnty. Sheriff's Dep't*, 447 F.3d 769 (9th Cir. 2006).
419. 17 U.S.C. § 117(c).
420. *Storage Tech. Corp. v. Custom Hardware Eng'g & Consulting, Inc.*, 421 F.3d 1307, 1311-12 (Fed. Cir. 2005) (quoting H.R. Rep. No. 105-551, pt. 1, at 27 (1998)).

"protect the class of companies that fix and maintain computer systems, as opposed to those that would make other commercial use of copyrighted material."[421]

4 *Reproductions for the Blind or Other People with Disabilities*

The exclusive reproduction right is not infringed by the reproduction (or distribution of copies or phonorecords) "of a previously published, nondramatic literary work if such copies or phonorecords are reproduced or distributed in specialized formats exclusively for use by blind or other persons with disabilities."[422] The exemption is specifically limited to "nondramatic literary works" reproduced in specialized formats, with appropriate notice, and does not apply to tests and testing material, or to computer programs.[423] Further, the exemption applies only to "a nonprofit organization or a governmental agency that has a primary mission to provide specialized services relating to training, education, or adaptive reading or information access needs of blind or other persons with disabilities."[424] Special exemption is provided for publishers of "print instructional materials for use in elementary or secondary schools" to create and distribute to the National Instructional Materials Access Center, under specified conditions, copies of certain electronic files that the publisher is entitled to distribute in print format.[425]

5 *Home Audio Taping*

The Act specifically immunizes from infringement actions "the noncommercial use by a consumer" of digital or analog recording devices or media "for making digital musical recordings or analog musical recordings."[426] Digital audio taping (DAT) technology provided the impetus for this exemption for noncommercial copying of musical works.

DAT technology, which preceded the introduction of inexpensive and easily usable devices for duplicating CDs, enabled the user to make extremely high fidelity copies of recorded works (particularly digitally encoded CDs). The recording industry, which had tolerated home analog tape recording, mounted a strong campaign against the importation of DAT equipment. The congressional response was the addition to Title 17 of Chapter 10—Digital Audio Recording Devices and Media,[427] which, while exempting such "noncommercial use by a consumer," prohibits the "importation, manufacture, and distribution" of digital audio recording devices unless such devices are so constructed as to prevent "serial copying," defined as "the duplication in a digital format of a copyrighted musical work or sound recording from a digital reproduction of

421. *Id.*
422. 17 U.S.C. § 121.
423. 17 U.S.C. § 121(b).
424. 17 U.S.C. § 121(d).
425. 17 U.S.C. § 121(c).
426. 17 U.S.C. § 1008.
427. 17 U.S.C. §§ 1001 et seq.

a digital musical recording."[428] The Act seeks to prevent the making of digital copies of a digitally recorded work; it is directed to wholesale copying of a work, rather than simple, even multiple copying from the original.[429]

A royalty obligation is imposed upon the manufacturer or importer of permitted digital audio equipment or media (i.e., DAT, discs, or other recording media). The Copyright Office distributes two-thirds of the royalty fund to the record companies and performers and one-third to publishers and composers.[430]

Time and technological developments have undermined the assumptions that underlay the congressional action. Focusing on digital tape technology, neither Congress nor the music industry was prepared either for the ease with which CDs may be directly copied onto other CDs or for the distribution of music through the Internet and the use of MP3 compression to facilitate such distribution. As the Ninth Circuit observed, neither Congress nor the interested parties contemplated a "revolutionary new method of music distribution made possible by digital recording and the Internet."[431] Indeed, there is a "brave new world of Internet music distribution."

Consequently, applying the specific statutory language in section 1008, the Ninth Circuit held that a computer hard drive is not a "digital audio recording device," nor is an MP3 player, and that therefore, the manufacturer of an MP3 player that records from a hard drive is not subject to the inhibitions and royalty provisions of Chapter 10.[432] Applying the same reasoning, the Ninth Circuit also held that the noncommercial downloading of copyrighted music from the Internet by means of a computer is not immunized by section 1008.[433]

6 *Compulsory License for Mechanical Reproduction*

The 1976 Act significantly expanded the use of compulsory licenses, and it continued the principal compulsory license created under the older, 1909 Act, the "compulsory license for making and distributing phonorecords."[434] Section 115, in essence, provides a statutory license to make "cover" recordings of previously recorded works. It permits, upon compliance with the compulsory license terms, the making and distribution of phonorecords of nondramatic musical works without the consent of the copyright owner of those works; the compulsory license can obviate the need for a specific "mechanical license" from the copyright owner of the work.

By its terms, the compulsory license applies to the making and distribution of mechanical copies, in the form of phonorecords, only of nondramatic musical works, phonorecords of which have theretofore been distributed to the public in the US under the authority of the copyright owner, and only if the primary purpose in making such

428. 17 U.S.C. § 1001.
429. 17 U.S.C. § 1002.
430. 17 U.S.C. §§ 1003–07.
431. *Recording Indus. Ass'n of Am. v. Diamond Sys., Inc.*, 180 F.3d 1072 (9th Cir. 1999).
432. *Id.*
433. *A&M Records v. Napster*, 239 F.3d 1004, 1024 (9th Cir. 2001) (concluding that "the Audio Home Recording Act does not cover the downloading of MP3 files [to computer hard drives]").
434. 17 U.S.C. § 115.

new phonorecords is to distribute them to the public for private use. The Digital Performance Right in Sound Recordings Act of 1995 extended the compulsory license to digital audio delivery of the nondramatic musical works.[435] In short, once the copyright owner of a nondramatic musical work has authorized the making and distribution of phonorecords of that work in the US, anyone else may similarly make phonorecords of that work for similar distribution to the public upon compliance with the compulsory license provisions. The provisions, limitations, and procedure for acquisition of the compulsory license, and for determination and payment of royalties are set out in detail in section 115 of the Act.[436]

Since the compulsory license is limited to nondramatic musical works, it cannot be used to make a recording of an opera, or the entirety of a musical play. So too, the compulsory license to make a new recording of an existing nondramatic musical work does not authorize, without the consent of the owner of copyright in the sound recording, the duplication of an existing sound recording in which that work may be embodied.[437] The license extends to only the making and distribution of "phonorecords" and not any and all other kinds of reproductions of the works. Thus, a CD or other device that includes both the music of songs and a visual display of their lyrics (e.g., for karaoke or sing-along purposes) is not a "phonorecord" for the purposes of the compulsory license.[438]

The license does include "the privilege of making a musical arrangement of the work to the extent necessary to conform it to the style or manner of interpretation of the performance involved," so long as such arrangement does "not change the basic melody or fundamental character of the work."[439] In any event, the arrangement itself cannot be protected as a derivative work without the express consent of the copyright owner.

Although the creation of the compulsory mechanical license was a significant factor in implementing a policy favoring the proliferation of recorded music, that statutory mechanism itself is not the primary means by which phonorecords are commercially made and distributed; indeed, it is rarely used. Rather, the bulk of such recordings are made under license from the copyright owner through a voluntary system (administered by the Harry Fox Agency, a subsidiary of the National Music Publishers Association), pursuant to which nonexclusive licenses of the copyright owners' right to make reproductions of nondramatic musical works are granted to those seeking to make "cover" recordings. These voluntary licenses are under essentially the same royalty terms as are provided by the statutory compulsory licenses, but

435. 17 U.S.C. § 114(d).
436. 17 U.S.C. § 115(b)–(c).
437. 17 U.S.C. § 115(a)(1).
438. *ABKCO Music, Inc. v. Stellar Records, Inc.*, 96 F.3d 60 (2d Cir. 1996). The court also noted that even if a compulsory license were otherwise applicable, it would not cover the visual display of the lyrics. *Id.*, at 64–65; *see also Leadsinger, Inc. v. BMG Music Publ'g*, 512 F.3d 522 (9th Cir. 2008) (concluding that compulsory license to make and distribute phonorecords does not also authorize a display of song lyrics in real time with song recordings).
439. 17 U.S.C. § 115(a)(2).

without the more onerous accounting provisions of the statute.[440] Of course, neither the statutory compulsory license nor these voluntary collective arrangements preclude direct negotiations between a copyright owner and one seeking to record the work.

7 *Compulsory License for Public Broadcasting*

Section 118 of the Act creates a compulsory license granting "public broadcasting entities" a limited right to reproduce published nondramatic musical works and published pictorial, graphic, and sculptural works in connection with the broadcast of the performance and display of such works. Rather than set the license fee, the Act contemplates negotiations setting voluntary royalty rates between public broadcasters and organized copyright owners—with the rate to be determined in the absence of agreement by a copyright arbitration royalty panel convened by the Librarian of Congress.[441]

II The Right to Prepare Derivative Works

The creation of a "derivative work" can raise two independent issues. As discussed above,[442] there is the question of the independent copyrightability of a noninfringing derivative work. This involves the issue of the quantum of creativity and originality distinguishing the derivative work from the original upon which it is based. On the other side of that coin is the question of whether one who creates a work based on a copyrighted work infringes the copyright owner's exclusive right under section 106(2) "to prepare derivative works based upon the copyrighted work."

The Act defines a "derivative work" as:

> a work based upon one or more pre-existing works, such as a translation, musical arrangement, dramatization, fictionalization, motion picture version, sound recording, art reproduction, abridgement, condensation, or any other form in which a work may be recast, transformed, or adapted. A work consisting of editorial revisions, annotations, elaborations, or other modifications which, as a whole, represent an original work of authorship, is a "derivative work."[443]

For the purposes of determining whether a purported "derivative work" is itself copyrightable, it must, as noted, pass the test of originality and must be fixed in a tangible medium of expression. Whereas, one may be found to have infringed the exclusive right to prepare derivative works without having made a copy of the original work or without having fixed the infringing work.[444] As the congressional Committee

440. *See* Howard B. Abrams, *Copyright's First Compulsory License*, 26 SANTA CLARA COMP. & HIGH TECH. L.J. 215 (2010).
441. 17 U.S.C. § 118.
442. *See supra* §3.II.B.2.
443. 17 U.S.C. § 101.
444. *Lewis Galoob Toys, Inc. v. Nintendo of Am., Inc.*, 964 F.2d 965 (9th Cir. 1992).

Reports make clear, "the preparation of a derivative work … may be an infringement even though nothing is ever fixed in tangible form."[445]

The exclusive right to prepare a derivative work is not an omnibus shield against any and all appropriation. It protects against the taking of the underlying work through one or another form of transformation, as in, for example, the transformation of a novel into a motion picture.[446]

To be an infringing derivative work, the infringing work must incorporate a portion of the copyrighted work in some form.[447] A detailed commentary on a work or a musical composition inspired by a novel would not normally constitute infringement. Moreover, it has been held that to be considered an infringing derivative work, the offending work must be "substantially similar" to the original, so that even if there is actual "incorporation" of the original, the new work would not be infringing if the final product is not "substantially similar" to the original.[448]

Just as it does in the case of the exclusive right to reproduce a copyrighted computer program, section 117 of the Act creates a limited exemption for "adaptation" of a copyrighted computer program by the lawful owner of a copy of the program if such adaptation "is created as an essential step in the utilization of the computer program in conjunction with a machine and that it is used in no other manner" and such adaptation may not be transferred without the consent of the copyright owner of the underlying work.[449] In reliance on section 117 and the CONTU report, it has been held that the owner of a copy of a computer program was entitled to make modifications to the program—i.e., create a derivative work—without consent of the copyright owner so long as the changes "were necessary measures in [the] continuing use of the software" for no purpose other than the owner's "internal business needs."[450]

Registration of a derivative work, whose underlying work has not been registered, may, in appropriate circumstances, serve constructively as registration of the underlying work, "even the aspects copied from an unregistered preexisting work, so long as the owner of both copyrights is the same."[451]

---

445. H.R. Rep. No. 94-1476, at 62 (1976), *as reprinted in* 1976 U.S.C.C.A.N. 5659, 5675.
446. 17 U.S.C. § 117. *See Wall Data, Inc. v. Los Angeles Cnty. Sheriff's Dep't*, 447 F.3d 769 (9th Cir. 2006); *Krause v. Titleserve, Inc.*, 402 F.3d 119 (2d Cir. 2005).
447. *See Lewis Galoob Toys, Inc. v. Nintendo of Am., Inc.*, 964 F.2d 965 (9th Cir. 1992) (holding that the defendant's device that allows the user to alter features of plaintiff's video games was not itself a "derivative" work because of the absence of actual physical incorporation of the underlying work).
448. *Castle Rock Entm't, Inc. v. Carol Publ'g Grp.*, Inc., 150 F.3d 132, 143 n.9 (2d Cir. 1998) (noting that "if the secondary work sufficiently transforms the expression of the original work such that the two works cease to be substantially similar, then the secondary work is not a derivative work and, for that matter, does not infringe the copyright of the original work"); *see also Atkins v. Fischer*, 351 F.3d 988 (D.C. Cir. 2003); *Well-Made Toy Mfg. v. Goffa Int'l Corp.*, 354 F.3d 112 (2d Cir. 2003); *Litchfield v. Spielberg*, 736 F.2d 1352 (9th Cir. 1984); *Micro Star v. Formgen*, 154 F.3d 1107 (9th Cir. 1998). *See infra* §9.III.A, for discussion of "substantial similarity."
449. 17 U.S.C. § 117. *See Wall Data, Inc. v. Los Angeles Cnty. Sheriff's Dep't*, 447 F.3d 769 (9th Cir. 2006); *Krause v. Titleserve, Inc.*, 402 F.3d 119 (2d Cir. 2005).
450. *Aymes v. Bonelli*, 47 F.3d 23, 26 (2d Cir. 1995).
451. *Oravec v. Sunny Isles Luxury Ventures, L.C.*, 527 F.3d 1218, 1231 (11th Cir. 2008) (citing *Streetwise Maps, Inc. v. VanDam, Inc.*, 159 F.3d 739 (2d Cir. 1998)).

III The Right to Distribute

A *The Right of First Publication*

A rightsholder of a copyrighted work has the exclusive right "to distribute copies or phonorecords of the copyrighted work to the public by sale or other transfer of ownership, or by rental, lease, or lending."[452] This public distribution right is, in essence, a recasting of the old common law right of first publication, the right of the creator of a work to determine when that work will first be exposed to the public.[453] As with each of the enumerated exclusive rights, the public distribution right is distinct from the other rights, so that permission, for example, to copy, or to perform a work, would not include permission to make public distribution of those copies.

"Distribution" is not defined in the Act, although for most purposes the definition of "publication" as the "distribution of copies or phonorecords of a work to the public by sale or other transfer of ownership, or by rental, lease or lending,"[454] would be sufficient. However, concern over the nature of infringement of works through digital transmission has provoked legislative efforts more specifically to recognize such transmission as an actionable "distribution." In the mid-1990s, the Working Group on Intellectual Property Rights of the Information Infrastructure Task Force, directed by the Commissioner of Patents and Trademarks, recommended an amendment to section 106(3) to include "transmission" as a "distribution," so that "transmission" of a work would be an infringing "distribution" even when the transmitter retains a copy of the work. It proposed conforming amendments to define "transmit" to include transmission of a reproduction of a work as well as of a performance or display of a work, to make a "transmission" from abroad an "importation" under section 602,[455] and to define "publication" to include "transmission." Although Congress did not act on these proposals, the courts have, as it has been held that internet transmission of a sound recording (as opposed to a television or radio "broadcast")[456] is an infringing "distribution" of the recording and of the copyrighted music contained therein.[457] In other words, while a "broadcast" or internet streaming of a work will be a "performance" of the work, the upload or download is a "distribution" and not a "performance."[458]

---

452. 17 U.S.C. § 106(3).
453. *Cf. Harper & Row Publishers, Inc. v. Nation Enters.*, 471 U.S. 539, 533 (1985) ("From the beginning, those entrusted with the task of revision recognized the 'overbalancing reasons to preserve the common-law protection of disseminated works until the author or his successor chooses to disclose them.'").
454. 17 U.S.C. § 101.
455. *See infra* §6.III.D.
456. The broadcast would be treated as a "performance," rather than a "distribution." *Agee v. Paramount Commc'ns, Inc.*, 59 F.3d 317 (2d Cir. 1995).
457. *A&M Records v. Napster*, 239 F.3d 1004 (9th Cir. 2001) (concluding that Napster users who upload file names to the search index for others to copy violate plaintiffs' distribution rights).
458. *United States v. American Soc'y of Composers, Authors & Publishers*, 627 F.3d 64, 71–73 (2d Cir. 2010) ("The downloads … are simply transfers of electronic files containing digital copies from an on-line server to a local hard drive. The downloaded songs are not performed in any perceptible manner during the transfers; the user must take some further action to play the songs after they are downloaded. Because the electronic download itself involves no recitation,

B *The First Sale Doctrine*

Section 109 of the Act provides: "The owner of a particular copy or phonorecord lawfully made ..., or any person authorized by such owner, is entitled ... to sell or otherwise dispose of the possession of that copy or phonorecord."[459] This provision codifies the prior case law which established the "first sale doctrine."[460] Through these provisions, the "first sale" or its equivalent by a copyright owner terminates the public distribution right. Of course, the first sale doctrine has no effect on rights other than the distribution right and, therefore, will not shield infringement of the right to reproduce the work or the right to perform the work.[461] In the case of foreign works which had fallen into the public domain in the US but whose copyright has been restored,[462] the owner of copies or phonorecords of such works which had been manufactured prior to the date of restoration may sell or otherwise dispose of them without the authorization of the owner of the restored copyright, but such disposition "for purposes of direct or indirect commercial advantage" may be made only during the twelve-month period following notice of restoration or publication of notice of intention to file for restoration.[463]

The right to distribute a copy or phonorecord of a copyrighted work by one other than the copyright owner is limited to the lawful "owner" of that copy or phonorecord. Therefore, a lease or license by the copyright owner, rather than a transfer of "title" to that copy or phonorecord, will not serve to invoke the first sale doctrine or to divest a copyright owner of the distribution right.[464] For these purposes, the substance, and not the form, of any transaction between the copyright owner and the recipient of a copy will be determinative. The matter can become quite difficult and complex in the context of computer programs acquired subject to shrink-wrap or click-wrap "licenses" that purport to restrict distribution by the purchaser. In *Vernor v. Autodesk, Inc.*, the Ninth Circuit unequivocally enforced such a license,[465] and later reaffirmed that holding as "a significant validation of license restrictions on transfer and use of software."[466] Moreover, as electronic distribution increasingly displaces transfer of physical media, the question of what is a "copy" of a work becomes more complicated.

Apart from the specific exceptions relating to record and computer program rental, discussed below, the first sale doctrine as embodied in section 109 broadly permits any and all kinds of distribution or transfer by the lawful owner of a copy or a

---

rendering, or playing of the musical work encoded in the digital transmission, we hold that such a download is not a performance of that work, as defined by § 101.").

459. 17 U.S.C. § 109.
460. *See*, e.g., *Bobbs-Merrill Co. v. Straus*, 210 U.S. 339 (1908); *Indep. News Co. v. Williams*, 293 F.2d 510 (3d Cir. 1961).
461. *See*, e.g., *Columbia Pictures Indus., Inc. v. Redd Horne, Inc.*, 749 F.2d 154 (3d Cir. 1984).
462. 17 U.S.C. § 104A.
463. 17 U.S.C. § 109(a).
464. 17 U.S.C. § 109(d) (the first sale doctrine "privileges ... do not ... extend to any person who has acquired possession of the copy or phonorecord from the copyright owner, by rental, lease, loan, or otherwise, without acquiring ownership of it").
465. *Vernor v. Autodesk, Inc.*, 621 F.3d 1102 (9th Cir. 2010).
466. *Apple, Inc. v. Psystar Corp.*, 658 F.3d 1150, 1156 (9th Cir. 2011).

phonorecord of a work. There is no US equivalent to the widely recognized public lending right of a copyright owner. The sale and rental of motion pictures on videotape, DVD, or other media, the dissemination of books by libraries, and similar activities involving the distribution of copyrighted works take place under the umbrella of the first sale doctrine.

C *The Record and Computer Program Rental Exceptions to the First Sale Doctrine*

In response first to pressure from the recording industry and then from computer software developers, Congress sought to inhibit the unauthorized copying of recordings and computer programs by excluding commercial lending of recordings and computer programs from "first sale" protection. The Record Rental Amendment of 1984 and the Computer Software Rental Amendment Act of 1990 amended section 109 to exclude from the shelter of the first sale doctrine the rental, lease, or lending, or their equivalent, "for the purposes of direct or indirect commercial advantage," of copies of computer programs or phonorecords without the consent of the owners of copyright in such programs and in the sound recordings and the musical works embodied in phonorecords.[467] This provision does not apply to the rental, lease, or lending of a phonorecord for nonprofit purposes by a nonprofit library or nonprofit educational institution,[468] or to the lending of a computer program for nonprofit purposes by a nonprofit library;[469] nor does it apply to computer programs "used in conjunction with a limited purpose computer that is designed for playing video games."[470] Moreover, it has been held that the record rental exception to the first sale doctrine applies only to musical works and therefore does not apply to "audiobooks" or other nonmusical sound recordings.[471] The Record Rental and Computer Software Rental Amendments originally were considered "experimental" and had limited terms; however, these sunset provisions were repealed as part of the implementation of the North American Free Trade Agreement (NAFTA) and GATT agreements.

D *Importation and the First Sale Doctrine*

Section 602(a) of the Act expressly makes importation without the authority of the owner of copyright "of copies or phonorecords of a work that have been acquired outside the United States," an act of "infringement of the exclusive right to distribute copies or phonorecords under section 106."[472] Excluded from the ban on importation are: copies or phonorecords imported for the use of the government of the US or of any state or political subdivision; one copy or phonorecord imported for the private use of

467. 17 U.S.C. § 109(b)(1)(A).
468. *Id.*
469. 17 U.S.C. § 109(b)(2)(A).
470. 17 U.S.C. § 109(b)(1)(B)(ii).
471. *Brilliance Audio, Inc. v. Haights Cross Commc'ns, Inc.*, 474 F.3d 365 (6th Cir. 2007).
472. 17 U.S.C. § 602(a).

the importer and not for further distribution or brought into the US as part of the personal baggage of an individual; and not more than five copies or phonorecords imported by or for an organization operated for scholarly, educational, or religious purposes for its library or archival purposes or one copy of an audiovisual work solely for archival purposes.[473]

This section makes it an act of infringement of the distribution right to import into the US copies of works acquired abroad even if those copies were lawfully made and acquired. The question that has caused considerable conflict and confusion is the extent to which, if any, the first sale doctrine of section 109 limits application of the section 602(a) restraint on importation. The issue arises in several contexts, but the most troublesome appears to be in connection with "grey goods," or "parallel importation" of genuine goods purchased in foreign countries and imported into the US for resale, generally at a price lower than that charged by authorized US dealers. So long as there is no misrepresentation as to the goods and they are "genuine," such importation would not be an act of trademark infringement or unfair competition. However, if the packaging of the goods contains copyrighted material, then importation of the goods, as so packaged, could invoke the bar of section 602(a).[474]

The conflict played out in a series of cases. In *Sebastian International, Inc. v. Consumer Contacts (PTY) Ltd.*,[475] the Third Circuit appeared to hold that the first sale doctrine limited the application of section 602(a) so long as the goods had been made in the US and then shipped abroad and subsequently imported back into the US. The important question for the court was the place where the goods were originally made.

On the other hand, the Ninth Circuit, in *Parfums Givenchy, Inc. v. Drug Emporium, Inc.*[476] held that the first sale doctrine did not apply to insulate importation of perfume boxes having a distinctive design if those boxes had been made and initially first sold abroad. The court noted that both the importer and the one who purchases for resale from that importer are liable under section 602(a) for infringing the distribution right. The Ninth Circuit amplified its holding two years later, pointing out that the effect of Parfums Givenchy was that "§ 109 applies to copies made abroad only if the copies have been sold in the US by the copyright owner or with its authority."[477] However, shortly thereafter, another Ninth Circuit panel added to the confusion, in *L'Anza Research International, Inc. v. Quality King Distributors*,[478] as it rejected Sebastian's distinctions based upon the original sale of the goods, and held explicitly that section 602(a) is not limited by the first sale doctrine (section 109(a)).

The US Supreme Court granted certiorari to resolve this issue. Reversing the Ninth Circuit, the Court held that the first sale doctrine, section 109(a), is applicable to imported copies of works, and therefore conditions section 602(a).[479] Noting that section 602(a) "does not categorically prohibit the unauthorized importation of

473. 17 U.S.C. § 602(a)(1)-(3).
474. *See, e.g., Sebastian Int'l, Inc. v. Consumer Contacts (PTY) Ltd.*, 847 F.2d 1093 (3d Cir. 1988).
475. *Sebastian Int'l, Inc. v. Consumer Contacts (PTY) Ltd.*, 847 F.2d 1093 (3d Cir. 1988).
476. *Parfums Givenchy, Inc. v. Drug Emproium, Inc.*, 38 F.3d 477 (9th Cir. 1994).
477. *Denbicare U.S.A., Inc. v. Toys "R" US, Inc.*, 84 F.3d 1143, 1150 (9th Cir. 1996).
478. *L'Anza Research Int'l v. Quality King Distribs., Inc.*, 98 F.3d 1109 (9th Cir. 1996).
479. *Quality King Distribs., Inc. v. L'anza Research Int'l, Inc.*, 523 U.S. 135 (1998).

copyrighted materials," but rather "provides that such importation is an infringement of the exclusive right to distribute copies 'under section 106'," and that section 106 is limited by section 109(a), Justice John Paul Stevens read the statutory language as clearly making the first sale doctrine applicable to importation of copies lawfully made "under the United States Copyright Act" and acquired abroad.[480] The Court found that the two sections can "retain significant independent meaning" and that section 602(a) is not swallowed up by section 109(a), in that the importation provisions would still be applicable with respect to copies that were not lawfully made under the United States Copyright Act. Justice Ruth Bader Ginsburg, concurring, suggested that "lawfully made" under the Copyright Act "must mean 'lawfully made in the United States',"[481] which is essentially the position taken in by the Third Circuit in Sebastian. Justice Ginsburg's opinion was echoed in the 2008 Ninth Circuit opinion, *Omega S.A. v. Costco Wholesale Corp.*;[482] however, although the Supreme Court affirmed that determination, it did so by an equally divided (4–4) Court, thereby leaving the matter open until it resolved the issue in 2012 in *Kirtsaeng v. John Wiley & Sons, Inc.*[483] The Court reviewed and rejected a Second Circuit opinion that had largely adopted Justice Ginsburg's and the Omega rationale.[484] The Supreme Court, over Justice Ginsburg's dissent, rejected the Second and Ninth Circuits' imposition of "geographical limitations" on the first sale doctrine. Today, once a copyright owner sells a lawfully made copy of a work, either abroad or in the US, the first sale doctrine applies.[485]

IV The Public Performance Right

A *Generally*

The rightsholder of the public performance right is vested with the exclusive authority "in the case of literary, musical, dramatic, and choreographic works, pantomimes, and motion pictures and other audiovisual works, to perform the copyrighted work publicly."[486] The public performance right does not apply to all copyrighted works; pictorial, graphic, and sculptural works, and, with a limited exception (discussed below), sound recordings do not have performance rights. The growth of radio, television, motion pictures, and instantaneous digital communications has made the copyright owner's public performance right valuable, as well as controversial.

Generally, the performance right vests in the creator of the copyrighted work. Accordingly, it has been assumed that the one who actually "performs" a work has no

480. *Id.*, at 144.
481. *Id.*, at 1135 (Ginsburg, J., concurring).
482. *Omega S.A. v. Costco Wholesale Corp.*, 541 F.3d 982 (9th Cir. 2008).
483. *Kirtsaeng v. John Wiley & Sons, Inc.*, 568 U.S. 519 (2012).
484. *Kirtsaeng v. John Wiley & Sons, Inc.*, 654 F.3d 210 (2d Cir. 2011).
485. *Impression Prods., Inc. v. Lexmark Intern., Inc.*, 137 S. Ct. 1523, 1528 (2017) ("Under the first sale doctrine, when a copyright owner sells a lawfully made copy of its work, it loses the power to restrict the purchaser's right 'to sell or otherwise dispose of … that copy.'") (quoting 17 U.S.C. § 109(a) and citing *Kirtsaeng v. John Wiley & Sons, Inc.*, 568 U.S. 519 (2012)).
486. 17 U.S.C. § 106(4).

"performance right," as such, by virtue solely of that performance.[487] In this regard, the law in the US differs from that of the European Union Member States and signatories of the Rome Treaty on Phonograms, which recognize a performer's right in his or her performance.

The performance right has been particularly important to the music industry, with the virtually continuous use of music in connection with radio and television broadcasting and other forms of public communication. The performance right, with respect to dramatic musical works ("grand performance rights"), is often dealt with quite differently from that with respect to nondramatic musical works ("small performance rights"). For example, certain exemptions apply only to performance of nondramatic musical works, and licenses may be limited to the "small performance rights." Because of this distinction, a license that applies only to the performance of a nondramatic musical work will not protect the performance of a dramatized version of that same work.[488] Similarly, a license for performance of individual songs from a musical play will not insulate performance of the original cast album of that play or any other performance in which the songs are rendered sequentially, as that would constitute a "dramatic" version of the work. Unfortunately, there is no clear line separating dramatic from nondramatic musical works or performances. The nature of the performance itself may be determinative—the relevant question being whether the musical work is "dramatized."

For the performance right to be implicated, there must be a "performance" of the copyrighted work and that performance must be "public." The way in which these terms are defined has enormous significance in setting the scope and value of the right. These definitions are discussed below.

B "Performance"

The Copyright Act defines "performance" broadly:

> To "perform" a work means to recite, render, play, dance, or act it, either directly or by means of any device or process or, in the case of a motion picture or other audiovisual work, to show its images in any sequence or to make the sounds accompanying it audible.[489]

"Performance" is not limited to the act of a human being physically conveying the work to another. Certainly, an individual singing a song is performing it; an orchestra playing a symphony performs it; actors in a play give a performance of that play. If the works involved are copyrighted and these performances are public, then the public performance right has been violated and an action for infringement will lie if the

487. *Garcia v. Google, Inc.*, 786 F.3d 733 (9th Cir. 2015) (en banc) (concluding that actress' performance in a movie was not a copyrightable work); *see id.*, at 743 ("Treating every acting performance as an independent work would not only be a logistical and financial nightmare, it would turn cast of thousands into a new mantra: copyright of thousands.").
488. *See*, e.g., *Robert Stigwood Grp., Ltd. v. Sperber*, 457 F.2d 50 (2d Cir. 1972).
489. 17 U.S.C. § 101.

copyright owners have not consented to the performances. In this context, the "performance" has been done by "performers" as that term is generally understood.

However, a "performer" in that sense is not essential to invocation of the performance right. If a recording of an individual singing a song is played, a "performance" takes place and the person performing the copyrighted work (i.e., the song) is the person who has caused the record to be played. While "performance" is broadly defined, simple use of a copyrighted work for its intended purpose may not necessarily constitute performance. Thus, a copyrightable game is not "performed" when it is played, even when played by large groups of people at a public tournament.[490]

Consistent with the broad definition of performance is the recognition of multiple performances arising out of a single event. If a performance of a play in a theater is simultaneously televised, then while the actors perform the play, the television station also "performs" it, as does a restaurant owner who shows the television broadcast to patrons by means of a television set in the restaurant. In short, the single event of the performance of the play gives rise to multiple performances, each one of which may separately amount to an act of infringement. And permission, which may have been granted by the copyright owner with respect to the underlying event, will not insulate the performances for which permission was not granted. Using the above example, the copyright owner may have consented to the theatrical performance of the play and to the broadcast of that play, but such consent will not shield the restaurant owner from liability for the performance that arises from turning on the television set in the restaurant.[491]

The issue of retransmission of a broadcast as a "performance" has been a troublesome one. The multiple performance concept, discussed above, in which separate public performances occur when an event is broadcast and the transmission simultaneously received and further communicated, or retransmitted, was first recognized by the US Supreme Court in *Buck v. Jewell-LaSalle Realty Co.*,[492] which involved a hotel "piping" radio broadcasts into guest rooms. However, more than thirty-five years later, the Supreme Court cast serious doubt on this doctrine in two cases involving the retransmission of broadcast signals by cable television systems,[493] and essentially eviscerated the doctrine in a case involving a radio broadcast heard in a fast-food restaurant.[494] The matter was put to rest, however, with the 1976 Act, which effectively reinstated *Buck v. Jewell-LaSalle* and reversed the later cases. The Act now makes clear that a separate and, if done without consent or if not within any of the specific exceptions, actionable "performance" occurs when there is a transmission or retransmission of a performance of a copyrighted work.

490. *Allen v. Academic Games League of Am.*, 89 F.3d 614 (9th Cir. 1996).
491. *See generally* David E. Shipley, *Copyright Law and Your Neighborhood Bar and Grill: Recent Developments in Performance Rights and the Section 110(5) Exemption*, 29 ARIZ. L. REV. 475 (1987).
492. *Buck v. Jewell-LaSalle Realty Co.*, 283 U.S. 191 (1931).
493. *Fortnightly Corp. v. United Artists Television, Inc.*, 392 U.S. 390 (1968); *Teleprompter Corp. v. Columbia Broad. Sys., Inc.*, 415 U.S. 394 (1974).
494. *Twentieth Century Music Corp. v. Aiken*, 422 U.S. 151 (1975).

C *"Public"*

To invoke the performance right, a performance must be "public." The Act attempts to be comprehensive in its definition:

> To perform or display a work "publicly" means—
> 1. to perform or display it at a place open to the public or any place where a substantial number of persons outside of a normal circle of a family and its social acquaintances is gathered; or
> 2. to transmit or otherwise communicate a performance or display of the work to a place specified by clause (1) or to the public, by means of any device or process, whether the members of the public capable of receiving the performance or display receive it in the same place or in separate places and at the same time or at different times.[495]

Thus, one alternative prong of the definition looks at the place at which the work is performed. If it occurs in a place that is open to the public, even a very limited space which can accommodate only a few people at any one time, it is nevertheless "public," and the performance will be actionable even if there was virtually no audience for it. Accordingly, in *Columbia Pictures Industries, Inc. v. Redd Horne, Inc.*,[496] a videocassette rental store was deemed to have publicly performed videocassettes by providing customers with private "screening" rooms, accommodating no more than four people at a time, to which a rented videocassette was transmitted. Since the store was "a place open to the public," the performance of the videocassette was public, irrespective of the size of the place or the composition of the audience.[497]

Alternatively, a performance that occurs in what is clearly a private place, one not open to the public, will nevertheless be considered "public" if the audience to whom the performance is directed consists of "a substantial number of persons outside of a normal circle of a family and its social acquaintances." There are no clear standards for determining what size group will be considered such a "substantial number," but that determination will depend upon not only the absolute size of the group but also the nature of the occasion and the relationship among the members of the group.[498]

Transmission of a performance to a place open to the public, as in Redd Horne, or generally to the public, as in the case of a radio or television broadcast, will constitute a public performance under the Act, whether the recipients receive it simultaneously or sequentially. Thus, a hotel that electrically transmits a copyrighted motion picture to individual rooms upon request of the guests would be publicly performing the work, as it would if it played tapes or discs of the motion picture on a

495. 17 U.S.C. § 106.
496. *Columbia Pictures Indus. v. Redd Horne, Inc.*, 749 F.2d 154 (3d Cir. 1984).
497. *Id.*, at 158–59.
498. *Compare Columbia Pictures Indus., Inc. v. Aveco, Inc.*, 800 F.2d 59 (3d Cir. 1986) (holding videocassette rental store liable as a contributory infringer for renting videocassettes to customers to be played on cassette players located in separate on premises screening rooms, rather than by means of transmission from a central location), *with Cartoon Network v. CSC Holdings, Inc.*, 536 F.3d. 121 (2d Cir. 2008) (holding that RS-DVR playback transmission from a "Remote Storage DVR System" made to a single subscriber using a single unique copy produced by that subscriber was not a performance "to the public").

monitor in the hotel lobby or other common room. On the other hand, if the hotel rented the motion picture individually to guests for use in the private guest rooms equipped with their own players, the performance would not be "public."[499]

Applying these principles, in Cartoon Network, the Second Circuit held that RS-DVR playback transmission from a "Remote Storage DVR System" made to a single subscriber using a single unique copy produced by that subscriber was not a performance "to the public."[500] Relying on this ruling, that court subsequently held that retransmissions of over the air broadcasts to subscribers by means of arrays of multiple tiny individually assigned antennas was similarly not a "public performance" by the provider of the service.[501] The Second Circuit's determination was reversed by the Supreme Court (in a majority opinion that does not comment on the Cartoon Network determination).[502]

D *Statutory Exemptions: Generally*

Under the 1909 Act, the public performance right for nondramatic musical works was limited to performances made "for profit." With the growth of broadcast of recorded music and the concomitant increasing importance of the performance right for nondramatic musical works, a rich body of case law developed over the issue of what constitutes a performance "for profit," with the courts making it clear that any benefit, direct or indirect, from the performance (such as a pianist playing background music in a restaurant or recorded music being played over the air) would be sufficient to constitute a performance "for profit."[503]

The 1976 Act eliminated the "for profit" limitation for nondramatic musical works. Section 106(4) makes the performance right applicable to all works (except for sound recordings and pictorial, graphic, and sculptural works) without conditioning any rights upon the "profit" nature of the performance. Rather, the Act creates a broad performance right and then provides an array of highly specific exemptions, defining specific noncommercial or nonprofit situations in which performances are exempt, many of which, as discussed below, are refinements of the older, broader general not-for-profit exemption.

E *The Specific Statutory Exemptions*

Exemptions are set out in sections 110, 111, 118, 119, 120, 121, 121A, and 122 of the Act. The section 110 exemptions cover a wide variety of situations; section 111

499. *See Columbia Pictures Indus., Inc. v. Professional Real Estate Investors, Inc.*, 866 F.2d 278 (9th Cir. 1989).
500. *Cartoon Network v. CSC Holdings, Inc.*, 536 F.3d. 121 (2d Cir. 2008). The court also held that the individual users, rather than the cable operator, made "copies" of the works, a holding that was the basis for a similar holding by the Ninth Circuit in *Fox Broadcasting Co. v. Dish Network LLC*, 747 F.3d 1060 (9th Cir. 2014).
501. *WNET Thirteen v. Aereo, Inc.*, 712 F.3d 676 (2d Cir. 2014).
502. *Am. Broad. Cos., Inc. v. Aereo, Inc.*, 574 U.S. 431 (2014).
503. *See*, e.g., *Herbert v. Shanley*, 242 U.S. 591 (1917).

exempts certain secondary transmissions; section 111, section 119, and section 122 create compulsory license mechanisms for certain secondary transmissions; section 118 exempts public performances by certain noncommercial broadcasting entities under negotiated licenses; section 120 exempts representations of architectural works; and section 121 and section 121A exempt accessible reproductions for people with visual disabilities.

Section 110 specifically exempts 11 closely defined performances.[504] Performances that come strictly within the literal terms of these exemptions "are not infringements of copyright."[505] Section 110(1)–(4), (6), and (8)–(11) are concerned with various types of not-for-profit performances, while section 110(5) and (7) are narrowly defined commercial exemptions.

1 *Section 110(1) and 110(2): Classroom Exemption*

An exemption is provided for "performance or display of a work by instructors or pupils in the course of face-to-face teaching activities of a non-profit educational institution, in a classroom or similar place devoted to instruction," provided that, if the work is a motion picture or other audiovisual work, the exemption will not apply if the performance is "by means of a copy that was not lawfully made" and if "the person responsible for the performance knew or had reason to believe" that it was not lawfully made.[506] In other words, the performance, by teachers or students, of copyrighted works as part of face-to-face teaching activities at nonprofit educational institutions are exempt from the public performance right. This exemption covers performances of all copyrightable subject matter and will apply to face-to-face teaching situations in nonprofit educational institutions. Accordingly, if an instructor, in the course of classroom instruction, plays on a player and video monitor in the classroom, a lawfully obtained copy of a copyrighted motion picture relating to the course of instruction, the instructor's performance of the motion picture will be exempt. The legislative history suggests that "teaching activities" are those that involve "systematic instruction," and exclude performance, "whatever their cultural value or intellectual appeal, that are given for the recreation or entertainment of any part of their audience."[507]

The focus of the exemption is the instructional, classroom nature of the performance. Any opening up of the situation, so that the performance becomes directed to a wider audience, for other purposes, would place it outside the protection of the exemption. So, too, the exemption would be lost, even if the audience were limited to the students in that instructor's class, if, instead of playing the copy in a player located in the classroom, the instructor arranged for the motion picture to be transmitted to that classroom from an external location.

Section 110(2) expands the instructional exemption from the face-to-face teaching context to instructional "transmissions." That exemption, as originally enacted,

504. 17 U.S.C. § 110.
505. *Id.*
506. 17 U.S.C. § 110(1).
507. H.R. Rep. No. 94-1476, at 81.

was limited to performances of nondramatic literary or musical works and would not include audiovisual works, motion pictures, or dramatic literary or musical works; so too, "transmission" of a performance of such works would be exempt only under limited circumstances related to classroom use. Note that section 110(2) does not exempt other uses, like adaptations and derivatives.

The growth of distance education, particularly through the internet, prompted reexamination of these instructional exemptions. Responding to a directive in the 1998 Digital Millennium Copyright Act (DMCA), the Register of Copyrights sent to Congress a Report on Copyright and Digital Distance Education, and in 2002 Congress enacted the "Technology, Education and Copyright Harmonization Act" (the TEACH Act) implementing some of the recommendations. Section 110(2), as so amended, broadens the "transmission" exemption to accommodate some of the exigencies of distance education by expanding the kinds of works to which the exemption applies, and broadening its scope beyond the classroom. But it retains several serious limitations; it is not a broad "educational" transmission exemption, and the educational institutions seeking to use the exemption must meet an array of stringent requirements.[508]

2 *Section 110(3): Religious Organizations*

The section exempts performance, as part of religious services, "of a nondramatic literary or musical work or of a dramatico-musical work of a religious nature."[509] Other works, like movies, are not within the exemption, even if they have a religious theme. The statutory exemption applies only to performances that occur "at a place of worship or other religious assembly." The legislative history suggests that "other" places could be where "services are conducted before a religious gathering," including auditoriums and outdoor theaters.[510] As the performance must occur "at a place of worship or other religious assembly," the House Report emphasized that "the exemption would not extend to religious broadcasts or other transmissions to the public at large, even where the transmissions were sent from the place of worship."[511]

3 *Section 110(4): General Not-for-Profit Exemption for Nondramatic Works*

The Copyright Act carves out a statutory exemption for nonprofit public performances of musical and nondramatic literary works. Section 110(4) attempts to preserve part of the 1909 Act "profit" limitation of the performance right. It exempts from liability performance of a nondramatic literary or musical work if that performance: (1) is not in a transmission to the public and (2) is given "without any purpose of direct or indirect commercial advantage and without payment of any fee or other compensation

508. 17 U.S.C. § 110(2).
509. 17 U.S.C. § 110(3).
510. H.R. Rep. No. 94-1476, at 84–85.
511. *Id.*, at 84.

for the performance to any of its performers, promoters, or organizers."[512] Further, the exemption requires either: (1) that there be no direct or indirect admission charge; or (2) that the proceeds from any direct or indirect admission charge (after deduction of expenses) be used "exclusively for educational, religious, or charitable purposes and not for private financial gain"; as to the latter, even if the proceeds are so dedicated, the exemption will not apply if the copyright owner of the work has served written notice of objection to the performance, with a statement of the reasons for the objection, upon the person responsible for that performance at least seven days before the performance date.[513] The Act does not require the sponsor of the event to notify the copyright owner of the intention to use the work.

4 *Section 110(5): Communication of Transmission of a Performance*

a The "*Aiken*" Exemption for "Home" Type Equipment

The 1976 Act resolved controversy over the application of the performance right to multiple performances and secondary transmissions by overturning the series of US Supreme Court opinions that had culminated in *Twentieth Century Music Corp. v. Aiken.*[514] The Act effectively reinstated *Buck v. Jewell-LaSalle Realty Co.*,[515] making each of the elements of the multiple performances of a single event a separate "performance" for the purposes of the Act. However, at the same time, Congress attempted to codify the result in Aiken by exempting performances occurring in a context similar to that of that case. Specifically, section 110(5)(A) exempts a performance which consists of the public reception "on a single receiving apparatus of a kind commonly used in private homes" of a transmission embodying a performance of a work, unless: (1) a direct charge is made to see or hear the transmission or (2) there is a further transmission of the work to the public.[516] In short, this section would exempt a performance consisting of having a simple radio or television receiver turned on in a restaurant. The exemption is limited specifically to communication of a transmission and, therefore, would not exempt playing of a CD or recording under the same circumstances and on a similarly simple device.

The crucial issue for determining applicability of the exemption is the characterization of the receiving apparatus as being "of a kind commonly used in private homes." The intention behind the exemption was to allow the use of ordinary radio and television sets in small commercial establishments. In considering the applicability of the exemption, one must consider both the size of the establishment and the nature of the receiving apparatus. The House Committee Report suggested that the factors to be considered are "the size, physical arrangement, and noise level of [the premises] and

512. 17 U.S.C. § 110(4).
513. 17 U.S.C. § 110(4)(B).
514. *Twentieth Century Music Corp. v. Aiken*, 422 U.S. 151 (1975).
515. *Buck v. Jewell-LaSalle Realty Co.*, 283 U.S. 191 (1931).
516. 17 U.S.C. § 110(5)(A).

the extent to which the receiving apparatus is altered or augmented."[517] The Report suggested that the exemption would not be applicable where "the commercial establishment is of sufficient size to justify ... a subscription to a commercial background music service."[518] For these purposes, the relevant "size" is that of the individual establishment, so that an installation in each small store of an affiliated chain will be evaluated on an individual store basis and the court will not aggregate the stores; so long as each store uses equipment "of a kind commonly used in private homes" the use will be exempt.[519]

b Nondramatic Musical Works in Licensed Broadcast Transmissions

Changing technology and increased sophistication of audio and video equipment have altered the boundaries of the definition of the statutory words. It is no longer so easy to differentiate "home" from "commercial" equipment. The result has been a lack of clear definitional rules or consistency in application.[520]

In response, both to the problem of technology and to concerns over the activities of ASCAP and the other performing rights societies, Congress enacted the "Fairness in Music Licensing Act of 1998," creating a further exemption with respect to performance or display of nondramatic musical works.[521] These provisions exempt communication by a business establishment of a transmission (or of a retransmission) originated by a licensed radio or television broadcast station, or, if an audiovisual transmission, by a cable system or satellite carrier, embodying a performance or display of a nondramatic musical work intended to be received by the general public if: no direct charge is made to see or hear the transmission or retransmission, and the transmission or retransmission is not further transmitted beyond the establishment where it is received, and the transmission or retransmission is licensed by the copyright owner of the work. The exemption is further limited by the requirement that if the establishment has 2,000 or more (or, in the case of a food service establishment, 3,750 or more) gross square feet of space, the communication may not involve: (i) in the case of an audio performance, or of the audio portion of an audiovisual performance, more than six loudspeakers (with no more than four located in any one room or adjoining outdoor space); and (ii) in the case of the visual portion of an audiovisual performance, more than four

517. H.R. REP. No. 94-1476, at 87 (1976), *as reprinted in* 1976 U.S.C.C.A.N. 5659, 5701.
518. *Id.*, at 75.
519. *See Broadcast Music, Inc. v. Claire's Boutiques, Inc.*, 949 F.2d 1482 (7th Cir. 1991).
520. *Id.*; *see also Cass Cnty. Music Co. v. Muedini*, 55 F.3d 263 (7th Cir. 1995) (examining and applying *Claire's Boutiques*, to a different conclusion, holding that the addition to a standard receiver of a sophisticated control panel and nine recessed speakers, connected with a powerful transformer, resulted in a system in defendant's restaurant that is not "commonly found in homes" and is therefore not exempt); *Nat'l Football League v. McBee & Bruno's, Inc.*, 792 F.2d 726 (8th Cir. 1986) (holding that the use of antenna dishes to receive blacked out television signals on a simple television set located in a bar was not exempt; while the receiving set meets the requirements, use of the large antenna to pick up the signal infringes).
521. 17 U.S.C. § 110(5)(B).

audiovisual devices (with no more than one located in any one room) having a diagonal screen size greater than fifty-five inches.[522]

The addition of section 110(5)(B) significantly expanded the exemption for communication of a transmission of a nondramatic musical work. This expansion put into bold relief the problem of harmonizing US copyright law, and its array of exemptions and compulsory licenses, with the Berne Convention. In general, the Berne Convention leaves room for some limitation of copyright owner rights, as member countries reserve the right to impose "minor reservations" on the public performance right. However, in June 2000, a WTO dispute resolution panel, responding to the complaint by copyright owners in Ireland about the scope of section 110(5)(B), found that the section placed the US in violation of the TRIPS Agreement, specifically Article 13, a recodification of Article 9.2 of the Berne Convention, which limits exemptions to those "that do not conflict with a normal exploitation of the work."[523] The panel held that the section, in its breadth and with its significant economic implications, did indeed conflict. By contrast, the panel upheld the section 110(5)(A) Aiken exemption for homestyle equipment as comparatively minimal and not inconsistent with the Berne Convention. No enforcement action has been taken against the US, and the Congress has not acted to amend the section.

With respect to the exemptions under section 110(5), a proprietor of an establishment[524] who asserts the exemption as a defense to an infringement claim, without reasonable grounds to believe it was applicable, will be liable, in addition to any other damages, for twice the license fee that should have been paid, for up to the preceding three years.[525]

5 *Section 110(6): Governmental Agricultural Organizations*

Performance of a nondramatic musical work is exempt if it is done by a governmental body or a nonprofit agricultural or horticultural organization in the course of an annual agricultural or horticultural fair or exhibition; the exemption extends to any vicarious liability which might otherwise be imposed upon the sponsoring organization for infringing activities of concessionaires or others at such agricultural fair or exhibition (but does not protect such individual infringers).[526]

6 *Section 110(7): Performance Ancillary to Retail Sales*

The Act exempts performance of a nondramatic musical work by a vending establishment open to the public at large without any direct or indirect admission charge, where

522. *Id.*
523. *United States—Section 110(5) of the United States Copyright Act*, WT/DS160/R; for a case comment *see* Phillip Johnson, *One Small Step or One Giant Leap? How Has the WTO Panel Decision on Section 110(5) of the United States Copyright Act Changed Our Understanding of the "Three-Step Test"?*, 26 EUROPEAN INTELL. PROP. REV. 265 (2004).
524. As these terms are defined in 17 U.S.C. § 101.
525. 17 U.S.C. § 504(d).
526. 17 U.S.C. § 110(6).

the sole purpose of the performance is to promote the retail sale of copies or phonorecords of the work, or of the audiovisual or other devices utilized in such performance, if the performance is not transmitted beyond the place where the establishment is located and is made "within the immediate area where the sale is occurring."[527] As is clear from the language, the exemption is designed to protect performance of a work to enhance sales of phonorecords of the work or associated equipment. Thus, playing a CD by means of a player and speakers located near the cash register of the music department of a department store would be exempt, whereas playing a videocassette of a motion picture through a cassette player and monitor located near the cash register of a video rental store would not be exempt, since the motion picture is not a nondramatic musical work. So, too, the exemption would be lost by the department store in the case of the CD if the music were further transmitted from the music department to other parts of the store.

7 *Section 110(8) and (9): Performance and Transmissions to Certain Handicapped Persons*

The performance of a nondramatic literary work will be exempt if it occurs in the course of a transmission specifically designed for and primarily directed to "blind or other handicapped persons who are unable to read normal printed material," or "deaf or other handicapped persons who are unable to hear the aural signals accompanying the transmission of visual signals," if the "performance is made without any purpose of direct or indirect commercial advantage" and its transmission is made through the facilities of: (i) a governmental body; or (ii) a noncommercial educational broadcast station; or (iii) a radio subcarrier; or (iv) a cable system.[528] The section 110(8) exemption applies only to nondramatic literary works and therefore will not cover the performance of a play or of any musical or audiovisual works.

A limited exemption is provided for a single performance, on only one occasion, of a dramatic literary work in a transmission "specifically designed for and primarily directed to blind or other handicapped persons who are unable to read normal printed material" if the performance is made without any purpose of direct or indirect commercial advantage and the transmission is made through the facilities of a radio subcarrier.[529] Moreover, for the exemption to apply, the work must have been published at least ten years before the date of the performance.

8 *Section 110(10): Fraternal and Veterans Organizations, for Charitable Purposes*

Performance of a nondramatic literary or musical work is exempt if it is done "in the course of a social function which is organized and promoted by a non-profit veterans'

527. 17 U.S.C. § 110(7).
528. 17 U.S.C. § 110(8).
529. 17 U.S.C. § 110(9).

organization or a non-profit fraternal organization to which the general public is not invited ... if the proceeds from the performance, after deducting the reasonable costs of producing the performance, are used exclusively for charitable purposes and not for financial gain."[530] For these purposes, a college or university fraternity or sorority will be included only if the social function "is held solely to raise funds for a specific charitable purpose." This exemption was added to the Act to give these organizations somewhat broader rights than they would have under section 110(4), the general not-for-profit exemption for nondramatic works.

9 *Section 110(11): Sanitizing Audio or Video Portions of Movies*

In 2005, the Family Entertainment and Copyright Act exempted "the making imperceptible, by or at the direction of a private household, of limited portions of audio or video content of a motion picture."[531] It is not an infringement for a member of a private household to make imperceptible limited portions of audio or video content of a motion picture, nor is it an infringement to create technology that enables such making imperceptible, so long as the technology is designed and marketed to be used at the direction of a member of a private household.[532] The term "making imperceptible" does not include the addition of audio or video content that is performed or displayed over or in place of existing content in a motion picture.

10 *Section 111: Exemptions for Secondary Transmissions*

Section 111 creates a limited exemption, under certain circumstances, for "secondary transmissions of a primary transmission embodying a performance or display of a work."[533] The exemption deals essentially with the retransmission of over the air broadcast signals. It specifically exempts a retransmission, other than one made by a cable system, in the form of relaying transmissions by licensed broadcast stations "by the management of a hotel, apartment house, or similar establishment," "to the private lodgings of guests or residents of such establishment," if no direct charge is made to see or hear that secondary transmission.[534] The Act here seeks to exempt the *Buck v. Jewell-LaSalle* situation of a simple relay of a broadcast signal to private rooms (simply placing a radio or television receiver in a private hotel room is not a public performance or actionable in any event).[535]

Section 111 further exempts the following: secondary transmissions as part of the systematic instructional activities of a governmental body or nonprofit educational institution under the circumstance set out in section 110(2) (discussed above);[536]

530. 17 U.S.C. § 110(10).
531. Pub. L. No. 109-9, § 202 (2005) (codified at § 110(11)).
532. 17 U.S.C. § 110(11).
533. 17 U.S.C. § 111(a).
534. 17 U.S.C. § 111(a)(1).
535. *See Buck v. Jewell-LaSalle Realty Co.*, 283 U.S. 191 (1931).
536. 17 U.S.C. § 111(a)(2).

secondary transmissions made by a "passive" carrier, one with no control over the content of the primary transmission or with the recipients of the secondary transmission, but merely a provider of hardware and communications channels for the use of others;[537] secondary transmissions "made by a satellite carrier for private home viewing pursuant to a statutory license under section 119 [of the Act]";[538] and secondary transmissions made by a governmental body or other nonprofit organization without charge to the recipients other than assessments necessary to defray the actual and reasonable costs of maintaining and operating the secondary transmission service.[539]

The foregoing exemptions under section 111(a) will not apply if the secondary transmission is of a primary transmission that is "controlled and limited to reception by particular members of the public" unless that primary transmission is made by a licensed broadcast station and the secondary transmitter is required under the rules of the Federal Communications Commission to carry that signal and the signal is not altered.[540]

Finally, section 111 deals with retransmissions by cable systems. Cable operators typically carry multiple broadcast signals, each containing protected works owned by dozens of copyright owners. Because of the logistical challenges of clearing rights with dozens of owners, section 111 set up a statutory licensing system. The compulsory licensing scheme, by which cable systems pay royalties, is based on the size of the respective systems. The statute outlined a detailed procedure for determining both the amount to be distributed and the proper parties to receive payment of the royalty fees.[541] These royalties are allocated and distributed by the Library of Congress, on recommendation from the Register of Copyrights. To be protected by the compulsory license, a cable system may not change the content of the primary broadcast.[542]

Peculiar problems have been created by new technologies, like satellite carrier companies, which retransmit television-programming signals by means of satellite to home satellite receiving dishes. If such companies are "cable systems," they would come within section 111, so long as they otherwise met its provisions. But if they are not a cable system, and absent some other exemption, their retransmissions would be infringing. It was initially left to the courts to decide if a satellite rebroadcast facility could also be a "cable system" under section 111. In 1991, the Eleventh Circuit held that such a carrier was a "cable system,"[543] but the next year the Copyright Office issued regulations providing that satellite carriers were not "cable systems" for the purposes of section 111. The Copyright Office's regulations were subsequently upheld

537. 17 U.S.C. § 111(a)(3).
538. 17 U.S.C. § 111(a)(4).
539. 17 U.S.C. § 111(a)(5).
540. 17 U.S.C. § 111(b).
541. 17 U.S.C. § 111(c)–(f).
542. U.S. Copyright Office, Satellite Home Viewer Extension and Reauthorization Act Section 109 Report 1 (June 2008), available at, https://www.copyright.gov/reports/section109-final-report.pdf.
543. *Nat'l Broad. Co., Inc. v. Satellite Broad. Network, Inc.*, 940 F.2d 1467 (11th Cir. 1991).

by the Eleventh Circuit.[544] While satellite is not included in section 111, in 1994, Congress amended the section to expressly include another new technology: microwave retransmissions.

Congress has yet to provide a compulsory license for internet-based retransmission services. Courts have generally held that such retransmission services are not a "cable system."[545] Thus far, internet-based retransmitters are ineligible for a compulsory license for retransmission of broadcast television networks' copyrighted works.[546]

11 *Section 118: Noncommercial Broadcasting*

The compulsory license for noncommercial broadcasters under section 118 of the Act includes the right to perform or display a work "in the course of a transmission made by a noncommercial educational broadcast station."[547] For the purposes of this statute, a "noncommercial educational broadcast station" is a television or radio station that is either: (1) owned and operated by a municipality and transmits only noncommercial programs for education purposes or (2) is eligible to be licensed as a noncommercial educational station and is owned and operated by a public agency or a nonprofit private foundation, corporation, or association.[548]

12 *Section 119: Exemptions for Secondary Transmissions of Distant Television Programming by Satellite*

Section 119, the Satellite Home Viewer Act, creates a statutory license for the secondary transmissions of network and nonnetwork television by satellite carriers, so long as they meet certain requirements.[549] This law was passed in response to the growing shift from broadcast and cable television to direct satellite television service, largely out of a desire by the American public for viewing options not available locally. For "secondary transmissions of a performance or display of a work embodied in a primary transmission made by a non-network station," the compulsory license is applied so long as: (1) the transmission is for either "private home viewing" or "viewing in a

544. *Satellite Broad. & Commc'ns Ass'n of Am. v. Oman*, 17 F.3d 344, 345 (11th Cir. 1994) ("Although the new regulations conflict with our interpretation of the term 'cable system' in [*Nat'l Broad. Co., Inc. v. Satellite Broad. Network, Inc.*, 940 F.2d 1467 (11th Cir. 1991)], they are neither arbitrary, capricious, nor in conflict with the clear meaning of the statute. They are therefore valid exercises of the Copyright Office's statutory authority to interpret the provisions of the compulsory licensing scheme, and are binding on this circuit.").

545. *Fox Television Stations, Inc. v. Aereokiller, LLC*, 851 F.3d 1002, 1007 n.1 (9th Cir. 2017) ("As of this writing, at least seven federal courts have weighed in on whether Internet-based retransmission services count as 'cable systems' under § 111. The district court here is the only one to conclude that they do.").

546. *See, e.g., Fox Television Stations, Inc. v. Aereokiller, LLC*, 851 F.3d 1002 (9th Cir. 2017); *WPIX, Inc. v. ivi, Inc.* 691 F.3d 275 (2d Cir. 2012); *Fox Television Stations, Inc. v. FilmOn X, LLC*, 150 F. Supp. 3d (D.D.C. 2015).

547. 17 U.S.C. § 118.

548. 47 U.S.C. § 397(6).

549. 17 U.S.C. § 119.

commercial establishment," (2) the satellite carrier acts in accordance with the mandates of the Federal Communications Commission, and (3) the "carrier makes a direct or indirect charge for each retransmission service to each subscriber receiving the secondary transmission" or to a contracted distributor.[550]

For a "network station" (as defined by the Federal Communications Commission) or for a "noncommerical educational broadcast station,"[551] section 119 imposes additional requirements to satisfy the statutory license. Unlike nonnetwork transmissions, a section 119 license will apply if (1) "the secondary transmission is made by a satellite carrier to the public for private home viewing," (2) the carrier acts in accord with the mandates of the Federal Communications Commission, (3) the carrier makes a direct or indirect charge for such retransmission service to each subscriber receiving the transmission, and (4) the carrier provides "local-into-local service to all [designated market area]s."[552] This network license is further limited to "secondary transmissions of the signals of no more than two network stations in a single day for each television network to persons who reside in unserved households" and, if the household is in a short market,[553] to "secondary transmissions of only those primary transmissions of network stations that embody the programming of networks not offered on the primary stream or the multicast stream transmitted by any network station in that market."[554] The satellite carrier is also required to regularly submit a list of subscribers to the network station.[555]

Both types of licenses established by section 119 are contingent on the satellite carrier meeting certain other requirements. Among other conditions, the carrier must timely pay royalty fees and provide relevant account statements; the carrier must neither willfully alter the transmission nor discriminate against a distributor.[556]

13 *Section 120: Architectural Works*

The Act exempts any pictorial representations (e.g., a picture, a painting, or a photograph) of an architectural work so long as the building is located in or is ordinarily visible from a public place.[557] This section also limits the power of the copyright owner of an architectural work by allowing the owner of the building embodying the architectural work to destroy or alter the building without the copyright owner's consent.[558] For the purposes of this statute, an "architectural work" is defined

550. 17 U.S.C. § 119(a)(1).
551. 17 U.S.C. § 119(d)(2).
552. 17 U.S.C. § 119(a)(2)(A).
553. "The term 'short market' means a local market in which programming of one or more of the four most widely viewed television networks nationwide is not offered on either the primary stream or multicast stream transmitted by any network station in that market or is temporarily or permanently unavailable as a result of an act of god or other force majeure event beyond the control of the carrier." 17 U.S.C. § 119(d)(16).
554. 17 U.S.C. § 119(a)(2)(B).
555. 17 U.S.C. § 119(a)(2)(C).
556. 17 U.S.C. § 119(a).
557. 17 U.S.C. § 120(a).
558. 17 U.S.C. § 120(b).

as " the design of a building as embodied in any tangible medium of expression, including a building, architectural plans, or drawings."[559] The exemptions do not, however, include pictorial, graphical, or structural works that are on the building but are not a part of the architectural work itself (i.e., a mural).[560]

14 *Section 121 and 121A: Reproductions for People with Visual Disabilities*

Section 121 and 121A of the Act create an exemption for reproducing and distributing certain works to people with visual disabilities. Section 121 states that it shall not be an infringement to reproduce or distribute "copies or phonorecords of a previously published literary work or of a previously published musical work that has been fixed in the form of text or notation" so long as they are distributed in an "accessible format" for the exclusive use by eligible persons within the US.[561] Here, an "eligible person" means an individual who: (1) is blind, (2) has a visual impairment or perceptual or reading disability such that they are unable to read printed works to substantially the same degree as a person without an impairment or disability, or (3) is otherwise unable to "hold or manipulate a book or to focus or move the eyes to the extent that would normally be acceptable for reading."[562] Section 121A creates the same exemption for the exportation of such materials to an authorized entity or eligible person within a country that is a party to the Marrakesh Treaty.[563]

15 *Section 122: Exemptions for Secondary Transmissions of Local Television Programming by Satellite*

Similar to section 119 (discussed above), section 122 creates a compulsory license for a satellite carrier to retransmit a broadcast from a television broadcast station into that station's local market so long as: (1) the satellite carrier is in compliance with the mandates of the Federal Communications Commission, and (2) the satellite carrier makes a direct or indirect charge for the transmission to each receiving subscriber or to their contracted distributor.[564] Additionally, if the Federal Communication Commission has determined a signal to be "significantly viewed" within a community, the

559. 17 U.S.C. § 101.
560. *See Falkner v. General Motors LLC*, 393 F. Supp. 3d 927, 937 (C.D. Cal. 2018).
561. 17 U.S.C. § 121(a). Section 121 also includes an exemption for a publisher to distribute "print instructional materials for use in elementary or secondary schools" to the National Instructional Materials Access Center as allowed by the Individuals with Disabilities Education Act so long as: (1) "the inclusion of the contents of such print instructional materials is required by any State educational agency or local educational agency," (2) "the publisher had the right to publish such print instructional materials in print format," and (3) "such copies are used solely for reproduction or distribution of the contents of such print instructional materials in accessible formats." 17 U.S.C. § 121(c).
562. 17 U.S.C. § 121(d)(3).
563. As used in the Act, the term "The Marrakesh Treaty" refers to the 2013 Marrakesh Treaty to Facilitate Access to Published Works by Visually Impaired Persons and Persons with Print Disabilities. 17 U.S.C. § 121A(f)(2).
564. 17 U.S.C. § 122(a)(1).

carrier is permitted to transmit that signal to a subscriber outside the station's local market.[565] The carrier may also retransmit "the primary transmission of a television broadcast station that is licensed as a low power television station" to a subscriber within that station's designated market area; however, this does not apply to a low power station that retransmits the signal of another station for more than two hours a day.[566] Unlike section 119's compulsory license, a satellite carrier's secondary transmissions that fall under these three categories do not have an obligation to pay a royalty for the transmissions.[567]

The Act also creates some special exemptions for states with limited television stations. If a state has a single full-power station that was a network station on January 1, 1995, the license under this section shall apply to the satellite retransmission of that station's primary transmission to any subscriber in nonmajor market within that state.[568] Similar exemptions apply to states when all stations are within the same local market or have local markets principally comprised of counties from another state.[569]

All licenses under section 122 are subject to additional conditions, including a prohibition against the willful alteration of the primary transmission and a requirement to regularly report a list of subscribers to the stations.[570]

F *Performing Rights Societies*

While the Act clearly recognizes the performance right, enforcement of the right can be difficult, particularly with respect to the "small performance right," the performance right with respect to nondramatic musical works. Quite apart from the difficulty of any copyright owner tracking live performances of copyrighted works, the ubiquity of broadcast recorded music makes individual enforcement of performance rights a virtual impossibility. The difficulty was recognized almost as soon as recorded music began, and the solution was found in collective action with the formation in 1914 of the ASCAP, primarily through the efforts of the well-known composer Victor Herbert and the lawyer Nathan Burkan.

ASCAP, the first and still largest of the performing rights societies,[571] is essentially a licensing, collection, and distribution body. Its members—composers, authors, and publishers of copyrighted musical works—assign to the society the nonexclusive right to license the small performance rights (the nondramatic musical performance rights) to their works collectively. With the license from the individual members, the society then negotiates blanket licenses with broadcast stations, restaurants, bars, health

565. 17 U.S.C. § 122(a)(2).
566. 17 U.S.C. § 122(a)(3).
567. 17 U.S.C. § 122(c).
568. 17 U.S.C. § 122(a)(4).
569. *Id.*
570. 17 U.S.C. § 122.
571. A "performing rights society" is "an association, corporation, or other entity that licenses the public performance of nondramatic musical works on behalf of copyright owners of such works, such as the American Society of Composers, Authors and Publishers (ASCAP), Broadcast Music, Inc. (BMI), and SESAC, Inc." 17 U.S.C. § 101.

clubs, and any other entities desiring to perform any of the works; in exchange for payment of the annual fee, the licensee then may exercise the nondramatic musical rights attaching to any and all of the society's works. The accumulated license fees, after expenses, are then distributed to the members more or less on the basis of the frequency of performance of their works, as determined by statistical samples.[572]

There was growing dissatisfaction by composers with the weighting distribution system employed by ASCAP, which allegedly favored older, more established composers. And broadcasters also were developing concerns about ASCAP's pricing practices. The alignment of these forces resulted in the formation, under the auspices of broadcasters, of a competing performing rights society: BMI. Several other, considerably smaller, special-purpose performing rights societies also exist. What they all have in common is collective action and a practice of blanket licenses. This inevitably invited scrutiny and attack under the US antitrust laws, with the result that ASCAP and BMI operate under consent decrees putting constraints on their activities. For example, ASCAP may acquire only nonexclusive licenses from its members, who remain free to negotiate licenses individually, and ASCAP must make available to users a per program license as well as a blanket license.[573]

The performing rights societies, and particularly ASCAP, vigorously enforce their rights and regularly institute litigation against entities who exercise the small performing rights without consent. The advent of internet-based music "streaming" services and downloading of music via the internet has brought into focus the distinction between streaming as a "performance" (with implications for the performance right, and performance rights societies interests) and downloading as a "distribution" outside the purview of the societies.[574]

Similarly with respect to motion pictures, the Motion Picture Association, while not a performing rights society, nevertheless quite actively monitors motion picture performances and arranges appropriate licenses. As discussed above,[575] there are other organizations that seek to facilitate licensing of various rights, although they are not licensing organizations as such but rather agents for copyright owners.

V The Display Right

The exclusive rights in copyrighted works include the right "to display the copyrighted work publicly."[576]

572. *See* Bernard Korman & I. Fred Koenigsberg, *Performing Rights in Music and Performing Rights Societies*, 33 J. Copy. Socy. 332 (1986).
573. *See*, e.g., Alan J. Hartnick, *The Newest Blanket License Triumphant: The Fourth Round of the ASCAP-BMI/CBS Litigation*, 2 Comm. & L. 49 (1980); Ralph Oman, *Source Licensing: The Latest Skirmish in an Old Battle*, 11 Colum.-VLA J.L. & Arts 251 (1987).
574. *See United States v. Am. Soc'y of Composers, Authors & Publishers*, 627 F.3d 64 (2d Cir. 2010).
575. *See supra* §6.I.B.
576. 17 U.S.C. § 106(5) ("in the case of literary, musical, dramatic, and choreographic works, pantomimes, and pictorial, graphic, or sculptural works, including the individual images of a motion picture or other audiovisual work, to display the copyrighted work publicly").

A The Nature of the Right

To "display" a work:

> means to show a copy of it, either directly or by means of a film, slide, television image, or any other device or process or, in the case of a motion picture or other audiovisual work, to show individual images nonsequentially.[577]

As with a performance, one may "transmit" the display, that is, "communicate it by any device or process whereby images or sounds are received beyond the place from which they are sent."[578]

The display right was not explicitly recognized prior to the 1976 Act. It arose largely from concern over the possibility of harm to copyright owners from exhibition of works on mass communication devices or other forms of communication which might not necessarily amount to performance or distribution of a work but could nevertheless result in wide dissemination of that work to the public. Explicit recognition of the right reflects an intention to give the copyright owner control over direct showings of copyrighted work, as well as the projection of images and electronic transmission of images of such work.

In many respects, the display right parallels the public performance right. The right is concerned with public display of a work; that term is defined, for the purposes of the display right, the same as it is defined for the purposes of the performance right. The display right is implicated when an internet website "displays" thumbnail images of copyrighted material—although it may be found that such display is a protected fair use. A split in the courts has arisen on whether embedding, or in-line linking, constitutes a public display.[579] In-line linking has become common, especially on social media, where a preview of a linked page is provided.[580] Under the "server test," in-line linking constitutes a public display only when the defendant hosts the photo on its server.[581] A minority trend rejected the server test, in favor of the "incorporation test," finding websites that displayed an "embedded" photo, residing on another server, were still liable for copyright infringement.[582] However, the Ninth Circuit subsequently

577. 17 U.S.C. § 101.
578. *Id.*
579. *Compare Perfect 10, Inc. v. Amazon.com, Inc.*, 508 F.3d 1146 (9th Cir. 2007) (holding that framed in-line linked full-size images of copyrighted photographs were not "display" of owner's works), *with Goldman v. Breitbart News Network, LLC*, 302 F. Supp. 3d 585 (S.D.N.Y. 2018) (holding that embedding messages constituted "display" of work under Copyright Act).
580. *See* Isabela M. Palmieri & Amanda Reid, *Copyright's Threat to Shareability: A Contractual Solution Via Platforms' User Agreement to Favor Free Embedding*, 28 COMM. L. & POL'Y 152 (2023), doi: 10.1080/10811680.2023.2185405.
581. *See Perfect 10, Inc. v. Amazon.com, Inc.*, 508 F.3d 1146 (9th Cir. 2007); *see also Flava Works, Inc. v. Gunter*, 689 F.3d 754 (7th Cir. 2012) (similar conclusion for embedding code containing a video).
582. *See, e.g.*, *Leader's Inst., LLC v. Jackson*, No. 3:14-CV-3572-B, 2017 WL 5629514, at *11 (N.D. Tex. Nov. 22, 2017) ("[T]o the extent *Perfect 10* makes actual possession of a copy a necessary condition to violating a copyright owner's exclusive right to display her copyrighted works, the Court respectfully disagrees with the Ninth Circuit."); *Goldman v. Breitbart News Network, LLC*, 302 F. Supp. 3d 585, 593 (S.D.N.Y. 2018) ("The plain language of the Copyright Act, the

reaffirmed that, under the server test, a website's practice of embedding images does not infringe the copyright in those images.[583]

B Limitations on the Display Right

To a large extent, the exemptions and limitations upon the display right parallel those attendant to the performance right. Specifically, the performance right exemptions in sections 110(1) (face-to-face teaching), 110(2) (instructional broadcast), 110(3) (religious services), 110(5) (communication of a transmission), 111(c) (secondary transmissions by cable systems), and 118 (activities of public broadcasting stations)[584] all apply equally to the display right.

Moreover, an analog to the first sale doctrine[585] limits the display right. In addition to the right to make transfers or dispositions, the owner of a lawfully made copy of a work may display that copy publicly, either directly or by the projection of no more than one image at time, to viewers present at the place where the copy is located.[586]

Thus, a museum that has purchased artwork (without acquiring the copyright in that work) need not have the consent of the copyright owner to display that work at the museum. Just as with the first sale doctrine, the person seeking the benefit of the exemption must be the owner of a lawfully made copy of the work. Further, so long as the display takes place where the copy of the work is located, it may be displayed either directly or indirectly, such as by projection. The exemption is also limited to the display of not more than "one image at a time," and therefore it would not apply to a transmission made available to a number of people by the use of multiple images or multiple receiving devices, such as computer terminals.

VI The Limited Performance Right for Sound Recordings

As discussed above,[587] the 1976 Act, in creating the sound recording copyright, explicitly refused to generally include performance rights as part of the exclusive rights of the owner of copyright in a sound recording.[588] Consequently, the US cannot adhere to the Rome Convention for the Protection of Performers, Producers of Phonograms, and Broadcasting Organizations.

---

legislative history undergirding its enactment, and subsequent Supreme Court jurisprudence provide no basis for a rule that allows the physical location or possession of an image to determine who may or may not have 'displayed' a work within the meaning of the Copyright Act."); *McGucken v. Newsweek LLC*, No. 19 CIV. 9617 (KPF), 2022 WL 836786, at *6 (S.D.N.Y. Mar. 21, 2022) ("In support of this argument, Defendant relies on the 'server test' established by the Ninth Circuit .... The [District] Court rejects Defendant's argument.").

583. *Hunley v. Instagram*, LLC, 73 F.4th 1060, 1076-77 (9th Cir. 2023).
584. *See supra* §6.IV.E.
585. *See supra* §6.III.B.
586. 17 U.S.C. § 109(c).
587. *See supra* §2.IV.F.
588. 17 U.S.C. § 114(a).

However, with the passage, in 1995, of the Digital Performance Right in Sound Recordings Act, there was created a limited performance right in sound recordings, directed essentially to those applications that displace the market for the recordings, as opposed to those (such as over the air broadcast) that could enhance the market. The 1995 Act effectively limited the right to subscription or interactive digital audio transmissions and a defined class of nonsubscription transmissions.

The Digital Performance Right in Sound Recordings Act granted to the owner of copyright in a sound recording the exclusive right "to perform the copyrighted work publicly by means of a digital audio transmission."[589] "Digital transmission" is defined as "a transmission in whole or in part in a digital or other nonanalog format,"[590] and therefore the performance right would not apply to an analog transmission of a sound recording, such as was usually done by radio broadcast stations. Similarly, the right is limited to "transmission" and therefore would not apply to other forms of performance of sound recordings, such as playing prerecorded music in restaurants or other public places, nor can the right apply to the transmission of any audiovisual work.[591] Most significant is the complex set of limitations and exceptions which effectively tailor the performance right in sound recordings to digital "subscription transmissions" (and selected "eligible nonsubscription transmissions"), transmissions to a controlled group of recipients who pay to receive them.[592]

The DMCA of 1998 significantly expanded the scope and complexity of section 114 (making it now one of the most complex and densely worded provisions of the 1976 Act), which now extends to internet performances and contains a statutory and voluntary compulsory licensing scheme and measures related to that Act's antipiracy provisions.[593] These amendments were part of an effort "to ensure that recording artists and record companies will be protected as new technologies affect the ways in which their creative works are used ... and to create fair and efficient licensing mechanisms that address the complex issues facing copyright owners and copyright users as a result of the rapid growth of digital audio services."[594]

Concerned over the economic impact of this limited performance right in sound recording on royalties payable to owners of the underlying musical works, Congress expressly provided: "It is the intent of Congress that royalties payable to copyright owners of musical works for the public performance of their works shall not be diminished in any respect as a result of the rights granted by section 106(6)."[595]

---

589. 17 U.S.C. § 106(6). *See generally* Lionel S. Sobel, *A New Music Law for the Age of Digital Technology*, 17 Ent. L. Rep. 3 (November 1995).
590. 17 U.S.C. § 101.
591. 17 U.S.C. § 114(j)(3).
592. 17 U.S.C. § 114(d)–(j).
593. *See infra* §11.
594. H.R. Rep. No. 105-796, 105th Cong., 2d Sess. (1998).
595. 17 U.S.C. § 114(i).

VII Moral Right

A *Background*

The so-called moral right is predicated on the idea that an artist invests his or her work with the artist's personality,[596,597] so that the creation of the work invokes personality rights which are independent of economic interests in the work. As so understood, the moral right in American society must conflict not only with rooted property principles but also with egalitarian norms. While we translate the French droit moral almost (but not quite) literally into the phrase "moral right," the translation of this Civil Law concept into its American incarnation cannot be nearly so literal.[598] The Civil Law's comfort and the common law's unease with the bundle of personality interests protected by the moral right are manifest.[599]

Although there are significant variations among the different Civil Law moral right schemes, there is no dichotomy, or mutual exclusivity in the Civil Law generally between "copyright" and "moral right." The moral right is an inherent part of the intellectual property scheme, a structure that accommodates, definitionally, both economic and noneconomic rights of the "creator." The law reflects a societal consensus with respect to artistic creation. At the very least, this consensus relates to a creator's rights of attribution and integrity, that is, the right to have one's name attached to one's work, with the corollary right not to have one's name attached to someone else's work, and the right to object to distortion of the work. These principal components of the moral right are set out in Article 6bis of the Berne Convention.[600]

In the US, there is not a similar consensus and American law has not been hospitable to the moral right construct. As a general matter, the common law in the US rejected moral right: (1) as an independent basis for recognition of creator's rights of attribution or integrity or (2) as legally actionable independent of ownership of

---

596. *See generally* Roberta Rosenthal Kwall, *How Fine Art Fares Post VARA*, 1 MARQ. INTELL. PROP. L. REV. 1, 3–4 (1997); Sheldon W. Halpern, *Of Moral Right and Moral Righteousness*, 1 MARQ. INTELL. PROP. L. REV. 65 (1997).

597. Martin A. Roeder, *The Doctrine of Moral Right: A Study in the Law of Artists, Authors and Creators*, 53 HARV. L. REV. 540 (1940):

> When an artist creates, be he an author, a painter, a sculptor, an architect, or a musician, he does more than bring into the world a unique object having only exploitive possibilities; he projects into the world part of his personality and subjects it to the ravages of public use.

598. The translation of the words leaves something to be desired. *See* Roberta Rosenthal Kwall, *Copyright and the Moral Right: Is an American Marriage Possible?*, 38 VAND. L. REV. 1 (1985). Professor Kwall suggests that "moral right" is not an adequate rendering of the term "*droit moral*," which connotes "a right that exists in an entity's ultimate being." *Id.*, at 3 n.6.

599. It was bountifully documented more than 70 years ago in Martin A. Roeder, *The Doctrine of Moral Right: A Study in the Law of Artists, Authors and Creators*, 53 HARV. L. REV. 540 (1940).

600. "Independently of the author's economic rights, and even after the transfer of the said rights, the author shall have the right to claim authorship of the work and to object to any distortion, mutilation or other modification of, or other derogatory action in relation to, the said work, which would be prejudicial to his honour or reputation." Berne Convention for the Protection of Literary and Artistic Property, Sept. 9, 1886, *as revised* in Paris on July 24, 1971.

copyright in a work.[601] Over time, the courts, through interpretation of contracts, construction of the copyright laws, and extension of the laws of trademark, have adopted cognates to enforce, by proxy, some of the essence of the moral right, without adopting the construct itself.[602]

By the late 1980s, there was significant interest in comprehensive moral right legislation, driven by the perceived need for the US to accede to the Berne Convention. Ultimately, the consortium of interests behind legislative action abandoned moral rights legislation upon being convinced that the judicial development of basic moral right cognates permitted US adherence to the Berne Convention without such legislation, and the Berne Convention Implementation Act of 1988 was adopted without reference to moral right or a counterpart to Article 6bis of the Berne Convention.[603]

Congress did take a step in the direction of preservation of works, in response to objections to the colorization of black and white films, with creation of the National Film Preservation Board,[604] which can add twenty-five films every year into a National Film Registry so that unaltered versions of those films will always be available. Then, in 1990, Congress adopted the VARA,[605] a tentative move toward incorporation of moral right principles into the federal copyright scheme.

B *The Visual Artists Rights Act*

Embodied in section 106A,[606] the VARA creates limited rights of attribution and integrity for certain works of visual art. These rights vest in the "author" rather than in the "copyright owner," and are designed to secure a personal right independent of the economic attributes of copyright ownership.[607] These are rights that would survive transfer of ownership of any copy of the work of visual art or transfer of the copyright in that work.[608] The "author" contemplated by these provisions is an individual (or individual coauthors). The definition of works of visual art to which the section is applicable specifically excludes "any work made for hire."[609] The VARA expressly preempts any state law claims equivalent to those created by section 106A.[610]

601. *See generally* Roberta Rosenthal Kwall, The Soul of Creativity: Forging a Moral Rights Law for the United States (2009).
602. *See*, e.g., *Gilliam v. American Broad. Cos.*, 538 F.2d 14 (2d Cir. 1976); *Lamothe v. Atlantic Recording Corp.*, 847 F.2d 1403 (9th Cir. 1988); *Granz v. Harris*, 198 F.2d 585 (2d Cir. 1952).
603. *See* Ralph S. Brown, *Adherence to the Berne Copyright Convention: The Moral Rights Issue*, 35 J. Copy. Soc'y. 196 (1988); *see also* Roberta Rosenthal Kwall, *How Fine Art Fares Post VARA*, 1 Marq. Intell. Prop. L. Rev. 1, 3–4 (1997).
604. Department of the Interior and Related Agencies Appropriations of 1988, Pub. L. No. 100-446, 102 Stat. 1774.
605. Judicial Improvements Act of 1990, Pub. L. No. 101-650, 104 Stat. 5089.
606. 17 U.S.C. § 106A.
607. 17 U.S.C. § 106A(b) ("Only the author of a work of visual art has the rights conferred by subsection (a) in that work, whether or not the author is the copyright owner.").
608. 17 U.S.C. § 106A(e).
609. 17 U.S.C. § 101.
610. 17 U.S.C. § 301(f).

1 *The Attribution and Integrity Rights*

The "author" of a work of visual art within that section is given the right "to claim authorship of that work," and "to prevent the use of his or her name as the author of any work of visual art which he or she did not create."[611]

The author is also given the right "to prevent the use of his or her name as the author of the work of visual art in the event of the distortion, mutilation, or other modification of the work which would be prejudicial to his or her honor or reputation." Further elaborating on this right of integrity, the author is given the right "to prevent any intentional distortion, mutilation, or other modification of that work which would be prejudicial to his or her honor or reputation"; and the author has the right "to prevent any destruction of a work of recognized stature."[612] The Second Circuit clarified that a work of recognized stature "is one of high quality, status, or caliber that has been acknowledged as such by a relevant community," and the willful destruction of such works can result in statutory damages up to USD 150,000 per work.[613]

The integrity right under VARA is rather convoluted, but it is clearly limited to acts which "would be prejudicial" to the author's "honor or reputation." This formula was taken directly from Article 6bis of the Berne Convention, but neither the Copyright Act nor any other constructs in US law provide a definition of "honor." Serious problems may arise in determining what is "prejudicial to ... honor and reputation" in order to fix liability. "Reputation" as used in the moral rights context has not been coextensive with its use in defamation, nor has American jurisprudence had much occasion to deal with the concept of "honor" as a juridical construct.[614]

2 *Exclusions and Limitations*

The Act defines a "work of visual art" quite narrowly, limiting it to single copies of "a painting, drawing, print, or sculpture" or "a still photographic image produced for exhibition purposes only" or to signed and numbered copies of such works in limited editions of not more than two hundred copies; motion pictures, books, periodicals, and a wide array of other types of work are specifically excluded, as are works made for hire.[615] It is clear that VARA was intended to be and is a limited subset of the broad European moral rights. It has been held that the creator of a living wildflower garden

611. 17 U.S.C. § 106A(a)(1).
612. 17 U.S.C. § 106A(a)(2), (3).
613. *Castillo v. G & M Realty L.P.*, 950 F.3d 155 (2d Cir. 2020). *See also Philips v. Pembroke Real Estate, Inc.*, 459 F.3d 128 (1st Cir. 2006); *Martin v. City of Indianapolis*, 192 F.3d 608 (7th Cir. 1999).
614. To date, there has been little judicial examination of VARA's terms. One district court attempted to define VARA's terms and relied on dictionary definitions. *Carter v. Helmsley-Spear, Inc.*, 861 F. Supp. 303 (S.D.N.Y. 1994) (relying on WEBSTER'S THIRD NEW INTERNATIONAL DICTIONARY (unabridged) (1971): "'Honor' is commonly understood to mean 'good name or public esteem.' ... 'Reputation' is commonly understood to mean 'the condition of being regarded as worthy or meritorious'."), *rev'd on other grounds*, 71 F.3d 77 (2d Cir. 1995).
615. 17 U.S.C. § 101.

is not an "author" protected by VARA, nor is the "work" (i.e., the garden) the kind of visual art contemplated by the statute.[616]

Moreover, the attribution and integrity rights will not apply "to any reproduction, depiction, portrayal, or other use of a work in, upon or in any connection with" any of the above excluded works, nor will any such reproduction, depiction, portrayal, or other use of a work in connection with such excluded works be considered violative of the integrity right.

The integrity right is further limited. Modification of a work of visual art "which is a result of the passage of time or the inherent nature of the materials is not distortion, mutilation or other modification" for the purposes of that right, nor is modification "which is the result of conservation, or of the public presentation, including lighting and placement, of the work ... unless the modification is caused by gross negligence."[617]

For a work of visual art that has been incorporated in or made part of a building "in such a way that removing the work from the building will cause the destruction, distortion, mutilation, or other modification of the work" contemplated by the integrity right, the integrity right will not apply to its removal, if a written instrument has been signed by the owner of the building and the author specifying that installation of the work may subject it to destruction or other modification upon removal (such consent need not be in writing if the work was installed prior to the effective date of the VARA).[618] Whereas, if "incorporation" takes the form of "site-specific" art, it has been held that the protections of VARA do not apply.[619]

If a work has been incorporated in or made part of a building and can be removed without destruction or other modification and the owner wishes to remove that work, the integrity right will apply to acts occurring during such removal unless the owner has "made a diligent, good-faith attempt without success to notify the author of the owner's intended action," or such notice has been given and the author has failed either to remove the work or to pay for its removal within ninety days after receipt of such notice (if the author does remove the work, then title to that copy of the work shall

---

616. *Kelley v. Chicago Park Dist.*, 635 F.3d 290, 300 (7th Cir. 2011). The Seventh Circuit explained:

> VARA's definition of "work of visual art" operates to narrow and focus the statute's coverage; only a "painting, drawing, print, or sculpture," or an exhibition photograph will qualify. These terms are not further defined, but the overall structure of the statutory scheme clearly illuminates the limiting effect of this definition. Copyright's broad general coverage extends to "original works of authorship," and this includes "pictorial, graphic, and sculptural works." 17 U.S.C. § 102(a)(5). The use of the adjectives "pictorial" and "sculptural" suggests flexibility and breadth in application. In contrast VARA uses the specific nouns "painting" and "sculpture." To qualify for moral-rights protection under VARA, Wildflower Works cannot just be "pictorial" or "sculptural" in some aspect or effect, it must actually *be* a "painting" or a "sculpture." Not metaphorically or by analogy, but *really*.

617. 17 U.S.C. § 106A(c).
618. 17 U.S.C. § 113(d)(1).
619. *Philips v. Pembroke Real Estate, Inc.*, 459 F.3d 128 (1st Cir. 2006).

be vested in the author).[620] For the purpose of such notice, the Register of Copyrights is required to maintain a system for recording the address and identity of the author of a work of visual art incorporated in a building.[621]

The rights will inhere in works created on or after June 1, 1991 (and to works created earlier if the title has not been transferred prior to that date), and rights will generally endure only for the lifetime of the author.[622] The statute, while prohibiting transfer of the rights, does expressly recognize their waivability by a properly executed instrument. The matter of waiver is one of the salient differences between the statute and "moral right" as it exists in most other countries, and Congress directed the Copyright Office to undertake a study of the impact of this provision.[623] The studies have proven inconclusive.

The VARA is a first tentative step by Congress to move expressly into the "moral rights" issue. As limited, of course, it does not apply to the motion picture "colorization" dispute nor does it appear, even within its own terms, to be coextensive with the Civil Law approach. Whether these provisions, together with the earlier judicial gloss creating moral right analogues,[624] amount to full compliance with the Berne Convention remains to be determined.

The right of integrity is under unique tension with regard to motion pictures. In 2005, Congress enacted the Family Movie Act, which shields from liability acts that filter out portions of a movie (e.g., scenes involving violence, drug use, sexual activity, or coarse language) during a performance, so long as: (1) performance is being made from a lawful copy of the movie and (2) no new copy is made.[625] Companies, like VidAngel, have sought immunity from infringement liability for filtering "mature content" from movies for consumers. Statutory immunity depends on the technological processes used, and the Ninth Circuit held that the filtered performance itself "must be 'from' an authorized copy of the motion picture."[626]

C *State Moral Rights Statutes*

Prior to the enactment of the VARA, several states adopted legislation purporting to create variants of the droit moral. None of the statutes approximates the broad sweep of the Civil Law concept. The New York[627] and California[628] statutes are exemplary. In

620. 17 U.S.C. § 113(d)(2). *See Martin v. City of Indianapolis*, 192 F.3d 608 (7th Cir. 1999).
621. 17 U.S.C. § 113(d)(3).
622. 17 U.S.C. § 106A(d).
623. 17 U.S.C. § 106A(e). *See* Roberta Rosenthal Kwall, *How Fine Art Fares Post VARA*, 1 Marq. Intell. Prop. L. Rev. 1 (1997) for analysis of the results of the first study.
624. The impact of these analogues, particularly the extension of Lanham Act § 43(a), may have been attenuated by the Supreme Court's language in *Dastar v. Twentieth Century Fox Film Corp.*, 539 U.S. 23 (2003). *See* Jane C. Ginsburg, *The Right to Claim Authorship in U.S. Copyright and Trademarks Law*, 41 Hous. L. Rev. 263 (2004).
625. 17 U.S.C. § 110(11). *See also Disney Enterprises, Inc. v. VidAngel Inc.*, 869 F.3d 848 (9th Cir. 2017).
626. *Disney Enterprises, Inc. v. VidAngel, Inc.*, 869 F.3d 848, 858 (9th Cir. 2017).
627. N.Y. Arts & Cult. Aff. Law §§ 14.01–08.
628. Cal. Civ. Code § 987.

these entertainment and artistic centers, this kind of legislation that balances the interests of the creative artist and the entrepreneur and dealer necessarily involves compromise.[629]

The New York and California statutes are limited to works of "fine art." California law further defines as "an original painting, sculpture, or drawing, or an original work of art in glass, of recognized quality."[630] The New York statute recognizes the attribution right with respect to "works of fine art or limited edition multiples of not more than three hundred copies knowingly displayed in a place accessible to the public, published or reproduced in this state," and limits the integrity right to the public display or publication of such works "in an altered, defaced, mutilated or modified form [if] damage to the artist's reputation is reasonably likely to result therefrom."[631] Approaching the problem from a different direction, the California statute is concerned principally with intentional physical defacement, mutilation, alteration, or destruction of works of fine art. Both statutes have numerous limitations and exceptions. As noted above, the VARA of 1990 contains explicit federal preemption provisions, and it is not clear how much of the existing state statutes remains operable.

D *Droit De Suite*

While the droit de suite—the right of an artist to share in the proceeds of subsequent resales of the artist's work—is explicitly part of the Berne Convention (Article 14ter) and is recognized widely in the European Union, and it is not recognized in the US, except in California, which has adopted a limited droit de suite statute. California's Resale Royalties Act of 1976[632] provides that when a work of fine art is sold and the seller resides in California or the sale takes place in California, and the resale price is more than USD 1,000 and more than the original price paid by the seller, "the seller or the seller's agent shall pay to the artist of such work of fine art or to such artist's agent [or, if the artist cannot be found, to the California Arts Council] 5% of the amount of such sale"; the right to such resale royalty is assignable by the artist, but is not waivable and, upon the artist's death, will inure to the benefit of the estate for a period of twenty years.

The California Resale Royalties Act, like the state moral rights statutes, raises a question of federal preemption under the moral right preemption provisions of the

629. For analysis of the legislation, *see* John G. Petrovich, *Artists' Statutory Droit Moral in California: A Critical Appraisal*, 15 LOYOLA L.A. L. REV. 29 (1981); Joseph Taubman, *New York Artists' Authorship Rights Act of 1983: Waiver and Fair Use*, 3 CARDOZO ARTS & ENT. L.J. 113 (1984); Edward J. Damich, *The New York Artists' Authorship Rights Act: A Comparative Critique*, 84 COLUM. L. REV. 1733 (1984). Statutes in Louisiana (LA REV. STAT. ANN. §§ 51:2151 et seq.), Maine (ME. REV. STAT. ANN. tit. 27, § 303), New Jersey (N.J. STAT. ANN. §§ 2A: 24A-1 et seq.), and Rhode Island (5 R.I. GEN. LAWS. §§ 5-62-2 et seq.) are modeled on the New York statute. Of the state statutes, only Massachusetts' is broader, covering "any original work of visual or graphic art of any media." MASS. GEN. LAWS ANN. Ch. 231 § 85S(b).

630. CAL. CIV. CODE § 987(b)(2).

631. N.Y. ARTS & CULT. AFF. LAW § 14.03; *see also Wojnarowicz v. Am. Family Ass'n*, 745 F. Supp. 130 (S.D.N.Y. 1990).

632. CAL. CIV. CODE § 986.

VARA. While the matter is not clear, the legislative history of the VARA appears to support the position that resale royalty rights are not preempted.[633]

§7 FAIR USE AS A LIMITATION ON THE SCOPE OF COPYRIGHT PROTECTION

I The Fair Use Concept

Section 106 enumerates the fundamental rights of a copyright owner, namely the bundle of exclusive rights, the unauthorized exercise of which gives rise to a claim of copyright infringement. Sections 108–122 provide highly detailed, narrowly tailored limitations upon the copyright owner's exclusive rights. To recapitulate, these specific exemptions concern:

- § 108: Libraries and Archives.
- § 109: "First Sale."
- § 110: Exempt Performances.
- § 111: Secondary Transmissions: Hotels, Cable Systems.
- § 112: Ephemeral Recordings.
- § 113: Useful Articles.
- § 114: Limitations on Sound Recordings.
- § 115: Compulsory Mechanical License.
- § 116: Jukeboxes.
- § 117: Copying Computer Programs.
- § 118: Public Broadcasting.
- § 119: Secondary Transmission: Super Stations.
- § 120: Pictures of Architectural Works.
- §§ 121 & 121A: Reproduction for People with Visual Disabilities.
- § 122: Secondary Transmission: Satellite Carriers.

Determination of infringement or noninfringement in cases involving these exemptions does not depend upon reasoning by analogy or application of common law or equitable principles—it is simply a matter of construing the specific words of the statute. However, those statutory words do not necessarily do all that is necessary to maintain the balance between the rights of the copyright owner and the public interest underlying the Copyright Act. To perform that function, the courts have developed, and the 1976 Act has attempted to codify, the doctrine of "fair use."

The Supreme Court has instructed: "From the infancy of copyright protection, [the fair use doctrine] has been thought necessary to fulfill copyright's very purpose,

633. H.R. Rep. No. 101-735 (1990), *as reprinted in* 1990 U.S.C.C.A.N. 6935. *See also* Gordon P. Katz, *Copyright Preemption under the Copyright Act of 1976: The Case of Droit de Suite*, 47 Geo. Wash. L. Rev. 200 (1978); Jennifer R. Clarke, Note, *The California Resale Royalties Act as a Test Case for Preemption*, 81 Colum. L. Rev. 1315 (1981). Congress has so far rejected proposals for federal *droit de suite* legislation.

'[t]o promote the Progress of Science and useful Arts'."[634] Lower courts agree: "The ultimate test of fair use ... is whether the copyright law's goal of 'promot[ing] the Progress of Science and useful Arts,' ... would be better served by allowing the use than by preventing it."[635] It is a safety valve, by means of which a court can find that, notwithstanding the absence of any specific exemption, the defendant's use of the copyrighted material is such that, as a matter of policy, society gains most by a finding of noninfringement.

The doctrine of fair use has been called "the most troublesome in the whole law of copyright."[636] It is a judge-made concept, with origins in American law going back to 1841,[637] but it was not until 1984 that a sharply divided US Supreme Court first dealt with the doctrine in *Sony Corp. of America v. Universal City Studios, Inc.*[638] This was followed by another divided opinion in *Harper & Row Publishers, Inc. v. Nation Enterprises,*[639] and by what appears to be a consensus in 1994 in *Campbell v. Acuff-Rose Music, Inc.*[640] These three cases are not necessarily consistent with one another, apart from the general agreement that "fair use is 'a rule of reason' fashioned by Judges to balance the author's right to compensation for his work, on the one hand, against the public's interest in the widest possible dissemination of ideas and information, on the other'."[641]

Although the law zealously protects the commercial interests of the artist from unscrupulous opportunistic interlopers, it recognizes that not all copying of artistic invention is necessarily undesirable piracy. Certain forms of copying of artistic creation are indispensable to education, journalism, history, criticism, humor, and other informative endeavors. The statute therefore allows latitude in appropriate circumstances for copying of protected artistic expression and exempts such copying from a finding of infringement. The doctrine of fair use identifies this category of permissible copying.[642]

The purpose of the doctrine is quite clear—it "permits and requires courts to avoid rigid application of the copyright statute, when, on occasion, it would stifle the very creativity which that law is designed to foster"[643]—as is its peculiar status as a court-developed "rule of reason" residing, with varying degrees of discomfort, within

634. *Campbell v. Acuff-Rose Music, Inc.*, 510 U.S. 569, 575 (1994) (quoting U.S. Const. Art. I, § 8, cl. 8); *see also id.* ("[I]n truth, in literature, in science and in art, there are, and can be, few, if any, things, which in an abstract sense, are strictly new and original throughout. Every book in literature, science and art, borrows, and must necessarily borrow, and use much which was well known and used before.").
635. *Arica Inst., Inc. v. Palmer*, 970 F.2d 1067, 1077 (2d Cir. 1992).
636. *Dellar v. Samuel Goldwyn, Inc.*, 104 F.2d 661, 662 (2d Cir. 1939).
637. *Folsom v. Marsh*, 9 F.Cas. 342 (C.C.D. Mass. 1841).
638. *Sony Corp. of Am. v. Universal City Studios, Inc.*, 464 U.S. 417 (1984).
639. *Harper & Row Publishers, v. Nation Enters.*, 471 U.S. 539 (1985).
640. *Campbell v. Acuff-Rose Music*, Inc., 510 U.S. 569 (1994).
641. *Triangle Publ'ns, Inc. v. Knight-Ridder Newspapers*, 626 F.2d 1171, 1174 (5th Cir. 1980) (quoting Lionel Sobel, *Copyright and the First Amendment: A Gathering Storm?*, 19 Ascap Copyright L. Symp. 43, 51 (1971) and Alan Latman, *Fair Use of Copyrighted Works* 5 (Sen. Comm. on Judiciary Study No. 141960)).
642. *New Era Publ'ns Int'l v. Henry Holt & Co.*, 695 F. Supp. 1493 (S.D.N.Y. 1988) (Leval, J.).
643. *Campbell v. Acuff-Rose Music, Inc.*, 510 U.S. 569, 577 (1994).

a complex and comprehensive statute. What is not clear are the boundaries, standards, and parameters of the doctrine necessary to a reasonable degree of predictability. The House Report on the 1976 Act succinctly describes the problem:

> Although the courts have considered and ruled upon the fair use doctrine over and over again, no real definition of the concept has ever emerged. Indeed, since the doctrine is an equitable rule of reason, no generally applicable definition is possible, and each case raising the question must be decided on its own facts.[644]

Judge Pierre Leval put it perhaps more forcefully:

> What is most curious about this doctrine is that neither the decisions that have applied it ..., nor its eventual statutory formulation, undertook to define or explain its contours or objectives .... Judges do not share a consensus on the meaning of fair use .... Confusion has not been confined to judges. Writers, historians, publishers, and their legal advisers can only guess and pray as to how courts will resolve copyright disputes.[645]

II Section 107: Codification of the Doctrine

A *Scope and Purpose*

Section 107, in its entirety, reads as follows:

> § 107. Limitations on Exclusive Rights: Fair Use
>
> Notwithstanding the provisions of sections 106 and 106A the fair use of a copyrighted work, including such use by reproduction in copies or phonorecords or by any other means specified by that section, for purposes such as criticism, comment, news reporting, teaching (including multiple copies for classroom use), scholarship, or research, is not an infringement of copyright. In determining whether the use made of a work in any particular case is a fair use the factors to be considered shall include—
>
> 1. the purpose and character of the use, including whether such use is of a commercial nature or is for nonprofit educational purposes;
> 2. the nature of the copyrighted work;
> 3. the amount and substantiality of the portion used in relation to the copyrighted work as a whole; and
> 4. the effect of the use upon the potential market for or value of the copyrighted work.
>
> The fact that a work is unpublished shall not itself bar a finding of fair use, if such finding is made upon consideration of all the above factors.[646]

The language makes clear that "fair use" conditions all of the exclusive rights granted by the Act ("notwithstanding the provisions of sections 106 and 106A, the fair use of a copyrighted work [for the purposes described] is not an infringement of copyright"). As the Supreme Court has observed: "Any individual may reproduce a

644. H.R. Rep. No. 94-1476, at 65 (1976), *as reprinted in* 1976 U.S.C.C.A.N. 5659, 5679.
645. Pierre Leval, *Toward a Fair Use Standard*, 103 Harv. L. Rev. 1105, 1107 (1990).
646. 17 U.S.C. § 107.

copyrighted work for a 'fair use'; the copyright owner does not possess the exclusive right to such a use."[647]

Congress intended that, under section 107, "courts continue the common law tradition of fair use adjudication."[648] "The statutory formulation of the defense of fair use in the Copyright Act reflects the intent of Congress to codify the common-law doctrine."[649] However, it is not always clear just what that judicial doctrine is, and the statutory language itself leaves much room for interpretation. The House Report contemplates such an open-ended approach to fair use: "Beyond a very broad statutory explanation of what fair use is, and some of the criteria applicable to it, the courts must be free to adapt the doctrine to particular situations on a case-by-case basis."[650] Fair use analysis, if not ad hoc, nevertheless ultimately "calls for case-by-case analysis."[651] However, both the human craving for order and the statutory language itself provide an impetus for the development of principles of general application.

B Parsing the Statute

1 The Preamble: Productive and Transformative Uses

The opening sentence of section 107 is quite rich: it says that "the fair use of a copyrighted work ... for purposes such as criticism, comment, news reporting, teaching ..., scholarship, or research, is not an infringement of copyright."[652] This language seems to suggest that the application of fair use requires a two-part analysis: one must first determine whether there is a "fair use" and then determine if that use is for an appropriate purpose. The "factors" which then follow seem to be directed to the first question, whether there is a "fair use," but the "purpose" analysis would appear to be central to the determination of whether such a "fair use" will be effective to insulate the activity. The US Supreme Court has been neither entirely consistent nor clear in providing guidance as to the appropriate analytic model.

Sony Corp. of America v. Universal City Studios, Inc.,[653] the first of the Supreme Court's statutory fair use cases, was a contributory infringement action brought on behalf of the major motion picture producers against the prominent maker of video-cassette recorders. Resolution of the contributory infringement issue depended upon whether videotaping the over the air broadcast of copyrighted motion pictures for the purposes of "time shifting" was infringing or a fair use. A slim majority (5-4) held

647. *Sony Corp. of Am. v. Universal City Studios, Inc.*, 464 U.S. 417, 433 (1984); *see also* 17 U.S.C. § 107 ("the fair use of a copyrighted work ... is not an infringement of copyright").
648. *Campbell v. Acuff-Rose Music, Inc.*, 510 U.S. 569, 577 (1994) ("Congress meant § 107 'to restate the present judicial doctrine of fair use, not to change, narrow, or enlarge it in any way' and intended that courts continue the common-law tradition of fair use adjudication") (quoting H.R. Rep. No. 94-1476, at 66 (1976), *as reprinted in* 1976 U.S.C.C.A.N. 5659, 5680).
649. *Harper & Row Publishers, Inc. v. Nation Enters.*, 471 U.S. 539, 549 (1985).
650. H.R. Rep. No. 94-1476, at 66 (1976), *as reprinted in* 1976 U.S.C.C.A.N. 5659, 5680.
651. *Campbell v. Acuff-Rose Music, Inc.*, 510 U.S. 569, 577 (1994).
652. 17 U.S.C. § 107 (emphasis added).
653. *Sony Corp. of Am. v. Universal City Studios, Inc.*, 464 U.S. 417 (1984).

time-shifting to be a fair use, so Sony was not contributorily liable for selling Betamax recorders. Justice John Paul Stevens, writing for the majority, described the character of fair use as an "equitable rule of reason."[654] The Court focused on the enumerated factor analysis, emphasizing the personal, noncommercial nature of home videotaping in finding the use "fair." While the majority's analysis did not hinge on the opening language of section 107, Justice Harry Blackmun, for the dissenters, focused heavily on the preamble's exemplary uses, characterizing such uses ("criticism, comment, news reporting, teaching ..., scholarship, or research") as "productive" uses, "resulting in some added benefit to the public beyond that produced by the first author's work."[655] The dissenters suggested that while not every "productive use" was a fair use, only a "productive use" could be "fair." The legacy of the Sony case has created a safe harbor for technology capable of substantial noninfringing uses.

A year later, the Supreme Court revisited the fair use question in a different context. In *Harper & Row Publishers, Inc. v. Nation Enterprises*,[656] a divided (6-3) Court rejected a fair use defense by the publisher of a magazine who had "scooped" the plaintiff by publishing excerpts from the not yet published memoirs of President Gerald Ford. Rejecting the idea that there is some overriding general "public interest" or First Amendment consideration that would shield as a fair use dissemination of copyrighted matter in which there was a strong public interest,[657] Justice Sandra Day O'Connor, for the majority, emphasized the general inapplicability of fair use to unpublished works.[658] Finding "that the unpublished nature of a work is '[a] key, though not necessarily determinative, factor' tending to negate a defense of fair use,"[659] she concluded that "the scope of fair use is narrower with respect to unpublished works."[660]

While the opinion said little about either "productive use" or the impact of the enumeration of purposes in the preamble, it did expressly note, in response to the claim that the defendant was entitled to special consideration because its activity was "news reporting," that the listing of "purposes" in section 107 are merely exemplary, not exhaustive, and not designed "to single out any particular use as presumptively a 'fair' use."[661] Rather than issues of productive or unproductive use, the distinction between published and unpublished works significantly colored the Court's application of the fair use factors. Note, that distinction produced a controversy exemplified in several notable Second Circuit opinions seeking to apply the Harper & Row limitation with respect to unpublished works.[662] Ultimately, after extensive hearings, Congress

654. *Id.*, at 448.
655. *Id.*, at 478 (Blackmun, J., dissenting).
656. *Harper & Row Publishers, Inc. v. Nation Enters.*, 471 U.S. 539 (1985).
657. *Id.*, at 558–59.
658. *Id.*, at 554 ("Under ordinary circumstances, the author's right to control the first public appearance of his undisseminated expression will outweigh a claim of fair use.").
659. *Id.*, at 554 (quoting from the Senate Report).
660. *Id.*, at 564.
661. *Id.*, at 561.
662. *See Salinger v. Random House, Inc.*, 811 F.2d 90 (2d Cir. 1987); *New Era Publ'ns Int'l., ApS v. Henry Holt & Co., Inc.*, 873 F.2d 576 (2d Cir. 1989); *Wright v. Warner Books, Inc.*, 953 F.2d 731 (2d Cir. 1991).

amended section 107 to read, as it now does, that "[t]he fact that a work is unpublished shall not itself bar a finding of fair use if such finding is made upon consideration of all the [enumerated] factors."

In sum, the majority in Sony deemphasized "productive use" for fair use analysis and the Harper & Row majority declined to grant it special consideration.[663] Nevertheless, lower courts continued to emphasize the importance of a fair use determination of the societal value derived from the defendant's use,[664] although not necessarily in terms of whether that use was "productive."[665] In 1994, the Supreme Court confronted the question directly in *Campbell v. Acuff-Rose Music, Inc.*[666] and firmly reinvigorated the productive use concept, under the rubric "transformative use," making it central to fair use analysis. The case itself, involving a rap music parody of a popular song, provided an opportunity for the Court to address a series of issues (the question of application of fair use to parody is discussed below).

Justice David Souter's opinion attempted to articulate and apply fundamental fair use principles. The opinion rested heavily on the opening language of section 107.[667] The preamble articulated "the central purpose" of fair use investigation, namely to determine if the new work "adds something new, with a further purpose or different character, altering the first with new expression, meaning, or message; it asks, in other words, whether and to what extent the new work is 'transformative'."[668] Echoing Justice Blackmun's observation in Sony with respect to "productive use," the opinion noted:

> Although such transformative use is not absolutely necessary for a finding of fair use, the goal of copyright, to promote science and the arts, is generally furthered by the creation of transformative works. Such works thus lie at the heart of the fair use doctrine's guarantee of breathing space within the confines of copyright, and the more transformative the new work, the less will be the significance of other factors, like commercialism, that may weigh against a finding of fair use.[669]

---

663. "The fact that an article arguably is 'news' and therefore a productive use is simply one factor in a fair use analysis." *Harper & Row Publishers, Inc. v. Nation Enters.*, 471 U.S. 539, 561 (1984).
664. *See*, e.g., *Los Angeles News Serv. v. Tullo*, 973 F.2d 791 (9th Cir. 1992); *Maxtone-Graham v. Burtchaell*, 803 F.2d 1253 (2d Cir. 1986); *Pacific & Southern Co. Inc. v. Duncan*, 744 F.2d 1490 (11th Cir. 1984).
665. *See*, e.g., *Hustler Magazine, Inc. v. Moral Majority, Inc.*, 796 F.2d 1148 (9th Cir. 1986) (holding that defendant's use of the copyrighted material for "self-defense" supported a fair use determination).
666. *Campbell v. Acuff-Rose Music, Inc.*, 510 U.S. 569 (1994).
667. *Id.*, at 577 ("The task is not to be simplified with bright-line rules, for the statute, like the doctrine it recognizes, calls for case-by-case analysis. [Moreover, the statute here] employs the terms 'including' and 'such as' in the preamble paragraph to indicate the illustrative and not limitative function of the examples given, which thus provide only general guidance about the sorts of copying that courts and the Congress most commonly had found to be fair uses.") (internal citation omitted).
668. *Id.*, at 580 (quoting from Pierre Leval, *Toward a Fair Use Standard*, 103 HARV. L. REV. 1105, 1111 (1990)). *See Ringgold v. Black Entm't Television, Inc.*, 126 F.3d 70, 79 (2d Cir. 1997) (rejecting a fair use defense in connection with the fleeting, background use in a television program of plaintiff's artwork because "the defendants have used [plaintiff's] work for precisely a central purpose for which it was created—to be decorative").
669. *Campbell v. Acuff-Rose Music, Inc.*, 510 U.S. 569, 580 (1994) (internal citations omitted).

Transformative copying remains a factor that weighs favorably in the fair use analysis.[670] Yet, transformativeness is not the sum total of the analysis. In *Andy Warhol Foundation (AWF) v. Goldsmith*, the Court (7-2) concluded that Andy Warhol's "Orange Prince"—one of the Prince Series that was derived from the photograph by Lynn Goldsmith—served essentially the same commercial purpose.[671] The Court, therefore, held that the purpose and character of the "Orange Prince" did not favor a finding of fair use of Goldsmith's original.

2 *The Enumerated Factors*

The Supreme Court has made clear that the four enumerated statutory factors are interrelated and are not to be "treated in isolation, one from another. All are to be explored, and the results weighed together, in light of the purposes of copyright."[672] As the Seventh Circuit observed:

> The important point is simply that ... the four factors are a checklist of things to be considered rather than a formula for decision; and likewise the list of statutory purposes.[673]

a The First Factor: Purpose and Character of the Use

The first statutory factor requires a consideration of "the purpose and character of the use, including whether such use is of a commercial nature or is for nonprofit educational purposes." In Sony, the majority used this factor to build a presumption: a use "for a commercial or profit-making purpose ... would presumptively be unfair," while a noncommercial use would raise a presumption of fairness.[674] The following year, in Harper & Row,[675] Justice O'Connor suggested further that the "crux of the profit/nonprofit distinction is not whether the sole motive of the use is monetary gain but whether the user stands to profit from exploitation of the copyrighted material without paying the customary price."[676]

670. *Google LLC v. Oracle Am., Inc.*, 141 S. Ct. 1183, 1204 (2021) ("the 'purpose and character' of Google's copying was transformative—to the point where this factor too weighs in favor of fair use").
671. Andy Warhol Found. for the *Visual Arts, Inc. v. Goldsmith*, 598 U.S. 508 (2023).
672. *Campbell v. Acuff-Rose Music, Inc.*, 510 U.S. 569, 578 (1994); *accord Castle Rock Entm't, Inc. v. Carol Publ'g Grp., Inc.*, 150 F.3d 132 (2d Cir. 1998).
673. *Ty, Inc. v. Publications Int'l, Ltd.*, 292 F.3d 512, 522 (7th Cir. 2002).
674. *Sony Corp. of Am. v. Universal City Studios, Inc.*, 464 U.S. 417, 449 (1984). Justice Stevens was quite forceful in asserting for the majority that "every commercial use of copyrighted material is presumptively an unfair exploitation of the monopoly privilege that belongs to the owner of the copyright." *Id.*, at 451.
675. *Harper & Row Publishers, Inc. v. Nation Enters.*, 471 U.S. 539, 562 (1985) ("The fact that a publication was commercial as opposed to nonprofit is a separate factor that tends to weigh against a finding of fair use").
676. *Id.*

The Sony "presumptions," buttressed by Harper & Row, caused considerable problems for the Courts of Appeal in analyzing fair use cases in which the defendant received some commercial benefit, and these courts attempted to ameliorate the impact of the presumptions by finding some social benefit attendant to the commercial use.[677]

The Supreme Court appears to have abandoned these presumptions and the special role of commerciality.[678] In Campbell, the Court reversed the lower court for "giving virtually dispositive weight to the commercial nature [of the defendant's use]":

> The language of the statute makes clear that the commercial or nonprofit educational purpose of a work is only one element of the first factor enquiry into its purpose and character .... Accordingly, the mere fact that a use is educational and not for profit does not insulate it from a finding of infringement, any more than the commercial character of a use bars a finding of fairness. If, indeed, commerciality carried presumptive force against a finding of fairness, the presumption would swallow nearly all of the illustrative uses listed in the preamble paragraph of § 107, including news reporting, comment, criticism, teaching, scholarship, and research, since these activities "are generally conducted for profit in this country."[679]

Rather, for the purposes of the first factor, the relevant issue is the overall one of "the purpose and character of the use," and the significant element in that analysis is the extent to which the use is "transformative." The Campbell Court noted, "the more transformative the new work, the less will be the significance of other factors, like commercialism, that may weigh against a finding of fair use."[680] Yet, in AWF, the Supreme Court held that Andy Warhol's painted portrait of music icon Prince—known as "Orange Prince"—was not a fair use of Lynn Goldsmith's reference image. The AWF argued that Warhol's artworks were transformative of Goldsmith's photo because the pop artist gave new meaning to the previous work. However, the Court's majority was unpersuaded, noting that "new expression may be relevant to whether a copying use has a sufficiently distinct purpose or character," but that it was not dispositive on its own.[681] In short, the lesson is that the fair use calculus involves balancing, and no single factor will create a presumptively fair or unfair use.

---

677. *See*, e.g., *Maxtone-Graham v. Burtchaell*, 803 F.2d 1253 (2d Cir. 1986); *Hustler Magazine, Inc. v. Moral Majority, Inc.*, 796 F.2d 1148 (9th Cir. 1986).
678. *Google LLC v. Oracle Am., Inc.*, 141 S. Ct. 1183, 1204 (2021) ("There is no doubt that a finding that copying was not commercial in nature tips the scales in favor of fair use. But the inverse is not necessarily true, as many common fair uses are indisputably commercial."). *See also Leibovitz v. Paramount Pictures Corp.*, 137 F.3d 109, 113 (2d Cir. 1998) ("In focusing the first factor inquiry upon the 'transformative' nature of the use, the Court in *Campbell* abandoned the statement in *Sony* ... that 'every commercial use of copyrighted material is presumptively ... unfair' ....").
679. *Campbell v. Acuff-Rose Music, Inc.*, 510 U.S. 569, 580 (1994). *See also Castle Rock Entm't, Inc. v. Carol Publ'g Grp., Inc.*, 150 F.3d 132, 142 (2d Cir. 1998) ("We ... do not give much weight to the fact that the secondary use was for commercial gain."); *Sony Computer Entm't Am., Inc. v. Bleem, LLC*, 214 F.3d 1022, 1026 (9th Cir. 2000) ("In this analysis, the commercial use of copyrighted material is not presumptively unfair; rather, commercial use is but one of four factors that we must weigh.").
680. *Campbell v. Acuff-Rose Music, Inc.*, 510 U.S. 569, 579 (1994). *But see* Andy Warhol Found. for the *Visual Arts, Inc. v. Goldsmith*, 598 U.S. 508 (2023).
681. *Andy Warhol Found. for the Visual Arts, Inc.*, 598 U.S. at 525-26.

b The Second Factor: Nature of the Copyrighted Work

The inquiry here requires categorizing the plaintiff's work; it calls for recognition that "some works are closer to the core of [copyright] than others."[682] As the Ninth Circuit has observed, this can mean that "fair use is more difficult to establish when the former works are copied."[683] Thus, the second factor will militate against a finding of fair use where the copyrighted work is creative art or literary fiction, or other forms of creative expression, as opposed to factual, historical data, or news reporting.[684] While this content-based categorization for the purposes of the second factor was elided by the Supreme Court in Harper & Row, which made a distinction between copyrighted works which had been published and those which had been unpublished, the Court in Campbell brought the analysis back to the fundamental distinction between those works which are "closer to the core" of copyright protection than those which are more removed.

In this analysis, the commercial use of copyrighted material is not presumptively unfair; rather, commercial use is but one of four factors that the courts must weigh. The Supreme Court expressly rejected the irrebutability of the presumption against fair use in commercial contexts in Campbell when the court flatly reversed the Sixth Circuit for making just such a presumption. The Court emphasized that, although the fourth factor may be the most important, all factors must be considered, and the commercial nature of the copies is just one element in the broader calculus.

c The Third Factor: The Amount Taken

Here, one must consider "the amount and substantiality of the portion used in relation to the copyrighted work as a whole." Asking how much the defendant took from the plaintiff, the question is both quantitative and qualitative; a quantitatively small amount may nevertheless be sufficient to encapsulate the copyrighted work and qualitatively be quite substantial.[685] As the Supreme Court illustrated: "If a defendant had copied one sentence in a novel, that copying may well be insubstantial. But if that single sentence set forth one of the world's shortest short stories—'When he awoke, the dinosaur was still there.'—the question looks much different, as the copied material

682. *Google LLC v. Oracle Am., Inc.*, 141 S. Ct. 1183, 1202 (2021) (quoting *Campbell v. Acuff-Rose Music, Inc.*, 510 U.S. 569, 586 (1994)).
683. *Leadsinger, Inc. v. BMG Music Publ'g*, 512 F.3d 522, 530, 585 (9th Cir. 2008).
684. *See*, e.g., *Stewart v. Abend*, 495 U.S. 207 (1990) ("in general, fair use is more likely to be found in factual works than in fictional works"); *Castle Rock Entm't, Inc. v. Carol Publ'g Grp., Inc.*, 150 F.3d 132, 143 (2d Cir. 1998) ("the scope of fair use is somewhat narrower with respect to fictional works ... than to factual works"); *Twin Peaks Prods., Inc. v. Publ'ns Int'l, Ltd.*, 996 F.2d 1366, 1376 (2d Cir. 1993) (the second factor "favor[s] ... creative and fictional work").
685. *Campbell v. Acuff-Rose Music, Inc.*, 510 U.S. 569, 579 (1994) ("this factor calls for thought not only about the quantity of the materials used, but about their quality and importance, too"); *see also Iowa State Univ. Research Found., Inc. v. Am. Broad. Cos., Inc.*, 621 F.2d 57 (2d Cir. 1980).

constitutes a small part of the novel but the entire short story."[686] Central to resolution of the third factor is the manner in which and purposes for which the copyrighted material is used by the defendant. By its terms, analysis under this factor focuses on the relationship between the material taken and the copyrighted work as a whole; whether the material taken constitutes a significant or insignificant portion of the defendant's work would seem to be irrelevant. However, since the analysis is qualitative, the fact that the defendant's work makes extensive use of material that is a quantitatively small part of the copyrighted work is evidence of the qualitative substantiality of the material taken.[687] Moreover, the extent to which the defendant has used the material in a "transformative" manner can have a significant bearing upon whether the taking is to be considered excessive; a transformative use can support a qualitatively greater taking than can a nontransformative use.[688] As discussed below, this issue has been particularly important in parody fair use analysis.

d The Fourth Factor: Market Effects

This factor is directed to "the effect of the use upon the potential market for or value of the copyrighted work." While the four factors are not specifically weighted, the economic impact of the taking upon the plaintiff's work has generally been considered a weighty factor.[689] The inquiry concerns the impact upon both the existing market for the plaintiff's work and potential markets for that work itself as well as for derivative works.[690] In short, the concern is with the present and future exploitative possibilities of the copyright in the work. In general, this factor "is concerned with secondary uses that, by offering a substitute for the original, usurp a market that properly belongs to the copyright-holder."[691] But, the Supreme Court noted, "a potential loss of revenue is not the whole story. We here must consider not just the amount but also the source of the loss."[692] The market effects analysis can present certain logical problems. For example, in any given case in which the defendant has taken some copyrighted material, that defendant, and the use to which that material was put, theoretically constitute a potential market with respect to which the copyright owner might license the work. In effect, since every use is potentially a market, this factor, if analyzed

686. *Google LLC v. Oracle Am., Inc.*, 141 S. Ct. 1183, 1205 (2021) (citing A. Monterroso, El Dinosaurio, *in* Complete Works & Other Stories 42 (E. Grossman transl. 1995) (in the original Spanish, the story reads: "Cuando despertó, el dinosaurio todavía estaba allí")).

687. *See Iowa State Univ. Research Found., Inc. v. Am. Broad. Cos., Inc.*, 621 F.2d 57 (2d Cir. 1980) (finding use of approximately 8% of a copyrighted film on three separate occasions did not constitute fair use where the defendant's use of the film had a profit-making character and the defendant usurped a significant market for the plaintiff's film).

688. *Campbell v. Acuff-Rose Music, Inc.*, 510 U.S. 569, 587–88 (1994) ("a work composed primarily of an original, particularly its heart, with little added or changed, is more likely to be a merely superseding use, fulfilling demand for the original").

689. "This last factor is undoubtedly the single most important element of fair use." *Harper & Row Publishers, Inc. v. Nation Enters.*, 471 U.S. 539, 566 (1985).

690. "This inquiry must take account not only of harm to the original but also of harm to the market for derivative works." *Harper & Row Publishers, Inc. v. Nation Enters.*, 471 U.S. 539, 568 (1985).

691. *Infinity Broad. Corp. v. Kirkwood*, 150 F.3d 104 (2d Cir. 1998).

692. *Google LLC v. Oracle Am., Inc.*, 141 S. Ct. 1183, 1206 (2021).

literally, would simply swallow fair use.[693] In practice, however, the courts avoid this logical extreme and focus on realistic potential markets for exploitation of the copyright.[694] The principal concern is whether the defendant's use can substitute for the copyrighted work or lawful derivative works based thereon. Since the focus is on displacement of the copyrighted work, a use in criticism, a use disparaging the copyrighted work, that harms the market by suppressing demand rather than usurping the work, would not constitute a cognizable market harm. As the Supreme Court noted in Campbell:

> the role of the courts is to distinguish between "[b]iting criticism [that merely] suppresses demand [and] copyright infringement[, which] usurps it." ... This distinction between potentially remediable displacement and unremediable disparagement is reflected in the rule that there is no protectible derivative market for criticism. The market for potential derivative uses includes only those that creators of original works would in general develop or license others to develop.[695]

Similarly, the fact that the infringing use might well serve to revive or create a market for the copyrighted work, and thereby benefit the copyright owner, is immaterial if the effect of the infringement is market usurpation.[696]

In Sony, the Supreme Court majority not only created and relied heavily upon presumptions of fairness or unfairness as a function of the commercial or noncommercial nature of the defendant's use but also extended these presumptions into the fourth-factor analysis. The majority appeared to hold that a commercial use creates a presumption of potential market harm, which the defendant is required to rebut, and a noncommercial use creates a presumption of lack of such harm, requiring a plaintiff to demonstrate the harm.[697] Limiting Sony, the Court in Campbell rejected these presumptions: "No 'presumption' or inference of market harm that might find support in Sony is applicable to a case involving something beyond mere duplication for commercial purposes .... No such evidentiary presumption is available to address either the first factor, the character and purpose of the use, or the fourth, market harm, in determining whether a transformative use ... is a fair one."[698]

693. *See*, e.g., *Ringgold v. Black Entm't Television, Inc.*, 126 F.3d 70, 81 (2d Cir. 1997) ("We have recognized the danger of circularity in considering whether the loss of potential licensing revenue should weight the fourth factor in favor of a plaintiff.").
694. *Id.* ("We have endeavored to avoid the vice of circularity by considering 'only traditional, reasonable, or likely to be developed markets' when considering the challenged use upon a potential market."); *Leibovitz v. Paramount Pictures Corp.*, 137 F.3d 109, 116–17 (2d Cir. 1998) ("[Plaintiff's] only argument for actual market harm is that the defendant has deprived her of a licensing fee by using the work. But she is not entitled to a licensing fee for a work that otherwise qualifies for the fair use defense ....").
695. *Campbell v. Acuff-Rose Music, Inc.*, 510 U.S. 569, 593 (1994) (quoting *Fisher v. Dees*, 794 F.2d 432, 438 (9th Cir. 1986)).
696. *See*, e.g., *Iowa State Univ. Research Found., Inc. v. Am. Broad. Cos., Inc.*, 621 F.2d 57 (2d Cir. 1980).
697. *Sony Corp. of Am. v. Universal City Studios, Inc.*, 464 U.S. 417, 449, 451 (1984) ("If the intended use is for commercial gain, [the] likelihood [of harm] may be presumed. But if it is for a noncommercial purpose, the likelihood must be demonstrated.").
698. *Campbell v. Acuff-Rose Music, Inc.*, 510 U.S. 569, 591, 594 (1994).

Grounds a fair use analysis on the section 107 preamble, lower courts have centralized the "transformative" purposes and weighed the four factors against the "transformative" use.[699] At the same time, the different Courts of Appeal have taken divergent paths in elaborating what makes a given use "transformative," and the role of a "repurposing" use in such analysis.[700]

III Parody as Fair Use

Parody has been defined as a "'literary or artistic work that imitates the characteristic style of an author or a work for comic effect or ridicule,' or as a 'composition in prose or verse in which the characteristic turns of thought and phrase in an author or class of authors are imitated in such a way as to make them appear ridiculous'."[701] By its very nature, to be at all effective, a parody must take qualitatively substantial and significant parts of the underlying work; if such work is protected by copyright, then, absent a fair use defense, the parody must necessarily be infringing. Since a parody, again, by its nature, serves to some extent as critical commentary, it would appear to be peculiarly susceptible to fair use analysis. The judicial treatment of parody and fair use, however, has been complex and inconsistent, exemplified by the different approaches of the Second and Ninth Circuits.

The Ninth Circuit initially, in 1956, rejected the proposition that the parodic nature of a use created any special significance for fair use analysis, a position that an equally divided US Supreme Court then left unresolved.[702] The Ninth Circuit modified its position in 1978, recognizing the particular applicability of fair use to parody, but focused analysis upon the third factor, the amount taken, holding that the parodist may take only so much as is necessary to "recall or conjure up" the original.[703]

The Second Circuit took a significantly different position when it dealt directly with the matter in 1980, seeming to rely upon dicta from an earlier Second Circuit case.[704] The court established a special place for parody in the fair use calculus, holding that "a parody is entitled at least to 'conjure up' the original. Even more extensive use

699. *See, e.g.*, *Bill Graham Archives v. Dorling Kindersley Ltd.*, 448 F.3d 605 (2d Cir. 2006) (analyzing all four factors with emphasis on the transformative use of the allegedly infringing work); *Perfect 10, Inc. v. Amazon.com, Inc.*, 508 F.3d 1146 (9th Cir. 2007) (holding that the use of thumbnail images in a search engine was "transformative" and a presumptive fair use).

700. *See Monge v. Maya Magazines*, 688 F.3d 1164, 1175–76 (9th Cir. 2012) ("the 'heart' of a claim for transformative use is 'the use of some elements of a prior author's composition to create a new one that, at least in part, comments on that author's works' … a 'difference in purpose is not quite the same thing as transformation'"); *see also Authors' Guild v. Hathitrust*, 755 F.3d 87 (2d Cir. 2014); *Cariou v. Prince*, 714 F.3d 694 (2d Cir. 2013); *Gaylord v. United States*, 595 F.3d 1364 (Fed. Cir. 2010); *Bill Graham Archives v. Dorling Kindersley Ltd.*, 448 F.3d 605 (2d Cir. 2006). *But see Fox News Network, LLC v. Tveyes, Inc.*, 883 F.3d 169, 174 (2d Cir. 2018) (rejecting fair use despite serving a transformative purpose).

701. *Campbell v. Acuff-Rose Music, Inc.*, 510 U.S. 569, 580 (1994) (quoting from *American Heritage Dictionary* 1317 (3d ed. 1992) and 11 *Oxford English Dictionary* 247 (2d ed. 1989)).

702. *Benny v. Loew's Inc.*, 239 F.2d 532 (9th Cir. 1956), *aff'd by an equally divided court*, 356 U.S. 43 (1958).

703. *Walt Disney Prods. v. Air Pirates*, 581 F.2d 751 (9th Cir. 1978).

704. *Berlin v. E.C. Publ'ns, Inc.*, 329 F.2d 541 (2d Cir. 1964).

would still be fair use, provided the parody builds upon the original, using the original as a known element of modern culture and contributing something new for humorous effect or commentary."[705]

Today it is well accepted that parody is a valued form of criticism; it is "encouraged because this sort of criticism itself fosters the creativity protected by the copyright laws."[706] A parodist's criticism need not be devastating: "A parodist need not demonstrate that the copyright owner would prohibit the use in order to qualify the copy as fair use."[707] The Second and Ninth Circuits are split on the extent to which a parodist must comment and criticize the underlying work.[708] A parodist is generally allowed to take enough of the original "to accomplish reasonably its parodic purpose."[709]

The Supreme Court, in Campbell, spoke definitively about the place of parody in fair use analysis:

> [P]arody has an obvious claim to transformative value ... Like less ostensibly humorous forms of criticism, it can provide social benefit, by shedding light on an earlier work, and, in the process, creating a new one. We thus line up with the courts that have held that parody, like other comment or criticism, may claim fair use under § 107.[710]

Moreover, the Court made clear that in applying the fair use factors to parody, the extent to which the parody is "transformative" will play a significant role in determining the impact of each of the factors. Thus, with respect to the third factor, the Court affirmed that "the parody must be able to 'conjure up' at least enough of [the] original to make the object of its critical wit recognizable .... Copying does not become excessive in relation to parodic purpose merely because the portion taken was the original's heart." Rather, in a parodic use, "context is everything, and the question of fairness asks what else the parodist did besides go to the heart of the original."[711]

For the purposes of the third factor, the amount of permissible taking is a function of the nature of the use: a transformative use can support a qualitatively greater taking than can a nontransformative use.[712] Similarly, for the fourth factor, a "transformative" commentary whose adverse market impact arises out of the fact of criticism or

705. *Elsmere Music, Inc. v. Nat'l Broad. Co.*, 623 F.2d 253 (2d Cir. 1980) (emphasis added).
706. *Rogers v. Koons*, 960 F.2d 301, 310 (2d Cir. 1992). *But see Cariou v. Prince*, 714 F.3d 694, 698 (2d Cir. 2013) (rejecting the proposition that a secondary work *must* comment on the original in order to qualify as fair use), *holding modified by* Andy Warhol Found. for the *Visual Arts, Inc. v. Goldsmith*, 992 F.3d 99 (2d Cir. 2021), *aff'd*, 598 U.S. __ (2023).
707. *Leibovitz v. Paramount Pictures Corp.*, 137 F.3d 109, 115 n.3 (2d Cir. 1998).
708. *Compare Dr. Seuss Enterprises, L.P. v. ComicMix LLC*, 983 F.3d 443, 452 (9th Cir. 2020) ("By definition, a parody must use some elements of a prior author's composition to create a new one that, at least in part, comments on that author's works."), *with Cariou v. Prince*, 714 F.3d 694, 698 (2d Cir. 2013) (rejecting the proposition that a secondary work *must* comment on the original in order to qualify as fair use), *holding modified by* Andy Warhol Found. for the *Visual Arts, Inc. v. Goldsmith*, 992 F.3d 99 (2d Cir. 2021), *aff'd*, 598 U.S. __ (2023).
709. *Fisher v. Dees*, 794 F.2d 432 (9th Cir. 1986).
710. *Campbell v. Acuff-Rose Music, Inc.*, 510 U.S. 569, 579 (1994).
711. *Id.*, at 588–89.
712. *Id.*, at 587–88.

disparagement may well be a fair use, as opposed to a blatant taking which simply usurps the market.[713] In assessing market impact, "the law looks beyond the criticism to the other elements of the work."[714]

With parody holding a preferred position in the fair use calculus, determining whether a given work is a "parody" is a significant task. As the Ninth Circuit observed, "Parody emerges from [the] 'joinder of reference and ridicule'."[715] The determination of whether a work is a "parody" is one for the court and is not a "factual" determination to be resolved by the weight of the evidence or other evidentiary factors: "The issue of whether a work is a parody is a question of law, not a matter of public majority opinion."[716]

Justice Souter's opinion in Campbell also is unequivocal in distinguishing "satire"—which uses the underlying work humorously to comment on societal matters without in some way ridiculing that work itself—from "parody." It is only the latter that may have special fair use protection:

> For the purposes of copyright law, the nub of the definitions, and the heart of any parodist's claim to quote from existing material, is the use of some elements of a prior author's composition to create a new one that, at least in part, comments on that author's works .... If, on the contrary, the commentary has no critical bearing on the substance or style of the original composition, which the alleged infringer merely uses to get attention or to avoid the drudgery in working up something fresh, the claim to fairness in borrowing from another's work diminishes accordingly (if it does not vanish), and other factors, like the extent of its commerciality, loom larger. Parody needs to mimic an original to make its point, and so has some claim to use the creation of its victim's (or collective victims') imagination, whereas satire can stand on its own two feet and so requires justification for the very act of borrowing.[717]

IV Fair Use of Utilitarian Works

Complex computer software cases have included issues resulting from the "dissection" and "disassembly" of a program for the purpose of reverse engineering to create a competing program. It has been held that while "disassembly is wholesale copying [that] falls squarely within the category of acts that are prohibited by the statute," such copying may be a fair use:

> We are not unaware of the fact that to those used to considering copyright issues in more traditional contexts, our result may seem incongruous at first blush.
>
> ...
>
> We conclude that where disassembly is the only way to gain access to the ideas and functional elements embodied in a copyrighted computer program and

713. *Id.*, at 593.
714. *Id.*, at 592.
715. *Mattel, Inc. v. Walking Mountain Prods.*, 353 F.3d 792, 802 (9th Cir. 2003) (quoting *Campbell v. Acuff-Rose Music, Inc.*, 510 U.S. 569, 591, 583 (1994)).
716. *Id.*, at 801.
717. *Campbell v. Acuff-Rose Music, Inc.*, 510 U.S. 569, 591, 580–81 (1994).

where there is a legitimate reason for seeking such access, disassembly is a fair use of the copyrighted work, as a matter of law.[718]

V Fair Use and Photocopying for Research and Academic Purposes

A *Library, Archival, and Research Copying*

Although the Copyright Act contains specific exemptions with respect to certain enumerated kinds of copying by archives and libraries, the scope of a broader, fair use exemption for library and archival photocopying is not clear.[719] Photocopying for research in a commercial context was the subject of *American Geophysical Union v. Texaco, Inc.*,[720] where the question was "whether it is lawful under the U.S. Copyright Act ... for a profit-seeking company to make unauthorized copies of copyrighted articles published in scientific and technical journals for use by the company's scientists employed in scientific research." The district court held that such copying was not a fair use. The divided Second Circuit affirmance focused on the nontransformative and "archival" nature of the copying: "to assemble a set of papers for future reference, thereby serving the same purpose for which additional subscriptions are normally sold, or ... for which photocopying licenses may be obtained." Such licenses are available from the Copyright Clearance Center, a central clearinghouse established in the late 1970s to license photocopying, thereby facilitating inexpensive copying for research and obviating a difficult fair use question.

B *Academic, Classroom Copying*

While the exemplary uses in section 107 include making "multiple copies for classroom use," there is no general exemption for copying either for academic research or for classroom distribution. In response to various concerns, an agreement was reached among representatives of publishers, authors, and educational institutions concerning Guidelines for Classroom Copying in Not-for-Profit Educational Institutions; these "guidelines" were incorporated into the House Committee Report underlying the 1976 Act. Without having the direct force of law, they nevertheless establish a minimum safe harbor for copying for academic research and for limited, brief, and spontaneous

718. *Sega Enters. Ltd v. Accolade, Inc.*, 977 F.2d 1510 (9th Cir. 1998). *Sega* was expressly adopted in *Bateman v. Mnemonics, Inc.*, 79 F.3d 1532 (11th Cir. 1996) ("We find the *Sega* opinion persuasive in view of the principal purpose of copyright—the advancement of science and the arts."); *see also Atari Games Corp. v. Nintendo of Am. Inc.*, 975 F.2d 832 (Fed. Cir. 1992) (concluding "reverse engineering object code to discern the unprotectable ideas in a computer program is a fair use"). *See Sony Computer Entm't Am., Inc. v. Connectix Corp.*, 203 F.3d 596 (9th Cir. 2000).

719. *See*, e.g., *Williams & Wilkins Co. v. United States*, 487 F.2d 1345 (Ct. Cl. 1973), a four to three Court of Claims decision, that was *affirmed by an equally divided* Supreme Court, 420 U.S. 376 (1975).

720. *Am. Geophysical Union v. Texaco, Inc.*, 802 F. Supp. 1 (S.D.N.Y. 1992), *aff'd*, 60 F.3d 513 (2d Cir. 1994).

copying for classroom distribution. There remains, however, the issue of the extent to which general fair use analysis applies to academic copying in excess of the guidelines. In that connection, it has been held that wholesale copying of copyrighted works for reproduction in "coursepacks" or "anthologies" is both outside the guidelines and not a fair use.[721] On the other hand, it has also been held that archiving of student essays in a database used to check for plagiarism is fair use.[722]

VI First Amendment Considerations

"The Copyright Clause and the First Amendment, while intuitively in conflict, were drafted to work together to prevent censorship; copyright laws were enacted in part to prevent private censorship and the First Amendment was enacted to prevent public censorship."[723] It has been argued that First Amendment concerns provide an additional, unstated fair use factor—in essence, an extra-statutory gloss on fair use.[724] In response, the Supreme Court has emphasized that "copyright law contains built-in First Amendment accommodations."[725] In particular, the idea/expression dichotomy and the fair use defense are embraced as traditional, built-in First Amendment protections.[726]

Thus, within the fair use analysis, courts "must remain cognizant of the First Amendment protections interwoven into copyright law."[727]

§8 DURATION OF COPYRIGHT PROTECTION

I General Overview

By its express terms, Article I, section 8, clause 8 of the US Constitution requires that the copyright monopoly may be granted only "for limited Times." Accordingly, in exercising its constitutional power, Congress may not grant a perpetual copyright, but

721. *Princeton Univ. Press v. Michigan Document Servs.*, 99 F.3d 1381 (6th Cir. 1996); *Basic Books, Inc. v. Kinko's Graphics Corp.*, 758 F. Supp. 1522 (S.D.N.Y. 1991); *cf. Cambridge University Press v. Becker*, 446 F. Supp. 3d 1145 (N.D. Ga. 2020) (concluding, on remand, that 37 of 48 infringement claims in the context of digital coursepacks were fair use), *remanded by*, *Cambridge University Press v. Albert*, 906 F.3d 1290 (11th Cir. 2018).
722. A.V. ex rel. *Vanderhye v. iParadigms LLC*, 562 F.3d 630 (4th Cir. 2009).
723. *Suntrust Bank v. Houghton Mifflin Co.*, 268 F.3d 1257, 1263 (11th Cir. 2001).
724. *See*, e.g., *Triangle Publ'ns v. Knight-Ridder Newspapers*, 626 F.2d 1171 (5th Cir. 1980) (Tate, J., concurring); *Maxtone-Graham v. Burtchaell*, 803 F.2d 1253 (2d Cir. 1986). *See also* Lawrence Lessig, *Copyright's First Amendment*, 48 UCLA L. Rev. 1057 (2001).
725. *Eldred v. Ashcroft*, 537 U.S. 186, 190 (2003). *See also Harper & Row Publishers, Inc. v. Nation Enters.*, 471 U.S. 539, 560 (1985) ("In view of the First Amendment protections already embodied in the Copyright Act's distinction between copyrightable expression and uncopyrightable facts and ideas, and the latitude for scholarship and comment traditionally afforded by fair use, we see no warrant for expanding the doctrine of fair use to create what amounts to a public figure exception to copyright.").
726. *Golan v. Holder*, 565 U.S. 302, 328 (2012).
727. *Suntrust Bank v. Houghton Mifflin Co.*, 268 F.3d 1257, 1265 (11th Cir. 2001).

must define and set limits to the term of copyright.[728] The determination of the copyright term, of course, has far-reaching consequences for the economic value of copyright.

A *The Pre-1976 Renewal Right and the Renewal Term*

In the first Copyright Act of 1790, Congress established a dual copyright term: an initial term (fourteen years) and a right in the copyright owner to renew the copyright for a second renewal term of equal duration. Over the succeeding years, the term of copyright under this dual-term scheme was extended; the 1909 Act set initial and renewal terms of twenty-eight years each.

Under the 1909 Act, copyright attached to a work upon its publication with appropriate notice and endured for an initial fixed term of twenty-eight years from the date of publication. If no further action was taken with respect to copyright in the work thereafter, the copyright ended, and the work fell into the public domain upon the expiration of that term. However, copyright in the work would continue for an additional renewal term of twenty-eight years if appropriate action was taken prior to the expiration of the initial term by the persons entitled to renew the copyright.

1 *Vesting of the Renewal Right*

The renewal right generally vested in the author of the work; the entity originally entitled to the initial copyright. Thus, an individual author who assigned and completely transferred his or her copyright interest in a work during the initial term would nevertheless own the renewal right and the transferee would have no interest with respect to the renewal term. In the case of an individual author, if that author did not survive the expiration of the initial term, then the right vested in specifically named and prioritized statutory successors, essentially the family, or the estate of the author.[729] There was some uncertainty as to how long the author had to survive for the renewal right, and the renewal term, to vest in the author or the author's assignee; that is, survival might be required up to the date of registration of the renewal application or through the initial term and to the beginning of the renewal term for the author or his or her assignee to own the copyright for the renewal term as against the statutory successors.[730] With the 1992 automatic renewal amendment, discussed below,[731] and its specific disposition of this question, the issue has become academic.

In the case of works made for hire, the employer was the entity entitled to renew. As for works that were within the first term, at the effective date of the 1976 Act, determination of whether a work is "a work made for hire" for these purposes will be

728. *See Eldred v. Ashcroft*, 537 U.S. 186 (2003) (holding that Congress was within its constitutional authority to extend the term of protection from 50 years to 70 years because the duration of copyright protection was still for "limited Times").
729. *See Marascalco v. Fantasy, Inc.*, 953 F.2d 469 (9th Cir. 1991).
730. *Id.*
731. *See infra* §8.I.A.4.

governed by the earlier 1909 Act standards, rather than the definition of work for hire under the 1976 Act.[732]

To be renewed, a work had to have been registered, and the application for renewal registration had to be filed with the Copyright Office by the person entitled thereto during the final year of the initial term. Upon expiration of the initial term, if proper renewal application had been filed, the renewal term would commence and vest in the person entitled thereto.[733]

2 *The Renewal Term as a New, Independent Term*

The renewal term was not simply an extension of the initial term. It was a completely new term, vesting only in the person entitled to renewal. Thus, assignments, transfers, licenses, and other rights granted by the author during the initial term would endure only for that term and would not encumber the renewal term. Similarly, as the Supreme Court made clear in *Stewart v. Abend*,[734] such rights could not continue to be exercised during the renewal term on the strength only of rights granted during the initial term; new arrangements would have to have been made with the owner of the renewal term.

3 *Assignment of the Renewal Right*

Since a grant, even of the entire copyright interest, endured only for the initial term of copyright, grantees often sought to secure for themselves rights in the renewal term. While it appeared to be the intent of Congress in creating a bifurcated duration structure to protect authors by limiting their transfers to the initial term, the US Supreme Court held that an assignment of the renewal right by an author during the initial term was binding, if otherwise a valid contract, and gave the assignee a right to renew superior to that of the author.[735]

However, since the author's right to renew was contingent upon survival of the author to effect that renewal, the assignee's right was similarly contingent; if the author did not survive to the appropriate time for vesting of the renewal term, then the assignee could not exercise the renewal right and would have no rights in the renewal term—the assignment was only of a "mere expectancy."[736] Accordingly, it became common practice for grantees of rights to get assignments with respect to the renewal

732. *See supra* §4.VI.
733. *See* 17 U.S.C. § 304(a)(3).
734. *Stewart v. Abend*, 495 U.S. 207 (1990).
735. *Fred Fisher Music Co. v. M. Witmark & Sons*, 318 U.S. 643 (1943).
736. *Stewart v. Abend*, 495 U.S. 207 (1990) (holding that the producer of a motion picture made during the initial term of the short story upon which it was based, the author of which had granted the producer motion picture rights in the story and had assigned to the producer rights in the renewal term, infringed the copyright in the short story by exhibiting the motion picture during the renewal term since the author had died prior to the time for registration for renewal and renewal had in fact vested in the statutory successor, for whom appropriate filing of renewal had been made).

term not only from the author but also from as many statutory successors as could be located.

4 *Automatic Renewal*

In 1992, Congress amended the Copyright Act to alleviate some of the technical concerns over renewal for works copyrighted under the 1909 Act. Section 304(a)[737] was amended to provide for automatic renewal, without registration, for works that were in their initial term at the effective date of the 1976 Act and were still in their initial term in 1992 (i.e., works whose copyright term commenced between January 1, 1963, and December 31, 1977).[738]

However, in an effort to encourage renewal by registration, the amendments provided differing consequences from renewal by registration and automatic renewal. Thus, in setting vesting rights, the statute distinguishes between automatic renewal and renewal by application and registration. If proper renewal registration is made, then the renewal term will vest (once the term begins) in the person entitled to renewal at the time the application is made; if renewal is automatic, without registration, the term will vest in the person entitled to renewal as of the last day of the original term.[739] Moreover, by virtue of these amendments, the creator of a derivative work authorized during the original term may continue to exploit that work during the renewal term if (and only if) the renewal is automatic, and not the result of registration, essentially limiting the rule of *Stewart v. Abend* to cases of renewal by registration.[740]

B *The 1976 Act Single Term*

One of the most significant changes made by the 1976 Act was the abandonment of this dual-term system, based upon absolutely fixed terms of years, and substitution of a single copyright term to endure, in general, for the life of the author plus a fixed term—originally fifty years. The 1998 Copyright Term Extension Act extended by twenty years the term for all works, including existing works then in copyright (for those works in which no real person is identified as the author and for works made for hire, the term was fixed originally at 100 years from creation (extended, in 1998, to 120 years) or, if the work is unpublished, seventy-five years (extended to ninety-five years) from publication, whichever expires earlier). The Supreme Court upheld the 1998 term extension, even with respect to existing copyrights, as within the constitutional "limited Times" restriction and as a proper exercise of Congress' constitutional power:[741]

737. 17 U.S.C. § 304(a).
738. 17 U.S.C. § 304(a)(2).
739. *Id.*
740. 17 U.S.C. § 304(a)(4)(A).
741. *Eldred v. Ashcroft*, 537 U.S. 186 (2003).

> Guided by text, history, and precedent, we cannot agree with petitioners' submission that extending the duration of existing copyrights is categorically beyond Congress' authority under the Copyright Clause.
>
> …
>
> [W]e find that the CTEA is a rational enactment; we are not at liberty to second-guess congressional determinations and policy judgments of this order, however debatable or arguably unwise they may be. Accordingly, we cannot conclude that the CTEA—which continues the unbroken congressional practice of treating future and existing copyrights in parity for term extension purposes—is an impermissible exercise of Congress' power under the Copyright Clause.[742]

The twenty-year extension adopted in October 1998 is applicable to all works whose copyright had not by then expired, but does not serve to restore copyright in works which had theretofore fallen into the public domain.

The 1976 Act's change to a fixed term was designed both to bring American law more closely into line with that of the Berne Convention states and, in the view of Congress, more adequately to protect US authors. As the House Committee Report noted:

> The present 56 year term is not long enough to insure an author and his dependents the fair economic benefits from the works. Life expectancy has increased substantially, and more and more authors are seeing their works fall into the public domain during their lifetimes, forcing later works to compete with their own early works in which copyright has expired.
>
> …
>
> One of the worst features of the present copyright law is the provision for renewal of copyright. A substantial burden and expense, this unclear and highly technical requirement results in incalculable amounts of unproductive work. In a number of cases it is the cause of inadvertent and unjust loss of copyright. Under a life-plus-50 system the renewal device would be inapplicable and unnecessary.
>
> …
>
> A very large majority of the world's countries have adopted a copyright term of the life of the author and 50 years after that author's death ….[743]

As is clear from a detailed analysis of the duration provisions,[744] the assumption underlying these provisions was that the practical effect of their application would be to produce, on average, a copyright term of seventy-five years. With movement of the European Union toward a term of life of the author plus seventy years, and the passage of conforming legislation in the US, adjustment of that assumption would appear to be necessary.

II Works Created on or after the Effective Date of the 1976 Act (January 1, 1978)

In general, for works created on or after January 1, 1978, copyright attaches from the time the work is fixed in a tangible medium of expression and endures for the life of the

742. *Id.*, at 187, 208.
743. H.R. Rep. No. 94-1476, at 135 (1976), *as reprinted in* 1976 U.S.C.C.A.N. 5659, 5751.
744. 17 U.S.C. §§ 302–305.

author plus seventy years.[745] In the case of works of joint authorship, the term is measured by the life of the last surviving joint author (plus seventy years).[746]

To aid in the determination whether a copyright in a given work has expired, the Copyright Office is required to maintain current records of information as to the death of authors of copyrighted works, and, for such purposes, any person having an interest in a copyright may record in the Copyright Office a statement of the date of death of the author of that work, or statement that the author is alive as of a particular date.[747] Further, in the absence of such records with respect to the author of a particular work, after the expiration of the earlier of ninety-five years from the year of first publication of that work, or 120 years from the year of its creation, it may be presumed that the author has been dead for at least seventy years and reliance upon that presumption is a complete defense to any action for infringement.[748]

For anonymous works, pseudonymous works, and works made for hire, the term is fixed at ninety-five years from the year of first publication or, if the work is unpublished, 120 years from the year of creation, whichever expires first.[749] With respect to anonymous or pseudonymous works, a person with an interest in the copyright in such works may record with the Copyright Office a statement identifying one or more authors of the work. If, prior to the expiration of the fixed term, such statement has been filed or the identity of one or more of the authors is otherwise revealed in records of registration for the work, then the term will be measured by the life of the last surviving author whose identity has been revealed (plus seventy years).[750]

III Works Created But Not Published or Copyrighted Before January 1, 1978

In abolishing the perpetual "common law" copyright for unpublished works, Congress provided protection under the 1976 Act for works created but not published or copyrighted[751] or in the public domain as of the effective date of the Act. Copyright in such works subsists from January 1, 1978, and endures for the later of: (a) the term that would apply had the work been created on or after January 1, 1978; (b) the period ending on December 31, 2002; and (c) the period ending on December 31, 2047, if the work is published on or before December 31, 2002.[752]

Thus, for example, copyright might attach to an unpublished manuscript created in 1920, even if the author had died by 1925, and such copyright would endure through 2002 and if published by that date, until 2047. Essentially, in exchange for removal of

745. 17 U.S.C. § 302(a).
746. 17 U.S.C. § 302(b).
747. 17 U.S.C. § 302(d).
748. 17 U.S.C. § 302(e).
749. 17 U.S.C. § 302(c).
750. 17 U.S.C. § 302(c).
751. Under the 1909 Act, it was possible to secure federal copyright protection for certain unpublished works (e.g., to secure protection for a play performed in the theater, which did not constitute "publication," prior to the time that the play itself might appear in book form).
752. 17 U.S.C. § 303.

the perpetual protection accorded to unpublished works pursuant to the "common law" copyright, the Act, for all practical purposes, treats the author of an unpublished work who had died prior to the effective date of the Act as if such author had died on that date.

IV Works with Subsisting Copyright Protection as of January 1, 1978

The intention of the Act with respect to copyright subsisting as of the effective date was to extend their term from fifty-six years to seventy-five (now ninety-five) years. Thus, for copyrights in their first term as of that date, the first term continued to the completion of its twenty-eight years, followed by the renewal term (effected either by registration or automatically), for a further period of sixty-seven years.[753] For works which were in the renewal term or had been registered for renewal before January 1, 1978, that renewal term continued and was extended, originally by nineteen years, and currently, if the work was still in its renewal term as of the end of October 1998, by thirty-nine years, to produce a total term of ninety-five years from the date copyright was originally secured.[754] As discussed above, in connection with termination of transfers,[755] it is this thirty-nine-year extension that may be recaptured by the author, free of any intervening grants or transfers.

V Restoration of Copyright in Certain Foreign Works

Legislation in 1993 implementing the NAFTA added a new provision, section 104A, restoring copyright in certain Mexican and Canadian works which had entered the public domain in the US. The GATT implementation amendments of 1994, effective January 1, 1996, substituted much broader language restoring copyright protection generally to foreign works under copyright protection in their "source" country but which had fallen into the public domain in the US as a result of noncompliance with then-existing statutory formalities, or for lack of subject matter protection. Restoration provides protection in the US for the remainder of the term the work would have had had it not entered the public domain. There are detailed provisions as to "eligible" countries, protection for "reliance" parties, continued exploitation of preexisting derivative works, and notice and procedural requirements.[756]

As noted above,[757] the constitutionality of section 104A has been challenged, and while the D.C. Circuit, relying on Eldred, upheld the constitutionality of the restoration provisions,[758] the Tenth Circuit initially held that, although section 104A is not inconsistent with the constitutional limitations on congressional power, by removing

753. 17 U.S.C. § 304(a)(1).
754. 17 U.S.C. § 304(b).
755. *See supra* §5.
756. 17 U.S.C. § 104A. *See Dam Things from Denmark v. Russ Berrie & Co., Inc.*, 290 F.3d 548 (3d Cir. 2002).
757. *See supra* §3.I.C.
758. *Luck's Music Library v. Gonzalez*, 407 F.3d 1262 (D.C. Cir. 2005).

material from the public domain it "has altered the traditional contours of copyright protection and requires First Amendment scrutiny."[759] Ultimately, the Tenth Circuit, reversing a district court determination on remand that the statute was not "narrowly tailored,"[760] upheld the statute's constitutionality.[761] In 2012, the US Supreme Court affirmed the Tenth Circuit determination that the provision is constitutionally permissible.[762]

§9 INFRINGEMENT

Anyone who violates any of the exclusive rights of the copyright owner as provided by sections 106 through 118 or of the author as provided in section 106A(a), or who imports copies or phonorecords into the US in violation of section 602, is an infringer of the copyright or right of the author, as the case may be.[763]

I Procedural Issues in Infringement Actions

A Registration

Registration, while not mandatory for the attachment of copyright to a work, is a prerequisite to the institution of actions for infringement.[764] Note that registration is not a prerequisite for actions involving copyright in works first published in a Berne Convention country other than the US.[765] If proper application for registration has been made and refused, the applicant may nevertheless institute an action for infringement if notice of such action, together with a copy of the complaint, is served on the Register of Copyrights.[766] Moreover, if the work was registered within five years after first publication, the certificate of registration is prima facie evidence of the validity of the copyright and of the facts stated in the certificate,[767] creating a rebuttable presumption of validity.[768] As noted above,[769] the Supreme Court has held that the Copyright Act registration requirement is "procedural," and not "jurisdictional."[770]

759. *Golan v. Gonzalez*, 501 F.3d 1179 (10th Cir. 2007).
760. *Golan v. Holder*, 611 F. Supp. 2d 1165 (Dist. Colo. 2009).
761. *Golan v. Holder*, 609 F.3d 1076 (10th Cir. 2010).
762. *Golan v. Holder*, 565 U.S. 302 (2012).
763. 17 U.S.C. § 501(a).
764. *Fourth Estate Pub. Benefit Corp. v. Wall-Street.com, LLC*, 139 S. Ct. 881 (2019) (holding a "United States work" must be registered with the Copyright Office before the rightsholder may sue for infringement). Note that this does not apply to claims for violation of the attribution and integrity rights of works of visual art protected by 17 U.S.C. § 106A.
765. 17 U.S.C. § 411.
766. *Id.*
767. 17 U.S.C. § 410(c).
768. *See Entm't Research Grp., Inc. v. Genesis Creative Grp., Inc.*, 122 F.3d 1211, 1217 (9th Cir. 1997).
769. *See supra* §3.I.D.3.
770. *Reed Elsevier, Inc. v. Muchnick*, 559 U.S. 154 (2010), *rev'g In re* Literary Works in Elec. Databases Copyright Litig., 509 F.3d 116 (2d Cir. 2007). *See also Brooks-Ngwenya v. Indianapolis Public Sch*, 564 F.3d 804 (7th Cir. 2009) ("Even though nonjurisdictional, the notification requirement is a prerequisite to suit. Congress wanted to ensure that the Copyright Office could

B *Subject Matter Jurisdiction*

1 *Exclusive Federal Jurisdiction*

Jurisdiction of civil actions "arising under" the Copyright Act is vested exclusively in the federal district courts; it is "exclusive of the courts of the states."[771] A copyright infringement action, therefore, must be brought in federal court. Since subject matter jurisdiction is involved, the parties may not circumvent this requirement to confer jurisdiction upon a state court; the court may, on its own motion, dismiss a claim as outside its jurisdiction.

The Supreme Court recently clarified that states have not abrogated sovereign immunity for copyright infringement liability.[772] This means an individual may not recover money damages against a state for copyright infringement. Creative attempts to avoid suing state actors in federal court have been unsuccessful. The Texas Supreme Court recently rejected an attempt to bring an unlawful taking claim in state court, rather than a copyright infringement claim.[773]

The jurisdictional language, however, is not limited to actions for copyright infringement. Rather, the conferring of jurisdiction on the federal courts, and the ousting of state court jurisdiction, requires that the action be one "arising under any Act of Congress relating to" copyright. While an action for copyright infringement based upon a claimed unauthorized reproduction of a copyrighted work clearly must be brought in a federal district court and may not be brought in a state court, other kinds of actions might also "arise under" the Copyright Act. So, too, not every claim that may involve a copyrighted work will be considered to "arise under" the Act so as to confer jurisdiction upon the federal court. The leading interpretive formulation for setting boundaries for subject matter jurisdiction is that of Judge Friendly in *T.B. Harms Co. v. Eliscu*:[774]

> [The] jurisdictional statute does not speak in terms of infringement, and the undoubted truth that a claim for infringement "arises under" the Copyright Act does not establish that nothing else can ....
>
> ...

---

intervene and defend its refusal to register a work"); *Perfect 10, Inc. v. Amazon.com, Inc.* 508 F.3d 1146 (9th Cir. 2007) ("Once a court has jurisdiction over an action for copyright infringement under section 411, the court may grant injunctive relief to restrain infringement of any copyright, whether registered or unregistered").

771. 25 U.S.C. § 1338(a) ("The district court shall have original jurisdiction of any civil action arising under any Act of Congress relating to patents, plant variety protection, copyrights and trademarks. Such jurisdiction shall be exclusive of the courts of the states in patent, plant variety protection and copyright cases").
772. *Allen v. Cooper*, 140 S. Ct. 994 (2020).
773. *See Jim Olive Photography v. Univ. of Houston Sys.*, No. 19-0605, 2021 WL 2483766, at *9 (Tex. June 18, 2021) (affirming dismissal of a photographer's inverse condemnation claim because "infringement does not equate to the 'theft' or 'conversion' of the copyright owner's exclusive rights" and "allegations of copyright infringement by the government do not constitute a per se taking").
774. *T.B. Harms Co. v. Eliscu*, 339 F.2d 823, 825, 828 (2d Cir. 1964).

> Mindful of the hazards of formulation in this treacherous area, we think that an action "arises under" the Copyright Act if and only if the complaint is for a remedy expressly granted by the Act, e.g., a suit for infringement or for the statutory royalties for record reproduction, or asserts a claim requiring construction of the Act ... or, at the very least and perhaps more doubtfully, presents a case where a distinctive policy of the Act requires that federal principles control the disposition of the claim.[775]

Thus, a claim, even if not for infringement, that would require interpretation or construction of the Copyright Act would be within the exclusive jurisdiction of the federal court. While it is not clear how and when jurisdiction would be conferred because of the requirements of "a distinctive policy" of the Copyright Act, it is clear that "the general interest that copyrights, like all other forms of property, should be enjoyed by the true owner is not enough to meet this last test."[776] The issue has been most clearly presented in litigation involving disputes over contracts and licenses relating to copyrighted works. Although it had been suggested, contrary to T.B. Harms Co., that the determinative factor is the centrality of Copyright Act interpretation to the principal dispute, "whether the plaintiff's infringement claim is only 'incidental' to the plaintiff's claim seeking a determination of ownership or contractual rights under the copyright,"[777] the Second Circuit has reasserted the continued viability of the T.B. Harms Co. test.[778]

2 *Pendent Jurisdiction*

If a district court properly has jurisdiction over a copyright claim, it may, in certain cases, also adjudicate related, noncopyright pendent claims. Statutorily, such jurisdiction is authorized specifically for "any civil action asserting a claim of unfair competition when joined with a substantial and related claim under the copyright, patent,

775. *Id.*, at 828.
776. *Id.*
777. *Schoenberg v. Shapolsky Publishers, Inc.*, 971 F.2d 926, 932–33 (2d Cir. 1992):

> [To determine] whether a suit "arises under" the Copyright Act when it alleges infringement stemming from a breach of contract [a] district court must first determine whether the plaintiff's infringement claim is only "incidental" to the plaintiff's claim seeking a determination of ownership or contractual rights under the copyright .... If ... the claim is not merely incidental, then a ... court must next determine whether the complaint alleges a breach of a condition to, or a covenant of, the contract licensing or assigning the copyright. [I]f a breach of a condition is alleged, then the district court has subject matter jurisdiction .... But if the complaint merely alleges a breach of a contractual covenant ... then the court must undertake a third step and analyze whether the breach is so material as to create a right of rescission in the grantor. If the breach would create a right of rescission, then the asserted claim arises under the Copyright Act.

778. *Bassett v. Mashantucket Pequot Tribe*, 204 F.3d 343 (2d Cir. 2000) ("When a complaint alleges a claim or seeks a remedy provided by the Copyright Act, federal jurisdiction is properly invoked.").

plant variety protection or trademark laws."[779] Thus, a district court having jurisdiction over a copyright claim may decide pendent nonfederal claims if the federal claim is both "substantial" and "related" to the nonfederal claims. The relationship need not be based on absolutely identical facts, although there must be a strong factual tie between the two types of claims. While the statute speaks only of pendent "unfair competition" claims, it has been construed more broadly to include other types of claims, where appropriate.[780]

3 *Suits in the US for Acts of Infringement Abroad*

Generally, a district court does not have jurisdiction to hear an infringement action based upon acts of infringement occurring in a foreign jurisdiction.[781] "It is settled that the Copyright Act does not apply extraterritorially."[782] It has been held that authorization within the US of these foreign acts of infringement is not a sufficient domestic act to support jurisdiction.[783] However, where there has been a completed act of infringement in the US, the plaintiff "is entitled to recover damages flowing from exploitation abroad of the domestic acts of infringement."[784]

C *Personal Jurisdiction and Venue*

There are no special personal jurisdictional rules for copyright infringement actions. Rather, jurisdiction over the person of the defendant is governed by the general in personam jurisdiction provisions of the Federal Rules of Civil Procedure. In *Penguin Group (USA) Inc. v. American Buddha,*[785] the New York Court of Appeals, responding to a certified question from the Court of Appeals for the Second Circuit, dealt with the applicability of New York's long-arm jurisdiction provisions in a federal copyright infringement action brought in New York and arising out of allegedly infringing uploading and downloading activities on internet websites based in Oregon and Arizona, by an Oregon corporation, whose principal place of business is in Arizona. The New York Court of Appeals reframed the certified question as:

779. 28 U.S.C. § 1338(b).
780. *See, e.g., Lone Ranger Television, Inc. v. Program Radio Corp.*, 740 F.2d 718 (9th Cir. 1984).
781. *See, e.g., Filmvideo Releasing Corp. v. Hastings*, 668 F.2d 91 (2d Cir. 1981); *Robert Stigwood Grp. Ltd. v. O'Reilly*, 530 F.2d 1096 (2d Cir. 1976).
782. *Los Angeles News Serv. v. Reuters Television Int'l, Ltd.*, 149 F.3d 987, 990 (9th Cir. 1998). This "predicate act" doctrine, allowing recovery of damages incurred abroad flowing from a predicate act of infringement in the US, enunciated in *Los Angeles News Service v. Reuters*, was reaffirmed by the Fourth Circuit in *Tire Eng'g v. Shandong Linglong Rubber Co.*, 682 F.3d 292 (4th Cir. 2012).
783. *Subafilms, Ltd. v. MGM—Pathe Commc'ns Co.*, 24 F.3d 1088 (9th Cir. 1994) ("when the assertedly infringing conduct consists solely of the authorization within the territorial boundaries of the United States of acts that occur entirely abroad ... such allegations do not state a claim for relief under the copyright laws of the United States"); *cf. Twin Books v. Walt Disney Co.*, 83 F.3d 1162 (9th Cir. 1996); *Societe Civile Succession Guino v. Renoir*, 549 F.3d 1182 (9th Cir. 2008).
784. *L. A. News Serv. v. Rueters TV Int'l, Ltd.*, 149 F.3d 987, 992 (9th Cir. 1998).
785. *Penguin Group (USA) Inc. v. American Buddha*, 16 N.Y.3d 295 (N.Y. 2011).

> In copyright infringement cases involving the uploading of a copyrighted printed literary work onto the Internet, is the situs of injury for purposes of determining long-arm jurisdiction under [New York's long arm statute] the location of the infringing action or the residence or location of the principal place of business of the copyright holder?

The court concluded that the situs of injury for the purposes of determining New York long-arm jurisdiction was the location of the principal place of business of the plaintiff copyright holder:

> [A]lthough it may make sense in traditional commercial tort cases to equate a plaintiff's injury with the place where its business is lost or threatened, it is illogical to extend that concept to online copyright infringement cases where the place of uploading is inconsequential and it is difficult, if not impossible, to correlate lost sales to a particular geographic area. In short, the out-of-state location of the infringing conduct carries less weight in the jurisdictional inquiry in circumstances alleging digital piracy and is therefore not dispositive.
>
> ...
>
> In sum, the role of the Internet in cases alleging the uploading of copyrighted books distinguishes them from traditional commercial tort cases where courts have generally linked the injury to the place where sales or customers are lost. The location of the infringement in online cases is of little import inasmuch as the primary aim of the infringer is to make the works available to anyone with access to an Internet connection, including computer users in New York. In addition, the injury to a New York copyright holder, while difficult to quantify, is not as remote as a purely indirect financial loss due to the broad spectrum of rights accorded by copyright law. The concurrence of these two elements–the function and nature of the Internet and the diverse ownership rights enjoyed by copyright holders situated in New York–leads us to ... conclude that the alleged injury in this case occurred in New York for purposes of [the long arm statute].

With respect to venue, copyright actions, as other actions, may be instituted "in the district in which the defendant or his agent resides or may be found."[786]

D *Standing*

Under the 1909 Act, standing to sue for infringement vested only in the owner of the entire copyright interest; a transferee of less than the whole was considered merely a licensee for these purposes. With the infinite divisibility of copyright under the 1976 Act,[787] any number of entities might own rights in a copyrighted work and the Act recognizes their right to sue for infringement. Subject to the registration requirements,[788] an action may be brought by "the legal or beneficial owner of an exclusive right under copyright ... for any infringement of the particular right committed while he or she is the owner of it."[789] The effect of this provision is to confer proper standing to sue for infringement on anyone owning any exclusive right in a copyright. For example,

786. 28 U.S.C. § 1400(a).
787. 17 U.S.C. § 201(d); *see supra* §4.II.
788. 17 U.S.C. § 411; *see supra* §3.I.D.
789. 17 U.S.C. § 501(b).

the owner of the exclusive right to make a motion picture version of a book may sue for infringement of that motion picture. So too, an exclusive licensee would have standing to object to infringement of the licensed right. The beneficial owner of an exclusive right, such as a composer who had assigned copyright in exchange for percentage royalties, would similarly have standing to sue.[790] Whereas, a nonexclusive licensee—whether the "legal" or "beneficial" holder of the license—would not be considered an "owner" for these purposes.[791] So, too, it has been held that the assignee of a cause of action for infringement does not have a sufficient interest by virtue alone of the assignment, to have standing to sue.[792]

To ameliorate the problem of multiplicity of litigation resulting from the divisibility of copyright "ownership," notice of a pending action must be served "upon any person whose interest is likely to be affected by a decision in the case," and the court may require notice to be served upon any person who is shown "to have or claim an interest in the copyright."[793]

E Statute of Limitations

A civil action under the Copyright Act must be "commenced within three years after the claim accrued."[794] The statute may be tolled by the defendant's concealment of the infringement or for the period during which the plaintiff could not reasonably have learned of the infringement.[795] Criminal proceedings under the Act must, except as expressly provided otherwise in the Act, be "commenced within five years after the cause of action arose."[796]

With respect to continuing acts of infringement, "each infringing act starts a new limitations period."[797] Unlike defamation, copyright does not have a single publication rule; the statute of limitations does not commence with the initial publication. Rather, it is the last instance of infringement that sets the limitation period. However, damages, under this separate-accrual rule, are limited to those flowing from infringement only within the three years preceding suit.[798] Where there has been such continuing conduct, notwithstanding the plaintiff's delay in bringing suit, the defense of laches (i.e., unreasonable prejudicial delay in commencing suit) may not be used to preclude

790. *See, e.g.*, *Cortner v. Israel*, 732 F.2d 267 (2d Cir. 1984).
791. *See Tresona Multimedia, LLC v. Burbank High Sch. Vocal Music Ass'n*, 953 F.3d 638 (9th Cir. 2020) (concluding plaintiff lacked standing under 17 U.S.C. § 501(b) because plaintiff received its interests from individual co-owners, without the consent of the other co-owners, and therefore held only nonexclusive licenses in those works).
792. *Silvers v. Sony Pictures Entm't, Inc.*, 402 F.3d 881, 890 (9th Cir. 2005) ("The bare assignment of an accrued cause of action is impermissible under 17 U.S.C. § 501(b). Because that is all [plaintiff's assignor] conveyed to Silvers, Silvers was not entitled to institute and may not maintain this action against Sony for alleged infringement of the copyright.").
793. 17 U.S.C. § 501(b).
794. 17 U.S.C. § 507(b).
795. *Taylor v. Meirick*, 712 F.2d 1112 (7th Cir. 1983); *cf. Roley v. New World Pictures, Ltd.*, 19 F.3d 479 (9th Cir. 1994).
796. 17 U.S.C. § 507(a).
797. *Petrella v. Metro-Goldwyn-Mayer, Inc.*, 572 U.S. 663, 671 (2014).
798. *Petrella*, 572 U.S. at 671–72.

claims for damages (as opposed to injunctive relief) for infringement to the extent brought within the statutory period.[799]

A copyright claim ordinarily accrues when an infringing act occurs.[800] In determining when such claims accrue, most Circuits have adopted the "discovery rule," rather than the "injury rule."[801] Under a discovery rule, an infringement claim does not "accrue" until the copyright holder discovers, or with due diligence should have discovered, the infringement. On the other hand, under the injury rule, a cause of action accrues at the time of the injury. Under the discovery rule, a rightsholder would be allowed to recover damages beyond the three-year lookback period so long as: (1) the rightsholder reasonably did not discover the infringement and (2) a suit is filed within three years of when the rightsholder should reasonably have discovered the infringing act.

F *Actions Against State Instrumentalities*

1 *Sovereign Immunity under the Eleventh Amendment*

The US government has waived its sovereign immunity from suits for patents and copyright infringement.[802] However, the Eleventh Amendment to the Constitution appears to shield states from suit. The Amendment provides: "The Judicial power of the United States shall not be construed to extend to any suit in law or equity, commenced, or prosecuted against one of the United States by Citizens of another State, or by Citizens or Subjects of any Foreign State." Under the Eleventh Amendment, states may claim immunity against copyright infringement damages claims.[803]

2 *Abrogation of Immunity*

In 1989, in *Pennsylvania v. Union Gas Co.*,[804] the US Supreme Court suggested that Congress could, by express resolution, abrogate a state's Eleventh Amendment immunity. Exercising that power, in 1990 Congress enacted the Copyright Remedy

799. *Id.*, at 667 ("courts are not at liberty to jettison Congress' judgment on the timeliness of suit"); *see also Evergreen Safety Council v. RSA Network, Inc.*, 698 F.3d 1221 (9th Cir. 2013).
800. *Petrella v. Metro-Goldwyn-Mayer, Inc.*, 572 U.S. 663, 670 (2014).
801. *See*, e.g., *Sohm v. Scholastic Inc.*, 959 F.3d 39, 49 (2d Cir. 2020); *William A. Graham Co. v. Haughey*, 568 F.3d 425, 433 (3d Cir. 2009); *Warren Freedenfeld Assocs., Inc. v. McTigue*, 531 F.3d 38, 44–46 (1st Cir. 2008); *Comcast v. Multi-Vision Elecs., Inc.*, 491 F.3d 938, 944 (8th Cir. 2007); *Roger Miller Music, Inc. v. Sony/ATV Publ'g, LLC*, 477 F.3d 383, 390 (6th Cir. 2007); *Polar Bear Prods., Inc. v. Timex Corp.*, 384 F.3d 700, 705–07 (9th Cir. 2004); *Gaiman v. McFarlane*, 360 F.3d 644, 653 (7th Cir. 2004); *Lyons P'ship, L.P. v. Morris Costumes, Inc.*, 243 F.3d 789, 796 (4th Cir. 2001); *Daboub v. Gibbons*, 42 F.3d 285, 291 (5th Cir. 1995).
802. 28 U.S.C. § 1498. Infringement suits against the federal government must be brought in the US Court of Federal Claims, and plaintiffs may receive only "reasonable" damages for the use, and neither injunctive relief nor costs or attorneys' fees. *See*, e.g., *Steve Altman Photography v. United States*, 18 Cl. Ct. 267, 282 (Cl. Ct. 1989) (awarding "plaintiff reasonable compensation of $1500.00").
803. *Allen v. Cooper*, 140 S. Ct. 994 (2020).
804. *Pennsylvania v. Union Gas*, 491 U.S. 1 (1989).

Clarification Act,[805] expressly stating that state instrumentalities "shall not be immune, under the Eleventh Amendment of the Constitution of the United States or under any other doctrine of sovereign immunity," from suit for copyright infringement.[806] However, in 1996, in *Seminole Tribe v. Florida*,[807] a case not involving copyright or patent issues, a sharply divided Supreme Court overruled *Pennsylvania v. Union Gas* and held that Congress could not use its powers under Article I to abrogate Eleventh Amendment immunity. Four years later, the Supreme Court held that similar attempts to abrogate state sovereign immunity in federal patent and trademark cases were an invalid exercise of Congress' constitutional powers.[808] In 2020, the Supreme Court invalidated Congress' attempt to abrogate state sovereign immunity in copyright cases.[809]

States may claim immunity against copyright infringement damages judgments under the Eleventh Amendment.[810] Congress may only abrogate a state's sovereign immunity under its power to enforce the Fourteenth Amendment.[811] To exercise this authority, Congress must: (1) identify state conduct that violates the Fourteenth Amendment and then (2) tailor a legislative scheme to remedying or preventing such conduct. In the copyright context, Congress failed to identify a pattern of state copyright infringement significant enough to justify wholesale abrogation of state sovereign immunity.[812]

G *Misuse of Copyright*

Borrowing a concept from patent law, some courts have held that the copyright owner may forfeit the right to sue for otherwise actionable infringement if the copyright has been "misused." The public policy behind the limited monopoly of copyright "forbids

805. Copyright Remedy Clarification Act of 1990, Pub. L. 101-553, 104 Stat. 2749 (codified at 17 U.S.C. §§ 501(a), 511).
806. 17 U.S.C. § 511.
807. *Seminole Tribe v. Florida*, 517 U.S. 44 (1996).
808. *Florida Prepaid Postsecondary Educ. Expense Bd. v. College Savings Bank*, 527 U.S. 627 (1999) (patents); *College Savings Bank v. Florida Prepaid Postsecondary Educ. Expense Bd.*, 527 U.S. 666 (1999) (trademarks).
809. *Allen v. Cooper*, 140 S. Ct. 994 (2020).
810. Note that local governments may not be covered by state sovereign immunity. *See*, e.g., *Owen v. City of Independence, Missouri*, 445 U.S. 622 (1980). Thus, municipalities may not be shielded from damage claims for copyright infringement. Also, state officials may be vulnerable to actions for injunctive relief. *See* Ex Parte Young, 209 U.S. 123 (1908). For example, university officials have been sued for prospective, injunctive relief for violating copyright. *See*, e.g., *Hairston v. N. Carolina Agr. & Tech. State Univ.*, No. 1:04 CV 1203, 2005 WL 2136923, at *10 (M.D.N.C. Aug. 5, 2005) (denying a motion to dismiss for plaintiff's prospective, injunctive relief for alleged copyright infringement); *Salerno v. City Univ. of New York*, 191 F. Supp. 2d 352, 357 (S.D.N.Y. 2001) ("Plaintiffs in this suit seek a prospective injunction to prevent a state official from violating federal law, which is precisely the type of relief which the *Ex Parte Young* exception was created to provide.").
811. *Allen v. Cooper*, 140 S. Ct. 994 (2020).
812. *Id.*, at 1007; ("the law's 'indiscriminate scope' is 'out of proportion' to any due process problem").

the use of the copyright to secure an exclusive right or limited monopoly not granted by the Copyright Office":[813]

> Put simply, our Constitution emphasizes the purpose and value of copyrights and patents. Harm caused by their misuse undermines their usefulness. Anticompetitive licensing agreements may conflict with the purpose behind a copyright's protection by depriving the public of the would-be competitor's creativity. In the licensing context, the Ninth Circuit held that copyright misuse prevents copyright holders from using license terms "to stifle competition," but it does not "prohibit using conditions to control use of copyrighted material."[814] The fair use doctrine and the refusal to copyright facts and ideas also address applications of copyright protection that would otherwise conflict with a copyright's constitutional goal. But it is possible that a copyright holder could leverage its copyright to restrain the creative expression of another without engaging in anticompetitive behavior or implicating the fair use and idea/expression doctrines.[815] Query how to draw the line between stifling competition and merely leveraging use of copyrighted material. This begs the question where the copyright monopoly should begin and end.

While the patent model has generally been concerned with use of the monopoly in ways that violate the antitrust laws, the misuse of copyright defense has been applied to prevent the use of the copyright monopoly for anticompetitive or restrictive purposes going beyond the subject of the copyright itself, whether or not antitrust activities are implicated:

> The question is not whether the copyright is being used in a manner violative of antitrust law ..., but whether the copyright is being used in a manner violative of the public policy embodied in the grant of copyright.[816]

II Copyright Alternative in Small-Claims Enforcement Act

In 2020, Congress enacted the Copyright Alternative in Small-Claims Enforcement Act (CASE Act). The CASE Act adds Chapter 15 to Title 17 of the United States Code (U.S.C.) and creates the Copyright Claims Board, which is "an alternative forum in which parties may voluntarily seek to resolve certain copyright claims."[817] In this

813. *Lasercomb Am., Inc. v. Reynolds*, 911 F.2d 970, 979 (4th Cir. 1990).
814. *Apple Inc. v. Psystar Corp.*, 658 F.3d 1150, 1157, 1159 (9th Cir. 2011).
815. *Video Pipeline, Inc. v. Buena Vista Home Entm't, Inc.*, 342 F.3d 191, 204–05 (3d Cir. 2003).
816. *Lasercomb Am., Inc v. Reynolds*, 911 F.2d 970, 978 (4th Cir. 1990). *See also Assessment Techs. of Wisconsin, LLC. v. WIREdata, Inc.*, 350 F.3d 640, 647 (7th Cir. 2003) ("The doctrine of misuse 'prevents copyright holders from leveraging their limited monopoly to allow them control of areas outside the monopoly.'"); *Video Pipeline, Inc. v. Buena Vista Home Entm't, Inc.*, 342 F.3d 191, 206 (3d Cir. 2003) ("Thus, while we extend the patent misuse doctrine to copyright, and recognize that it might operate beyond its traditional anti-competition context, we hold it inapplicable here. On this record Disney's licensing agreements do not interfere significantly with copyright policy (while holding to contrary might, in fact do so)."); *Practice Mgmt. Info. Corp. v. Am. Med. Ass'n*, 121 F.3d 516, 521 (9th Cir. 1997), *modified*, 133 F.3d 1140 (9th Cir. 1998) ("a defendant in a copyright infringement suit need not prove an antitrust violation to prevail on a copyright misuse defense").
817. 17 U.S.C. § 1502(a).

alternative forum, claimants may seek up to USD 30,000 in actual or statutory damages.[818] Participation in a proceeding before the Board is "voluntary":[819] a claimant may choose to commence a proceeding with the Board instead of filing a lawsuit in federal court,[820] and the respondent has sixty days after service of notice within which to "opt out" of the Board proceeding in writing.[821] However, if the respondent fails to timely "opt out," then the Board's determination is binding.[822]

Under the CASE Act, the Board may render final determinations with respect to the following claims, counterclaims, and defenses:[823]

- a claim for infringement of an exclusive § 106 right;
- declaration of noninfringement of an exclusive § 106 right;
- a claim under § 512(f) for misrepresentation in connection with a DMCA notification or a counter notification;
- a counterclaim arising under § 106 or § 512(f) and out of the same transaction or occurrence that is the subject of a claim; and
- a legal or equitable copyright defense (e.g., fair use or first sale) or otherwise available under law (e.g., implied license), in response to a claim or counterclaim.

The CASE Act excludes certain claims; for example, the statute specifies that claimants may not seek damages for infringement from federal or state governmental entities.[824] While not expressly excluded, libraries and archives may prospectively and preemptively opt out of all Board proceedings.[825]

In proceedings before the Board, discovery is generally limited to: (1) the production of relevant information and documents, (2) written interrogatories, and (3) written requests for admission.[826] Parties may elect to proceed pro se or may be represented by an attorney (or a qualified law student on a pro bono basis).[827] A final determination must be reached by a majority of the three-member Board, and the written determination must be published on a "publicly accessible website."[828] A request for reconsideration must be made within thirty days of the issuance of the final determination and only on the basis of "a clear error of law or fact material to the outcome, or a technical mistake."[829] If the Board denies a request for reconsideration,

818. 17 U.S.C. § 1502(c). For timely registered works, the maximum statutory damage award is USD 15,000 per work and USD 30,000 per claim. On the other hand, unregistered copyrighted works are eligible for half those amounts. 17 U.S.C. § 1504(e).
819. 17 U.S.C. § 1504(a).
820. 17 U.S.C. § 1502(a).
821. 17 U.S.C. § 1506(i).
822. A final determination precludes litigation of all claims asserted and determined by the Board. 17 U.S.C. § 1507.
823. 17 U.S.C. § 1504(c).
824. 17 U.S.C. §1504(d)(3).
825. 17 U.S.C. § 1506(aa).
826. 17 U.S.C. § 1506(n).
827. 17 U.S.C. § 1506(d).
828. 17 U.S.C. § 1506(t).
829. 17 U.S.C. § 1506(w).

that party has thirty days within which to request review by the Register of Copyrights.[830] A losing party may challenge a final determination in federal district court if: (1) the determination was issued as a result of fraud, corruption, misrepresentation, or other misconduct or (2) the Board exceeded its authority.[831]

III Substantive Issues in Infringement Actions

When it is claimed that the defendant has copied the plaintiff's work, or created a derivative work, the plaintiff must prove: "(1) ownership of a valid copyright, and (2) copying the constituent elements of the work that are original"[832] (although issues of "copying" may arise in actions involving the distribution right, the performance right, or the display right, in the usual course in such actions there is no real dispute as to whether the defendant has actually employed the plaintiff's work). Ownership issues are generally straightforward. However, frequently, there is little or no direct evidence of copying available. Rather, the copying necessary to establish infringement must be demonstrated circumstantially by presenting proof of the defendant's access to the copyrighted work and of the "substantial similarity" between that work and the defendant's allegedly infringing copy.[833] "Substantial similarity" is an "elusive concept, not subject to precise definition."[834] In a recent case claiming that the classic Led Zeppelin rock song "Stairway to Heaven" infringed a song called "Taurus," the Ninth Circuit held that a high degree of access to copyrighted work does not justify a lower standard of proof to show substantial similarity.[835] The court emphasized that copyright infringement requires copying, and if there are no similarities between the two works, there has been no copying.

A Substantial Similarity

1 Generally

Inasmuch as infringement consists of the copying of protected expression, in determining whether there is substantial similarity between two works so as to create an inference of copying, the analysis must be limited to a determination of substantial similarity of protectible expression. "When we determine that a work contains both protectible and unprotectible elements, we must take care to inquire only whether 'the

830. 17 U.S.C. § 1506(x).
831. 17 U.S.C. § 1508(c).
832. *Feist Publ'ns, Inc. v. Rural Telephone Serv. Co.*, 499 U.S. 340, 361 (1991); *Stenograph L.L.C. v. Bossard Assocs., Inc.*, 144 F.3d 96, 99 (D.C. Cir. 1998).
833. "To prove copyright infringement, the plaintiff must show (1) ownership of the copyright; (2) access to the copyrighted work; and (3) substantial similarity between the copyrighted work and the defendant's work." *Litchfield v. Spielberg*, 736 F.2d 1352, 1355 (9th Cir. 1984) (noting, as well, that "a work is not a derivative work unless it has been substantially copied from the prior work").
834. *Concrete Mach. Co. v. Classic Lawn Ornaments, Inc.*, 843 F.2d at 606 (1st Cir. 1988).
835. *Skidmore v. Led Zeppelin*, 952 F.3d 1051 (9th Cir. 2020).

protectible elements, standing alone, are substantially similar'."[836] However, as noted above,[837] protectable "expression" can embrace structural elements and other matter beyond the literal text of a work. As the Eleventh Circuit explained: "Two works need not be identical in order to be deemed 'substantially similar' for purposes of copyright infringement .... Both literal and nonliteral similarity may warrant a finding of copyright infringement."[838]

It has become necessary, therefore, for the courts to develop analytic tools to aid in the determination of whether the similarities between two works can be found at the level of "expression" rather than "idea." These tools provide only the starting point for analysis. The fundamental analytic concepts were set out by Judge Learned Hand, who nevertheless observed that "the test for infringement of a copyright is of necessity vague .... Decisions must therefore inevitably be ad hoc."[839]

2 *Modes of Analysis*

Judge Hand suggested that in attempting to determine if there is "substantial similarity" between two works, in the absence of literal copying, the allegedly taken nonliteral elements must be positioned on a spectrum ranging from "idea" to "expression," the position varying with the degree of "abstraction" or "concreteness" of the material.[840] To draw the distinction between ideas and their expressions, courts use the abstraction test first described by Judge Learned Hand with respect to a theatrical play. This test only will place a work's elements on a spectrum from more expression-like to more idea-like. It does not pick the point on the spectrum at which elements cease to be unprotected ideas and become protectible expressions. Nevertheless, it serves as a useful, if not dispositive, analytical tool in drawing these distinctions.[841]

The "abstraction analysis" has been used in a variety of circumstances, involving a wide array of copyrightable material, and, as noted above, has been the center of the dispute over the proper approach to take in dealing with issues of nonliteral copying of computer programs.[842] Although Hand's analysis "has often been referred to as Hand's

836. *Williams v. Crichton*, 84 F.3d 58, 81 (2d Cir. 1996) (quoting *Knitwaves v. Lollytogs, Ltd.*, 71 F.3d 996, 1002 (2d Cir. 1995)). *See also Jacobsen v. Deseret Book Co.*, 287 F.3d 936, 942–43 (10th Cir. 2002) ("In order to prove copying of legally protectible material, a plaintiff must typically show substantial similarity between legally protectible elements of the original work and the allegedly infringing work.").
837. *See supra* §2.III.
838. *Bateman v. Mnemonics, Inc.*, 79 F.3d 1532, 1543 n.25 (11th Cir. 1996); *see also Twin Peaks Prods., Inc. v. Publications Int'l Ltd.*, 996 F.2d 1366, 1372 (2d Cir. 1993) ("substantial similarity can take the form of 'fragmented literal similarity' or 'comprehensive nonliteral similarity'").
839. *Peter Pan Fabrics, Inc. v. Martin Weiner Corp.*, 274 F.2d 487, 489 (2d Cir. 1960).
840. *See Nichols v. Universal Pictures Corp.*, 45 F.2d 119 (2d Cir. 1930); *Sheldon v. Metro-Goldwyn Pictures Corp.*, 81 F.2d 49 (2d Cir. 1936).
841. *Murray Hill Publ'ns, Inc. v. Twentieth-Century Fox*, 361 F.3d 312, 319 (6th Cir. 2004).
842. *See supra* §2.IV.A.3. As the Ninth Circuit observed in *Apple Computer, Inc. v. Microsoft Corp.*, 35 F.3d 1435, 1445 (9th Cir. 1994), "graphical user interface audiovisual works are subject to the same process of analytical dissection as are other works."

'abstractions test,' in fact, as Judge Hand and others have noted, it is no test at all, but merely a way of perceiving the problem."[843]

Parallel with, and sometimes in opposition to the "abstraction" model, is the "total concept and feel" construct, in which the inquiry is predicated not so much on dissection of the works at issue and close comparison of their details, as it is on examining the similarities and differences in the total concept and feel of the works.[844] That "test" is not always appropriate:

> The total concept and feel test ... is simply not helpful in analyzing works that, because of their different genres and media, must necessarily have a different concept and feel. Indeed, many "derivative" works of different genres, in which copyright owners have exclusive rights, ... may have a different total concept and feel from the original work.[845]

3 *Extrinsic/Intrinsic Tests, "Probative Similarity," and the Roles of Experts, Judge, and Jury*

In its 1946 opinion in *Arnstein v. Porter*,[846] the Second Circuit adopted a two-step analytic scheme for determining substantial similarity. In the first step, the two works are analyzed and compared in detail, a process of dissection, to determine if there are similarities of expression; this stage involves objective analysis of the works, an "extrinsic" test, for which purpose expert testimony is appropriate. It has been suggested that the initial issue is the existence of "probative" similarity, the search for similarities that are probative of copying.[847] If such analysis produces a reasonable basis for finding similarity of expression, then the inquiry moves to the second step, in which the trier of fact determines the substantiality of the similarity; this is a subjective process, an "intrinsic" test, in which the use of experts gives way to the subjective judgment of the "ordinary" lay observer. Building on the Second Circuit's analysis, the First Circuit articulated the "probative similarity" model as the first step in a two-step "substantial similarity" analysis:

> Proof of wrongful copying is a two-step process. First, the plaintiff must show that copying actually occurred. This showing entails proof that, as a factual matter, the

843. *CCC Info. Servs., Inc. v. Maclean Hunter Market Reports, Inc.*, 44 F.3d 61, 69 (2d Cir. 1994). For a more modern application of this "dissection" approach, *see Blehm v. Jacobs*, 702 F.3d 1193 (10th Cir. 2012).

844. *See*, e.g., *Litchfield v. Spielberg*, 736 F.2d 1352, 1356, 1357 (9th Cir. 1984) (finding, listing, and comparing similarities and differences is "inherently subjective and unreliable," thus the court concludes that "[t]o constitute infringement of expression, the total concept and feel of the works must be substantially similar"); *Hartman v. Halmark Cards, Inc.*, 833 F.2d 117, 120–21 (8th Cir. 1987) ("Infringement of expression occurs only when the total concept and feel of the works in question are substantially similar."); *see also Williams v. Crichton*, 84 F.3d 581, 589 (2d Cir. 1996) ("consideration of the total concept and feel of a work").

845. *Castle Rock Entm't v. Carol Publ'g Grp., Inc.*, 150 F.3d 132, 140 (2d Cir. 1998).

846. *Arnstein v. Porter*, 154 F.2d 464 (2d Cir. 1946).

847. *Castle Rock Entm't v. Carol Publ'g Grp., Inc.*, 150 F.3d 132, 137 (2d Cir. 1998); *Repp v. Webber*, 132 F.3d 882, 889 (2d Cir. 1998).

> defendant copied the plaintiff's copyrighted material. [T]he plaintiff may satisfy his "first step" obligation indirectly by adducing evidence that the alleged infringer enjoyed access to the copyrighted work and that a sufficient degree of similarity exists between the copyrighted work and the allegedly infringing work to give rise to an inference of actual copying ... We have referred to that degree of similarity as "probative similarity." ... This requirement ... is somewhat akin to but different than [sic], the requirement of substantial similarity that emerges at the second stage in the progression ....
>
> The substantial similarity requirement focuses holistically on the works in question and entails proof that the copying was so extensive that it rendered the works so similar that the later work represented a wrongful appropriation of expression.[848]

The bifurcated extrinsic/intrinsic model of analysis has generally been followed, albeit with a confusing detour in the Ninth Circuit. That court, while purporting to follow Arnstein, at first described the extrinsic test as an analysis of similarity of ideas and the intrinsic test as an analysis of similarity of expression.[849] After a series of opinions in which it expanded the scope of the constituent parts of protected expression,[850] the Ninth Circuit ultimately conformed its approach more closely to that of the Second Circuit as it articulated an "extrinsic" test comprised of an objective analysis of expression and an "intrinsic" test in the form of a subjective analysis of expression.[851] The Ninth Circuit, even more strongly than the Second, makes clear that the subjective judgment of the trier of fact, without the use of expert testimony, is the ultimate determinant of infringement. Accordingly, once the objective extrinsic test is satisfied, summary judgment is precluded and the case must proceed to the subjective intrinsic stage.[852]

---

848. *Johnson v. Gordon*, 409 F.3d 12 (1st Cir. 2005).
849. *Sid & Marty Krofft Television Prods., Inc. v. McDonald's Corp.*, 562 F.2d 1157 (9th Cir. 1977).
850. *See*, e.g., *Olson v. National Broad. Co., Inc.*, 855 F.2d 1446 (9th Cir. 1988); *Narell v. Freemen*, 872 F.2d 907 (9th Cir. 1989).
851. *Shaw v. Lindheim*, 919 F.2d 1353 (9th Cir. 1990). The *Shaw* formulation was reaffirmed by the Ninth Circuit in *Brownbag Software v. Symantec Corp.*, 960 F.2d 1465 (9th Cir. 1992) and in *Smith v. Jackson*, 84 F.3d 1213 (9th Cir. 1996). *See also L.A. Printex Indus., Inc. v. Aeropostale, Inc.*, 676 F.3d 841 (9th Cir. 2012); *Benay v. Warner Bros. Entm't, Inc.*, 607 F.3d 620 (9th Cir. 2010); *Apple Computer, Inc. v. Microsoft Corp.*, 35 F.3d 1435, 1442 (9th Cir. 1994) ("the extrinsic test now objectively considers whether there are substantial similarities in both ideas and expression, whereas the intrinsic test continues to measure expression subjectively"); *Kouf v. Walt Disney Pictures & Television*, 16 F.3d 1042 (9th Cir. 1994); *Funky Films v. Time Warner Entm't Co.*, 462 F.3d 1072 (9th Cir. 2006); *Dr. Seuss Enters., L.P v. Penguin Books*, 109 F.3d 1394 (9th Cir. 1997).
852. *Shaw v. Lindheim*, 919 F.2d 1353, 1359–60 (9th Cir. 1990) ("[S]atisfaction of the extrinsic test creates a triable issue of fact .... Once a court has established that a triable question of objective similarity of expression exists, ... its inquiry should proceed no further. What remains is a subjective assessment of the 'concept and feel' of two works of literature—a task no more suitable for a judge than for a jury."); *Amini Innovation Corp. v. Anthony California, Inc.*, 439 F.3d 1365 (Fed. Cir. 2006) ("In this case, the trial court erred in expanding its application of the 'extrinsic' part of the infringement test to encompass an examination of 'the total concept and feel of the works.' Thus, the trial court mistakenly expanded the extrinsic elements of the infringement test to encompass the intrinsic elements as well. The trial court's error is significant because on summary judgment the Ninth Circuit places the extrinsic part of the infringement test within the court's purview, but disfavors application of the subjective-intrinsic part.").

Although the Ninth Circuit's reaffirmation of Arnstein should eliminate any conflict among the circuits, the Fourth and Eighth Circuits appear still to follow the now superseded older Ninth Circuit rule,[853] while another purports to "apply a more stringent standard regarding when to allow expert testimony on the first part of the test."[854]

In applying the subjective, intrinsic test, the courts reiterate the primacy of the "ordinary" observer.[855] However, it has been suggested that it is more appropriate to consider the "intended audience" rather than the "ordinary observer": "The undisputed principles of copyright law ... require orientation of the ordinary observer test to the works' intended audience, permitting an ordinary lay observer characterization of the test only where the lay public fairly represents the works' intended audience."[856] Where the intended audience is specialized, expert testimony relating to that specialization is appropriate.[857]

B Access

In the absence of direct evidence of copying, a determination of infringement requires not only that there be substantial similarity of expression between the copyrighted work and the allegedly infringing work but also evidence that the alleged infringer had access to the copyrighted work. Such access, as other elements of a claim, can be demonstrated circumstantially by a showing of a reasonable possibility of access, either because of the wide dissemination of the work or because of the availability of the work to the defendant via third parties.[858] However, clear evidence of independent creation by the alleged infringer (or by a third party from whom the alleged infringer in fact copied),[859] irrespective of circumstantial evidence of access, would defeat the infringement claim.[860]

853. *See*, e.g., *Towler v. Sayles*, 76 F.3d 579, 584 (4th Cir. 1996) ("First, a plaintiff must show—typically with the aid of expert testimony—that the works in question are extrinsically similar because they contain substantially similar ideas that are subject to copyright protection. Second, a plaintiff must satisfy the subjective, or intrinsic, portion of the test by showing substantial similarity in how those ideas are expressed."); *Schoolhouse, Inc. v. Anderson*, 275 F.3d 726, 729 (8th Cir. 2002) ("[W]e must first analyze the similarity of ideas extrinsically, focusing on any objective similarities in the details of the works. If the ideas behind the works are substantially similar, we must then evaluate similarity of expression intrinsically, according to the response of the ordinary, reasonable person.").
854. *Murray Hill Publ'ns, Inc. v. Twentieth Century Fox Film Corp.*, 361 F.3d 312, 318 (6th Cir. 2004).
855. *See*, e.g., *Baxter v. MCA, Inc*, 812 F.2d 421 (9th Cir. 1987); *Concrete Mach. Co., Inc. v. Classic Lawn Ornaments*, 843 F.2d 600 (1st Cir. 1988) ("whether there is substantial similarity between copyrightable expressions is determined by the 'ordinary observer' test").
856. *Dawson v. Hinshaw Music Inc.*, 905 F.2d 731, 733 (4th Cir. 1990).
857. *Id.*; *see also Whelan Assocs., Inc. v. Jaslow Dental Lab., Inc.*, 797 F.2d 1222 (3d Cir. 1986).
858. *Selle v. Gibb*, 741 F.2d 896, 901 (7th Cir. 1984).
859. *Mag Jewelry Co. v. Cherokee, Inc.*, 496 F.3d 108 (1st Cir. 2007).
860. *See*, e.g., *Benson v. Coca-Cola Co.*, 795 F.2d 973 (11th Cir. 1986). *See also La Resolana Architects, PA v. Reno, Inc*, 555 F.3d 1171, 1178 (10th Cir. 2009) ("[W]hile a plaintiff is not required to demonstrate the defendant's actual access to the work, 'evidence that only creates a bare possibility that the defendant had access is not sufficient'").

A reciprocal relationship, an "inverse ratio rule," appears to exist between substantial similarity and access. Thus, it has been suggested that conceded or overwhelming proof of access may reduce the requisite quantum of proof of similarity,[861] although the subjective nature of the proof of similarity inhibits quantification. The Second and Seventh Circuits have explicitly rejected such a "rule" as to reduction of quantum of proof of substantial similarity.[862] On a more practical level, convincing evidence of substantial similarity can serve to reduce the requisite quantum of proof of access. Where the similarity is "striking" access may be inferred; where the nature of the works and the similarities between them are such as reasonably to preclude coincidence or independent creation, "striking similarity" can support a determination of infringement even in the absence of any proof of access:[863]

> [A] similarity that is so close as to be highly unlikely to have been an accident of independent creation is evidence of access .... Access (and copying) may be inferred if two works are so similar to each other and not to anything in the public domain that it is likely that the creator of the second work copied the first, but the inference can be rebutted by disproving access or otherwise showing independent creation.[864]

IV "Innocent" Infringement

The Act imposes liability for infringement on "anyone who violates any of the exclusive rights of the copyright owner."[865] The Act makes no distinction, for the purposes of liability (as opposed to damages), among the willful copier who takes from another with knowledge of the infringing nature of the taking, the copier who believes either

---

861. *Sid & Marty Krofft Television Prods., Inc. v. McDonald's Corp.*, 562 F.2d 1157, 1172 (9th Cir. 1977). *See also Benay v. Warner Bros. Entm't, Inc.*, 607 F.3d 620, 625 (9th Cir. 2010) ("Under the 'inverse ratio' rule, if a defendant had access to a copyrighted work, the plaintiff may show infringement based on a lesser degree of similarity between the copyrighted work and the allegedly infringing work").

862. In *Peters v. West*, 692 F.3d 629 (7th Cir. 2012), the Seventh Circuit questioned the "rule" as such and the Ninth Circuit's purported adoption of it with respect to access lowering proof of similarity, noting that it had been explicitly rejected by the Second Circuit; the court notes that while, as in *Selle v. Gibb* and *Ty, Inc. v. GMA Accessories*, below, a high degree of similarity can reduce the required quantum of proof of access, there is no reason for a converse "rule."

863. *Ty, Inc. v. GMA Accessories, Inc.*, 132 F.3d 1167 (7th Cir. 1997); *Repp v. Webber*, 132 F.3d 882 (2d Cir. 1997); *Gaste v. Kaiserman*, 863 F.2d 1061 (2d Cir. 1988). *See also Murray Hill Publ'ns, Inc. v. Twentieth Century Fox Film Corp.*, 361 F.3d 312, 317 (6th Cir. 2004) (making clear that although "a bare possibility of access" is insufficient and "access may not be inferred through mere speculation or conjecture," striking similarity "carries the burden of proof that the infringing work is sufficient[ly] similar as to intrude into the copyrighted work's protection *and* that the defendant must have had access to the copyrighted work, even if the plaintiff can provide no extrinsic proof of that fact").

864. *Ty, Inc. v. GMA Accessories, Inc.*, 132 F.3d 1167, 1170–71 (7th Cir. 1997) (attempting to harmonize *Gaste v. Kaiserman* with its earlier opinion in *Selle v. Gibb* which had held that even striking similarity cannot dispense totally with the need for some evidence of reasonable possibility of access).

865. 17 U.S.C. § 501(a). Infringement is essentially a strict liability offense. *But see* Patrick R. Goold, *Is Copyright a Strict Liability Tort*, 30 Berkeley Tech. L.J. 305 (2015) (arguing that copyright infringement is a fault-based tort and not a strict liability tort).

that the work is not protected or that the copying is defensible, and the copier who was unaware that he or she was in fact copying the work of another. In short, intention to infringe is not a necessary predicate for liability. Rather, the "innocent" infringer, one whose copying may be the product of a subconscious retention of the copyrighted work, will nevertheless be liable for infringement: "when a defendant's work is copied from the plaintiff's, but the defendant in good faith has forgotten that the plaintiff's work was the source of his own, such 'innocent copying' can nevertheless constitute an infringement. [C]opyright infringement can be subconscious."[866]

"Innocent" infringement, arising from either subconscious copying or copying predicated on a good faith belief that the material was not protected, will not shield the infringer from liability. It may, however, serve to mitigate damages or otherwise have an impact on the remedies available to the copyright owner.[867]

V Criminal Infringement

It is a criminal offense to infringe a copyright "willfully either (1) for purposes of commercial advantage or private financial gain; or (2) by the reproduction or distribution, including by electronic means, during any 180-day period, of one or more copies or phonorecords of one or more copyrighted works, which have a total retail value of more than USD 1,000."[868] Depending upon the nature of the offense, the criminal infringer is subject to fines and/or imprisonment for terms ranging from one year to ten years.[869] Moreover, "all infringing copies or phonorecords and all implements, devices, or equipment used in the manufacture of such infringing copies of phonorecords" are subject to forfeiture and destruction.[870] As with other criminal offenses, the prosecution has the burden of proving the elements of the crime, including willfulness; for these purposes, "evidence of reproduction or distribution of a copyrighted work, by itself, shall not be sufficient to establish willful infringement."[871]

It is also a criminal offense, subject to a fine of up to USD 2,500, for one, acting with "fraudulent intent," knowingly to place a false notice of copyright on an article or knowingly to distribute publicly an article with such notice, or to remove or alter a notice of copyright, or knowingly to make a false representation of a material fact in an

866. *ABKCO Music, Inc. v. Harrisongs Music, Ltd.*, 722 F.2d 988, 998–99 (2d Cir. 1983); *see also Sheldon v. Metro-Goldwyn Pictures Corp.*, 81 F.2d 49, 54 (2d Cir. 1936) ("unconscious plagiarism is actionable quite as much as deliberate"); *Three Boys Music Corp. v. Bolton*, 212 F.3d 477, 482 (9th Cir. 2000) ("Proof of widespread dissemination is sometimes accompanied by a theory that copyright infringement of a popular song was subconscious.").

867. The court, in its discretion, may award an appropriate amount of statutory damages: ordinary damages (between USD 750 and USD 30,000), increased damages for willful infringement (up to USD 150,000), or reduced damages for innocent infringement (not more than USD 250). 17 U.S.C. § 504. For further discussion *see* Pamela Samuelson & Tara Wheatland, *Statutory Damages in Copyright Law: A Remedy in Need of Reform*, 51 WM. & MARY L. REV. 439 (2009).

868. 17 U.S.C. § 506(a).

869. 18 U.S.C. § 2319.

870. 17 U.S.C. § 506(b).

871. 17 U.S.C. § 506(a).

application for copyright registration.[872] In 2005, Congress made it acts of criminal infringement to record a motion picture in a theater and to distribute a work not then otherwise distributed but "being prepared for commercial distribution."

VI Vicarious Liability and Contributory Infringement

In a variety of circumstances, a person not directly involved in infringing activity may be held liable as an infringer for the infringing conduct of another. Such liability may arise vicariously through the relationship between the infringer and the person sought to be held liable or, in the special case of contributory infringement, it may arise through a person's activities that facilitate another's infringing conduct.[873] The issue has become particularly difficult with the development and growth of digital communication and dissemination of material through the Internet. The courts have been struggling with the application of principles of vicarious liability and contributory infringement to Internet Service Providers (ISPs) as a result of infringing activities by individuals using these facilities.

A *Vicarious Liability*

In accordance with general principles of respondeat superior, an employer will be held liable for the infringing acts of an employee acting within the scope of employment.[874] However, for copyright infringement purposes, vicarious liability has a much broader scope than the narrow tort concept of respondeat superior. Rather, liability for the infringing acts of another will be imposed upon one who has power to supervise or control the infringer and a financial interest in the fruits of the infringer's activities. Such liability will be imposed, where these conditions exist, irrespective of the knowledge, or lack of knowledge, of the infringing activity.[875]

872. 17 U.S.C. § 506(c)–(e).

873. *Compare Metro-Goldwyn-Mayer Studios Inc. v. Grokster, Ltd.*, 545 U.S. 913, 930 (2005) ("One infringes contributorily by intentionally inducing or encouraging direct infringement, and infringes vicariously by profiting from direct infringement while declining to exercise a right to stop or limit it."), *with Ellison v. Robertson*, 357 F.3d 1072, 1076 (9th Cir. 2004) ("We recognize three doctrines of copyright liability: direct copyright infringement, contributory copyright infringement, and vicarious copyright infringement.").

874. *See Shapiro, Bernstein & Co. v. H.L. Green Co.*, 316 F.2d 304, 307 (2d Cir. 1963) ("It is quite clear … that the normal agency rule of *respondeat superior* applies to copyright infringement by a servant within the scope of his employment.").

875. *See*, e.g., *Ellison v. Robertson*, 357 F.3d 1072, 1076 (9th Cir. 2004) ("A defendant is vicariously liable for copyright infringement if he enjoys a direct financial benefit from *another's* infringing activity and 'has the right and ability to supervise' the infringing activity.") (quoting *A & M Records v. Napster, Inc.*, 239 F.3d 1004, 1022 (9th Cir. 2001)); *Shapiro, Bernstein & Co. v. H. L. Green Co.*, 316 F.2d 304, 307 (2d Cir. 1963) ("When the right and ability to supervise coalesce with an obvious and direct financial interest in the exploitation of copyrighted materials—even in the absence of actual knowledge that the copyright monopoly is being impaired—the purposes of copyright law may be best effectuated by the imposition of liability upon the beneficiary of that exploitation.").

Accordingly, owners of premises rented to others for use as bars and music halls, at which infringing performances of copyrighted music can take place, will not be liable for those acts of infringement where the owners receive a fixed rental and exercise no supervision. But liability will be imposed where such performances can have an impact upon the proprietor's income. Similarly, the operators of those premises will be held liable for infringing performances "whether the bandleader is considered, as a technical matter, an employee or independent contractor, and whether or not the proprietor has knowledge of the compositions to be played or any control over their selection."[876] Applying these principles, the operators of a "swap meet" flea market were held vicariously liable for the infringement by vendors selling counterfeit sound recordings.[877] "Control" was found from the operators' active promotion of the swap meet and ability to control and patrol the premises and to terminate the occupancy of any vendors, and "financial benefit" came from admission fees, concession stand sales, and parking fees, "all of which flow directly from customers who want to buy the counterfeit recordings at bargain basement prices."[878]

B *Contributory Infringement*

Contributory infringement arises when "one who, with knowledge of the infringing activity, induces, causes, or materially contributes to the infringing conduct of another."[879] Liability under these circumstances is imposed upon one who knows and provides the wherewithal for another to infringe. However, not everyone whose conduct may facilitate another's infringing activities will incur liability. The crucial issue will be the nature of that conduct, the person's awareness of its consequences for infringement, and the extent to which that conduct is otherwise permissible. Clearly, the fact alone that copying equipment is used by some people to make infringing copies would not be sufficient to impose liability upon the manufacturer of that equipment for those acts of infringement.

The US Supreme Court attempted to provide standards and guidance in *Sony Corp. of America v. Universal City Studios, Inc.*[880] Borrowing from the "staple article of commerce" doctrine of patent law, the Court held that contributory infringement liability could not be imposed solely on the basis that the defendant sold equipment with constructive knowledge that customers may use that equipment to make unauthorized copies of copyrighted material; there must be a closer relationship between the direct infringer and the alleged "contributory" infringer, and some ability to control

876. Shapiro, Bernstein & Co., 316 F.2d 304, 307 (2d Cir. 1963) (reviewing cases).
877. *See, e.g., Fonovisa, Inc. v. Cherry Auction, Inc.*, 76 F.3d 259, 263 (9th Cir. 1996).
878. *Fonovisa, Inc. v. Cherry Auction, Inc.*, 76 F.3d 259, 263 (9th Cir. 1996). *See also RCA/Ariola v. Thomas & Grayston*, 845 F.2d 773 (8th Cir. 1988).
879. *Gershwin Publishing v. Columbia Artists Mgmt.*, 443 F.2d 1159, 1162 (2d Cir. 1971); *see also Ellison v. Robertson*, 357 F.3d 1072, 1076 (9th Cir. 2004) ("We have interpreted the knowledge requirement for contributory copyright infringement to include both those with *actual knowledge* and those who *have reason to know* of direct infringement.").
880. *Sony Corp. of Am. v. Universal City Studios, Inc.*, 464 U.S. 417 (1984).

the activity. Contributory infringement cannot be found if the article at issue is "capable of substantial noninfringing uses":

> The staple article of commerce doctrine must strike a balance between a copyright holder's legitimate demand for effective—not merely symbolic—protection of the statutory monopoly, and the rights of others freely to engage in substantially unrelated areas of commerce. Accordingly, the sale of copying equipment, like the sale of other articles of commerce, does not constitute contributory infringement if the product is widely used for legitimate, unobjectionable purposes. Indeed, it need merely be capable of substantial noninfringing uses.[881]

In contrast, providing the "site and facilities for known infringing activity" is sufficient to establish contributory liability,[882] as is the purported sale of the right to copyrighted material with knowledge by the seller of the seller's lack of rights to that material.[883] In such cases, liability arises when the defendant materially contributes to the infringing conduct of another.[884]

The growth of the internet, together with technology facilitating the digital distribution of copyrighted music, motion pictures, and other material, has put a strain on the accepted definitions of vicarious and contributory infringement. Thus, in *A & M Records v. Napster, Inc.*,[885] the Ninth Circuit held that, at least for the purposes of the pending preliminary injunction, a sufficient showing had been made to hold the operator of the Napster website that was used for the uploading and downloading by users of copyrighted music both vicariously and contributorily liable for the infringing activities of the users. The situation became more complicated with the proliferation of "peer-to-peer networking software," allowing for the distribution among users without the use of a centralized entity that actually stores the material. In actions against the providers of the software,[886] the circuits split over the issue of whether liability can be avoided by a showing of "capability" of noninfringing use alone or if the defendant

881. *Id.*, at 442.
882. *Fonovisa, Inc. v. Cherry Auction, Inc.*, 76 F.3d 259, 264 (9th Cir. 1996).
883. *Casella v. Morris*, 820 F.2d 362 (11th Cir. 1987).
884. *Matthew Bender & Co. v. West Publishing Co.*, 158 F.3d 693, 706 (2d Cir. 1998) ("Two types of activities that lead to contributory liability are: (i) personal conduct that encourages or assists the infringement; and (ii) provision of machinery or goods that facilitate the infringement.").
885. *A&M Records v. Napster, Inc.*, 239 F.3d 1004 (9th Cir. 2001).
886. *See*, e.g., *Perfect 10, Inc. v. Amazon.com, Inc.*, 508 F.3d 1146 (9th Cir. 2007) (examining the nature and scope of contributory and vicarious liability arising out of search engine links to websites containing infringing material). As to contributory liability, the court held "that a computer system operator can be held contributorily liable if it 'has actual knowledge that specific infringing material is available using its system,' and can 'take simple measures to prevent further damage' to copyrighted works, yet continues to provide access to infringing works." And concluding that because "Perfect 10 has not shown a likelihood of establishing Google's right and ability to stop or limit the directly infringing conduct of third-party websites," it has not provided the basis for the imposition of vicarious liability. *Perfect 10, Inc. v. Amazon.com, Inc.*, 508 F.3d 1146, 1175 (9th Cir. 2007). In related litigation, a majority of the panel found the relation between the Visa credit card service and the infringing websites that used the service to charge for their activities too tenuous for the imposition of either contributory or vicarious liability on Visa. *Perfect 10, Inc. v. CCBill, LLC.*, 488 F.3d 1102 (9th Cir. 2007).

must demonstrate the probability or quantitative significance of such use.[887] In its 2005 decision in *Metro-Goldwyn-Mayer Studios, Inc. v. Grokster, Ltd.*,[888] the Supreme Court declined the invitation to broadly reexamine the issue. Instead, it held that contributory liability may properly be imposed on "one who distributes a device" (e.g., peer-to-peer software) with the object of promoting its use to infringe copyright, as shown by clear expression or other affirmative steps taken to foster infringement.[889] Since Grokster, courts typically classify secondary liability into three headings: (1) contributory copyright infringement, (2) vicarious copyright infringement, and (3) inducement (liability for inducing copyright infringement). However, inducement may simply be a subset of contributory liability, rather than a distinct species of secondary liability.

C Online Infringement Liability Limitation

1 Generally

As part of the DMCA, Congress enacted the Online Copyright Infringement Liability Limitation Act, embodied in section 512 of the Copyright Act.[890] This section creates four separate safe harbors to protect eligible online service providers from copyright liability based on actions by users of their online services: (1) serving as a conduit for transmitting material; (2) system caching; (3) storing information at the direction of users; and (4) providing links to infringing locations.[891] To qualify for a safe harbor, online service providers must act expeditiously to remove infringing materials, or access thereto, upon receipt of proper notice of claimed infringement (e.g., takedown notice).[892] The statute sets out detailed takedown notice[893] and counter-notice[894] provisions.

For qualifying providers, a safe harbor shields the online service provider from all monetary liability for copyright infringement, and limits relief to only those specific remedies set out in the DMCA.[895] The safe harbor can protect an online service provider from both direct and indirect copyright infringement claims.[896] The limitations on liability apply only to a service provider who "accommodates and does not interfere

887. *Compare In re* Aimster Copyright Litig., 334 F.3d 643 (7th Cir. 2003), *with Metro-Goldwyn-Mayer Studios, Inc. v. Grokster Ltd.*, 380 F.3d 1154 (9th Cir. 2004), *rev'd*, 545 U.S. 913 (2005).
888. *MGM Studios, Inc. v. Grokster, Ltd.*, 545 U.S. 913 (2005).
889. *Id.*, at 936–37.
890. 17 U.S.C. § 512. For a recent assessment of the law *see* s. 512 of Title 17: A Report of The Register of Copyrights, U.S. Copyright Office (May 2020) https://www.copyright.gov/policy/section512/section-512-full-report.pdf.
891. 17 U.S.C. § 512(a)–(d).
892. The nature and elements of effective "notification" are set out in detail in 17 U.S.C. § 512(c)(3).
893. 17 U.S.C. § 512(c)(3) (process for a copyright owner to provide notice of alleged infringement).
894. 17 U.S.C. § 512(g)(3) (process for an alleged infringer to provide notice objecting to its material being taken down).
895. 17 U.S.C. § 512(a)–(d), (j), and (k)(2).
896. *See Viacom Int'l, Inc. v. YouTube, Inc.*, 676 F.3d 19 (2d Cir. 2012); *Perfect 10, Inc. v. Amazon.com, Inc.*, 508 F.3d 1146, 1175 (9th Cir. 2007).

with standard technical measures," and who has adopted and reasonably implemented, and informs subscribers and account holders of, "a policy that provides for the termination in appropriate circumstances of subscribers and account holders of the service provider's system or network who are repeat infringers."[897] To be eligible for a safe harbor, a service provider must have a policy for terminating repeat infringers' use of its service.[898] It must reasonably implement such policy, and inform its users of the policy.[899] If a service provider does not qualify for safe harbor protection, traditional copyright laws apply.[900]

In a notable instance, a service provider failed to qualify for safe harbor protection because it failed to reasonably implement a policy of terminating service to repeat infringers.[901] The service provider's implementation failed "as a deterrent to copyright infringement" in a number of ways:[902] (1) subscribers who were terminated under a 13-strike process were allowed, shortly thereafter, to reactivate their Internet service accounts; (2) shortly after the service provider "abandoned its practice of routine reactivation," it adopted a practice of nontermination, on average terminating fewer than one subscriber per month; (3) the service provider automatically reset the 13-strike counter every six months; and (4) the service provider categorically deleted and disregarded DMCA notices that contained a settlement offer. The Fourth Circuit rejected the service provider's argument that a repeat infringer policy applied only to adjudicated infringers: "[T]he risk of losing one's Internet access would hardly constitute a 'realistic threat' capable of deterring infringement if that punishment applied only to those already subject to civil penalties and legal fees as adjudicated infringers."[903] After being denied DMCA safe harbor protection, a jury awarded a USD 1 billion verdict against the service provider for contributory and vicarious liability arising from ISP subscribers' unauthorized download and distribution of rightsholders' works.[904]

The DMCA sets out complex and highly technical provisions. To effectuate the purposes of these provisions,[905] copyright owners must provide an appropriate notice

897. 17 U.S.C. § 512(c); *see Perfect 10, Inc. v. CCBill, LLC.*, 488 F.3d 1102 (9th Cir. 2007).
898. 17 U.S.C. § 512(i)(1)(A). *See also Ventura Content, Ltd. v. Motherless, Inc.*, 885 F.3d 597, 614 (9th Cir. 2018) ("Even if a website deletes infringing material as soon as it learns about it, the safe harbor is unavailable unless the site has a policy of excluding repeat infringers").
899. *See Perfect 10, Inc. v. CCBill LLC*, 488 F.3d 1102, 1109–10 (9th Cir. 2007) ("We hold that a service provider 'implements' a policy if it has a working notification system, a procedure for dealing with DMCA-compliant notifications, and if it does not actively prevent copyright owners from collecting information needed to issue such notifications").
900. But failing to qualify for a safe harbor does not limit any traditional defenses a service provider may have. *See* 17 U.S.C. § 512(l).
901. *BMG Rights Mgmt. LLC v. Cox Commc'ns, Inc.*, 881 F.3d 293 (4th Cir. 2018).
902. *BMG Rights Mgmt.*, 881 F.3d at 299.
903. *Id.*, at 302.
904. *Sony Music Ent. v. Cox Commc'ns, Inc.*, 464 F. Supp. 3d 795 (E.D. Va. 2020).
905. *Capitol Records, LLC v. Vimeo, LLC*, 826 F.3d 78, 82 (2d Cir. 2016) (The DMCA's safe harbor system "undertake[s], through complex provisions, to establish a compromise, which, on the one hand, augments the protections available to copyright owners, and, on the other, insulates service providers from liability for infringements of which they are unaware, contained in material posted to their sites by users, so as to make it commercially feasible for them to provide valuable Internet services to the public.").

of infringing activity.[906] And service providers must designate an agent to receive such notices of alleged infringement to be eligible for the safe harbors.[907] A takedown notice must be in writing, be sent to the service provider's designated agent, identify the infringed work, include complaining party's contact information, signature, a statement of good faith belief that the material is not authorized by law, and statement that the information in the notice is accurate.[908] A copyright owner is then empowered to request the issue of a subpoena to the service provider to disclose the identity of the alleged infringer.[909]

To maintain the safe harbor protection, upon receipt of a substantially compliant takedown notice, a service provider generally must expeditiously take down the infringing material. To protect against potential abuse of this extrajudicial system, the DMCA authorizes a counter-notice whereby a subscriber may object to the removal of the allegedly infringing content.[910] Like the takedown notice, the counter-notice must substantially comply with similar statutory requirements: in writing, send to the service provider's designated agent, identify the removed work, include subscriber's contact information, signature, a statement of good faith belief that the material was removed as a result of mistake or misidentification of the material, and consent to jurisdiction of the appropriate federal district court.[911]

Upon receipt of a substantially compliant counter-notice, a service provider must promptly provide the complaining party with a copy of the counter-notice, and inform the complaining party that the removed material will be restored within ten business days.[912] Unless the service provider receives notice that the complaining party has filed suit seeking to restrain the infringing behavior, the service provider must restore the material between ten and fourteen days after receipt of the counter-notice.[913]

To guard against fraudulent notices and counter-notices, the DMCA imposes liability upon one who knowingly materially misrepresents that online material or activity is infringing or was mistakenly removed or disabled.[914] An alleged infringer,

906. Defects in the notice may not be fatal if the copyright owner has "substantially complied" with the notice provisions. *Compare ALS Scan, Inc. v. Remarq Communities, Inc.*, 239 F.3d 619, 620 (4th Cir. 2001) ("Because we conclude that the service provider was provided with a notice of infringing activity that *substantially* complied with the Act, it may not rely on a claim of defective notice to maintain the immunity defense provided by the safe harbor."), *with Perfect 10, Inc. v. CCBill LLC*, 488 F.3d 1102, 1111–13 (9th Cir. 2007) (substantial compliance with the notice of infringement "means substantial compliance with all of § 512(c)(3)'s clauses, not just some of them").

907. 17 U.S.C. § 512(c)(2); *see also* 37 C.F.R. § 201.38 (designation of agent to receive notification of claimed infringement).

908. 17 U.S.C. § 512(c)(3)(A).

909. 17 U.S.C. § 512(h). Cf. *Recording Indus. Ass'n of Am., Inc. v. Verizon Internet Servs., Inc.*, 351 F.3d 1229, 1236–37 (D.C. Cir. 2003) (concluding "the subpoena power of § 512(h) applies only to ISPs engaged in storing copyrighted material and not to those engaged solely in transmitting it on behalf of others").

910. 17 U.S.C. § 512(g)(3).

911. *Id.*

912. 17 U.S.C. § 512(g)(2)(B).

913. 17 U.S.C. § 512(g)(2)(C).

914. 17 U.S.C. § 512(f).

copyright owner, or service provider may recover damages, costs, and attorneys' fees incurred as a result of such misrepresentation.[915]

The Ninth Circuit has held that section 512(f) requires the complaining party to consider fair use before sending a takedown notice in order to support a subjective good faith belief that the use was not authorized by law.[916] The court concluded that the "statute unambiguously contemplates fair use as a use authorized by the law."[917] And, as such, "if a copyright holder ignores or neglects our unequivocal holding that it must consider fair use before sending a takedown notification, it is liable for damages, under § 512(f)."[918]

2 *Transmission*

Section 512(a) provides a safe harbor for service providers who serve as a conduit for transmitting material through their system. Specifically, a service provider[919] will not be liable for monetary relief for infringement of copyright resulting from that provider's "transmitting, routing, or providing connections for material" through a system if the service provider was involved neither in the initiation of the transmission nor in the selection of the material or of the recipients of the material, and if no intermediate or transient storage copy is maintained on the system longer than is necessary or is ordinarily accessible to anyone other than anticipated recipients, and if the material is transmitted without modification.[920] This safe harbor for transitory communications is intended to protect service providers acting as a mere conduit, like broadband networks and ISPs. Unlike the other safe harbors, the notice, takedown, and counter-notice provisions do not apply here because there is no material within the conduit's control to either take down or put back. But a qualifying service provider must have a repeat infringer policy that it reasonably implements.

915. *Id.*
916. *Lenz v. Universal Music Corp.*, 815 F.3d 1145, 1148–49 (9th Cir. 2015) ("We hold that the statute requires copyright holders to consider fair use before sending a takedown notification, and that in this case, there is a triable issue as to whether the copyright holder formed a subjective good faith belief that the use was not authorized by law").
917. *Id.*, at 1151.
918. *Id.*, at 1154. Such recovery includes actual monetary damages and nominal damages. *Id.*, at 1156 ("We hold a plaintiff may seek recovery of nominal damages for an injury incurred as a result of a § 512(f) misrepresentation.").
919. Defined, for this purpose, as "an entity offering the transmission, routing, or providing of connections for digital online communications, between or among points specified by a user, of material of the user's choosing, without modification to the content of the material as sent or received." 17 U.S.C. § 512(k)(1)(A). For other purposes, it is defined more broadly as "a provider of online services or network access, or the operator of facilities therefor ...." 17 U.S.C. § 512(k)(1)(B). These are indeed capacious definitions. *See In re* Aimster Copyright Litig., 252 F. Supp. 2d 634, 658 (N.D. Ill. 2002) ("A plain reading of both definitions reveals that 'service provider' is defined so broadly that we have trouble imagining the existence of an online service that *would not* fall under the definitions, particularly the second.").
920. 17 U.S.C. § 512(a).

Injunctive relief with respect to a qualifying service provider is limited to an order preventing access by terminating the accounts of the subscriber or account holder engaged in infringing activity.[921]

3 *System Caching*

Section 512(b) provides a safe harbor for service providers who cache material; caching is the intermediate and temporary storage of material on a system. A service provider will not be liable for monetary relief for infringement of copyright resulting from system caching if: (1) the material is made available online by a person other than the service provider; (2) it is transmitted from such person to another at the direction of that other person; and (3) the storage is done through an automatic process that makes the material available to users of the system who request access to it from the person providing the material.[922] The safe harbor is further conditioned by requirements that the material be transmitted without modification, and that the service provider acts expeditiously to remove material upon notification of claimed infringement if it was made available online without authorization of the copyright owner.[923]

Injunctive relief with respect to a qualifying service provider under these, and the limitation on liability provisions discussed below, is limited to an order restraining the service provider from providing access to infringing material or activity, or providing access to a subscriber or account holder by terminating such person's accounts, or such other relief as is least burdensome to the service provider and necessary to prevent or restrain infringement of copyright.[924]

4 *Storage*

Section 512(c) provides a safe harbor for service providers storing material on their systems at the direction of a user, like social media sites. A service provider will not be liable for monetary relief for infringement resulting from the storage of material on the system or network if: (1) the storage was done at the direction of a user of the system; (2) the operator has, in accordance with the statutory provisions, designated an agent to receive notification of claimed infringement, and neither has knowledge of infringement nor awareness of facts or circumstances from which infringing activity is apparent, or acts expeditiously to remove or disable access to the material upon obtaining such knowledge or awareness or notice of claimed infringement; and (3) the operator, with the right and ability to control the infringing activity, does not receive a financial benefit directly attributable thereto.[925] To disqualify from the safe harbor, courts have required a service provider to have actual knowledge of infringement,

921. 17 U.S.C. § 512(j)(1)(B).
922. 17 U.S.C. § 512(b)(1).
923. 17 U.S.C. § 512(b)(2). The service provider must also comply with additional statutory conditions on how it caches the material and makes it available to subsequent requesters. *Id.*
924. 17 U.S.C. § 512(j)(1)(A).
925. 17 U.S.C. § 512(c).

rather than "general knowledge that one's services could be used to share infringing material."[926] To have disqualifying "red flag" knowledge of infringement, the service provider must have actually known facts that would make the specific infringement claimed objectively obvious to a reasonable person.[927] And while a provider cannot be willfully blind to "red flag" knowledge of infringement,[928] service providers are not required to affirmatively monitor or investigate for infringement.[929]

5 *Links*

Section 512(d) provides a safe harbor for service providers linking users to another location that contains infringing material, like search engines and directories. A service provider will not be liable for monetary relief for infringement resulting from the linking of users to another online location containing infringing material or infringing activity: (1) if the service provider neither has knowledge of infringement nor awareness of facts or circumstances from which infringing activity is apparent; (2) acts expeditiously to remove or disable access to the material upon obtaining such knowledge or awareness or notice of claimed infringement; and (3) if the operator, with the right and ability to control the infringing activity, does not receive a financial benefit directly attributable thereto.[930]

6 *Further Limitations on Liability of Nonprofit Educational Institutions*

If the service provider is a nonprofit educational institution, faculty members and graduate students who are employees of the institution and who perform teaching or research functions will be considered persons "other than the institution."[931] The knowledge or awareness by faculty members and graduate students of infringing

926. *UMG Recordings, Inc. v. Shelter Capital Partners LLC*, 718 F.3d 1006, 1022 (9th Cir. 2013). *See id.*, at 1023 ("[W]e hold that Veoh's general knowledge that it hosted copyrightable material and that its services could be used for infringement is insufficient to constitute a red flag."). *Accord Capitol Records, Inc. v. MP3tunes, LLC* 821 F. Supp. 2d 627, 644 (S.D.N.Y 2011) ("General awareness of rampant infringement is not enough to disqualify a service provider of protection.").
927. *Capitol Records, LLC v. Vimeo, LLC*, 826 F.3d 78, 93 (2d Cir. 2016). *Accord EMI Christian Music Grp., Inc. v. MP3tunes, LLC*, 844 F.3d 79 (2d Cir. 2016).
928. *Viacom Int'l v. YouTube, Inc.*, 676 F.3d 19, 35 (2d Cir. 2013) ("[W]e hold that the willful blindness doctrine may be applied, in appropriate circumstances, to demonstrate knowledge or awareness of specific instances of infringement under the DMCA.").
929. 17 U.S.C. § 512(m)(1) ("Nothing in this section shall be construed to condition the applicability of [the DMCA safe harbors] on a service provider monitoring its service or affirmatively seeking facts indicating infringing activity."); *see also Ventura Content, Ltd. v. Motherless, Inc.*, 885 F.3d 597, 604 (9th Cir. 2018) ("The copyright owner, not the service provider, has the burden of policing infringement."); *Capitol Records, LLC v. Vimeo, LLC*, 826 F.3d. 78, 94 (2d Cir. 2016) ("service provider's personnel are under no duty to 'affirmatively seek[]' indications of infringement"); *Perfect 10, Inc. v. CCBill LLC*, 488 F.3d 1102, 1114 (9th Cir. 2007) ("We do not place the burden of determining whether photographs are actually illegal on a service provider.").
930. 17 U.S.C. § 512(d).
931. 17 U.S.C. § 512(e).

activity will not be attributed to the institution if: (1) such persons' infringing activities do not relate to instructional materials required or recommended within the preceding three-year period for courses taught by such persons, (2) the institution has not received more than two valid notifications of claimed infringement by such persons within that three-year period, and (3) the institution provides to all users "materials that accurately describe, and promote compliance with, the laws of the United States relating to copyright."[932]

7 *Limitation on Liability for Removal of Material*

In general, a service provider will not incur liability for any claim based upon the good faith disabling of access to, or removal of, material or activity claimed to be infringing or based on facts or circumstances from which infringing activity is apparent.[933] There are detailed statutory provisions with respect notifying one who posted material that was removed, and to a duty to replace removed material upon proper "counter notification."[934]

§10 REMEDIES

I Injunctive Relief

The Copyright Act expressly empowers the district court to "grant temporary and final injunctions on such terms as it may deem reasonable to prevent or restrain infringement of a copyright."[935] As an equitable remedy, injunctive relief is subject to the discretion of the court and the general principles governing such relief: the need for a showing of irreparable harm, the comparative threatened injury to the plaintiff, and of the harm an injunction might inflict on the defendant, and (in the case of preliminary relief) the reasonable likelihood of plaintiff's success.[936] So too, the equitable defense of laches (unreasonable, prejudicial delay in commencing suit) may bar injunctive relief.[937]

However, while injunctive relief is not automatic, it is quite common and follows from a generally accepted presumption that copyright infringement produces irreparable harm.[938] While it had been held that, once infringement has been found, the district court does not retain broad discretion to deny injunctive relief on general public

932. *Id.*
933. 17 U.S.C. § 512(g)(1).
934. 17 U.S.C. § 512(g)(2), (3).
935. 17 U.S.C. § 502(a).
936. *See*, e.g., *Atari, Inc. v. North Am. Philips Consumer Elecs. Corp.*, 672 F.2d 607 (7th Cir. 1982).
937. *Petrella v. Metro-Goldwyn-Mayer*, 572 U.S. 663, 667–68 (2014) ("As to equitable relief, in extraordinary circumstances, laches may bar at the very threshold the particular relief requested by the plaintiff. And a plaintiff's delay can always be brought to bear at the remedial stage, in determining appropriate injunctive relief, and in assessing the 'profits of the infringer ... attributable to the infringement.'") (quoting 17 U.S.C. § 504(b)).
938. *Apple Computer, Inc. v. Franklin Computer Corp.*, 714 F.2d 1240 (3d Cir. 1983).

interest grounds,[939] the court does retain discretion to balance harm.[940] The Supreme Court has since noted the propriety of public interest considerations to temper the grant of injunctive relief, at least in close cases or where serious questions of fair use are involved:

> [W]hile in the "vast majority of cases, [an injunctive] remedy is justified because most infringements are simple piracy," such cases are "worlds apart from many of those raising reasonable contentions of fair use" where "there may be a strong public interest in the publication of the secondary work [and] the copyright owner's interest may be adequately protected by an award of damages for whatever infringement is found."[941]

In *eBay, Inc. v. MercExchange*,[942] the Supreme Court clearly rejected a categorical rule favoring injunctive relief in patent infringement cases. In 2010, the Second Circuit held that the eBay reasoning applied equally to the copyright context and to both preliminary and final injunctions.[943] The Ninth Circuit expressly followed the Second Circuit in holding that the Supreme Court's eBay opinion is applicable to copyright infringement cases. Injunctions are to be based upon the totality of equitable considerations rather than on any presumption of irreparable harm.[944]

II Damages

Section 504 of the Act sets out alternative bases for the award of monetary damages. An infringer of copyright is liable for either: (1) the copyright owner's actual damages and any additional profits of the infringer or (2) statutory damages.[945] A plaintiff may choose between actual damages or statutory damages at any time before the court renders a final judgment.[946] But if a plaintiff elects statutory damages, the plaintiff may no longer seek actual damages.[947]

A *Actual Damages and Profits*

"The copyright owner is entitled to recover the actual damages suffered by him or her as a result of the infringement, and any profits of the infringer that are attributable to the infringement and are not taken into account in computing the actual damages."[948]

939. *New Era Publ'ns Int'l, ApS v. Henry Holt & Co.*, 873 F.2d 576 (2d Cir. 1989).
940. *Abend v. MCA, Inc.*, 863 F.2d 1465, 1479 (9th Cir. 1988) (finding "special circumstances" that would cause "great injustice" to defendants and "public injury" were injunction to issue), *aff'd sub nom. Stewart v. Abend*, 495 U.S. 207 (1990) (the Supreme Court did not reach this issue).
941. *Campbell v. Acuff-Rose Music, Inc.*, 510 U.S. 569, 578 n.10 (1994).
942. *eBay, Inc. v. MercExchange, L.L.C.*, 547 U.S. 388 (2006).
943. *Salinger v. Colting*, 607 F.3d 68 (2d Cir. 2010).
944. *Perfect 10, Inc. v. Google, Inc.*, 653 F.3d 976 (9th Cir. 2011).
945. 17 U.S.C. § 504(a).
946. 17 U.S.C. § 504(c)(1).
947. *See, e.g.*, *Twin Peaks Prods., Inc. v. Publications Int'l, Ltd.*, 996 F.2d 1366, 1380 (2d Cir. 1993); *EarthCam, Inc. v. OxBlue Corp.* 49 F. Supp. 3d 1210, 1240 (N.D. Ga. 2014).
948. 17 U.S.C. § 504(b).

That is, the successful plaintiff in an infringement action may recover proven actual damages attributable to the infringement, which may also include profits lost by the plaintiff as a result thereof, and any nonduplicative profits of the infringer. As the House Report notes, this provision "recognizes the different purposes served by awards of damages and profits."[949]

1 *Provable Damages*

The plaintiff must prove damage attributable to the act of infringement, the injury caused by the infringer to the value of the copyrighted work.[950] While the fact of harm and the amount of damages may not be purely speculative, once the plaintiff does in fact demonstrate harm, the precise amount of damages need not be established with certainty and the burden will shift to the infringer to demonstrate the extent to which the harm was the result of circumstances other than the acts of infringement. To the extent provable, potential profits on demonstrated lost sales are recoverable as part of the plaintiff's damages, as is proven loss of licensing royalties. In short, if loss and causation—injury to the copyrighted work attributable to the acts of infringement—are established, the loss is compensable.

In the case of a proprietor of an establishment[951] who asserts, as a defense to a claim of violation of the performance right, the exemptions provided by section 110(5),[952] without reasonable grounds to believe it was applicable, will be liable, in addition to any other damages, for twice the license fee that should have been paid, for up to the preceding three years.[953]

2 *Infringer's Profits*

As noted above, to the extent that they are not duplicated in the plaintiff's lost profits,[954] the plaintiff may, in addition to provable damages, recover the defendant's profits arising out of the acts of infringement.

Damages are awarded to compensate the copyright owner for losses from the infringement, and profits are awarded to prevent the infringer from unfairly benefiting from a wrongful act. Where the defendant's profits are nothing more than a measure of the damages suffered by the copyright owner, it would be inappropriate to award damages and profits cumulatively, since in effect they amount to the same thing. However, section 504(b) authorizes the award of both actual damages and profits in cases where the copyright owner has suffered damages not reflected in the infringer's

949. H.R. REP. NO. 94-1476, at 161 (1976), *as reprinted in* 1976 U.S.C.C.A.N. 5659, 5777.
950. *Frank Music Corp. v. Metro-Goldwyn-Mayer, Inc.*, 772 F.2d 505 (9th Cir. 1985); *see also Mary Ellen Enters. v. Camex, Inc.*, 68 F.3d 1065 (8th Cir. 1995).
951. As these terms are defined in 17 U.S.C. § 101.
952. *See supra* §6.IV.E.4.
953. 17 U.S.C. § 504(d).
954. *See, e.g., Taylor v. Meirick*, 712 F.2d 1112 (7th Cir. 1983).

profits, or where there have been profits attributable to the copyrighted work but not used as a measure of damage.[955]

Consistent with the purpose of the Act, a plaintiff might recover the infringer's profits significantly in excess of the plaintiff's actual losses; the deterrent effect of such a result is of greater significance than the unearned benefit derived by the plaintiff.[956] The more serious problem in dealing with the infringer's profits is the difficulty of determining with exactitude both the amount of "profits" realized by the infringer from a given act and how much of those profits are specifically allocable to the act of infringement. Difficult and complex questions are frequently presented with respect to the nature and the amount of appropriate deductions and the allocation of profits to infringing and noninfringing activity.[957] The Act is clear in placing the burden with respect to both of these issues on the alleged infringer:

> In establishing the infringer's profits, the copyright owner is required to present proof only of the infringer's gross revenue, and the infringer is required to prove his or her deductible expenses and the elements of profits attributable to factors other than the copyrighted work.[958]

Although the burden is placed on the infringer to present proof of appropriate deductions from gross revenues in arriving at net profits and of "the elements of profit attributable to factors other than the copyrighted work," meeting that burden does not necessarily require exact proof: "where it is clear ... that not all the profits are attributable to the infringing material, the copyright owner is not entitled to recover all of those profits merely because the infringer fails to establish with certainty the portion attributable to the non-infringing elements."[959] The court will make such apportionment as it deems proper.

B *Statutory Damages*

It is frequently quite difficult to prove actual damages, even when infringement is clearly established. The Copyright Act provides for alternative monetary relief, statutory damages in lieu of proven actual damages. "[T]he copyright owner may elect, at any time before final judgment is rendered, to recover, instead of actual damages and profits, an award of statutory damages ...."[960]

---

955. H.R. Rep. No. 94-1476, at 161 (1976), *as reprinted in* 1976 U.S.C.C.A.N. 5659, 5777 ("allowing the plaintiff to recover 'the actual damages suffered by him or her as a result of the infringement,' plus any of the infringer's profits 'that are attributable to the infringement and are not taken into account in computing the actual damages'").
956. *See, e.g.*, *Taylor v. Meirick*, 712 F.2d 1112 (7th Cir. 1983).
957. *Id.*; *see also Frank Music Corp. v. Metro-Goldwyn-Mayer, Inc.*, 772 F.2d 505 (9th Cir. 1985).
958. 17 U.S.C. § 504(b).
959. *Cream Records, Inc. v. Joseph Schlitz Brewing Co.*, 754 F.2d 826, 828 (9th Cir. 1985); *Frank Music Corp. v. Metro-Goldwyn-Mayer, Inc.*, 772 F.2d 505 (9th Cir. 1985); *see Sheldon v. Metro-Goldwyn Pictures Corp.*, 106 F.2d 45, 51 (2d Cir. 1939), *aff'd*, 309 U.S. 390 (1940) ("we are resolved to avoid the one certainly unjust course of giving the plaintiffs everything, because the defendants cannot with certainty compute their own share").
960. 17 U.S.C. § 504(c)(1).

1 *Registration as a Condition*

The alternative of electing to recover statutory damages is not available as a remedy for infringement of copyright which commenced after the first publication of a work and prior to the effective date of its registration, "unless such registration is made within three months after the first publication of the work";[961] nor are statutory damages available for infringement of copyright in an unpublished work commenced before the effective date of its registration.[962] The requirement of timely registration for recovery of statutory damages is equally applicable to actions for infringement of works originating from the Berne Convention countries (notwithstanding the fact that registration is not a condition to the institution of infringement actions for such works).

2 *Amount of Damages: Range of Discretion*

Generally, statutory damages with respect to infringement for any one work (for which purposes, all the parts of a compilation or derivative work constitute one work) are recoverable in a range from USD 750 to USD 30,000, "as the court considers just."[963] Where multiple acts of infringement are involved, the award can be quite substantial. Thus, infringement of a television series, with each episode being considered a separate work, resulted in an award of USD 9 million in statutory damages.[964] More recently, a jury verdict awarding USD 1 billion in statutory damages was upheld by a district court against an ISP for contributory infringement and vicarious liability infringement arising from ISP subscribers' unauthorized download and distribution of rightsholders' songs.[965]

Since statutory damages are awarded "for all infringements involved in the action, with respect to any one work," there has been confusion as to the application of the language in cases of multiple acts of infringement, the issue being whether statutory damages are to be applied to each infringed work or to each infringement of a given work. The First Circuit has held that, in accord with its view of the prevailing reading in the circuits, "under § 504(c) the total number of 'awards' of statutory damages that a plaintiff may recover in any given action against a single defendant depends on the number of works that are infringed and the number of individually liable infringers and is unaffected by the number of infringements of those works."[966]

961. 17 U.S.C. § 412(2).
962. 17 U.S.C. § 412(1). *See Bouchat v. Bon-Ton Dep't Stores, Inc.*, 506 F.3d 315, 329 (4th Cir. 2007) ("Not every copyright owner is eligible to seek statutory damages. The Act provides that 'no award of statutory damages ... shall be made for (1) any infringement of copyright in an unpublished work commenced before the effective date of its registration.'") (quoting 17 U.S.C. § 412).
963. 17 U.S.C. § 504(c)(1).
964. *MCA Television Ltd. v. Feltner*, 89 F.3d 766 (11th Cir. 1996); *Feltner v. Columbia Pictures Television*, 523 U.S. 340 (1998).
965. *Sony Music Ent. v. Cox Commc'ns, Inc.*, 464 F. Supp. 3d 795 (E.D. Va. 2020).
966. *Venegas-Hernandez v. Sonolux Records*, 370 F.3d 183 (1st Cir. 2004).

So too, the concluding language of section 504(c) that "all parts of a compilation or derivative work constitute one work" does not limit statutory damages when the infringer copies several different musical works and bundles them together in a single CD; rather, each of the separately copied works included on the infringing CD gives rise to statutory damages.[967] The "unauthorized compilation of multiple separate copyrights did not trigger the last sentence of § 504(c)."[968]

Moreover, if the plaintiff proves that the defendant committed the acts of infringement "willfully," the court in its discretion may award statutory damages up to "USD 150,000."[969] However, a finding that an infringer acted "willfully" requires more than a showing of conscious copying. It requires knowledge that the act constitutes an infringement or action in reckless disregard of the copyright owner's rights:

> Willfulness, under [the] statutory scheme, has a rather specialized meaning .... "In other contexts [willfulness] might simply mean an intent to copy, without necessarily an intent to infringe. It seems clear that as here used, 'willfully' means with knowledge that the defendant's conduct constitutes copyright infringement. Otherwise, there would be no point in providing specially for the reduction of minimum awards in the case of innocent infringement, because any infringement that was nonwillful would necessarily be innocent. This seems to mean, then, that one who has been notified that his conduct constitutes copyright infringement, but who reasonably and in good faith believes the contrary, is not 'willful' for these purposes." ...
>
> [T]he issue is whether the copyright law supported the plaintiffs' position so clearly that the defendants must be deemed as a matter of law to have exhibited a reckless disregard of the plaintiffs' property rights.[970]

The willful infringement provisions of section 504(c) were strengthened in connection with infringing activities conducted via the internet, as a new subsection 504(c)(3) was added at the end of 2004, providing in part:

> In a case of infringement, it shall be a rebuttable presumption that the infringement was committed willfully for purposes of determining relief if the violator, or a person acting in concert with the violator, knowingly provided or knowingly caused to be provided materially false contact information to a domain name registrar, domain name registry, or other domain name registration authority in registering, maintaining, or renewing a domain name used in connection with the infringement.[971]

Whereas, if the infringer proves "that such infringer was not aware and had reason to believe that his or her acts constituted an infringement of copyright, the court in its discretion may reduce the award of statutory damages to a sum of not less than

---

967. Each downloaded song file can support its own statutory damage, but "compilations" only get one statutory damages award. *Sony Music Ent. v. Cox Commc'ns, Inc.*, 464 F. Supp. 3d 795 (E.D. Va. 2020).
968. *WB Music Corp. v. RTV Commc'ns Grp.*, 445 F.3d 538 (2d Cir. 2006).
969. 17 U.S.C. § 504(c)(2).
970. *Princeton Univ. Press v. Michigan Document Servs.*, 99 F.3d 1381, 1392 (6th Cir. 1996); *see also Peer Int'l Corp. v. Pausa Records, Inc.*, 909 F.2d 1332, 1335 (9th Cir. 1990) ("'willful' [means] with knowledge that the defendant's conduct constitutes copyright infringement").
971. 17 U.S.C. § 504(c)(3).

$200."[972] In certain limited circumstances, involving a reasonable belief that the act of infringement was a fair use in the case of infringing copying by employees or agents of nonprofit educational institutions, libraries, or archives, or infringing performance, or transmission by a public broadcasting entity, statutory damages are to be totally remitted.

3 *Right to Jury Determination*

Statutory damages are to be determined within a range "as the court considers just"; thus, the court retains a great deal of discretion in fixing the amount. Statutory damages serve as an alternative form of compensation; while the statute refers to the court's discretion, a conflict developed among the Courts of Appeal as to the right of either party in an infringement action to a jury trial with respect to the amount of statutory damages. This conflict was resolved in 1998 when the US Supreme Court in 1998 ruled that although the Copyright Act itself creates no right to a jury trial with respect to statutory damages, "the Seventh Amendment provides a right to a jury trial on all issues pertinent to an award of statutory damages under section 504(c) of the Copyright Act, including the amount itself."[973] However, it has been held that if the plaintiff seeks only the minimum statutory damages, then there is no Seventh Amendment right to a jury trial.[974]

III Costs and Counsel Fees

The court, in its discretion, may allow the recovery of full costs by or against any party (other than the US or an officer thereof).[975] The Supreme Court has clarified that "full costs" do not include expenses like expert witness fees, e-discovery expenses, and jury consultant fees.[976] In awarding full costs, a court is not authorized to award litigation expenses beyond the six categories of "costs" specified by Congress in the general costs statute.[977] In addition to full costs, a district court may also award a reasonable attorney's fee to the prevailing party.[978] However, as with statutory damages, attorney's fees are not available to a prevailing plaintiff who has failed to make timely registration of the copyrighted work at issue (i.e., where infringement occurs prior to

972. 17 U.S.C. § 504(c)(2).
973. *Feltner v. Columbia Pictures Television, Inc.*, 523 U.S. 340, 355 (1998).
974. *BMG Music v. Gonzalez*, 430 F.3d 888 (7th Cir. 2005).
975. 17 U.S.C. § 505.
976. *Rimini Street, Inc. v. Oracle USA, Inc.*, 139 S. Ct. 873 (2019).
977. 28 U.S.C. §§ 1821, 1920. The six categories that a federal court may award as costs are: (1) fees of the clerk and marshal; (2) fees for printed or electronically recorded transcripts necessarily obtained for use in the case; (3) fees and disbursements for printing and witnesses; (4) fees for exemplification and the costs of making copies of any materials where the copies are necessarily obtained for use in the case; (5) docket fees under s. 1923 of this title; and (6) compensation of court-appointed experts, compensation of interpreters, and salaries, fees, expenses, and costs of special interpretation services. 28 U.S.C. § 1920. In addition, § 1821 provides particular reimbursement rates for witnesses' "[p]er diem and mileage" expenses.
978. 17 U.S.C. § 505.

registration, unless infringement occurs after first publication and registration is made within three months after first publication).[979]

While the Act authorizes discretionary award of attorney's fees to the prevailing party, there was disagreement among the Courts of Appeal as to whether prevailing plaintiffs and prevailing defendants were to be subject to the same standards.[980] In 1994, the US Supreme Court resolved the matter by adopting an "even-handed" model in which prevailing plaintiffs and prevailing defendants are to be treated alike:[981]

> Because copyright law ultimately serves the purpose of enriching the general public through access to creative works, it is peculiarly important that the boundaries of copyright law be demarcated as clearly as possible. To that end, defendants who seek to advance a variety of meritorious copyright defenses should be encouraged to litigate them to the same extent that plaintiffs are encouraged to litigate meritorious claims of infringement. [A] successful defense of a copyright infringement action may further the policies of the Copyright Act every bit as much as a successful prosecution of an infringement claim by the holder of a copyright.
>
> ...
>
> [W]e reject both the "dual standard" adopted by several of the Courts of Appeals, and petitioner's claim that § 505 enacted the British Rule for automatic recovery of attorney's fees by the prevailing party. Prevailing plaintiffs and prevailing defendants are to be treated alike, but attorney's fees are to be awarded to prevailing parties only as a matter of the court's discretion.[982]

When there is a material dispute of fact to be resolved or discretion to be exercised in selecting a financial award, then either side is entitled to a jury; if there is no material dispute and a rule of law eliminates discretion in selecting the remedy, then summary judgment is permissible.

The Supreme Court recently confirmed that there are a number of nonexclusive factors that courts may consider in determining whether a proposed award of attorney's fees "advances the Copyright Act's goals" of "encouraging and rewarding authors' creations while also enabling others to build on that work."[983] These factors include motivation, the objective unreasonableness of the losing party's factual and legal arguments, the degree of success obtained, the need, in particular circumstances, to advance considerations of compensation and deterrence, and frivolousness.[984] The objective-reasonableness approach is intended to encourage parties with strong legal positions "to stand on their rights" and to deter those with weak ones from proceeding with litigation.[985]

979. 17 U.S.C. § 412.

980. *See*, e.g., *Lieb v. Topstone Indus., Inc.*, 788 F.2d 151 (3d Cir. 1986) (reviewing distinctions).

981. *Fogerty v. Fantasy, Inc.*, 510 U.S. 517 (1994); *accord Perfect 10, Inc. v. CCBill LLC*, 488 F.3d 1102, 1120 (9th Cir. 2007).

982. *Fogerty v. Fantasy, Inc.*, 510 U.S. 517, 527–28, 534 (1994).

983. *Kirtsaeng v. John Wiley & Sons, Inc.*, 136 S. Ct. 1979, 1986 (2016).

984. *Id.*, at 1985; *see also Fogerty v. Fantasy, Inc.*, 510 U.S. 517, 534 n.19 (1994); *Omega S.A. v. Costco Wholesale Corp.*, 776 F.3d 692, 695–96 (9th Cir. 2015).

985. *Kirtsaeng v. John Wiley & Sons, Inc.*, 136 S. Ct. 1979, 1986 (2016).

IV Impoundment and Disposition

While an action is pending, the court may, at any time, order the impoundment of infringing articles and devices used to produce them: "all copies or phonorecords claimed to have been made or used in violation of the exclusive right of the copyright owner, and ... all plates, and molds, matrices, masters, tapes, film negatives, or other articles by means of which such copies or phonorecords may be reproduced."[986] It is not clear what procedures must be followed in connection with impoundment orders and what showing one seeking impoundment must make; that is, the propriety of ex parte or summary impoundment orders.

At the conclusion of the action, as part of its final judgment, the court may similarly "order the destruction or other reasonable disposition" of all infringing articles and the devices used to produce them (as above defined).[987] This provision contemplates the alternative of destruction or a sale to the public, delivery to the plaintiff, or other appropriate disposition.

§11 COPYRIGHT PROTECTION SYSTEMS AND COPYRIGHT MANAGEMENT INFORMATION

I Generally

The DMCA was enacted on October 28, 1998, to implement certain provisions of the WIPO Copyright Treaty and Performances and Phonograms Treaty, which had been adopted by WIPO in Geneva in December 1996. The centerpiece of this legislation is the addition to the Copyright Act of Chapter 12—"Copyright Protection and Management Systems."[988] These are antipiracy provisions directed: (i) to the circumvention of technological protection measures taken by copyright holders to limit access to copyrighted material; and (ii) to the facilitation of such circumvention and of circumvention of technological measures that inhibit infringing activities; there are also provisions designed to protect the integrity of "copyright management information." The legislation directs the Register of Copyrights and the Assistant Secretary for Communications and Information to evaluate, and to report thereon to Congress within twenty-four months, the effect of the legislation and the development of electronic commerce and associated technology on sections 109 ("first sale") and 117 (computer programs) of the Copyright Act and the relation between existing and emergent technology and the operation of those sections. The resultant report did not recommend significant change.

986. 17 U.S.C. § 503(a).
987. 17 U.S.C. § 503(b).
988. 17 U.S.C. §§ 1201–1205.

II Circumvention of Copyright Protection Systems

A *Actionable Conduct*

Chapter 12 enumerates as actionable specific conduct, both direct and contributory, relating to the circumvention of technology designed to limit access to or to protect all or portions of copyrighted works. These provisions are not intended either to enlarge or diminish rights or defenses with respect to copyright infringement or vicarious or contributory liability for copyright infringement as such, or to set standards for the design of consumer electronics, telecommunications, or computer products.[989]

1 *Circumvention of Access Control*

"No person shall circumvent a technological measure that effectively controls access to a [copyright protected] work."[990] The prohibition relates, essentially, to the circumvention of encryption or scrambling schemes that limit access to a work; it does not deal directly with circumvention of technological copy protection or other schemes that inhibit infringing activities. More specifically, to "circumvent a technological measure" means "to descramble a scrambled work, to decrypt an encrypted work, or otherwise to avoid, bypass, remove, deactivate, or impair a technological measure, without the authority of the copyright owner."[991] For these purposes, "a technological measure 'effectively controls access to a work' if the measure, in the ordinary course of its operation, requires the application of information, or a process or a treatment, with the authority of the copyright owner, to gain access to the work."[992]

Application of this prohibition was deferred until October 28, 2000 (the expiration of two years from the enactment date of the legislation).[993] During the two-year deferral period, and during each succeeding three-year period, the Librarian of Congress was required to institute a rulemaking proceeding to determine the existence of persons who are, or are likely to be, adversely affected by the prohibition in their ability to make noninfringing uses of a particular class of works.[994] If the rulemaking proceeding concludes that there are classes of copyrighted works with respect to which noninfringing uses are, or are likely to be, adversely affected, then, with respect to each succeeding three-year period, the prohibition will not apply to users of those classes of works.[995]

989. 17 U.S.C. § 1201(c).
990. 17 U.S.C. § 1201(a)(1)(A).
991. 17 U.S.C. § 1201(a)(3)(A).
992. 17 U.S.C. § 1201(a)(3)(B).
993. 17 U.S.C. § 1201(a)(1)(A).
994. 17 U.S.C. § 1201(a)(1)(B), (C).
995. 17 U.S.C. § 1201(a)(1)(D).

2 *Facilitating Circumvention of Technological Protection Measures*

There is a separate specific prohibition with respect to providing the means for circumvention of technological protection measures. It is a violation to "import, offer to the public, provide, or otherwise traffic in any technology, product, service, device, component, or part thereof, that": (a) is primarily designed or produced for the purpose of: (i) "circumventing a technological measure that effectively controls access" to a copyrighted work or (ii) "circumventing protection afforded by a technological measure that effectively protects a right of a copyright owner ... in a work or a portion thereof"; or (b) has only limited commercially significant purpose or use other than to (i) "circumvent a technological measure that effectively controls access" to a copyrighted work or (ii) "circumvent protection afforded by a technological measure that effectively protects a right of a copyright owner ... in a work or a portion thereof"; or (c) is knowingly marketed for use in "circumventing a technological measure that effectively controls access" to a copyrighted work, or "circumventing protection afforded by a technological measure that effectively protects a right of a copyright owner ... in a work or a portion thereof."[996]

This language appears to create an express and specifically defined contributory infringement analog with respect to technology and devices used to circumvent technology either limiting access to copyrighted works or protecting copyrighted works from infringing activities. The provisions relating to facilitating circumvention essentially create a form of contributory liability independent of the standards for determining contributory copyright infringement generally with respect to copyrighted works.[997] In the words of the statute, "to 'circumvent protection afforded by a technological measure' means avoiding, bypassing, removing, deactivating or otherwise impairing a technological measure." And "a technological measure 'effectively protects a right of a copyright owner ....' if the measure, in the ordinary course of its operation, prevents, restricts, or otherwise limits the exercise of a right of a copyright owner:"[998]

> [T]he DMCA applies ... when the product manufacturer prevents all access to the copyrightable material and the alleged infringer responds by marketing a device that circumvents the technological measure designed to guard access to the copyrightable material.
>
> ...
>
> Nowhere in its deliberations over the DMCA did Congress express an interest in creating liability for the circumvention of technological measures designed to prevent consumers from using consumer goods while leaving the copyrightable content of a work unprotected.[999]

996. 17 U.S.C. § 1201(a)(2), (b)(1).
997. *See supra* §9.VI.B.
998. 17 U.S.C. § 1201(b)(2).
999. *Lexmark Int'l, Inc. v. Static Control Components, Inc.*, 387 F.3d 522, 548–49 (6th Cir. 2004). *See also The Chamberlain Grp., Inc. v. Skylink Techs., Inc.*, 381 F.3d 1178, 1183 (Fed. Cir. 2004) ("Chamberlain's proposed construction of the DMCA ignores the significant differences between defendants whose accused products enable copying and those, like Skylink, whose accused products enable only legitimate uses of copyrighted software").

These provisions of the DMCA have been upheld against constitutional, First Amendment, challenge.[1000]

3 *Limitation on Analog Videocassette Recorders*

While the use of "black box" devices to defeat copy protection embedded in prerecorded videotaped motion pictures would appear clearly to be violative of section 1201(b)(2), discussed above, Chapter 12 further attempts to inhibit copying of copyrighted audiovisual works essentially by penalizing: (i) new analog videocassette recorders that are not equipped with specified copy control technology;[1001] and (ii) analog videocassette recorders whose design has been modified to eliminate preexisting conformity to copy control technology.[1002] The provisions as to new recorders became effective at the end of April 2000 (eighteen months after the enactment of Chapter 12), and violations are to be treated as violations of section 1201(b)(1); the provisions with respect to modification of preexisting conformity are effective immediately and violations will be deemed an "act of circumvention."[1003] The various technical terms are defined in detail.[1004]

The requirement of conformity to copy control technology does not apply to "professional" analog videocassette recorders or to the trafficking in legally manufactured, unmodified, previously owned cassette recorders, and is not required with respect to video signals received through a camera lens.[1005] Moreover, the use of copy control technology on consumer videocassette recorders is limited[1006] to the prevention of "the making of a viewable copy of a pay-per-view, near video on demand, or video on demand transmission or prerecorded tape or disk containing one or more motion pictures or other audiovisual works," without impairing the ability of consumers to make analog copies of other types of programming. "The basic and extended basic tiers of programming services ... may not be encoded with these technologies at all."[1007]

1000. *Universal City Studios, Inc. v. Corley*, 273 F.3d 429, 441 (2d Cir. 2001).
1001. 17 U.S.C. § 1201(k)(1)(A). Such recorders must conform to the "automatic gain control copy control technology." The prohibition covers analog videocassette recorders in VHS, 8 mm, Beta, and National Television System Committee analog television color system formats. But the statutory prohibition would not apply to Beta until US sales in any one calendar year are at least 1,000 units or to an 8 mm format analog videocassette recorder that is not an analog camcorder until US sales in any one calendar year equal 20,000 units.
1002. 17 U.S.C. § 1201(k)(1)(B). Specifically, this provision refers to preexisting conformity to the "automatic gain control copy control technology" or to the "four-line colorstripe copy control technology." The prohibition covers analog videocassette recorders in VHS or 8 mm formats but the prohibition concerning modification of preexisting four-line colorstripe copy control technology does not apply to 8 mm analog videocassette recorders that are not also 8 mm analog videocassette camcorders.
1003. 17 U.S.C. § 1201(k)(5).
1004. 17 U.S.C. § 1201(k)(4).
1005. 17 U.S.C. § 1201(k)(3).
1006. 17 U.S.C. § 1201(k)(2).
1007. H.R. REP. NO. 105-796, at 70 (1998).

Once again, as with the audio home taping issues,[1008] the technological replacement of analog with digital recording equipment has outpaced the statute.

B *Exceptions and Limitations*

As detailed below, section 1201 contains a number of highly specific exemptions to the circumvention liability provisions. There is no general "fair use" exemption for circumvention activities, and, other than in connection with the specific exemptions, the purpose for otherwise actionable circumvention is not relevant to determination of liability:

> [T]he DMCA targets the circumvention of digital walls guarding copyrighted material (and trafficking in circumvention tools), but does not concern itself with the use of those materials after circumvention has occurred. Subsection 1201(c)(1) ensures that the DMCA is not read to prohibit the "fair use" of information just because that information was obtained in a manner made illegal by the DMCA.
>
> ...
>
> It would be strange for Congress to open small, carefully limited windows for circumvention to permit fair use in subsection 1201(d) if it then meant to exempt in subsection 1201(c)(1) any circumvention necessary for fair use.
>
> ...
>
> Fair use has never been held to be a guarantee of access to copyrighted material in order to copy it by the fair user's preferred technique or in the format of the original.[1009]

1 *Nonprofit Libraries, Archives, and Educational Institutions*

Nonprofit libraries, archives, and educational institutions are exempt from liability with respect solely to circumvention of access limitation technology engaged in for the purpose of determining whether to acquire a copy of a commercially exploited copyrighted work for noninfringing purposes if an unprotected copy of the identical work is not reasonably available.[1010] Repeated nonexempt circumvention of access limitations by an institution can result in forfeiture of the exemption.[1011]

2 *Law Enforcement, Intelligence, and Other Government Activities*

A broad exemption with respect to all otherwise prohibited circumvention activity is provided for law enforcement, intelligence, and other governmental activities, including "activities carried out in order to identify and address the vulnerabilities of a government computer, computer system, or computer network."[1012]

1008. *See supra* §6.I.B.
1009. *Universal City Studios v. Corley*, 273 F.3d 429, 443, 444 n.13, 459 (2d Cir. 2009).
1010. 17 U.S.C. § 1201(d).
1011. 17 U.S.C. § 1201(d)(3)(B).
1012. 17 U.S.C. § 1201(e).

3 *Reverse Engineering of Computer Programs to Achieve Interoperability*

Circumvention of access limitation technology by one with the lawful right to use an access-protected copy of a computer program is exempt from liability if it is not otherwise infringing and if done "for the sole purpose of analyzing those elements of the program that are necessary to achieve interoperability of an independently created computer program with other programs …."[1013] For the purposes of enabling such analysis, or achieving interoperability, the development and use of technological means to circumvent technological access limitation or protection are exempt from liability.[1014]

4 *Encryption Research on Published Works*

It is not a violation of the prohibition on circumvention of technological access limitation applied to a copy, phonorecord, performance, or display of a published work if that circumvention is done by one in lawful possession of the encrypted work "in the course of an act of good faith encryption research."[1015] For the exemption to apply, the act of circumvention must be necessary to conduct such encryption research, a good faith effort had to have been made to obtain authorization for it, and the act may not otherwise constitute an act of infringement.[1016] "Encryption research" is defined as:

> activities necessary to identify and analyze flaws and vulnerabilities of encryption technology applied to copyrighted works, if these activities are conducted to advance the state of knowledge in the field of encryption technology or to assist in the development of encryption products.[1017]

Exemption is also provided with respect to the development and use of technological means to circumvent technological measures in order to perform such acts of encryption research.[1018]

Factors to be considered in determining whether a person qualifies for the "encryption research" exemption include the extent and manner of dissemination of the information derived from the research—dissemination that is "reasonably calculated to advance the state of knowledge or development of encryption technology," as opposed to that which may facilitate infringement or violations of law; whether the person involved "is engaged in a legitimate course of study, is employed, or is appropriately trained or experienced, in the field of encryption technology"; and

1013. 17 U.S.C. § 1201(f)(1). "Interoperability" means "the ability of computer programs to exchange information, and of such programs mutually to use the information which has been exchanged." 17 U.S.C. § 1201(f)(4).
1014. 17 U.S.C. § 1201(f)(2).
1015. 17 U.S.C. § 1201(g)(2).
1016. *Id.*
1017. 17 U.S.C. § 1201(g)(1)(A). "Encryption technology" means "the scrambling and descrambling of information using mathematical formulas or algorithms." 17 U.S.C. § 1201(g)(1)(B).
1018. 17 U.S.C. § 1201(g)(4).

whether the person provides notice of the findings of the research, and appropriate documentation, to the copyright owner of the work involved.[1019]

5 *Protection of Personally Identifying Information*

It is not a violation of the prohibition on circumvention of technological measures that control access to work: (i) if those measures, or the protected work, contain "the capability of collecting or disseminating personally identifying information reflecting the online activities of a natural person who seeks to gain access to the work protected," and collect and disseminate such information "without providing conspicuous notice of such collection of dissemination to such person, and without providing such person with the capability to prevent or respect such collection of dissemination"; and (ii) the only effect of the act of circumvention is identifying and disabling the capability of so collecting or disseminating personally identifying information, and is carried out solely for the purpose of preventing such collection or dissemination, and is not otherwise in violation of any law.[1020]

6 *Security Testing*

It is not a violation of the prohibition on circumvention of technological measures that control access to work, "to engage in an act of security testing," that does not otherwise constitute infringement or a violation of law,[1021] or to develop or use technological means solely to perform such acts of security testing.[1022] For these purposes, "security testing" means "accessing the computer, computer system, or computer network, solely for the purpose of good faith testing, investigating, or correcting a security fall vulnerability, with the authorization of the owner or operator of such computer, computer system, or computer network."[1023]

III Copyright Management Information

"Copyright management information" refers to information identifying a copyrighted work, such as the name of the author, the title of the work, such information as is set forth in notice of copyright, terms, and conditions for use of the work, identifying numbers or symbols linking referring to such information, the names of performers, writers, directors, and others credited with a work (except with respect to public

1019. 17 U.S.C. § 1201(g)(3).
1020. 17 U.S.C. § 1201(i)(1).
1021. 17 U.S.C. § 1201(j)(2).
1022. 17 U.S.C. § 1201(j)(4).
1023. 17 U.S.C. § 1201(j)(1). Two factors are to be considered in determining whether an exemption applies: (1) whether the information derived from the security testing was used solely to promote the security of the owner or operator of such computer, computer system or computer network; and (2) whether that information was used or maintained in a manner that does not facilitate infringement or other violation of law. 17 U.S.C. § 1201(j)(3).

performances of works by radio and television broadcast stations), and such other information as the Register of Copyrights prescribes by regulation.[1024]

A *Impairment of Copyright Management Information*

Section 1202 subjects to liability: (i) one who provides or distributes false copyright management information, knowingly and with the intent to induce, enable, facilitate or conceal infringement;[1025] and (ii) one who, without authority, and with knowledge or reasonable grounds to know that such action will induce, enable, facilitate, or conceal infringement, intentionally removes or alters any copyright management information, distributes or imports for distribution copyright management information with knowledge that such information has been removed or altered, or distributes, imports for distribution, or publicly performs works with knowledge that copyright management information has been removed or altered.[1026]

B *Exemptions and Limitations*

1 *Law Enforcement and Other Government Activities*

These provisions do not apply so as to prohibit "lawfully authorized investigative, protective, information security, or intelligence activity" of governmental bodies.[1027]

2 *Transmissions*

No liability will attach to analog transmissions of broadcast stations, or cable systems, or those who provide programming to broadcast stations or cable systems that impair copyright management information if avoidance of the prohibited activity "is not technically feasible or would create an undue financial hardship" and if it was not intended by such activity to "induce, enable, facilitate, or conceal infringement."[1028] Separate exemption is provided for digital transmissions, dependent upon the development of a voluntary industry standard for the placement of copyright management information (interim, tightly circumscribed exemptions are provided).[1029]

1024. 17 U.S.C. § 1202(c).
1025. 17 U.S.C. § 1202(a).
1026. 17 U.S.C. § 1202(b).
1027. 17 U.S.C. § 1202(d).
1028. 17 U.S.C. § 1202(e)(1).
1029. 17 U.S.C. § 1202(e)(2).

IV Enforcement and Remedies

A Civil Remedies

"Any person injured by a violation of section 1201 or 1202 may bring a civil action in an appropriate United States district court for such violation."[1030]

1 Injunctive and Related Relief

The court may, in its discretion, grant temporary and permanent injunctive relief to prevent or restrain a violation, "but in no event shall [the court] impose a prior restraint on free speech or the press protected under the first amendment to the Constitution."[1031]

During the pendency of an action, the court may order the impounding "of any device or product that is in the custody or control of the alleged violator and that the court has reasonable cause to believe was involved in a violation."[1032] As part of its final judgment or decree, where a violation is found, the court may order "the remedial modification or the destruction of any device or product involved in the violation that is in the custody or control of the violator or has been impounded."[1033]

2 Damages: Actual and Statutory

The successful plaintiff is entitled to actual damages suffered as a result of the violation, and "any profits of the violator that are attributable to the violation and are not taken into account in computing the actual damages."[1034]

In lieu of actual damages, the successful plaintiff may elect, at any time before final judgment is entered, to recover statutory damages ranging from USD 200 to USD 2,500 for each violation of section 1201 (relating to circumvention of technological measures) and ranging from USD 2,500 to USD 25,000 for each violation of section 1202 (copyright management information), the specific amount to be determined "as the court considers just."[1035] Given the similarity of statutory language, the US Supreme Court holding of a constitutional right to jury determination in claims involving statutory damages for copyright infringement[1036] presumably is applicable to these statutory damages claims.

1030. 17 U.S.C. § 1203(a).
1031. 17 U.S.C. § 1202(b)(1).
1032. 17 U.S.C. § 1203(b)(2).
1033. 17 U.S.C. § 1203(b)(6).
1034. 17 U.S.C. § 1203(c)(2).
1035. 17 U.S.C. § 1203(c)(3).
1036. *See supra* §10.II.B.3.

3 *Increasing or Reducing Damages*

Where the injured party proves that the defendant violated section 1201 or 1202 within three years after entry of a final judgment for another violation of those sections, "the court may increase the award of damages up to triple the amount that would otherwise be awarded, as the court considers just."[1037]

Conversely, the court may, in its discretion, reduce or remit the total award of damages in any case in which the violator proves that it was not aware and had no reason to believe that its acts constituted a violation.[1038] In the special case of violation by a nonprofit library, archives, or educational institution, the court shall remit damages if the library, archives, or educational institution proves that it was not aware and had no reason to believe that its acts constituted a violation.[1039]

4 *Costs and Counsel Fees*

The court, in its discretion, may allow the recovery of costs by or against any party other than the US or an officer thereof, and may award to the prevailing party reasonable attorneys' fees.[1040] The US Supreme Court's determination that prevailing plaintiffs and prevailing defendants are to be treated alike in the exercise of the court's discretion in awarding attorney's fees[1041] would appear to be applicable here.

B Criminal Penalties

Willful violation, "for purposes of commercial advantage or private financial gain" (except by a nonprofit library, archives, or educational institution) may result in fines and/or imprisonment; criminal proceedings must be commenced within five years after the cause of action arose.[1042]

1037. 17 U.S.C. § 1203(c)(4).
1038. 17 U.S.C. § 1203(c)(5)(A).
1039. 17 U.S.C. § 1203(c)(5)(B).
1040. 17 U.S.C. §§ 1203(b)(4), (5).
1041. *See supra* §10.III.
1042. 17 U.S.C. § 1204. The fine may be up to USD 500,000 and/or imprisonment up to 5 years, or both, for the first offense; the fine may be up to USD 1,000,000 and/or imprisonment up to 10 years, for any subsequent offense.

PART II Patent

CHAPTER 1

Sources of US Patent Law

§1 CONSTITUTIONAL FOUNDATION

The foundation for American patent law, as for copyright law, is embodied in Article I, section 8, clause 8 of the US Constitution.[1043,1044] This constitutional provision empowers Congress:

> To promote the Progress of Science and useful Arts, by securing for limited Times to Authors and Inventors the exclusive Right to their respective Writings and Discoveries.[1045]

The US Supreme Court understands this clause to be "both a grant of power and a limitation."[1046] According to the Court:

> This qualified authority, unlike the power often exercised in the sixteenth and seventeenth centuries by the English Crown, is limited to the promotion of advances in the "useful Arts." It was written against this backdrop of the practices—eventually curtailed by the Statute of Monopolies—of the Crown in granting monopolies to court favorites in goods or businesses which had long before been enjoyed by the public ... The Congress in the exercise of the patent power may not overreach the restraints imposed by the stated constitutional purpose.[1047]

James Madison, one of America's more prominent founders, wrote in The Federalist No. 43 that:

1043. I would like to thank the West Virginia College of Law Hodges Research Fund for partially funding this work.

1044. Much of the material of this section is adapted from DONALD S. CHISUM ET AL., PRINCIPLES OF PATENT LAW (3rd ed. 2004).

1045. U.S. CONST. Art. 1, § 8, cl. 8.

1046. *Id.*; *Graham v. John Deere Co.*, 383 U.S. 1, 5 (1966).

1047. *Graham*, 383 U.S. at 5–6.

> [T]he utility of [Article I, § 8, cl. 8] will scarcely be questioned. The copyright of authors has been solemnly adjudged, in Great Britain, to be a right of common law. The right to useful inventions seems with equal reason to belong to the inventors. The public good fully coincides in both cases with the claims of individuals.[1048]

Thus, the drafters of the American Constitution understood that patent law seeks to strike a balance between the promotion of technological creativity and the dissemination of its fruits.

§2 STATUTORY FOUNDATION

The present statutory scheme for American patent law is embodied in Title 35 of the U.S.C. A brief history of the numerous statutory enactments may be helpful to fully appreciate what led up to Title 35.

The Patent Act of 1790, America's first patent statute, was signed into law on April 10, 1790, by President George Washington.[1049] The 1790 Act authorized the issue of patents for "any useful art, manufacture, engine, machine, or device, or any improvement therein not before known or used."[1050] The Act did not create a patent office, but instead designated a patent board that would examine patent applications, comprising a specification and drawings, to determine if "the invention or discovery [was] sufficiently useful and important"[1051] so as to merit a patent. The Board, self-dubbed the "Commissioners for the Promotion of the Useful Arts," consisted of the Secretary of State (Thomas Jefferson), Secretary of War (Henry Knox), and the Attorney General (Edmund Randolph). The first patent under the 1790 Act was issued to Samuel Hopkins for a method of "making Pot ash and Pearl ash by a new apparatus and Process."[1052]

The examination system under the 1790 Act proved to be too burdensome on the three-member patent board, and, in 1793, a new Patent Act was on the books. Although the 1793 Act contained several fundamental patent law concepts that are extant today, the Act did away with the patent board and the examination proceedings and implemented a registration system, clerical in nature, like that which existed in England.[1053] Needless to say, the lack of an examination requirement attracted several

1048. *The Federalist*, No. 43 (James Madison).
1049. Act of Apr. 10, 1790, Ch. 7, 1 Stat. 109.
1050. A total of fifty-five patents were issued under the 1790 Act. It is interesting to note that the Patent Act of 1790 was passed, on Apr. 5, 1790, by the Congress of 12 states. Rhode Island did not join the Union as the thirteenth state until May 29, 1790, forty-nine days after President Washington signed the bill. *See* KENNETH W. DOBYNS, THE PATENT OFFICE PONY: A HISTORY OF THE EARLY PATENT OFFICE 22 (1994).
1051. Act of Apr. 10, 1790, Ch. 7, 1 Stat. 109.
1052. *See* David W. Maxey, *Samuel Hopkins, the Holder of the First U.S. Patent: A Study of Failure*, The Pennsylvania Magazine of History and Biography 3–37 (January/April 1998).
1053. Dobyns, *supra* n. 1050, at 35 ("The Act of 1793 went from the extreme of rigid examination to the opposite extreme of no examination at all. The Patent Board was abolished. The State Department was to register patents, and the courts were to determine whether the patents were valid").

fraudulent or duplicative patents.[1054] Nevertheless, the registration system lasted for forty-three years, until, on July 4, 1836, Congress enacted what is generally acknowledged to be the foundation of the modern patent system in the US.[1055] The 1836 Patent Act reintroduced the requirement under the 1790 Act that patent applications be examined for novelty and utility.[1056] In 1850, the Supreme Court, in *Hotchkiss v. Greenwood*,[1057] established what is presently referred to as the nonobviousness requirement of patentability.[1058] Applicants, as under the 1790 and 1793 Acts, were required to submit a specification, drawings, and models with their application. In addition to the examination requirement, the 1836 Act, by law, made the Patent Office a distinct and separate bureau in the Department of State and created the position of Commissioner of Patents.[1059] The Act also created the present patent numbering system[1060] and allowed for a patent applicant to appeal an examiner's refusal to issue a patent. The appeal was heard by a three-member board appointed by the Secretary of State.

The next major statutory revisions came in 1870 and 1952. The 1870 Act essentially retained the 1836 Act's provisions. But because the courts found it increasingly difficult to discover what the invention was and the distinction between new and old was sometimes blurred, the 1870 Act placed more emphasis on the importance of the patent claim and required the patent applicant to define more distinctly what the invention was.[1061]

1054. *See* Edward C. Walterscheid, *To Promote the Progress of Useful Arts: American Patent Law and Administration, 1787–1836 (Part I)*, 79 J. PAT. & TRADEMARK OFF. SOC'Y 61, 73–74 (1997); BRUCE BUGBEE, GENESIS OF AMERICAN PATENT AND COPYRIGHT LAW 150–53 (1967).
1055. *See* Bugbee, *supra* n. 1054, at 152 (1967) ("With the Act of 1836, the United States patent system came of age"); Walterscheid, *supra* n. 1054, at 61.
1056. As noted, the 1793 Act did away with the examination requirement of the 1790 Act which in turn led to fraudulent and duplicative patents. A Senate Report accompanying the 1836 Act cited these fraudulent and duplicative patents as some of the "evils" that existed under the 1793 Act. *See* Senate Report Accompanying Senate Bill No. 239, 24th Cong., 1st Sess. (April 1836).
1057. 52 U.S. (11 How.) 248 (1850).
1058. *See infra* Ch. 2, §4.
1059. Henrey Leavitt Ellsworth (1791–1858), one of the twin sons of Justice Oliver Ellsworth, was appointed as the first Commissioner of Patents in 1836.
1060. Patent Number 1 was issued to Senator John Ruggles of Maine, who was primarily responsible for the passage of the 1836 Act. Prior to 1836, patents were identified by the date they were issued.
1061. *See* Risdale Ellis, Patent Claims 3 (1949) (explaining that claims under the 1836 Act "served merely to call attention to what the inventor considered the salient features of his invention. The drawing and description were the main thing, the claims were a mere adjunct thereto … The idea that the claim is just as important if not more important than the description and drawings did not develop until the Act of 1870 or thereabouts"). Another commentator adds:

> Along with the development of the importance of the claim, there was another far-reaching change in the attitude of both the Patent Office and the courts as to the way in which claims should be drawn and interpreted. To appreciate this change, it is necessary to go back to the fundamental principles underlying the definition of what is new and the various modes of distinguishing what is new from what is old. Generally speaking, compliance with the requirements of the early statutes for a distinction between new and the old was not perfect. The problem of discovering in the early patents what invention was involved was a burden which was carried by the courts and

A brief discussion of the Supreme Court's attitude toward patents prior to the 1952 Act will shed light on the Act itself as well as the driving forces behind the Act. From 1890 to 1930, patents were viewed favorably by the Court; but from about 1930–1950, the Court approached patents with a great deal of suspicion, emphasizing the monopolistic and social costs aspects of patents.

The 1952 Act was largely a response to the previous twenty years of the Supreme Court's antipatent attitude. A significant portion of the 1952 Act, codified in Title 35 of the U.S.C., governs American patent law to the present day. Further amendments to the patent laws occurred in 1984, and in the mid-1990s, important changes were ushered in by the GATT and the NAFTA. For example, the term for patents filed on or after June 8, 1995, is now twenty years from the date of filing.[1062] Prior to GATT, the term of a patent was seventeen years from the date of issue. Furthermore, evidence of inventive activity (i.e., conception and reduction to practice (RTP)) outside of the US may be used to establish the date of invention, whereas before, only inventive activity within the US could be used. The next significant amendment to the patent law came in 1999 with the American Inventors Protection Act (AIPA). Prior to the AIPA, patents were kept secret by the Patent and Trademark Office (PTO). Now, most patent applications publish eighteen months after the earliest effective filing date.[1063]

The most recent amendment to the patent law is the America Invents Act (AIA).[1064] The AIA, which culminates six years of legislative activity, became law on September 16, 2011. The major substantive changes to the patent laws are the conversion of the US from a first-to-invent to a first-inventor-to-file patent system (including a fully international definition of prior art)[1065] and the abolition of the failure to disclose the best mode as a defense to patent infringement.[1066] The major administrative changes include the allowance of third-party submissions during patent examination[1067] and Post-Grant Review (PGR), Inter Partes Review (IPR) and Covered Business Method (CBM) Review.[1068] The AIA represents the most comprehensive revision to US patent law since the Patent Act of 1952. Given that the AIA provisions apply to patent applications filed on or after March 16, 2013, the pre-AIA and post-AIA regimes will run parallel for the next twenty years.

---

the public. The desirability of shifting this burden to the Patent Office and to the patentee himself soon became apparent.

1 Anthony William Deller, Patent Claims 11 (2d ed. 1971).

1062. If the application contained a specific reference to an earlier-filed application or applications under 35 U.S.C. §120, 121 or 365(c), then the expiration date is 20 years from the filing date of the earliest of such application.
1063. *See* 35 U.S.C. §122(b)(1); *infra* Ch. 3, §2.II.G.
1064. *See* Leahy-Smith America Invents Act, Pub. L. No. 112-29, 125 Stat. 284 (2011).
1065. *See infra* Ch. 2, §2.VIII.A and B.
1066. *See infra* Ch. 2, §1.II.
1067. *See infra* Ch. 3, §2.II.B.
1068. *See infra* Ch. 3, §3.III.

§3 THE US COURT OF APPEALS FOR THE FEDERAL CIRCUIT

A particularly significant development in American patent law was the creation of the US Court of Appeals for the Federal Circuit. The Federal Circuit was created by Congress in 1982 and is America's thirteenth federal appellate court.[1069] The court was created primarily in response to a spree of forum shopping in patent litigation, a lack of uniformity in our patent laws, and a high invalidity rate among litigated patents.[1070]

The Federal Circuit sits in Washington, D.C., and in any place where the other regional circuit courts may sit pursuant to 28 U.S.C. § 48(a) and is comprised of 12 active judges. Unlike the regional circuit courts, the Federal Circuit has unlimited geographic jurisdiction nationwide with broad subject matter jurisdiction. As such, the court enjoys exclusive jurisdiction over cases arising "under any Act of Congress relating to patents," as well as over cases in several other areas of the law.[1071] Furthermore, the court's jurisdiction includes appeals of nonpatent claims that accompany patent claims. For example, an appeal regarding antitrust claims will go to the Federal Circuit if the case in the district court also involved claims arising under the patent laws. In this type of situation, although the court applies its own law when reviewing the patent claims, it applies the substantive law of that district court's regional circuit court when reviewing the antitrust claims.[1072] Also, the Federal Circuit

---

1069. Federal Courts Improvement Act of 1982, Pub. L No. 97-164, 96 Stat. 25 (Apr. 2, 1982). This Act merged the Court of Claims, which had seven judges, and the Court of Customs and Patent Appeals, which had five judges. The Federal Circuit came into existence on Oct. 1, 1982. *See The United States Court of Appeals for the Federal Circuit: A History* (1991).

1070. As stated in the legislative history:

> [S]ome circuit courts are regarded as "pro-patent" and others "anti-patent," and much time and money is expended in "shopping for a favorable venue. [Furthermore,] the validity of a patent is too dependent upon geography (i.e., the accident of judicial venue) to make effective business planning possible ... A single Court of Appeals for patent cases will promote certainty where it is lacking to a significant degree and will reduce, if not eliminate, the forum-shopping that now occurs."

H.R. Rep. No. 312, 97th Cong., 1st Sess. 20–22 (1981); *see also* S. Rep. No. 275, 97 Cong., 1st Sess. 5 (1981) ("The creation of the Court of Appeals for the Federal Circuit will produce desirable uniformity in this area of [patent] law. Such uniformity will reduce the forum-shopping that is common to patent litigation.").

1071. *See* 28 U.S.C. §§ 1295, 1338; *see also* H.R. Rep. No. 312, *supra* n. 1070, at 19 ("The proposed new court is not a 'specialized court.' Its jurisdiction is not limited to one type of case, or even to two or three types of cases. Rather, it has a varied docket spanning a broad range of legal issues and types of cases."); S. Rep. No. 275, *supra* n. 1070, at 6 ("[The Federal Circuit's] rich docket assures that the work of the ... court will be a broad variety of legal problems. Moreover, the subject matter of the new court will be sufficiently mixed to prevent any special interest from dominating it."). "The court's jurisdiction consists of administrative law cases (55%), intellectual property cases (31%), and cases involving money damages against the United States government (11%). The administrative law cases consist of personnel and veterans claims. Nearly all of the intellectual property cases involve patents. Suits for money damages against the United States government include government contract cases, tax refund appeals, unlawful takings, and civilian and military pay cases." http://www.cafc.uscourts.gov/the-court/court-jurisdiction.

1072. *See Atari, Inc. v. JS & A Group, Inc.*, 747 F.2d 1422, 1438–40 (Fed. Cir. 1984).

decides procedural issues that are unrelated to the patent issues in dispute by applying the law of the relevant regional circuit court.[1073]

While all appeals will first go through the Federal Circuit, forum shopping at the district court level is becoming more common. For example, the US District Court for the Western District of Texas under Judge Alan Albright has become one of the most popular venues for patent plaintiffs. Before Judge Albright was confirmed in 2018 there were less than 10 patent cases filed in the Waco district in its entire history. In 2020 alone, Judge Albright took almost 800 new patent cases, which accounts for almost 20% of all new patent cases filed in 2020. The Western District of Texas is considered a patentee-friendly forum due to its patent rules and decisions.

1073. *See Panduit Corp. v. All States Plastic Mfg. Co.*, 744 F.2d 1564, 1574–75 (Fed. Cir. 1984). *Accord CoreBrace LLC v. Star Seismic LLC*, 566 F.3d 1069, 1072 (Fed. Cir. 2009).

CHAPTER 2

Conditions of Patentability

Before the particulars of American patent law are discussed, it should be noted, as an initial matter, that inventors may opt for trade secret protection in lieu of patent protection. Trade secret law offers an extremely important means of protecting a firm's commercial information. Indeed, many industries rely heavily on trade secrecy vis-à-vis patent law, particularly for process-related inventions.[1074] There are important distinctions between patent law and trade secret law. First, information eligible for trade secret protection may or may not be eligible for patent protection. Trade secrets include not only technological information but also customer lists, business plans, and marketing strategies. Also, there is no novelty requirement for trade secret protection, only that the commercial information provides an economic advantage. Second, trade secret protection can last in perpetuity as long as the information remains secret and maintains its value, whereas a patent expires twenty years from its filing date.[1075] Third, with the exception of the Economic Espionage Act, trade secret protection is a creature of state law and is recognized in one form or another by every jurisdiction. Patent law is a strictly federal regime.

A patent applicant is entitled to a patent only if the invention is new,[1076] adequately disclosed,[1077] enabled,[1078] useful,[1079] nonobvious,[1080] and fits within statutorily defined subject matter.[1081] These patentability requirements secure a quid pro

1074. *See* Wesley M. Cohen, Richard R. Nelson & John P. Walsh, *Protecting Their Intellectual Assets: Appropriability Conditions and Why U.S. Manufacturing Firms Patent (Or Not)* (Nat'l Bureau of Econ. Research, Working Paper No. 7552, 2000).
1075. If the application contained a specific reference to an earlier-filed application or applications under 35 U.S.C. § 120, 121 or 365(c), then the expiration date is 20 years from the filing date of the earliest of such application.
1076. 35 U.S.C. § 102.
1077. 35 U.S.C. § 112.
1078. *Id.*
1079. 35 U.S.C. § 101.
1080. 35 U.S.C. § 103.
1081. 35 U.S.C. § 101.

quo for society. The disclosure requirements ensure that the patentee discloses to the public how to make and use the patented invention so that others, namely persons of ordinary skill in the art, can improve upon or design around the patentee's claimed invention. Because it would be nonsensical to grant a patent on an invention that already exists, the novelty requirement ensures that the inventor has contributed something new to society, something not previously known or used.[1082] The utility requirement is fairly straightforward and requires that in exchange for patent protection, the patent applicant discloses an invention that is useful and operative. The nonobviousness requirement builds upon the novelty requirement and raises the patentability hurdle by denying patent protection to inventions that are "obvious" to a person of ordinary skill in the art. Thus, even if an invention is novel, it may nevertheless be unpatentable. Lastly, the invention must fall within statutorily classified subject matter (e.g., process or composition of matter) and, for example, cannot be a naturally occurring substance or a fundamental mathematical formula (e.g., $E = mc^2$). Taken collectively, these requirements assure that a patent applicant has made a genuine contribution to society in exchange for patent protection.[1083]

§1 DISCLOSURE REQUIREMENTS

It would be difficult to overstate the importance of the patent law's disclosure requirements, which are contained in the first two paragraphs of 35 U.S.C. § 112. The patent's disclosure provides the foundation for the claims and hence for the scope of patent protection.[1084] Specifically, § 112 provides in part:

> [a] The specification shall contain a written description of the invention, and of the manner and process of making and using it, in such full, clear, concise, and

---

1082. *See Kewanee Oil Co. v. Bicron Corp.*, 416 U.S. 470, 481 (1974). Judge Pauline Newman elaborates:

> Although it is accepted that prior art is knowledge that is available to the public, it has been unusual that opinions have explained the real reason for the denial of patent rights, which is the basic principle (to which there are minor exceptions) that no patent should be granted which withdraws from the public domain technology already available to the public. It is available, in legal theory at least, when it is described in the world's accessible literature, including patents, or has been publicly known or in the public use or on-sale "in this country."

Lamb-Weston, Inc. v. McCain Foods Ltd., 78 F.3d 540, 549 (Fed. Cir. 1996) (J. Newman dissenting) (quoting *Kimberly-Clark Corp. v. Johnson & Johnson and Personal Prods. Co.*, 745 F.2d 1437, 1453 (Fed. Cir. 1984)).

1083. *See Kewanee*, 416 U.S. at 480–81. Patent law promotes the constitutional provision for the progress of the useful arts "by offering a right of exclusion for a limited period as an incentive to inventors to risk the often enormous costs in terms of time, research, and development." *Id.*, at 480. Further, patent law not only introduces new product and process technology into the economy but also provides "employment and better life ...." *Id.*

1084. *Compare O'Reilly v. Morse*, 56 U.S. (15 How.) 62, 62–63 (1854) (finding Morse's eighth claim too broad because specification was not enabling and not shown to have been invented, which claimed "every improvement where the motive power is the electric or galvanic current, and the result is the marking or printing intelligible characters, signs, or letters at a distance"), *with* The Telephone Cases, 126 U.S. 1, 536 (1888) (upholding as enabling, Bell's

exact terms as to enable any person skilled in the art to which it pertains, or with which it is most nearly connected, to make and use the same, and shall set forth the best mode contemplated by the inventor or joint inventor of carrying out the invention.

[b] The specification shall conclude with one or more claims particularly pointing out and distinctly claiming the subject matter which the inventor or a joint inventor regards as the invention.[1085]

The following four requirements:

(1) enablement;
(2) best mode;
(3) written description; and
(4) clear claiming (definiteness)

must be satisfied for a patent to issue. The disclosure must support the scope of the patent claim. Section 112 requires the patentee to give the public "fair notice of what the patentee and the PTO have agreed constitute the metes and bounds of the claimed invention"[1086] and to disseminate to the public information concerning the patented subject matter. This dual notice/dissemination function allows third parties to avoid conduct that would infringe the patent while providing the interested public with information that enlarges the storehouse of knowledge and may also help others to improve upon or design around the claimed invention—thus leading to further technological progress. As the Supreme Court stated in *Markman v. Westview Instruments, Inc.*:

> [t]he limits of a patent must be known for the protection of the patentee, the encouragement of the inventive genius of others and the assurance that the subject of the patent will be dedicated ultimately to the public. Otherwise, a zone of uncertainty which enterprise and experimentation may enter only at the risk of infringement claims would discourage invention only a little less than unequivocal foreclosure of the field, and [t]he public [would] be deprived of rights supposed to belong to it, without being clearly told what it is that limits these rights.[1087]

I Enablement

The enablement requirement of § 112 requires the inventor to provide sufficient information in the specification to enable a person skilled in the relevant art to make

claim to the "method of, an apparatus for, transmitting vocal or other sounds telegraphically ... by causing electrical undulation" because the invention was limited to a method and apparatus).

1085. 35 U.S.C. § 112(b).

1086. *London v. Carson Pirie Scott & Co.*, 946 F.2d 1534, 1538 (Fed. Cir. 1991).

1087. 517 U.S. 370, 390 (1996).

and use the claimed invention without undue experimentation.[1088] The enablement requirement is often considered to be at the heart of the quid pro quo between the government and the inventor. In exchange for the powerful right to exclude, the inventor must inform the public how to make and use the invention so others, namely competitors of the inventor, can improve upon the claimed invention.[1089]

Although § 112 does expressly resolve the question of at what time the disclosure must be enabling, the Federal Circuit and its predecessor court have held that the sufficiency of the patent's disclosure must be judged as of its filing date.[1090] Information that is developed or becomes available after that date cannot be considered in determining disclosure sufficiency. Similarly, post-filing date developments that enable previously unknown variations cannot be relied upon to establish nonenablement.[1091]

Enablement is a question of law that is based on underlying factual findings.[1092] The test for compliance with the enablement requirement is whether "undue experimentation" is required to make and use the claimed invention.[1093] In determining what constitutes undue experimentation, the Federal Circuit has set forth several factors relevant to the enablement analysis in In re Wands.[1094] They are:

(1) the quantity of experimentation necessary;
(2) the amount of direction or guidance presented;
(3) presence or absence of working examples;
(4) the nature of the invention;
(5) the state of the prior art;
(6) the relative skill of those in the art;
(7) the predictability or unpredictability of the art; and
(8) the breadth of the claims.[1095]

1088. Although the term "undue experimentation" does not appear in the statute, "it is well established that enablement requires that the specification teach those in the art to make and use the invention without undue experimentation." *In re* Wands, 858 F.2d 731, 737 (Fed. Cir. 1988).

1089. This policy was first expressed by Chief Justice Marshall. *See Grant v. Raymond*, 31 U.S. (6 Pet.) 218, 219 (1832) (stating the enablement requirement "is necessary in order to give the public, after the privilege shall expire, the advantage for which the privilege is allowed, and is the foundation of the power to issue the patent").

1090. *See In re* Glass, 492 F.2d 1228, 1232 (C.C.P.A. 1974); *accord Enzo Biochem, Inc. v. Calgene, Inc.*, 188 F.3d 1362, 1371–72 (Fed. Cir. 1999) (explaining that in both patent examination and litigation the enablement determination "is made retrospectively, i.e., by looking back to the filing date of the patent application and determining whether undue experimentation would have been required to make and use the claimed invention at that time."); *In re* Hogan, 559 F.2d 595, 607 (C.C.P.A. 1977) (reaffirming rule).

1091. *See United States Steel Corp. v. Phillips Petroleum Co.*, 865 F.2d 1247, 1251 (Fed. Cir. 1989); *Hogan*, 559 F.2d at 604.

1092. *In re* Vaeck, 947 F.2d 488, 495, 20 U.S.P.Q.2d 1438, 1444 (Fed. Cir. 1991); *Atlas Powder Co. v. E.I. du Pont de Nemours & Co.*, 750 F.2d 1569, 1576, 224 U.S.P.Q. 409, 413 (Fed. Cir. 1984).

1093. *In re* Wright, 999 F.2d 1557, 1561 (Fed. Cir. 1993); *see also Sitrick v. Dreamworks, LLC*, 516 F.3d 993, 999 (Fed. Cir. 2008) (reaffirming the standard).

1094. 858 F.2d 731, 737 (Fed. Cir. 1988).

1095. *See id.*

While not mandatory,[1096] the Wands factors are ubiquitous in evaluating enablement because they touch on issues that are important in virtually all enablement determinations.

In addition to serving as an information dissemination device, the enablement requirement also requires the specification's enablement to be commensurate with the scope of the claims. The claim scope sought cannot be any broader than the disclosure.[1097] An example of the claim limiting function of the enablement requirement can be found in the famous case of *O'Reilly v. Morse*.[1098] Though he invented a telegraph that used his code, Samuel Morse obtained a patent with a claim that covered "the exclusive right to every improvement where the motive power is [electromagnetism], ... and the result is the marking or printing intelligible characters, signs, or letters at a distance."[1099] In striking down the claim, the Supreme Court stated:

> It is impossible to misunderstand the extent of this claim.
>
> If this claim can be maintained, it matters not by what process or machinery the result is accomplished .... [S]ome future inventor, in the onward march of science, may discover a mode of writing or printing at a distance [with electromagnetism] without using any part of the process or combination set forth in the plaintiff's specification ...
>
> In fine, he claims an exclusive right to use a manner and process which he has not described and indeed had not invented[.][1100]

So, while Morse's specification taught and enabled telegraphy with his device, had the claim survived, it would have dominated other technological innovations that only subsequent workers in the field could teach and enable.[1101]

Recently, the Supreme Court upheld the idea that the specification must enable the claimed invention through its entire scope. Thus, a skilled artisan must disclose how to make and use the claimed invention without undue experimentation, especially if the claimed invention covers a broad genus claim that embraces thousands of species.[1102]

II Best Mode

Compliance with § 112 requires that "[t]he specification ... set forth the best mode contemplated by the inventor or joint inventor of carrying out the invention."[1103]

1096. *See Amgen, Inc. v. Chugai Pharm. Co.*, 927 F.2d 1200, 1213 (Fed. Cir. 1991) (noting that the *Wands* factors are illustrative and not mandatory).
1097. *See National Recovery Technologies, Inc. v. Magnetic Separation Systems, Inc.*, 166 F.3d 1190, 1195 (Fed. Cir. 1999).
1098. 56 U.S. 62 (1853). For a fuller discussion of Morse and interesting tidbits surrounding the case, *see* KENNETH SILVERMAN, LIGHTNING MAN: THE ACCURSED LIFE OF SAMUEL F.B. MORSE 319–24 (2003).
1099. *O'Reilly*, 56 U.S. (15 How.) at 112 (emphasis added).
1100. *Id.*, at 112–13.
1101. Sean B. Seymore, *The Teaching Function of Patents*, 85 NOTRE DAME L. REV. 621, 660 (2010).
1102. *Amgen Inc. v. Sanofi* 598 US 594 (2023).
1103. 35 U.S.C. § 112(a). The Federal Circuit has explained why the best mode requirement is distinct from the enablement requirement:

Compliance with the best mode requirement is a question of fact, but the scope of the invention to which the best mode applies is a question of law, which is reviewed de novo.[1104]

The best mode requirement prohibits an inventor from applying for a patent while concealing from the public a preferred embodiment of the invention, which the inventor has in fact conceived.[1105]

The best mode analysis involves two inquiries, one subjective and the other objective: the first inquiry is whether the inventor subjectively contemplated and disclosed the best mode of practicing the claimed invention at the time of filing; and the second inquiry is whether, objectively, the specification adequately discloses the best mode such that a person of ordinary skill in the art could practice it.[1106]

Because "Congress ... specifically limited the best mode requirement to that contemplated by the inventor," the best mode requirement is based upon the inventor's knowledge at the time that the patent application is filed.[1107] Consequently, the Federal Circuit has held that there is no best mode violation even though the specification did not disclose a superior process that was known by the patentee's employees, but unknown to the actual inventor of the patented process.[1108] Because only the inventor's knowledge is relevant for a best mode violation, it is improper to impute a third party's knowledge of a preferred embodiment onto the inventor.[1109] In addition, there is no duty to update the best mode disclosure after the application is filed, unless the applicant introduces new matter, in which case he or she would have to file a continuation-in-part application.[1110]

Even when an inventor discloses the best mode, a § 112 violation will occur if the disclosure is so objectively inadequate that it effectively conceals the best mode from the public.[1111] That is, the "quality of an applicant's best mode disclosure is so poor" that those skilled in the art could not practice it.[1112]

> Enablement looks to placing the subject matter of the claims generally in the possession of the public .... Best mode looks to whether specific instrumentalities and techniques have been developed by the inventor and known to him at the time of filing as the best way of carrying out the invention ... The enablement requirement, thus, looks to the objective knowledge of one of ordinary skill in the art, while the best mode inquiry is a subjective, factual one, looking to the state of the mind of the inventor.
>
> *Glaxo Inc. v. Novopharm Ltd.*, 52 F.3d 1043, 1050 (Fed. Cir. 1995).

1104. *Bayer AG v. Schein Pharms.* 301 F.3d 1306 (Fed. Cir. 2002).
1105. *See Chemcast Corp. v. Arco Indus. Corp.*, 913 F.2d 923, 926 (Fed. Cir. 1990); *Spectra-Physics, Inc. v. Coherent, Inc.*, 827 F.2d 1524, 1532 (Fed. Cir. 1987); *Dana Corp. v. IPC Ltd. P'ship*, 860 F.2d 415, 419 (Fed. Cir. 1988).
1106. *See Great Northern Corp. v. Henry Molded Prods., Inc.*, 94 F.3d 1569, 1571 (Fed. Cir. 1996); *United States Gypsum Co. v. National Gypsum Co.*, 74 F.3d 1209, 1212 (Fed. Cir. 1996); *Transco Prods., Inc. v. Performance Contracting, Inc.*, 38 F.3d 551, 560 (Fed. Cir. 1994).
1107. *Glaxo*, 52 F.3d at 1052.
1108. *Id.*
1109. *Id.*
1110. *See Transco*, 38 F.3d at 557–59.
1111. *See U.S. Gypsum Co.*, 74 F.3d at 1215; *Transco Prods.*, 38 F.3d at 560.
1112. *U.S. Gypsum*, 74 F.3d at 1215.

Notwithstanding the best mode disclosure requirement, an inventor is not required to disclose "commercial considerations" or "production details" like particular materials, sources of materials, manufacturing methods, or specific techniques if the information is readily known in the art. For example, in *Wahl Instruments, Inc. v. Acvious, Inc.*,[1113] Acvious defended an infringement suit on the ground that Wahl's patent failed to disclose "manufacturing techniques[,] materials and sources of supply for materials used in [the invention]."[1114] The district court ruled that the claims were invalid for failure to disclose the best mode; however, the Federal Circuit reversed, holding that "there is no mechanical rule that a best mode violation occurs because the inventor failed to disclose particular manufacturing techniques beyond that information sufficient for enablement."[1115]

In addition to inquiring into the inventor's beliefs, the scope of an invention, and the skill in the art, one must consider whether any missing information would be readily known by those skilled in the art.[1116] If it is known, then there is no best mode violation.

At the patent examination stage, the applicant is assumed to have complied with the best mode requirement. Although a patent examiner may reject an application for failure to disclose the best mode, it is rarely done. Failure to disclose the best mode has been frequently asserted to challenge patent validity, but this changed on September 16, 2011, when the AIA was signed into law. For proceedings commenced on or after that date, "the failure to disclose the best mode shall not be a basis on which any claim of a patent may be canceled or held invalid or otherwise unenforceable."[1117]

III Written Description

The first paragraph of § 112 requires that the specification contains a "written description of the invention ...."[1118] Unlike the enablement requirement, which demands that an inventor discloses how to make and use an invention, the purpose of the written description requirement is to convey with reasonable clarity to those skilled in the art that an inventor was in possession of the claimed subject matter when the

1113. 950 F.2d 1575 (Fed. Cir. 1991).
1114. *Id.*, at 1580.
1115. As stated by the Federal Circuit:

> [A] requirement for routine details to be disclosed because they were selected as the "best" for manufacturing or fabrication would lay a trap for patentees whenever a device has been made prior to filing for the patent. The inventor would merely have to be interrogated with increasing specificity as to steps or material selected as "best" to make the device. A fortiori, he could hardly say the choice is not what he thought was "best" in some way. Thus, at the point he would testify respecting a step or material or source or detail which is not in the patent, a failure to disclose the best mode would, ipso facto, be established.
>
> *Id.*

1116. *Id.*
1117. 35 U.S.C. § 282(b)(3)(A).
1118. 35 U.S.C. § 112 ¶1.

patent application was filed.[1119] To comply with the written description requirement, the specification must clearly allow persons of ordinary skill in the art to recognize that the inventor invented what is claimed. Yet, in *Ariad Pharmaceuticals, Inc. v. Eli Lilly*,[1120] the Federal Circuit recognized that the term possession "has never been very enlightening"[1121] because "[i]t implies that as long as one can produce records documenting a written description of a claimed invention, one can show possession."[1122] The court expressly anchored the written description requirement within the "four corners of the specification," and held that compliance is based on whether the specification conveys to a person of ordinary skill in the art "that the inventor actually invented the invention claimed."[1123] Under proper circumstances, drawings alone may provide an adequate written description.[1124]

But simply describing a large body of information is not sufficient to satisfy the written description requirement as to a particular subset of information contained therein.[1125] To use a metaphor set out in In re Ruschig:

> It is an old custom in the woods to mark trails by placing blaze marks on the trees. It is no help in finding a trail ... to be confronted simply by a large number of unmarked trees .... We are looking for blaze marks which single out particular trees.[1126]

Following this reasoning, the Federal Circuit, in *Fujikawa v. Wattanasin*,[1127] held that describing a large genus of compounds is not sufficient to satisfy the written description requirement as to a particular species of subgenus; a blanket disclosure does not reveal that the inventor knew the value of an exact subset of information.[1128] Another example is where the patent applicant discloses a numerical range of 30%–70% of a compound X, but claims, as the invention, a specific numerical value within that range (e.g., 37.5%). A court is likely to hold that the written description requirement is not satisfied as to that claim.[1129]

IV Definiteness Requirement

Section 112 requires the patentee to "particularly point[] out and distinctly claim[]" the invention. The purpose of the definiteness requirement is to put the public, namely

1119. *See Vas-Cath, Inc. v. Mahurkar*, 935 F.2d 1555, 1560 (Fed. Cir. 1991).
1120. 598 F.3d 1336 (Fed. Cir. 2010).
1121. *Id.*, at 1351.
1122. *Id.*
1123. 598 F.3d 1336, 1343 (Fed. Cir. 2010).
1124. *See Vas-Cath*, 935 F.2d at 1563.
1125. *See Fujikawa v. Wattanasin*, 93 F.3d 1559, 1570 (Fed. Cir. 1996).
1126. 379 F.2d 990, 994–95 (C.C.P.A. 1967).
1127. 93 F.3d 1559 (Fed. Cir. 1996).
1128. *Id.*, at 1570 ("[S]imply describing a large genus of compounds is not sufficient to satisfy the written description requirement as to particular species or sub-genuses.").
1129. *See id.* ("Specific claims to single compounds require reasonably specific supporting disclosure and while ... naming [each species] is not essential, something more than the disclosure of a class of 1000, or 100, or even 48 compounds is required." (quoting *Ruschig*, 379 F.2d at 994)).

competitors, and the PTO on notice of what exactly is being claimed by the patentee.[1130] An assertion of indefiniteness requires an analysis of whether persons skilled in the art would understand the metes and bounds of the claim when read in light of the specification. A claim is indefinite if its legal scope is not clear enough that a person of ordinary skill in the art could determine whether a particular product or method infringes or not. The definiteness requirement entails a delicate balance which takes into account the inherent limitations of language while also ensuring that the language is precise enough to give clear notice of what is claimed, thereby allowing the public to elucidate what is still open to them. The Supreme Court announced the test for definiteness in *Nautilis, Inc. v. Biosig Instruments, Inc.*:

> [We read §112(b)] to require that a patent's claims, viewed in light of the specification and prosecution history, inform those skilled in the art about the scope of the invention with reasonable certainty. The definiteness requirement, so understood, mandates clarity, while recognizing that absolute precision is unattainable. The standard we adopt accords with opinions of this Court stating that "the certainty which the law requires in patents is not greater than is reasonable, having regard to their subject-matter."[1131]

In a situation where claim language is subject to two plausible interpretations, one narrower than the other, but both supported by the specification, the Federal Circuit will adopt the narrower interpretation rather than invalidating the claim.[1132]

§2 NOVELTY AND LOSS OF RIGHT

I Requirements for Anticipatory Prior Art

A basic requirement of American patent law is that an invention, to be patentable, must be novel. It makes no sense to grant someone a patent on an invention that already exists and is available to the public. The novelty requirement, as it is appropriately known, is embodied in subsections (a), (e), and (g) of 35 U.S.C. § 102. If an invention is not new, it is said to be anticipated by the prior art. The term "prior art" refers to preexisting knowledge and technology already available to the public.[1133] For example, if an inventor claims an apparatus comprising elements A, B, and C and a certain relationship among these three elements, and the prior art discloses explicitly or inherently the same apparatus comprising the same elements in the same relationship, the invention is said to be anticipated by the prior art.

To qualify as novelty-defeating prior art, a reference must satisfy three conditions. First, it must predate the applicant's invention or have existed more than one year before the applicant's filing date. Second, the strict identity requirement mandates

1130. *All Dental Prox LLC v. Advantage Dental Prods.*, 309 F.3d 774, 770–80 (Fed. Cir. 2002).
1131. 134 S. Ct. 2120, 2129 (2014).
1132. *Athletic Alternatives, Inc. v. Prince Mfg., Inc.*, 73 F.3d 1573 (Fed. Cir. 1996).
1133. *Kimberly-Clark Corp. v. Johnson & Johnson*, 745 F.2d 1437, 1453 (Fed. Cir. 1984) (citing *Graham v. John Deere*, 383 U.S. 1, 6 (1966)); 35 U.S.C. § 102 (2006) (defining the documents and activities that can serve as prior art).

that each and every element of the claimed invention be identically disclosed, either expressly or inherently, within the four corners of a single prior art reference. Third, the prior art reference must be enabling.

A *Date of Invention: Relevant for Pre-AIA Disclosures (Patent Applications Filed Before March 16, 2013)*

For a prior art reference to anticipate an invention, it must have existed prior to the patent applicant's date of invention (thus, the name prior art). Therefore, it is important to understand how one establishes the date of invention. In the US, the date of invention is the date when the inventor reduces the invention to practice.[1134] There are two types of RTP: (1) actual RTP; and (2) constructive RTP. The latter occurs when a patent application is filed, regardless of whether anything is actually built as long as the applicant satisfies the disclosure requirements of § 112. Actual RTP occurs when the invention is shown to be suitable for its intended purpose.[1135]

Alternatively, a "person 'who conceives, and, in a mental sense, first invents ... may date his patentable invention back to the time of its conception, if he connects the conception with its reduction to practice by reasonable diligence on his part, so that they are substantially one continuous act'."[1136] In short, "priority of invention 'goes to the first party to reduce an invention to practice unless the other party can show that it was the first to conceive the invention and that it exercised reasonable diligence in later reducing that invention to practice'."[1137] Conception occurs when the inventor has "a definite and permanent idea of the complete and operative invention, as it is thereafter applied in practice."[1138] Corroboration is required when the inventor seeks to establish conception through oral testimony rather than physical exhibits.[1139] Without

---

1134. *See Mahurkar v. C.R. Bard, Inc.*, 79 F.3d 1572, 1577–78 (Fed. Cir. 1996).

1135. *See id.* ("Depending on the character of the invention and the problem it solves, this showing may require test results. Less complicated inventions and problems do not demand stringent testing. In fact, some invention are so simple and their purpose and efficacy so obvious that their complete construction is sufficient to demonstrate workability."); *see also Estee Lauder Inc. v. L'Oreal S.A.*, 129 F.3d 588, 593 (Fed. Cir. 1997).

1136. *Mahurkar*, 79 F.3d at 1577. Diligence only comes into play when a party is the first to conceive, but the second to reduce to practice. The patent law favors prompt public disclosure, and therefore wants to know what this party was doing given the fact that another was the second to conceive, but the first to reduce practice. Thus, the party who was the first to conceive must show "reasonably continuous activity" from just prior to the other party's date of conception to the reduction to practice date of the party who was the first to conceive. *Burns v. Curtis*, 172 F.2d 588, 591 (C.C.P.A. 1964).

1137. *Mahurkar*, 79 F.3d at 1577.

1138. *Id.* ("The idea must be 'so clearly defined in the inventor's mind that only ordinary skill would be necessary to reduce the invention to practice, without extensive research or experimentation'." (quoting *Burroughs Wellcome Co. v. Barr Labs., Inc.*, 40 F.3d 1223, 1228 (Fed. Cir. 1994))).

1139. *Id.* (The courts assess corroboration of oral testimony with a rule of reason analysis, which evaluates "all pertinent evidence must be made so that a sound determination of the credibility of the inventor's story may be reached." (quoting *Price v. Symsek*, 988 F.2d 1187, 1195 (Fed. Cir. 1993))).

evidence of conception or actual RTP, the filing date (i.e., constructive RTP) acts as the date of invention.[1140]

B Strict Identity

To serve as anticipatory prior art, there must be identity of invention.[1141] The rule is that "[a]nticipation is established only when a single prior art reference discloses, expressly or under principles of inherency, each and every element of a claimed invention."[1142] In other words, every element of the claimed invention[1143] must be identically disclosed or described within the four corners of the prior art reference.[1144] This is referred to as the "strict identity" requirement.[1145] So, for example, if an applicant seeks to claim a paper clip made with titanium and nickel, the reference must also disclose a paper clip made with titanium and nickel.[1146]

Anticipation can be proven inherently. Under the doctrine of inherency, "[i]f an inventor seeks to claim an advantage or modification that flows necessarily from a prior art reference, the reference inherently anticipates the inventor's claim."[1147] The inherent feature must occur with certainty, and may not be established by probabilities or possibilities.[1148] Furthermore, the inherent feature does not need to be recognized at the time of the invention, but only that the subject matter is in fact inherent in the prior art reference.[1149] Under § 102, the strict identity rule proscribes the use of multiple references to furnish claim elements.[1150] In other words, for a prior art reference to anticipate an invention, "all the claimed elements must be found in exactly the same

1140. *See Hybritech Inc. v. Monoclonal Antibodies, Inc.*, 802 F.2d 1367, 1374 (Fed. Cir. 1986).
1141. *See Minnesota Mining & Mfg. Co. v. Johnson and Johnson*, 976 F.2d 1559, 1565 (Fed. Cir. 1992).
1142. *RCA Corp. v. Applied Digital Data Systems, Inc.*, 730 F.2d 1440, 1444 (Fed. Cir. 1984); *see also Scripps Clinic & Research Foundation v. Genetech, Inc.*, 927 F.2d 1565, 1576 (Fed. Cir. 1991) ("There must be no difference between the claimed invention and the reference as viewed by a person of ordinary skill in the field of the invention").
1143. A patent claim must define "the subject matter which the applicant regards as his invention." 35 U.S.C. § 112, ¶ 2. A claim element further limits the breadth of the claim. 1 Donald S. Chisum, Chisum on Patents, at Gl-3 (2011).
1144. *In re* Skvorecz, 580 F.3d 1262, 1266 (Fed. Cir. 2009); *Richardson v. Suzuki Motor Co.*, 868 F.2d 1226, 1236 (Fed. Cir. 1989) ("The identical invention must be shown in as complete detail as is contained in the patent claim."); *see also Structural Rubber Prods. Co. v. Park Rubber Co.*, 749 F.2d 707, 716 (Fed. Cir. 1984) (explaining that another reference or knowledge in the art cannot supply missing elements).
1145. *Trintec Indus., Inc. v. Top-U.S.A. Corp.*, 295 F.3d 1292, 1296 (Fed. Cir. 2002) (noting the "strict identity" test for novelty); *see also Jamesbury Corp. v. Litton Indus. Prods., Inc.*, 756 F.2d 1556, 1560 (Fed. Cir. 1985) (explaining that "a prior art disclosure which is only 'substantially the same' as the claimed invention" is insufficient to defeat novelty).
1146. In this hypothetical, titanium and nickel are claim elements.
1147. *Glaxo, Inc. v. Novopharm Ltd.*, 830 F. Supp. 871, 874 (E.D.N.C. 1993), *aff'd*, 52 F.3d 1043 (Fed. Cir. 1995); *see also In re* Paulsen, 30 F.3d 1475, 1479–80 (Fed. Cir. 1994).
1148. *Continental Can Company USA Inc. v. Monsanto Company*, 948 F.2d 1264 at 1269 (Fed. Cir. 1991).
1149. *Schering Corp. v. Geneva Pharm. Inc.*, 339 F.3d 1373, 1377 (Fed. Cir. 2003).
1150. Multiple references, however, may be used in a § 103 nonobviousness determination. *See infra* §4.

situation and united in the same way to perform the identical function" in a single piece of prior art.[1151] However, courts have held that the rule is not violated when the decision-maker uses additional references to clarify, interpret, or explain the asserted prior art's teachings;[1152] or, as discussed below, to show that the prior art was sufficiently enabling.[1153]

C Anticipatory Enablement

Novelty-defeating prior art must be enabling.[1154] This means that the reference must disclose the subject matter in sufficient detail to enable a person having ordinary skill in the art to make the invention without undue experimentation[1155] (the latter being a fact-intensive inquiry which depends on interrelated technical issues such as the presence or absence or working examples in the reference, the skilled artisan's knowledge at the time of the reference, and the nature of the technology).[1156]

Although similar to § 112 enablement,[1157] anticipatory enablement is a narrower doctrine.[1158] A prior art reference need not demonstrate utility in order to anticipate.[1159] Also, an anticipatory reference need only enable what falls precisely within the scope of the claim-at-issue and nothing more.[1160] By comparison, an enabling description for patent-supporting purposes must enable the full scope of the claimed subject matter. These differing standards reveal a curious asymmetry: a description that is sufficient to anticipate a claim for patent-defeating purposes might be insufficient to enable a claim for patent-supporting purposes.[1161]

1151. *Studiengesellschaft Kohle, m.b.H. v. Dart Indus., Inc.*, 762 F.2d 724, 726 (Fed. Cir. 1984).
1152. *Scripps Clinic & Research Foundation v. Genetech, Inc.*, 927 F.2d 1565, 1576 (Fed. Cir. 1991) ("It is sometimes appropriate to consider extrinsic evidence to explain the disclosure of a reference."); *see also In re* Baxter Travenol Labs., 952 F.2d 388, 390 (Fed. Cir. 1991) ("[E]xtrinsic evidence may be considered when it is used to explain, but not expand, the meaning of a reference.").
1153. *In re* Samour, 571 F.2d 559 (C.C.P.A. 1978); *see also Cont'l Can Co. v. Monsanto Co.*, 948 F.2d 1264, 1269 (Fed. Cir. 1991) (discussing the "modest flexibility" in the single-reference rule that allows a secondary reference to accommodate situations in which the skilled artisan's knowledge cannot be gleaned from the primary reference).
1154. *Amgen Inc. v. Hoechst Marion Roussel, Inc.*, 457 F.3d 1293, 1306 (Fed. Cir. 2006) ("In order to anticipate, a prior art reference must not only disclose all of the limitations of the claimed invention, but also be enabled.").
1155. *Impax Labs., Inc. v. Aventis Pharm., Inc.*, 545 F.3d 1312, 1314 (Fed. Cir. 2008).
1156. *See id.*, at 1314–15 (discussing the factors set forth in *In re* Wands, 858 F.2d 731, 737 (Fed. Cir. 1988)).
1157. *See supra* Ch. 2, §1.I.
1158. *Verizon Servs. Corp. v. Cox Fibernet Va., Inc.*, 602 F.3d 1325, 1337 (Fed. Cir. 2010) ("The standard for what constitutes proper enablement of a prior art reference for purposes of anticipation under §102 ... differs from the enablement standard under §112." (quoting *Rasmusson v. SmithKline Beecham Corp.*, 413 F.3d 1318, 1325 (Fed. Cir. 2005))).
1159. *In re* Gleave, 560 F.3d 1331, 1335 (Fed. Cir. 2009) (citing *Rasmusson*, 413 F.3d at 1326).
1160. *Schering Corp. v. Geneva Pharm., Inc.*, 339 F.3d 1373, 1381 (Fed. Cir. 2003).
1161. *See Vas-Cath Inc. v. Mahurkar*, 935 F.2d 1555, 1562 (Fed. Cir. 1991) (recognizing the distinction); *In re* Lukach, 442 F.2d 967, 970 (C.C.P.A. 1971) (same).

II Section 102(a) Prior Art

Section 102(a) of the patent code states that a person is entitled to a patent unless "the invention was known or used by others in [the United States], or patented or described in a printed publication in [the United States] or a foreign country, before the invention thereof by the applicant …."[1162] Subsection (a) entails three significant limitations. A patent will not issue if someone other than the applicant:

(1) knew of or used the invention in the US before the applicant's date of invention;
(2) patented the invention in the US or a foreign country before the applicant's date of invention; or
(3) described the invention in a printed publication before the applicant's date of invention.[1163]

While at first glance these limitations seem fairly straightforward, a closer inspection reveals several underlying questions: how precisely does a reference need to coincide with the claimed invention to qualify as anticipatory prior art? Under what conditions is an invention known or used? What considerations determine the foreign equivalent to a patent? What constitutes a printed publication? To answer these questions, one must turn to common law principles.

A *"Known or Used by Others"*

As stated above, a patent applicant is entitled to a patent under § 102(a) unless the invention was "known or used by others" (i.e., by someone other than the inventor).[1164]

Courts have interpreted the "known or used" clause as publicly known or used; that is, knowledge or use will not anticipate a claimed invention unless such knowledge or use is publicly accessible.[1165] One reason for this interpretation may be the public policy favoring the person who is the first to disclose the invention to the public,

1162. 35 U.S.C. § 102(a).
1163. The "date of invention" is used for pre-AIA applications (patent applications filed before Mar. 16, 2013). For post-AIA applications (patent applications filed on or after Mar. 16, 2013), the relevant date is the "effective filing date" of the invention. *See infra* §2.I.A.
1164. As explained by Justice Story:

> What then is the true meaning of the words "known or used before the application"? They cannot mean that the thing invented was not known or used before the application by the inventor himself, for that would prohibit him from the only means to obtain a patent … These words, then, to have any rational interpretation, must mean, "not known or used by others before the application." In other words, to put it somewhat awkwardly, an inventor cannot invent before he or she invents.
>
> *Pennock v. Dialogue*, 27 U.S. (2 Pet.) 1, 18 (1829).

1165. *Gayler v. Wilder*, 51 U.S. (10 How.) 477, 498 (1850).

even though someone else may have made the discovery earlier. Public disclosure is a firmly embedded policy underlying our patent system.[1166]

Under this view, a previously invented, but unknown invention should not act as an anticipatory reference against one who was the first to disclose the invention to the public.

However, there is no requirement that a prior inventor makes an effort to publicize an invention. Even if an invention is hidden from view, if it is used in the usual course of business without efforts to conceal it, the use qualifies as public.[1167]

B *"Printed Publication"*

A patent will not issue if the patent applicant's invention was, prior to the date of invention, described in a "printed publication." The term "printed publication,"[1168] in the light of data storage and retrieval technologies, has been interpreted to mean any reference that is "sufficiently accessible to the public interested in the art";[1169] indeed, there is no requirement that a person of ordinary skill in the art actually obtains the

---

1166. According to the Supreme Court:

> But if the [prior] discovery is not patented, nor described in any printed publication, it might be known or used in remote places for ages, and the people of this country be unable to profit by it. The means of obtaining knowledge would not be within their reach; and as their interest is concerned, it would be the same thing as if the improvement had never been discovered. It is the inventor here that brings [the invention] to [the public], and places it in their possession.
>
> *Id.* at 497.

1167. *See Rosaire v. Baroid Sales Division*, 218 F.2d 72, 74 (5th Cir. 1955) (explaining that § 102(a) does not "require some affirmative act to bring the work to the attention to the public at large"); *W.L. Gore & Assoc., Inc. v. Garlock, Inc.*, 721 F.2d 1540, 1562 (Fed. Cir. 1983) ("The non-secret use of a claimed process in the usual course of producing articles for commercial purposes is a public use."); *Egbert v. Lippmann*, 104 U.S. 333, 337 (1881) ("public use" found where the invention was corset steels which were hidden from public view by the clothing worn over the corset).

1168. In 1836, when the term "printed" first appeared in § 102(a), actual printing was the only known means for disseminating or making information available. Today, however, there are obviously other means available. As the Court of Customs and Patent Appeals eventually stated:

> The traditional dichotomy between "printing" and "publication" is no longer valid. Given the state of technology in document duplication, data storage, and data-retrieval systems, the "probability of dissemination" of an item very often has little to do with whether or not it is printed in the same sense of the word when it was introduced into the patent statute in 1836.
>
> *In re* Wyer, 655 F.2d 221, 226 (C.C.P.A. 1981).

1169. *Constant v. Advanced Micro-Devices, Inc.*, 848 F.2d 1560, 1568 (Fed. Cir. 1988); *see also In re* Hall, 781 F.2d 897, 899 (Fed. Cir. 1986) ("'public accessibility' has been called touchstone in determining whether a reference constitutes a 'printed publication'").

reference.[1170] To be a printed publication, a source must be cataloged or indexed in a library, or other places reasonably accessible, such that the material would be accessible with a reasonably diligent search.[1171] Likewise, a publication cannot become prior art before the public has access to it. Thus, the reference becomes prior art on the date it becomes accessible to the relevant public (e.g., indexed, cataloged, or published).[1172]

C *Geographical Limitations (Pre-AIA)*

Section 102(a) reads that an invention will be anticipated if it was "known or used in this country."[1173] However, foreign patents and foreign printed publications may act as prior art. Why is knowledge and use limited to the US? This geographic distinction did not make its way into US patent law until 1836, but the Senate Report accompanying the 1836 Act offers little, if any, explanation.

Common sense tells us that unpublished knowledge and use are less difficult for a US inventor to discover in the US as opposed to Europe or Japan. How does one search for unpublished knowledge in foreign lands without incurring a great deal of expense (i.e., search costs). It is difficult enough to obtain such knowledge in the US, let alone a foreign country. At least with many foreign publications and most foreign patents, there exist databases that one can search relatively cheaply today. The Supreme Court has addressed the geographic distinction issue:

> If the foreign invention had been printed or patented, it was already given to the world and open to the people of this country, as well as of others, upon reasonable inquiry. They would therefore derive no advantage from the invention here. It would confer no benefit upon the community, and the inventor therefore is not considered to be entitled to the reward. But if the foreign discovery is not patented, nor described in any printed publication, it might be known and used in remote places for ages, and the people of this country be unable to profit by it. The means of obtaining knowledge would not be within their reach; and, as far as their interest is concerned, it would be the same thing as if the improvement had never been discovered.[1174]

1170. *See Constant*, 848 F.2d at 1568 ("[D]issemination and public accessibility are the keys to the legal determination whether a prior art reference was published … If accessibility is proved, there is no requirement to show that particular members of the public actually received the information").
1171. *See In re* Cronyn, 890 F.2d 1158, 1161 (Fed. Cir. 1989); *In re* Klopfenstein, 380 F.3d 1345, 1352 (Fed. Cir. 2004) (finding printed publication for slide show when confidentiality agreements were not secured).
1172. *See In re* Bayer, 568 F.2d 1357, 1361 (C.C.P.A. 1978) ("The date on which the public actually gained access to the invention by means of the publication is the focus of the inquiry.").
1173. Under AIA 35 U.S.C. § 102(a)(1), there is no geographic limitation on where prior public use, public availability, sale or offer for sale may occur. Furthermore, a public use would need to occur before the effective filing date of the claimed invention to constitute prior art under the AIA 35 U.S.C. § 102(a)(1). *See also* MPEP 2152.02. *See also infra* §2.VIII.B.
1174. *Gayler*, 51 U.S. at 497.

III Section 102(e) Prior Art

Under § 102(e), prior art may assume two forms. First, the AIPA of 1999 amended the patent code to require, with certain exceptions, patent applications filed on or after November 29, 2000, to be published "promptly after the expiration of a period of eighteen months from the earliest filed date."[1175] As such, § 102(e)(1) was added to permit published applications to serve as prior art. This subsection reads:

> A person shall be entitled to a patent unless:
>
> > (e)(1) an application for patent, published under Section 122(b), by another filed in the United States before the invention by the applicant for patent, except that an international application filed under the treaty defined in Section 351(a) [Patent Cooperation Treaty] shall have the effect under this subsection of a national application published under Section 122(b) only if the international application designating the United States was published under Article 21(2)(a) of such treaty in the English language.

Under § 102(e)(1), once a US patent application is published in the US, its prior art effect is triggered, and its effective date reverts to its date of filing.

Of perhaps greater significance, however, is that an international patent application filed pursuant to the Patent Cooperation Treaty (PCT) that designates the US and is ultimately published in English will have prior art effect under § 102(e)(1) as of its international filing date, which is the date the PCT application is filed. The international filing date is no more than twelve months from the priority date (i.e., the date of first filing in a PCT member country). Under Article 21(2)(a) of the PCT, a PCT application is published eighteen months after its priority date. Note that a PCT application, which satisfies the English language and designation requirements, can serve as a prior art reference as of its international filing date, even though an application is never subsequently filed in the US.[1176]

The second form of § 102(e) prior art falls under § 102(e)(2). Under this section, international (or PCT) applications have no prior art effect, but US patent applications are certainly eligible. A US patent application that is not subject to publication (e.g., the applicant certifies that he or she is not filing in a foreign country) is kept in confidence by the PTO under § 122(a). As a result, pending patent applications are not "known" (i.e., "publicly accessible" in the § 102(a) sense); yet, such applications can serve as prior art references as of their filing date under § 102(e)(2) if the application eventually issues as a patent. Why? According to Justice Holmes in *Alexander Milburn Co. v. Davis-Bournonville Co.*,[1177] "delays in the Patent Office ought not to cut down the effect of what has been done."[1178] That is, but for the administrative delays present within the PTO in examining and ultimately issuing the patent, the basic fact is that someone other than the inventor previously disclosed the inventor's claimed invention.

1175. 35 U.S.C. § 122(b) (under 37 C.F.R. § 1.219, an applicant can have his or her application published earlier than 18 months from the earliest filing date).
1176. *See* 35 U.S.C. § 374.
1177. 270 U.S. 390 (1926).
1178. *Id.*, at 401.

Accordingly, information which is not known and is unknowable may act as anticipatory prior art so long as the patent does issue. The fact that the patent must issue before it can be used as prior art indicates that § 102(e)(2) does have a publicity requirement, but it simply comes later in the game, acting as a condition precedent.

Three points should be made with respect to § 102(e) prior art. First, documents are prior art only for what they disclose, not what they claim. If a previously filed patent application claims the same subject matter as a later filed application, § 102(g)(1) would be applicable because now the issue is who invented first or who has priority of invention.[1179] Second, a US application which publishes is available as § 102(e) prior art even if the application is abandoned after publication. Third and relatedly, a PCT application which publishes in English and designates the US is available as § 102(e) prior art, even if the application is abandoned after publication and/or the applicant chooses not to file an application in the US.

A *The Hilmer Doctrine*

For those US patent applications filed before March 16, 2013, another source of § 102(e) prior art to consider are US patents or published patent applications which claim priority to an application filed abroad under the Paris Convention.[1180] In what is known as the Hilmer rule,[1181] the § 102(e) date is the US filing date, not the date of the earlier-filed foreign application.[1182] The Hilmer rule states that a US patent or US patent application § 102(e) date (pre-AIA) is its US filing date, and not any earlier foreign priority date. The Hilmer rule requires applicants to distinguish between patent-obtaining (shield) and patent-defeating (sword) uses of foreign priority under 35 U.S.C. § 119(a). Under the Hilmer rule, only patent-obtaining (shield) uses of foreign priority are allowed, while patent-defeating uses are not permitted.

An example of the Hilmer rule is as follows: (1) X files a Swiss patent application on January 24, 1957; (2) Y files a German patent application on July 31, 1958; (3) X files a US patent application on January 23, 1958; and (4) Y files a US patent application on July 25, 1958. Y can overcome X's earlier US filing date by claiming priority to the German priority date via 35 U.S.C. § 119(a). This is because Y is using the German application as a shield (patent-obtaining use) to obtain his patent. X may try to argue that the Swiss application should count as prior art because the Swiss application was filed before the German application. However, under the Hilmer rule, the Swiss application cannot be used as a sword to defeat X's US patent filing. Accordingly, under the Hilmer rule, foreign priority can be used as a shield to obtain a patent, but foreign priority cannot be used as a sword for patent-defeating uses.

1179. *See infra* §2.VI.
1180. *See infra* Ch. 3, §2.II.H.
1181. *See In re* Hilmer, 359 F.2d 859 (C.C.P.A. 1966).
1182. *Id.*, at 862; *accord In re* Giacomini, 612 F.3d 1380, 1384–85 (Fed. Cir. 2010) (reaffirming rule).

The AIA repealed the Hilmer rule, so those US applications filed on or after March 16, 2013, can use foreign priority as a shield to obtain a patent and a sword for patent-defeating uses.[1183]

IV Section 102(g)(2) Prior Art (Pre-AIA)

For those applications filed before March 16, 2013, section 102(g) serves dual purposes.[1184] First, § 102(g)(2) is the basis for what is known as a priority dispute or "interference."[1185] When an application is made for a patent claiming the same subject matter as another application or an issued patent, the PTO can declare an interference.[1186] An interference is a procedural mechanism to determine who is the first inventor (i.e., who has priority of invention).[1187] Second, § 102(g)(2) provides statutory grounds for "secret" prior art that may have a patent-defeating effect.[1188] This section allows for patent-defeating inventive activity that is not subject to an interference, but the inventive activity must be "in this country" (i.e., the US). For example, imagine that Smith, instead of filing a patent application, practices his invention, that he made in the United States, as a trade secret. A third party can use Smith's trade secret as a prior art reference against Mary's claimed invention if Smith invented Mary's claimed invention before she did.

Although it may look like § 102(g) incorporates § 102(a) prior art, one basic distinction is that § 102(a) does not require continued use like § 102(g); that is, under § 102(g), the prior invention must not be abandoned, suppressed, or concealed. Some factors that the court may consider include "[t]he failure to file a patent application, to describe the invention in a published document, or to use the invention publicly, within a reasonable time after first making the invention."[1189]

V Derivation: Section 102(f) (Pre-AIA)

Section 102(f) of Title 35 is known as the "derivation" provision. It provides that a person is entitled to a patent unless "he did not himself invent the subject matter sought to be patented." In other words, the named inventor derived the claimed subject matter from a third party and is, therefore, not the original inventor.

1183. 35 U.S.C. § 102(d)(2).
1184. Generally § 102(g) is no longer prior art under the AIA.
1185. *See* 35 U.S.C. § 135.
1186. *See id.*
1187. Under the first-to-invent system, when two parties claimed the same invention, a PTO tribunal known as the Board of Patent Appeals and Interferences institutes an "interference" proceeding to determine priority (i.e., which party is entitled to a patent). The party that reduced the invention to practice usually wins; however, a party that was "first to conceive the invention but last to reduce it to practice" (either actively or constructively) will win if that party "demonstrates reasonable diligence [toward] reduction to practice." *Cooper v. Goldfarb*, 240 F.3d 1378, 1382 (Fed. Cir. 2001) (citing 35 U.S.C. § 102(g)).
1188. *Thomson, S.A. v. Quixote Corp.*, 166 F.3d 1172, 1175 (Fed. Cir. 1999).
1189. *Dow Chemical Co. v. Astro-Valcour, Inc.*, 267 F.3d 1334, 1342 (Fed. Cir. 2001).

To show derivation, the party asserting invalidity must prove: (1) prior conception of the invention by another; and (2) communication of that conception to the patentee such that the communication enabled one of ordinary skill in the art to make the patented invention.[1190] It is important to note that § 102(f) applies to derivation that occurs in the US or in a foreign country.

The AIA repeals § 102(f) and implements a new procedure (derivation proceedings) for stolen inventions or patent applications filed by those who did not invent the subject matter disclosed in the application.[1191]

VI Priority (Pre-AIA)

Priority of invention is based on a first-to-invent system and thus applies to applications filed before the implementation of the AIA (applications filed before March 16, 2013). It allows a party who is second to file to nevertheless be awarded the patent if he or she can prove that he or she was the first-to-invent. As previously discussed, the procedure by which priority (who invented first) is determined is called an interference.[1192]

As a general rule, priority is awarded to the inventor who first reduced the invention to practice. However, there are two exceptions to this rule: (1) an inventor who was the first to conceive the invention but the last to reduce it to practice will be awarded priority if he or she can show that he or she exercised reasonable diligence in reducing to practice from a time just prior to when the first person who reduced to practice conceived the invention; and (2) the second inventor will be awarded priority if the first inventor abandoned, suppressed, or concealed the invention (after reducing it to practice). As the Federal Circuit has stated, the person "who first conceives, and, in a mental sense, first invents ... may date his patentable invention back to the time of its conception, if he connects the conception with its reduction to practice by reasonable diligence on his part, so that they are substantially one continuous act."[1193]

A *Conception*

In the 1897 case of *Mergenthaler v. Scudder*,[1194] the Court of Appeals for District of Columbia laid down a definition for conception that has been adopted by the Federal Circuit:

> The conception of the invention consists in the complete performance of the mental part of the inventive act. All that remains to be accomplished in order to perfect the act or instrument belongs to the department of construction, not invention. It is, therefore, the formation in the mind of the inventor of a definite and permanent idea of the complete and operative invention as it is thereafter to be

1190. *See Gambro Lundia AB v. Baxter Healthcare Corp.*, 110 F.3d 1573, 1576 (Fed. Cir. 1997).
1191. *See* America Invents Act § 3; *infra* Ch. 3, §2.II.J.
1192. *See supra* IV.
1193. *Mahurkar v. C.R. Bard, Inc.*, 79 F.3d 1572, 1577 (Fed. Cir. 1996).
1194. 1897 C.D. 724 (1897).

> applied in practice that constitutes an available conception within the meaning of the patent law.[1195]

Similarly, the Federal Circuit has stated:

> To have conceived of an invention, an inventor must have formed in his or her mind "a definite and permanent idea of the complete and operative invention, as it is hereafter to be applied in practice." The idea must be "so clearly defined in the inventor's mind that only ordinary skill would be necessary to reduce the invention to practice, without extensive research or experimentation."[1196]

Subsequently, in *Amgen, Inc. v. Chugai Pharmaceutical Co., Ltd.*,[1197] the Federal Circuit added that:

> [i]n some instances, an inventor is unable to establish a conception until he has reduced his invention to practice through a successful experiment. This situation results in simultaneous conception and reduction to practice.[1198]

Because conception "is a mental act, courts require corroborating evidence of a contemporaneous disclosure that would enable one skilled in the art to make the invention."[1199] Using a rule of reason analysis, the court evaluates all pertinent evidence "so that a sound determination of the credibility of the inventor's story may be reached."[1200]

B *Reduction to Practice*

There are two types of RTP: constructive and actual. Constructive RTP results when the patent application is filed. Constructive RTP may occur even if the applicant never built or tested the invention as long as the applicant satisfies § 112.[1201] The policy behind

1195. *Id.*, at 731.
1196. *Mahurkar*, 79 F.3d at 1577 (citing *Burroughs Wellcome Co. v. Barr Laboratories, Inc.*, 40 F.3d 1223, 1228 (Fed. Cir. 1994)).
1197. 927 F.2d 1200 (Fed. Cir. 1991).
1198. *Id.*, at 1206. The doctrine of simultaneous conception and reduction to practice (SCRTP) is a narrow exception to the rule that "[r]eduction to practice follows conception," *Mahurkar* 79 F.3d at 1578; *see also Smith v. Bousquet*, 111 F.2d 157, 159 (C.C.P.A. 1940) (establishing the doctrine). SCRTP arises in the rare instance where an inventor cannot formulate a complete picture of the invention until "reduc[ing] the invention to practice through a successful experiment." *Burroughs Wellcome*, 40 F.3d at 1229; *cf. Alpert v. Slatin*, 305 F.2d 891, 894 (C.C.P.A. 1962) (explaining that the doctrine is reserved for "a residuum of cases where results at each step do not follow as anticipated, but are achieved empirically by what amounts to trial and error"). For an example of the doctrine's application, *see Amgen*, 927 F.2d at 1206, which held that for an invention claiming a purified DNA sequence for encoding a protein, conception did not occur until after the fragment had been isolated and characterized. In sum, SCRTP arises when actual experimentation (which is also sufficient to fulfill the requirements of RTP) is necessary to supply the knowledge to complete conception. *See* 2 R. Carl Moy, Moy's Walker on Patents § 8:54 (4th ed. 2007).
1199. *Burroughs Wellcome*, 40 F.3d at 1228.
1200. *Mahurkar*, 79 F.3d at 1577.
1201. *See Fiers v. Revel*, 984 F.2d 1164, 1169 (Fed. Cir. 1993) ("While one does not need to have carried out one's invention before filing a patent application, one does need to be able to describe that invention with particularity.").

constructive RTP is to encourage early disclosure of the invention. Requiring actual testing may delay disclosure. Actual RTP occurs when the invention is shown to be suitable for its intended purpose, that is when the invention is physically made and tested (e.g., a prototype).[1202]

To prove actual RTP, an inventor must construct the invention (e.g., prototype) and test it to determine if it works for its intended purpose. There must be some recognition of successful testing for an invention to be actually reduced to practice.[1203] It is clear that actual working conditions are not required. Indeed, laboratory tests may be sufficient if they simulate actual working conditions. The Federal Circuit referred to a "common sense approach" with respect to sufficiency of testing:

> This common sense approach prescribes more scrupulous testing under circumstances approaching actual use conditions when the problem includes many uncertainties. On the other hand, when the problem to be solved does not present myriad variables, common sense similarly permits little or no testing to show the soundness of the principles of operation of the invention.[1204]

There is a difference between proving that the invention works for its intended purpose and proving that the invention works in the commercial sense. Neither perfection nor commercial viability is required to show actual RTP.[1205]

As with conception, an inventor must be able to corroborate independently an actual RTP. This can be done through the submission of affidavits analyzing and describing the experiments, the dates of the experiments, etc. As with conception, the Federal Circuit applies a "rule of reason" standard when evaluating the sufficiency of the corroborating evidence.[1206]

1202. According to the Federal Circuit:

> [P]roof of actual reduction to practice requires a showing that "the embodiment relied upon as evidence of priority actually worked for its intended purpose." ... On the other hand, tests performed outside the intended environment can be sufficient to show reduction to practice if the testing conditions are sufficiently similar to those of the intended environment.
>
> *DSL Sciences, Ltd. v. Union Switch & Signal, Inc.*, 928 F.2d 1122, 1124 (Fed. Cir. 1991).

1203. *Estee Lauder Inc. v. L'Oreal S.A.*, 129 F.3d 588 (Fed. Cir. 1997).

1204. *Scott v. Finney*, 34 F.3d 1058, 1063 (Fed. Cir. 1994). The court has also explained that:

> To show actual reduction to practice, an inventor must demonstrate that the invention is suitable for its intended purpose .... Depending on the character of the invention and the problem it solves, this showing may require test results .... Less complicated inventions and problems do not demand stringent testing .... In fact, some inventions are so simple and their purpose and efficacy so obvious that their complete construction is sufficient to demonstrate workability.
>
> *Mahurkar*, 79 F.3d at 1578.

1205. *DSL Sciences*, 928 F.2d at 1126.

1206. *Holmwood v. Balasubramanyan Sugavanam*, 948 F.2d 1236, 1238 (Fed. Cir. 1991).

C *Abandonment, Suppression, and Concealment*

Consistent with the patent policy favoring prompt disclosure, an inventor who was the first to reduce to practice may lose priority if he or she abandons, suppresses, or conceals his or her invention. Consider the following scenario:

> Inventor 1 reduces to practice invention X, but neither files a patent application, nor markets invention X. A year later, inventor 2, ignorant of inventor 1 and his invention X, invents X and files a patent application. Upon learning of inventor 2, inventor 1 is "spurred" into activity and claims that he is the first to invent X.

The law favors inventor 2 in this instance because it is he or she who brought invention X to the public, whereas inventor 1 abandoned, suppressed, and concealed invention X and only came to the fore once he or she found out about inventor 2. However, if inventor 2 never came into the picture, or if inventor 1 resumed inventive activity prior to inventor 2's inventive activity, inventor 1 may still apply for and obtain a patent, even though there was a delay.[1207] Indeed, there is no duty to file a patent application.[1208]

Diligence comes into play only when a party is the first to conceive but the second to reduce to practice. The patent law favors prompt disclosure and, therefore, wants to know what this party was doing, given the fact that another was the second to conceive, but the first to reduce to practice. The party who was the first to conceive but the second to reduce to practice must show continuous and reasonable diligence from a date just prior to the other party's conception to its RTP. As the Board of Patent Appeals & Interferences explained:

> A party that seeks to establish reasonable diligence must account for the entire period during which diligence is required; that period commences from a time just prior to the senior party's [party who was the first to RTP] date to the junior party's [party who was the second to RTP] reduction to practice, either actual or constructive .... Public policy favors early disclosure, ... and thus the law is reluctant to displace an inventor who was the first to disclose to the public his invention .... During this period there must be "reasonably continuous activity." ... Evidence which is of a general nature to the effect that work was continuous and which has little specificity as to dates and facts does not constitute the kind of evidence required to establish diligence in the critical period.[1209]

While a showing of constant effort is not required to prove diligence, the inventor must account for the entire critical period. The question is whether the applicant was pursuing his or her goal "in a reasonable fashion."[1210] Thus, periods of inactivity may not be fatal to a showing of diligence if the inventor has an adequate excuse such as:

1207. *Paulik v. Rizkalla*, 760 F.2d 1270, 1276 (Fed. Cir. 1985) (en banc); *Fujikawa v. Wattanasin*, 93 F.3d 1559, 1568 (Fed. Cir. 1996).
1208. *See Checkpoint Sys., Inc. v. U.S. Int'l Trade Comm'n*, 54 F.3d 756, 762 (Fed. Cir. 1995).
1209. *Hunter v. Beissbarth*, 230 U.S.P.Q. 365, 368 (Bd. Pat. App. & Int'f 1986).
1210. *Hybritech, Inc. v. Abbott Laboratories*, 4 U.S.P.Q.2d 1001, 1006 (C.D. Calif. 1987), *aff'd*, 849 F.2d 1446 (Fed. Cir. 1988).

(1) poverty or illness of the inventor;[1211] (2) obligations of the inventor's regular employment;[1212] or (3) excessive workload of the inventor's patent attorney, provided the attorney "takes up work in a reasonable order—for example, handling applications in the chronological order in which they are submitted."[1213]

D Inventorship

US patent law requires that a patent issue to the correct inventive entity, and there is a rebuttable presumption that the inventors named on an issued patent are correct. With multiple inventors, the "theory of inventorship entity" postulates that "the joint work of two or more persons is treated as being by an 'inventorship entity' separate and distinct from the work of each person solely or in other joint entities."[1214] The Patent Act requires an "inventor" to be a natural person and does not include Artificial Intelligence.[1215]

This requirement does not mean that joint inventors must make equal contributions or that each inventor must contribute to the subject matter in each and every claim. Section 116 of Title 35, as amended in 1984, reads:

> When an invention is made by two or more persons jointly, they shall apply for a patent jointly and each make the required oath .... Inventors may apply for a patent jointly even though (1) they did not physically work together or at the same time, (2) each did not make the same type or amount of contribution, or (3) each did not make a contribution to the subject matter of every claim of the patent.[1216]

The Manual of Patent Examining Procedure (MPEP) states that "[s]ome quantum of collaboration or connection is required in order for persons to be 'joint' inventors under 35 U.S.C. § 116, and thus individuals who are completely ignorant of what each other has done until years after their individual independent efforts cannot be considered joint inventors."[1217]

E Inventive Activity Abroad

Prior to 1994, § 104 of the patent code precluded an inventor from using inventive activity abroad (i.e., conception and RTP) to establish priority under § 102(g). However, GATT/TRIPS and NAFTA amended § 104 to allow applicants to rely on

1211. *See Christie v. Seybold*, 55 F. 69, 77 (6th Cir. 1893) ("the sickness of the inventor, his poverty, and his engagement in other inventions of similar kind are all circumstances which may affect the question of reasonable diligence").
1212. *See Gould v. Schawlow*, 363 F.2d 908, 919 (C.C.P.A. 1966) ("reasonable diligence does not require that one abandon his means of livelihood to further his reduction to practice").
1213. Donald S. Chisum et al., Principles of Patent Law (3rd ed. 2004), §10.07[4][e].
1214. *Id.*, at Ch. 8, §3.II.
1215. *Thaler v. Vidal.* 43 F.4th 1207 (Fed. Circ. 2022).
1216. Prior to 1984, courts applied the "all-claims rule," which required each named inventor to contribute to every claim. The 1984 Amendments to § 116 eliminated this requirement.
1217. U.S. Patent & Trademark Office, Manual of Patent Examining Procedure, § 605.07 (8th edn, 8th rev. 2010).

foreign inventive activity to prove the date of invention.[1218] For GATT/TRIPS, the amendment is effective as of January 1, 1996; the effective date for reliance on inventive activity in a NAFTA country is December 8, 1993.

VII Loss of Right: Statutory Bars

A *Section 102(b): On-Sale and Public Use Bars*

According to § 102(b), an inventor may be statutorily barred from obtaining a patent, even though he or she was the first-to-invent, if "the invention was ... in public use or on sale in [the United States], more than one year prior to the date of application for patent in the United States."[1219] Such a statutory bar may be viewed as a backhanded grant of a one-year grace period "during which an inventor may perfect his invention and prepare and file his application, testing it in public, if necessary. Section 102(b) actually encourages earlier disclosure, publication, or public use of the invention, through which the public may gain knowledge of it."[1220]

These restrictions differ significantly from § 102(a) in that § 102(b) also includes the inventor's conduct. Consequently, an inventor's own acts may preclude patentability under § 102(b). Furthermore, § 102(b) focuses on the filing date, rather than the date of invention. If an inventor does not file for a patent within twelve months of the on-sale or public use activity, a patent will be statutorily barred. Thus, the critical date under § 102(b) is one year prior to the date of application.

Four policies underlying § 102(b) have been recognized:

> These underlying policies include: (1) discouraging removal of inventions from the public domain which the public justifiably comes to believe are freely available; (2) favoring prompt and widespread disclosure of inventions; (3) giving the inventor a reasonable amount of time following the sales activity to determine the value of a patent[;] and (4) prohibiting an extension of the period for exploiting the invention.[1221]

1218. *See* 35 U.S.C. § 104 (as amended by Pub. L. 103–82, Dec. 8, 1993, § 331, 107 Stat. 2113; Pub. L. 103–465, Dec. 8, 1994, § 531(a), 108 Stat. 4982).

1219. 35 U.S.C. § 102(b). In other words, an applicant loses the right to obtain a patent when he or she or a third party: (1) patents the claimed subject matter in the United States or a foreign country more than one year before the filing date; (2) describes the claimed subject matter in a printed publication in the United States or a foreign country more than one year before the filing date; (3) publicly uses the invention in the United States more than one year before the filing date; or (4) sells or offers to sell the invention in the United States more than one year before the filing date. *Id.*

1220. *Palmer v. Dudzik*, 481 F.2d 1377, 1387 (C.C.P.A. 1973); *see also LaBounty Mfg., Inc. v. U.S. Int'l Trade Comm'n*, 958 F.2d 1066, 1071 (Fed. Cir. 1992) ("The general purpose behind § 102(b) bars is to require inventors to assert with due diligence their right to a patent through the prompt filing of a patent application."); *Woodland Trust v. Flowertree Nursery, Inc.*, 148 F.3d 1368, 1370 (Fed. Cir. 1998) (explaining that § 102(b), "unlike §102(a), is primarily concerned with the policy that encourages an inventor to enter the patent system promptly, while recognizing a one year period of public knowledge or use ... before the patent application must be filed").

1221. *King Instrument Corp. v. Otari Corp.*, 767 F.2d 853, 860 (Fed. Cir. 1985).

The one-year grace period strikes a balance between the needs of the inventor and the needs of the public.[1222]

1 *Public Use*

"Public use" in the US by the inventor or a third party occurring more than one year prior to filing precludes the grant of a patent.[1223] As with the on-sale bar, the one-year grace period allows an inventor a reasonable amount of time to test an invention, gauge its sales activity, and determine its potential economic value.[1224]

Thus, public use is any nonsecret, nonexperimental use of the invention. Additionally, a public use includes any use of a claimed invention "by a person other than the inventor who is under no limitation, restriction or obligation of secrecy to the inventor."[1225] A public use has been found even where the third party improperly obtained the idea from the inventor.[1226] To escape qualifying as a public use, a use must be private, under the inventor's control, and not for commercial purposes.[1227] The court determines whether an invention was in public use by considering the totality of the circumstances in light of the policies underlying the public use bar.[1228]

2 *Experimental Use*

A patent applicant may defeat a showing of public use by presenting evidence that the use was for experimental purposes.[1229] An inventor, or any person under the inventor's direction, may experiment with an invention in order to perfect it without defeating patentability.[1230] Even a blatantly public display of an invention will qualify under the

1222. *General Elec. Co. v. United States*, 654 F.2d 55, 61 (Ct. Cl. 1981).
1223. 35 U.S.C. § 102(b).
1224. As famously stated by the Supreme Court:

> When the subject of invention is a machine, it may be tested and tried in a building, either with or without closed doors. In either case, such use is not a public use, within the meaning of the statute, so long as the inventor is engaged, in good faith, in testing its operation .... And though, during all that period, he may not find that any changes are necessary, yet he may be justly said to be using his machine only by way of experiment .... So long as he does not voluntarily allow others to make it and use it, and so long as it is not on-sale for general use, he keeps the invention under his own control, and does not lose his title to a patent.
>
> *City of Elizabeth v. Am. Pavement Co.*, 97 U.S. 126, 134–35 (1877).

1225. *In re* Smith, 714 F.2d 1127, 1134 (Fed. Cir. 1983).
1226. *See Lorenze v. Colgate-Palmolive-Peet Co.*, 167 F.2d 423, 429 (3d Cir. 1948).
1227. *See Moleculon Research Corp. v. CBS, Inc.*, 793 F.2d 1261, 1266–67 (Fed. Cir. 1986).
1228. *Tone Bros. v. Sysco Corp.*, 28 F.3d 1192, 1198 (Fed. Cir. 1994).
1229. *See Lough v. Brunswick Corp.*, 86 F.3d 1113, 1119 (Fed. Cir. 1996).
1230. *See* City of Elizabeth, 97 U.S. at 135; *Seal-Flex, Inc. v. Athletic Track and Court Construction*, 98 F.3d 1318, 1324 (Fed. Cir. 1996) ("When an evaluation period is reasonably needed to determine if the invention will serve its intended purpose, the [on-sale] bar does not start to accrue while such determination is being made.").

exception if, due to the nature of the invention, only a public use will adequately test the invention.[1231]

Although in determining whether a use is experimental one looks to the totality of the circumstances,[1232] factors that a court will consider are "the length of the test period ..., whether payment is made for the device, whether a user agreed to use secretly, whether records were kept of progress, whether persons other than the inventor conducted the asserted experiments, how many tests were conducted, how long the testing period was in relationship to tests of other similar devices."[1233]

3 *On-Sale Bar*

According to § 102(b), an inventor is barred from obtaining a patent if the patent application claims subject matter that was sold or offered for sale more than one year before filing the application or is obvious in the light of what was sold or offered for sale more than one year before filing the patent application.[1234] This restriction is known as the "on-sale" bar. An offer to sell an invention is sufficient to invoke the bar regardless of whether the offer is accepted.[1235]

In *UMC Electronics Co. v. United States,*[1236] the Federal Circuit determined that RTP of the claimed invention "has not been and should not be made an absolute requirement of the on-sale bar."[1237] The court used the term "substantial embodiment" when referring to the level of development of the invention, but did not attempt "to formulate a standard for determining when something less than a complete embodiment of the invention will suffice under the on-sale bar."[1238] At the same time, the court noted:

> We hasten to add ... that we do not intend to sanction attacks on patents on the ground that the inventor or another offered for sale, before the critical date [i.e., more than one year before the filing date of the patent application], the mere concept of the invention ....
>
> All of the circumstances surrounding the sale or offer to sell, including the stage of development of the invention and the nature of the invention, must be considered and weighed against the policies underlying § 102(b).[1239]

There was a great deal of inconsistency at the Federal Circuit with respect to this issue, with some panels embracing the UMC standard and others adhering to an RTP standard.[1240]

1231. *See,* e.g., City of Elizabeth, 97 U.S. at 134–35.
1232. *See* Tone Bros., 28 F.3d at 1198; *Lough,* 86 F.3d at 1119.
1233. *TP Laboratories, Inc. v. Professional Positioners, Inc.*, 724 F.2d 965, 972 (Fed. Cir. 1984).
1234. 35 U.S.C. § 102(b).
1235. *Scaltech, Inc. v. Retec/Tetra, LLC,* 269 F.3d 1321, 1328 (Fed. Cir. 2001).
1236. 816 F.2d 647 (Fed. Cir. 1987).
1237. *Id.*, at 656.
1238. *Id.*, at 657.
1239. *Id.*, at 656.
1240. *Compare Seal-Flex v. Athletic Track,* 98 F.3d 1318 (Fed. Cir. 1996), *with Micro Chemical v. Great Plains Chemical,* 103 F.3d 1538 (Fed. Cir. 1997).

In light of this intra-circuit conflict and uncertainty surrounding the on-sale bar determination, the Supreme Court granted certiorari in *Pfaff v. Wells Electronics*[1241] and addressed the following question:

> In view of the longstanding statutory definition that the one-year grace period to an "on sale" bar can start to run only after an invention is fully completed, should the Pfaff patent have been held invalid under 35 U.S.C. §102(b) when Mr. Pfaff's invention was admittedly not "fully completed" more than one year before he filed his patent application?[1242]

The Court rejected both the RTP standard and the substantial embodiment standard. According to the Court:

> The word "invention" must refer to a concept that is complete, rather than merely one that is "substantially complete." It is true that reduction to practice ordinarily provides the best evidence that an invention is complete. But just because reduction to practice is sufficient evidence of completion, it does not follow that proof of reduction to practice is necessary in every case.
>
> ...
>
> We conclude, therefore, that the on-sale bar applies when two conditions are satisfied before the critical date. First, the product must be the subject of a commercial offer for sale .... Second, the invention must be ready for patenting. That condition may be satisfied in at least two ways: by proof of reduction to practice before the critical date; or by proof that prior to the critical date the inventor had prepared drawings or other descriptions of the invention that were sufficiently specific to enable a person skilled in the art to practice the invention.[1243]

Recently, in *Helsinn Healthcare SA v. Teva Pharmaceuticals USA Inc.*,[1244] the Supreme Court held that the on-sale bar applies even to secret sales. Thus, under Helsinn, inventors must continue to exercise caution when engaging in transactions involving their patented inventions prior to filing applications to those inventions.

4 *Third-Party Activity*

Third-party public use or on-sale activity may bar a patent applicant from obtaining a patent.[1245]

1241. 525 U.S. 55 (1998).
1242. Petition for *Writ of Certiorari, Pfaff v. Wells Elec., Inc.*, 124 F.3d 1429 (Fed. Cir. 1997), *cert. granted*, 523 U.S. 1003, 66 U.S.L.W. 3474 (U.S. Mar. 9, 1998).
1243. *Pfaff v. Wells Elec., Inc.*, 525 U.S. 55, 66–67 (1998).
1244. *Helsinn Healthcare SA v. Teva Pharmaceuticals USA Inc.*, 139 S. Ct. 628 (2019).
1245. As explained by one court:

> Where the sale is by one other than the inventor (one not under the inventor's control), it would seem that the policy against extended commercial exploitation and the policy favoring the filing of only worthwhile inventions could be said not to apply. Nevertheless, it is well established that a placing of the invention "on sale" by an unrelated third party more than 1 year prior to the filing of an application for patent by another has the effect under §102(b) of invalidating a patent directed to that invention.

In *Evans Cooling Systems, Inc. v. General Motors Corp.*,[1246] the patentee argued that the on-sale bar should not apply when an invention is misappropriated by the alleged infringer which led to an offer for sale by third parties not involved in the theft.[1247] The Federal Circuit disagreed and held that a patent is barred when "a public use arises from any source whatsoever."[1248] But the court was particularly persuaded by the fact that the offers were made by innocent third parties:

> Even if we were to create an exception to the on sale bar such that third parties accused of misappropriating an invention could not invalidate a patent based upon sales by the guilty third party, GM correctly asserts that ... activities of third parties uninvolved in the alleged misappropriation raise the statutory bar, even if those activities are instigated by the one who allegedly misappropriated the invention.[1249]

B Section 102(d): Bar on Foreign Applicants (Pre-AIA)

Section 102(d) is a type of statutory bar which precludes a foreign patent applicant (which may be an American company) from obtaining a US patent if: (1) the US application is filed more than one year after the foreign application is filed; and (2) the foreign patent issues before the US patent issues.[1250] Thus, even if a foreign patent applicant files in the US more than one year after the foreign patent filing, the applicant may still obtain a US patent if the foreign patent issues after the US patent.

This section has been eliminated under the AIA effective March 16, 2013.[1251]

VIII Changes to Novelty, Prior Art, and the Grace Period under the AIA

The AIA replaces § 102 in its entirety. The changes described below will apply to all patent applications filed on or after March 16, 2013. Briefly, the AIA: (1) moves the US from a first-to-invent system to a first to file system; (2) narrows the scope of the one-year grace period for filing a patent application; and (3) eliminates the Hilmer rule. Furthermore, the AIA eliminated the § 102(c) abandonment rules, § 102(d) rules

General Elec. Co. v. United States, 654 F.2d 55, 61 (Ct. Cl. 1981); see also Lorenz v. Colgate-Palmolive-Peet Co., 167 F.2d 423 (3rd Cir. 1948); Baxter Int'l, Inc. v. Cobe Labs, Inc., 88 F.3d 1054 (Fed. Cir. 1996). But see W.L. Gore & Associates, Inc. v. Garlock, Inc., 721 F.2d 1540, 1550 (Fed. Cir. 1983) (noting that if the details of an inventive process cannot be ascertained from the product sold or displayed and the third party has kept the invention as a trade secret then that use is not a § 102(b) public use).

1246. 125 F.3d 1448 (Fed. Cir. 1997).
1247. *See id.*, at 1450.
1248. *Id.*, at 1453.
1249. *Id.*
1250. 35 U.S.C. § 102(d). *See In re* Kathawala, 9 F.3d 942, 945 (Fed. Cir. 1993) (foreign applicant barred under § 102(d) from obtaining a U.S. patent).
1251. *See* America Invents Act § 3.

dealing with the foreign patenting statutory bar,[1252] and § 102(f) which addresses originality and inventorship.[1253] Finally, the AIA added a new section of novelty-destroying prior art to § 102, which includes references that are "otherwise available to the public before the effective filing date of the claimed invention."[1254]

A First Inventor to File

The most dramatic change brought about by the AIA is the conversion of the US from a first-to-invent system to a first-inventor-to-file system. The new § 102(a) reveals that the date for determining prior art and priority is the effective filing date of claimed invention rather than the date of invention:

> § 102. Conditions for Patentability; novelty
>
> a. Novelty; Prior Art.—A person shall be entitled to a patent unless—
>   1. the claimed invention was patented, described in a printed publication, or in public use, on sale, or otherwise available to the public before the effective filing date of the claimed invention; or
>   2. the claimed invention was described in a patent issued under § 151, or in an application for patent published or deemed published under § 122(b), in which the patent or application, as the case may be, names another inventor and was effectively filed before the effective filing date of the claimed invention.[1255]

The AIA also abolishes the § 102(g) priority rules. It will now be given to the first-inventor-to-file a patent application or publicly disclose the invention (if they file an application within a year). Applicants will no longer be able to antedate (or "swear behind") a prior art reference or establish priority by proving an earlier date of invention.

B Expansion of Prior Art

The AIA expands the universe of prior art from that which "was known or used by others in this country, or patented or described in a printed publication in this or a foreign country before the invention thereof by the applicant for patent,"[1256] to that where "the claimed invention was patented, described in a printed publication, or in public use, on-sale, or otherwise available to the public before the effective filing date

1252. *See* Ch. 2, §2.VII.B. *supra*.
1253. Although the AIA eliminated § 102(f), the AIA introduced a new procedure, the derivation proceeding, to address "stolen" inventions, or patent applications filed by those who did not invent the subject matter disclosed within those applications. Additionally, inventors are still required to sign an oath or declaration that states that she believes "herself to be the original inventor of a claimed invention in the application." 35 U.S.C. 115(b)(2).
1254. 35 U.S.C. § 102(a); *See infra* Ch. 2, §2.VIII.B.
1255. *Id.*
1256. 35 U.S.C. § 102(a).

of the claimed invention."[1257] These amendments eliminate the geographic distinction for public use, on-sale or "otherwise available to the public" between acts occurring in the US ("in this country") and those occurring abroad ("in this or a foreign country")—thereby making these activities prior art regardless of where in the world they occur. Congress did not define "otherwise available to the public," which may make it a catchall for prior art. Ultimately it will be up to the courts to decide its scope.

C *The New Section 102(b) Grace Period*

Although the AIA retains a one-year grace period, it is substantially weaker than before. Most notably, there is no grace period relative to third parties who arrived at the invention independently of the inventor. Under the new law, such disclosures can be used against the inventor. The new § 102(b) grace period has provisions for the inventor's own disclosures and for those derived from the inventor.

New § 102(b)(1)(A) addresses the inventor's or joint inventor's own disclosure. A disclosure made less than one year prior to the effective filing date of the invention will not be considered prior art if it was made by the inventor or joint inventor or "by another who obtained the subject matter disclosed directly or indirectly from the inventor or joint inventor."[1258]

By contrast, new § 102(b)(1)(B) addresses disclosures made by someone other than the inventor. These disclosures will not bar a patent if "the subject matter disclosed had, before such disclosure, been publicly disclosed by the inventor or a joint inventor or another who obtained the subject matter disclosed directly or indirectly from the inventor or a joint inventor" less than one year prior to the effective filing date.[1259] Thus, this new provision protects the true inventor's public disclosure from a second disclosure made by another provided that the true inventor files a patent application within one year of the initial disclosure.

Given the expansion of prior art and weakened grace period, inventors might consider several options to secure an early filing date including the filing of a provisional patent application[1260] or perhaps to simply make an early, prefiling disclosure. The latter option, however, could hinder an inventor's ability to obtain protection outside the US since many other countries still require absolute novelty and do not grant a grace period for any public disclosure. The ultimate choice of whether or when to file or disclose will depend on the inventor's overall patenting strategy.

D *Elimination of the Hilmer Doctrine*

Before the AIA, under In re Hilmer,[1261,1262] US patents and published patent applications claiming priority to a patent application filed in a foreign country were considered

1257. America Invents Act § 3.
1258. *Id.*
1259. *Id.*
1260. *See supra* VI. Priority (Pre-AIA).
1261. *See* Ch. 2, §2.IV *supra* for the pre-AIA rules.
1262. 359 F.2d 859 (C.C.P.A. 1966).

prior art as of the US filing date, not the foreign priority date.[1263] New § 102(d) eliminates the Hilmer doctrine and affords US applications claiming foreign priority a prior art effect as of their foreign priority date.[1264]

§3 NONOBVIOUSNESS

In addition to the patentability requirements of novelty and utility, an invention must also be nonobvious. The nonobviousness requirement, embodied in § 103 of the patent code, lies at the heart of our patent system and, in many ways, is the most significant obstacle that a patent applicant faces.[1265] The nonobviousness requirement casts a broader net than the novelty requirement because it recognizes that the limitations of a claimed invention may be scattered throughout more than one prior art reference, and it would not be unduly difficult for a person of ordinary skill in the art to assemble these elements in the form of the claimed invention. In such a situation, it could reasonably be said that the claimed invention was already in the public domain, albeit not in one single prior art reference.[1266] Thus, even if an invention is novel, it may nevertheless be unpatentable if it is not significantly different (although not necessarily better than) than the prior art.[1267]

By constitutional command, a patent can neither remove such knowledge from the public domain nor limit free access to those materials already available.[1268] Rather, a patent can only be awarded for technical advances which add to the storehouse of useful knowledge.[1269] As the Supreme Court recently explained:

1263. *See supra* §2.III.
1264. *See* America Invents Act § 3.
1265. *See generally* NONOBVIOUSNESS: THE ULTIMATE CONDITION OF PATENTABILITY (JOHN F. WITHERSPOON ed., 1980); Glynn S. Lunney, Jr., *Patent Law, the Federal Circuit, and the Supreme Court: A Quiet Revolution*, 11 SUP. CT. ECON. REV. 1, 19 (2004) (noting that "nonobviousness has traditionally represented the principal substantive hurdle for patentability" due to the scope and flexible nature of the inquiry). Nonobviousness is the most common issue raised on appeal in patent cases. Dennis D. Crouch, *Understanding the Role of the Board of Patent Appeals: Ex Parte Rejection Rates on Appeal* 10 (Univ. of Mo. Sch. of Law Legal Studies Research Paper No. 2009-16, 2009), available at http://ssrn.com/abstract=1423922 (finding that 87%–90% of cases decided a nonobviousness issue).
1266. *See* ROCHELLE COOPER DREYFUSS & ROBERTA ROSENTHAL KWALL, INTELLECTUAL PROPERTY 648 (1996).
1267. *See* Pasquale Joseph Federico, *Commentary on the New Patent Act*, 75 J. PAT. & TRADEMARK OFF. SOC'Y 160, 179–80 (1993) ("An invention which has been made, and which is new in the sense that the same thing has not been made before, may still not be patentable if the difference between the new thing, and what was known before is not considered sufficiently great to warrant a patent.").
1268. *Graham v. John Deere Co.*, 383 U.S. 1, 6 (1966); *see also* Edmund W. Kitch, *The Nature and Function of the Patent System*, 20 J.L. & ECON. 265, 277 (1977) (arguing that patents should not be granted for the use and development of known technical information because "proper incentives for its acquisition and use exist without a property right").
1269. *Graham*, 383 U.S. at 6 ("Innovation, advancement, and things which add to the sum of useful knowledge are inherent requisites in a patent system which by constitutional command must 'promote the Progress of useful Arts.'"); *cf. Great Atl. & Pac. Tea Co. v. Supermarket Equip. Corp.*, 340 U.S. 147, 152 (1950) ("The conjunction or concert of known elements must contribute something; only when the whole in some way exceeds the sum of its parts is the accumulation of old devices patentable.").

> We build and create by bringing to the tangible and palpable reality around us new works based on instinct, simple logic, ordinary inferences, extraordinary ideas, and sometimes even genius. These advances, once part of our shared knowledge, define a new threshold from which innovation starts once more. And as progress beginning from higher levels of achievement is expected in the normal course, the results of ordinary innovation are not the subject of exclusive rights under the patent laws. Were it otherwise patents might stifle, rather than promote, the progress of useful arts.[1270]

Thus, the nonobviousness requirement denies patents for inventions that would come about through ordinary technological progress[1271] and, as a corollary, seeks to "to weed[] out those inventions that would not be disclosed or devised but for the inducement of a patent."[1272]

Whether an invention is obvious is a question of law with several underlying factual inquiries, which were set forth in the seminal obviousness case of *Graham v. John Deere Co.*[1273] The factual inquiries are: (1) the scope and content of the prior art; (2) the differences between the prior art and the claims at issue in the patented invention; (3) the level of ordinary skill in the art; and (4) any available objective evidence of nonobviousness (i.e., so-called secondary considerations).[1274]

I Scope of the Prior Art

The scope of the nonobviousness inquiry is much broader than the one for novelty. Two differences are worth highlighting. First, since nonobviousness does not target identically disclosed inventions, the inquiry extends beyond that of a single reference and contemplates that the person having ordinary skill in the art will combine and modify the teachings of multiple references.[1275] Second, the prior art for nonobviousness as a whole must be enabling—not any single reference.[1276] As the Federal Circuit

1270. *KSR Int'l Co. v. Teleflex Inc.*, 550 U.S. 398, 427 (2007).

1271. *See* Peter K. Yu, Intellectual Property and Information Wealth 2 (2007) ("It is socially wasteful for us to pay a patent-backed premium for an innovation that we are almost certain to receive for free and just as early."); Michael J. Meurer & Katherine J. Strandburg, *Patent Carrots and Sticks: A Model of Nonobviousness*, 12 Lewis & Clark L. Rev. 547, 549 (2008) ("The nonobviousness threshold may be used as a 'stick' to induce researchers to pursue more difficult, socially preferred research projects.").

1272. *Graham*, 383 U.S. at 11.

1273. *Id.*, at. 17.

1274. *Id.* Although *Graham* states that secondary considerations can serve as "as indicia of obviousness or nonobviousness," the Federal Circuit has since treated secondary considerations as a fourth element. *See Stratoflex, Inc. v. Aeroquip Corp.*, 713 F.2d 1530, 1538 (Fed. Cir. 1983) ("It is jurisprudentially inappropriate to disregard any relevant evidence on any issue in any case, patent cases included. Thus evidence rising out of the so-called '*secondary considerations' must always when present be considered en route to a determination of obviousness.*") (emphasis added).

1275. 35 U.S.C. § 103(a); *see also Cohesive Technologies, Inc. v. Waters Corp.*, 543 F.3d 1351, 1364 (2008) ("Obviousness can be proven by combining existing prior art references, while anticipation requires all elements of a claim to be disclosed within a single reference.").

1276. *Therasense v. Becton, Dickinson & Co.*, 593 F.3d 1289, 1297 (Fed. Cir. 2010) ("In order to render a claimed [invention] obvious, the cited prior art as a whole must enable one skilled in the art to make and use [it]." (citing *Symbol Techs., Inc. v. Opticon, Inc.*, 935 F.2d 1569, 1578

has stated, a reference "is prior art for all that it teaches" because a person having ordinary skill in the art can possibly extract something from it.[1277] This explains why such references can play a powerful role in defeating patentability.

Even though § 102 is the only source of prior art for § 103 determinations, not just any § 102 reference can be used for § 103 purposes. The courts have developed what is known as the analogous art doctrine.[1278] Only prior art that is considered to be analogous to the subject matter sought to be patented can be used under § 103:[1279]

> Two criteria have evolved for determining whether prior art is analogous: (1) whether the art is from the same field of endeavor, regardless of the problem addressed, and (2) if the reference is not within the field of the inventor's endeavor, whether the reference still is reasonably pertinent to the particular problem with which the inventor is involved.[1280]

The reason for the analogous art doctrine is that while it is a difficult enough burden to presume that an inventor is knowledgeable of prior art in his or her own inventive field and fields related thereto, it is not only unfair but also unrealistic to require an inventor to be presumptively aware of nonanalogous prior art.[1281]

This analogous art requirement highlights a key distinction between a § 102 novelty determination and a § 103 obviousness inquiry. With respect to the former, a reference's analogous nature or lack thereof to the claimed subject matter is entirely irrelevant. To prove anticipation under § 102, one could point to any single prior art reference so long as it discloses the same invention including each and every limitation of the claimed invention, not so for § 103 purposes. To prove obviousness under § 103, one can combine the teachings of several prior art references.

II Content of the Prior Art

The Federal Circuit and its predecessor, the C.C.P.A., stated on numerous occasions that before prior art references can be combined under § 103, the references must Teach, Suggest, or Motivate (TSM) a person of ordinary skill in the art to make the

---

(Fed. Cir. 1991) ("While a reference must enable someone to practice the invention in order to anticipate[,] a non-enabling reference may qualify as prior art for the purpose of determining obviousness under §103."))).

1277. *Beckman Instruments, Inc. v. LKB Produkter AB*, 892 F.2d 1547, 1551 (Fed. Cir. 1989); *accord Amgen Inc. v. Hoechst Marion Roussel, Inc.*, 314 F.3d 1313, 1357 (Fed. Cir. 2003) ("Under §103[,] a reference need not be enabled; it qualifies as a prior art, regardless, for whatever is disclosed therein.").
1278. *In re* Kahn, 441 F.3d 977, 986–87 (Fed. Cir. 2006) (citing *Graham v. John Deere Co.*, 383 U.S. 1, 35 (1966)).
1279. *See In re* Clay, 966 F.2d 656, 659 (Fed. Cir. 1992) ("Although §103 does not, by its terms, define the 'art to which [the] subject matter [sought to be patented] pertains,' this determination is frequently couched in terms of whether the art is analogous or not, i.e., whether the art is 'too remote to be treated as prior art'.").
1280. *Id.*
1281. *In re* Wood, 599 F.2d 1032, 1036 (C.C.P.A. 1979); *see also Union Carbide Corp. v. Am. Can Co.*, 724 F.2d 1567, 1572 (Fed. Cir. 1984).

invention and, once made, have a reasonable expectation of success.[1282] According to the Federal Circuit:

> Where claimed subject matter has been rejected as obvious in view of a combination of prior art references, a proper analysis under § 103 requires, inter alia, consideration of two factors: (1) whether the prior art would have suggested to those of ordinary skill in the art that they should make the claimed composition or device, or carry out the claimed process; and (2) whether the prior art would also have revealed that in so making or carrying out, those of ordinary skill would have a reasonable expectation of success.[1283]

But in *KSR v. Teleflex*[1284] the Supreme Court criticized the Federal Circuit's rigid application of the TSM test. Although the KSR Court rejected the rigid application of the TSM test, it did not provide a bright-line test for obviousness or a clear indication of what exactly its "expansive and flexible approach" has been over the years. Rather, the Court focused on broad themes such as the role of common sense, predictability, and the importance of the person having ordinary skill in the art. With these themes in mind, the KSR Court offered a number of considerations that may be relevant to an obviousness inquiry. These considerations are captured in the following passages from the opinion:

(1) Often, it will be necessary for a court to look to interrelated teachings of multiple patents; the effects of demands known to the design community or present in the marketplace; and the background knowledge possessed by a person having ordinary skill in the art, all in order to determine whether there was an apparent reason to combine the known elements in the fashion claimed by the patent at issue.
(2) *Common sense* teaches … that familiar items may have obvious uses beyond their primary purposes, and in many cases a person of ordinary skill will be able to fit the teachings of multiple patents together like pieces of a puzzle.
(3) In many fields it may be that there is little discussion of obvious techniques or combinations, and it often may be the case that *market demand, rather than scientific literature, will drive design trends.*
(4) [T]he analysis need not seek out precise teachings directed to the specific subject matter of the challenged claim, for a court can take account of the *inferences and creative steps that a person of ordinary skill in the art would employ.*
(5) *[A]ny need or problem known in the field of endeavor* at the time of invention and addressed by the patent can provide a reason for combining the elements in the manner claimed.

1282. *See*, e.g., *In re* Dow Chemical Co., 837 F.2d 469, 473 (Fed. Cir. 1988).
1283. *In re* Vaeck, 947 F.2d 488, 493 (Fed. Cir. 1991) (citing *Dow Chemical*, 837 F.2d at 473).
1284. 550 U.S. 398 (2007).

(6) *[F]amiliar items may have obvious uses beyond their primary purposes*, and in many cases a person of ordinary skill will be able to fit the teachings of multiple patents together like pieces of a puzzle.[1285]

In *Perfect Web Technologies, Inc. v. Infousa, Inc.*,[1286] the court—while stressing the need for a district court to "articulate its reasoning with sufficient clarity for review"—affirmed these themes, noting that the examiner's analysis "may include recourse to logic, judgment, and common sense available to a person of ordinary skill that do not necessarily require explication in any reference or expert opinion."[1287] And in *TriMed, Inc. v. Stryker Corp.*,[1288] the Federal Circuit captured the obviousness test by noting KSR requires that we "ask whether the improvement is more than the predictable use of prior art elements according to their established functions."[1289] To answer this question necessitates several factual inquiries, such as the "interrelated teachings of multiple patents; the effects of demands known to the design community or present in the marketplace; and the background knowledge possessed by a person having ordinary skill in the art, all in order to determine whether there was an apparent reason to combine the known elements in the fashion claimed by the patent at issue."[1290]

Another factor weighing in favor of an obviousness finding is "simultaneous invention" by another party. In *Geo. M. Martin Co. v. Alliance Machine Systems International LLC.*,[1291] the court—to support a finding of obviousness—relied on a third party's development of the claimed invention "only a year later than the earliest possible reduction-to-practice date of the claimed invention."[1292] According to the court, "[i]ndependently made, simultaneous inventions, made 'within a comparatively short space of time,' are persuasive evidence that the claimed apparatus 'was the product only of ordinary mechanical or engineering skill'."[1293]

Occasionally, instead of suggesting a course of action leading to a claimed invention, the prior art will teach away from it. That is, upon reading a reference, a person of ordinary skill would be discouraged from following the path set out in the claimed invention.[1294] Such a reference indicates nonobviousness and is a significant factor for a court to consider in making its nonobviousness determination.[1295]

1285. *See id.*, at 418–21 (emphasis added).
1286. 587 F.3d 1324 (Fed. Cir. 2009).
1287. *Id.*, at 1329.
1288. 608 F.3d 1333 (Fed. Cir. 2010).
1289. *Id.*, at 1341.
1290. *Id.*
1291. 618 F.3d 1294 (Fed. Cir. 2010).
1292. *Id.*, at 1306.
1293. *Id.*, at 1305.
1294. *See In re* Gurley, 27 F.3d 551, 553 (Fed. Cir. 1994) ("[I]n general, a reference will teach away if it suggests that the line of development flowing from the reference's disclosure is unlikely to be productive of the result sought by the applicant.").
1295. *Id.* ("Although a reference that teaches away is a significant factor to be considered in determining nonobviousness, the nature of the teaching is highly relevant, and must be weighed in substance. A known or obvious composition does not become patentable simply because it has been described as somewhat inferior to some other product for the same use.").

III Persons of Ordinary Skill in the Art

The trier of fact does not consider whether a claimed invention was obvious to just anyone. Rather, the test of obviousness is an objective one, viewed through the eyes of a hypothetical person having ordinary skill in the art.[1296] Although this imaginary person's level of skill in the art is ordinary, he or she is presumed to have complete knowledge of all pertinent prior art.[1297] When determining the appropriate level of ordinary skill, a court may consider the inventor's level of education, the types of problems encountered in the art, typical solutions to those problems, rapidity with which innovations are made, sophistication of the technology involved, and the educational background of those working in the field.[1298] Finally, a person of ordinary skill in the art is also a person of ordinary creativity, and is not an automaton.[1299]

IV Secondary Considerations

Secondary considerations are relevant to, and sometimes determinative of, a § 103 obviousness determination. The "real world" considerations, thought to be objective in nature, include commercial success, long-felt need/failure of others, copying, and licensing/acquiescence. Applicants using these secondary factors have to establish a nexus between the secondary considerations and the merits of the claimed invention.[1300] As the Graham Court noted, these considerations "focus our attention on economic and motivational, rather than technical issues and are, therefore, more susceptible of judicial treatment than are the highly technical facts often present in patent litigation."[1301] Indeed, the Federal Circuit, perhaps more adamantly than the Supreme Court, has recognized the importance of secondary considerations, sometimes elevating them to a fourth Graham factor.[1302]

1296. The Federal Circuit has explained that the person having ordinary skill in the art is not the inventor, "but an imaginary being possessing 'ordinary skill in the art' created by Congress to provide a standard of patentability, a descendant of the 'ordinary mechanic acquainted with the business' of [*Hotchkiss v. Greenwood*, 52 U.S. (How.) 246, 267 (1851)]." *Kimberly-Clark Corp. v. Johnson & Johnson Co.*, 745 F.2d 1437, 1454 (Fed. Cir. 1984). Further, "[r]ealistically, courts never have judged patentability by what the real inventor/applicant/patentee could or would do. Real inventors, as a class, vary in their capacities from ignorant geniuses to Nobel laureates; the courts have always applied a standard based on an imaginary worker of their own devising whom they have equated with the inventor." *Id.*

1297. *See Custom Accessories, Inc. v. Jeffrey-Allan Industries, Inc.*, 807 F.2d 955, 962 (Fed. Cir. 1986) ("The person of ordinary skill is a hypothetical person who is presumed to be aware of all the pertinent prior art."). As Judge Learned Hand stated, "[w]e must suppose the inventor to be endowed, as in fact no inventor is endowed; we are to impute to him knowledge of all that is not only in his immediate field, but in all fields nearly akin to that field." *Int'l Cellucotton Prod. Co. v. Sterilek Co.*, 94 F.2d 10, 13 (2d Cir. 1938).

1298. *Envtl. Designs, Ltd. v. Union Oil Co.*, 713 F.2d 693, 696 (Fed. Cir. 1983).

1299. *KSR Int'l Co. v. Teleflex Inc.*, 550 U.S. 398, 427 (2007).

1300. *Classco Inc. v. Apple Inc.*, 838 F.3d 1214 (Fed. Cir. 2016).

1301. *Graham v. John Deere Co.*, 383 U.S. 1, 35–36 (1966)).

1302. In *Stratoflex*, the court stated:

A *Commercial Success*

Commercial success is the most important and most often asserted of the secondary considerations. When a patentee asserts commercial success, he or she is essentially saying, "if my invention is obvious, why did not any of my competitors have success making the invention given its significant consumer demand?" The reason, the argument goes, is that the competitors tried and failed, thus leading to the conclusion that the invention was nonobvious.

The assumption of the importance of the market is not self-evident. Commercial success may be due to, and consumer demand may be a result of, factors unrelated to the technical quality of the claimed invention (e.g., clever advertising, aggressive marketing, business acumen, or significant market share). In fact, the Federal Circuit has held that raw sales data is insufficient to prove commercial success.[1303] For evidence of commercial success to be persuasive, the patentee must show comparative success with other products on the market,[1304] and "a nexus must be established between [commercial success] and the merits of the claimed invention."[1305]

B *Long-Felt Need and Failure of Others*

The fact that there is a long-felt need in an industry and others in the industry have tried and failed to satisfy that need may imply nonobviousness.[1306] Consider Judge Easterbrook's comments in In re Mahurkar Patent Litigation:

> It is jurisprudentially inappropriate to disregard any relevant evidence on any issue in any case, patent cases included. Thus evidence rising out of the so-called "secondary considerations" must always when present be considered en route to a determination of obviousness ....
>
> En route to a conclusion on obviousness, a court must not stop until all pieces of evidence on that issue have been fully considered and each has been given its appropriate weight. Along the way, some pieces will weigh more heavily than others, but decision should be held in abeyance, and doubt maintained, until all the evidence has had its say. The relevant evidence on the obviousness-nonobviousness issue, as the Court said in Graham, and as other courts had earlier emphasised, includes evidence on what has now been called "secondary considerations." It is error to exclude that evidence from consideration.
>
> 713 F.2d 1530, 1538–39 (Fed. Cir. 1983).

1303. *Vandenberg v. Dairy Equip. Co.*, 740 F.2d 1560, 1567 (Fed. Cir. 1984).
1304. *In re* Mageli, 470 F.2d 1380, 1384 (C.C.P.A. 1973).
1305. *Pentec, Inc. v. Graphic Controls Corp.*, 776 F.2d 309, 315 (Fed. Cir. 1985); *see also Windsurfing Int'l, Inc. v. AMF, Inc.*, 782 F.2d 995, 1000 (Fed. Cir. 1986).
1306. *See Graham*, 383 U.S. at 17 (recognizing "failure of others" as a secondary consideration); *Advanced Display Sys., Inc. v. Kent State Univ.*, 212 F.3d 1272, 1285 (Fed. Cir. 2000) (explaining that "failure of others" may be "the most probative and cogent evidence of nonobviousness"). The rationale is that the claimed invention is not a mere trivial advance over the prior art if many have tried to solve the problem but failed. *In re* Dow Chemical Co., 837 F.2d 469, 472 (Fed. Cir. 1985) ("Recognition of need, and difficulties encountered by those skilled in the field, are classical indicia of unobviousness."); *Boehringer Ingelheim Vetmedica, Inc. v. Schering-Plough Corp.*, 320 F.3d 1339, 1354 (Fed. Cir. 2003) ("While absolute certainty is not necessary to establish a reasonable expectation of success, there can be little better evidence negating an expectation of success than actual reports of failure.").

> The existence of an enduring, unmet need is strong evidence that the invention is novel, not obvious, and not anticipated. If people are clamoring for a solution, and the best minds do not find it for years, that is practical evidence—the kind that can't be bought from a hired expert, the kind that does not depend on fallible memories or doubtful inferences—of the state of knowledge.[1307]

As the Federal Circuit has noted, "the failure of others to provide a feasible solution to a long standing problem is probative of nonobviousness."[1308]

However, the fact that there was a failure to achieve the patented solution may simply be the result of a company's complacency toward its existing technology even though such technology is not state of the art. Furthermore, certain firms may not be willing to commit the time and resources to solve identified problems within the industry. That is, economic and business decisions must be considered when one analyzes long-felt need and failure of others. Finally, "the mere passage of time without the claimed invention is not evidence of nonobviousness."[1309]

C *Copying*

Frequently, patentees assert that a competitor copied the claimed invention, thus manifesting nonobviousness. This argument is perhaps strongest, however, when there is evidence that the competitor initially attempted to design around the patent.[1310]

D *Licensing/Acquiescence*

Lastly, a patentee may assert that the acceptance of a license by the defendant or other competitors is an implicit recognition that the patent is nonobvious. The rationale is that firms would not pay royalties on a patent unless it thought the patent was valid. As the Federal Circuit stated, "such real world considerations provide a colorful picture of the state of the art, what was known by those in the art, and a solid evidentiary foundation on which to rest a nonobviousness determination."[1311]

However, the Federal Circuit has noted:

> [Licensing] programs are not infallible guides to patentability. They sometimes succeed because they are mutually beneficial to the licensed group or because of business judgments that it is cheaper to take licenses than to defend infringement suits, or for other reasons unrelated to the unobviousness of the licensed subject matter.[1312]

1307. 831 F. Supp. 1354, 1377–78 (N.D. Ill. 1993), *aff'd*, 71 F.3d 1573 (Fed. Cir. 1995).
1308. *Uniroyal, Inc. v. Rudkin-Wiley Corp.*, 837 F.2d 1044, 1054 (Fed. Cir. 1988).
1309. *In re* Kahn, 441 F.3d 977, 991–92 (Fed. Cir. 2006) (quoting *Iron Grip Barbell Co. v. USA Sports, Inc.*, 392 F.3d 1317, 1325 (Fed. Cir. 2004)).
1310. *Vandenberg v. Dairy Equipment Co.*, 740 F.2d 1560, 1567 (Fed. Cir. 1984).
1311. *Minnesota Mining & Mfg. Co. v. Johnson & Johnson Orthopaedics, Inc.*, 976 F.2d 1559, 1575 (Fed. Cir. 1992).
1312. *EWP Corp. v. Reliance Universal, Inc.*, 755 F.2d 898, 907–08 (Fed. Cir. 1985).

In other words, sometimes it just makes business sense not to contest the validity of a patent even though you may have strong evidence of obviousness. As a result, the patentee must show a "nexus between the merits of the invention and the licenses of record."[1313]

V Modifications under the AIA

The AIA amends § 103 to reflect that nonobviousness is gauged as of the effective filing date of the invention rather than the date of invention:

> § 103. Conditions for patentability; non-obvious subject matter
>
> A patent for a claimed invention may not be obtained, notwithstanding that the claimed invention is not identically disclosed as set forth in § 102, if the differences between the claimed invention and the prior art are such that the claimed invention as a whole would have been obvious before the effective filing date of the claimed invention to a person having ordinary skill in the art to which the claimed invention pertains. Patentability shall not be negated by the manner in which the invention was made.[1314]

§4 UTILITY

Section 101 of the patent code restricts patentable inventions to those which are useful. Only one who "invents or discovers [a] new and useful process, machine, manufacture, or composition of matter, or any new and useful improvement thereof, may obtain a patent …."[1315] At first glance, the utility requirement in patent law appears to be somewhat superfluous. Indeed, it is a rare occasion that lack of utility is raised as an invalidating defense in a patent litigation context. However, there is a purpose behind the utility requirement in that it secures a quid pro quo for society. We require the claimed invention to function for its intended purpose. Thus, before an inventor is granted the right to exclude others from practicing or selling his or her invention, society must be provided with an invention that operates in accordance with its intended purpose or a purpose discernible by a person of ordinary skill in the art. As the noted nineteenth-century patent law scholar William C. Robinson stated:

> In order that an invention may be patentable it must not only be bestowed upon the public by its inventor, but when bestowed it must confer on them a benefit …. No recompense can properly be made to one from whom the community receives no consideration.[1316]

As one might imagine, the utility requirement is not usually an obstacle for mechanical and electrical applications. These types of inventions have a certain

1313. *In re* GPAC, Inc., 57 F.3d 1573, 1580 (Fed. Cir. 1995).
1314. America Invents Act § 3.
1315. 35 U.S.C. § 101 (2006) (emphasis added).
1316. 1 William Robinson, Treatise on the Law of Patents for Useful Inventions 462–63 (1890).

physicality, the utility of which is manifested through the use of drawings and diagrams. In contrast, utility poses a greater concern for chemical and biological inventions. First, it is difficult to convey the utility of a chemical composition or a pharmaceutical invention by employing drawings, diagrams, or formulae. Second, unlike mechanical and electrical inventions which usually have an end result and use in mind, chemical and pharmaceutical inventions possess an evolving utility. In short, they are more like building blocks rather than a completed building. Therefore, there is a spectrum of utility, whose breadth is especially apparent in the case of chemical and biological inventions. At one end of the spectrum, some of these inventions may be viewed as having a general usefulness in basic research; while at the other end, some may provide specific and immediate societal utility. Whether a patent application satisfies the utility requirement depends upon where the claimed invention lies on this spectrum.

The utility requirement is a question of fact,[1317] and as the Federal Circuit has stated, "The threshold [for] utility is not high."[1318] While an invention must adequately carry out its intended purpose, an invention need not be fully operational.[1319] Indeed, the invention can be partially operable,[1320] perform crudely,[1321] be inferior to others,[1322] or even be deceptive/immoral.[1323] All § 101 requires of an invention is that it be capable of performing the proposed function.[1324] A lack of practical utility can only be sustained by a showing of total incapacity.[1325]

1317. *Raytheon v. Roper*, 724 F.2d 951 (Fed. Cir. 1983).
1318. *Juicy Whip, Inc. v. Orange Bang, Inc.*, 185 F.3d 1364, 1366 (Fed. Cir. 1999).
1319. *See Stiftung v. Renishaw PLC*, 945 F.2d 1173, 1180 (Fed. Cir. 1991).
1320. An invention is inoperable only if it is "totally incapable of achieving a useful result." *Brooktree Corp. v. Advanced Micro Devices, Inc.*, 977 F.2d 1555, 1571 (Fed. Cir. 1992). Thus, an applicant satisfies § 101 as long as the invention accomplishes at least one stated objective. *Raytheon Co. v. Roper Corp.*, 724 F.2d 951, 958 (Fed. Cir. 1983).
1321. *Hildreth v. Mastoras*, 257 U.S. 27, 34 (1921) ("The machine patented may be imperfect in its operation; but if it embodies the generic principle[] and works ... though only in a crude way ... it is enough."); *see also Nat'l Recovery Techs., Inc. v. Magnetic Separation Sys., Inc.*, 166 F.3d 1190, 1196 (Fed. Cir. 1999) (explaining that operability still exists even if the invention does not work perfectly under all conditions).
1322. *See Stiftung v. Reinshaw PLC*, 945 F.2d 1173, 1180 (Fed. Cir. 1991) ("An invention need not be the best or the only way to accomplish a certain result, and it need only be useful to some extent and in certain applications ...."); *Custom Accessories, Inc. v. Jeffrey-Allan Indus.*, 807 F.2d 955, 960 n. 12 (Fed. Cir. 1986) ("It is possible for an invention to be less effective than existing devices but nevertheless meet the statutory requirements for patentability."); *In re* Ratti, 270 F.2d 810, 814 (C.C.P.A. 1959) (rejecting the PTO's contention that an invention "[must] possess some definite advantage over the prior art" in order to be patentable).
1323. Previously the U.S. courts interpreted the utility requirement to include a morality component. However, the modern standard for utility does not include this morality standard. The utility standard only requires some minimal real-world use. The court has recognized that the USPTO should not be the arbiter of an invention's morality, and that this judgment should be left to other agencies (e.g., the Food and Drug Administration, or the Federal Trade Commission, or the Environmental Protection Agency), or to Congress. *See Juicy Whip, Inc. v. Orange Bang, Inc.* 185 F.3d 1364 (Fed. Cir. 1999).
1324. *Brooktree*, 977 F.2d at 1573.
1325. *See Envirotech Corp. v. Al George, Inc.*, 730 F.2d 753, 762 (Fed. Cir. 1984).

For pharmaceutical inventions, an applicant can demonstrate practical utility by presenting adequate proof of pharmacological activity.[1326] Because it is difficult to predict whether a novel compound will exhibit pharmacological activity, testing is often required to establish practical utility.[1327] "[T]here must be a sufficient correlation between the tests and an asserted pharmacological activity so as to convince those skilled in the art, to a reasonable degree, that the novel compound will exhibit the asserted pharmacological behavior."[1328]

The Federal Circuit has articulated a two-step test for determining whether the utility requirement has been met. First, the PTO "has the initial burden of challenging a presumptively correct assertion of utility in the disclosure." Second, "[o]nly after the PTO provides evidence showing that one of ordinary skill in the art would reasonably doubt the asserted utility does the burden shift to the applicant" to prove utility.[1329]

§5 STATUTORY SUBJECT MATTER

Statutory subject matter addresses the kinds of things that may be patented. Specifically, 35 U.S.C. § 101 authorizes the issuance of patents for "any new and useful process, machine, manufacture, or composition of matter, or any new and useful improvement thereof."[1330] In *Diamond v. Chakrabarty*,[1331] the Supreme Court stated

1326. *See Fujikawa v. Wattanasin*, 93 F.3d 1559, 1564 (Fed. Cir. 1996).
1327. *Id.*, at 1564.
1328. *Id.*
1329. *In re* Brana, 51 F.3d 1560, 1566 (Fed. Cir. 1995). In *Cross v. Iizuka*, the Federal Circuit held that in vitro testing of a claimed invention coupled with in vivo testing of structurally similar compounds satisfied the utility requirement because in vitro data is:

> [p]resumably ... the accepted practice in the pharmaceutical industry, ... and we note that this practice has an inherent logical persuasiveness. In vitro testing, in general, is relatively less complex, less time consuming, and less expensive than in vivo testing. Moreover, in vitro results with respect to the particular pharmacological activity are generally predictive of in vivo test results, i.e., there is reasonable correlation there between. Were this not so, the testing procedures of the pharmaceutical industry would not be as they are. [We agree with the Board that] there is a reasonable correlation between the disclosed in vitro utility and an in vivo activity, and therefore a rigorous correlation is not necessary where the disclosure of the pharmacological activity is reasonable based upon the probative evidence.

753 F.2d 1040, 1050 (Fed. Cir. 1985). According to the court, the utility requirement was satisfied because the in vitro data possessed "pharmacological activity," which in turn is "generally predictive" of in vivo test results. *Id.* That is, utility is satisfied if there is a "reasonable correlation between the disclosed in vitro utility and an in vivo activity." *Id.*

1330. 35 U.S.C. § 101. In the first patent statute (in 1790), Congress authorized patents for "any useful art, manufacture, engine, machine, or device, or any improvement therein not before known or used." Act of Apr. 4, 1790. Then, in 1793, Congress authorized patents for "any useful art, machine, manufacture, or composition of matter, or any new and useful improvement, not known or used before the application." Act of Feb. 21, 1793. The four categories recited in the 1793 statute are still used to describe the classes of patentable subject matter, except that the term "process" replaced "art" in the 1952 Patent Act. "Art" and "process" are considered to have the same meaning. *See Diamond v. Diehr*, 450 U.S. 175, 181–82 & nn. 6–7 (1981) ("Although the term 'process' was not added to 35 U.S.C. § 101 until 1952 a process has

that these four categories of patentable subject matter "include anything under the sun that is made by man."[1332] There are, however, exceptions such as "laws of nature, natural phenomena, … [and] abstract ideas."[1333] Currently, 35 U.S.C. § 101 is one of the most unsettled areas of patent law. In order to give better guidance over this area, the PTO has created a set of examples illustrating how the Office applies eligibility guidance in fact-specific situations, including: abstract ideas, nature-based products, life science examples, and business method examples.[1334]

Patent claims can generally be separated into products and processes. Further, a single patent may encompass both product claims and process claims.

I Products

A *Machines, Articles of Manufacture, and Compositions of Matter*

Product claims encompass machines, manufactures,[1335] and compositions of matter. Each is a distinct category of invention, but generally the distinctions have little substantive impact on patentability. For instance, "[t]he term machine includes every mechanical device or combination of mechanical powers and devices to perform some function and produce a certain effect or result."[1336] In other words, machines are often used to affect another object or entity by way of transferring force or energy. A "manufacture" is typically anything human-made that is not a machine or composition of matter. Further, the Supreme Court stated that a manufacture is interpreted "in accordance with its dictionary definition to mean 'the production of articles for use from raw or prepared materials by giving to these materials new forms, qualities, properties, or combinations, whether by hand-labor or by machinery'."[1337] The general

historically enjoyed patent protection because it was considered a form of 'art' as that term was used in the 1793 Act."); *Corning v. Burden*, 56 U.S. (15 How.) 252, 267 (1853) ("A process … is included under the general term 'useful art'."); H.R. Rep. No. 1923, 82d Cong., 2d Sess. (1952).

1331. 447 U.S. 303 (1980).
1332. *Id.*, at 309 (citing the Committee Reports, S. Rep. No. 1979, 82d Cong., 2d Sess. 5 (1952); H.R. Rep. No. 1923, 82d Cong. 2d Sess., 6 (1952); Hearings on H.R. 3760 Before Subcomm. No. 3 of the House Comm. on the Judiciary, 82d Cong. 1st Sess. 37 (1951) (testimony of P.J. Federico)).
1333. *Chakrabarty*, 447 U.S. at 309 ("[A] new mineral discovered in the earth or a new plant found in the wild is not patentable subject matter. Likewise, Einstein could not patent … $E=mc^2$; nor could Newton have patented the law of gravity."); *Diehr*, 450 U.S. at 185 ("A principle, in the abstract, is a fundamental truth; an original cause; a motive; these cannot be patented, as no one can claim in either of them an exclusive right.") (quoting *Le Roy v. Tatham*, 55 U.S. (14 How.) 156, 175 (1853)); *Rubber-Tip Pencil Co. v. Howard*, 87 U.S. (20 Wall.) 498, 507 (1874) ("An idea is itself not patentable.").
1334. https://www.uspto.gov/patent/laws-and-regulations/examination-policy/subject-matter-eligibility.
1335. The term "manufacture" is synonymous with "article of manufacture." *In re* Hruby, 373 F.2d 997, 1001–02 (C.C.P.A. 1967).
1336. *Corning*, 56 U.S. (15 How.) at 267 (distinguishing a machine from a process).
1337. *Chakrabarty*, 447 U.S. at 308 (quoting *Am. Fruit Growers, Inc. v. Brogdex Co.*, 283 U.S. 1, 11 (1931)).

distinction between machines and manufactures is that machines typically involve moving parts,[1338] where manufactures are static. A machine or manufacture is often referred to as an apparatus.

Generally, a composition of matter is a new substance resulting from the combination of known or new ingredients.[1339] A "'composition of matter' has been construed consistent with its common usage to include 'all compositions of two or more substances and ... all composite articles, whether they be the results of chemical union, or of mechanical mixture, or whether they be gases, fluids, powders, or solids'."[1340] In the chemical and pharmaceutical fields composition of matter claims are considered to be among the most powerful patent claims because of their broad application. An example of a composition of matter is a drug comprising a combination of two known molecules that creates something that is different from anything made before.

In sum, products are "things" made by man whether static, dynamic, or chemical. These classes of "products" are useful in determining exactly what the invention is, but do not have any procedural or substantive legal significance during the application process or during infringement litigation.

One lingering question has been whether isolated DNA molecules are either patent-eligible compositions of matter or patent-ineligible products of nature. The Supreme Court addressed this question in *Association for Molecular Pathology v. Myriad Genetics, Inc.*[1341] The Court addressed two specific issues in Myriad: (1) the patentability of "naturally occurring" DNA fragments isolated from the rest of the genome; and (2) the patentability of synthetically created DNA known as cDNA. As to the first, the Court held that isolated DNA does not constitute patentable subject matter:

> In Chakrabarty, scientists added four plasmids to a bacterium, which enabled it to break down various components of crude oil .... The Court held that the modified bacterium was patentable. It explained that the patent claim was "not to a hitherto unknown natural phenomenon, but to a nonnaturally occurring manufacture or composition of matter—a product of human ingenuity ...." The Chakrabarty bacterium was new "with markedly different characteristics from any found in nature," [Diamond v. Chakrabarty, 447 U.S. 303, 310 (1980)] .... In this case, by contrast, Myriad did not create anything. To be sure, it found an important and useful gene, but separating that gene from its surrounding genetic material is not an act of invention.[1342]

In reaching this conclusion, the Court pointed out that Myriad's claims were not "saved by the fact that isolating DNA from the human genome severs chemical bonds and thereby creates a non-naturally occurring molecule ... [Its] claim is concerned

1338. "The term machine includes every mechanical device or combination of mechanical powers and devices to perform some function and produce a certain result." *Corning*, 56 U.S. (15 How.) at 267.
1339. *Chakrabarty*, 447 U.S. at 308.
1340. *Id.*
1341. 133 S. Ct. 2107 (2013).
1342. *Id.*, at 2116–17.

primarily with the information contained in the genetic sequence, not with the specific chemical composition of a particular molecule."[1343]

As to the second, the Court held that cDNA can be patent-eligible because it does not present the same obstacles to patentability as naturally occurring DNA fragments:

> [T]he lab technician unquestionably creates something new when cDNA is made. cDNA retains the naturally occurring exons of DNA, but it is distinct from the DNA from which it was derived. As a result, cDNA is not a "product of nature" and is patent eligible under § 101, except insofar as very short series of DNA may have no intervening introns to remove when creating cDNA. In that situation, a short strand of cDNA may be indistinguishable from natural DNA.[1344]

Given the Court's focus on DNA's information content, one question left unanswered in Myriad is whether other classes of naturally occurring biological molecules remain patent-eligible subject matter.

B Living Organisms

The boundaries of patentable subject matter are tested by new technologies, including biotechnology. Biotechnology is a booming field, and patent law plays an important role in its growth and development.[1345] One must begin with the Supreme Court case of *Diamond v. Chakrabarty*[1346] when discussing the fields of biotechnology and genetics. Although the Court pointed out that a naturally occurring product cannot be patented even if its existence was unknown, it held that a genetically engineered, living microorganism constituted patentable subject matter.[1347] According to the Court, "the relevant distinction was not between living and inanimate things, but between products of nature, whether living or not, and human-made inventions."[1348]

II Processes

Process claims are directed "to an act or a series of acts, performed upon the subject matter to be transformed and reduced to a different state or thing."[1349] Section 100(b)

1343. *Id.*, at 2118.
1344. *Id.*, at 2119.
1345. *See, e.g., In re* O'Farrell, 853 F.2d 894 (Fed. Cir. 1988); *Amgen, Inc. v. Chugai Pharmaceutical Co., Ltd.*, 927 F.2d 1200 (Fed. Cir. 1991); *In re* Bell, 991 F.2d 781 (Fed. Cir. 1993); *In re* Deuel, 51 F.3d 1552 (Fed. Cir. 1995).
1346. 447 U.S. 303 (1980).
1347. *Id.*, at 309 ("[A] new mineral discovered in the earth or a new plant found in the wild is not patentable subject matter."). Earlier, the Court stated that "[h]e who discovers a hitherto unknown phenomenon of nature has no claim to a monopoly of it which the law recognizes." *Funk Bros. Seed Co. v. Kalo Inoculant Co.*, 333 U.S. 127, 130 (1948) (quoted in *Gottschalk v. Benson*, 409 U.S. 63, 67–68 (1972)).
1348. *Chakrabarty*, 447 U.S. at 313.
1349. *Cochrane v. Deener*, 94 U.S. 780, 787–88 (1876). More recently, the Federal Circuit has attempted to clarify the definition of process by stating that "[a] process ... is a manipulation according to an algorithm, ... doing something to or with something according to a schema." *In re* Durden, 763 F.2d 1406, 1410 (Fed. Cir. 1985).

provides that "[t]he term 'process' means process, art or method, and includes a new use of a known process, machine, manufacture, composition of matter, or material."[1350] Thus, a process may entail a new use for a known product.[1351]

Perhaps the principal controversy surrounding patentable subject matter today concerns the mathematical characteristics of computer software and business methods.[1352] Patentable subject matter issues arise with digital computers because it is essentially a process that includes steps involving mathematical formulas or algorithms. In *Diamond v. Diehr*,[1353] the Supreme Court affirmed the potential patentability of such a method. Specifically, the Court stated that "[w]hile a scientific truth, or the mathematical expression of it, is not a patentable invention, a novel and useful structure created with the aid of knowledge of scientific truth may be."[1354] In determining whether the use of a particular mathematical algorithm is patentable, the Court held that a claim satisfies § 101 "when a claim containing a mathematical formula implements or applies that formula in a structure or process which, when considered as a whole, is performing a function which the patent laws were designed to protect (e.g., transforming or reducing an article to a different state or thing)."[1355]

The Federal Circuit, in *State Street Bank & Trust Co. v. Signature Financial Group Inc.*,[1356] took an expansive view of patentable subject matter, specifically process patent inventions that include mathematical algorithms. According to the court, any process, including a business method, is statutory subject matter if it possesses practical utility in producing a "useful, concrete and tangible result."[1357]

1350. 35 U.S.C. § 100(b).
1351. A known product with a newly discovered use, on its own, would not be patentable as a product because of a lack of novelty. However, the inventor might acquire a patent for a new method of using a known product so long as the new use can be distinguished from the known use. *Titanium Metals Corp. v. Banner*, 778 F.2d 775, 780–81 (Fed. Cir. 1985); *In re* Bergstrom, 427 F.2d 1394, 1402–03 (C.C.P.A. 1970). For example, a new treatment for Alzheimer's disease using a previously known drug that was previously only used to treat breast cancer. An applicant could not get a composition of matter patent on the drug because of novelty issues; however, the applicant could get a process claim directed to the use of the drug for the treatment of Alzheimer's disease.
1352. Besides computer-related process difficulties, other areas have experienced challenges. For example, from at least 1862 a patent could not be acquired for medical procedures. *See Morton v. New York Eye Infirmary*, 17 F. Cas. 879, 882–84 (C.C.S.D.N.Y. 1862) (No. 9,865) (implying that medical procedures were not patentable despite the invention being "one of the great discoveries of modern time"). In 1954, the PTO Board of Appeals ruled that a patent may be attained for a medical procedure. Ex parte Scherer, 103 U.S.P.Q. 107, 108 (Pat. & Tm. Off. Bd. App. 1954). Then from 1954 to 1996, medical procedures were, theoretically, patentable and enforceable. However, after a patentee attempted to enforce a medical procedure patent, in *Pallin v. Singer*, 36 U.S.P.Q.2d 1050 (D. Vt. 1995) (Opinion and Order), 1996 WL 274407 (D. Vt. 1995), Congress and medical associations rallied and legislation was passed to render medical procedure patents unenforceable. *See* 35 U.S.C. § 287(c).
1353. 450 U.S. 175 (1981).
1354. *Id.*, at 188.
1355. *Id.*, at 192.
1356. 149 F.3d 1368 (Fed. Cir. 1998).
1357. *Id.*, at 1373 ("Today, we hold that the transformation of data, representing discrete dollar amounts, by a machine through a series of mathematical calculations into a final share price, constitutes a practical application of a mathematical algorithm, formula, or calculation, because it produces 'a useful, concrete and tangible result'.").

But State Street Bank has effectively been overruled by the *Supreme Court in Bilski v. Kappos*.[1358] The Bilski opinion—including language from Justice Breyer's concurrence—made clear that State Street Bank's "useful, concrete, and tangible" test is no longer applicable.[1359] The Court recognized the importance of another test, which focuses on whether the claimed process relates to a "machine or transformation."[1360] But what is the machine-or-transformation test?

In Federal Circuit Bilski,[1361] the court stated that subject matter is eligible for patent protection if: "(1) it is tied to a particular machine or apparatus, or (2) it transforms a particular article into a different state or thing."[1362] The court added two additional filters in unpacking this test, namely that the claimed machine-or-transformation of an article "must impose meaningful limits on the claim's scope" to satisfy § 101's eligibility requirements, and the specific machine-or-transformation "must not merely be insignificant extra-solution activity." Accordingly, the machine-transformation test can be viewed as a rule-like framework that is broad and inclusive, but not without underlying considerations or filters that can inform the subject matter analysis. The question remains how aggressively will the Federal Circuit and PTO apply the machine-transformation framework.

What is a "Machine"? The Federal Circuit did not elaborate on the machine component, but other cases have stated "a machine is a concrete thing, consisting of parts, or of certain devices and combination of devices," which "includes every mechanical device or combination of mechanical powers and devices to perform some function and produce a certain effect or result."[1363]

The Federal Circuit left open the question "whether or when recitation of a computer suffices to tie a process claim to a particular machine." The obvious question is: what is a "particular machine"? The common law will have to play itself out and draw the line at the appropriate level of abstraction, but one can plausibly argue that according to the Supreme Court opinion in *Gottschalk v. Benson*,[1364] a claimed process tied to a computer may not satisfy the machine prong unless the claim is geared toward a real-world application, something concrete, not overly abstract.[1365] In other words, a computer is not a "particular machine."[1366] As the Federal Circuit noted, in Benson "the limitations tying the process to a computer were not actually limiting because the

1358. 130 S. Ct. 3218 (2010).

1359. *See id.*, at 3231.

1360. *See id.*, at 3227 (explaining that the machine-or-transformation test, while not the exclusive test, "is a useful and important clue, an investigative tool, for determining whether some claimed inventions are processes under §101.").

1361. 545 F.3d 943 (Fed. Cir. 2008).

1362. *Id.*, at 954.

1363. *In re* Nuijten, 500 F.3d 1346, 1355 (Fed. Cir. 2007) (denying patent eligibility for a claim to an encoded signal used for reducing distortion in, for example, a digital audio file); *see also In re* Ferguson, 558 F.3d 1359, 1364 (Fed. Cir. 2009) (denying patent eligibility based on *Bilski* for a claim for marketing a product because "applicants' method claims are not tied to any concrete parts, devices, or combination of devices").

1364. 409 U.S. 63 (1972).

1365. *Id.*, at 71–72.

1366. *Id.*, at 70.

fundamental principle at issue, a particular algorithm, had no utility other than operating on a digital computer."[1367]

But this may be too broad a reading of Benson. Federal Circuit Bilski recognized that "Benson presents a difficult case" because "the claimed process operated on a machine, a digital computer, but was still held to be ineligible subject matter." Thus, the claimed process in Benson arguably satisfies the machine-transformation test. One way to reconcile Benson with the machine-transformation test, therefore, is to find another reason why the Benson claims were deemed ineligible. This other reason may be that Benson's claimed invention would have preempted a fundamental principle, particularly because the only use of the claimed algorithm was on a digital computer.[1368] That is, the claims "purported to cover any use of the claimed method in a general-purpose digital computer of any type."[1369] Thus, a claim to an algorithm tied to a computer may be eligible if the algorithm has additional computer-related uses beyond what is claimed.

In ex parte Gupta,[1370] a precedential opinion from the USPTO Board of Patent Appeals and Interferences, the Board created a two-part test for determining whether a machine that makes use of a mathematical algorithm satisfies § 101.[1371] Claim 1 recited:

> A method for identifying one or more mean items for a plurality of items, J, each of the items having a symbolic value of a symbolic attribute, the method comprising:
>
> computing a variance of the symbolic values of the plurality of items relative to the symbolic value of each of the items; and selecting at least one mean item that has the symbolic value that minimizes the variance.[1372]
>
> The two-part test, which closely tracked the Federal Circuit *Bilski* decision, is:
>
> 1. Is the claim limited to a tangible practical application, in which the mathematical algorithm is applied, that results in a real-world use (e.g., "not a mere field-of-use label having no significance")?
> 2. Is the claim limited so as to not encompass substantially all practical applications of the mathematical algorithm either "in all fields" of use of the algorithm or even in "only one field?"
>
> If the machine (or article of manufacture) claim fails either prong of the two-part inquiry, then the claim is not directed to patent eligible subject matter.[1373]

The Board held that claim 1 did not recite eligible subject matter because the invention was not limited to a machine. According to the Board:

> "[A] machine is a concrete thing, consisting of parts, or of certain devices and combination of devices. This includes every mechanical device or combination of mechanical powers and devices to perform some function and produce a certain

1367. *Bilski*, 545 F.3d at 955.
1368. *See id.*, at 955 n. 9.
1369. *Id.*
1370. 93 U.S.P.Q.2d 1025 (B.P.A.I. 2009).
1371. *Id.*, at 1026–27.
1372. *Id.*, at 1027.
1373. *Id.*, at 1026–27.

> effect or result." Claim 1 computes a variance and selects a mean item (FF 4 and 5) without tying these steps to any concrete parts, devices, or combinations of devices. In fact, one can compute the variance and select the mean item in one's mind. Such mental steps are patentably excluded under § 101. See [Gottschalk v. Benson, 409 U.S. 63, 67 (1972)]. Thus, while we agree with Appellants that the method of claim 1 does not recite a law of nature we do not find claim 1 recites any machine, let alone a particular machine, under this prong of the machine-or-transformation test.[1374]

What Is a "Transformation"? Regarding the transformation component, in Bilski the Federal Circuit made clear that the transformation "must be central to the purpose of the claimed process" and must transform an "article."[1375] It is hard to know what the court meant by the former other than the transformation imposes "meaningful limits" on claim scope.[1376] Regarding the latter, the court endeavored to clarify what sorts of things constitute "articles." For instance, it can include a claimed process that is directed toward "a chemical or physical transformation of physical objects or substances."[1377] Also, a claimed process that employs electronic signals and electronically manipulated data is eligible if the data represents physical or tangible objects.[1378] But the issue becomes more difficult as you move away from physicality. What about data transformations that do not represent physical or tangible information on a computer screen, in other words, the transformation of data that results in an intangible representation. Thus, the physicality of the representation seems to play an important role in the transformation test.

In the closely watched case of *Mayo Collaborative Servs. v. Prometheus Laboratories*,[1379] the question was whether a method for calibrating a drug dosage satisfied was eligible for patent protection. In particular, the patent claimed "a method of optimizing therapeutic efficiency for treatment of an immune-mediated gastrointestinal disorder."[1380] This included "administering" a drug to a patient and thereafter "determining" the patient's metabolic response. A subsequent dosage is then provided based on the measurement of the patient's metabolic response to the first dosage. The Federal Circuit rejected the argument that the claims merely relate to natural correlations and data-gathering steps, and it held that the "administering" and "determining" steps satisfy the transformation prong of the machine-transformation test.[1381] Mayo petitioned the Supreme Court for review. In light of its recent holding in Bilski, the Supreme Court vacated and remanded the Federal Circuit's first Prometheus decision. On remand, the Federal Circuit explained that Supreme Court Bilski did not undermine its earlier analysis and reaffirmed the validity of the asserted claims.[1382] However, on

1374. *Id.*, at 1029.
1375. *In re* Bilski, 545 F.3d 943, 962 (Fed. Cir. 2008) (en banc).
1376. *Id.*, at 961.
1377. *Id.*, at 962 (emphasis in original).
1378. *Id.*
1379. 132 S. Ct. 1289 (2012).
1380. *Id.*, at 1295.
1381. *Prometheus*, 581 F.3d 1336, 1345–46 (Fed. Cir. 1999).
1382. *Prometheus Laboratories, Inc. v. Mayo Collaborative Servs.*, 628 F.3d 1347, 1355 (Fed. Cir. 2010).

appeal, the Supreme Court sided unanimously with Mayo.[1383] It held that the claims to the blood test were invalid because they merely recited a law of nature. According to the Court, the claims fail to do "significantly more than simply describe ... natural relations[hips]"[1384] and do not "add enough to their statements of the correlations to allow the processes they describe to qualify as patent-eligible processes that apply natural laws."[1385] And since a law of nature is not patentable, "then neither is a process reciting a law of nature, unless that process has additional features that provide practical assurance that the process is more than a drafting effort designed to monopolize the law of nature itself."[1386] What remains unclear from Prometheus is exactly what additional application of a law of nature is sufficient to define patent-eligible subject matter.

In *Alice Corp. Pty. Ltd. v. CLS Bank Int'l*,[1387] the Supreme Court again addressed the question of the patent eligibility of software and business methods. The patents at issue claimed computerized methods for mitigating "settlement risk" (the risk that one party will fail to meet its obligations) in a financial transaction. In particular, the patent claims are designed to facilitate the exchange of financial obligations between two parties by using a computer system as a third-party intermediary. The patents in suit claim: (1) a method for exchanging financial obligations (method claims); (2) a computer system configured to carry out the method for exchanging obligations (system claims); and (3) a computer-readable medium containing program code for performing the method of exchanging obligations (media claims).[1388] Mayo, according to the Court, provides the analytical framework to gauge patent eligibility:

> First, we determine whether the claims at issue are directed to one of those patent-ineligible concepts. If so, we then ask, "[w]hat else is there in the claims before us?" To answer that question, we consider the elements of each claim both individually and "as an ordered combination" to determine whether the additional elements "transform the nature of the claim" into a patent-eligible application. We have described step two of this analysis as a search for an "inventive concept"—i.e., an element or combination of elements that is "sufficient to ensure that the patent in practice amounts to significantly more than a patent upon the [ineligible concept] itself."[1389]

A unanimous Court in Alice determined that all three claims were patent-ineligible subject matter. Applying the first step, the Court concluded that intermediated settlement was a patent-ineligible abstract idea. "Like the risk hedging in Bilski, the concept of intermediated settlement is 'a fundamental economic practice long prevalent in our system of commerce'."[1390] Turning to step two, the court determined

1383. *Mayo Collaborative Servs. v. Prometheus Laboratories*, 132 S. Ct. 1289, 1305 (2012).
1384. *Id.*, at 1297.
1385. *Id.* (emphasis in original).
1386. *Id.*
1387. 134 S. Ct. 2347 (2014).
1388. *Id.*, at 235.
1389. *Id.*, at 2345.
1390. *Id.*, at 2356 (quoting *Bilski v. Kappos*, 130 S. Ct. 3218, 3231 (2010)).

that the claims failed to transform an abstract idea into patent-eligible subject matter. The method claims, for example, did not add "enough" to the abstract idea:

> The method claims do not, for example, purport to improve the functioning of the computer itself ... Nor do they effect an improvement in any other technology or technical field. Instead, the claims at issue amount to "nothing significantly more" than an instruction to apply the abstract idea of intermediated settlement using some unspecified, generic computer. Under our precedents, that is not "enough" to transform an abstract idea into a patent-eligible invention ....[1391]

The system and media claims failed for essentially the same reason.[1392]

Alice reiterated that "the mere recitation of a generic computer cannot transform a patent-ineligible abstract idea into a patent-eligible invention." And using claim language like "creating," "obtaining," "adjusting," and "issuing" was not enough to do so because the Court "has long 'warn[ed] ... against interpreting § 101 in ways that make patent eligibility depend simply on the draftsman's art'."[1393]

1391. *Id.*, at 2360.
1392. *Id.*, at 2360.
1393. *Id.*, at 2359 (quoting *Mayo*, 132 S. Ct. at 1294).

CHAPTER 3
Formalities

The US PTO plays a crucial role in the US patent system. Patent rights do not exist unless granted by the federal government.[1394] To obtain a patent, an inventor must file a patent application with the PTO. Then, the Commissioner of Patents and Trademarks is required to "cause an examination to be made of the application and the alleged new invention; and if on such examination it appears that the applicant is entitled to a patent under the law, the Commissioner shall issue a patent therefor."[1395] Examination is conducted to ensure that the claimed invention is adequately disclosed (35 U.S.C. § 112), new (35 U.S.C. § 102), nonobvious (35 U.S.C. § 103), useful (35 U.S.C. § 101), and within the statutory classes of patentable subject matter (35 U.S.C. § 101). The process of obtaining a patent is called patent prosecution.[1396] The writing necessary for a patent application is very technical and a degree in the relevant scientific discipline or other appropriate technical background is helpful. Indeed, the patent prosecutor has an obligation to know and comprehend not only the law but also the pertinent

1394. In contrast, for example, copyright subsists in a work once it is "fixed in any tangible medium of expression," 17 U.S.C. § 102(a), and federal registration is needed only to obtain certain remedies, 17 U.S.C. § 412. Similarly, property rights in trademarks are initially created by using the mark in trade, not by governmental grant or registration, while federal registration gives the owner the benefit of additional federal rights and remedies. *See In re* DC Comics 689 F.2d 1042, 1046–55 (Fed. Cir. 1982) (opinions by Judges Rich and Nies concurring in result and reviewing the life cycle of a trademark—beginning with initial use and ending with abandonment or genericness).

1395. 35 U.S.C. § 131.

1396. Broadly, patent prosecution generally includes all of the steps up to and including the grant of a patent (writing, filing, and registering a patent application with the PTO). Patent litigation, in contrast, represents events that occur after the grant of a patent (suing another party for violating patent rights). In general, to prosecute patents one needs to have a scientific background.

technology. Thus, specialized training is generally required, with a few notable exceptions, for registration to practice before the PTO.[1397]

The patent application, and the resulting issued patent, contains two major components: (1) the written description; and (2) the claims. These two components together make up the specification.[1398] The process by which the patent specification and especially the patent claims are shaped is of primary importance because the claims of the issued patent establish the metes and bounds of the patent owner's right to exclude:

> The US is strictly an examination country and the main purpose of the examination, to which every application is subjected, is to try and make sure that what each claim defines is patentable. To coin a phrase, the name of the game is the claim [and] the function of claims is to enable everyone to know, without going through a lawsuit, what infringes the patent and what does not.[1399]

§1 THE PATENT APPLICATION AND ISSUED PATENT

Although the patent application process may be thought of as beginning with the drafting of the application itself, this is usually preceded by other events. For example, an inventor usually documents and records his or her conception of the invention as well as the ensuing development of the invention toward a practical embodiment—this development process is called "reduction to practice." In addition, substantial dialogue may occur between the inventor and the person preparing the patent application.

Another probable prefiling event is a prior art search. "Prior art" is a term used in patent law to refer broadly to known technical information.[1400] Although an applicant is under no obligation to conduct a search prior to filing an application,[1401] a search is usually done in view of the significant cost associated with filing a patent application. A thorough search may avoid the unnecessary costs of attempting to patent a preexisting invention. It may also help give the applicant an opportunity to make informed arguments about the patentability of the invention, and to present the written description and claims in a way favorable to patentability. This search for relevant prior patents and other technical literature may be carried out in the Public Search Room maintained by the PTO in its Arlington, Virginia, location or various satellite search

1397. *See* 37 C.F.R. §§ 10.5, 10.6, 10.7, wherein the regulations governing the individuals practicing before the PTO are set forth. The PTO issues a pamphlet entitled "General Requirements for Admission to the Examination for Registration to Practice in Patent Cases Before the U.S. Patent and Trademark Office."

1398. *See* 35 U.S.C. § 112. Although often, and incorrectly, used interchangeably, the terms "written description" and "specification" are *not* coextensive. The specification contains the claims as well as the written description.

1399. Giles S. Rich, *The Extent of the Protection and Interpretation of Claims: American Perspectives*, 21 INT'L REV. INDUS. PROP. & COPYRIGHT L. 497, 499, 501 (1990).

1400. The term is "prior" art because the only relevant references included are those references that predate the invention date (for pre-AIA applications, applications filed before Mar. 16, 2013) or those references that predate the earliest filing date (for applications filed under the AIA, applications filed on or after Mar. 16, 2013).

1401. *See American Hoist & Derrick Co. v. Sowa & Sons*, 725 F.2d 1350, 1362 (Fed. Cir. 1984).

locations scattered throughout the US, or in libraries or other repositories. Today, one may conduct a prior art search using various electronic media, including online services and the Internet.

Each application consists of: (1) a specification (i.e., the written description and at least one claim); (2) one or more drawings (if necessary); (3) an oath or declaration;[1402] and (4) the required filing fees.[1403] The filing date of such an application, known as a nonprovisional application,[1404] is the date on which the specification and drawings, including at least one claim, are received at the PTO or the date they were deposited in a US post office as Express Mail, provided that the mailing day was one on which the PTO was open.

While there is some flexibility as to the presentation of the patent application, the PTO prefers the application to be filed as follows:

(1) title;
(2) cross-reference to related inventions;
(3) statement regarding federally sponsored research;
(4) background of the invention;
(5) summary;
(6) brief description of the drawings;
(7) detailed description of the invention;
(8) claims;
(9) abstract of the disclosure;
(10) drawings;
(11) oath or declaration.

I The Written Description

A *Background of the Invention*

The Background section of a patent usually accomplishes three things: (1) it sets the stage for the applicant's invention by describing the state of the prior art; (2) it directly addresses the most important aspect of the invention; and (3) it points out why that aspect was an improvement over the prior art. Skilled practitioners disagree about

1402. The oath or declaration must usually be signed by the inventor, and must state that the inventor: (1) has read the application; (2) believes he or she is the first inventor; and (3) acknowledges the duty to disclose any material information. *See* 37 C.F.R. §§ 1.63(b), 1.77; MPEP, § 601.

1403. *See* 35 U.S.C. § 111(a)(2), (3).

1404. Instead of *initially* filing a nonprovisional application, an applicant, as of June 8, 1995, may opt to file a "provisional application." As a provisional application does not require claims, it is not examined and cannot mature into a patent. § 111(b). Nevertheless, priority can still be claimed from the date of the provisional application by filing a nonprovisional application within one year from the provisional application's filing date.

whether to introduce the invention's improvements over the prior art in the Background section, or whether to limit the Background section to a discussion of the prior art.

The Background section should use as simple language as the invention permits, especially with respect to commercial issues. Although the law provides that a patent application should provide technical information to a "person of ordinary skill in the art" to which the invention pertains, some argue that every patent should be written with an eye to the judge, jury, investment banker, present and future competitors as well as the patent examiner.

B Summary of the Invention

The Summary states the invention broadly, tracking the broadest claim, but requires sufficient detail to explain and distinguish from the prior art. The "MPEP" points out that "[s]ince the purpose of the brief summary of invention is to apprise the public, and more especially those interested in the particular art to which the invention relates, of the nature of the invention, the summary should be directed to the specific invention being claimed, in contradistinction to mere generalities which would be equally applicable to numerous preceding patents."[1405] The MPEP also suggests that "[t]he brief summary, if properly written to set out the exact nature, operation, and purpose of the invention, will be of material assistance in aiding ready understanding of the patent in future searches."[1406]

Although no one particular way to write the Summary exists, it is recommended that section 608.01(d) of the MPEP be followed so that the patent examiner, as well as the public, knows where to look for various kinds of information.

C Detailed Description of the Invention

The Detailed Description focuses on the details of the invention. Because of its comprehensiveness, it constitutes the bulk of the specification. The Detailed Description must contain a written description of the invention and must be in terms sufficiently full, clear, concise, and exact as to enable any person skilled in the art to which the invention pertains to make and use the invention.[1407] The patent applicant must also disclose the best mode of carrying out the invention known to the inventor at the time of filing.[1408] The best mode is usually described in the detailed description and may also be represented in the drawings.

1405. MPEP § 608.01(d).
1406. *Id.*
1407. *See* 35 U.S.C. § 112 ¶ 1.
1408. *Id.*

D *The Drawings*

35 U.S.C. § 113 requires the applicant to "furnish a drawing where necessary for the understanding of the subject matter sought to be patented." Drawings are often instructive in teaching the essence of the invention and are typically necessary for mechanical devices and other forms of invention. If the invention is for a process or method, then drawings usually are not required. If drawings are required, there are formal rules governing their acceptability. Black and white drawings are normally required when submitting figures; however, the office will accept color drawings if an explanation is provided for why a color drawing is necessary. Additionally, photographs are not accepted, except in very limited situations.

II The Claims

The 1790 and 1793 Patent Acts made no mention of claims. The invention was discerned from the written description, often with a claim-like summary at the end. It was not until the 1836 Act that "claims" were mentioned by statute.

Our present patent statute requires that "[t]he specification shall conclude with one or more claims particularly pointing out and distinctly claiming the subject matter which the applicant regards as his invention."[1409] Today, the claim is the most important part of the patent, setting forth the metes and bounds of the patentee's right to exclude. The Federal Circuit has stated time and again that "[i]t is the claims that measure the invention" and "[c]laims are infringed, not specifications."[1410] Indeed, claim drafting is truly an art, the importance of which cannot be overstated.[1411]

Claims are usually made up of three parts: a preamble, a transition phrase, and a body. The preamble identifies the invention or the technical field of the invention. The preamble usually does not limit the invention, unless limiting language is used that gives "life, meaning and vitality" to the claim, or if the preamble recites essential structure(s) or step(s).[1412]

The transition phrase joins the preamble to the body of the claim. Three common transition phrases are: (1) "comprising"; (2) "consisting of"; and (3) "consisting essentially of." The transition phrase defines the scope of the claim, and helps determine what unrecited additional components or steps, if any, are included or excluded from the scope of the claim.[1413]

1409. 35 U.S.C. § 112 ¶ 2.
1410. *SRI Int'l v. Matsushita Electric Corp. of Am.*, 775 F.2d 1101, 1121 (Fed. Cir. 1985).
1411. Books have been devoted to teaching the patent practitioner how best to draft claims. *See*, e.g., Robert C. Faber, Faber on Mechanics of Patent Claim Drafting (6th ed. 2010); Morgan D. Rosenberg, The Essentials of Patent Claim Drafting (2011); Ronald D. Slusky, Invention Analysis and Claiming: A Patent Lawyer's Guide (2007). Giles Rich famously stated that "the name of the game is the claim." Giles S. Rich, *The Extent of the Protection and Interpretation of Claims: American Perspectives*, 21 Int'l Rev. Indus. Prop. & Copyright L. 497 (1990).
1412. *Catalina Marketing Int'l, Inc. v. CoolSavings.com, Inc.*, 289 F.3d 801, 808 (Fed. Cir. 2002).
1413. *See* MPEP § 2111.03.

The broadest transition phrase is usually made up only of the word "comprising,"[1414] which means that the invention includes the listed elements, but does not exclude others.[1415] The word "comprising" creates an "open" claim that can be infringed when the competitor's product includes each of the specifically listed elements of the claim, plus anything else.[1416] In contrast, the narrowest transition phrase "consisting of" creates a "closed" claim, which can only be infringed by a product that includes each of the specifically listed elements of the claim, but nothing else. Thus, the transitional phrase "consisting of" excludes any element, step or ingredient not specified in the claim.[1417] Finally, the transitional phrase "consisting essentially of" is a partially closed claim, and it limits the scope of a claim to the specified materials or steps and "those that do not materially affect the basic and novel characteristic(s)" of the claimed invention.[1418]

The body of the claim includes a recitation of the "elements": the steps or parts that make up the invention. It also includes the structural, physical, or functional relationship among the elements. The elements and their relationship usually define the claim, at least for apparatus or device claims. Process claims may require additional detail.

Words in a patent are not necessarily held to their ordinary meaning. Each inventor can be his or her own lexicographer. However, the application must define words being used in an uncommon manner.[1419] As with the rest of the patent, the author of the patent can punctuate and fashion the claim in whatever manner he or she desires, except that each claim must be one sentence, so there can be only one period, at the end of the sentence.

A patent application generally has more than one claim. The claims of a patent may vary in scope or method of description or expression. Broad claims include fewer limitations than do narrow claims and therefore cover a wider scope. Claims are often arranged in order of decreasing scope, that is, the broadest first and the narrowest last. Claims can be in independent, dependent, or multiple dependent forms. An independent claim is completely self-contained. A dependent claim refers back to an earlier claim and thus it incorporates by reference all limitations of the claim to which it refers and also includes its own limitations. A multiple dependent claim refers back in the

1414. "Including," "containing," "characterized by," or "having" sometimes replace the word "comprising." *See*, e.g., *Mars, Inc. v. H.J. Heinz Co.*, 377 F.3d 1369, 1376 (Fed. Cir. 2004).

1415. *See Moleculon Res. Corp. v. CBS, Inc.*, 793 F.2d 1261, 1271 (Fed. Cir. 1986).

1416. Thus, one cannot escape infringement of an open claim by simply adding elements to the claimed invention.

1417. *See* MPEP § 2111.03. *See also In re Gray*, 53 F.2d 520 (CCPA 1931). Thus, one can escape infringement liability of a closed claim by simply adding additional elements or structures not specifically recited in the claim.

1418. *See* MPEP § 2111.03. *See also In re Hertz*, 537 F.2d 549 (CCPA 1976) and *Norian Corp. v. Stryker Corp.*, 363 F.3d 1321 (Fed. Cir. 2004).

1419. *See Lear Siegler, Inc. v. Aeroquip Corp.*, 733 F.2d 881, 888 (Fed. Cir. 1984); *W.L. Gore & Assocs., Inc. v. Garlock, Inc.*, 721 F.2d 1540, 1558 (Fed. Cir. 1983); *Autogiro Co. of America v. United States*, 384 U.S. F.2d 391, 376–97 (Ct. Cl. 1967).

alternative to two or more claims and is considered to include all of its own limitations as well as those of any one of the referenced claims.[1420]

There are five principal ways of claiming the statutory classes of invention set forth in 35 U.S.C. § 101: composition of matter claims, process claims, apparatus claims, product-by-process claims, and means-plus-function claim elements.

A *Composition of Matter Claims*

Although in practice the usage is not precise, chemical compounds are viewed as "compositions of matter," whereas chemical combinations or mixtures of ingredients are more accurately called "compositions." They may be claimed by naming the compound or the ingredients. If necessary, the proportions or other parameters of the composition are stated. For example:

A plasticizer composition, comprising:

a. about 50%–55% A;
b. about 10%–15% B;
c. about 15%–30% C; and
d. a pH-modifying substance in an amount sufficient to adjust the pH to a value of about 3 to 4.5.[1421]

B *Process Claims*

Process or method claims can be divided into: (1) processes or methods of making; and (2) processes or methods of using. As to the former, the typical method of making claim involves acts or steps performed on an object(s) or substance(s) to achieve some result. For example:

A process for making chemical compound X, comprising the steps of:

a. *mixing* water with compound Z to form a mixture;
b. *heating* the mixture at a temperature of about 150°C–160°C;
c. *distilling* the mixture; and
d. *permitting* the mixture to cool to room temperature.[1422]

Notice the importance of gerunds in process claims.

It is the combination or sequence of acts or steps that are patented in a process claim, not the resulting product. Where there is a sequence of steps, the sequence

1420. For other examples of an independent claim, *see* Robert C. Faber, Faber on Mechanics of Patent Claim Drafting, 17–18 (6th ed. 2010). For examples of a dependent claim, *see id.*, at 163. For examples of multiple dependent claims, *see* MPEP § 608.01(n). One exception is that a multiple dependent claim cannot depend on any other multiple dependent claim, *see* MPEP § 608.01(n).
1421. *See* Robert C. Faber, Faber on Mechanics of Patent Claim Drafting, 49 (6th ed. 2010).
1422. *Id.*, at 37.

should be described. However, nonessential or unnecessary steps and sequences should not be recited in a process claim lest the claim be too easily circumvented.[1423]

The only way to patent a new use of an old or new product is in the form of a method claim—this would be a method of using claim. Consider the following typical method of use claim:

> The method of treating baldness, which comprises applying to the scalp an aqueous solution of sodium chloride having a concentration of 30%–40% by weight of sodium chloride.

C *Apparatus Claims*

Apparatus claims generally are directed to mechanical structure. The preamble usually recites the purpose of the apparatus. After the transition (e.g., "comprising"), each essential element of the apparatus is set forth, in outline form. The claim must sufficiently recite the connection among the elements to clearly define the apparatus. The following example illustrates a simple apparatus claim:

> Apparatus for shaking articles, which comprises:
>
> a. a container having at least two ends for the articles;
> b. a base; and
> c. a plurality of parallel legs, each leg connected pivotally at one end to the container and at the other end to the base to support the container for oscillating movement with respect to the base.[1424]

D *Product-by-Process Claims*

Product-by-process claims are hybrid claims designed to facilitate the claiming of complex products whose structure or other characteristics are insufficiently known to permit adequate description of the product itself. They indirectly claim a product by reciting the process of creating the product. However, for examination purposes, these claims are considered product claims, and are not limited by the process steps recited in the claim. They usually take the form "a product prepared by a process comprising the steps of …."[1425] For example:

> The product of a process comprising the steps of:
>
> a. *mixing* water with compound Z to form a mixture;
> b. *heating* the mixture at a temperature of about 150°C–160°C;
> c. *distilling* the mixture; and

1423. *See id.*, at 39. Alternatively, nonessential steps may be included in a dependent claim.
1424. *Id.*, at 14.
1425. Jeffrey D. Sheldon, How to Write a Patent Application § 6.4.5 (2d ed. 2010). The PTO views product-by-process claims as product claims. Therefore, the MPEP and several cases require that the product itself meets the requirements of patentability.

d. *permitting* the mixture to cool to room temperature.

Federal Circuit precedent is inconsistent as to whether such products are limited to the process described and claimed in the patent.[1426]

E *Means-Plus-Function Claims*

Title 35, section 112, paragraph 6, specifically permits "an element in a claim for a combination [to] be expressed as a means or step for performing a specified function." These claim elements are called means-plus-function elements.[1427] Such a claim element defines the function of the element, rather than its structure. The statute then provides that the claim element "shall be construed to cover the corresponding structure, material, or acts described in the specification and equivalents thereof." Consider the sample apparatus claim stated above, with the added means-plus-function element:

Apparatus for shaking articles, which comprises:

a. a container for the articles;
b. a base;
c. a plurality of parallel legs, each leg is connected pivotally at one end to the container and at the other end to the base to support the container for oscillating movement with respect to the base; and
d. means for oscillating the container on the legs to shake the articles.[1428]

Whether a claim element may properly be considered under § 112, paragraph 6, is sometimes a difficult question.[1429] Although not just limited to means-plus-function claims, the Federal Circuit held that broad functional claims, which are especially common in the pharmaceutical industry, will not meet the enablement requirement.[1430]

1426. *Compare Scripps Clinic & Research Foundation v. Genentech, Inc.*, 927 F.2d 1565 (Fed. Cir. 1991) (product-by-process claims not limited by process set forth in claim), *with Atlantic Thermoplastics Co. v. Faytex Corp.*, 970 F.2d 834 (Fed. Cir. 1992) (process set forth serves as limitation in determining infringement).

1427. Section 112, para. 6 applies only to combination claims, which necessarily have two or more distinct elements, only one of which might be defined in means-plus-function language.

1428. Robert C. Faber, Faber on Mechanics of Patent Claim Drafting, 14 (6th ed. 2010).

1429. *See*, e.g., *York Prods., Inc. v. Central Tractor Farm & Family Center*, 99 F.3d 1568, 1574 (Fed. Cir. 1996) (explaining that while "the use of the word 'means' triggers a presumption that the inventor used this term advisedly to invoke the statutory mandates for means-plus-function clauses[,] … mere incantation of the word 'means' in a clause reciting predominantly structure cannot evoke section 112, ¶6"); *Sage Products, Inc. v. Devon Indus., Inc.*, 126 F.3d 1420, 1427 1428 (Fed. Cir. 1997) (explaining that "where a claim recites a function, but then goes on to elaborate sufficient structure, material, or acts within the claim itself to perform entirely the recited function, the claim is not in means-plus-function format").

1430. *Amgen Inc. v. Sanofi*, 987 F.3d 1080 (Fed. Cir. 2021) (holding that the enablement requirement is not met for antibody claims that are defined "not by structure, but by meeting functional limitations").

§2 PROCEDURES BEFORE THE US PTO

The Patent Office, renamed the PTO in 1975, is recognized as the oldest federal agency in the US, created by statute in 1836 and now one of 14 bureaus in the Department of Commerce.[1431]

I Initial Processing of the Application

New applications are initially processed by the Application Division, which decides if an application is complete and meets all formal requirements. Any drawings accompanying the application are forwarded to the official draftsman, who checks to see if the drawings comply with the formal requirements. Any assignment of the application is forwarded to the Assignment Division, which records the assignment in its computer and microfilm records and returns it to the applicant with a notification of the reel and frame numbers in the microfilm records.

The PTO maintains a detailed classification system by which all technologies are broken down into specific categories (e.g., chemical, electrical, etc.).[1432] Within the classification system are hundreds of classes, each class having at least dozens of subclasses. The Application Division determines the appropriate technological class and subclass of the application. It then forwards the application to the examining group in charge of that class and subclass. These documents are kept in a file jacket known as a file wrapper.

II Examination and Prosecution

A *Formalities and Search by the Examiner*

When an application reaches an examining group, it is assigned to the appropriate art (i.e., technology) unit and then to a particular examiner. The examiner first ascertains

1431. Although it was the 1836 Act that officially created the Patent Office, it is difficult to say exactly when it was started. It was not part of the 1790 or 1793 Patent Acts. However, in 1802, Secretary of State James Madison, who was instrumental in the development of patent and copyright law during the early years of the American republic, made the Patent Office a distinct division of the Department of State and appointed the highly regarded Dr. William Thorton, the designer of the U.S. Capitol, at a salary of USD 1,400 a year to the full-time position of supervising the issuance of patents. Some say that it was with the appointment of Dr. Thorton in 1802 that the Patent Office was created. For a brief history of the name of the Patent and Trademark Office *see* S. Rep. No. 93-1399 (1974), *reprinted in* 1974 U.S.C.C.A.N. 7113.

1432. There are two major patent classification systems. The PTO uses the U.S. Patent Classification System (USPC), which divides all technical subject matter into over 400 main classes and approximately 152,000 subclasses. *See* MANUAL OF PATENT CLASSIFICATION, www.uspto.gov/patents/resources/classification. Most other countries use the World Intellectual Property Organization's International Patent Classification System (IPC), which divides patentable technologies into 8 main sections, 21 subsections, 120 classes, 628 subclasses and over 69,000 groups. *See* INTERNATIONAL PATENT CLASSIFICATION (IPC), www.wipo.int/classifications/ipc/en/. Both systems are regularly revised and amended to follow technological progress.

that the application contains the elements required to obtain a filing date: (1) written description; (2) claim; and (3) any required drawing.[1433]

After determining that an application satisfies the basic requirements needed for a filing date, the examiner then conducts a search for prior art relevant to the claimed subject matter. Much of the relevant prior art is usually set forth in the patent applicant's Information Disclosure Statement submitted to the PTO along with or shortly after the filing of the application.[1434] The quality and thoroughness of the examiner's search is a function of his or her searching skill, the time allocated for the search, and the completeness of the libraries searched.

B *Third-Party Submissions of Prior Art under the AIA*

Presently, PTO regulations allow any member of the public to submit prior art (up to ten references) within two months of the publication of the application.[1435] However, the third party "[may] not include any explanation of the patents or publications, or any other information."[1436] The AIA greatly expands a third party's ability to submit information relevant to patentability at the examination.[1437] Under the AIA, any third party can submit prior art for consideration and inclusion in the file. Importantly, the third party must "set forth a concise description of the asserted relevance of each submitted document."[1438] Submissions must be made within six months of publication or before the date of the first rejection.[1439] This provision becomes effective on September 16, 2012, and applies to any patent application filed before, on, or after that date.

C *Office Action*

After this initial activity by the examiner, the examiner then communicates in writing to the applicant or to his or her attorney or agent, if one has been appointed. This communication is called an Office Action, which includes a form cover letter, on which the examiner summarizes the action by checking the appropriate boxes and filling in the correct blanks, and an explanation of the action. This is where the examiner

1433. *See* 37 C.F.R. § 1.53(b)(1). To receive a filing date for a nonprovisional application, other formalities such as the transmittal form, the application data sheet, and the declaration or oath by the inventor are required. To receive a filing date for a provisional application, the three main elements needed are: (1) a written description of the invention (complying with all requirements of 35 U.S.C. § 112(a)); (2) any necessary drawings; and (3) the USPTO filing fee. Additional elements include: (1) the name(s) of all inventors; (2) inventor residence(s); (3) title of the invention; (4) name and registration number of attorney or agent (if applicable); (5) correspondence address; and (6) any U.S. government agency that has a property interest in the application.
1434. *See* 37 C.F.R. § 1.56.
1435. *See* 37 C.F.R. § 1.99.
1436. *See* 37 C.F.R. § 1.99(d).
1437. *See* America Invents Act § 8 (amending 35 U.S.C. § 122(e)).
1438. *Id.*
1439. *See id.*

explains the substantive rejections[1440] and/or objections[1441] (s)he has to the application. Alternatively, the examiner may allow some or all of the claims without any rejections or objections.

D Applicant's Response

After receiving the first Office Action, the applicant must respond to all of the examiner's rejections and/or objections or the application will be held abandoned. The applicant will usually have three months to respond to the application, which usually can be extended up to the maximum statutory period of six months upon payment of a fee.

Applicants may respond to claim rejections and objections by amendment of the claims and/or arguments specifically addressing the examiner's Office Action. Usually, a response includes both claim amendments and arguments designed to distinguish the invention as claimed from any prior art cited by the examiner.[1442]

The applicant may also respond by amending the written description to include the language of an originally filed claim if the examiner rejects or objects to a claim as not being supported by the written description. In addition, the applicant may amend the written description in response to an objection asserting that it does not describe the invention with sufficient clarity, provided that the applicant does not introduce "new matter."[1443] New matter is substantive information not contained in the originally filed application that is added after the application's filing date.[1444] For the most part, there is very little an applicant can do to the written description after he or she files the application.

E Reconsideration and Allowance

After the applicant submits a response to the first Office Action, the examiner reconsiders the application. Generally, the examiner has three options: (1) allow the case; or (2) reject the case based on new arguments and/or new prior art; or (3) reject the case based on a previous rejection and/or objection. If the examiner is satisfied with the response, he or she issues a Notice of Allowance, a form letter, the primary purpose of which is to inform the applicant of allowance of the application.

If the examiner is not satisfied with the response, he or she may issue a second Office Action. Unless a second or subsequent Office Action is based on a new ground

1440. A "rejection" is used by the patent examiner when the substance of the claims is unallowable under Title 35 of the U.S. code (usually a rejection under 35 U.S.C. § 101, 102, 103 and/or 112).
1441. An "objection" is used by the patent examiner when the form of the claim is improper.
1442. Although the amendment may be self-explanatory, as a rule of practice the applicant should accompany the amendment with an explanation of its relevance.
1443. *See* 35 U.S.C. § 132. *See also* MPEP § 608.04(A).
1444. "New matter includes not only the addition of wholly unsupported subject matter, but may also include adding specific percentages, or compounds after a broader original disclosure, or even the omission of a step from a method." MPEP § 706.03(O).

of rejection, such as newly discovered prior art, the examiner may make the rejection "final."[1445]

At any time from the issuance of the first Office Action until the issuance of a final Office Action, the applicant or applicant's representative is entitled to a personal or telephonic interview with the examiner for the purposes of clarifying the issues and of reaching an agreement leading to the allowance of the application. After a final Office Action is issued, it is within the examiner's discretion to allow interviews and to consider responses.[1446] The examiner must make the substance of the interview of record by completing an Examiner Interview Summary Record form and, unless excused by the examiner, the applicant must also file a summary of the interview.[1447] Generally, examiner interviews are not permitted after the submission of an appeal brief or after a notice of allowability for the application has been mailed.[1448]

F Responses to a Final Office Action

After a final rejection by the examiner, the applicant is faced with a choice. The applicant can: (1) abandon the application; (2) file an appeal with the Patent Trial and Appeal Board (PTAB);[1449] (3) take allowed claims and cancel the others; or (4) file a continuing application.

1 Appeals

If the applicant files an appeal with the Board, he or she is given two months, extendable to six months, to file an Appeal Brief. After the Appeal Brief has been filed, the examiner must file an Examiner's Answer. There is no statutory or regulatory time limit for filing the Examiner's Answer. Within one month of the Examiner's Answer, the applicant may file a Reply Brief directed only to any new points that were raised in the Examiner's Answer.

The applicant may request an oral hearing. The appeal is then placed on the Board's calendar and assigned to a panel of three Administrative Patent Judges (APJs). When an appeal is set for oral hearing, the applicant is given notice of the date of the hearing and, at that point, may waive the hearing.

1445. A "non-final" Office Action raises an issue for the first time. A "final" Office Action issues when the applicant's response to the prior Office Action fails to address or overcome all issues. MPEP § 2271.
1446. Normally, one interview after final rejection is permitted in order to place the application in condition for allowance or to resolve issues prior to appeal. Such an interview may be granted if the examiner is convinced that disposal or clarification for appeal may be accomplished with only nominal further consideration. MPEP § 713.09.
1447. *See* 37 C.F.R. § 1.133(b). For a discussion of interview practice, *see Magnivision v. Bonneau Co.*, 115 F.3d 956, 958 (Fed. Cir. 1997).
1448. MPEP § 713.05.
1449. The Patent Trial and Appeal Board is an Article I adjudicative board within the PTO, and it replaced what was formerly known as the Board of Patent Appeals and Interferences on Sept. 16, 2012. *See* America Invents Act § 3 (eliminating inference proceedings and all references to "interferences" in the patent code).

After oral hearing, or if no oral hearing is requested, the appeal is considered by the Board. The Board may affirm the decision of the examiner in whole or in part, or may reverse it. If the Board affirms the examiner's decision, the applicant may abandon the application, file a continuing application, bring a civil action to obtain a patent in the US District Court for the Eastern District of Virginia,[1450] or appeal the Board's decision directly to the Federal Circuit. If the Board reverses the examiner's decision, the examiner must issue a Notice of Allowance. The Board can also order further examination or other procedures, if the case warrants.[1451]

2 *Cancelation of Claims*

If an applicant faces final rejection of some claims, but allowance of others, whether or not the result of an appeal, he or she may decide to take the allowed claims and cancel the others. A Notice of Allowance so limited would then be issued.

3 *Continuing Applications*

"Continuing application" is a generic term for three types of patent applications that are entitled to the filing date of an earlier (parent) application. The three types of continuing applications are continuation applications, continuation-in-part applications, and divisional applications. The requirements for claiming continuing status are that the application be filed while the parent application is still pending (copendency), at least one inventor must be common to the two applications, and the text of the second application must refer back to the first.[1452]

If an applicant faces a final rejection of all claims in an application, or a final rejection of claims that were canceled to allow other claims to issue, the applicant may wish to file a continuing application directed to the canceled claims. In addition, there may be other reasons for filing a continuing application, as discussed below.

A continuation application is an application whose written description is the same as that of the parent application, but whose claims may be the same or different from those of the parent application. A continuation application is entitled to the parent's filing date as to all subject matter contained in it. A continuation might be filed to obtain further prosecution if all claims are finally rejected in the parent, but the applicant has new amendments or arguments to present. A continuation application is often appropriate if the new amendments or arguments were presented in the parent after final rejection and were not entered because they raised new issues or required further searching, but the examiner gave some indication that the amendments or

1450. *See* 35 U.S.C. § 145 (applicable for actions commencing on or after Sept. 16, 2011). The former venue was the U.S. District Court for the District of Columbia.

1451. The Board may issue a new ground of rejection under 37 C.F.R. § 41.50. When the Board issues a new ground for rejection, the applicant must either: (1) reopen prosecution and submit an appropriate amendment of the claims and/or submit new evidence addressing the new rejection or (2) request rehearing. *See* 37 C.F.R. § 41.50.

1452. *See* MPEP §§ 201.06, 201.07, 201.08, 201.11.

arguments had some merit. A continuation might also be filed if only some claims were finally rejected in the parent. Those claims might be canceled from the parent, allowing the other claims to issue. The canceled claims may then be pursued, with or without change, in the continuation application.

A continuation-in-part application is an application that has some subject matter in common with the parent but also has new subject matter. A continuation-in-part is entitled to the parent's filing date as to any subject matter in common, but only to its own filing date as to the new matter. A continuation-in-part might be filed if the applicant wished to add limitations to the parent claims to distinguish a reference or references, but the added limitations were not supported by the written description of the parent and the examiner would not allow supporting material to be added to the written description because it introduced new matter. The applicant could file a continuation-in-part to include the new matter. A continuation-in-part, including newly developed information, might also be filed if the applicant has improved the invention described in the parent. A continuation-in-part may be filed at any time, regardless of the status of prosecution of the parent case, as long as the parent is still pending.

A divisional application is a continuing application that is based on a parent application and has the same written description except that the claims differ, usually because of a restriction requirement. An examiner issues a restriction requirement when he or she believes the application claims more than one invention. When an examiner issues a restriction requirement the applicant is forced to elect which invention he or she wants to prosecute. This does not mean that the applicant is precluded from seeking patent protection for the nonelected invention. In fact, the nonelected invention may be prosecuted by filing a divisional application. If the claims of the divisional application, however, are not patentably distinct (nonobvious) from the claims of the parent application, the examiner may reject the divisional claims based on obviousness-type double patenting.[1453] In essence, the examiner is preventing the applicant from extending his or her patent rights beyond the statutory term. This type of rejection had significantly more power prior to the GATT amendments to the patent law, which now measure a patent's term from the date of filing (i.e., twenty years from the date of filing) as opposed to the date of issuance (i.e., seventeen years from the date of issuance). Because a divisional application by definition is entitled to the same filing date as the parent application, both will terminate twenty years from the filing date of the parent application.

1453. *See Symbol Technologies Inc. v. Opticon Inc.*, 936 F.2d 1569, 1581 (Fed. Cir. 1991). However, if the divisional application was filed as a result of an examiner's restriction requirement, then the PTO is prohibited from making an obviousness-type double patenting rejection based on that application. *See* 35 U.S.C. § 121 and MPEP § 804.01. This prohibition does not apply to divisional applications that were voluntarily filed by the applicant and not in response to a restriction requirement.

4 *Request for Continued Examination*

Request for Continued Examination (RCE) practice allows the applicant to continue examination for a fee, without requiring the applicant to file a continuation application. Upon filing of the RCE, the finality of the last Office Action is withdrawn, and any previously filed unentered amendments, amendments filed with the RCE, and any amendments filed prior to the mailing of the next Office Action (after the RCE) are entered.

G *Publication*

Prior to the AIPA of 1999, patents were kept secret by the PTO. Now, subject to some exceptions, 35 U.S.C. § 122(b)(1) authorizes that "each application for a patent shall be published … promptly after the expiration of a period of eighteen months from the earliest filing date."[1454] The principal exception to publication is when the applicant agrees to not seek foreign patent protection.[1455]

H *Foreign Priority*

An applicant can claim the benefit of the filing date of an application filed abroad. Under the terms of the Paris Convention for the Protection of Industrial Property,[1456] implemented in the US under 35 U.S.C. § 119, the benefit of the filing date (referred to as "priority") from the first application for an invention filed in any member country can be claimed in a US application as long as it is filed within one year of the first application.[1457] Priority can be claimed at any time during the pendency of an application. A claim of priority is perfected by filing a certified copy of the foreign application. Whether benefit is claimed from a domestic or foreign application, materials published between the priority date and the application filing date are not prior art to the application. However, the one-year period of 35 U.S.C. § 102(b) is counted from the earliest effective US filing date, not from a foreign priority date.[1458]

1454. 35 U.S.C. § 122(b)(1).
1455. *See* 35 U.S.C. § 122(b)(2) (listing exceptions).
1456. Priority is also available under the GATT-WTO Treaty or under bilateral agreements with individual countries. For example, the US now has an agreement with Taiwan, as of Apr. 10, 1996, allowing patent applications filed in Taiwan to claim priority based on the filing date of the corresponding U.S. patent applications. *See* Daisy Wang, *Taiwan-U.S. Agreement Permits Claim to Priority Based on U.S. Filing Date*, World Intellectual Property Report 10 (1996): 173.
1457. In addition to the application filed in a member country, an applicant (in certain circumstances) may rely on an "international application" filed pursuant to the PCT, which is administered by the WIPO. The PCT is a multilateral treaty among more than 50 nations that is designed to simplify the patenting process when an applicant seeks a patent on the same invention in more than one nation. *See* 35 U.S.C. Ch. 35–37, and World Intellectual Property Organization, *PCT Applicant's Guide* (1992, rev. 1994).
1458. What effect the GATT-based provisional application's domestic priority date will have if invoked is unknown.

I *Interferences (Pre-AIA)*

If two or more applications claim the same subject matter, the applications are said to be "interfering" and the examiner, after determining patentability of the invention to each applicant, can declare an "interference" between them.[1459] A patent interference is an inter partes proceeding in the PTO to determine which of two or more parties was the first-to-invent. An interference can also be declared between a pending application and an issued patent. If the examiner does not declare the interference, the applicant can provoke an interference. An interference can relate to some or all of the claims in the application or patent. Since the AIA changes the US from a first-to-invent system to a first to file system, applications filed on or after March 16, 2013, are not subject to interference proceedings.

J *Derivation Proceedings under the AIA*

As the AIA transforms the US patent system from a first-to-invent to a first-inventor-to-file regime, it abolishes interference proceedings since there is no longer a need to determine priority of invention. In lieu of interference proceedings, the AIA institutes derivation proceedings. The new § 135(a) reads in pertinent part:

> § 135. Derivation proceedings
>
> An applicant for patent may file a petition to institute a derivation proceeding in the Office. The petition shall set forth with particularity the basis for finding that an inventor named in an earlier application derived the claimed invention from an inventor named in the petitioner's application and, without authorization, the earlier application claiming such invention was filed.[1460]

Thus, derivation proceedings will be used to determine whether the inventor of an earlier-filed application derived the claimed invention from the inventor of an application filed later. As for timing, the petitioner must initiate a derivation proceeding within one year from "the date of first publication of a claim to an invention that is the same or substantially the same as the earlier application's claim to the invention."[1461]

III Appeals to the Courts

Once all administrative remedies are exhausted, the applicant can then appeal through the federal court system. Thus, if an applicant is dissatisfied with a decision of the PTAB in an appeal from a final rejection by the examiner, he or she may initiate a civil action against the Commissioner of Patents and Trademarks in the US District Court for the Eastern District of Virginia.[1462] A party to an interference that is dissatisfied with the

1459. *See* 37 C.F.R. § 1.605; MPEP § 2305.
1460. 35 U.S.C. § 145.
1461. *Id.*
1462. *See* America Invents Act § 9 (applicable for actions commencing on or after Sept. 16, 2011). The former venue was the U.S. District Court for the District of Columbia.

decision of the Board may have remedy by civil action against the other party.[1463] In the district court, the question of the applicant's or the interfering parties' right to a patent is tried de novo. Appeal from the decision of the district court is taken exclusively to the Federal Circuit.[1464] Alternatively, an applicant may appeal directly from the PTO to the Federal Circuit.[1465] In practice, a vast majority of appeals are taken directly to the Federal Circuit, which reviews the PTO's conclusions of law de novo and affirms its findings of fact if they are supported by substantial evidence.[1466] Decisions of the Federal Circuit are subject to the certiorari jurisdiction of the Supreme Court.

§3 POST-ISSUANCE PROCEDURES

There are procedures whereby the terms of a patent may be reconsidered after the patent issues. The procedures are complex and should not be relied upon to correct major flaws in prosecution. The two main procedures that the patent code has established to accomplish this renegotiation and correction are reissue and reexamination.

I Reissue

Reissue's objective is to allow the patent owner to correct an inadvertent mistake.[1467] As such, this process is made available only to the patent owner. Unlike a reexamination proceeding, neither a third party nor the PTO can institute a reissue proceeding.

The patent code requires that the mistake sought to be corrected by reissue must be such that its presence causes the patent to be "deemed by the owner wholly or partially inoperative or invalid."[1468] The courts have interpreted this requirement to include everything from a typographical error to an error in the scope of the claims.

An inventor is required to show that the mistake was unintentional or unavoidable, and before the passage of the AIA, "without any deceptive intention."[1469] The AIA amended the statute to remove the latter limitation,[1470] thereby expanding the types of errors that can be corrected by the reissue process.

As one may expect, the time frame for requesting reissue depends upon the nature of the request itself. Thus, an inventor who wishes to narrow his or her claim scope may do so at any time during the life of the patent. However, an inventor who attempts to broaden the scope of his or her claims through reissue may harm the

1463. *See* 35 U.S.C. §§ 145, 146.
1464. *See* 28 U.S.C. § 1295.
1465. *See* 35 U.S.C. § 141.
1466. *In re* Bass, 314 F.3d 575, 576 (Fed. Cir. 2002); *see also Dickinson v. Zurko*, 527 U.S. 150, 152 (1999) (holding that 5 U.S.C. § 706 governs the court's review of findings of fact made by the PTO); *In re* Zurko, 258 F.3d 1379, 1384 (Fed. Cir. 2001) (defining "substantial evidence" as evidence that "a reasonable person might accept as adequate to support a conclusion").
1467. *In re* Hounsfield, 699 F.2d 1320, 1323 (Fed. Cir. 1982).
1468. 35 U.S.C. § 251.
1469. *See id.*
1470. *See* America Invents Act § 20.

public's expectations, including competitors of the patentee, who have relied on the original claim language. Therefore, a broadening reissue may be requested only within the first two years of the original patent grant. Even this two-year limitation, however, may unfairly impact a third party who began to make and use (or, at least, made preparations for such) the invention as originally claimed and all of a sudden finds himself or herself infringing the reissue patent.[1471] To guard against such an occurrence, the doctrine of intervening rights may protect the competitor's investment.[1472]

II Ex Parte and *Inter Partes* Reexamination

Reexamination is a procedure whereby the patentee or a third party may request that the PTO reexamine any patent claim during the life of the patent. The purpose of the reexamination statute, enacted in 1980, is to strengthen "investor confidence in the certainty of patent rights by creating a system of administrative re-examination of doubtful patents."[1473] Reexamination differs from reissue in several other significant ways: (1) reexamination is limited to anticipation and obviousness arguments based on prior art references;[1474] (2) anyone can request reexamination;[1475] (3) claims in a reexamination cannot be broadened;[1476] and (4) a reexamination can be filed anytime during the life of the patent.[1477] There are two types of reexamination: (1) ex parte reexamination; and (2) inter partes reexamination.

Ex parte reexamination can be instituted by anyone (e.g.,: patentee, USPTO director, or a third party) at any time during the lifetime of the patent. If a third party requests reexamination, he or she will challenge the validity of the patent based only on prior art consisting of patents or printed publications.[1478] The third party will submit the prior art to the USPTO and before the USPTO institutes the reexamination, the USPTO must find that the request raises a "substantial new question of patentability."[1479] If the USPTO institutes the reexamination, then the patent owner can respond to the statement by amending the claims, adding new claims, and/or proffering arguments against the prior art. The third-party requester then has the ability to file a response to the patent owner's response.[1480] However, from that point forward, the third-party requester does not participate in the prosecution of the patent. Thus, if

1471. For example, a patentee's competitor may capitalize on an area left unclaimed by the patent. The competitor may begin to make a significant investment within the first two years of the patent's life, only to have the reissue lay claim to this previously unoccupied area.
1472. *See* 35 U.S.C. § 252.
1473. H.R. Rep. 96–1307.
1474. *See* 35 U.S.C. §§ 301, 302.
1475. *See* 35 U.S.C. § 302. Only the patentee can institute a reissue proceeding.
1476. *See* 35 U.S.C. § 305.
1477. *See* 35 U.S.C. § 302. This is in contrast to a broadening reissue, which can only be instituted within two years from the grant of the original patent. A narrowing reissue, however, can be instituted any time during the life of the patent.
1478. *See* 35 U.S.C. § 302. Even patents that were previously cited by the USPTO or that were previously considered by the Office during the original prosecution can be used to create a substantial new question of patentability. *See* 35 U.S.C. § 303(a), 312(a).
1479. *See* 35 U.S.C. §§ 303, 304.
1480. *See* 35 U.S.C. § 304.

further amendments are made, or if further arguments are proffered by the patent owner, the third-party requestor cannot respond to the arguments made by the patent owner. Ex parte review is still available to post-AIA.[1481]

Inter partes reexamination (pre-AIA) is no longer available under the AIA, and replaced with IPR. Thus, after September 15, 2012, no one can file for inter partes reexamination. Inter partes reexamination is similar to ex parte reexamination, but allows the third-party requestor to participate more during the prosecution of the patent. Accordingly, the third-party requestor was allowed to file a response to each statement filed by the patentee throughout the entire reexamination. One major limitation with IPR was that the third-party requestor could not raise the same validity issues in any subsequent litigation of the patent in federal court.[1482]

III PGR, IPR, and CBM Review under the AIA

The AIA creates three new methods for post-grant reconsideration of patents: (1) IPR, which replaces inter partes reexamination; (2) PGR; and (3) CBM review.

A *Post-Grant Review*

PGR is a post-grant opposition system which allows a third party to seek the cancelation of one or more claims in an issued patent.[1483] PGR is similar to European "opposition" practice. PGR is instituted by anyone who is not the patent owner and has not previously filed a civil action challenging the validity of a claim of the patent. Additionally, all real parties in interest must be identified.[1484] One key difference between reexamination and PGR is that the petitioner must file a PGR not later than nine months after the date of the grant of a patent or the issuance of a reissue patent.[1485] PGR will be conducted by the PTAB.[1486]

Unlike reexamination, the petitioner can base the PGR not only on prior art but also on "any ground that could be raised under paragraph (2) or (3) of [35 U.S.C.] section 282(b)."[1487] Thus, 35 U.S.C. §§ 101, 102, 103, 112 or double patenting (but not best mode) can be used to institute the PGR.[1488] The threshold showing is that it is "more likely than not" that at least one claim is unpatentable.[1489] Furthermore, the PTO Director can grant the PGR if it "raises a novel or unsettled legal question that is important to other patents or patent applications."[1490]

1481. *See* 35 U.S.C. §§ 301–07.
1482. *See* 35 U.S.C. § 315(c).
1483. *See* America Invents Act § 6 (codified at 35 U.S.C. §§ 321–29).
1484. 37 C.F.R. § 42.8(b)(1).
1485. 35 U.S.C. § 324(c).
1486. *See id.*
1487. 35 U.S.C. § 321(b).
1488. Failure to satisfy the best mode requirement is specifically excluded from a ground to institute a PGR. *See* 35 U.S.C. § 321(b)(3)(A).
1489. *See id.*
1490. 35 U.S.C. § 324(b).

There is, however, a significant estoppel issue: the third party may not assert invalidity in a civil action "on any ground that the petitioner raised or reasonably could have raised during that post-grant review." Estoppel is applied to subsequent USPTO, district court or International Trade Commission (ITC) actions.

B Inter Partes *Review*

Under the AIA, IPR is a second method by which a petitioner can request review of a previously granted patent.[1491] Starting on September 16, 2012, IPR replaces the pre-AIA inter partes reexamination. An IPR action cannot be filed during the first nine-month window after the grant of a patent (the PGR process is used for patents during this first nine-month period). IPRs are adjudicated by a three-judge panel of the PTAB and should conclude within one year of the institution of the IPR.[1492] These PTAB judges are Article I APJs appointed by the Secretary of Commerce. Additionally, judicial review of whether to institute an IPR is unavailable under 35 U.S.C. §314(d), which states that the decision to institute at the PTAB will be final and nonappealable.[1493] Similar to PGR, IPR must be completed within twelve months from institution of the IPR, with six months good cause exception. Finally, decisions by APJs are subject to review by the Director, which can then be appealed to an Article III court.[1494]

The petitioner for an IPR must be a person who is not the patent owner, who has not previously filed a civil action challenging the validity of a claim of the patent and has not been served with a complaint alleging infringement of the patent more than one year prior.[1495] Furthermore, a petitioner cannot file an IPR if the petitioner already has filed a civil action challenging the validity of a claim of the patent.[1496] If, however, the petitioner first files an IPR, and then files a civil action, the civil action is automatically stayed.[1497] The civil action will be stayed until: (1) the patent owner moves the court to lift the stay; (2) the patent owner files a civil action or counterclaim alleging that the petitioner (or real party in interest) has infringed the patent; or (3) the petitioner (or real party in interest) moves the court to dismiss the civil action.[1498]

The basis for an IPR is limited to prior art (patents or printed publications) under section 35 U.S.C. § 102 or 103.[1499] Unlike the previous inter partes reexamination, the threshold used to grant an IPR is "a reasonable likelihood that the petitioner would prevail with respect to at least 1 of the claims challenged in the petition."[1500] In 2020,

1491. 35 U.S.C. §§ 311–19 (effective Sept. 16, 2012).
1492. 35 U.S.C. § 316(a). The one-year period may be extended by no more than six months if good cause is shown. *See also* 35 U.S.C. § 316(a)(11).
1493. *Thryv Inc. v. Click-To_Call Technologies LP*, 140 S. Ct. 1367 (2020).
1494. *United States v. Arthrex*, 141 S. Ct. 549 (2021).
1495. 35 U.S.C. § 315(b) requires that a party must file a petition to institute an IPR within one year of being served with a complaint alleging patent infringement.
1496. 35 U.S.C. § 315(a)(1).
1497. 35 U.S.C. § 315(a)(2).
1498. *Id.*
1499. 35 U.S.C. § 311(b).
1500. 35 U.S.C. § 314(a).

the Federal Circuit reaffirmed that only sections 102 and 103 can be used to invalidate a patent in an IPR.[1501]

Similar to inter partes reexamination, IPR has an estoppel provision.[1502] Unlike inter partes reexamination, the estoppel provisions for IPR are limited to "any ground that the petitioner raised or reasonably could have raised during that inter partes review."[1503] Estoppel is applied to subsequent USPTO, district court, and ITC actions. Any claims and grounds that were raised in an IPR, or reasonably could have been raised, are grounds for estoppel.[1504]

C *CBM Review*

CBMs Review is available for use after September 16, 2012, and is available for first-inventor-to-file applications. This type of proceeding will be available until September 15, 2020.[1505] Similar to both IPR and PGR, CBM requires the petitioner to identify all real parties in interest. CBMs are adjudicated by a three-judge panel of the PTAB and should conclude within one year of the institution of the IPR.[1506] Similar to PGR, IPR must be completed within twelve months from institution of the IPR, with six months good cause exception.

The scope of CBM review is, however, more limited than either PGR or IPR. Specifically, CBM review is available only to patents that the PTAB determines are "covered business method patents." CBM patents are defined as claims that: (1) are used in the practice, administration, or management of a financial product or service; and (2) do not claim a "technological invention."[1507]

Similar to IPR, CBM is an adversarial proceeding where the petitioner can participate in the prosecution after filing the petition.[1508] Similar to PGR, CBM allows the petitioner to challenge the validity of a patent on any ground that is a condition for patentability.[1509] The standard for granting the CBM is identical to the standard used for PGR, namely, that at least one claim is "more likely than not" unpatentable. CBM review also includes estoppel provisions that are narrower than PGR. Specifically, estoppel under CBM extends only to grounds actually asserted, but not to grounds that reasonably could have been asserted.[1510]

1501. *Samsung Electronics America v. Prisua Engineering Corp,* 948 F.3d 1342 (Fed. Cir. 2020).
1502. 35 U.S.C. § 315(e).
1503. 35 U.S.C. § 315(e)(2).
1504. *Cal. Inst. Of Tech. v. Broadcom Ltd.* 25 F.4th 976 (Fed. Cir. 2022).
1505. 37 C.F.R. § 42.300(d).
1506. 37 C.F.R. § 42.300(c).
1507. 37 C.F.R. § 42.301(a). *See also Secure Axcess v. PNC Bank* 848 F.3d 1370 (Fed. Cir. 2017).
1508. 37 C.F.R. § 42.300(a).
1509. 37 C.F.R. § 42.304(b)(2).
1510. 35 U.S.C. § 315(e)(1)–(2); 352(e)(1)–(2).

CHAPTER 4
Ownership and Transfer

Patent law acknowledges the distinction between ownership and inventorship and deals with each differently.[1511] Patent rights are a form of personal property[1512] and, although proprietary rights in an invention initially vest in the inventor,[1513] such rights may be transferred.[1514] Ownership rests with whomever owns legal title to the subject matter, regardless of who actually invented it.[1515] Likewise, inventorship belongs to the person or persons who actually invented the subject matter claimed in a patent. Innovation is dominated not by the lone inventor, but by collaborative research teams, who usually work in some sort of corporate structure. Accordingly, patents are usually invented by a research team working together, and assigned to corporations that assemble a portfolio of related patents.

A person, corporation, commercial laboratory, or other legal entity may be an owner of a patent. Joint ownership is recognized and "[i]n the absence of any agreement to the contrary, each of the joint owners of a patent may make, use, offer, or sell the patented invention within the United States, ... without the consent of and without an accounting to the other owners."[1516] Thus, co-owners of a patent are tenants in common. The proportion of the co-owners' shares only enters into the equation when an award is recovered for infringement. In such a circumstance, each co-owner is given his or her proportionate share.[1517]

1511. *See Beech Aircraft Corp. v. EDO Corp.*, 990 F.2d 1237, 1248 (Fed. Cir. 1993) ("[I]nventorship is a question of who actually invented the subject matter in a patent. Ownership, however, is a question of who owns legal title to the subject matter claimed in a patent, patents having the attributes of personal property.").
1512. 35 U.S.C. § 261.
1513. *See Teets v. Chromalloy Gas Turbine Corp.*, 83 F.3d 403, 407 (Fed. Cir. 1996).
1514. 35 U.S.C. § 261; *see also GAIA Technologies, Inc. v. Reconversion Techs., Inc.*, 93 F.3d 774, 777 (Fed. Cir. 1996) ("Patents[,] like other personal property, may be conveyed from the inventor ... to others.").
1515. *Sewall v. Walters*, 21 F.3d 411, 417 (Fed. Cir. 1994).
1516. 35 U.S.C. § 262.
1517. *See Lemelson v. Synergistics Research Corp.*, 669 F. Supp. 642, 645 (S.D.N.Y. 1987).

The patent code requires the actual inventor of the claimed subject matter to make or authorize the application for a patent and sign a statement, under oath, that acknowledges the duties attendant to obtaining a patent.[1518] Although inventorship is held in great esteem, inventorship in itself does not carry with it the ability to grant a license, assign a share in a patent, or sue for infringement. These are characteristics of ownership.[1519] The proprietary rights in a patent rest with the owner and can be conveyed to another by mutual agreement even before the invention is conceived. Thus, an owner of a patent may parcel out the rights of the patent by either assignment or license.[1520] Questions relating to ownership and licensing of patent rights are matters of state contract law.[1521]

Before the 1952 Patent Act, patents ran a great risk of invalidation based on: (1) nonjoinder of an inventor; or (2) misjoinder of an inventor. Nonjoinder of an inventor involves a failure to include someone who was truly an inventor of the claimed subject matter. Misjoinder involves improperly including a person as an inventor when the person is not an inventor. After the 1952 Patent Act, under 35 U.S.C. § 256, invalidation of the patent could be avoided by correcting the inventors. Under pre-AIA rules, a nonjoined inventor could be added only if there was no deceptive intention on the part of the nonjoined inventor. Additionally, under pre-AIA rules, no intent analysis is needed to remove the misjoined inventor. The AIA has removed the deceptive intent limitation for nonjoinder. Thus, under the AIA, a court may grant relief for both misjoinder and nonjoinder without considering the inventor's state of mind.

Under 35 U.S.C. § 256, correction of inventorship on an issued patent can occur in one of two ways. First, if all parties agree to the correction, then they may simply petition the Director of the USPTO for the correction. However, if all parties do not agree to the correction, then this issue may be resolved by going to court so long as "notice and hearing of all parties concerned" are provided. Under 35 U.S.C. § 116, correction of inventorship on a pending patent application can occur only by petition to the Director of the USPTO.

1518. 35 U.S.C. §§ 111, 115.

1519. *See Rite-Hite Corp. v. Kelley Co.*, 56 F.3d 1538, 1551–52 (Fed. Cir. 1995).

1520. *See Waterman v. MacKenzie*, 138 U.S. 252, 255–56 (1891). Under 35 U.S.C. § 261, the assignment must be recorded in the PTO within three months "from its date" or it will "be void as against any subsequent purchaser or mortgagee for a valuable consideration."

1521. *See Jim Arnold Corp. v. Hydrotech Sys., Inc.*, 109 F.3d 1567, 1572 (Fed. Cir. 1997) ("[T]he question of who owns the patent and on what terms typically is a question exclusively for state courts."); *McCoy v. Mitsuboshi Cutlery, Inc.*, 67 F.3d 917, 920 (Fed. Cir. 1995) ("Whether express or implied, a license is a contract 'governed by ordinary principles of state contract law'.").

CHAPTER 5
The Rights and Limitations of the Patent Grant

§1 THE BASIC EXCLUSORY RIGHT

A patent grant gives the patentee several rights, but there are also certain statutory and common law limitations that circumscribe these rights. Section 154 sets forth the basic exclusory right:

> [A] patent shall contain … a grant … of the right to exclude others from making, using, offering for sale, or selling the invention throughout the United States or importing the invention into the United States.[1522]

Section 271(a) provides that:

> whoever, without authority makes, uses, offers to sell, or sells any patented invention within the United States or imports into the United States any patented invention during the term of the patent therefor, infringes the patent.[1523]

Thus, a patentee has five basic rights of exclusion: (1) making; (2) using; (3) selling; (4) offering for sale; and (5) importing.[1524] Note that the patent grant does not give the patentee the right to make, use, sell, offer for sale, or import, but rather it provides a right to exclude.

1522. 35 U.S.C. § 154.
1523. 35 U.S.C. § 271(a).
1524. The "importing" and "offering for sale" provisions became effective on Jan. 1, 1996, and these were added to § 154 and § 271(a) as part of the Uruguay Round agreement of the GATT on Trade-Related Aspects of Intellectual Property.

§2 THE SCOPE OF THE RIGHT TO EXCLUDE

I Temporal Scope: The Patent Term

Prior to June 8, 1995, the term for a US patent was seventeen years from the date the patent was issued.[1525] In April 1994, the US and several other countries concluded the Uruguay Round trade negotiation under GATT, which included an "Agreement on Trade-Related Aspects of Intellectual Property" (TRIPS). The TRIPS patent section provided: "The term of protection available shall not end before the expiration of a period of twenty years counted from the filing date."[1526] To effectuate this language, § 154(a)(2) of the patent code was amended to read:

> Term.—Subject to the payment of fees under this title, such grant shall be for a term beginning on the date on which the patent issues and ending 20 years from the date on which the application for the patent was filed in the United States, or, if the application contains a specific reference to an earlier filed application or applications ... from the date on which the earliest such application was filed.

The TRIPS legislation also affects patent applications filed before its effective date, June 8, 1995. The patent term for applications filed before June 8, 1995, is: (1) seventeen years from the date of issuance; or (2) twenty years measured from the filing date of the earliest referenced application, whichever is greater. For applications filed on or after June 8, 1995, the patent term is twenty years measured from the earliest referenced application filing date. Earlier referenced applications may include, for example, continuation applications under § 120, divisional applications under § 121, or PCT applications under § 365(c).

A patent is effective and enforceable only upon issuance.[1527] Section 154 specifically states that the patent's term shall begin "on the date on which the patent issues." Therefore, activity prior to issuance that would have resulted in a finding of infringement during the life of the patent is not actionable. Also, just as a patent is unenforceable prior to issuance, it is unenforceable after it expires.[1528]

1525. The patent term of the Patent Act of 1790 was "for any term not exceeding fourteen years." The term of 14 years was derived from the English Statute of Monopolies, which provided a patent term of 14 years. *See* Edward C. Walterscheid, *Defining the Patent and Copyright Term: Term Limits and the Intellectual Property Clause*, 7 J. INTELL. PROP. L. 315, 367 (2000); Pascquale Joseph Federico, *Origin and Early History of Patents*, 11 J. PAT. OFF. SOC'Y 292, 304 (1929).

1526. The patent term for design patents was not affected and remains 14 years from the date of issuance. *See* 35 U.S.C. § 173.

1527. *Marsh v. Nichols*, 128 U.S. 605, 612 (1888); *see also GAF Building Materials Corp. v. Elk Corp. of Dallas*, 90 F.3d 479, 483 (Fed. Cir. 1996) ("[A] patent does not exist until it is granted .... Patent rights are created only upon the formal issuance of the patent; thus, disputes concerning patent validity and infringement are necessarily hypothetical before patent issuance.").

1528. However, expiration of a patent during pending litigation does not deprive the court of jurisdiction. *See Beedle v. Bennett*, 122 U.S. 71, 75 (1887).

II Geographic Scope

Section 154(a)(1) grants a patentee the right to exclude others from making, using, offering for sale, or selling the claimed invention "within" or "throughout" the US or importing the invention "into" the US. Thus, activity in a foreign country, in and of itself, does not constitute an infringing act. However, acts relating to the export from the US to a foreign country or importation into the US from a foreign country may give rise to an infringement action. These issues present difficult questions of statutory construction.

A *Exporting a Claimed Invention*

Clearly, a person who makes a patented invention in the US and exports it for use or sale infringes the patent because the act of making in this situation is itself an infringement under US patent law (the product was actually made in the US). A more difficult scenario is where a person makes an incomplete version of the patented product for export, or makes only the parts of a patented machine, and thereafter exports them for assembly abroad.

As the word "make" is not defined in the patent code, the task of giving it meaning has been left to the courts. The Supreme Court, in *Deepsouth Packing Co. v. Laitram Corp.*,[1529] addressed this issue, holding essentially that one who manufactured the parts of a patented machine and shipped them to customers in a foreign country who would then assemble an entire machine was not an infringer.[1530] Competitors of the patentee could manufacture, with impunity, the parts of a patented machine in the US and export them to a foreign country for assembly.

In 1984, Congress responded to Deepsouth and this apparent loophole in the patent code by adding subsection (f) to § 271, making the export of unassembled components an act of infringement when it is known that the components will be reassembled in an infringing way.[1531]

In recent years, § 271(f) has been the subject of a small, but important group of cases. In *Pellegrini v. Analog Devices, Inc.*,[1532] for example, the patent related to brushless motor drive circuits that used integrated circuit chips. It was undisputed that the accused infringer, Analog, manufactured and sold the circuit chips outside the US.

1529. 406 U.S. 518 (1972).
1530. *Id.*, at 527, 531.
1531. *See* "Section-by-Section Analysis of H.R. 6286, Patent Law Amendments Act of 1984," Congressional Record, Oct. 1, 1984, H10525-26 ("The ... change ... will prevent copiers from avoiding U.S. patents by supplying components of a patented product in this country so that the assembly of the components may be completed abroad."). *The Federal Circuit in Pellegrini v. Analog Devices, Inc.*, 375 F.3d 1113 (Fed. Cir. 2004) suggested that § 271(f) only applies when the exported components are physical. But the case of *Eolas Technologies v. Microsoft Corp.*, 399 F.3d 1225 (Fed. Cir. 2005) appears to have expanded the US patent's geographic reach by suggesting there is no physicality requirement.
1532. 375 F.3d 1113 (Fed. Cir. 2004).

The chips in question—the Analog Motor Drive Circuit (ADMC) chips—were manufactured in Ireland by two independent contractors hired by Analog in Taiwan. Also, most of the chips were shipped and sold to customers outside the US. Pellegrini sued Analog for direct and indirect infringement, asserting that certain claims of its patent read on a combination of ADMC chips and other components in brushless motors. The district court granted Analog's motion for summary judgment of noninfringement because US patent laws do not have an extraterritorial effect. The court rejected Pellegrini's argument that, because Analog's headquarters are located in the US and instructions for the production and disposition of the ADMC chips emanate from the US, the chips should be regarded as having been "supplie[d] or cause[d] to be supplied in or from the United States" and Analog should be liable as an infringer under § 271(f)(1).

The Federal Circuit affirmed the district court, and characterized the issue—one of first impression—as "whether components that are manufactured outside the United States and never physically shipped to or from the United States may nonetheless be 'supplie[d] or cause[d] to be supplied in or from the United States' within the meaning of § 271(f)(1) if those components are designed within the United States and the instructions for their manufacture and disposition are transmitted from within the United States."[1533] According to the court, § 271(f) was inapplicable because "Analog did not make, use, sell, or offer to sell ADMC products in the United States, and it did not import ADMC products into the United States. Analog also does not supply ADMC chips in or from the United States, and does not cause ADMC chips to be supplied in or from the United States."[1534] The court wrote:

> §271(f) applies only where components of a patent invention are physically present in the United States and then either sold or exported "in such a manner as to actively induce the combination of such components outside the United States in a manner that would infringe the patent if such combination occurred within the United States." ... The plain language of § 271(f)(1) focuses on the location of the accused components, not the accused infringer. Pellegrini contends that it is irrelevant that the chips within the scope of the partial summary judgment never enter the United States, because to impose a location requirement would lead to a "seemingly contradictory construction of §271(f)(1)." According to Pellegrini, "it is difficult to understand how the combination of such components outside the United States can occur if they are inside the United States." However, the language of §271(f) clearly contemplates that there must be an intervening sale or exportation; there can be no liability under §271(f)(1) unless components are shipped from the United States for assembly.[1535]

The Supreme Court addressed two questions in *Microsoft v. AT&T*:[1536] Was the software a "component" under § 271(f), and, were "components" of a foreign-made computer "supplied" by Microsoft "from the United States"?

1533. *Id.*, at 1115–16.
1534. *Id.*, at 1118.
1535. *Id.*, at 1117.
1536. 550 U.S. 437 (2007).

In interpreting the term "components" in § 271, the Court noted that the statute refers to components that are combined to form the patented invention, which is AT&T's speech-processing computer. As such, "[u]ntil [the software] is expressed as a computer-readable 'copy,' e.g., on a CD-ROM, Windows software—indeed any software detached from an activating medium—remains uncombinable."[1537] The Court also rejected AT&T's argument that "[b]ecause it is so easy to encode software's instructions onto a medium that can be read by a computer, that extra step should not play a decisive role under § 271(f)."[1538] But, wrote the Court, the extra step is what renders the software a usable, combinable part of a computer; easy or not.[1539] In short, "copy-producing step is essential."[1540] Justice Stevens, in his dissent, was not persuaded of the importance of "copy-producing step." For him, "if a disk with software inscribed on it is a 'component,' I find it difficult to understand why the most important ingredient of that component is not also a component."[1541] That the majority opinion was too formalistic was implicit in Justice Stevens' dissent. As he wrote, liability under § 271(f) would attach only if Microsoft "sends individual copies of its software directly from the United States with the intent that each copy would be incorporated into a separate infringing computer."[1542]

In addressing whether Microsoft "supplied" components, the Court refused to read § 271(f) expansively. For example, the Court expressly rejected the "easy" to copy argument, stating "[s]ection 271(f) contains no instruction to gauge when duplication is easy and cheap enough to deem a copy in fact made abroad nevertheless 'supplie[d] ... from the United States'."[1543] This reasoning eschews, absent congressional intervention, a technology-specific approach to patent law, at least with regard to § 271(f). In an exercise of judicial restraint, the Court stated that "[o]ur decision leaves to Congress' informed judgment any adjustment of § 271(f) it deems necessary or proper."[1544]

The Court's reading of § 271(f) permits a US producer to evade liability by shipping components abroad to have them copied, and thereafter have the copies used or installed by a foreign entity to create another product. But lurking behind the legal issues and questions of statutory construction was whether an affirmance of the Federal Circuit would induce software companies (and companies in other industries) to move their manufacturing facilities outside the US. This argument was raised in the briefs, including amici briefs. In addition, Microsoft also highlights the importance of obtaining foreign patent protection; § 271(f) can be circumvented if the actual production occurs abroad, even though the product design occurred in the US or if instructions on how to produce the product were shipped from the US. Perhaps the lack

1537. *Id.*, at 438.
1538. *Id.*, at 451.
1539. *Id.*
1540. *Id.*
1541. *Microsoft Corp. v. AT & T Corp.*, 550 U.S. 437, 463–64 (2007) (Stevens, J., dissenting).
1542. *Id.*, at 464 (Stevens, J., dissenting).
1543. *Id.*, at 439.
1544. *Id.*, at 442.

of patent protection in Europe reflects the less than sympathetic environment in Europe vis-à-vis the US for software patents.

Most recently, in *Life Technologies v. Promega Corp.*, the Court interpreted the § 271(f)(1) requirement that creates liability for supplying from the US "all or a substantial portion of the components of a patented invention" to be combined abroad in a manner that would infringe the US patent, if the components were combined in the US.[1545] Supreme held that the "supply of a single component of a multicomponent invention for manufacture abroad does not give rise to §271(f) liability." Thus, the "substantial component" requirement must include more than one single component in a multicomponent invention.

B Importing a Claimed Invention or Products Made by a Claimed Process Invention

Importation of a patented invention, in and of itself, is an act of infringement.[1546] Moreover, since February 23, 1989, importation of an unpatented product that is made in a foreign country by a US patented process constitutes infringement.[1547] This provision, part of the Process Patent Amendments Act of 1988, "was enacted to close a perceived loophole in the statutory scheme for protecting owners of United States patents."[1548] Prior to this Act, process patent owners could only sue for infringement if others used the patented process in the US, but not if it was used in a foreign country and the product made from the process was imported into the US.[1549]

The linchpin to protection under § 271(g) is that the imported product is "made by" a process patented in the US.[1550] Section 271(g) provides that an imported product is not "made by" a patented process if: "(1) it is materially changed by subsequent processes; or (2) it becomes a trivial and nonessential component of another product."[1551] Thus, the statute "permits the importation of an item that is derived from a product made by a patented process as long as that product is 'materially changed' in the course of its conversion into the imported item."[1552] To construe whether an

1545. *Life Technologies Corp. v. Promega Corp.*, 137 S. Ct. 734 (2017).
1546. 35 U.S.C. § 154. This provision was revised to conform to the TRIPS Agreement from the Uruguay Round in April 1994.
1547. 35 U.S.C. § 271(g). Previously, a patentee had to petition the United States International Trade Commission under § 337 of the Tariff Act of 1930 for an exclusionary order that prohibited importation of the product. Also, in order to recover under § 337, petitioners had the burden of showing that their patented process was used "in manufacturing the imported products, that an efficiently and economically operated industry utilizing the patent exists in the United States, and that the imported product had the effect or tendency of destroying or substantially injuring the domestic industry." Senate Comm. on the Judiciary, Process Patents Amendments Act of 1987, S. Rep. No. 100-83, at 37. Further, under § 337, patentees could not collect damages. Today, the revised § 271(g) provides for the patentee to exclude others from using or selling throughout the US and importing into the US.
1548. *See Eli Lilly and Co. v. Am. Cyanamid Co.*, 82 F.3d 1568, 1571 (Fed. Cir. 1996).
1549. *Id.*
1550. 35 U.S.C. § 271(g).
1551. *Id.*
1552. *See Eli Lilly*, 82 F.3d at 1572.

imported product is "materially changed," the Federal Circuit looks to "the substantiality of the change between the product of the patented process and the product that is being imported."[1553]

The legislative history reflects the evolution of tests that Congress thought would provide guidance for the courts to determine whether there had been a material change. Specifically, the Senate Reports set forth a two-part test: a product will be considered to be made by the patented process: (1) "if it would not be possible or commercially viable to make that product but for the use of the patented process"; and (2) "if the additional processing steps ... do not change the physical or chemical properties of the product in a manner which changes the basic utility of the product [produced] by the patented process."[1554]

1553. *Id.*, at 1573.
1554. S. Rep. No. 83, 100th Cong., 1st Sess. 51 (1987).

CHAPTER 6
Infringement and Remedies

§1 INFRINGEMENT

Section 271 of the patent code declares that "whoever without authority makes, uses, offers to sell, or sells any patented invention ... infringes the patent."[1555]

Analyzing a patent infringement action involves determining the meaning and scope of the patent claims asserted to be infringed, and comparing the properly construed claims to the infringing device.[1556] The first step, known as claim construction or claim interpretation, is decided by the court, while the second step is determined by the finder of fact.[1557]

I Claim Interpretation

Although claim interpretation is a matter of law, since a judge may not possess the requisite knowledge pertaining to the technology used in a patent, the judge may utilize supplementary sources to ascertain the meaning of obscure words or phrases. The Federal Circuit divides potential evidence into two categories: intrinsic evidence (i.e., the written description, the claims, and the prosecution history); and extrinsic evidence (e.g., dictionaries, technical treatises, and expert testimony).[1558] Both intrinsic and extrinsic evidence are deemed proper; however, a court must look first to intrinsic evidence in interpreting a claim.[1559] Intrinsic evidence is part of the public record and thus enables others to take notice of a claim's scope.[1560] Only if ambiguity persists after a court has considered all available intrinsic evidence may a court consider extrinsic

1555. 35 U.S.C. § 271(a).
1556. *See Markman v. Westview Instruments, Inc.*, 52 F.3d 967, 976 (Fed. Cir. 1995).
1557. *See CVI/Beta Ventures, Inc. v. Tura*, 112 F.3d 1146, 1152 (Fed. Cir. 1997).
1558. *See Vitronics Corp. v. Conceptronic, Inc.*, 90 F.3d 1576, 1584 (Fed. Cir. 1996).
1559. *Id.*, at 1582.
1560. *Id.*, at 1583.

evidence.[1561] Any extrinsic evidence which is inconsistent with the intrinsic evidence should be afforded little or no weight.[1562]

In *Phillips v. AWH Corp.*,[1563] the Federal Circuit outlined the hierarchy of evidentiary sources in claim construction.[1564] When construing claims, the court first looks to the asserted and nonasserted claims to define the scope of the patent.[1565] Second, claims are given their ordinary and customary meaning, which is "the meaning that the term would have to a person of ordinary skill in the art in question at the time of the invention,"[1566] unless it appears from the intrinsic evidence that the inventor chose to be his or her own lexicographer and used them differently.[1567] Special construction of words must be clearly stated in the patent's written description or prosecution history.[1568] In other words, the written description acts as a dictionary when it expressly defines terms used in the claims or when it defines terms by implication.[1569] Third, the court looks to the prosecution history, which contains a complete record of all the proceedings during patent prosecution, including express representations made by the applicant regarding the scope of the claims.[1570] Finally, only if the public record ambiguously describes the scope of the claims, the court may look to extrinsic evidence.[1571]

Because claim construction is a matter of law, the Federal Circuit reviews claim interpretation de novo[1572] and thus has complete discretion to accept or reject a district court's interpretation of a claim. The Federal Circuit can make an independent analysis of any intrinsic evidence on record, and can adopt or completely disregard any extrinsic evidence.[1573]

1561. *Id.*, at 1584.
1562. *See Markman*, 52 F.3d at 983.
1563. 415 F.3d 1303 (Fed. Cir. 2005) (en banc).
1564. *See id.*, at 1311–19.
1565. *See Vitronics*, 90 F.3d at 1582.
1566. *Phillips*, 415 F.3d at 1313.
1567. *See Vitronics*, 90 F.3d at 1582.
1568. *Id.*
1569. *See Markman*, 52 F.3d at 979.
1570. *See Vitronics*, 90 F.3d at 1582.
1571. *See id.*
1572. *Lighting Ballast Control LLC v. Philips Elecs. N.A. Corp.*, 744 F.3d 1272, 1276–77 (Fed. Cir. 2014) (en banc); *Cybor Corp. v. FAS*, 138 F.3d 1448, 1454–55 (Fed. Cir. 1998) (en banc). *See also Teva Pharmaceuticals, Inc. v. Sandoz, Inc.*, where the court stated that the review of factual matters in claim construction is for clear error, and that the ultimate inquiry is de novo.
1573. According to the court:

> [Our] review of a district court's claim construction, albeit without deference, nonetheless is not an independent analysis in the first instance. Moreover, in order to perform such a review, this court must be furnished sufficient findings and reasoning to permit meaningful appellate scrutiny. This requirement for sufficient reasoning applies with equal force to issues of law, such as claim construction, and issues of fact, such as infringement.
>
> *Nazomi Communications, Inc. v. Arm Holdings, PLC*, 403 F.3d 1364, 1371 (Fed. Cir. 2005) (internal citations omitted).

II Literal Infringement

Patent infringement is said to occur where there is either literal infringement or infringement under the Doctrine of Equivalents (DOE). Literal infringement of a patent is very basic and occurs when "every limitation recited in the claim is found in the accused device."[1574] For example, patentee 1 has a patent claiming a product comprising elements A, B, and C and competitor 2 makes a product comprising A, B, and C. It would then be said that patentee 1's patent claim "reads on" competitor 2's product. Literal infringement is analogous to anticipation. As discussed above, to anticipate a patent, a prior art reference must disclose each and every claim limitation. In an infringement context, however, it is the accused device, not a prior art reference, that must embody each and every claim limitation. Thus, the fundamental patent law maxim: "that which infringes, if later, would anticipate, if earlier."[1575]

III Infringement under the Doctrine of Equivalents

Although 35 U.S.C. § 112 requires the patentee to particularly point out and distinctly claim his or her invention, courts do not always limit the patentee to the literal meaning of the claims. To do so "would convert the protection of a patent into a hollow and useless thing."[1576] The courts have, therefore, established the DOE, which permits infringement to be found even where the accused product or process does not literally infringe the patent claim, if each element of the claimed invention has a substantial equivalent in the accused product or process or if the difference between each element in the accused product or process and the claim elements are insubstantial. Thus, in determining infringement under the DOE, the fact finder must employ an element by element analysis. According to the Supreme Court in *Warner-Jenkinson Co. Inc. v. Hilton Davis Chem. Co.*:[1577]

> Each element contained in a patent claim is deemed material to defining the scope of the patented invention, and thus the doctrine of equivalents must be applied to individual elements of the claim, not to the invention as a whole .... An analysis of the role played by each element in the context of the specific patent claim will thus inform the inquiry as to whether a substitute element matches the function, way, result of the claimed element, or whether the substitute element plays a role substantially different from the claimed patent.[1578]

The Federal Circuit has stated that "[t]o be a substantial equivalent, the element substituted in the accused product for the element set forth in the claim must not be such as would substantially change the way in which the function of the claimed invention is performed."[1579]

1574. *Engel Industries, Inc. v. Lockformer Company*, 96 F.3d 1398, 1405 (Fed. Cir. 1996).
1575. *Peters v. Active Mfg. Co.*, 129 U.S. 530, 537 (1889).
1576. *Graver Tank & Mfg. Co. Inc. v. Linde Air Products Co.*, 339 U.S. 605, 607 (1950).
1577. 520 U.S. 17 (1997).
1578. *Id.*, at 40.
1579. *Pennwalt Corp. v. Durand-Wayland, Inc.*, 833 F.2d 931, 935 (Fed. Cir. 1987) (en banc).

The application of the DOE is, however, subservient to the doctrine of prosecution history estoppel and the public dedication rule. With respect to prosecution history estoppel, the Supreme Court has established the following rule:

> When the patentee has chosen to narrow a claim, courts may presume the amended text was composed with awareness of this rule and that the territory surrendered is not an equivalent of the territory claimed. In those instances, however, the patentee still might rebut the presumption that estoppel bars a claim of equivalence. The patentee must show that at the time of the amendment one skilled in the art could not reasonably be expected to have drafted a claim that would have literally encompassed the alleged equivalent.[1580]

The patentee can meet this burden by showing that: (1) the equivalent was unforeseeable at the time of amendment, and therefore, could not have been claimed; (2) the rationale underlying the amendment was only tangentially related to the equivalent; or (3) some other reason suggesting the patentee could not reasonably be expected to have claimed the equivalent.[1581] The public dedication rule further limits the DOE. This rule states that subject matter disclosed in a patent specification, but not claimed, is dedicated to the public domain.[1582] For public dedication to occur, the specification must be specific enough for a person having ordinary skill in art to identify and understand the disclosed unclaimed subject matter.[1583] A generic reference to in the specification does not necessarily give rise to dedication.[1584]

IV Indirect Infringement: Inducing Infringement and Contributory Infringement

In addition to direct infringement, the patent code, under § 271(b) and (c), imposes liability for indirect infringement. Section 271(b) pertains to "active inducement," that is, where a party encourages or aids another directly to infringe a patent by taking affirmative steps like providing instructions on how to practice a patented invention.[1585] Two elements must be established to show inducement of infringement: (1) direct infringement by another;[1586] and (2) "knowledge that the induced acts constitute

1580. *Festo Corporation v. Shoketsu Kinzoku Kogyo Kabushiki Co., Ltd.*, 535 U.S. 722, 741 (2002).
1581. *Id.*, at 740–41.
1582. *Miller v. Bridgeport Brass Co.*, 104 U.S. 350, 352 (1881) ("[T]he claim of a specific device or combination, and an omission to claim other devices or combinations apparent on the face of the patent, are, in law, a dedication to the public of that which is not claimed."); *Johnson & Johnson Associates, Inc. v. R.E. Service Co., Inc.*, 285 F.3d 1046, 1054 (Fed. Cir. 2002) (en banc) ("[W]hen a patent drafter discloses but declines to claim subject matter ... this action dedicates that unclaimed subject matter to the public.").
1583. *PSC Computer Prods., Inc. v. Foxconn Int'l, Inc.*, 355 F.3d 1353, 1360 (Fed. Cir. 2004); *Toro Co. v. White Consolidated Industries, Inc.*, 383 F.3d 1326, 1334 (Fed. Cir. 2004) (explaining that the requisite level of teaching is less than that required to satisfy § 112).
1584. *PSC Computer*, 355 F.3d at 1360.
1585. *See Hewlett-Packard Co. v. Bausch & Lomb, Inc.*, 909 F.2d 1464 (Fed. Cir. 1990).
1586. *Limelight Networks, Inc. v. Akamai Technologies, Inc.*, 134 S. Ct. 2111, 2117 (2014) ("[O]ur case law leaves no doubt that inducement liability may arise 'if, but only if, [there is] ... direct infringement'." (quoting *Aro Mfg. Co. v. Convertible Top Replacement Co.*, 365 U.S. 336, 341 (1961))).

patent infringement."[1587] Regarding the first element, in *Limelight Networks, Inc. v. Akamai Technologies, Inc.*,[1588] the Supreme Court held that in the case of a method claim, there is direct infringement only if the performance of each step in the method is attributable to one person.[1589] Regarding the second element, in *Global-Tech Appliances, Inc. v. SEB, S.A.*,[1590] the Supreme Court held that "knowledge" could be satisfied by a showing of actual knowledge or "willful blindness"[1591]—which is present if the defendant "subjectively believes" that there is a "high probability" of infringement and that the defendant takes "deliberate actions" to avoid learning of that fact.[1592] Additionally, a defendant's good faith belief in a patent's invalidity is not a defense to an induced infringement claim under § 271(b).[1593]

In contrast to inducement under § 271(b), section 271(c) concerns itself with contributory infringement. For example, the sale of a component of a patented device or composition or the sale of a component for use in practicing a patented process. Contributory infringement applies, therefore, to the supply of a "nonstaple" component of a claimed invention to third party, who makes, uses or sells the entire invention. That section requires that the alleged contributory infringer sells his or her component "knowing the same to be especially made or especially adapted for use in an infringement of such patent." In *Aro Mfg. v. Convertible Top Replacement Co.*,[1594] the Supreme Court stated that "§271(c) does require a showing that the alleged contributory infringer knew that the combination for which his component was especially designed was both patented and infringing."[1595] The same knowledge needed for induced infringement must be shown for contributory infringement.[1596] Section 271(c) codifies prior case law which refused to find contributory infringement where the component sold had a noninfringing use.[1597] The statute uses the phrase "substantial non-infringing use," which "relates ... to whether the portion of the invention supplied by the contributory infringer ... has a use other than to be combined with other items that together fall within the metes and bounds of the claims of the patent."[1598]

1587. *Global-Tech Appliances, Inc. v. SEB, S.A.*, 131 S. Ct. 2060, 2070 (2011).
1588. 134 S. Ct. 2111 (2014).
1589. *Id.*, at 2117. In an earlier inducement case, the Federal Circuit held that a method's steps have not been performed as claimed unless they are all attributable to the same defendant, either because the defendant actually performed all of the steps or because he directed or controlled others who performed them. *Muniauction, Inc. v. Thomson Corp.*, 532 F.3d 1318, 1329–30 (Fed. Cir. 2008).
1590. 131 S. Ct. 2060 (2011).
1591. *See id.*, at 2068–71.
1592. *Id.*, at 2070.
1593. *Commil USA, LLC v. Cisco Sys., Inc.*, 135 S. Ct. 1920 (2015).
1594. 377 U.S. 476 (1964).
1595. *Id.*, at 488–90.
1596. *Global-Tech*, 131 S. Ct. at 2068.
1597. As the Supreme Court stated, "Undoubtedly a bare supposition that by a sale of an article which, though adopted to an infringing use, is also adopted to other and lawful uses, is not enough to make the seller a contributory infringer. Such a rule would block the wheels of commerce." *Sidney Henrey v. A.B. Dick Co.*, 224 U.S. 1, 48 (1912).
1598. *Lucas Aerospace, Ltd. v. Unison Indus.*, 899 F. Supp. 1268, 1287 (D.Del. 1995).

§2 DEFENSES TO PATENT INFRINGEMENT

I Noninfringement and Invalidity

The most common defenses to patent infringement are noninfringement and invalidity. With respect to noninfringement, the general rule is that "[t]he patentee bears the burden of proving infringement by a preponderance of the evidence."[1599] When the patentee fails to meet that burden, "the patentee loses regardless of whether the accused comes forward with any evidence to the contrary."[1600]

Through an invalidity defense, an accused infringer often argues that the patent-in-suit is invalid for failure to comply with one or more of the statutory patentability requirements. However, an issued patent enjoys a statutory presumption of validity.[1601] To overcome the presumption, the challenger must come forward with clear and convincing evidence of invalidity.[1602]

II Patent Misuse

In general, a patent may be considered misused if it is used in a way that violates the antitrust laws or when it is used to expand the scope of the patent rights in an anticompetitive fashion.[1603] Such patent-related antitrust violations comprise three general categories. First, they may involve fraudulent procurement of a patent.[1604] Second, an antitrust violation can occur if there is bad faith enforcement of a patent (e.g., enforcing a patent known to be invalid).[1605] Finally, a violation can occur where patent-related conduct violates any other antitrust law. Antitrust violations are limited by the Noerr-Pennington doctrine, which precludes liability when private entities solicit government action to exercise a legal right.[1606]

Congress, however, narrowed the patent misuse defense when it stated that a patent owner would not be denied relief for infringement or deemed guilty of patent misuse by:

> (1) deriv[ing] revenue from acts which if performed by another without his consent would constitute contributory infringement[;] (2) licens[ing] or authoriz-[ing] another to perform acts which if performed without his consent would constitute contributory infringement[;] (3) [seeking] to enforce his patent rights

1599. *SRI Int'l v. Matsushita Elec. Corp.*, 775 F.2d 1107, 1123 (Fed. Cir. 1985).
1600. *Creative Compounds, LLC v. Starmark Laboratories*, 651 F.3d 1303, 1314 (Fed. Cir. 2011).
1601. 35 U.S.C. § 282.
1602. *See, e.g., Pfizer, Inc. v. Apotex, Inc.*, 480 F.3d 1348, 1359–60 (Fed. Cir. 2007); *Hybritech Inc. v. Monoclonal Antibodies, Inc.*, 802 F.2d 1367, 1375 (Fed. Cir. 1986). The Supreme Court reaffirmed the standard of proof. *See Microsoft Corp. v. i4i Ltd. P'ship*, 131 S. Ct. 2238, 2242 (2011).
1603. *See Windsurfing Int'l, Inc. v. AMF, Inc.*, 782 F.2d 995 (Fed. Cir. 1986).
1604. *See Walker Process Equipment, Inc. v. Food Machinery & Chemical Corp.*, 382 U.S. 172 (1965).
1605. *See Handgards, Inc. v. Ethicon, Inc.*, 601 F.2d 986 (9th Cir. 1979); *Handgards, Inc. v. Ethicon, Inc.*, 743 F.2d 1282 (9th Cir. 1984).
1606. *See Eastern R. Conf. v. Noerr Motors*, 365 U.S. 127, 145 (1961); *United Mine Workers v. Pennington*, 381 U.S. 657, 670 (1965).

> against infringement or contributory infringement; (4) refus[ing] to license or use any rights to the patent; or (5) condition[ing] the license of any rights to the patent or the sale of the patented product on the acquisition of a license to rights in another patent or purchase of a separate product, unless in view of the circumstances, the patent owner has market power in the relevant market for the patent or patented product on which the license or sale is conditioned.[1607]

When a patent is deemed to have been misused, it is unenforceable until the improper conduct ceases and the effects are dissipated.[1608]

III First Sale, Implied License, and Repair/Reconstruction

Section 271(a) gives rise to an infringement cause of action when certain acts are conducted "without authority."[1609] Authority may be express or implicit. Express authority may arise, for example, in a license[1610] or settlement contract.[1611] Implicit authority exists, generally, under three circumstances: after the first sale of the patented invention (also known as the principle of patent exhaustion); where the circumstances necessitate an implied license; and where a patented product has merely been repaired, as opposed to being reconstructed.

After the first sale of a patented product, the buyer is free to use or resell that patented product, unless there is a special agreement between the buyer and seller.[1612] In general, the sale of patented products follow general contract law. The sale or license contract may contain provisions that restrict conduct after the sale of the patented product. Otherwise, the sale contract of a patented product is considered to contain implied contract terms that free the buyer from the rights afforded to patent owners with respect to further sale or transfer of the product. Additionally, the "patentee's decision to sell a product exhausts all of its patent right in that item, regardless of any restrictions the patentee purports to impose or the location of the sale."[1613] It is important to point out that the first sale doctrine "restricts a patentee's rights only as to the particular article sold; it leaves untouched the patentee's ability to prevent a buyer from making new copies of the patented item."[1614] In a recent Supreme Court case,

1607. 35 U.S.C. § 271(d).
1608. *Senza-Gel Corp. v. Sieffhart*, 803 F.2d 661, 668 n.10 (Fed. Cir. 1986).
1609. 35 U.S.C. § 271(a) (2006) ("[W]hoever without authority makes, uses, offers to sell, or sells any patented invention, within the United States or imports into the United States any patented invention during the term of the patent therefor, infringes the patent.").
1610. *See McCoy v. Mitsuboshi Cutlery, Inc.*, 67 F.3d 917 (Fed. Cir. 1995).
1611. *See Gjerlov v. Schuyler Labs.*, 131 F.3d 1016 (Fed. Cir. 1997).
1612. *See Adams v. Burke*, 84 U.S. (17 Wall.) 453, 456 (1873) ("The [patented] article passes without the limit[s] of the monopoly."); *Quanta Computer, Inc. v. LG Electronics, Inc.*, 553 U.S. 617, 625 (2008) ("The longstanding doctrine of patent exhaustion provides that the initial authorised sale of a patented item terminates all patent rights to that item.").
1613. *Impression Products, Inc. v. Lexmark International, Inc.*, 137 S. Ct. 1523 (2017). However, "if the patentee negotiates a contract restricting the purchaser's right to use or resell the item, it may be able to enforce that restriction as a matter of contract law, but may not do so through a patent infringement lawsuit." *Id.*
1614. *Bowman v. Monsanto*, 133 S. Ct. 1761, 1766 (2013) (internal citation and quotation marks omitted). In *Bowman*, the Court held that the first sale doctrine did not enable a farmer to

Impression Products, Inc. v. Lexmark International, Inc., the Supreme Court held that foreign sales trigger the doctrine of exhaustion just as a sale within the US does.[1615]

Second, the facts and circumstances may cause a court to apply the equitable doctrine of implied license.[1616] The categories of conduct that give rise to an implied license include acquiescence, conduct, equitable estoppel, or legal estoppel.[1617] The sale of nonpatented equipment to practice a patented invention may arise if two requirements are met: "First, the equipment involved must have no non-infringing uses"; and "[s]econd, the circumstances of the sale must 'plainly indicate that the grant of a license should be inferred'."[1618]

Finally, the legal doctrine of repair/reconstruction provides for an inferred grant of authority without an express contractual grant.[1619] Generally, the authorized purchaser may repair or replace damaged or worn parts necessary for use.[1620] The authorized purchaser, however, may not reconstruct a patented product from the parts of worn-out products.[1621] According to the Federal Circuit:

> The authority to use and sell a purchased device, however, does not include the right to make a new device or to reconstruct one which has been spent. Reconstruction, i.e., the re-creation of a patented combination, is an infringement because such activity is beyond the implied authorization to use and sell a patented device.[1622]

IV Experimental Use Doctrine

Mere use of a patented product usually constitutes infringement under § 271(a). However, there is a line of authority suggesting that use of a patented product for

make additional copies of patented soybeans (with self-replicate to make a new generation of soybeans genetically identical to the seeds from which they were grown) without express or implied permission from the patentee. *Id.*, at 1766.

1615. *Impression Products, Inc. v. Lexmark International, Inc.*, 137 S. Ct. 1523 (2017).
1616. *See Deforest Radio Tel. & Tel. Co. v. United States*, 273 U.S. 236, 241 (1927) ("No formal granting of a license is necessary to give it effect. Any language used by the owner of the patent or any conduct on his part exhibited to another from which that other may properly infer that the owner consents to his use of the patent in making or using it, or selling it, upon which the other acts, constitutes a license and a defense to an action for a tort."); *Wang Laboratories v. Mitsubishi Electronics*, 103 F.3d 1571, 1580 (Fed. Cir. 1997) ("[A]n implied license merely signifies a patentee's waiver of the statutory right to exclude others from making, using, or selling the patented invention.").
1617. *See Wang Laboratories*, 103 F.3d at 1580.
1618. *Met-Coil Systems Corp. v. Korners Unlimited, Inc.*, 803 F.2d 684, 686 (Fed. Cir. 1986).
1619. *See generally* Mark D. Janis, *A Tale of the Apocryphal Axe: Repair, Reconstruction, and the Implied License in Intellectual Property Law*, 58 Md. L. Rev. 423 (1999).
1620. *See Aro Mfg. Co. v. Convertible Top Replacement Co.*, 365 U.S. 365 U.S. 338, 342–46 (1961); *Wilbur-Ellis Co. v. Kuther*, 377 U.S. 422, 424–25 (1964).
1621. *See American Cotton-Tie Co. v. Simmons*, 106 U.S. (16 Otto.) 89 (1882).
1622. *Hewlett-Packard Co. v. Repeat-O-Type Stencil Mfg. Corp., Inc.*, 123 F.3d 1445, 1451 (Fed. Cir. 1997). "On the other hand, one does have authority to repair a patented device that he has purchased .... A reconstruction occurs after the patented combination, as a whole, has been spent, when 'the material of the combination ceases to exist'." *Id.*, at 1451–52 (quoting *Wilson v. Simpson*, 50 U.S. (9 How.) 109, 123 (1850)).

noncommercial, experimental purposes is not an act of infringement. This "experimental use doctrine" is particularly germane to the pharmaceutical industry. Ideally, a generic drug should be available to the public immediately upon expiration of a patent claiming the drug. However, given the lengthy Food and Drug Administration (FDA) approval requirements, to accomplish this result would require the generic drug companies to test and use the patented drug before the patent expires.

In *Roche Products, Inc. v. Bolar Pharmaceutical Co.*,[1623] the Federal Circuit held that the experimental use doctrine did not apply to "limited use of a patented drug for testing and investigation strictly related to FDA drug approval requirements during the last six months of the term of the patent."[1624]

Shortly after Roche was decided, Congress responded by enacting the Drug Price Competition and Patent Term Restoration Act of 1984, also known as the Hatch-Waxman Act, which added § 271(e) to the patent code. That provision abrogated the holding in Roche. Section 271(e)(1) hastened the introduction of generic equivalents into the marketplace by exempting from infringement the making, using, or selling of "a patented invention ... solely for uses reasonably related to the development and submission of information under a Federal law which regulates the manufacture, use, or sale of drugs."[1625] The Act also created the "Abbreviated New Drug Application" or ANDA, a streamlined application process for entities seeking FDA Administration approval and wishing to market a generic equivalent of an FDA-approved patented product. Further, the Act, under § 271(e)(2), provides a patent owner with a special infringement remedy against entities filing an ANDA seeking FDA approval to market a generic equivalent before expiration of the patent. Finally, it provided for extensions of patent terms that result from delays and the rigors of the FDA approval process.[1626]

The Act was designed to promote technological innovation while at the same time enhance the public welfare, a balancing act that is at the very heart of the patent system.

V Governmental Use

A *Federal Government*

When the US government makes or uses a patented invention, the patent owner's exclusive remedy resides in the US Court of Federal Claims, not federal district court. According to 28 U.S.C. § 1498(a):

> Whenever an invention described in and covered by a patent of the United States is used or manufactured by or for the United States without license of the owner thereof or lawful right to use or manufacture the same, the owner's remedy shall

1623. 733 F.2d 858 (Fed. Cir. 1984).
1624. *Id.*, at 861.
1625. 35 U.S.C. § 271(e)(1) (emphasis added).
1626. For a discussion of the interrelationship between the Hatch-Waxman Act provisions on patent term extension, exemption of FDA data gathering for generic equivalents, and the filing of ANDAs, *see Eli Lilly and Co. v. Medtronic, Inc.*, 496 U.S. 661, 676–78 (1990).

> be by action against the United States in the United States Court of Federal Claims for the recovery of his reasonable and entire compensation for such use and manufacture.
>
> ...

For the purpose of this section, the use or manufacture of an invention described in and covered by a patent of the US by a contractor, a subcontractor, or any person, firm, or corporation for the Government and with the authorization or consent of the Government, shall be construed as use or manufacture for the US.[1627]

The second paragraph of § 1498(a) states that the "use or manufacture" of a patented invention by an entity "with the authorization or consent of the Government shall be construed as use or manufacture for the United States." The requirement that the use or manufacture has the "authorization or consent" of the government can involve both a "product manufactured for actual delivery to the United States or a product, machine, or process used by a contractor or subcontractor doing work for the United States."[1628] In the first situation, courts have held that acceptance by the government of a patented product manufactured by a contractor or subcontractor invokes § 1498, even absent a specified authorization.[1629]

The second situation poses greater difficulties. According to Professor Chisum:

> [t]he standard clause in United States Government supply contracts is limited, extending authorization and consent only where the invention is "utilized in the machinery, tools, or methods the use of which necessarily results from compliance by the Contractor or the using subcontractor with (a) specifications or written provisions now or hereafter forming a part of this contract, or (b) specific written instructions given by the Contracting Officer directing the manner of performance." On the other hand, in contracts for research and development, the government extends "greater latitude," extending authorization and consent for "all use and manufacture of any patented invention in the performance" of a contract.[1630]

1627. Some courts have suggested that § 1498 is actually based on "takings" jurisprudence, wherein the government is exercising its power of eminent domain. In *W.L. Gore & Associates Inc. v. Garlock Inc.*, the Federal Circuit stated that:

> The patentee takes his patent from the United States subject to the government's eminent domain rights to obtain what it needs from manufacturers and to use the same. The government has graciously consented, in the same statute, to be sued in the Claims Court for reasonable and entire compensation, for what would be infringement if by a private person.
>
> 842 F.2d 1275, 1283 (Fed. Cir. 1988).

1628. DONALD S. CHISUM ET AL., PRINCIPLES OF PATENT LAW (3rd ed. 2004), §16.06[3][c].

1629. *See TVI Energy Corp. v. Blane*, 806 F.2d 1057, 1059 (Fed. Cir. 1986) (holding that a demonstration of a product pursuant to a Government bidding procurement scheme was covered by § 1498, despite the fact that the government had not issued an "authorization and consent" letter).

1630. DONALD S. CHISUM ET AL., PRINCIPLES OF PATENT LAW (3rd ed. 2004), §16.06[3][c] quoting *Stelma, Inc. v. Bridge Elec. Co.*, 300 F.2d 761 (Fed. Cir. 1962).

B *State Government*

Generally, state governments and their agencies are subject to the patent law. However, Eleventh Amendment to the US Constitution immunity issues present significant impediments to an infringement suit. The Amendment states:

> The Judicial power of the United States shall not be construed to extend to any suit in law or equity, commenced or prosecuted against one of the United States by Citizens of another State, or by Citizens or Subjects of any Foreign State.[1631]

In 1992, Congress enacted the Patent and Plant Variety Protection Remedy Clarification Act (Patent Remedy Act).[1632] This Act added § 271(h) and abrogated state immunity as it relates to the patent law. However, four years later, in *Seminole Tribe of Florida v. Florida*,[1633] the Supreme Court cast the constitutionality of abrogating state immunity. In Seminole Tribe, the Court addressed the Indian Gaming Regulatory Act, which was "passed by Congress under the Indian Commerce Clause [which, according to the Court, is not distinguishable from the Interstate Commerce Clause], U.S. Const., Art I, §8, cl. 3."[1634] The Act "imposes upon the States a duty to negotiate in good faith with an Indian tribe toward the formation of a compact, ... and authorizes a tribe to bring suit in federal court against a State in order to compel performance of that duty."[1635] The Court held that Congress' attempt to abrogate the state of Florida's immunity was not passed pursuant to a valid exercise of congressional power, and was therefore unconstitutional. According to the Supreme Court, the only legitimate avenue available to Congress in abrogating State immunity was the Fourteenth Amendment:

> Even when the Constitution vests in Congress complete law-making authority over a particular area, the Eleventh Amendment prevents congressional authorization of suits by private parties against unconsenting States. The Eleventh Amendment restricts the judicial power under Article III, and Article I cannot be used to circumvent the constitutional limitations placed upon federal jurisdiction.[1636]

Since the fundamental power to regulate patents derives from Article I, section 8, clause 8 of the US Constitution, the question is whether the 1992 abrogation of immunity for patent infringement claims is constitutional. This question was resolved by the Supreme Court in *Florida Prepaid Postsecondary Ed. Expense Board v. College Savings Bank*.[1637] The Court determined that the purpose of the Patent Remedy Act was not to enforce the guarantees of the Fourteenth Amendment but rather to serve the Article I concerns of "provid[ing] a uniform remedy for patent infringement and ... plac[ing] States on the same footing as private parties under that regime."[1638] Consistent with Seminole Tribe, the Court held that Congress could not use its Article I powers

1631. U.S. Const. amend. XI.
1632. Pub. L. No. 102-560, 106 Stat 4230.
1633. 517 U.S. 44 (1996).
1634. *Id.*, at 47.
1635. *Id.*
1636. 517 U.S. 44, 72–73 (1996).
1637. 527 U.S. 627 (1999).
1638. *Id.*, at 647–48.

under the Intellectual Property Clause to abrogate State sovereign immunity;[1639] thus, the Eleventh Amendment abrogation provision in the Patent Remedy Act was unconstitutional.[1640]

State sovereign immunity does not apply to IPRs.[1641] In *Regents of the University of Minnesota v. LSI Corp*, the Federal Circuit held that IPRs are similar to an agency enforcement action, in contrast to civil litigation. Accordingly, the court held that state sovereign immunity does not apply to IPR proceedings. Furthermore, in *St. Regis Mohawk Indian Tribe v. Mylan Pharms. Inc.*, the Federal Circuit held that tribal sovereign immunity does not protect the tribe from being named as a party in an IPR.[1642]

VI Inequitable Conduct

A duty of candor and good faith is owed to the PTO in prosecuting patent applications "which includes a duty to disclose to the Office all information known to that individual to be material to patentability."[1643] The duty extends not only to applicants, but to "each attorney or agent who prepares or prosecutes an application and on who is substantively involved in the preparation or prosecution of the application and who is associated with the inventor, with the assignee, or with anyone to whom there is an obligation to assign the application."[1644] The duty to disclose information exists with respect to each pending claim until the claim is canceled or withdrawn from consideration, or the application becomes abandoned.[1645] A breach of the duty of candor and good faith constitutes inequitable conduct and renders the entire patent unenforceable.[1646] By obliging the applicant to fully cooperate with patent examination, the duty of candor and good faith helps the PTO combat its information deficit.

Inequitable conduct is an equitable doctrine which requires a finding of both intent to deceive the PTO and the misrepresentation or omission of information material to patentability.[1647] Until recently the standards for materiality and intent were sufficiently low that a charge of inequitable conduct was alleged in almost every patent case.[1648] It became the "atomic bomb" of patent law because: (1) it could not be cured;

1639. *Id.*, at 636 (citing *Seminole Tribe*, 517 U.S. at 72–73).
1640. *Id.*, at 640.
1641. *Regents of the University of Minnesota v. LSI Corp.*, 926 F.3d 1327 (Fed. Cir. 2019).
1642. *Saint Regis Mohawk Tribe v. Mylan Pharms. Inc.*, 896 F.3d 1332 (Fed. Cir. 2018).
1643. 37 C.F.R. § 1.56(a).
1644. 37 C.F.R. § 1.56(c).
1645. 37 C.F.R. § 1.56(a).
1646. *See Warner-Lambert Co. v. Teva Pharms. USA, Inc.*, 418 F.3d 1326, 1342 (Fed. Cir. 2005); *Molins PLC v. Textron, Inc.*, 48 F.3d 1172, 1178 (Fed. Cir. 1995).
1647. *Star Scientific Inc. v. R.J. Reynolds Tobacco Co.*, 537 F.3d 1357, 1365 (Fed. Cir. 2008).
1648. *See Therasense, Inc. v. Becton, Dickinson and Co.*, 649 F.3d 1276, 1288 (Fed. Cir. 2011) (en banc); *see also Burlington Indus., Inc. v. Dayco Corp.*, 849 F.2d 1418, 1422 (Fed. Cir. 1988) (recognizing that "the habit of charging inequitable conduct in almost every major patent case has become an absolute plague").

(2) inequitable conduct involving one claim rendered the entire patent unenforceable; (3) the finding of inequitable conduct could spread to an entire family of patents.[1649]

In *Therasense v. Becton, Dickinson and Co.*,[1650] the Federal Circuit addressed these issues en banc by raising the standards of proof for both intent and materiality. Regarding intent, "the accused infringer must prove that the patentee acted with the specific intent to deceive the [PTO]."[1651] Specifically, "the accused infringer must prove by clear and convincing evidence that the applicant knew of the reference, knew that it was material, and made a deliberate decision to withhold it."[1652] For materiality, it is now a "but-for materiality"[1653] such that the accused infringer must show by a preponderance of the evidence that "the [PTO] would not have allowed a claim had it been aware of the undisclosed reference."[1654] Practically, the heightened standard will oblige the accused infringer to adduce prior art that would invalidate the patent anyway for a lack of novelty or nonobviousness.

VII Laches

A laches is a judicially created defense developed by courts of equity to protect defendants against "unreasonable, prejudicial delay in commencing suit."[1655] The laches defense is asserted by the accused infringer when the plaintiff fails to bring a patent infringement suit within a reasonable time frame. The remedy for laches is to prevent recovery of damages prior to the filing of the action. Thus the laches defense only diminishes the amount of recovery by the plaintiff, and does not bar the plaintiff from recovery.

To assert the laches defense, the accused infringer must establish that: (1) the plaintiff delayed filing suit for an unreasonable and inexcusable length of time from the time the plaintiff knew or reasonably should have known of its claim against the defendant; and (2) the delay operated to the prejudice or injury of the defendant.[1656] If the plaintiff sues within six years of learning about the infringement, then the burden of proof is on the defendant to show these two elements. In contrast, if the plaintiff files suit more than six years after he or she knew or should have known about the alleged infringement, then there is a presumption of laches that is created in the defendant's favor. The burden of production then shifts to the plaintiff, who can then provide evidence to rebut the presumption. In *SCA Hygiene v. First Quality Baby Products*, the Supreme Court held that laches cannot be invoked as a defense against a claim for damages brought within the six-year limitations period of § 286.[1657]

1649. *Therasense*, 649 F.3d at 1288–89.
1650. 649 F.3d 1276 (Fed. Cir. 2011) (en banc).
1651. *Id.*, at 1290.
1652. *Id.*
1653. 649 F.3d 1276, 1291 (Fed. Cir. 2011) (en banc).
1654. *Id.*
1655. *Petrella, v. Metro-Goldwyn-Mayer, Inc.*, 134 S. Ct. 1962 (2014).
1656. *A.C. Aukerman Co. v. Chaides Constr. Co.*, 960 F.2d 1028 (Fed. Cir. 1992) (en banc).
1657. *SCA Hygiene Products Aktiebolag v. First Quality Baby Products, LLC.*, 137 S. Ct. 954 (2017).

VIII Equitable Estoppel

Equitable estoppel is an independent defense that is based on the idea that the plaintiff's misleading actions led the defendant to believe that they would not be sued. In contrast to the laches defense, equitable estoppel bars the plaintiff's claim of infringement.[1658]

To assert the equitable estoppel defense, the defendant must establish that: (1) the patentee, through misleading conduct, leads the alleged infringer to reasonably infer that the patentee does not intend to enforce its patent against the alleged infringer; (2) the alleged infringer relies on that conduct; and (3) due to its reliance, the alleged infringer will be materially prejudiced if the patentee is allowed to proceed with its claim.[1659]

§3 REMEDIES

Once liability in an infringement action has been found, the focus turns to an assessment of damages or equitable relief. An infringement remedy may take the form of compensatory relief (lost profits or reasonable royalties), equitable relief (preliminary and permanent injunctions), and an award of attorney fees. Section 284 of the patent code allows a successful patent owner to recover "damages adequate to compensate for the infringement."[1660] Although computing the exact damage caused by an infringing product can be complex, the patentee is entitled to no less than a "reasonable royalty."[1661]

I Compensatory Damages

A patent owner may seek any reasonably foreseeable damages that were proximately caused by an infringing product.[1662] A reasonably foreseeable damage may entail lost profits due to captured sales, eroded prices, or increased expenses in producing the patented invention.[1663] In addition, recovery is sometimes available for component parts normally sold with a patented invention if the parts act to complete a functional machine under the "entire market rule."[1664] Calculation of monetary damages is generally measured as lost profits or reasonable royalty. The burden of proving damages is on the patentee.[1665]

1658. *Scholle Corp. v. Blackhawk Molding Co.*, 133 F.3d 1469 (Fed. Cir. 1998).
1659. *A.C. Aukerman Co. v. Chaides Constr. Co.*, 960 F.2d 1020 (Fed. Cir. 1992) (en banc).
1660. 35 U.S.C. § 284.
1661. *Id.*
1662. *See Rite-Hite Corp. v. Kelley Co.*, 56 F.3d 1538, 1549 (Fed. Cir. 1995).
1663. *See Lam, Inc. v. Johns-Manville Corp.*, 718 F.2d 1056, 1065 (Fed. Cir. 1983).
1664. *See Rite-Hite*, 56 F.3d at 1549–50.
1665. *Lucent Techs, Inc. v. Gateway, Inc.*, 580 F.3d 1301, 1324 (Fed. Cir. 2009).

To recover the lost profits, a patent owner must show a causal link between the lost profits and the infringement.[1666] *Panduit Corp. v. Stahlin Bros.* Fibre Works[1667] set forth four elements that must be proven in a lost profit analysis: (1) a demand for the patented product; (2) the absence of acceptable noninfringing substitutes for the patented product; (3) the patent owner's manufacturing and marketing capability to exploit the demand for the patented product; and (4) the amount of profit the patent owner would have expected in the absence of infringement.[1668] A patent holder must establish each criterion to recover lost profits.[1669]

In the event that a patent owner cannot show lost profits, a court may impose a reasonable royalty to provide adequate compensation.[1670] A district court has discretion in choosing a method to calculate a reasonable royalty.[1671] The court may calculate a reasonable royalty based on an established royalty, or rely on the standards of the pertinent industry.[1672] This method is commonly referred to as the analytical approach.[1673]

The alternative more common approach referred to as the "hypothetical negotiation" or the "willing licensor-willing licensee" approach[1674] "attempts to ascertain the [reasonable] royalty upon which the parties would have agreed had they successfully negotiated an agreement just before infringement began."[1675] A court must be flexible in applying this approach, for to focus solely on a standard fictitious negotiation "would be to pretend that the infringement never happened."[1676] When establishing a reasonable royalty, a court should consider the specific factors that "normally prudent businessmen would, under similar circumstances take into consideration."[1677]

1666. *Lam*, 718 F.2d at 1065.
1667. 575 F.2d 1152 (6th Cir. 1978).
1668. *Id.*, at 1156.
1669. *See Smithkline Diagnostics, Inc. v. Helena Laboratories Corp.*, 926 F.2d 1161, 1165 (Fed. Cir. 1991).
1670. *See Dowagiac Mfg. Corp. v. Minnesota Moline Plow Co.*, 235 U.S. 641, 648–49 (1915).
1671. *See TWM Mfg. Co. v. Dura Corp.*, 789 F.2d 895, 900 (Fed. Cir. 1986).
1672. *See Armco, Inc. v. Republic Steel Corp.*, 707 F.2d 886, 891 (6th Cir. 1983).
1673. *See TWM*, 789 F.2d at 899 (describing the analytical method as "subtract[ing] the infringer's usual or acceptable net profit from its anticipated net profit realized from sales of infringing devices").
1674. *See Lucent*, 580 F.3d at 1324.
1675. *Id.*; *see also Radio Steel & Mfg. Co. v. MTD Prods., Inc.*, 788 F.2d 1554, 1557 (Fed. Cir. 1986) ("The determination of a reasonable royalty, however, is based not on the infringer's profit, but on the royalty to which a willing licensor and a willing licensee would have agreed at the time the infringement began.").
1676. *TWM*, 789 F.2d at 900.
1677. *Georgia-Pacific Corp. v. United States Plywood Corp.*, 318 F. Supp. 1116, 1121 (S.D.N.Y. 1970); *see also Panduit*, 575 F.2d at 1159 ("Among the relevant facts are: what plaintiff's property was, to what extent defendant has taken it, its usefulness and commercial value as shown by its advantages over other things and by the extent of its use, and the commercial situation." (internal citations and quotation marks omitted)).

II Exemplary Damages

A district court may award up to three times the assessed damages in the event of willful infringement.[1678] To establish willful infringement, "a patentee must show by clear and convincing evidence that the infringer acted despite an objectively high likelihood that its actions constituted infringement of a valid patent."[1679] Deliberately copying the invention of another, bypassing a reasonable investigation to determine the validity of a patent, and behaving improperly during litigation suggest bad faith on the part of an infringer.[1680] "For a finding of willfulness, once the threshold objective standard is satisfied, the patentee must also demonstrate that this objectively-defined risk ... was either known or so obvious that it should have been known to the accused infringer."[1681] Once a district court finds clear and convincing evidence of willful infringement, it looks to the totality of the circumstances to assess the appropriate increase in damages.[1682]

Although not specifically mentioned under § 284 of the patent code, a district court has the discretion to award prejudgment interest.[1683] Notwithstanding this grant of discretion, it has been held that a court should award prejudgment interest unless there is a sound reason to withhold the interest.[1684] Also, adequate compensation for infringement customarily entails post-judgment interest, which is controlled by 28 U.S.C. § 1961.

III Injunctive Relief

A district court can prevent possible ongoing infringement of a patent prior to a finding of infringement by granting a preliminary injunction.[1685] The Federal Circuit has set forth four factors a district court must weigh before granting a preliminary injunction.[1686] First, whether the party seeking the injunction (the movant) has sufficiently established a reasonable likelihood of success on the merits. This requirement includes a showing that the patent is not invalid and is infringed. Second, whether the movant would suffer irreparable harm if an injunction was not granted. A presumption of irreparable harm can be made by a strong showing of both validity and infringement, regardless of the solvency of the infringer.[1687] Third, whether a balance of hardships tips in the movant's favor. This analysis entails comparing the potential harm to the

1678. *See* 35 U.S.C. § 284.
1679. *In re* Seagate Technologies., LLC, 497 F.3d 1360, 1371 (Fed. Cir. 2007) (en banc).
1680. *See Liquid Dynamics Corp. v. Vaughan Co.*, 449 F.3d 1209, 1225 (Fed. Cir. 2006) (citing *Read Corp. v. Portec, Inc.*, 970 F.2d 816, 826–27 (Fed. Cir. 1992)).
1681. *Seagate*, 497 F.3d at 1371.
1682. *ACCO Brands, Inc. v. ABA Locks Mfrs. Co., Ltd.*, 501 F.3d 1307, 1311–12 (2007).
1683. *Group One, Ltd. v. Hallmark Cards, Inc.*, 407 F.3d 1297, 1308 (Fed. Cir. 2005) (citing *General Motors Corp. v. Devex Corp.*, 461 U.S. 648, 656–57 (1983)).
1684. *See General Motors*, 461 U.S. at 656.
1685. *See* 35 U.S.C. § 283.
1686. *See, e.g.*, *Abbott Laboratories v. Andrx Pharms., Inc.*, 452 F.3d 1331, 1334 (Fed. Cir. 2006); *Ranbaxy Pharm., Inc. v. Apotex, Inc.*, 350 F.3d 1235, 1239 (Fed. Cir. 2003).
1687. *Smith Int'l, Inc. v. Hughes Tool Co.*, 718 F.2d 1573, 1581 (Fed. Cir. 1983).

patent owner if the injunction is withheld, with the potential harm to the alleged infringer if the injunction is granted. The final consideration is whether an injunction will impair the public interest. Although the public interest is generally concerned with protecting patent rights, the true focus of this element is whether the public would be injured by granting preliminary relief.[1688] None of the four factors is dispositive. Rather a "district court must weigh and measure each factor against the other factors and against the form and magnitude of the relief requested."[1689] The Federal Circuit reviews the trial courts' grant or denial of a preliminary injunction for an abuse of discretion.[1690]

After finding infringement, a court generally grants a permanent injunction unless there is a sufficient countervailing reason.[1691] Similar to preliminary injunctions, a patentee seeking a permanent injunction must establish: "(1) that it has suffered an irreparable injury; (2) that remedies available at law, such as monetary damages, are inadequate to compensate for that injury; (3) that, considering the balance of hardships between the plaintiff and defendant, a remedy in equity is warranted; and (4) that the public interest would not be disserved by a permanent injunction."[1692] A public interest concern may delay or prevent a permanent injunction; e.g., a transition period may be required to allow the industry to adjust,[1693] or the defendant to respond to an injunction.[1694]

1688. *See Hybritech Inc. v. Abbott Lab.*, 849 F.2d 1446, 1458 (Fed. Cir. 1988).
1689. *Id.*, at 1451.
1690. *Amazon.com, Inc. v. Barnesandnoble.com, Inc.*, 239 F.3d 1343, 1350 (Fed. Cir. 2001).
1691. *See Richardson v. Suzuki Motor Co.*, 868 F.2d 1226, 1246–47 (Fed. Cir. 1989).
1692. *eBay Inc. v. MercExchange, L.L.C.*, 547 U.S. 388, 391 (2006).
1693. *See*, e.g., *Schneider AG v. SciMed Life Sys, Inc.*, 852 F. Supp. 813, 850–51, 860–61 (D. Minn. 1994).
1694. *See*, e.g., *Polaroid Corp. v. Eastman Kodak Co.*, 228 U.S.P.Q. 305, 343–44 (D. Mass. 1985), *aff'd*, 789 F.2d 1556 (Fed. Cir. 1986).

CHAPTER 7

Design Patents

One may obtain a design patent on a "new, original, and ornamental design for an article of manufacture."[1695] The Patent & Trademark Office has defined a design patent as follows:

> The design of an object consists of the visual characteristics or aspects displayed by the object. It is the appearance presented by the object which creates an impression, through the eye upon the mind of the observer.[1696]

The term of a design patent is fourteen years from the date of issuance.[1697] Like a utility patent, a design patent must meet the requirements of patentability (e.g., novelty, etc.).

Section 171 requires that a design patent be ornamental, "the product of aesthetic skill and artistic conception[,]"[1698] but not necessarily "pleasing to the eye." Although one may obtain a design patent on a useful invention,[1699] a design is unpatentable if it is "primarily functional rather than ornamental" or "is 'dictated by' the use or purpose of the article."[1700]

A court will first construe the claim of the design patent, and then compare it to the accused device.[1701] Infringement occurs:

> if, in the eye of an ordinary observer, giving such attention as a purchaser usually gives, two designs are substantially the same, if the resemblance is such as to deceive such an observer, inducing him to purchase one supposing it to be the other, the first one patented is infringed by the other.[1702]

1695. 35 U.S.C. § 171.
1696. MPEP § 1502.
1697. *See* 35 U.S.C. § 173.
1698. *Blisscraft of Hollywood v. United Plastics Co.*, 294 F.2d 694, 696 (2d Cir. 1961).
1699. *See Avia Group Int'l, Inc. v. L.A. Gear California, Inc.*, 853 F.2d 1557, 1563 (Fed. Cir. 1988).
1700. *Power Controls Corp. v. Hybrinetics, Inc.*, 806 F.2d 234, 237 (Fed. Cir. 1986); *see also Bonito Boats, Inc. v. Thunder Craft Boats, Inc.*, 489 U.S. 141, 148 (1989).
1701. *See Elmer v. ICC Fabricating, Inc.*, 67 F.3d 1571, 1577 (Fed. Cir. 1995).
1702. *Gorham Co. v. White*, 81 U.S. (14 Wall.) 511, 528 (1871).

The Federal Circuit has held that "[b]eyond the substantial similarity requirement[,] design patent infringement requires that the accused product 'appropriate the novelty in the patented device which distinguishes it from the prior art'."[1703] The substantial similarity must pertain to the novel features of the design.

Only the ornamental features of the patented design can be infringed.[1704] If the patented design comprises both ornamental and functional elements, "to prove infringement a patent owner must establish that an ordinary person would be deceived by reason of the common features in the claimed and accused designs which are ornamental."[1705]

A person who: (1) applies the patented design to any article of manufacture; or (2) sells any article of manufacture to which [a patented] design or colorable imitation has been applied shall be liable to the owner to the extent of his total profit.[1706] However, the Supreme Court has stated that an "article of manufacture" for design patent damages can be less than the end product sold to consumers.[1707]

1703. *Sun Hill Indus., Inc. v. Easter Unlimited, Ltd.*, 48 F.3d 1193, 1197 (Fed. Cir. 1995) (quoting *Litton Sys. v. Whirlpool Corp*, 728 F.2d 1423, 1444 (Fed. Cir. 1984)).
1704. *See Lee v. Dayton-Hudson Corp.*, 838 F.2d 1186, 1188 (Fed. Cir. 1988); *KeyStone Retaining Wall Sys., Inc. v. Westrock, Inc.*, 997 F.2d 1444, 1450 (Fed. Cir. 1993).
1705. Read *Corp. v. Portec, Inc.*, 970 F.2d 816, 825 (Fed. Cir. 1992).
1706. 35 U.S.C. § 289. *See also Samsung Electronics Co., LTD. v. Apple Inc.*, 137 S. Ct. 429 (2016).
1707. *Samsung Electronics Co., LTD. v. Apple Inc.*, 137 S. Ct. 429 (2016).

PART III Trademark

CHAPTER 1
Sources of Power

§1 COMMON LAW APPROACH

As a common law jurisdiction, trademark protection in the US is premised upon prior adoption and use rather than prior registration as is generally the case in Civil Law jurisdictions. The concept of trademark protection in the US is also completely distinct from either patents or copyrights in the US. Whereas the US Constitution provides the grounding foundation for both patents and copyrights,[1708] trademarks do not enjoy such recognition. In fact, when confronted with the issue, the US Supreme Court expressly held that the Patent and Copyright Clause of the Constitution did not envision protection of trademarks.[1709]

Rather than being based on the Patent and Copyright Clause, federal trademark protection in the US is premised upon Congress' authority to regulate commerce via the Commerce Clause of the US Constitution.[1710] This is why interstate commerce or "use" of a trademark is necessary for federal protection.[1711] In the US, trademark protection is a common law concept that exists independent of any statute. In fact, the legislative history of the Lanham Act,[1712] the current trademark law, suggests that it purports to be only a registration statute codifying common law and not a statute that creates new rights.[1713] The US Supreme Court has reasoned that trademarks do not "depend upon

1708. U.S. Const. Art. I, § 8, cl. 8.
1709. *In re* The Trade-mark Cases, 100 U.S. 82, 94 (1879).
1710. U.S. Const. Art. I, § 8, cl. 3.
1711. In 1988, the Lanham Act was amended to provide registration and significant rights to be established based on a bona fide "intent" to use a mark in commerce. 15 U.S.C. § 1051(b). *See also infra* Ch. 4 §2.II. ITU Applications.
1712. 15 U.S.C. §§ 1051 et seq.
1713. In fact, the first draft of the Lanham Act included s. 34 which stated:

> Nothing in the Act shall entitle the registrant to interfere with or restrain the use by any person of the same trade-mark or of a similar trade-mark for the same or like goods or services when such person by himself or his predecessors in business has continuously

novelty, invention, discovery, or any work of the brain. It requires no fancy or imagination, no genius, no laborious thought. Trademarks are simply founded on priority of appropriation."[1714]

Trademark jurisprudence has developed over centuries of time. The use of a mark to identify the source of a product actually began at least 3,500 years ago when potters made scratchings on the bottom of their creations to identify the source. The first judicial recognition of trademarks in a common law system did not come, however, until 1584 in what is known as "Sandforth's Case."[1715] From this rather inauspicious beginning where a mark owner was protected from economic loss due to the deceit of another, it soon became a well-accepted judicial notion in England that a mark deserved protection at common law to indicate source or origin of goods.

§2 THE LANHAM ACT

The American concept of trademark law followed this English common law notion.[1716] Today, the common law has been codified in the Lanham Act. The Lanham Act defines trademarks as any "word, name, symbol, or device or any combination thereof ... used ... to indicate the source of the goods ...."[1717]

Although the Lanham Act was primarily intended as a registration statute codifying common law rights, in reality, the Act has engendered the creation of rights for two concepts that were not widely accepted at common law: a right of incontestability,[1718] and now dilution.[1719]

---

used such trade-mark from a date prior to the use or registration, whichever is earlier, by the registrant or his predecessors.

Trade-mark: Hearings on H.R. 9041 Before Subcomm. on Trade-marks of the House Comm. on Patents, 75th Cong. 3d Sess. 6 (1938) (reading of the bill H.R. 9041 into the record). The United States Trademark Association interpreted this to mean that "nothing in this Act shall affect any common-law rights acquired by a third party prior to the use or registration of the registrant." *Id.* at 64.

1714. *In re Trade-mark Cases*, 100 U.S. at 94.
1715. Sandforth's Case, Cory's Entries, BL MS. Hargrave 123, fo. 168 (1584) (providing a fairly complete portion of the complaint), *reprinted in* JOHN H. BAKER & S.F.C. MILSOM, SOURCES OF ENGLISH LEGAL HISTORY: PRIVATE LAW TO 1750, 615–18 (1986); HLS MS. 2071, fo. 86 (providing a brief abstract of the case), *reprinted in* Baker & Milsom, *supra*, at 615–18; HLS MS. 5048 fo. 118v. (formerly cataloged as HLS MS. Acc. 704755, fo 118v.) (providing another brief abstract of the case), *reprinted in* Baker & Milsom, *supra*, at 615. Other unpublished references to the case are found in CUL MS. Ii 5. 38, fo. 132; HLS MS. 2074, fo. 84v.; and BL MS. Lansdowne 1086, fo. 74v. For an extremely helpful analysis of the history and significance of this case, *see* Keith M. Stolte, *How Early Did Anglo-American Trademark Law Begin? An Answer to Schechter's Conundrum*, 8 FORDHAM INTELL. PROP. MEDIA & ENT. L.J. 505 (1998) (relying on the above cited research to correct the erroneous, but well accepted, view that *Southern v. Howe*, 79 Eng. Rep. 1244 (1618) had been the first Common Law trademark case) *See generally* FRANK I. SCHECHTER, THE HISTORICAL FOUNDATIONS OF THE LAW RELATING TO TRADE-MARKS (1925).
1716. *Trademark Cases*, 100 U.S. at 92.
1717. 15 U.S.C. § 1127 (Lanham Act § 45).
1718. 5 U.S.C. §§ 1064, 1065, 1115. *See* Kenneth L. Port, *The Illegitimacy of Trademark Incontestability*, 26 IND. L. REV. 519 (1993) (arguing that incontestability was not recognized at common law and a codification of such a concept was an expansion of the common law).

With the common law overlay on the statute, there are essentially two parallel avenues of concern for trademark owners. The first is whether the common law would recognize a mark as a valid trademark; the second is whether such a mark is registrable. Although today validity for registration on the Principal Registry and validity for enforcement purposes in a federal court receive essentially the same analysis, there are times when the common law will still prevail. For example, a decision to register a mark by the USPTO Examining Attorneys is not binding on a court that is faced with the question of the mark's validity, and a federal court has the power to correct the registry by canceling marks as it deems appropriate.[1720]

Even though the source of trademark protection in the US is state common law, the Lanham Act does provide many meaningful additional protections that make registration necessary for anyone seeking the fullest protection of their trademarks in the US.

I Nationwide Protection

Once a trademark is registered, nationwide protection is conferred on the owner of the registration as of the date of the filing of the registration application, even if the use has not been nationwide. Intent-to-Use (ITU)[1721] registrations similarly enjoy a constructive nationwide first-use date. This date is the date of the filing of the application with the USPTO.

II Evidentiary Presumptions

A registered trademark is also prima facie evidence of the validity of the registered mark, of the registration, of the registrant's ownership of the mark, and of the registrant's exclusive right to use the registered mark in commerce on or in connection with the goods or services specified in the registration.[1722] Once a mark is used for five years and a section 15 affidavit is filed appropriately with the USPTO—or becomes "incontestable"[1723]—the registration, subject to statutory exceptions, becomes conclusive evidence of the validity of the registered mark, of the registration, of the registrant's ownership of the mark, and of the registrant's exclusive right to use the registered mark in commerce on or in connection with the goods or services specified in the registration.[1724]

1719. 15 U.S.C. § 1125(c) (Lanham Act § 42). *See* Kenneth L. Port, *The "Unnatural" Expansion of Trademark Rights: Is a Federal Dilution Statute Necessary*?, 18 SETON HALL LEGIS. J. 433 (1994) (arguing that the federal dilution statute is not justified in a common law system and converts the trademark right to a property right when the common law never treated it as such).
1720. 15 U.S.C. § 1119 (Lanham Act § 37).
1721. *See infra* at Ch. 4, §2.II. ITU Applications.
1722. 15 U.S.C. § 1115(a) (Lanham Act § 33(a)).
1723. 15 U.S.C. § 1065 (Lanham Act § 15).
1724. 15 U.S.C. § 1115(b) (Lanham Act § 33(b)).

III Warning Function

Once a trademark is registered, the owner may use the symbol® or "Registered Trademark" to designate that the mark is registered with the USPTO. This clearly notifies all other would-be users of the mark of the first comer's rights. It should therefore act as a general deterrent to prevent innocent and unintentional infringing.

IV Damages

In very egregious cases, the statute allows for a trebling of damages if the mark infringed is a registered trademark.

Therefore, although the US is a use-based, priority system grounded in common law and not a registration-based system, there are still extremely important reasons why any trademark user in the US should seriously consider filing for a federal registration.

§3 SIGNIFICANT AMENDMENTS TO THE LANHAM ACT

I Trademark Clarification Act of 1984

The Trademark Clarification Act of 1984[1725] added the following language to the Lanham Act:

> The primary significance of the registered mark to the relevant public rather than purchaser motivation shall be the test for determining whether the registered mark has become the generic name of goods or services on or in connection with which it has been used.[1726]

This amendment was added to the Lanham Act because the Ninth Circuit insisted on using the purchaser motivation test to arrive at a result that made the famous trademark MONOPOLY[1727] for a board game to be generic and therefore unenforceable. It is one of the rare instances where the US Congress has specifically overruled a court on a trademark matter using an amendment to the Lanham Act.

II Trademark Counterfeiting Act of 1984

The Trademark Counterfeiting Act of 1984[1728] was the most extensive set of amendments to the Lanham Act in its first forty years.[1729] Congress amended the Lanham Act to provide both federal prosecutors and trademark holders with the "essential tools" for

1725. Trademark Clarification Act of 1984, Pub. L. No. 98-620, § 102, 98 Stat. 3335 (1984) (codified at 15 U.S.C. § 1064(c)).
1726. 15 U.S.C. § 1064(c).
1727. *Anti-Monopoly, Inc. v. General Mills Fun Grp.*, 684 F.2d 1316 (9th Cir. 1982), *cert. denied*, 459 U.S. 1227 (1983), *superseded by statute*, 15 U.S.C. § 1064(c).
1728. Trademark Counterfeiting Act of 1984, Pub. L. No. 100-667, 102 Stat. 3935 (1988) (codified at 15 U.S.C. §§ 1117, 1118, 1119) (Lanham Act §§ 35, 36, 37).
1729. *See* S. Rep. No. 100-515, at 2 (1988), *reprinted in* 1988 U.S.C.C.A.N. 5577, 5578.

combating counterfeiters.[1730] In what is called the "insidious and rapidly growing form of commercial fraud,"[1731] the Act changed sections 34, 35, and 36 of the Lanham Act and granted the courts the power to grant ex parte seizure orders and monetary remedies in cases of counterfeiting of registered marks, including lessening the burden to establish treble damages.[1732] It did this in a new paragraph of section 35 that states that a court shall award "three times ... profits or damages, whichever is greater" in the case of any violation that consists of "intentionally using a mark or designation, knowing such mark or designation is a counterfeit mark ... in connection with the sale, offering for sale, or distribution of goods or services."[1733] It created a presumption of damages in cases of counterfeiting toward an award of treble damages and placed the burden upon the potential defendant to demonstrate the defense of "extenuating circumstances."[1734] It also added criminal trademark anti-counterfeiting penalties for the first time.[1735]

III Trademark Revision Act of 1988

The Trademark Revision Act of 1988[1736] made two rather profound changes to the Lanham Act and the way trademarks are protected in the US, by redefining "use" and allowing for an "ITU" registration.

A *New Definition of Use*

Until the Trademark Revision Act of 1988, mere "token" use was sufficient to establish that the applicant had used a mark in interstate commerce and had therefore met one of the primary prerequisites to federal registration. The Revision Act did away with token use and now requires "bona fide use ... in the ordinary course of trade."[1737] This is a flexible standard. It requires use that is commensurate with the goods or services identified on the application. Therefore, if one sold candy bars, significantly more sales would be necessary compared to an applicant who claimed use of a mark on or in connection with the sale of highly sophisticated machine tools.

1730. S. Rep. No. 98-526, at 1 (1984), *reprinted in* 1984 U.S.C.C.A.N. 3627, 3627.
1731. *Id.*
1732. S. Rep. No. 98-526, at 2–3 (1984), *reprinted in* 1984 U.S.C.C.A.N. 3627, 3628–29.
1733. 15 U.S.C. § 1117(b) (Lanham Act § 35(b)). *See also* Thomas P. Olson, *An Analysis of the Trademark Counterfeiting Act of 1984*, in *New and Extraordinary Relief in Intellectual Property Cases*, at 21 (*PLI Pat., Copyrights, Trademarks, and Literary Prop. Course, Handbook Series* No. G4 3765, 1985).
1734. 15 U.S.C. § 1117(d) (Lanham Act § 35(d)).
1735. 18 U.S.C. § 2320.
1736. Trademark Revision Act of 1988, Pub. L. No. 100-667 § 132, 102 Stat. 3935, 3946 (codified at 15 U.S.C. § 1125).
1737. 15 U.S.C. § 1127 (Lanham Act § 45).

B *ITU Registration*

The more significant change, concomitant with abolition of token use, was to adopt an ITU registration system.[1738] Because use (even though it was token use) was required prior to the amendment, some companies were prejudiced by having to wait until they actually got some sort of product to market before they could obtain a USPTO ruling on whether the mark was valid. This delay was considered excessive and made American industries less competitive.

Also, under the language of section 44 of the Lanham Act in effect at that time, a mark registered in a foreign country could be used as the basis for priority and for registration in the US if that application is filed in the US within one year of the issuance of the registration in the foreign country.[1739] Therefore, owners of trademark registrations in many Civil Law countries could obtain a federal registration in the US based on that foreign registration without ever using the mark in commerce in the US. Foreign trademark owners, therefore, received an undue advantage over US applicants.

For these reasons and many more, it was perceived that a US trademark owner should be able to reserve rights in a mark it intends to use as well as a mark it actually uses. Consequently, section 1051(b) was added to the Lanham Act, which allows for the federal registration of marks for which the owner had a "bona fide intention" to use.[1740] Bona fide means real and actual intent to use a mark in commerce. It does not mean merely making convenient business decisions regarding the mark with no intent to actually use it as a trademark to distinguish source.[1741]

IV NAFTA Implementation Act

Prior to the NAFTA Implementation Act,[1742] if a mark was determined to have secondary meaning, it could be placed on the Principal Register even if it was "primarily geographically deceptively misdescriptive." Additionally, it could be placed on the secondary register without a showing of secondary meaning. The NAFTA Implementation Act amended section 2 of the Lanham Act[1743] to no longer allow such registrations.[1744]

1738. *See infra* Ch. 4, §2.II. ITU Applications. Naturally, both foreign and domestic corporations may file intent-to-use applications.
1739. 15 U.S.C. § 1126.
1740. 15 U.S.C. § 1051(b) (Lanham Act § 1).
1741. *M.Z. Berger & Co. v. Swatch AG*, 787 F.3d 1368 (Fed. Cir. 2015) (denying the intent-to-use application of IWATCH as the applicant could not show actual evidence of its intent to use the mark as a trademark).
1742. North American Free Trade Agreement Implementation Act of 1993, Pub. L. No. 103-182, 107 Stat. 2057 (codified at 15 U.S.C. § 1052(f)).
1743. 15 U.S.C. § 1052(f) (Lanham Act § 2(f)).
1744. *See infra* Ch. 4, §2.I. Use Applications.

V Uruguay Round Agreements Act

Congress enacted the Uruguay Round Agreements Act[1745] to bring the Lanham Act in accordance with the TRIPS Agreement.[1746] The Act amended the Lanham Act section 2[1747] to prohibit registration of a geographical mark for wine or liquor that identifies a place other than the actual origin of the product.[1748] The Act also amended section 45[1749] to bring abandonment definitions in-line with international norms as set by the TRIPS Agreement.[1750]

VI Federal Trademark Dilution Act of 1995

In 1996, President Clinton signed into law the Federal Trademark Dilution Act (FTDA) of 1995.[1751] This law essentially provided for a new section to be added to the Lanham Act and requires courts to recognize a new cause of action never recognized by the Lanham Act before. In the new section 43(c) of the Lanham Act, injunctive relief may be granted if a trademark (registered or not) is "diluted" by the use of another mark. Section 43(c) is available only to owners of "famous" marks. Whereas trademark infringement is available only when there is competition between the parties' products or services, section 43(c) allows for injunctive relief even when there is no competition and therefore no confusion is possible. Examples from legislative history include Buick Brand Aspirin and the like. Where the owners of Buick may not be able to establish confusion because of the lack of competition between the manufacturer of an automobile and a pain reliever, they may be able to show a likelihood that there would be a lessening of the distinctive qualities of the famous mark.[1752]

Although prior documentation of the concept exists,[1753] Frank Schechter is generally given credit for raising the idea of dilution within the US. Schechter's revolutionary claim was that trademarks themselves sell products and therefore trademarks themselves deserve protection. That is, Schechter's implicit claim is that there is an unacceptable gap in trademark protection. Section 43(c) was intended to plug this gap. Certainly, section 43(c) grants new trademark rights not previously contemplated by the Lanham Act. It remains to be seen how significant section 43(c) will actually be on the practice of trademark law in the US. However, in the Trademark Amendments Act of 1999, the Lanham Act was amended to allow dilution to be a grounds for opposition to the registration of a mark as follows: "any person who

1745. Uruguay Round Agreements Act of 1994, Pub. L. No. 103-465, 108 Stat. 489 (codified as amended at 15 U.S.C. §§ 1052(f), 1127).
1746. Uruguay Round Agreements Act, S. Rep. No. 103-412, at 226 (1994).
1747. 15 U.S.C. § 1052(f) (Lanham Act § 2(f)).
1748. Uruguay Round Agreements Act, S. Rep. No. 103-412, at 226 (1994).
1749. 15 U.S.C. § 1127.
1750. Uruguay Round Agreements Act, S. Rep. No. 103-412, at 226 (1994).
1751. Federal Dilution Act of 1995, Pub. L. No. 104-98, 109 Stat. 985 (codified at 15 U.S.C. §§ 1051, 1125–27).
1752. 15 U. S. C. § 1125(c) (Lanham Act § 43(c)).
1753. *See* Judgment of Sept. 11, 1924, Landgericht Elberfeld, 25 Juristiche Wochemschrift 502, XXV Markenschutz and Wettbewerb (M.U.R.) 264.

believes that he would be damaged by the registration of a mark upon the principal register, including as a result of dilution under section 1125(c) of this title, may ... file an opposition."[1754] Prior to the Anticybersquatting Consumer Protection Act (ACPA),[1755] the dilution provisions of the Lanham Act were the main method of preventing cybersquatting. As discussed in §4, *infra*, the federal dilution provisions were further amended by the Trademark Dilution Revision Act (TDRA) of 2006.

VII Anticounterfeiting Consumer Protection Act of 1996

The ACPA[1756] strengthened the remedies created under the Trademark Counterfeiting Act of 1984.[1757] Congress created the Act to supplement the Trademark Counterfeiting Act of 1984 because the Trademark Counterfeiting Act of 1984 had proven to be an inadequate remedy for the explosive growth of criminal commercial counterfeiting.[1758]

The Act amended section 34(d) of the Lanham Act[1759] to ensure that any federal law enforcement or local law enforcement agent can execute a seizure order in a civil action. The Act's legislative history indicates that it had also granted courts the extreme authority, under certain conditions, to seize an aircraft, vehicle, or vessel used in connection with a violation of the Lanham Act.[1760] In addition, the Act created a new section 34(a) of the Lanham Act that requires the seizure and destruction of counterfeit goods imported into the US.[1761] It also provides for civil fines against persons who aid in the importation of counterfeit goods that are seized.[1762]

The Act also amends section 35 of the Lanham Act to allow trademark owners to opt for judicially determined statutory damages in civil cases, rather than actual damages and profits.[1763]

VIII Trademark Law Treaty Implementation Act of 1998

In 1994, the international community bound together to create a treaty that would standardize and simplify trademark registration in all signatory countries. The result of

1754. 15 U.S.C. § 1063(a).
1755. *See infra* Ch. 1, §3.VII. Anticybersquatting Consumer Protection Act of 1999.
1756. Anticounterfeiting Consumer Protection Act of 1996, Pub. L. No. 104-153, 110 Stat. 1386 (codified as amended at U.S.C. §§ 1116(d), 1117(c)).
1757. *See supra*, Ch. 1, §3.III. Trademark Revision Act of 1988; *infra* Ch. 8, §3.II.B. Damages for Counterfeiting.
1758. Anticounterfeiting Consumer Protection Act of 1996, H.R. REP. NO. 556, at 2, *reprinted in* 1996 U.S.C.C.A.N. 1074, 1075.
1759. 15 U.S.C. § 1116(d)(9) (Lanham Act § 34).
1760. *See* Anticounterfeiting Consumer Protection Act of 1996, H.R. REP. NO. 104-556, at 11, *reprinted in* 1996 U.S.C.C.A.N. 1074, 1084.
1761. A part of the Act that was not codified into the Lanham Act allowed for an altruistic alternative to destroying the counterfeit goods: "Where the counterfeit goods do not present a health risk and the trademark owner consents, the goods (or proceeds from the sales of the goods) may be distributed to an appropriate charity or governmental agency." H.R. REP. NO. 104-556, at 8, *reprinted in* 1996 U.S.C.C.A.N. 1074, 1081.
1762. Anticounterfeiting Consumer Protection Act of 1996, Pub. L. No. 104-153, 110 Stat. 1386.
1763. *Id.*

these efforts was the Trademark Law Treaty of 1994 (TLT). The TLT was ratified by the US Senate in June 1998.[1764] The legislation implementing the TLT and amending the Lanham Act in compliance with the requirements of the TLT was signed into law by President Clinton on October 30, 1998.[1765]

Most of the Lanham Act was already in compliance with the TLT provisions; however, some technical amendments were required to sections 1, 8, 9, 10, 12(b), and 44 of the Lanham Act.[1766]

For example, section 10 of the Lanham Act[1767] was amended to clarify that documents filed with the USPTO pursuant to the requirements of TLT Article 11 would be "recorded" for the purposes of section 10. Currently, the USPTO requires that a complete copy of the assignment document be filed for recording. Under the TLT (Article 11(b)(2)), only an extract from the assignment document need be recorded as evidence of the change in ownership. This amendment to section 10 of the Lanham Act was necessary to allow an assignee to file a mere extract of the assignment document rather than the entire document for recording purposes with the USPTO.

Section 9[1768] of the Lanham Act was amended to delete the requirement of continued use as the basis for a renewal of the registration. Article 13 of the TLT specifically prohibits any member from requiring proof of use as an element necessary for the renewal of a registration. In order to accommodate this provision and still eliminate "deadwood" from the Principal Register, sections 8 and 9 of the Lanham Act were both amended. Pursuant to the amendments, section 9 renewals will now issue without proof of continued use; however, section 8 now requires that Continuing Use Affidavits be filed not only between the fifth and sixth years of registration but also between the ninth and tenth year, nineteenth and twentieth year, etc. By separating these two requirements, the intent is to allow the US to remain faithful to its use-based system while adhering to the technical language of Article 13 of the TLT.

Section 44(e) of the Lanham Act[1769] was also amended. That section previously required that a certified copy of the foreign certificate of registration accompanies the application for registration in the US. Article 3 of the TLT sets out a comprehensive list of filing requirements. All applications filed with Contracting States must be granted a filing date if the application satisfies the requirements of Article 3. Article 3 does not include a certified copy of a foreign certificate of registration. Therefore, to be in compliance with Article 3, section 44(e) was amended to no longer require that a certified copy of the foreign certificate of registration accompanies the application in the US.[1770]

1764. 56 Patent, Trademark and Copyright Journal 278 (1998).
1765. 57 Patent, Trademark and Copyright Journal 12 (1998).
1766. 15 U.S.C. §§ 1051, 1058, 1059, 1060, 1062(b), and 1126.
1767. 15 U.S.C. 1060.
1768. 15 U.S.C. § 1059.
1769. 15 U.S.C. 1126(e).
1770. Section 44(e) now reads as follows: "Such applicant shall submit, within such time period as may be prescribed by the Commissioner, a certification or a certified copy of the registration in the country of origin of the applicant."

IX Trademark Amendments Act of 1999

The Trademark Amendments Act of 1999[1771] intended to clarify and broaden existing trademark law.[1772] The Trademark Amendments Act was signed into law by President Clinton on August 5, 1999.[1773] First, the Act amends section 43(c) of the Lanham Act to include dilution as a ground for opposition under section 13(a) and a ground for cancelation under section 14.[1774] While dilution is not a basis for an ex parte refusal to register a mark under section 2 of the Lanham Act,[1775] the Act provides that injunctive relief[1776] is available in dilution action, but that monetary recovery[1777] and/or destruction of infringing articles[1778] will be available only in the case of "willful violations."[1779]

Second, the Act eliminates the federal government's immunity from suit for violation of the Lanham Act. It expands the definition of "any person" in sections 32 and 45 to include the US, its agencies, instrumentalities, and any entities or persons acting for it.[1780] The Act specifically changes section 40 to expressly state that the US waives sovereign immunity.[1781]

Third, the Act amends section 43(a) to provide that, in a civil action for infringement of trade dress not registered on the Principal Register, the party that asserts trade dress protection has the burden to prove nonfunctionality.[1782]

X ACPA of 1999

In 1999, Congress passed a bill that, in effect, extended trademark law into cyberspace. On November 29, 1999, President Clinton signed into law an appropriations bill that included the Intellectual Property and Communications Omnibus Reform Act of 1999.[1783] The ACPA[1784] was Title III of this omnibus appropriations bill. Congress created the ACPA to:

1771. Trademark Amendments Act of 1999, Pub. L. No. 106-43, 113 Stat. 218 (1999) (codified at 15 U.S.C. §§ 1051, 1052, 1060, 1063, 1064, 1092, 1114, 1116, 1117, 1118, 1122, 1125, 1127, 1501). This Act also eliminated the old use of the word "trade-mark" in the Lanham Act and replaced all uses with "trademark."
1772. *See generally* John L. Welch, *Modernizing for the Millennium: The 1999 Amendments to the Trademark Law*, 13 Intl. L. Practicum 34 (New York State Bar Assoc. 2000).
1773. *Id.*, at 34.
1774. *See infra* Ch. 6, §4.III.
1775. 15 U.S.C. § 1052; *see* John L. Welch, *Modernizing for the Millennium: The 1999 Amendments to the Trademark Law*, 13 Intl. L. Practicum 34 (New York State Bar Assoc. 2000).
1776. 15 U.S.C. § 1116(a) (Lanham Act § 34(a)).
1777. 15 U.S.C. § 1117 (Lanham Act § 35).
1778. 15 U.S.C. § 1118 (Lanham Act § 36).
1779. The Lanham Act refers to counterfeiting as a "willful violation" under § 43(c). *See* 15 U.S.C. § 1118.
1780. *See* Trademark Amendments Act of 1999, Pub. L. No. 106-43, 113 Stat. 218.
1781. *Id.*
1782. *Id.*
1783. Steven R. Borgman, *The New Federal Cybersquatting Laws*, 8 Tex. Intell. Prop. L.J. 265, 265 (2000).
1784. Anticybersquatting Consumer Protection Act of 1999, Pub. L. No. 106-113, § 3002(a), 113 Stat. 1501, 1537 (codified at 15 U.S.C. §§ 1114, 1116, 1117, 1125(d), 1127 & 1129).

> protect consumers and American businesses, to promote the growth of online commerce, and to provide clarity in the law for Trademark owners by prohibiting the bad-faith and abusive registration of distinctive marks as Internet domain names with the intent to profit from the goodwill associated with such marks.[1785]

The ACPA aims to protect trademark owners against a new harm in cyberspace—"cybersquatting."[1786] Cybersquatting occurs when a party registers a domain name that is identical or confusingly similar to a trademark for the purpose of creating confusion as to the source of the domain name. The ACPA added a new section 43(d)[1787] to the Lanham Act, which again pushed the Lanham Act beyond its common law origins.[1788] The most obvious change that section 43(d) brings to the Lanham Act is that it designates domain names for Lanham Act protections. Section 43(d) of the Lanham Act does not give trademark-like protections to domain names; however, for holders of registered trademarks, section 43(d) gives them protections against those who register identical or confusingly similar domain names in bad faith:[1789] Section 43(d)(1) creates this new "bad faith" cause of action against cybersquatters;[1790] section 43(d)(2) creates an in rem cause of action for cybersquatting;[1791] and section 43(d)(3) expressly provides that the new causes of action under section 43(d)(1) and 43(d)(2) may be brought in addition to any other civil action or remedy otherwise applicable.[1792]

XI Madrid Protocol Implementation Act of 2002

Introduced in 2001, the Madrid Protocol Implementation Act of 2002[1793] serves as the implementing legislation for the Madrid Protocol. In general terms, the Madrid Protocol reformed the earlier international effort to allow international trademark registration—called the Madrid Agreement. The Madrid Protocol Implementation Act of 2002 gives a succinct explanation of how: (1) the Madrid Protocol would make up for the shortcomings of the Madrid Agreement; and (2) how the Lanham Act would need to change to accommodate the Madrid Protocol:

> Practically speaking, the Protocol "updated" the Madrid Agreement, in many respects by conforming its contents to existing provisions in U.S. law. For example, under the Protocol, applications for international trademark extension can be completed in English; ..., applications under the Agreement are required to be

1785. Anticybersquatting Consumer Protection Act, S. Rep. No. 106-140, at 4 (1999).
1786. *See infra* Ch. 2, §2.VI.
1787. 15 U.S.C. § 1125(d).
1788. *See supra*, Ch. 1, §1 and Ch. 1, §3.V.
1789. 15 U.S.C. § 1125(d). Anticybersquatting Consumer Protection Act of 1999, Pub. L. No. 106-113, § 3002(a), 113 Stat. 1501, 1537. *See infra* Ch. 6, §5.
1790. 15 U.S.C. § 1125(d)(1). Anticybersquatting Consumer Protection Act of 1999, Pub. L. No. 106-113, § 3002(a), 113 Stat. 1501, 1537. *See infra* Ch. 6, §5.I.
1791. 15 U.S.C. § 1125(d)(2). Anticybersquatting Consumer Protection Act of 1999, Pub. L. No. 106-113, § 3002(a), 113 Stat. 1501, 1537. *See infra* Ch. 6, §5.II.
1792. 15 U.S.C. § 1125(d)(3). Anticybersquatting Consumer Protection Act of 1999, Pub. L. No. 106-113, § 3002(a), 113 Stat. 1501, 1537. *See infra* Ch. 8, §3.II.C.
1793. Madrid Protocol Implementation Act of 2002, Pub. L. No. 107-273, § 13401, 116 Stat. 1758, 1913–20 (codified at 15 U.S.C. § 1141).

> completed in French. Moreover, under the Protocol, an international application may be based on a country of origin application—as opposed to an actual registration—thus allowing U.S. applicants to seek international protection at the same time they file a U.S. application, including an application based on a bona fide intention to use a mark in commerce. The Protocol also permits an extended eighteen month period in which a country may refuse to give effect to an international registration and allows for higher filing and renewal fees, both of which conform to the effective pendency and fee structure of the U.S. Patent and Trademark Office.
>
> Finally, the Protocol modifies the so-called "central attack" provision of the Madrid Agreement. Under the Madrid Agreement, if during the first five years of an international registration, the national application or registration upon which the international registration is dependent is limited or cancelled, all rights obtained in the member countries of the Madrid Agreement based on extensions of that registration are similarly limited or cancelled. This is known as "central attack." With the Protocol, in the event of a "central attack" on the home mark and the subsequent cancellation of the international registration, the international registration may be "transformed" into a series of national applications in the designated countries, all of which will retain the original filing date (i.e., the international registration date) and any priority claimed. So, a U.S. trademark owner whose mark is cancelled in the United States will still be able to retain a priority in other countries in which it is seeking protection.[1794]

In essence, the Act adds Title XII, sections 60–74 of the Lanham Act, to allow for trademark filers to make international trademark registrations through the USPTO.[1795]

XII Singapore Treaty

In 2006, the Singapore Treaty on Trademarks was concluded.

Although many thought this new treaty was the dawning of a new age in trademark harmonization, this was not the result. Old tensions took over and a watered-down document was the result. Although the Treaty does, for the first time in an international setting, recognize color and scent marks as within the definition of trademarks, otherwise, the treaty falls short. There are no substantive changes. Instead, the Treaty acts as another tiny step toward the procedural harmonization of trademark law.

In fact, the Singapore Treaty is heavily criticized:

> The Singapore Treaty sets out to "improve" the state of international trademark law, but does so in an extremely haphazard fashion. Instead of setting out a concrete goal and working to best achieve that goal, the framers of the Treaty seem to have entered into the treaty with the best of intentions, but with no clear outline of what the end result of the Treaty was supposed to resemble. The resulting treaty reflects this. Rather than making clear rules, or even addressing real problems of moving between various systems, the Singapore Treaty establishes broad outlines of behavior, which may or may not improve the lives of Interested Parties or

1794. Madrid Protocol Implementation Act of 2002, S. Rep. No. 107-46, at 3 (2001), 1991 WL 84058, at *3.

1795. 15 U.S.C. § 1441.

> trademark officials. This cannot be characterized as "harmonization" in any way. Instead, the New Treaty is comprised of superficial changes made to create the impression of progress. This "fluff" in the place of real harmonization is the reason countries like Brazil and Argentina have been pushing the new Agenda for WIPO. If the Singapore Treaty is any guide, however, that agenda may just be another piece of window dressing while WIPO continues to neglect the harmonization of trademark law.[1796]

Therefore, although it should be recognized as an important effort, no real substantive changes can be expected as a result of the Singapore Treaty.

XIII Anti-Counterfeiting Trade Agreement of 2011

In a controversial move, the Obama Administration negotiated and signed the Anti-Counterfeiting Trade Agreement (ACTA). ACTA was signed in October 2011 by Australia, Canada, Japan, Morocco, New Zealand, Singapore, South Korea, and the US. Although the US is a signatory country, it has not been implemented in the US because it became unclear whether the President had the constitutional authority to bind the US in this manner or whether he needed ascension from Congress. ACTA has been even more controversial in the European Union.

If implemented, ACTA would provide very rigid border measures which allow the arrest of individuals carrying certain quantities of counterfeit goods and allow the imposition of criminal penalties. It remains controversial.[1797]

XIV Trademark Modernization Act of 2020

The Trademark Modernization Act of 2020 (TMA) was enacted on December 27, 2020, as part of the Consolidated Appropriations Act, 2021.[1798] The majority of the changes implemented in the TMA went into effect on December 27, 2021—one year after the act was passed. The TMA put forth a number of procedural changes intended to help to increase efficiency at the USPTO and clear unused marks from the Principal and Supplemental Register. The TMA formalized a procedure for allowing third parties to submit evidence regarding potential grounds for refusal of a trademark application.[1799] The TMA also created new expedited and ex parte proceedings that may be used to "expunge a registration of a mark on the basis that the mark has never been used in commerce on or in connection with some or all of the goods or services recited in the registration."[1800] These petitions for cancelation can be brought against section 1(a)

1796. Legislative Update: *Singapore Sling: WIPO Passes the Buck on Meaningful Reform of International Trademark Law*, 17 DEPAUL-LCA J. ART & ENT. L. 305, 336–37 (2007).

1797. *See*, e.g., Kenneth L. Port, *A Case Against ACTA*, 33 CARDOZO L. REV. 1131 (2012).

1798. Trademark Modernization Act of 2020, enacted within Consolidated Appropriations Act, 2021, PL 116-260, Dec. 27, 2020, 134 Stat 1182, Div. Q, Title II, §§ 223(a), 224, 225(a)–(d), 226(a), 228(a), 134 Stat. 2201, 2202, 2208, 2209 (codified at 15 U.S.C. §§ 1051, 1062, 1064, 1065, 1066a, 1066b, 1068, 1070, 1071, 1092, 1094, 1116).

1799. *Id.*, at § 223(a) (revising 15 U.S.C. § 1051).

1800. *Id.*, at § 225 (adding 15 U.S.C. § 1066a).

(use-based) registrations where the specimen of use can be shown to be false and against marks registered under section 44(e) or 66(a) where evidence can be provided to show that the marks have never been used in commerce.[1801] Additionally, the TMA clarified that a plaintiff seeking an injunction "shall be entitled to a rebuttable presumption of irreparable harm."[1802] This change was made to resolve a circuit split about whether the presumption of irreparable harm survived the Supreme Court's ruling in *eBay v. MercExchange* that irreparable harm cannot be presumed in instances of patent infringement.[1803] The TMA also gave increased flexibility to USPTO Examining Attorneys by allowing them to alter the standard six-month deadline for responses to office actions.[1804] Effective December 1, 2022, applicants now only have three months to respond to an office action (provided that an applicant can receive a one-time extension of three months upon the payment of a fee).

§4 STATE TRADEMARK PROTECTION

In addition to the federal scheme of protection, each state in the US also has its own common law as well as statutory schemes of registration and protection of trademarks. Most state registration statutes still do not give the registrant priority of use statewide,[1805] require no substantive review of the marks they register,[1806] and frequently are not taken as seriously as federal registrations. The three types of state statutes most relevant are the state trademark protection statutes, deceptive trade practices acts, and state dilution statutes.

I State Trademark Protection Statutes

Most state trademark statutes follow the Model State Trademark Bill.[1807] This Bill is not significantly different from the protections recognized at common law and under the Lanham Act. The purpose of state trademark statutes is to protect marks that are not utilized sufficiently to be deemed used in interstate commerce for the purposes of the Lanham Act. That is, the state statutes operate as a fallback position for most trademark owners in the event they fail to obtain protections granted in federal court under the Lanham Act. There has been a renewed interest in state trademark protections and

1801. *Id.*
1802. Trademark Modernization Act of 2020, enacted within Consolidated Appropriations Act, 2021, PL 116-260, Dec. 27, 2020, 134 Stat 1182, Div. Q, Title II, § 226 (amending 15 U.S.C. § 1116a).
1803. *EBay Inc. v. MercExchange, L.L.C.*, 547 U.S. 388, 126 S. Ct. 1837 (2006).
1804. Trademark Modernization Act of 2020, *supra* footnote 92, § 224 (revising 15 U.S.C. § 1062).
1805. *See Burger King of Fla, Inc. v. Hoots*, 403 F.2d 904 (7th Cir. 1968) (common law trademark rights limited to a small geographical area surrounding defendant's existing business establishment).
1806. *See*, e.g., *Leon's Frozen Custard, Inc. v. Leon Corp.*, 513 N.W.2d 636 (Wis. Ct. App. 1994) (Wisconsin does not review trademark registration applications for similarity to existing registrations).
1807. *See* J. Thomas McCarthy, 3 McCarthy on Trademarks and Unfair Competition § 22:5 (5th ed 2021) (with various, full-text versions of the model act available at § 22:9).

registration schemes following the legalization of marijuana (or cannabis) by some US states.[1808] Because cannabis is still illegal at the federal level, the cannabis businesses in those legalized states are unable to sell or ship their products across state lines; as such, the USPTO will typically deny federal trademark registrations for marks used on cannabis products.[1809] State trademark registrations and common law protection may be the only options available for such businesses as long as cannabis products remain illegal at the federal level.

II Deceptive Trade Practices Statutes

State statutes based on the Model State Deceptive Trade Practices Act have slightly more teeth than the state trademark statutes. These statutes not only contemplate protection against conduct not necessarily prohibited by common law trademark law or the Lanham Act but also usually provide a possibility (if not a requirement) that the appropriate State Attorney General enforces the Act.[1810] The Illinois Uniform Deceptive Trade Practice Act is perhaps representative of these types of statutes. Not all states have adopted these statutes but most have. The Illinois statute states that:

> A person engages in a deceptive trade practice when, in the course of his business, vocation or occupation, he:
> 1. passes off goods or services as those of another;
> 2. causes likelihood of confusion or of misunderstanding as to the source, sponsorship, approval or certification of goods or services;
> 3. causes likelihood of confusion or of misunderstanding as to affiliation, connection or association with or certification by another;
> 4. uses deceptive representations or designations of geographic origin in connection with goods or services;
> 5. represents that goods or services have sponsorship, approval, characteristics, ingredients, uses, benefits or quantities that they do not have or that a person has a sponsorship, approval, status, affiliation or connection that he does not have;
> 6. represents that goods are original or new if they are deteriorated, altered, reconditioned, reclaimed, used or secondhand;
> 7. represents that goods or services are a particular standard, quality or grade or that goods are a particular style or model, if they are of another;
> 8. disparages the goods, services or business of another by false or misleading representation of fact;
> 9. advertises goods or services with intent not to sell them as advertised;
> 10. advertises goods or services with intent not to supply reasonably expectable public demand, unless the advertisement discloses a limitation of quantity;
> 11. make false or misleading statements of fact concerning the reasons for, existence of or amounts of price reductions;

1808. *See*, e.g., Spencer Keller, *How Small Cannabis Businesses Can Survive the Hurdles of IP Protection*, 8 TEX. A&M L. REV. 199 (2020).
1809. *See*, e.g., In re JJ206, LLC, dba JuJu Joints, 120 U.S.P.Q.2d. 1568 (T.T.A.B. 2016) (affirming refusals to register two marks for smokeless marijuana vaporizers because such product are illegal under the federal Controlled Substances Act and therefore such products could not be sold in interstate commerce).
1810. *See*, e.g., Illinois Uniform Deceptive Trade Practices Act, 815 ILL. COMP. STAT. 510/2.

12. engages in any other conduct which similarly creates a likelihood of confusion or of misunderstanding.

In order to prevail in an action under this Act, a plaintiff need not prove competition between the parties, actual confusion, or misunderstanding.[1811]

III State Dilution Statutes

Thirty-eight states recognize trademark dilution as an actionable harm.[1812] Twelve states offer no cause of action, either statutory or through the common law, for trademark dilution.[1813]

The typical state dilution statute states that the court "may consider" whether the mark is registered or whether a likelihood of confusion exists[1814] in granting injunctive relief to the holder of a trademark.[1815]

1811. Illinois Uniform Deceptive Trade Practices Act, 815 ILL. COMP. STAT. 510/2. *See also Defined Space, Inc. v. Lakeshore E., LLC,* 797 F. Supp. 2d 896 (N.D. Ill. 2011) (holding that plaintiff's claim under the Illinois Uniform Deceptive Trade Practices Act was preempted by the Copyright Act, but plaintiff's claim under the Lanham Act was not preempted).

1812. Alabama: ALA. CODE § 8-12-17 (1998); Alaska: ALASKA STAT. § 45.50.180 (2014); Arizona: ARIZ. REV. STAT.§ 44-1448.01 (2002); Arkansas: ARK. CODE ANN.§ 4-71-213 (2002); California: CAL. BUS. & PROF. CODE § 14247 (Deering 2007); Connecticut: CONN. GEN. STAT.§ 35-11i(c) (2006); Delaware: DEL. CODE ANN. tit. 6, § 3313 (2003); Florida: FLA. STAT. ANN.§ 495.151 (West, Westlaw through 2014 sess.); Georgia: GA. CODE ANN.§ 10-1-451(b) (2012); Hawaii: HAW. REV. STAT.§ 482-32 (2003); Idaho: IDAHO CODE § 48-501 (Michie 2004); Indiana: IND. CODE 24-2-1-13.5 (2004); Illinois: 765 ILL. COMP. STAT.1036/65 (2004); Iowa: IOWA CODE § 548.113 (West, Westlaw through 2014 sess.); Kansas: KAN. STAT. ANN. § 81-214; Louisiana: LA. REV. STAT. ANN. § 51:223.1 (West 2004); Maine: ME. REV. STAT. ANN. tit. 10, § 1530 (West, Westlaw through 2013 sess.); Massachusetts: MASS. GEN. L. ANN. Ch. 110H, § 12 (West, Westlaw through 2013 sess.); Minnesota: MINN. STAT. 333.285 (1998); Mississippi: MISS. CODE ANN. § 75-25-25 (2011); Missouri: MO. ANN. STAT.§ 417.061 (West, Westlaw through 2014 sess.); Montana: MONT. CODE ANN. § 30-13-334 (2003); Nebraska: NEB. REV. STAT. ANN. § 87-14 (Michie 2000); Nevada: NEVADA REV. STAT. 600.435 (West, Westlaw through 2013 sess.); New Hampshire: N.H. REV. STAT. ANN. § 350-A:12 (1992); New Jersey: N.J.S.A. 56: 3-13.20 (West, Westlaw through 2014); New Mexico: N.M. STAT. ANN. § 57-3B-15 (Michie 1997); New York: N.Y. GEN. BUS. LAW § 360(1) (West, Westlaw through 2014 sess.); Oregon: OR. REV. STAT. § 647.107 (2003); Pennsylvania: 54 PA. CONS. STAT. ANN. § 1124 (West, Westlaw through 2014 sess.); Rhode Island: R.I. GEN. LAWS R.I. § 6-2-12 (West, Westlaw through 2014 sess.); South Carolina: S.C. CODE ANN. § 39-15-1165 (Law. Co-op. 2004); Tennessee: TENN. CODE ANN. § 47-25-513 (2000); Texas: TEX. BUS. & COM. CODE ANN. § 16.29 (Vernon 2002); Washington: WASH. REV. CODE ANN. § 19.77.160 (West, Westlaw through 2014 sess.); West Virginia: W. VA. CODE § 47-2-13 (1996); Wyoming: WYO. STAT. ANN. § 40-1-115 (Michie 1997).

1813. Colorado, Kentucky, Maryland, Michigan, North Carolina, North Dakota, Oklahoma, South Dakota, Utah, Vermont, Virginia and Wisconsin.

1814. The typical state dilution statute lists a number of factors in considering dilution: these factors mirror the likelihood of confusion factors used in considering infringement.

1815. *See*, e.g., the Illinois dilution statute, which reads as follows:

> (a) The owner of a mark which is famous in this State shall be entitled, subject to the principles of equity and upon such terms as the court deems reasonable, to an injunction against another person's commercial use of a mark or trade name, if the use begins after the mark has become famous and causes dilution of the distinctive quality of the mark, and to obtain such other relief as is provided in this Section. In determining whether a mark is distinctive and famous, a court may consider factors such as, but not limited to: (1) the degree of inherent or acquired distinctiveness of

Unfortunately, statutory dilution language is not applied consistently from state to state. For example, some New York courts today require evidence of confusion even though the New York statute clearly dictates that dilution may be found regardless of confusion,[1816] while Illinois courts will refuse to find dilution if there is confusion because "[a] trademark likely to confuse is necessarily a trademark likely to dilute."[1817] Therefore, New York courts require confusion while Illinois courts, until 2011, precluded dilution remedies when there is confusion. To make matters worse, the New York dilution statute and the Illinois dilution statute were identical until 1997.[1818] In addition, many other states have identical dilution statutes.[1819]

The state statutes are consistent in requiring that the marks be famous prior to protecting them from dilution.

> the mark in this State; (2) the duration and extent of use of the mark in connection with the goods and services with which the mark is used; (3) the duration and extent of advertising and publicity of the mark in this State; (4) the geographical extent of the trading area in which the mark is used; (5) the channels of trade for the goods or services with which the mark is used; (6) the degree of recognition of the mark in the trading areas and channels of trade in this State used by the mark's owner and the person against whom the injunction is sought; (7) the nature and extent of use of the same or similar mark by third parties; and (8) whether the mark is the subject of a State registration in this State, or a federal registration under the Act of 3 March 1881, or under the Act of February 20, 1905, or on the Principal Register. 765 Ill. Comp. Stat. 1036/65 (1998).

1816. *See* Beverly Pattishall, *The Dilution Rationale for Trademark-Trade Identity Protection, Its Progress and Prospects*, 71 Nw. U. L. Rev. 618, 624, n.47 (1976) (citing cases).

1817. *James Burrough Ltd. v. Sign of the Beefeater, Inc.*, 540 F.2d 266, 274–75 n.16 (7th Cir. 1976), *superseded by statute*, the Federal Trademark Dilution Act, Pub. L. No. 109-312, 120 Stat. 1730, 15 U.S.C. § 1125(c), *as recognized in Cottonwood Fin. Ltd. v. Cash Store Fin. Servs.*, 778 F. Supp. 2d 726 (N.D. Tex. 2011) (claims for confusion and dilution examined on an economic basis and both claims considered to be within the same economic context).

1818. *Compare* 765 Ill. Comp. Stat. 1035/15 (repealed 1998) *with* N.Y. Gen. Bus. Law § 368-d (repealed in 1997).

1819. *See*, e.g., Ariz. Rev. Stat. § 44-1448.01 (2002); Ark. Code Ann. § 4-71-213 (1999); 765 Ill. Comp. Stat. 1036/65 (1998); Kan. Stat. Ann. § 81-214 (West, Westlaw through 2003 sess.); Minn. Stat. § 333.285 (2004); Mont. Code Ann. § 30-13-334 (2003); Neb. Rev. Stat. Ann. § 87-140 (Michie 2000); 54 Pa. Cons. Stat. Ann. § 1124 (West 1996); Tenn. Code Ann. § 47-25-513 (2000).

CHAPTER 2

Subject Matter of Protection

§1 INTRODUCTION

The Lanham Act defines trademarks as "word, name, symbol, or device[1820] or any combination thereof ... used ... to indicate the source of the goods ...."[1821] US courts have been taking this statement more and more literally. If "any" aspect of a product indicates the source or origin of that product, courts today in the US are very likely to recognize it as a trademark. Hence, the scope of trademark protection is theoretically unlimited, confined only by the requirement that the trademark acts to identify source (and otherwise not be violative of the Lanham Act). Thus, the inside of a restaurant might be distinctive enough to warrant trademark protection,[1822] the color alone of a product or a feature of a product,[1823] or even the sound a motorcycle makes when idling[1824] might warrant protection if it has come to identify a consistent source of that product.

US trademark law generally protects trademarks, collective marks, certification marks, service marks, trade and business names if they indicate source and are used on products, and trade dress.[1825]

1820. For a discussion on the history and development of the word "symbol or device," *see* Kenneth Port, *On Nontraditional Trademarks*, 38 N. KENT. L. REV. 1 (2011).

1821. 15 U.S.C. § 1127.

1822. *Two Pesos, Inc., v. Taco Cabana, Inc.*, 505 U.S. 763 (1992) ("Mexican theme" of bright colors, paintings and artifacts has acquired secondary meaning and is distinctive).

1823. *Qualitex Co. v. Jacobson Prod. Co.*, 514 U.S. 159 (1995).

1824. *See* U.S. Trademark Application Serial No. 74/485,223, in the name of Harley-Davidson (filed Feb. 1, 1994) (claiming the sound of a Harley-Davidson motorcycle to be distinctive and indicating Harley-Davidson, Inc. as the source of motorcycles in the minds of consumers) (on file with the USPTO); *see also Kawasaki Motors Corp., U.S.A. v. H-D Mich., Inc.*, 43 U.S.P.Q.2d 1521 (T.T.A.B. 1997) (attacks against Harley-Davidson's bid to register sound of motorcycle exhaust).

1825. 15 U.S.C. §§ 1127, 1053 (service marks); § 1054 (collective and certification marks).

A trademark serves to identify the source of goods or services. The source itself need not be known; rather, it is important that a source is consistently recognized and associated with a particular good or service.[1826] In addition to the identification of source, a trademark represents the goodwill of a business. Goodwill represents the reputation of the producer of goods or services. The consumer comes to rely upon an established level of quality in purchasing a particular good or service.[1827] Trademarks become the embodiment of this goodwill.

§2 CATEGORIES OF MARKS

I Trademarks

The Lanham Act defines trademarks as "any word, name, symbol, or device, or any combination thereof (1) used by a person; or (2) which a person has a bona fide intention to use in commerce and applies to register on the principal register established by this chapter to identify or distinguish his or her goods …."[1828]

A mark may be registered on the Principal Register, provided it satisfies 15 U.S.C. § 1052. Section 1052 actually serves as a list identifying marks that are prohibited from being registered. Thus, any mark which is not statutorily prohibited by section 1052 should be registrable.

Section 1052 prohibits the following types of marks from being registered:

(a) Marks which comprise immoral, deceptive, scandalous, or disparaging matter (or which may falsely suggest a connection with persons, living or dead, institutions, beliefs, or national symbols).

Although this provision has been in effect for 70 years and countless marks have been refused registration or successfully challenged using the disparaging or scandalous provisions,[1829] in 2017, the United State Supreme

1826. 15 U.S.C. § 1127; *see also Int'l Kennel Club of Chicago, Inc. v. Mighty Star, Inc.*, 846 F.2d 1079 (7th Cir. 1988) (International Kennel Club is distinctive and recognized as a source of information on pure bred dogs and registrations).

1827. A particular level of quality is not specified by the Lanham Act. The quality expectation of the consumer is one of continuity. The association between the consumer and the business is developed by the businesses efforts in establishing and maintaining a particular level of quality. Quality itself may be high or low, but the consumer knows that it will always be the same when identified by the trademark associated with a particular product. It is this expectation and fulfillment which establishes the goodwill that is protected by trademark law. *See Coca-Cola Co. v. Koke Co.*, 254 U.S. 143, 146 (1920) (holding that the expectation behind the COCA-COLA name is "a single thing coming from a single source"); *Mishawaka Rubber & Woolen Mfg. Co. v. S.S. Kresge Co.*, 316 U.S. 203, 205 (1942) ("The protection of trade-marks is the protection of symbols … A trade-mark is a merchandising short-cut which induces a purchaser to select what he wants, or what he has been led to believe he wants … Once this is attained, the trade-mark owner has something of value. If another poaches upon the commercial magnetism of the symbol he has created, the owner can obtain legal redress").

1828. 15 U.S.C. § 1127 (Lanham Act § 45).

1829. *See In re* McGinley, 660 F.2d 481 (C.C.P.A. 1981) (mark of nude woman and man kissing and embracing in manner that exposed the man's genitalia held scandalous); *In re* Mavely Media Group Ltd., 33 F.3d 1367 (Fed. Cir. 1994) (for marks considered scandalous under 15 U.S.C. § 1052(a)).

Court held that the "disparagement clause" of Section 2(a) was unconstitutional in light of the First Amendment.[1830] The Court reasoned that the disparagement clause was not a content-neutral regulation and as such was facially unconstitutional. In 2019, the United States Supreme Court determined that the "scandalousness" and "immoral" provisions should meet the same fate. In *Iancu v. Brunetti*, the Court struck down the scandalous clause and the immoral clause for violating the First Amendment.[1831] The Court reasoned that the USPTO should not be attempting to control content-specific speech. Therefore, the current status of the law in the United States is that the USPTO is powerless to prevent disparaging, scandalous or immoral marks from being registered.[1832] However, the prohibition on the registration of "deceptive" marks and on the registration of marks that falsely suggest a connection with persons, institutions, beliefs, or national symbols under this section of the statute remains in effect.

(b) A mark that consists of or comprises a flag or coat of arms of the United States, any State in the United States or any other foreign nation.

(c) A mark that consists of or comprises a name, portrait or signature identifying a particular living individual except with that individual's consent or the name, signature or portrait of a deceased President of the United States during the life of the Widow without the Widow's consent.

(d) Marks that are likely to cause confusion with a mark previously registered on the Principal Register. Marks that are likely to cause confusion as to the source of the goods or services or appear to create some false sense of sponsorship are also not registrable.[1833]

(e) Marks that are merely descriptive,[1834] merely geographic terms, are primarily merely of surname significance and primarily geographically deceptively misdescriptive terms are not registrable. Merely geographic marks are not registrable.[1835] However, words that also have geographic significance are registrable if there is no "goods/place" association in the minds of the consumers. Therefore, the mark NANTUCKET for use on T-shirts is registrable because the place called Nantucket is not generally associated as the place from where T-shirts emanate.[1836]

Marks which are merely of surname significance are not registrable unless they also act to identify the source or origin of some good or service. Although Taylor is the name of a person once connected with the manufacture and sale of wine, the mark TAYLOR WINE also acts to identify source and therefore constitutes a valid trademark.[1837] Titles of single creative works, no matter the length, are not registrable.[1838] The USPTO defines singular work to

1830. *Matal v. Tam*, 137 S. Ct. 1744 (2017).
1831. *Iancu v. Brunetti*, 139 S. Ct. 2294 (2019).
1832. *See*, e.g., USPTO registrations for REAL NIGGAS (Reg. No. 6,006,281) and CITY SLUTZ (Reg. No. 6,131,532). Applicants applied for these marks and received the registrations shortly after the Supreme Court's decisions on disparaging and scandalous marks.
1833. *See infra* Ch. 8, §1.
1834. Merely descriptive marks are marks which simply describe the product or attribute of the product and do not connote source to the relevant consuming public. *See Park 'N Fly, Inc. v. Dollar Park & Fly, Inc.*, 469 U.S. 189 (1985).
1835. *See* Donald S. Chisum & Michael A. Jacobs, Understanding Intellectual Property Law § 5C[1][c][ii](2) (1992).
1836. *In re* Nantucket, Inc., 677 F.2d 95 (C.C.P.A. 1982).
1837. *The Taylor Wine Co., Inc. v. Bully Hill Vineyards, Inc.*, 590 F.2d 701 (2d Cir. 1978).
1838. *See* 15 U.S.C. §§ 1051, 1052, 1127; *Herbko Int'l Inc. v. Kappa Books Inc.*, 308 F.3d 1156, 1163 (Fed. Cir. 2002) (singular creative works are incapable of creating an association to their

be any work in which the content does not change.[1839] Whereas, titles of creative works in a series, and creative works where the content changes with each new edition are registrable.[1840] Therefore, while The Empire Strikes Back is a singular work not eligible for registration, the series name STAR WARS[1841] is registrable as it identifies the source of goods, in this case a collection of films, books, and merchandise.

(f) Secondary meaning

The term used to describe when a mark which is otherwise violative of Section 1052(e) is registrable is "secondary meaning." A mark is said to have secondary meaning when the mark has two functions. One function may be to be descriptive of the goods or services, to merely be of geographic significance, or to merely name a surname. The other function may be to identify source. It is this second function that is necessary for any mark to overcome a Section 1052(e) rejection and still be registrable.[1842]

Generally speaking, a trademark must exhibit three qualities: it must embody the definition provided in section 1127 and be determined allowable by the Patent and Trademark Board; it must be in use or be intended for use in commerce; and it must be able to distinguish the goods or services of the manufacturer.[1843]

II Collective Marks

Collective marks may be registered on the Principal Register under 15 U.S.C. § 1054. A collective mark is defined as a trademark or service mark:

> (1) used by a person other than its owner; or (2) which its owner has a bona fide intention to permit a person other than the owner to use in commerce and files an application to register on the Principal Register established by this Act, to certify regional or other origin, material, mode of manufacture, quality, accuracy, or other characteristics of such person's goods or services or that the work or labor on the goods or services was performed by members of a union or other organization.[1844]

Collective marks are unique in certain respects. A collective mark must be registered by the group which exercises or intends to exercise control over use of the mark.[1845] An individual member of the collective is not allowed to register the mark.[1846] A collective mark may be either a collective membership mark or a collective

---

source); U.S. Patent & Trademark Office, Trademark Manual of Examination Procedure (TMEP) 1202.08 (October 2013).

1839. U.S. Patent & Trademark Office, Trademark Manual of Examination Procedure (TMEP) 1202.08(a) (October 2013).
1840. *Id.* 1202.08(b).
1841. STAR WARS, Registration No. 3301078.
1842. *Int'l Kennel Club of Chicago, Inc. v. Mighty Star, Inc.*, 846 F.2d 1079 (7th Cir. 1988) (concluding International Kennel Club has acquired secondary meaning).
1843. 1 Anne Gilson LaLonde & Jerome Gilson, Gilson on Trademarks§ 1.02[1] (2021).
1844. 15 U.S.C. § 1127 (Lanham Act § 45).
1845. Control and registration are indicative of ownership.
1846. *F.R. Lepage Bakery v. Roesch Bakery Products Co.*, 851 F.2d 351 (Fed. Cir. 1988) (collective trademark canceled upon assignment to an individual), *vacated on other grounds*, 863 F.2d 43 (Fed. Cir. 1988).

organization mark. A collective membership mark is used by a group to signify membership in an organization. A collective organization mark is used by a group which serves as an umbrella over other groups. The umbrella group may promote goods on behalf of its members.[1847] As opposed to a trademark, a collective mark may be geographically descriptive.

III Certification Marks

Certification marks should not be confused with collective marks. A certification mark serves a very specific and unique purpose and is owned and registered by an entity that exists to provide certification of other products or services. Certification marks cannot be used as trademarks by the entity that owns the mark.[1848] A certification mark may be used (under the authority of the owner) by others on products or services which meet the standards and specifications established by the owner of the mark. A good example of a certification mark is Underwriters Laboratory (UL). UL specifies standards that must be met by manufacturers in order to affix the UL mark to their product. This certification is relied upon by consumers to indicate a consistent level of quality. The use of the UL mark on goods and services is a great advantage in the marketplace.

Certification may only be used for certifying the goods or services of others. In addition, a certification mark owner must exercise control over the use of the mark. Failure to exercise control may result in cancelation of the mark.[1849]

IV Service Marks

Service marks have the same rights to registration as trademarks.[1850] The definition applied to service marks is nearly identical to that of a trademark.[1851] The primary distinction is that a service mark is specifically designated to cover services. Service marks, like trademarks, must be used in commerce in order to qualify for registration. Unlike trademarks, use in advertising is generally sufficient to constitute use of a service mark. Some courts, however, have held that advertisement is sufficient use to avoid a finding of abandonment, but use of the service mark through actual sales is still necessary to secure registration of service marks.[1852]

1847. J. Thomas McCarthy, 3 McCarthy on Trademarks and Unfair Competition § 19.99 (5th ed.) (2021).
1848. *See Consol. Dairy Prods. Co. v. Gildner & Schimmel Inc.*, 101 U.S.P.Q. 465, 467 (Comm'r Pat. 1954) (stating it is incompatible to use a mark as both a trademark and as a certification mark). *See also* J. Thomas McCarthy, 3 McCarthy, on Trademarks and Unfair Competition § 19.94 (5th ed.) (2021).
1849. 15 U.S.C. § 1064(e)(1) (Lanham Act § 14(e)(1)).
1850. 15 U.S.C. § 1053 (Lanham Act § 3); *In re* Dr. Pepper, 836 F.2d 508 (U.S. App. 1987) (lottery does not constitute a "service").
1851. 15 U.S.C. § 1127 (Lanham Act § 45).
1852. *Kinark Corp. v. Camelot Inc.*, 548 F. Supp. 429 (D.N.J. 1982) (advertising sent out prior to use for new hotel not yet in operation is not sufficient to confer rights).

Trademarks and service marks are essentially interchangeable. A business may choose to use an identical mark for both its products and its services.[1853] It is important to note, however, that a service mark must be used on services and a trademark on products.[1854] It is simple to define what a product is. A product constitutes any tangible article sold by the owner in commerce. A service, however, is more difficult to define. A service mark is being used when title to the goods in question is not transferred but only molded, fit, or otherwise worked upon.

V Trade Names

Trade names are the actual names of corporations which themselves might own a host of trademarks or service marks. Trademark protection is technically not available to trade names unless they are also used on, or in the connection with the sale of some goods or services in interstate commerce.[1855] Trade names must adhere to the same requirements as trademarks in order to gain protection.[1856] Simply registering a corporate name with the Secretary of State where business is conducted (also known as "qualifying to do business") does not result in the creation of any trademark rights. Only use as a trademark can result in trademark rights.[1857]

The owner of a trade name may prevail in a suit for infringement when the trade name is used by another as a trademark if confusion is likely in the minds of the relevant consumer. This remains true even if the trade name owner has not actually used its trade name as a trademark. Conversely, the owner of a trademark may prevail in a suit for infringement if its trademark is used as a trade name by a third party and would confuse purchasers as to source. Protection extends to related businesses which may not be direct competitors, provided there is a likelihood the plaintiff will bridge the gap between the products.[1858] In all cases, likelihood of confusion is the standard upon which a determination of infringement will be made.

Names used in noncommercial manners are also protectable. Religious groups, professional associations, fraternal, and benevolent groups are included in this category. The basis for protection in this instance is to maintain an established reputation

1853. Anne Gilson LaLonde & Jerome Gilson, GILSON ON TRADEMARKS § 1.02[1][b] (2021).
1854. *In re* Forbes, 31 U.S.P.Q. 1315 (T.T.A.B. 1983).
1855. *American Steel Foundries v. Robertson*, 269 U.S. 372 (1926) (use of trademark "Simplex" when applied to actual goods is sufficient to secure rights); Anne Gilson LaLonde & Jerome Gilson, GILSON ON TRADEMARKS § 2.15 (2021).
1856. *Goodyear's India Rubber Glove Mfg. Co. v. Goodyear Rubber Co.*, 128 U.S. 598 (1888) (generic names not protected); *Safeway Stores, Inc. v. Safeway Properties, Inc.*, 307 F.2d 495 (2d Cir. 1962) (descriptive marks have limited protection); *North American Aircoach Sys., Inc. v. North American Arats, Inc.*, 231 F.2d 205 (9th Cir. 1955) (geographically descriptive marks not protected).
1857. *George Washington Mint, Inc. v. Washington Mint, Inc.*, 349 F. Supp. 255 (S.D.N.Y. 1972) (prior establishment as corporation name does not confer rights).
1858. *Standard Oil Co. v. Standard Oil Co.*, 56 F.2d 973 (10th Cir. 1932) (second-comer activity in Mexico not sufficiently distant from senior user's reasonable geographical expansion when both users engage in manufacturing, production and marketing of petroleum products).

and to prevent confusion among persons wishing to associate with or make contributions to such groups.[1859]

VI Domain Names

A domain name is not a trademark.[1860] The Lanham Act defines a domain name as:

> any alphanumeric designation which is registered with or assigned by any domain name registrar, domain name registry, or other domain name registration authority as part of an electronic address on the Internet.[1861]

Trademark law encounters problems in cyberspace. Before delving into trademark law on the Internet, one must understand how the symbols of the Internet work. The Internet has its own lexicon that hinders analysis of relevant legal issues.[1862]

Now that the Internet has become a household tool, everyone in the US understands that the "Internet is not a physical or tangible entity, but rather a giant network which interconnects innumerable smaller groups of linked computer networks."[1863] Unlike other communications utilities, no single person, commercial or government entity controls the operation of the Internet.[1864] The Internet "exists and functions as a result of the fact that hundreds of separate operators … independently decided to use common data transfer protocols to exchange communications and information."[1865] "The resulting whole is a decentralized, global medium of communications … that links people, institutions, corporations, and governments around the world."[1866]

This computer network relies on consistent standards to communicate and share data. Each computer accessing the Internet has a corresponding Internet Protocol (IP) address, which is comprised of four groups of numbers, with each group separated by a decimal point—Deployment of the IPv6 protocol began in 1999. IPv6 addresses are 128-bit numbers and are conventionally expressed using hexadecimal strings, for example, 1080:0:0:0:8:800: 200C:417A—taken from http://www.iana.org/ipaddress/

1859. *Am. Gold Star Mothers, Inc. v. Nat'l Gold Star Mothers, Inc.*, 191 F.2d 488 (D.C. Cir. 1951) (uses which tend to divert membership and gifts are injurious); *American Legal Aid, Inc. v. Legal Aid Services, Inc.*, 176 U.S.P.Q. 131 (Wyo. 1972) (use of "legal aid" went beyond defendant's description of business in incorporation papers and was injurious to established association); *Nat'l Board of YWCA v. YWCA of Charleston, S.C.*, 335 F. Supp. 615 (D.S.C. 1971) (ability to raise money and maintain established reputation is undermined when there is a confusing mark in use).
1860. However, a domain name can develop sufficient secondary meaning to serve as both an electronic address and a signifier of the course of goods or services. *See*, e.g., *United States Patent and Trademark Office v. Booking.com B.V.*, 140 S.Ct. 2298 (2020).
1861. 15 U.S.C. § 1127 (Lanham Act § 45).
1862. Colby B. Springer, *Master of the Domain (Name): A History of Domain Name Litigation and the Emergence of the Anticybersquatting Consumer Protection Act and Uniform Dispute Resolution Policy*, 17 Santa Clara Computer & High Tech. L.J. 315, 317 (2001).
1863. *Am. Civil Liberties Union v. Reno*, 929 F. Supp. 824, 830 (E.D. Pa.), *aff'd*, 521 U.S. 844 (1997).
1864. *Id.*, at 832.
1865. *Id.*
1866. *Am. Civil Liberties Union v. Reno*, 929 F. Supp. 824, 831(E.D. Pa.), *aff'd*, 521 U.S. 844 (1997).

ip-addresses.htm.[1867] Instead of requiring Internet users to use IP addresses, the developers of the Internet devised a system of domain names.

A domain name "identifies a more specific area on the Internet, and as with IP numbers, is separated by a 'dot'."[1868] For example, in the US Supreme Court's domain name, supremecourtus.gov, ".gov" is the generic top-level domain (gTLD), and is a country code or identifier that may signify the country or, in the case of some gTLDs, the type of information at the resultant website. The "supremecourtus" portion of the domain name is the second-level domain. "All second level domains are unique, and frequently contain the corporate or trade name of the domain name holder."[1869] This is because domain names do not yet teach the Internet-user the precise context of use, which is what makes trademarks unique. Second-level domains are selected and requested by the domain name registrant.[1870]

Under trademark law, more than one party may hold the rights to the same mark,[1871] but in cyberspace only one party may hold the registration for a particular domain name.[1872] To cite a frequently noted example, although United Airlines and United Van Lines both have valid trademark rights in "United" for their respective goods and services, only one party can register as united.com.[1873]

The conceptual underpinnings of the nature of harm on the Internet hold certain assumptions about how commerce operates in the Internet. The ACPA presupposes two things. First, it presupposes that consumers seeking a good or service will use second-level domains[1874] as an indicator of source:

> If an internet user knows the domain name for a particular Web site ... the user can type the name into a Web browser and access that site directly without having to conduct what may be a time-consuming search.[1875]

Second, the ACPA presupposes that holders of trademarks, specifically work marks, will want to create domain names using the word mark as the second-level domain in a domain name.[1876]

1867. *See NSI v. Umbro Int'l, Inc.*, 529 S.E.2d 80, 83 (Va. 2000).
1868. *Id.*
1869. *MTV Networks v. Curry*, 867 F. Supp. 202, 204 n.2 (S.D.N.Y. 1994) (finding that domain names are unique).
1870. *NSI v. Umbro Int'l, Inc.*, 529 S.E.2d 80, 83 n.6 (Va. 2000).
1871. *See infra* Ch. 6, §2.IV.
1872. *MTV Networks v. Curry*, 867 F. Supp. 202, 204 n.2 (S.D.N.Y. 1994) (finding that domain names are unique).
1873. Example from Lisa M. Sharrock, *The Future of Domain Name Dispute Resolution: Crafting Practical Legal Solutions from Within the UDRP Framework*, 51 Duke L.J. 817, 820 (2001).
1874. "Second-level domains are selected and requested by the domain name registrant." *NSI v. Umbro Int'l, Inc.*, 529 S.E.2d 80, 83 n.6 (Va. 2000).
1875. *Id.*, at 83.
1876. For example, Microsoft holds the registration to microsoft.com, Coca-cola holds the registration to coca-cola.com, and Burger King holds the registration to burgerking.com. *See* Dan L. Burk, *Trademarks along the Infobahn: A First Look at the Emerging Law of Cybermarks*, 1 Rich. J.L. & Tech. 1 (1995).

In other words, domain names are valuable because they can concurrently function not only as an address but also as a symbol of the information to which they point.[1877]

§3 SIGNS WHICH MAY SERVE AS TRADEMARKS

I Words, Letters, and Slogans

Words, letters, and slogans may act as trademarks when they designate the source of a good or service.[1878] All three categories are sufficiently similar and allow discussion as a common group. Words or letters which merely designate differences in colors, grades, styles, or types of products are not eligible for protection as trademarks.[1879] Such designations are not capable of distinguishing source as they are used to describe a particular attribute of a specified product.

In the instance that a letter alone, or in combination with others, serving to identify grade or style is recognized as an identification of source, it will receive trademark protection to the extent it identifies the source of the good or service. In addition, an arbitrary number which does not indicate grade, style or type is eligible for protection.[1880] This is true of single letter and combination letter marks as well. If it is merely descriptive of the product, as to ingredients or merely an abbreviation, it will not be protected.[1881]

A Personal Names

Because a personal name is inherently descriptive (i.e., it describes the person not the source or origin of a good or service), it cannot function as a trademark unless it has acquired secondary meaning. In some instances, a celebrity may register his or her name with the USPTO, usually to brand a line of goods that the celebrity sponsors (George Foreman for use on propane and natural gas barbeque grills and stands for grills (Reg. No. 2,566,646)).

In the context of abusive registration of domain names, both the federal ACPA[1882] and the international Uniform Dispute Resolution Policy (UDRP) specifically mention

1877. *See NSI v. Umbro Int'l, Inc.*, 529 S.E.2d 80, 82 (Va. 2000).
1878. 15 U.S.C. § 1127 (Lanham Act § 45).
1879. Anne Gilson LaLonde & Jerome Gilson, GILSON ON TRADEMARKS § 2.05 (2021).
1880. *Worthington Prod, Inc. v. Lister Indus., Inc.*, 215 N.Y.S.2d 783 (1961) (random number system created by plaintiff for particular colors is confusing when used by defendant); *Shaw Stocking Co. v. Mack*, 21 Blatchf. 1, 12 F. 707 (C.C.D.N.Y. 1882) (use of arbitrary numbering system is protected).
1881. *Singer Mfg. Co. v. Singer Upholstering & Sewing Co.*, 130 F. Supp. 205 (D. Pa. 1955) (Singer's use of "S" is an indication of source); *Hypertherm Inc. v. Precision Products Inc.*, 832 F.2d 697 (1st Cir. 1987) (use of imaginative designations protected); *Shaw Stocking Co. v. Mack*, 12 F. 707 (N.D.N.Y. 1882) (numbering system not indicative of any particular ingredient or quality and therefore protected as trademarks).
1882. *See* Intellectual Property and Communications Omnibus Reform Act of 1999, H.R. Conf. Rep. No. 106-464 (1999), 1999 WL 1095089, at *109:

protecting personal names. To receive protection, they both require the personal name to function as an indicator of source.[1883]

With personal names, a fair use defense arises to allow one to use one's own name. In the face of a strong mark, this defense is very limited.

II Nonverbal Marks

A *Alphanumeric Symbols*

Letters and numbers are sometimes combined to create marks and, when not descriptive of the product, can be protected. Arbitrary combinations of numbers and letters are given the highest protection.[1884] Alphanumeric marks are infringed when another user adopts nearly the identical mark on a similar good or service.[1885]

Telephone mnemonics, a telephone number that has replaced some numerals with letters, are becoming more and more popular in advertising. For example, the phone number 800-DENTIST would most likely be descriptive of dental services and therefore not registrable. There is currently a split within the circuits on whether this type of mark can be protected.[1886] The USPTO has determined that it will deny

---

> Protection under Section 43 of the Lanham Act has been applied by the courts to personal names which function as marks, such as service marks, when such marks are infringed. Infringement may occur when the endorsement of products or services in interstate commerce is falsely implied through the use of a personal name, or otherwise, without regard to the goods or services of the parties. This protection also applies to domain names on the Internet, where falsely implied endorsements and other types of infringement can cause greater harm to the owner and confusion to a consumer in a shorter amount of time than is the case with traditional media.

1883. WIPO, Report of the Second WIPO Internet Domain Name Process, *The Management of Internet Names and Addresses: Intellectual Property Issues*, para. 199 (Sept. 3, 2001), available at http://arbiter.wipo.int/processes/process2/report/html/report.html ("Persons who have gained eminence and respect, but who have not profited from their reputation in commerce, may not avail themselves of the UDRP to protect their personal names against parasitic registrations").

1884. *Standard Brands, Inc. v. Smidler*, 151 F.2d 34 (2d Cir. 1945) ("V-8" arbitrary for vegetable juice).

1885. *Nabisco Brands, Inc., v. Kaye*, 760 F. Supp. 25 (D. Conn. 1991) (substituting the number "2" for the number one in "A-1" for meat sauce is confusing with "A-1").

1886. *Dial-A-Mattress Franchise Corp. v. Page*, 880 F.2d 675 (2d Cir. 1989) (telephone number spelling a generic term is protected); *Murrin v. Midco Communications, Inc.*, 726 F. Supp. 1195 (D. Minn. 1989) (telephone number spelling LAWYER is protected in a particular geographic area); *Dranoff-Perlstein Associates v. Sklar*, 967 F.2d 852 (3d Cir. 1992) (telephone numbers spelling generic terms are not protectable; secondary meaning must be demonstrated with descriptive terms). However, the Supreme Court held in *USPTO v. Booking.com B.V.*, 140 S.Ct. 2298 (2020) that a generic term combined with a generic internet domain name suffix (here, "booking" combined with ".com" for an online hotel reservation service) does not automatically yield a generic composite. Because a specific domain name, even one composed of generic terms, can only be used by a single entity, the Court held that such domain names could establish secondary meaning to consumers entitling the domain name to protection as a trademark.

registration for any mnemonic that is generic.[1887] However, a mnemonic that, as a composite, contains a generic word and a numeral may acquire protection if it has secondary meaning.[1888]

B Color

Historically, a color alone was not protected as a trademark. A general belief that the number of colors would become depleted and that it is impossible for the human eye to distinguish between fine shades of colors provided the basis for denying protection.[1889] The courts reasoned that allowing the use of a color as a trademark would prevent another manufacturer from utilizing a necessary tool in marketing a product. In the mid-1980s, a split in the circuits developed over this issue.[1890] The split was resolved in 1995 when the Supreme Court ruled that a color alone was capable of protection.[1891]

However, a color that is functional[1892] is not protected.[1893] More specifically, a color which is used on a product to enhance a particular feature will not be protected.[1894] The Second Circuit has qualified the Qualitex ruling by stating that a color is protected only after acquiring secondary meaning.[1895]

1887. TMEP § 1209.03(i) (3rd ed. 2002).
1888. *Dranoff-Perlstein Assocs. v. Sklar*, 967 F.2d 852 (3d Cir. 1992) (sufficient evidence of secondary meaning in telephone number spelling INJURY-1 justifies its protection as a trademark).
1889. *Nutra-Sweet Co. v. Stadt Corp.*, 917 F.2d 1024 (7th Cir. 1990), *cert. denied*, 499 U.S. 983 (1991) (blue color of packaging for "Nutra-Sweet" not distinguishable from blue color of packaging for "Equal").
1890. *In re* Owens-Corning Fiberglass Corp., 774 F.2d 1116 (Fed. Cir. 1985) (use of the color pink for insulation is distinctive); *Nutra-Sweet Co. v. Stadt Corp.*, 917 F.2d 1024 (7th Cir. 1990) (inability to distinguish between similar colors of blue packaging for artificial sweeteners precludes protection).
1891. *Qualitex Co. v. Jacobson Prods. Co.*, 514 U.S. 159 (1995) (green-gold color of press pads is distinctive).
1892. Functionality may be aesthetic or utilitarian. Aesthetic functionality is concerned with color that is used merely to "decorate" products and not as a source indicator. Functionality can also be described as utilitarian, application of a color only to serve a useful purpose. *Brunswick Corp. v. British Seagull*, 35 F.3d 1527 (Fed. Cir. 1994), *cert. denied*, 514 U.S. 1049 (1995) (black color of motor used to de-emphasize size not protectable).
1893. *Id.*, at 1162–63.
1894. *Deere & Co. v. Farmland, Inc.*, 560 F. Supp. 85 (S.D. Iowa 1982) (customer preference for matching implements is not sufficient to confer rights in use of a particular color); *Sazerac Co. v. Skyy Spirits*, 37 U.S.P.Q.2d 1731 (E.D. La. 1995) (no distinctiveness in blue color is used to attract customers' attention).
1895. *Fabrication Enters. v. Hygenic Corp.*, 64 F.3d 53 (2d Cir. 1995) (color scheme on rubber bands to denote resistance has acquired secondary meaning and is protectable); *Mana Prods. v. Columbia Cosmetics Mfg.*, 65 F.3d 1063 (2d Cir. 1995) (no secondary meaning for black compacts in ordinary shapes used within the industry as a whole); *Knitwaves Inc. v. Lollytogs Ltd.*, 71 F.3d 996 (2d Cir. 1995) (ecological design on sweaters is distinctive).

Color has been and continues to be protected when used in combination with other colors or as part of a design.[1896] It is important to note that when assessing a combination of colors or color(s) and designs, the general rule of trademark distinctiveness applies.[1897] The greater the distinctiveness, the greater the likelihood of protection. In addition, the more arbitrary the symbol used in association with the color, the greater the likelihood of protection.[1898]

A unique extension of color protection can be found in the application of protection to nonspecified colors. A color or one of several colors used consistently with a nonspecified color as part of a product design may be protected.[1899]

As with numbers and letters, colors cannot be used to differentiate grade or size if other manufacturers require the same colors to make the same differentiation.[1900] If different colors are used by different manufacturers of the same type of products, the use of color to distinguish grade and style is acceptable.[1901]

The inquiry into color protection is highly factual and hinges upon consideration of several factors, including the type of use, the association of the color with source, and the availability of color to other producers.

C *Fragrance*

In 1990, fragrance was added to the list of types of marks which can be registered.[1902] Fragrance is limited in application to use as an additive to a product.[1903] It may not in and of itself be protected. This limitation prevents product scents from obtaining registration. A product which is manufactured and sold as a scent or primarily associated with a scent is not allowed registration.[1904]

D *Designs*

A design that is not inherently distinctive must have acquired secondary meaning[1905] to be registered on the Principal Register. A design which is not sufficiently distinctive to

1896. *Barbasol Co. v. Jacobs*, 160 F.2d 336 (7th Cir. 1947) (combination of blue-white-red-white is protectable); *Brunswick-Balke-Collender Co. v. American Bowling & Billiard Corp.*, 150 F.2d 69 (2d Cir. 1945) (use of red crown design on neck of pin is protectable).
1897. *See infra* Ch. 3, §1 Distinctiveness.
1898. *Radio Corp. Of America v. Decca Records, Inc.*, 51 F. Supp. 493 (S.D.N.Y. 1943) (red color of phonograph label is not sufficiently distinctive for "RED SEAL" records).
1899. *A.T. Cross Co. v. TPM Distributing, Inc.*, 226 U.S.P.Q. 521 (D. Minn. 1985). *But see Keystone Camera Products Corp. v. Ansco Photo-Optical Corp.*, 667 F. Supp. 1221 (N.D. Ill. 1987) (unspecified combination of colors is not protectable when there is not a consistent design utilizing the color combination).
1900. *Coats v. Merrick Thread Co.*, 149 U.S. 562 (1893) (designation on embroidery floss denoting length and ply thickness is not infringed).
1901. *Barnes Group, Inc., v. Connell Ltd.*, 15 U.S.P.Q.2d (BNA) 1100 (D. Del. 1990) (color of die springs which denotes particular load strength is not protected).
1902. *In re* Clarke, 17 U.S.P.Q.2d 1238 (T.T.A.B. 1990) (scented yarn is held to be distinctive).
1903. *Id.*
1904. *Id.*
1905. *See infra* Ch. 3, §1.II. Noninherently Distinctive Marks.

obtain registration on the Principal Register may be registered on the Supplemental Register.[1906]

A design may be either pictorial or three dimensional.[1907] Either embodiment must meet the distinctiveness test. Pictorial designs may be used as backgrounds for word marks provided the background design creates a "separate commercial image" apart from the word mark itself.[1908] A background design utilizing a commonly used shape is unlikely to obtain protection due to the extensive use of such shapes in the promotion of products. Such shapes are generally not considered to have inherent distinctiveness.[1909]

Designs that are merely descriptive of a product are not eligible for registration.[1910] If a design meets the definition of fanciful,[1911] it need not acquire secondary meaning to be registered. A fanciful background design, which is not normally associated with a particular type of product, may be registered without secondary meaning, provided it also meets the separate commercial impression test.[1912]

A repeated design used to cover a package or label may also be registered, provided it meets the separate commercial impression test and is inherently distinctive.[1913]

E *Nontraditional Marks*

Since the 1992 Supreme Court holding in the Qualitex,[1914] many different types of nontraditional trademarks have been registered with the USPTO, including such things as the vertical opening motion of Lamborghini car doors[1915] or the vertical spray of water from the backs of Yamaha personal watercraft.[1916]

1906. *In re* David Crystal, Inc. 296 F.2d 771 (C.C.P.A. 1961); *In re* Dassler, 134 U.S.P.Q. 265 (T.T.A.B. 1962) (design of shoe had acquired sufficient secondary meaning for registration).
1907. In re *Yahama Int'l Corp. v. Hoshino Gakki Co.*, 231 U.S.P.Q. 926 (T.T.A.B. 1986) (registration is allowed for guitar peg head configuration), *aff'd*, 840 F.2d 1572 (Fed. Cir. 1988).
1908. *In re* Hillerich & Bradsby Co., 204 F.2d 287 (C.C.P.A. 1953) (oval line on baseball and softball bats is not protected).
1909. Seabrook Foods, Inc., Bar-Well Foods, Ltd., 568 F.2d 1342 (C.C.P.A. 1977) (stylized leaf background is not protected).
1910. *Ginger Group, Ltd., v. Beatrice Cos.*, 678 F. Supp. 555 (E.D.Pa. 1988) (background with half or whole apple for juice is not protected); *In re* Underwater Connections, Inc., 221 U.S.P.Q. 95 (T.T.A.B. 1983) (illustration of underwater air tank descriptive for diving equipment).
1911. *See* Ch. 3, §1.I. Inherently Distinctive Marks.
1912. *Hygenic Prod. Co. v. Coe*, 85 F.2d 264 (D.C. Cir. 1936) (yellow rectangle with blue border used as background is not descriptive of toilet cleaning powder).
1913. *Vuitton et Fils S.A. v. J. Young Enterprises, Inc.*, 644 F.2d 769 (9th Cir. 1981) (design comprised of letters "LV" and surrounded by flower-like symbols repeated over fabric is distinctive).
1914. *Qualitex Co. v. Jacobson Products Co., Inc.*, 514 U.S. 159 (1995).
1915. Automobile Lamborghini Holding S.p.A., United States Patent and Trademark Office Reg. No. 2793439 ("The mark consists of the unique motion in which the door of a vehicle is opened. The doors move parallel to the body of the vehicle but are gradually raised above the vehicle to a parallel position").
1916. Yamaha Motor Corp., Ltd., USPTO Reg. No. 1946170 ("The mark is comprised of a three dimensional spray of water issuing from the rear of a jet propelled watercraft and is generated during the operation of the watercraft"). *See generally*, Lesley Matty, Note, *Rock, Paper,*

In fact, USPTO application statistics indicate that there were only ninety-three nontraditional trademarks on record prior to the Qualitex decision. In the first forty-eight years of the existence of the Lanham Act, there were ninety-three nontraditional trademarks filed (1.93 per year). In the first fourteen years after the Qualitex decision, there were 688 trademark applications filed for nontraditional trademarks (approximately forty-nine a year). This is an explosion of interest in nontraditional trademarks.

Yet, much is made of this ability in the US to register nontraditional trademarks,[1917] and the US has even placed pressure on other countries to expand the scope of other countries' trademark laws to include the protection of nontraditional trademarks.[1918] The Singapore Treaty on Trademarks in 2006 was the first treaty explicitly to recognize nontraditional trademarks, although it also stated that signatory states are under no obligation to adopt "new types" of trademarks.[1919] This interest in and support for nontraditional trademarks is paying off as Japan has moved to adopt nontraditional trademarks. Even WIPO's Standing Committee on the Law of Trademarks, Industrial Designs and Geographic Indications has recently taken this up in the form of a major study and report.[1920]

Scissors, Trademark? A Comparative Analysis of Motion as a Feature of Trademarks in the United States and Europe, 14 CARDOZO J. INTL. & COMP. L. 557 (2006). A personal water craft is more commonly called a "jet ski." However, JET SKI is actually the registered trademark of the Kawasaki Company, Registration No. 1394547. Of course, this is not to be confused with Honda's AQUA TRAX (Reg. No. 2737518) or Bombardier Recreational Products' SEA-DOO (applied for but not yet registered at serial number 78560060).

1917. Jerome Gilson & Anne Gilson LaLonde, *Cinnamon Buns, Marching Ducks and Cherry-Scented Racecar Exhaust: Protecting Nontraditional Trademarks*, 95 TRADEMARK REP. 773 (2005).

1918. This pressure comes in the form of free trade agreements. If a country wants a free trade agreement, the US's agreement contains a provision to require partner nations to protect sound and scent marks. To date, no other nontraditional marks are protected in the free trade agreements. *See*, e.g., US-Australia Free Trade Agreement s. 17.2 which reads in its entirety as follows: "Neither Party may require, as a condition of registration, that marks be visually perceptible, nor may a Party deny registration of a mark solely on the ground that the sign of which it is composed is a sound or a scent" www.ustr.gov/sites/default/files/uploads/agreements/fta/australia/asset_upload_file469_5141.pdf. The free trade agreements with 13 other nations contain similar requirements. *See generally* www.ustr.gov/trade-agreements/free-trade-agreements. For more analysis of nontraditional trademarks, *see* Kenneth L. Port, *On Nontraditional Trademarks*, 38 N. KENT. L. REV. 1 (2011).

1919. Singapore Treaty on Trademarks, Rule 3(5): "(5) [*Hologram Mark, Motion Mark, Color Mark, Position Mark*] Where the application contains a statement to the effect that the mark is a hologram mark, a motion mark, a color mark or a position mark, a Contracting Party may require one or more reproductions of the mark and details concerning the mark, as prescribed by the law of that Contracting Party" www.wipo.int/edocs/mdocs/mdocs/en/tlt_r_dc/tlt_r_dc_30.pdf. The US position on nontraditional trademarks seems to be that the USPTO will support international efforts in this regard because there is so little else where cooperation seems possible at this given moment.

1920. WIPO (World Intellectual Property Organization): Standing Committee on the Law of Trademarks, Industrial Designs and Geographical Indications, Summary of Replies to the Questionnaire on Trademark Law and Practice (SCT/11/6) (Jan. 24, 2006).

III Trade Dress

A *Generally*

Trade dress may be registered and protected if it satisfies the definition of trademark under section 45 of the Lanham Act.[1921] Protection for unregistered trade dress is available under section 43(a) of the Lanham Act and state law on unfair competition. Trade dress protection extends to the total compilation and image presented by a product configuration or packaging.[1922] "'[T]rade dress' includes the total look of a product and its packaging and even includes the design and shape of the product itself."[1923]

Trade dress protection does not extend to promotion and advertising.[1924] Further, the unique "style" depicted in a particular expression of a product is not protected.[1925] In addition, trade dress protection must satisfy the parameters established by trademark law. Trade dress must be distinctive, either inherently or through secondary meaning, and it must identify the source of the product.

In *Wal-Mart Stores v. Samara Bros., Inc.*, the Supreme Court limited what constitutes protectable trade dress and distinguished three trade dress categories: product design, product packaging, and a third category, called the "Tertium quid." The Court further stated that a showing of secondary meaning was required in all cases of product design trade dress, and such a showing was only sometimes required for product packaging trade dress. To reconcile this decision with the Court's earlier holding in Two Pesos, the Court determined that Two Pesos was a case of product packaging and some other undefined third category, or Tertium quid.[1926] If the trade dress sought to be protected is the configuration or design of a product itself, secondary meaning will have to be shown as a prerequisite for registration or protection.

If one claims the design or portion of the trade dress as a trademark, it must be nonfunctional. If the trade dress is not registered as a trademark with the USPTO, the party claiming trade dress rights has the burden to show that the trade dress is nonfunctional.[1927]

1921. *Two Pesos, Inc. v. Taco Cabana*, Inc. 505 U.S. 763 (1992) ("Mexican theme" of a restaurant protected); *Blue Bell Bio-Medical v. Cin-Bad, Inc.*, 864 F.2d 1253 (5th Cir. 1989) (blue and off-white medical carts not protected due to absence of confusion); *John H. Harland Co. v. Clarke Checks, Inc.*, 711 F.2d 966 (11th Cir. 1983) (overall style of memory check stub products protected).
1922. *Compco Corp. v. Day-Brite Lighting, Inc.*, 376 U.S. 234 (1964); *Sears, Roebuck & Co. v. Stiffel Co.*, 376 U.S. 225 (1964).
1923. J. Thomas McCarthy, 1 McCarthy on Trademarks and Unfair Competition § 8:4 (2021).
1924. *Haagen-Dazs, Inc. v. Frusen Gladje, Ltd.*, 493 F. Supp. 73 (S.D.N.Y. 1980) (Scandinavian theme used in advertising and marketing is not protected).
1925. *Contra Romm Art Creations, Ltd. v. Simcha Int'l, Inc.*, 786 F. Supp. 1126 (E.D.N.Y. 1992) (posters and limited editions are protected when they are not merely an established "style" of expression).
1926. *See Wal-Mart Stores, Inc. v. Samara Bros., Inc.*, 529 U.S. 205 (2000) (holding that a line of children's clothing with decorative features was not distinctive).
1927. 15 U.S.C. § 1125(a)(3).

If one seeks to protect the design or the configuration of the product, and that feature is the subject of a utility patent, then there will be a strong presumption that the feature is functional and, therefore, not protectable as trade dress.[1928]

B Functionality

Trade dress, which is functional, is not protected. Functionality is determined in light of the "utility" that the trade dress may play on any given product. The utility of any given trade dress is determined by considering the superiority of design, and this determination is based on whether the trade dress is essential to competition. The factors that courts will consider to determine if a trade dress is functional include: (1) the existence of an expired utility patent which discloses the utilitarian advantage of the design sought to be registered as trade dress; (2) the trade dress owner's claim that there are no alternatives available;[1929] and (3) the trade dress contributes to more efficient use, adds durability, or aids in manufacturing or distribution.[1930] Common use of an item on packaging, referred to as "utilitarian functionality," will also limit trade dress protection.[1931]

Whether a particular trade dress is functional or not is determined by whether or not competitors need that specific trade dress to compete effectively in the market or if granting the trade dress to one entity would result in essentially a virtual monopoly on the goods in question and thereby grant a "backdoor" patent to the claimant. Courts view trade dress as a whole in determining whether it is functional.[1932] There are two types of functionality: utilitarian functionality and aesthetic functionality.

Unlike utilitarian functionality, aesthetic functionality is not protectable if the design feature contributes to or enhances a product's consumer appeal.[1933] In the

1928. *See TraffFix Devices, Inc. v. Marketing Displays, Inc.*, 532 U.S. 253 (2001).
1929. *In re* Morton-Norwich, 671 F.2d 1332 (C.C.P.A. 1982) (shape of spray bottle is not functional).
1930. *Bayline Partners L.P. v. Weyerhaeuser Co.*, 31 U.S.P.Q.2d 1051 (N.D. Cal. 1994) (box features related to efficiency of use and are functional).
1931. *Mana Prods. v. Columbia Cosmetics Mfg.*, 65 F.3d 1063 (2d Cir. 1995) (black cosmetic compacts used throughout the industry are not protected).
1932. *Fuddruckers Inc. v. Doc's B.R. Others Inc.*, 826 F.2d 837, 843 n.7 (9th Cir. 1987) (overall decor including menus, layout, and style of service is protected). The Federal Circuit has found that the rounded corners of the iPhone are functional and cannot act as Apple's trade dress. *Apple Inc. v. Samsung Elecs. Co.* 786 F.3d 983 (Fed. Cir. 2015), reversed and remanded by 137 S. Ct. 429 (2016) on other grounds. For the unregistered trade dress of the rounded corners of the phone, Apple failed to rebut the evidence that the trade dress is functional. The court reversed the denial of Samsung's motion for judgment as a matter of law that the trade dress is functional and not protectable. For the registered trade dress of the rounded icon corners, Apple also failed to provide sufficient evidence in the record to show that the registered trade dress of the rounded edges is nonfunctional. The court stated that the individual claimed elements are clearly functional and the trade dress as a whole is functional, so the registration loses its evidentiary significance. With the burden shifting back to Apple to prove nonfunctionality, the court found a lack of evidence to support the jury finding of nonfunctionality. The court reversed the DC for the same reasons as the unregistered trade dress.
1933. *See Pagliero v. Wallace China Co. Ltd.*, 198 F.2d 339, 343 (9th Cir. 1952) (designs which are a response to consumer demand are not protected).

rather famous *Pagliero*[1934] case, the Ninth Circuit held that if the particular feature was an important ingredient in the commercial success of the product, the interest in free competition would permit its imitation in the absence of a patent or copyright. However, if the feature or design was a mere arbitrary embellishment, a form of dress for the goods primarily adopted for the purposes of identification and individuality and therefore was unrelated to any need of a competitor to market or sell the same or similar product, imitation may be actionable if the owner can show secondary meaning is made.

Recently, however, some courts have rejected the important ingredient test and have preferred a more general analysis of competitive need. If the plaintiff is seeking protection "for a precise expression of a decorative style,"[1935] it is more likely to prevail than if it is attempting to protect "basic elements of style that are part of the public domain."[1936] After all, the Restatement (Third) of Unfair Competition states that a "design is functional because of its aesthetic value only if it confers a significant benefit that cannot be practically duplicated by the use of alternative designs."[1937] Therefore, although still alive and strong, analysis under the aesthetic functionality doctrine is more likely to be focused on overall competitive need for the trade dress and less on whether or not the claimed trade dress is an important ingredient of a product or service.

1934. *Id.*
1935. *Wallace Int'l Silversmiths, Inc. v. Godinger Silver Art Co.*, 916 F.2d 76 (2d Cir. 1990) (no protection for basic elements of style that are necessary to create common type of silverware), *cert. denied*, 499 U.S. 976 (1991).
1936. *Id.*
1937. Restatement (Third) Unfair Competition, Ch. 3 § 17 (1995).

CHAPTER 3
Conditions of Protection

§1 DISTINCTIVENESS

The first consideration in determining whether a trademark is protectable in the US is to determine whether or not the mark is distinctive of the products or services on which the mark is used. Distinctiveness is either "inherent" in the trademark itself or acquired through secondary meaning.[1938] A trademark that merely describes the product or service it is used on is not distinctive, but merely descriptive.[1939] Marks that are inherently distinctive may be immediately registered on the Principal Register provided they do not violate any of the prohibitions as stated in section 2 of the Lanham Act.

Most US courts look to the "continuum" of trademarks. That is, all trademarks fit somewhere on a continuum from generic words (and not protectable at all) to inherently distinctive marks (the most distinctive marks and the ones that deserve the most protection). Inherently distinctive marks include those that are arbitrary, fanciful, or suggestive.[1940] Marks that are not inherently distinctive require secondary meaning to be registered.[1941] All marks fall somewhere on this continuum. The categories include generic marks, descriptive marks, suggestive marks and fanciful/arbitrary inherently distinctive marks.

Where a trademark falls within this continuum will determine how much protection it will be afforded by the courts. This determination is a question of fact.[1942]

1938. *See infra* Ch. 3, §1.II.A. Descriptive Marks.
1939. *Id.*
1940. 15 U.S.C. § 1052 (Lanham Act § 2).
1941. 15 U.S.C. § 1052(f) (Lanham Act § 2(f)).
1942. *G. Heileman Brewing Co. v. Anheuser-Busch, Inc.*, 873 F.2d 985, 992 (7th Cir. 1989) (characterizing a mark is an issue of fact).

I Inherently Distinctive Marks

A *Arbitrary Marks*

Arbitrary marks are words or symbols that already exist in the language, but are used as trademarks on goods or services with which they are not normally associated. For example, "APPLE" for computers, or "IVORY" for soap. Arbitrary marks do not describe the good or service in any manner and do not convey any characteristic, ingredient, or function of the good. Arbitrary marks are considered inherently distinctive and do not require secondary meaning to be registered.[1943]

An arbitrary mark is created by using a common word, symbol, or name in association with a good in an arbitrary manner. Use of a common word in an arbitrary manner does not diminish the strength of the trademark.[1944] In fact, arbitrary marks are considered strong.[1945]

A mark is arbitrary if the consumer makes no association between the mark and the product/service. Although the word or words that comprise an arbitrary mark may appear in a dictionary and therefore actually be a common part of the English (or other) language, the mere fact that the word(s) appears in the dictionary is not dispositive in determining whether a mark is arbitrary.[1946] Rather, the key is whether the consumer makes a mental association between the mark and the goods or services upon viewing the mark for the first time. If there is such a mental association, the mark is not arbitrary.

B *Fanciful Marks*

Fanciful marks are "coined" or "invented" words that do not exist in any language. Fanciful marks, like arbitrary marks, do not require secondary meaning to be registered or protected because they are considered inherently distinctive. A fanciful mark is created solely for the purpose of using the term as a trademark. Fanciful marks are considered to be the strongest type of mark because they have no relation whatsoever to the good or service on or in connection with which they are used.[1947] Fanciful marks are purely made-up words.[1948]

1943. *Mobil Oil Corp. v. Pegasus Petroleum Corp.*, 818 F.2d 254 (2d Cir. 1961).
1944. *Fleischman Distilling Corp. v. Maier Brewing Co.*, 314 F.2d 149 (9th Cir. 1963) ("Black and White" for Scotch whiskey is held to be arbitrary).
1945. *Abercrombie & Fitch Co. v. Hunting World, Inc.*, 537 F.2d 4 (2d Cir. 1976) (stating arbitrary marks are strong marks).
1946. *Wynn Oil Co. v. Thomas*, 839 F.2d 1183 (6th Cir. 1988) (words that are found in the dictionary are not per se weak).
1947. *Abercrombie & Fitch Co. v. Hunting World, Inc.*, 537 F.2d 4 (2d Cir. 1976) (fanciful marks do not relate to the goods or services with which they are associated).
1948. Fanciful marks are not limited to words. They may be symbols, numbers, or letters as well.

Examples of fanciful marks include KODAK[1949] for photographic equipment, EXXON[1950] for oil and gas products, and CLOROX[1951] for bleach. Coined terms are considered to be the strongest mark possible because they are not only distinctive of the product or service on which they are used but also distinctive of any other words in any language. For this reason, fanciful marks are accorded the strongest protection available to trademarks.[1952]

C *Suggestive Marks*

A mark is "suggestive" when it suggests the goods or services but does not go so far as actually to describe them. To be suggestive, a mark must be one that requires the consumer to "conjure up" an image of the product, and the consumer does not think of the product or service immediately upon confronting the mark.[1953] This important distinction separates merely descriptive marks[1954] from suggestive marks. A suggestive mark can also be registered on the Principal Register without establishing secondary meaning, provided it is not violative of section 1052.

As with all marks in determining which category is appropriate, one must also consider the goods and services on which the mark is used because a mark may be suggestive if used on one type of good but descriptive or even arbitrary if used on another type of good. For example, ORANGE CRUSH has been held to be suggestive (not merely descriptive) when used on a flavored soda beverage[1955] and BROWN-IN-BAG has been held to be suggestive when used on a plastic bag used to cook meat.[1956]

The line between suggestive marks and descriptive marks is, of course, not clearly drawn.[1957] An underlying consideration in making this determination is whether or not the mark is necessary for competition. This fundamental policy decision will often be rather influential for courts when they determine whether a specific mark is suggestive or descriptive. If the mark is a word necessary in the industry for effective

1949. *Spraying Sys. Co. v. Delavan, Inc.*, 975 F.2d 387 (7th Cir. 1992) (coined words such as "Kodak" are fanciful).
1950. *Exxon Corp. v. Xoil Energy Resources, Inc.*, 552 F. Supp. 1008 (S.D.N.Y. 1981) (stating "Exxon" is a coined term).
1951. *Sara Lee Corp. v. Kayser-Roth Corp.*, 81 F.3d 455 (4th Cir. 1996) (stating but not holding that "Clorox" is a fanciful mark).
1952. *Id.*, at 464.
1953. *Stix Products, Inc. v. United Merchants & Manufacturers, Inc.*, 295 F. Supp. 479, 488 (S.D.N.Y. 1968) (suggestive terms require imagination; descriptive terms give an immediate idea of produce composition).
1954. Descriptive marks must have acquired secondary meaning to be registered on the principal register. *See infra* Ch. 3, §1.II. Noninherently Distinctive Marks.
1955. *Orange Crush Co. v. California Crushed Fruit Co.*, 297 F. 892 (D.C. Cir. 1924).
1956. *In re* Reynolds Metals Co., 480 F.2d 902 (C.C.P.A. 1973) ("Brown-In-Bag" bags were used for other purposes and as such could not be construed to conjure up the sole descriptive use of the good).
1957. *Franklin Knitting Mills, Inc. v. Fashonit Sweater Mills, Inc.*, 297 F. 247 (S.D.N.Y. 1923) (no clear demarcation exists between suggestive and descriptive marks, but "the validity of the mark ends where suggestion ends and description begins").

competition in the industry, it is much more likely to be found descriptive by the courts.[1958]

II Noninherently Distinctive Marks

A *Descriptive Marks*

Descriptive marks are not registrable and will not be afforded protection without establishing secondary meaning. The Lanham Act states:

> No trademark by which the goods of the applicant may be distinguished from the goods of others shall be refused registration on the principal register on account of its nature unless it—
>
> - consists of a mark which, (1)when used on or in connection with the goods of the applicant is merely descriptive ...
> - ... nothing herein shall prevent the registration of a mark used by the applicant which has become distinctive of the applicant's goods in commerce.[1959]

A descriptive mark is one that immediately conveys information regarding qualities, characteristics, or ingredients of the product without requiring any imagination on the part of the consumer.[1960]

Descriptive marks are not protectable because they consist of information that competitors need in order to sell the relevant goods or services. In this sense, descriptive marks are said to be incapable of identifying a consistent source for the goods or services because the mark may appear on the goods or services of others in order to describe the goods or an attribute of the goods or services. The trademark DOUBLE CERTIFIED ORGANIC was refused registration by the USPTO because it describes what the service accomplishes. If the mark was registrable, other producers wishing to use a repetitive certification process may be prevented from labeling the product as such.[1961] Giving one producer the right to use a descriptive term as a trademark stifles competition, which is contrary to the fundamental purpose of the Lanham Act.

Composite marks may escape designation as descriptive if the combination of their parts is not in totality descriptive. In other words, when terms normally considered descriptive on their own are combined to create a mark, the total image of

1958. *Miller Brewing Co., v. Heileman Brewing Co.*, 561 F.2d 75 (7th Cir. 1977) ("light" held to be descriptive for low calorie beer and necessary for other beer brewers to use in describing the nature of low calorie beer).

1959. 15 U.S.C. § 1052 (Lanham Act § 2).

1960. *Franklin Knitting Mills, Inc. v. Fashonit Sweater Mills, Inc.*, 297 F. 247 (S.D.N.Y. 1923) ("FASHIONIT" is merely descriptive of fashionable knit clothing).

1961. *In re* Eden Foods, 24 U.S.P.Q.2d 1757 (T.T.A.B. 1992) (refusal to register "DOUBLE CERTIFIED ORGANIC" as suggestive because it prevents other producers form claiming the same process for their pasta products).

the mark will be examined.[1962] In addition, if there are parts of a mark that are not descriptive, the mark as a whole will not be held to be descriptive.[1963]

Abbreviations or acronyms are not exempt from the analysis used to determine whether marks are descriptive. If an abbreviation or acronym merely describes a good or produces an immediate association with a characteristic or quality of the good, it will be held descriptive.[1964]

B *Secondary Meaning*

Descriptive marks may qualify for registration under the Lanham Act if they have acquired secondary meaning. Secondary meaning may be statutorily acquired through continuous and exclusive use of the mark for a period of five years.[1965] Use of the mark over a period of years creates the opportunity for an association as to source to be established between the good and the mark. If consumers come to know the mark as an indication of a source and immediately associate the mark in this manner, secondary meaning has been successfully created at any time and the registrant/owner need not wait five years to prove it.

A mark has secondary meaning when, in addition to the descriptive usage of the term, it has also come to indicate source.

The burden of proving secondary meaning is always the responsibility of the party asserting it. Proof must be clear and convincing in order to succeed in registration.[1966] Courts will consider the following evidence in determining whether a mark has secondary meaning:

- Consumer surveys.
- Success in the market.
- Duration of continuous use.
- Duration of exclusive use.
- Attempts to imitate.
- Amount spent on advertising.[1967]

1962. *In re* Disc Jockey, 23 U.S.P.Q.2d 1715 (T.T.A.B. 1992) ("DJDJ" is determined to be nondescriptive based upon the combination of the two separate DJ terms. Other users would still be able to utilize the well-known acronym "DJ" in reference to Disc Jockey).
1963. *Minnesota Mining & Mfg. Co. v. Johnson & Johnson*, 454 F.2d 1179 (C.C.P.A. 1972) ("SKINVISIBLE" tape, a combination of two descriptive terms, skin and invisible, held not to be descriptive as a combination term).
1964. *Bristol-Meyers Squibb Co. v. McNeil-P.P.C., Inc.*, 973 F.2d 1033 (2d Cir. 1992) ("PM" is determined to be descriptive of the use of the cold remedy at night).
1965. 15 U.S.C. § 1052(f) (Lanham Act § 2). A mark may acquire secondary meaning prior to the five years required under 2(f) if sufficient evidence is presented. Marks which are merely descriptive, and thus not able to be registered on the Principle Register, may be registered on the Supplemental Register if they are capable of distinguishing the owners' goods. *See infra* Ch. 4, §2.III Supplemental Register.
1966. Application of Meyer & Wenthe, Inc., 267 F.2d 945 (C.C.P.A. 1959) (level of proof required to show secondary meaning is clear and convincing).
1967. *International Kennel Club of Chicago v. Mighty Star, Inc.*, 846 F.2d 1079 (7th Cir. 1988); *Eagle Snacks v. Nabisco Brands, Inc.*, 625 F. Supp. 571 (D.N.J. 1985) (expenses in promoting

None of these factors on their own are dispositive in the determination of secondary meaning. Courts will look at this range of elements and make their determination based upon the impact on competition and whether or not the attempts to create secondary meaning have actually been effective.

C *Generic Marks*

Another noninherently distinctive mark is a generic mark. Generic marks are words that are found in the English (or other) language and amount to the very noun required for a specific product. Trademarks can be generic from inception or they can become generic through use. To make matters even more interesting, a mark can move over time on the continuum from generic to distinctive and then back again. The resolution of the precise position depends on the consumer's perception.

Regardless of whether the mark was generic from inception or became generic through use, the test today is: what is the primary significance to the relevant consumer? If the primary significance to the consumer is to identify source, the mark is valid; if the primary significance of the mark is to identify the product, the mark is generic and invalid.[1968]

Generic terms are never granted protection; acquisition of secondary meaning will not serve to make a generic mark distinctive. Granting protection to a generic term will prevent competitors from using a term necessary to identify their own goods. In the famous case involving the SHREDDED WHEAT mark, the court determined that the term "shredded wheat" was generic for the product itself and that other producers needed this term to sell their own version of the same good.[1969] To deny other competitors the right to use the word for the product itself would essentially grant a new patent to the owner. The trademark LITE for use on a beer with allegedly fewer calories is also another example of a mark that was deemed generic from its inception.[1970]

Marks can also become generic through use. This happens when the relevant mark comes to identify the goods themselves and not the producer. Examples of this are many. The most famous include the mark ASPIRIN[1971] for use on a pain reliever and CELLOPHANE[1972] for use on a plastic wrap. Trademark owners in the US must be vigilant to avoid genericism of their marks because courts are not concerned with the

goodwill lend credibility to the claim of secondary meaning, but will not necessarily prove it exists); *Mattel, Inc. v. Azrak-Hamway Int'l, Inc.*, 724 F.2d 357 (2d Cir. 1983) (surveys as an important way to determine secondary meaning); *Maternally Yours, Inc. v. Your Maternity Shop, Inc.*, 234 F.2d 538 (2d Cir. 1956) (secondary meaning is found even though there was rapid development in a short period of time).

1968. 15 U.S.C. § 1064 (Lanham Act § 14).
1969. *Kellogg Co. v. National Biscuit Co.*, 305 U.S. 111 (1938).
1970. *See Miller Brewing Co., v. Heileman Brewing Co.*, 561 F.2d 75 (7th Cir. 1977) ("light" held to be descriptive for low calorie beer and necessary for other beer brewers to use in describing the nature of low calorie beer).
1971. *Bayer Co. v. United Drug. Co.*, 272 F. 505 (S.D.N.Y. 1921).
1972. *DuPont Cellophane Co. v. Waxed Prods. Co.*, 85 F.2d 75 (2d Cir. 1936).

intent of the trademark owner; they are concerned with the effect on the marketplace and the minds of the consumers.

For example, the Court of Appeals for the Federal Circuit reversed a Trademark Trial and Appeals Board (TTAB) decision finding PRETZEL CRISPS generic in 2015 as the TTAB used a test to determine genericism where the mark was dissected into two components, "pretzel" and "crisps." The CAFC held that the appropriate analysis is to consider the mark in total and determine its impact on the consuming public. If the primary significance of the total mark is to identify source and not the product, it is a valid trademark.[1973]

The consuming public was also the focus of the analysis in *USPTO v. Booking-.com B.V.*, which was decided by the Supreme Court in 2020.[1974] In that case, the USPTO argued that combining a generic term ("booking") with a generic top-level domain (".com") will always produce a generic composite. As such the USPTO denied registration of BOOKING.COM for online hotel reservation services.[1975] However, the Supreme Court disagreed with the USPTO's analysis and stated that "whether 'Booking.com' is generic turns on whether that term, taken as a whole, signifies to consumers the class of online hotel reservation services."[1976] As the prior courts determined, and the USPTO no longer disputed, that consumers do not view the mark as a generic term for this class of services, the Court held that the mark was not generic.[1977] Therefore, the mark could be classified as descriptive and proceed to registration upon a showing of sufficient secondary meaning. This is a firm statement in support of the importance of consumer perception to classifying the strength of a trademark.

1973. *Princeton Vanguard, LLC v. Frito-Lay North Am., Inc.*, 786 F.3d 960 (Fed. Cir. 2015). However, the mark was still found to be generic by the United States District Court for the Western District of North Carolina in July 2021. *Snyder's Lance, Inc. v. Frito-Lay N. Am., Inc.*, No. 317CV00652KDBDSC, 2021 WL 2322931 (W.D.N.C. June 7, 2021).
1974. *USPTO v. Booking.com B.V.*, 140 S. Ct. 2298 (2020).
1975. *Id.*, at 2301.
1976. *Id.*, at 2304.
1977. *Id.*, at 2301.

CHAPTER 4
Formalities

§1 ADOPTION AND USE

Federal trademark rights in the US are premised upon the adoption and use of the mark in interstate commerce.[1978] Priority of rights is determined by first use, not registration (although the ITU registration is the singular exception to this rule). Therefore, the first party to use a mark in the ordinary course of trade will have priority over others who may want to use that same or similar mark on the same or similar goods. However, concurrent use is possible in remote geographic locations where no consumers will be confused. Federal registration is considered to be codification of those rights obtained via common law through priority of adoption and use.

I Priority: First to Use

Because the US trademark system is based upon use, it is important to establish priority in the use of a mark in order to obtain and enforce trademark rights. The first to use requirement is strict. Prior common law rights, based on prior use, will not be defeated by subsequent federal registrations. Use sufficient to establish priority for the purposes of the Lanham Act requires that the use be made in the ordinary course of trade and not be merely to secure or maintain trademark rights.[1979] Merely picking out or creating a mark without actually using it in commerce is not sufficient to acquire use-based rights in the mark.[1980]

1978. 15 U.S.C. § 1051(a) (Lanham Act § 1(a)).
1979. *Proctor & Gamble Co. v. Johnson & Johnson, Inc.*, 485 F. Supp. 1185 (S.D.N.Y. 1979) (trademarks may not be reserved for future use), *aff'd*, 636 F.2d 1203 (2d Cir. 1980).
1980. *Hanover Star Milling Co. v. Metcalf*, 240 US 403 (1916) (tea rose on flour limited to the geographic area where actual use is established).

Constructive nationwide first use will be conferred upon the successful applicant of an ITU application. Use priority is conferred by the Lanham Act.[1981] This is addressed in more detail in §2.II below.

II Sufficient Use

In order to gain priority in a mark, use of the mark must be "sufficient" to confer rights. For sales to constitute the requisite use, sales must be at "arm's length," meaning that the sale is actually one representing a commercial transaction and not merely an internal business deal.[1982]

Sale of a product to which the mark is attached may or may not be sufficient, depending upon the purpose and circumstances of the sale. A minimal number of sales spread over a long period of time is not necessarily sufficient to confer priority.[1983] Initial sales of a product in an effort to establish a market for the good may be sufficient to acquire rights if that use is in the ordinary course of trade.[1984] A transaction undertaken only to get the mark before the public but not an actual sale will not be enough to confer rights.[1985]

Under the 1988 Trademark Revision Act, the threshold for "use" under the Lanham Act was heightened. Prior to 1988, "token use" was sufficient to establish rights under the Act. After November 16, 1989, the effective date of the 1988 amendments, use must be "bona fide" and "in the ordinary course of trade" before rights will be established under the Lanham Act. Because the Act reads "ordinary course of trade," there is no objective amount of sales that any trademark user must attain before registration is allowed. Instead, each product in each industry will be analyzed to determine if the use in question amounts to the subjective amount of use of the applicant's product in that relevant market. For example, many thousands of candy bars would have to be sold to constitute "in the amount ordinary" for the candy bar industry; however, in the machine tool industry, only a sale of a single USD 1 million machine tool may be sufficient to establish use.

III Affixation

To satisfy the affixation requirement, a mark need only be used on or in connection with the sale of a good or service. At common law, it was necessary to "mark" or

1981. 15 U.S.C. § 1057(c) (Lanham Act § 7).
1982. *Florida v. Real Juices, Inc.*, 330 F. Supp. 428, 433 (M.D. Fla. 1971) (shipment of six cans of grapefruit juice not at arm's-length transaction is sufficient to establish use).
1983. *Sweetarts v. Sunline, Inc.*, 380 F.2d 923 (8th Cir. 1967) (minimal mail order sales of candy made in several states is not enough to confer rights in those states).
1984. *Int'l Tel. and Tel. Corp. v. Int'l Mobile Machines Corp.*, 800 F.2d 1118, 231 U.S.P.Q. 142 (Fed. Cir. 1986) (single sale is sufficient to confer rights).
1985. *Blue Bell v. Farah Mfg. Co.*, 765 F.2d 1097 (Fed. Cir. 1985) (use of trademark on goods not intended to be sold under that trademark does not confer rights in the trademark).

physically affix the trademark to the good itself.[1986] With the adoption of the Lanham Act, this requirement became much more liberal in its application. A mark need not be actually affixed to the product, but it could be part of the packaging, attached tags, or prominently displayed close to the product.[1987] A further relaxation in the requirement came with the 1988 Trademark Revision Act. If the mark is used on "documents associated with the goods or their sale" when "the nature of the goods makes such placement impracticable,"[1988] this would still be sufficient affixation for the purposes of the Lanham Act.

IV Interstate and Foreign Commerce

The Lanham Act is grounded in the Commerce Clause of the US Constitution.[1989] The Commerce Clause states that the US Congress has the authority to regulate interstate and foreign commerce.[1990] Therefore, to establish or protect trademark rights under the Lanham Act, there must not only be use of a mark but also that use must be in interstate (or foreign) commerce; mere intrastate use is insufficient.[1991]

Interstate commerce is often defined as the sale of goods over state lines. This is the easiest and most obvious case. The definition of interstate commerce, however, is broader than that for the purposes of the Lanham Act. Under the Act, one point sale of restaurant goods and services could constitute interstate commerce if the goods sold were transported across state lines and thereby "effected" interstate commerce.[1992] A good imported for sale in the US is judged by its movement through commerce once it enters the US market.[1993]

V Eleventh Amendment Concerns

Trademark law encounters special problems when a state is a party to a Lanham Act claim.[1994] Under the Eleventh Amendment states are guaranteed immunity from being sued in federal court.[1995] However, sovereign immunity is not absolute, and there are two ways a state can be sued in federal court.[1996]

1986. *Western Stove Co. v. George D. Roper Corp.*, 82 F. Supp. 206 (S.D. Cal. 1949) (affixation on goods held to have priority over use of mark in promotion).
1987. 15 U.S.C. § 1127 (Lanham Act § 45); *In re* Castelton China, Inc., 156 U.S.P.Q. 691 (T.T.A.B. 1968) (display close to goods and instantly associated with the goods sufficient to meet the affixation requirement; mere advertising not sufficient).
1988. S. Rep. No. 100-515, 100th Cong., 2d Sess. 45 (1988).
1989. U.S. Const. Art. I, § 8, cl. 3.
1990. *Heart of Atlanta Motel, Inc. v. United States*, 379 U.S. 241 (1964) (intrastate commerce which has an effect on interstate commerce is subject to regulation by Congress).
1991. 15 U.S.C. § 1051 (Lanham Act § 1).
1992. *Larry Harmon Pictures Corp. v. Williams Restaurant Corp.*, 929 F.2d 662 (Fed. Cir. 1991), *cert. denied*, 502 U.S. 823 (1991).
1993. *In re* Application of Silenus Wines, Inc., 557 F.2d 806 (C.C.P.A. 1977).
1994. *See generally*, 4 McCarthy on Trademarks and Unfair Competition §§ 25.64–66 (5th ed.).
1995. U.S. Const. amend. XI.
1996. *Coll. Sav. Bank v. Fla. Prepaid Postsecondary Educ. Expense Bd.*, 527 U.S. 666, 670 (1999).

The first circumstance in which a state can be sued in federal court is if Congress authorizes legislation to enforce the Fourteenth Amendment.[1997] In 1992, Congress passed the Trademark Remedy Clarification Act (TRCA) which attempted to remove the Eleventh Amendment immunity of a state or state agency from being sued in federal court for trademark infringement under the Lanham Act.[1998] However, in the 1999 *College Savings v. Florida Prepaid* case, the Supreme Court struck down the portion of the TRCA that authorized Lanham Act false advertising claims against a state.[1999] The Court held that a state could not be sued in federal court for false advertising in violation of Lanham Act section 43(a) because the TRCA did not validly abrogate state sovereign immunity.[2000]

The second circumstance in which a state can be sued in federal court is when a state waives its sovereign immunity.[2001] A state is generally found to waive sovereign immunity if it voluntarily invokes federal jurisdiction, or if it clearly declares that it will submit to federal jurisdiction.[2002] In *College Savings v. Florida Prepaid*, the Court rejected the argument that the state waived its Eleventh Amendment immunity by participating in commercial activities.[2003]

Waiver of sovereign immunity is not easy to show if the state is the plaintiff in a trademark case. In 2008, a Western District of Wisconsin court dismissed a nonstate defendant's counterclaim for trademark infringement against a state plaintiff based upon sovereign immunity.[2004] Even though the state plaintiff initiated the lawsuit in federal court, the court held that the state did not voluntarily invoke federal jurisdiction because it was appealing a TTAB decision canceling its mark.[2005]

§2 LANHAM ACT REGISTRATION

Registration of trademarks is accomplished through the Lanham Act, either as an application based on actual use or as an application based on the owner's intent to use the mark. Prior to the 1988 amendments, only use-based applications were allowed in the US. Subsequent to the implementation date of the 1988 amendments, a trademark

1997. *Id.*
1998. Trademark Remedy Clarification Act of 1992 (TRCA), Pub. L. No. 102-542, 106 Stat. 3567 (codified at 15 U.S.C. § 1122(b) (2006)), amending Trademark Act of 1946 (Lanham Act), 60 Stat. 441 (codified as amended at 15 U.S.C. §§ 1051–1141).
1999. 527 U.S. at 666.
2000. *Id.*, at 675. Congress can validly abrogate state sovereign immunity provided by the Eleventh Amendment in order to enforce the Fourteenth Amendment. *Id.*, at 671. In this case the plaintiff argued that the state defendant deprived the plaintiff of its property rights, guaranteed under the Due Process Clause of the Fourteenth Amendment, as a result of false advertising and a general loss of business interest security. *Id.*, at 672. However, the Court held that these were not property rights protected by the Fourteenth Amendment, and therefore Congress did not validly abrogate state sovereign immunity by the TRCA. *Id.*
2001. *Id.*, at 670.
2002. *Id.*, at 675–76.
2003. *Id.*, at 691.
2004. *Bd. of Regents of the Univ. of Wis. Sys. v. Phoenix Software, Int'l, Inc.*, 565 F. Supp. 2d 1007 (W.D. Wis. 2008).
2005. *Id.*, at 1014.

owner can either claim actual use as grounds for the federal registration or a bona fide intention to use the mark as grounds for the application. Both types of registrations confer nationwide protection and constructive notice of trademark rights to others. The applicant must choose and clearly state whether its application is a use-based application or an ITU application. Applications made under both provisions will be rejected.[2006]

I Use Applications

Application for a use-based registration may be made when a mark has already been adopted and used in commerce in the US. The user (or licensor of such use) is the only eligible party who can register a mark.[2007] All applications are filed with the USPTO in Washington, D.C. Applications must be in writing and include the following:

(1) The date of first use.
(2) The date of first use in commerce.
(3) A description of the goods on which the mark is used.
(4) A statement by the owner or a qualified representative that the mark is owned by the applicant and is not confusing with another mark.[2008]
(5) A drawing of the mark.
(6) A specimen or reproduction of the mark.
(7) The required fee.[2009]

The description of the goods on which the mark is used is critical. The scope of the registration once issued is determined by the "identification" of the goods or services. Although at common law, when enforcing a trademark against an alleged infringer, this identification of the goods or services, and the International Classification to which the mark is assigned, is not binding on any court and plays no role in the determination of infringement, claiming the appropriate goods or services are significant for many reasons. Perhaps the most important reason involves incontestability. Once a trademark has been registered and used for five years, the registration may become incontestable. Once the registration becomes incontestable, the registration itself serves as "conclusive proof" of, among other things, the owner's right to use the mark on or in connection with the sale of the goods or services identified in the registration. Clearly, if inappropriate goods are claimed in the identification of goods, the scope of the conclusive proof may be significantly narrowed.

All applications are reviewed by the USPTO to determine whether the mark meets the requirements for registration. Only trademarks which are barred by section 2 of the Lanham Act will be denied registration. The statutory bars to registration include:

2006. *In re* Gillier, 18 U.S.P.Q.2d 1973 (Comm'r of Pat. & TM 1991).
2007. 15 U.S.C. § 1051(a) (Lanham Act § 1(a)).
2008. *See infra* Ch. 6, §2.IV Concurrent Lanham Act Registration.
2009. 15 U.S.C. § 1051(a)(1–2) (Lanham Act § 1(a)(1–2)).

(a) Deceptive marks and marks that falsely suggest a connection with persons, institutions, beliefs, or national symbols.[2010]
(b) Marks which represent any national insignia.[2011]
(c) Marks which represent a living individual without that person's permission[2012] or represent a deceased President of the US during the lifetime of his widow without the widow's consent.[2013]
(d) Marks which are confusingly similar to another registered mark.[2014]
(e) Marks which are merely descriptive, deceptively misdescriptive,[2015] geographically misdescriptive[2016] or geographically deceptively misdescriptive[2017] of the applicant's goods or are of merely surname significance.[2018]
(f) Marks that are functional.[2019]

Marks which are merely descriptive, deceptively misdescriptive, or geographically misdescriptive may be registered on the Principal Register upon acquiring secondary meaning.[2020] Geographically descriptive terms may not be used as an appellation of origin for wines pursuant to the GATT Uruguay Round Treaty.[2021] Geographically deceptively misdescriptive marks cannot be registered even if secondary meaning can be shown, pursuant to the NAFTA Implementation Act.[2022] None of the other statutory bars can be overcome with secondary meaning.

Foreign applicants or US citizens not possessing US postal addresses are required to appoint a representative from the US. Any such designation is required to be identified in the application.

Upon review and acceptance by the USPTO, a mark will be published in the Official Gazette.[2023] Any party who believes that they will be damaged by a registration may file an opposition.[2024] Absent opposition, or a successful attempt to oppose a mark, the mark will be registered.[2025] The entire registration process, from application

2010. 15 U.S.C. § 1052(a) (Lanham Act § 2(a)). *See infra* Ch. 2, §2 for a discussion of why disparaging, immoral, and scandalous marks are no longer prohibited under this section of the Lanham Act.
2011. 15 U.S.C. § 1052(b) (Lanham Act § 2(b)).
2012. 15 U.S.C. § 1052(c) (Lanham Act § 2(c)).
2013. *Id.*
2014. 15 U.S.C. § 1052(d) (Lanham Act § 2(d)).
2015. 15 U.S.C. § 1052(e)(1) (Lanham Act § 2(e)(1)).
2016. 15 U.S.C. § 1052(e)(2) (Lanham Act § 2(e)(2)).
2017. 15 U.S.C. § 1052(e)(3) (Lanham Act § 2(e)(3)).
2018. 15 U.S.C. § 1052(e)(4) (Lanham Act § 2(e)(4)).
2019. 15 U.S.C. § 1052(e)(4) (Lanham Act § 2(e)(5)).
2020. *See infra* Ch. 3, §1.II.B. Secondary Meaning.
2021. Agreement on Trade-Related Aspects of Intellectual Property Rights, Apr. 15, 1994, 33 I.L.M. 81 (1994).
2022. *See supra*, Ch. 1, §3.IV.
2023. 15 U.S.C. § 1062 (Lanham Act § 12).
2024. 15 U.S.C. § 1063(a) (Lanham Act § 13(a)). Oppositions must be filed within 30 days of publication in the Official Gazette. Additional 30-day extensions may be granted by the USPTO for good cause. *Id.*
2025. 15 U.S.C. § 1063(b) (Lanham Act § 13(b)).

to registration, usually takes about eighteen months. Occasionally, marks are registered more quickly, and if any problems or oppositions are raised the process may take even longer.

II ITU Applications

The Trademark Revision Act of 1988 created an opportunity to obtain trademark rights based upon ITU applications.[2026] This represents a significant change from the previous statutory codification of common law. Prior to the 1988 amendments, there were no courts which expressly recognized a common law ITU claim. Although all other rights in the US system are based on actual use, this provision alone is based on the applicant's intent to use the mark in commerce. In ITU situations, all rights are created upon the registration of that intent, not on the actual use. Subsequent to the 1988 amendments, only one court had adopted a common law ITU cause of action where the intent to use the mark was implicitly protected without a registration.[2027]

The ITU application is similar to the actual use application. All of the information required in the use application is also required in the ITU application, except that the dates for first use and first use in commerce are omitted. Instead, the applicant must state a bona fide intention to use the mark.[2028] Naturally, because no actual use has occurred, the applicant may also not be able to provide a specimen of use.

If actual use occurs before any action on the application by an examiner (usually within three months of the actual filing date), the applicant may file an amendment to the ITU application claiming that actual use has taken place[2029] and convert the application to a standard use-based application.

All ITU applications are examined and published by the USPTO in the same manner as actual use applications and, if there is no successful opposition, a Notice of Allowance is issued rather than a Certificate of Registration.[2030]

Within six months of the date of the Notice of Allowance, the applicant must either file an affidavit claiming actual use (known as a "Statement of Use") or file a Request for an Extension of Time in which to file a Statement of Use. This time period can be extended for an additional six months without showing cause and an additional aggregate of twenty-four additional months by showing cause (for a total of thirty-six months) if the Requests for Extension of Time are timely filed.[2031] Upon completion of the review process, all ITU applications are also published in the Official Gazette[2032]

2026. 15 U.S.C. § 1051(b) (Lanham Act § 1(b)).
2027. *Maryland Stadium Authority v. Becker*, 806 F. Supp. 1236 (D. Md. 1992), *aff'd*, 36 F.3d 1093 (4th Cir. 1994) (use of "Camden Yards" in advertising and promotion prior to baseball stadium being built is held to be sufficient to confer rights), *aff'd*, 36 F.3d 1093 (4th Cir. 1994) (unpublished table decision).
2028. *Id.*
2029. 15 U.S.C. § 1051(c) (Lanham Act § 1(c)).
2030. 15 U.S.C. § 1063(b)(2) (Lanham Act § 13(b)(2)).
2031. 15 U.S.C. § 1051(d)(2) (Lanham Act § 1(d)(2)).
2032. 15 U.S.C. § 1062(a) (Lanham Act § 12(a)).

and are at that point open for opposition by parties who believe they will be harmed by the registration.

III Supplemental Register

Trademarks which are "capable of distinguishing applicants' goods or services and not registrable on the Principal Register" may be registered on the Supplemental Register.[2033] Generally speaking, marks which are not inherently distinctive and do not yet possess secondary meaning are considered appropriate for the Supplemental Register. Of course, in the US system, use of the trademark determines how courts will categorize the mark. Therefore, even if a mark is only registered on the Supplemental Register, this has no binding effect on a court's determination of whether the mark has, through use subsequent to the registration, obtained secondary meaning or even become inherently distinctive.[2034]

The Supplemental Register is available only to use-based applications and not ITU applications. Once use is claimed in a Statement of Use, the applicant can amend its application and choose the Supplemental Register instead of the Principal Register. A mark which is placed on the Supplemental Register is not published for opposition but is published in the Official Gazette. As any other trademark, a mark registered on the Principal Register is subject to cancelation upon a finding of confusion with another registered mark. A mark on the Supplemental Register which is found to have been abandoned will be canceled and removed from the Register.[2035]

§3 MAINTENANCE

Marks registered on the Principal Register must be maintained or they will be canceled by the USPTO.

I Registration Duration and Initial Renewal

The term of protection provided today under the Lanham Act is ten years. Marks registered under the Lanham Act prior to the effective date of the 1988 amendments (November 16, 1989) were valid for twenty years. Provided the registered mark is used on or in connection with the goods or services identified in the registration, the registration may be renewed for an unlimited number of ten-year period. If a renewal application is not filed with the USPTO during the period that commences six months

2033. 15 U.S.C. § 1091(a) (Lanham Act § 23(a)).
2034. *California Cooler, Inc. v. Loretto Winery, Ltd.*, 774 F.2d 1451 (9th Cir. 1985) (registration of "California Cooler" on Supplemental Register does not preclude owner from asserting proof of secondary meaning later).
2035. 15 U.S.C. § 1092 (Lanham Act § 24).

prior to the expiration date of the registration and ends three months after the expiration date of the registration, the USPTO will cancel the registration.[2036]

II Continuing Use Affidavits

In the initial term of registration, each registrant must file a Continuing Use Affidavit (also known as a "Section 8 Affidavit") during the fifth year of registration. Effective October 30, 1999, section 8 Affidavits are also now required in the final year of registration prior to an application to renew the mark on the Principal Register. If a section 8 Affidavit is not timely filed, the USPTO will cancel the registration.[2037] A section 8 Affidavit must claim that the mark is still being used in commerce on or in connection with the goods or services identified in the registration. Any gaps in continued use must be explained by the owner. Only nonuse due to special circumstances will be excusable.[2038] A section 8 Affidavit must be filed only in the initial term of registration. During subsequent terms of registration, section 8 Affidavits are not required.

III Loss of Trademark Rights

A *Abandonment*

Abandonment of a mark is ground for any party to move the USPTO to cancel a registered trademark. Abandoned trademarks are also not protectable under the common law. Abandonment is defined under the Lanham Act as discontinuing use of a mark with an intent not to resume such use.[2039] An intent to abandon will be inferred if the mark is not used for a period of three years. Use of a mark means the bona fide use of a mark in the ordinary course of trade and not mere token use to reserve rights in or to a mark. As discussed below, "abandonment" may also result from a mark becoming generic, or from failure of the owner to "police" the mark, or from assignment of the mark "in gross."

Abandonment differs from acquiescence. Acquiescence is a claim made by one party in a particular suit, while abandonment represents a complete loss of trademark rights and commits the trademark at issue to the public domain.[2040]

B *Voluntary Termination*

Any trademark registration may be voluntarily surrendered by voluntary cancelation[2041] or an intentional discontinuation of use.[2042] If the registrant specifically intends

2036. 15 U.S.C. § 1059 (Lanham Act § 9).
2037. 15 U.S.C. § 1058(a) (Lanham Act § 8(a)).
2038. 15 U.S.C. § 1058(b)(2) (Lanham Act § 8(b)(2)).
2039. 15 U.S.C. § 1127 (Lanham Act § 45).
2040. *Defiance Button Machine Co. v. C & C Metal Products Corp.*, 759 F.2d 1053 (2d Cir. 1985) (explaining abandonment as a complete loss of rights).
2041. 15 U.S.C. § 1057(e) (Lanham Act § 7).

to terminate the registration, the registrant need only surrender the registration to the USPTO for cancelation and the USPTO will correct the Principal Register accordingly.

C *Involuntary Termination: Genericism*

Involuntary termination of a registration occurs primarily when a registered mark becomes a generic term and ceases to indicate source. As stated above, a mark is generic when it primarily identifies the product on which it is used and not the source.[2043]

A petition to cancel a registered trademark must be filed within five years of the date of registration. It may be filed by anyone who feels they will be damaged by the registration. Such cancelation petition may be filed more than five years after the date of registration if it is based on the following grounds:

(1) The registered mark has become the generic term for the goods or services identified in the registration.
(2) The mark has been abandoned.
(3) The registration was obtained fraudulently.
(4) If a collective mark, the mark has been used by the collective on its own goods or services; if a certification mark, the registrant does not control the mark, the registrant engages in the production or marketing of goods on which the certification mark is used, permits use of the certification mark for reasons other than to certify and/or discriminately refuses to certify.
(5) The mark violates sections: (a) (deceptive marks); (b) (marks consisting of or comprising a flag, coat of arms or other national insignia); and (c) (marks which comprise or consist of the name or portrait of a particular living individual or the name, signature or portrait of a deceased president without the widow's consent) of section 1052 of the Lanham Act.

D *Expungement and Reexamination*

The TMA of 2020 created two new ex parte proceedings through which third parties can challenge trademark registrations based on allegations of nonuse.[2044] Such petitions can be based on allegations that the registrant has not used the mark at all, or has not used the mark in some of the listed goods or services classifications.

2042. *La Maur v. Block*, 176 U.S.P.Q. 218 (T.T.A.B. 1972) (mark abandoned for tax reasons).
2043. 15 U.S.C. § 1127 (Lanham Act § 45).
2044. 15 U.S.C. § 1066(a).

CHAPTER 5
Ownership and Transfer

§1 INITIAL OWNERSHIP

As indicated above, trademarks in the US are "owned" by the entity that first adopts, fixes and uses a trademark in commerce. However, in a common law system such as the US, the mark itself is not subject to property ownership. Rather, the first user of a mark in the US owns the right to exclude others from using the mark to the extent they have used the mark themselves.

The federal trademark registration issues to the owner of this trademark right (the right to exclude others). If a registration issues to a second user, the first user can oppose the application or move the USPTO within five years of the date of registration to cancel the registration. Once the mark is canceled, the first user can then file its own trademark registration application.

Although the proper owner of the trademark right is usually determined simply by ascertaining who used the mark in interstate commerce first, occasionally two or more entities may have concurrently used a trademark. For example, if a musical band adopts a trademark, writes and records songs, and then splits up, often times the issue of who owns the rights to the mark is an open question. In most instances, the party that controlled the mark would be considered the owner. However, in *Bell v. Streetwise Records, Ltd.*,[2045] the court determined that in such a situation, if neither party had registered the mark, ownership should be determined by the consuming public. Therefore, if the consuming public came to associate the band members themselves, for example, as the source of the goods or services, rather than the producer, the band members would be considered the owners of the mark regardless of how much time and money the producer invested in promoting the band.

2045. 640 F. Supp. 575 (D. Mass. 1986).

§2 ASSIGNMENT OF TRADEMARKS

Contrary to many Civil Law systems such as Japan,[2046] France, and Germany, trademarks in the US are not assignable in gross. That is, in most Civil Law systems, the trademark can be assigned without assigning the goodwill associated with the specific trademark. In the US, an assignment of a trademark without the appurtenant goodwill is invalid, and, if coupled with a cessation of use by the assignor, will usually result in an abandonment of the trademark.

An ITU application may not be assigned until a statement of use is filed with the USPTO and it is converted to a use-based application. The trademark in the US is a right to use a mark and the right to exclude others from using the mark. Therefore, unless actual use occurs and at least some goodwill is established, there is nothing to assign because all rights in the US are said to be premised on use, not registration.

§3 LICENSING OF TRADEMARKS

Trademarks may be licensed to third parties, but the licensor must retain the right to control the quality of the resulting products. This provision is known as "quality control" and must be expressly included in the language of any license agreement. If the licensor does not expressly retain quality control rights, a "naked" license results. A naked license may be inferred if a trademark owner does not police the use of its mark and allows others to use it without providing oversight.[2047] In either case, an abandonment will result and the trademark owner will lose all trademark rights.

The quality control requirement envisioned in the Lanham Act does not require that the licensor actually controls the business of the licensee.[2048] Rather, it is merely necessary to either have the latent ability to control the use of the mark or actually control the use of the mark to the extent reasonably necessary to ensure that the consumer will be able to rely on an established level of quality.[2049]

2046. *See* Kenneth L. Port, Japanese Trademark Jurisprudence (1998).

2047. *Yokum v. Covington*, 216 U.S.P.Q. 210 (T.T.A.B. 1982) (original owner of mark "Pied Pipers" abandoned the trademark by failing to monitor the mark's use by others).

2048. *Oberlin v. Marlin American Corp.*, 596 F.2d 1322 (7th Cir. 1979) (Lanham Act did not intend to create an agency requirement for licensors; day to day oversight is not required).

2049. *Kentucky Fried Chicken Corp. v. Diversified Packaging Corp.*, 549 F.2d 368 (5th Cir. 1977) (KFC's monitoring of packaging producers is sufficient to show control).

CHAPTER 6
Scope of Exclusive Rights

§1 EXTRATERRITORIALITY

In its 2023 decision in the case of *Arbitron Austria GmbH v. Hetronic International, Inc.*, the Supreme Court confirmed that the Lanham Act is only intended to apply to trademark infringement where the allegedly infringing "use in commerce" is domestic.[2050] This resolved a circuit split about the ability of US courts to address trademark infringement where the allegedly infringing sales and confusion occurred abroad but harm to the trademark owner was felt within the United States.[2051] While extraterritorial conduct may be regulated in some instances by Congress under the Commerce Clause, the Supreme Court clarified that the Lanham Act did not include an intent to be applied to extraterritorial conduct. As such, the presumption against extraterritorial application of US statutes applies.

§2 INCONTESTABILITY

"Incontestability" under the Lanham Act is premised on the notion that at some point, trademark owners essentially should be able to quiet title and rely on the registration as proof that no other party has superior rights in or to the relevant trademark. Therefore section 33(a) of the Lanham Act states that once a trademark has been registered for at least five years and certain formalities, addressed below, are completed by the registrant, the registration becomes conclusive evidence of the validity of the mark, the validity of the registration, the registrant's ownership of the mark and the registrant's exclusive right to use the mark on or in connection with the identified goods or services.[2052] As will be made clear below, there are many strategic reasons

2050. *Arbitron Austria GmbH v. Hetronic International, Inc.*, 600 U.S. _ (2023).
2051. The Arbitron Court expressly rejected the "effects test" promulgated by the Supreme Court in 1952 in *Steele v. Bulova Watch Co.*, 344 U.S. 280 (1952).
2052. 15 U.S.C. § 1115(b) (Lanham Act § 33(b)).

why all trademark registrants should take the necessary steps to take advantage of incontestability.

I Mechanics

A trademark registration may become incontestable if the mark is used for five continuous years in commerce in the US and the registrant files what is known as a section 15 Affidavit after section 15 of the Lanham Act.[2053] Section 15 Affidavits are not reviewed in the same manner as an application. The USPTO acknowledges the affidavit and records the filing but does not substantively review the claims in the section 15 Affidavit for accuracy and requires no supporting documentation or other evidence corroborating the claim made.[2054] Although actual abuse of this fact appears rare, many significant rights are granted to the registrant via an incontestable registration in response to the section 15 Affidavit.

II Defensive Use of Incontestable Registrations

There are two ways a registrant might use an incontestable registration:

(1) offensively to claim the mark is strong; and
(2) defensively to claim that the mark is beyond certain attacks.[2055]

The rationale behind the defensive use of incontestability centers on the fact that incontestability was originally envisioned as a way to insulate registered trademarks from frivolous claims of invalidity. Although the word "incontestable" is used, it is not intended to be absolutely incontestable. The following conditions apply even to incontestable registrations:

(1) The registration may be canceled if it or the incontestable right was obtained fraudulently.
(2) The registration may be canceled if the mark has been abandoned by the registrant.
(3) The registration may be canceled if the mark is being used to misrepresent the source or origin of the identified goods or services.
(4) An incontestable mark may still be used by any third party if such use is in a fair use, descriptive manner.
(5) The owner of an incontestable registration may not interfere with rights created in third parties via use by the third party prior to the registration of the mark.

2053. 15 U.S.C. § 1065 (Lanham Act § 15).
2054. TMEP § 1605.
2055. *Park 'N Fly, Inc. v. Dollar Park & Fly, Inc.*, 469 U.S. 189 (1985) (a mark which is incontestable is not subject to cancelation on "merely descriptive" challenges).

(6) The owner of an incontestable registration does not have absolute rights over a previously registered and used trademark in regional areas.
(7) The owner of an incontestable registration may not use the mark to violate the antitrust laws of the US.
(8) Equitable principles such as laches, estoppel and acquiescence apply to incontestable registrations as well.
(9) Incontestability will not apply to a trademark that has become generic or functional.[2056]

III Offensive Use of Incontestability

The mere use of an incontestable mark by a defendant is not per se infringement. Rather, even incontestable marks are subject to proof of infringing conduct. In considering whether a mark is infringed, US courts consider whether there is a likelihood of confusion as to the source, origin, or sponsorship of goods or services. To determine if there is a likelihood of confusion, courts consider, among other things, whether the plaintiff's trademark is strong or weak. Clearly, a strong mark should be afforded more protection than a weak mark.

There is uncertainty in the federal circuits regarding the offensive use of an incontestable trademark.[2057] Some circuits find that if the plaintiff's registered trademark is incontestable, the mark is presumptively a strong mark;[2058] some other circuits find that incontestability has no bearing on whether a mark is strong or weak during an infringement analysis.[2059]

Therefore, based on the evidentiary advantage that incontestability provides a registrant with regard to challenges to the registration's validity, the registrant is strongly advised to seek incontestability as soon as possible. Also, there is enough uncertainty in the application of incontestability in an offensive manner in infringement litigation that all plaintiffs should be encouraged to obtain incontestability before filing suit to claim whatever advantages that may be possible in that given jurisdiction.

§3 TERRITORIAL SCOPE OF TRADEMARK RIGHTS

I The Common Law Market Penetration Rule

Under the common law, the first user of a trademark has the right to use the mark and exclude others from using a trademark to the extent the first comer has both

2056. 15 U.S.C. § 1115(b) (Lanham Act § 33(b)).
2057. Kenneth L. Port, *The Illegitimacy of Trademark Incontestability*, 26 IND. L. REV. 519, 570 (1993).
2058. *Dieter v. B. & H. Indus. of Southwest Fla.*, 880 F.2d 322 (11th Cir. 1989) ("Shutterworld" as an incontestable mark is held to be at least "descriptive with secondary meaning and therefore a relatively strong mark").
2059. *Munters Corp. v. Matsui America, Inc.*, 909 F.2d 250 (7th Cir. 1990) (incontestability of trademark registration is not conclusive evidence of mark's strength).

horizontally and vertically used the mark.[2060] Vertical use refers to market analysis. Different vertical use implies that one party uses the mark, for example, in the retail market and the other party uses the mark in the wholesale market.[2061] Horizontal use implies geographic or regional use. Therefore, a subsequent user under the common law could enter the market using the same or similar mark on the same or similar goods and not infringe the first comer's rights if the use was either horizontally or vertically remote. Unless there is a showing of intentional adoption of another's mark to injure the prior user, there is no infringement at common law.[2062]

Therefore, even if a first user adopted a mark in the eastern part of the US on certain drugs, the common law would not prevent the use of the same or similar mark on the same or similar goods by a third party, for example, in the southern part of the US if such adoption and use were not done intentionally for the purposes of unfair competition.[2063] Similarly, if a mark is used only in wholesale, such prior use may not be a bar to a subsequent user from adopting the same or similar mark for use on the same or similar goods or services in the retail market for those goods or services.[2064]

II Scope of Concurrent Use Common Law Rights

A *Good Faith*

If a junior user adopts the same or similar mark with the intention of unfair competition, its rights to the mark may be limited despite the market penetration rule. Analysis of good faith is made at the point of adoption and first use of the mark.[2065] Good faith has not been unanimously defined within the circuits. The Tenth Circuit states that knowledge alone is not indicative of bad faith in adopting a mark, and that some evidence of intent to confuse must be present in order to find bad faith.[2066]

2060. *Hanover Star Milling Co. v. Metcalf*, 240 U.S. 403 (U.S. 1916) (territory where use has been established carves out rights in all segments of trade).
2061. *Dawn Donut Co. v. Hart's Food Stores, Inc.*, 267 F.2d 358 (2d Cir. 1959) (sales in retail and wholesale markets).
2062. *Hanover Star Milling Co. v. Metcalf*, 240 U.S. 403 (U.S. 1916).
2063. *United Drug Co. v. Theodore Rectanus Co.*, 248 U.S. 90 (1918) (adoption of "Rexall" by junior user was in an area distant to senior user and done without intention to trade on the goodwill of the senior user).
2064. *Dawn Donut Co. v. Hart's Food Stores, Inc.*, 267 F.2d 358 (2d Cir. 1959) (senior user may expand into a different segment of the market at a later time once rights are established).
2065. *Allied Telephone Co., Inc. v. Allied Telephone Systems Co.*, 565 F. Supp. 211 (S.D. Ohio. 1982) (at the time the junior user adopted the mark, the senior user was using another name). For a thorough discussion of the good faith requirement of a remote, junior user when such use occurred prior to registration, *see Stone Creek, Inc. v. Omnia Italian Design, Inc.*, 2017 U.S. App. LEXIS 12393 (9th Cir. Ariz. July 11, 2017).
2066. *GTE Corp. v. Williams*, 904 F.2d 536 (10th Cir. 1990) (intent to benefit from a senior user is required).

B Remoteness

Remoteness has taken on a different meaning as time has passed. At the time of the Hanover Star Milling decision,[2067] the ability to transport goods and the ability to communicate with the consumers were limited. In 1916, Tennessee may have appeared to be "remote" from the Northeast. Today, remoteness is much more difficult to establish because almost all consumers are extremely mobile in their pursuit of goods or services. Furthermore, the Internet also allows virtually immediate presence for any competitor in any market. The north woods of Minnesota is no longer "remote" if one has a cellular telephone and a computer. Therefore, many businesses today will be conferred a rather large geographic area of expansion and the common law market penetration rule may soon become obsolete.[2068]

C Market Penetration

The common law scope of protection is defined by the degree to which the trademark owner has penetrated the market. Each circuit court tends to use different factors in analyzing the extent to which the market has been penetrated. For example, the Eighth Circuit implements the following four-factor test: volume of sales; customer ratio to population; growth potential; and duration of any lapse in significant sales.[2069] On the other hand, the Fourth Circuit will analyze sales volume; identification of any growth trends; population in relation to potential customers; and product advertising.[2070]

In the end, the analysis is essentially the same: the common law allows trademark owners the right to exclude others, but only to the extent that the owner itself has used the mark. Therefore, there needs to be some objective criteria to determine to what extent the owner of the mark has penetrated the market and, therefore, the extent to which it deserves common law protection.

D Natural Zone of Expansion

In addition to the actual extent of market penetration, most courts in the US will also allow for a natural zone of expansion to protect not only the actual extent of the trademark owner's use but also the next logical step in the marketing and selling of its goods or services. However, all circuit courts are not in accord with what factors to analyze when considering the natural zone of expansion and what weight to give each element. For example, the Eleventh Circuit draws the boundary for trademark rights rather liberally and draws the line of natural expansion rather broadly. This court has

2067. *Hanover Star Milling Co. v. Metcalf*, 240 U.S. 403 (1916).
2068. *Travelodge Corp. v. Siragusa*, 228 F. Supp. 238 (N.D. Ala. 1964) (expansion "concept" held to be sufficient to prove expansion is likely).
2069. *Sweetarts v. Sunline, Inc.*, 436 F.2d 705 (8th Cir. 1971) (Sweetarts market penetration into several states was not sufficient to usurp Sunline's concurrent expansion).
2070. *Natural Footwear, Ltd., v. Hart, Schaffner & Markx*, 760 F.2d 1383 (3d Cir. 1985) (no market penetration is established by junior user).

stated that if a senior user can demonstrate that the junior user resides in an area which they can reasonably expand, the senior user even reserves rights in that area.[2071] A more narrow view is stated by the First Circuit, which has held that if a senior user fails to register its trademark, and it is subsequently innocently adopted by a junior user, the senior user's rights will be very narrowly construed.[2072]

E Relevance of State Boundaries

Although the court in Hanover Star Milling claimed that state boundaries had some significance in determining the scope of rights in common law marks, today, state boundaries will be rather inconsequential in setting the scope of protection for unregistered trademarks.[2073] Today, the real consideration is the extent to which consumers have been exposed to the relevant trademark. Because the nature of commerce in the US has changed so radically in the last fifty years due to the implementation of technological advances in transportation, communication, and marketing, state boundaries are becoming less and less relevant in determining the geographic scope of unregistered trademarks.[2074]

F Secondary Meaning Marks

Trademarks without secondary meaning are merely descriptive marks. As such, they are not afforded the various protections of either the common law or the Lanham Act. Therefore, if a mark lacks secondary meaning, it will not be afforded any expansion of protection considered above. Just as secondary meaning must be established to gain protection of the mark, it must also be established in order to form a basis for expansion of the rights in or to that mark.[2075]

If a mark is inherently distinctive (a suggestive, fanciful or, arbitrary mark), courts are likely to give the mark broad protection even if the mark lacks secondary meaning;[2076] however, the courts have been inconsistent in articulating a definition of inherently distinctive trade dress. In *Wal-Mart Stores, Inc. v. Samara Bros., Inc.*,[2077] the Supreme Court created at least two categories of trade dress: product design and product packaging. It held that a showing of secondary meaning was required in all

2071. *Tally-Ho, Inc. v. Coast Community College District*, 889 F.2d 1018 (11th Cir. 1989) (proof of a natural bridge to "related use" markets solidifies the rights of the senior user).
2072. *Raxton Corp. v. Anania Associates, Inc.*, 635 F.2d 924 (1st Cir. 1980), *on remand*, 668 F.2d 662 (1st Cir. 1982) (senior user was unable to establish any prior use or reputation in the area of the junior user's business).
2073. *Burger King of Florida Inc. v. Hoots*, 403 F.2d 904 (7th Cir. 1968) (senior user in Illinois limited to a small geographic area of priority).
2074. *Spartan Food Systems, Inc. v. HFS Corp.*, 813 F.2d 1279 (4th Cir. 1987).
2075. *Shoppers Fair of Arkansas, Inc. v. Sanders Co.*, 328 F.2d 496 (8th Cir. 1964) (lack of secondary meaning in the new market will preclude a finding of rights in the mark).
2076. *Two Pesos, Inc. v. Taco Cabana Int'l, Inc.*, 505 U.S. 763 (1992), *reh'g denied*, 505 U.S. 1244 (1992).
2077. 529 U.S. 205, 120 (2000).

cases of product design trade dress, and such a showing was only sometimes required for product packaging trade dress.

III Effects of Federal Registration

Federal registration affords important benefits to the registrant, affecting the power and scope of the mark.

A *Constructive Notice: Post Registration Use*

Registration of a trademark on the Principal or Supplemental Registers provides nationwide constructive notice of the owner's claim to rights in the mark.[2078] Once registered, all subsequent applications for registration that would cause confusion, mistake, or deception (as well as all other bars enumerated in section 2 of Lanham Act) should be denied registration by the USPTO. For ITU applications, the effective date of the notice reverts back to the date the application was filed once a Notice of Allowance issues. Once a plaintiff's mark is registered, the defense of innocent infringement is usually no longer available to the defendant in an infringement cause of action. Some courts apply a strict interpretation to the effect of registration. The Second Circuit has held that if the plaintiff's mark is registered, it is impossible for a subsequent user to adopt the same or similar mark for use on the same or similar goods in good faith.[2079] That is, in some settings, courts will infer bad faith or wrongful intent for adopting a mark that was previously registered by another party. It is thought that this evidentiary advantage reduces the number of conflicting marks by encouraging applicants to search the USPTO's records prior to filing their trademark applications, thereby reducing the number of conflicts over use of marks.

B *Freezing the Junior User's Market*

One of the most effective important results of registration under the Lanham Act is that five years after registration is effected, a trademark registration may become incontestable as discussed above.[2080] Once a registration is incontestable, the provisions of section 33(b)(5) apply. Therefore, if party A is the first to use a mark in commerce in the US and party B subsequently uses the same or similar mark on the same or similar goods, and party A registers the mark after party B first uses the mark but before party B registers the mark, then the full effect of nationwide rights granted under the Lanham Act takes effect on the date A's trademark application is published for opposition. Accordingly, on the date of publication, B's common law rights to use the mark are terminated except to the extent that B has continuously used the mark up to the date

2078. 15 U.S.C. § 1072 (Lanham Act § 22).
2079. *Dawn Doughnut Company, Inc. v. Hart's Foods Stores, Inc.*, 267 F.2d 358 (2d Cir. 1959) (§ 1072 eliminates the good faith defense by providing constructive notice of use).
2080. *See supra*, Ch. 6, §1 Incontestability.

that A's mark is published. B will be required to relinquish all market shares and use that it may have obtained[2081] subsequent to that date.

IV Concurrent Lanham Act Registration

If two different entities establish rights in the same or similar mark on the same or similar goods through concurrent use of a mark but no confusion is likely because the relevant uses have been geographically remote, the Lanham Act allows two or more parties to own such "concurrent" registrations.[2082] The test in this regard remains whether the consumer is likely to be confused. Given the nature of markets and consumers today, concurrent registrations should probably be granted only in the most extreme cases.

A First User's Rights

If a subsequent user attempts or even succeeds in registering its trademark prior to the first user, the first user can oppose the application or petition the USPTO to cancel the mark within five years from the date of the registration. In the US, all rights are supposed to be derived from use. Therefore, the first party to use a mark in commerce should have the right to register the mark first. However, in some rare instances, if both parties have established mark awareness in geographically remote areas, the USPTO may grant a concurrent use registration. A concurrent use registration effectively carves up the nation and assigns each party a particular area in which they can use the mark.[2083]

B Correction of the Register by Federal Courts

Contrary to most Civil Law jurisdictions where the courts do not have the authority to cancel registered trademarks or issue orders affecting the relevant trademark registry,[2084] the Lanham Act allows any federal court to order that the Principal Register be corrected to conform to its holdings regarding concurrent use.[2085] The Sixth Circuit has held that federal courts may hear and decide concurrent use controversies.[2086] Once a court has ordered the issuance of a concurrent use registration, the USPTO enforces the decision by issuing the necessary concurrent use registrations.[2087]

2081. *Burger King of Florida, Inc. v. Hoots*, 403 F.2d 904 (7th Cir. 1968) (junior user limited to the small geographic area where they have established business); *Thrifty Rent-A-Car System v. Thrift Cars, Inc.*, 831 F.2d 1177 (1st Cir. 1987) (limited exception of use in remote area established by junior user after senior user but prior to senior user's federal registration).
2082. 15 U.S.C. § 1052(d) (Lanham Act § 2(d)).
2083. *In re* Beatrice Foods Co., 429 F.2d 466 (C.C.P.A. 1970).
2084. Kenneth L. Port, Japanese Trademark Jurisprudence (1998).
2085. 15 U.S.C. § 1052(d) (Lanham Act § 2(d)).
2086. *Old Dutch Foods, Inc. v. Dan Dee Pretzel & Potato Chip Co.*, 477 F.2d 150 (6th Cir. 1973).
2087. *Holiday Inn v. Holiday Inns, Inc.*, 534 F.2d 312 (C.C.P.A. 1976).

§4 PRODUCT AND SERVICE SCOPE

The trademark rights in the US are premised on the basic common law understanding that mark users may exclude others from using the mark to the extent that they, the first user, have used the mark. Therefore, as discussed above, the scope of trademark protection is not absolute. Rather, if a second-comer's use is geographically remote, the prior user may not be able to interfere with that use. Likewise, if the products on which a third party uses the mark are sufficiently distinct so that no competition is likely between the sellers of the two relevant products, the first comer should not be able to prevent such use either.

That is, in the US, confusion is supposed to be impossible unless the two parties are in competition.[2088] This is because trademark law is a subset of the larger unfair competition law. Trademark protection is justified in the US only in connection with the basic mandate that producers must compete fairly so that consumers are not harmed by the resulting confusion as to the source or origin of the relevant goods or services.

§5 DILUTION

The only exception to this common law rule is found in the provisions of section 43(c)[2089] of the Lanham Act, which creates a federal cause of action for trademark dilution. As stated above, dilution is defined as the lessening of the capacity of a famous mark to identify or distinguish the good or services regardless of competition between the parties or the likelihood of confusion, mistake, or deception.[2090] If a second-comer's mark is likely to cause dilution, the owner of a famous mark may sue to obtain an injunction to such use.

Unlike trademark infringement, which has its roots in common law, trademark dilution is a creature of statute. The current version of the Lanham Act was modified to recognize dilution first by the FTDA of 1995, and then again by the TDRA of 2006. Thirty-eight states have also adopted dilution statutes.[2091] These statutes are an

2088. Determining when two parties are in competition has been a particularly vexing issue for courts. Initially, head-to-head competition was required before trademark infringement was allowed. This changed with *Aunt Jemima Mills Co. v. Rigney & Co.*, 247 F. 407 (2d Cir. 1917). Now known as the "Aunt Jemima Doctrine," this case stands for the proposition that two companies need not be in head-to-head competition for precisely the same products. Rather, if the consumer believes the two products at issue come from the same source, the definition of competition for confusion analysis has been satisfied. This has now been expanded into the "bridging the gap" doctrine where even if a company is not selling in the defendant's market at all, if it had real plans to do so, this would be sufficient to satisfy the definition of competition for the confusion analysis. Therefore, the use of the word "competition" in this sentence must be considered in this context.

2089. 15 U.S.C. § 1125(c) (Lanham Act § 43(c)).

2090. 15 U.S.C. § 1127 (Lanham Act § 45).

2091. Most states base their dilution statutes on the relevant provisions of the 1964, 1992, 1996 or 2007 versions of the Model State Trademark Bill.

important departure from the historical roots of trademark protection in that they serve to protect the rights of the mark owner, not the consuming public.

The Lanham Act identifies two kinds of dilution: dilution by blurring and dilution by tarnishment. Blurring involves the "whittling away of an established trademark's selling power through unauthorized use by others upon dissimilar products."[2092] Tarnishment occurs when a plaintiff's trademark is associated with products of lesser quality or is presented to the consumer in some derogatory manner.[2093] In such a case, the plaintiff's reputation may suffer in the minds of its consumers.

The drafters of section 43(c) considered the use of "Buick" on aspirin or "Kodak" on pianos as examples of dilution. Once a mark has become very well known, if others merely use the mark on unrelated products, such use will drastically lessen the distinctiveness of the well-known mark. Kodak is a very distinctive mark for the very reason that one sees no other use of the mark on products not emanating from Kodak. If there were many examples of Kodak brand pianos, Kodak brand bicycles, Kodak brand tires, etc., the distinctiveness of Kodak as a trademark to identify one source would be lessened and its value as a trademark would correspondingly decrease.

I Fame

Like all trademark rights, the right to claim one's mark has been diluted is not absolute. The most important fact requirement is that only "famous" marks can take advantage of section 43(c). Under that section, a mark is famous if it is "widely recognized by the general consuming public of the United States."[2094] It is important to note that there are three elements to this definition: wide recognition, recognition by the general consuming public, and recognition in the US. The wide recognition requirement is, of course, amorphous.[2095] However, it does indicate that fame within a geographically limited market is insufficient to merit the protection of the Act.[2096] The requirement that the mark be recognized by the general consuming public specifically does away with "niche fame."[2097] The requirement that the consuming public must be in the US means that marks famous outside of the US will not be eligible for dilution protection.

The TDRA lays out four nonexclusive factors for courts to consider when determining whether a mark has the requisite degree of distinctiveness:

(1) The duration, extent, and geographic reach of advertising and publicity of the mark, whether advertised or publicized by the owner or third parties.

2092. *Mead Data Central, Inc. v. Toyota Motor Sales, U.S.A., Inc.* 875 F.2d 1026, 1031 (2d Cir. 1989).
2093. *Acad. of Motion Picture Arts and Scis. v. Creative House Promotions, Inc.*, 944 F.2d 1446, 1457 (9th Cir. 1991) (if the appearance of the defendant's STAR award is poor or cheap, the Oscar's value as a "symbol of excellence ... is threatened").
2094. 15 U.S.C. § 1125(c)(2)(A) (Lanham Act § 43(c)(2)(A)).
2095. Some state dilution statutes also have "famous in this state" language or no fame requirement at all, which further complicates matters.
2096. *USTA Report*, 77 Trademark Rep. at 460; 1995 House Rep. at 7 ("[t]he geographic fame of a mark must extend throughout a substantial portion of the U.S.").
2097. *USTA Report*, 77 Trademark Rep. at 460.

(2) The amount, volume, and geographic extent of sales of goods or services offered under the mark.
(3) The extent of actual recognition of the mark.
(4) Whether the mark was registered under the Act of March 3, 1881, or the Act of February 20, 1905, or on the Principal Register.[2098]

Unfortunately, past applications of the rule that marks need to be famous before the dilution principles apply have been, to say the least, rather inconsistent. For example, the Ninth Circuit has found that "Fruit" as in "Fruit of the Loom" is not famous for the purposes of dilution; whereas, the district court in Pennsylvania has held that the mark "WAWA" for use on convenience stores is famous enough to apply the dilution rationale. It remains to be seen what effect, if any, TDRA will have on bringing a measure of uniformity to fame analysis.

II Dilution Likelihood

The test for whether or not the injunction contemplated under section 43(c) should issue was first articulated in a concurring opinion (discussing New York law) in *Mead Data Central v. Toyota Motor Sales, U.S.A., Inc.*[2099]

Today, proving dilution is still difficult, and the dilution doctrine remains puzzling. Before *Moseley v. V Secret Catalogue,*[2100] the federal circuits were split on two points concerning dilution: (1) whether the Dilution Act requires proof of "actual dilution"; and (2) whether dilution (actual dilution or likelihood of dilution) must be proven directly or by circumstantial evidence.[2101]

To determine a likelihood of dilution, courts had looked at the following factors:

(1) Renown of senior mark.
(2) Similarity of marks.
(3) Similarity of products.
(4) Predatory intent.
(5) Renown of junior mark.
(6) Sophistication of buyers.

In Moseley, the Supreme Court held that the Dilution Act "unambiguously requires a showing of actual dilution, rather than a likelihood of dilution."[2102] However, the Court also stated "that direct evidence of dilution such as surveys will not

2098. 15 U.S.C. § 1125(c)(2)(A) (Lanham Act § 43(c)(2)(A)). These four factors are from the TDRA, and replaced the original eight factors of the FTDA.
2099. 875 F.2d 1026 (2d Cir. 1989).
2100. 537 U.S. 418 (2003).
2101. *See* Thomas R. Lee, *Demystifying Dilution*, 84 B. U. L. Rev. 859, 863 (2004).
2102. *Moseley*, 537 U.S. at 434.

be necessary if actual dilution can reliably be proved through circumstantial evidence."[2103]

Apparently dissatisfied with this result, Congress specified in the TDRA that actual dilution was not required.[2104] The TDRA does not address the type of evidence needed to prove likelihood of dilution, however, so Moseley would appear to still be good law in this respect.

On remand, Victoria's Secret finally prevailed in showing that the use of the term "Victor's Little Secret" on sex toys tarnished Victoria's Secret mark.[2105]

III Dilution by Blurring

As discussed above, the fame of a trademark is blurred when used by a junior party who "whittles away" at the associations the general public has toward the mark. The TDRA defines dilution by blurring as "association arising from the similarity between a mark or trade name and a famous mark that impairs the distinctiveness of the famous mark."[2106] The TDRA also provided six nonexclusive factors for courts to consider when determining dilution by blurring:

- The degree of similarity between the mark or trade name and the famous mark.
- The degree of inherent or acquired distinctiveness of the famous mark.
- The extent to which the owner of the famous mark is engaging in substantially exclusive use of the mark.
- The degree of recognition of the famous mark.
- Whether the user of the mark or trade name intended to create an association with the famous mark.
- Any actual association between the mark or trade name and the famous mark.[2107]

The definition and multifactor test show that the TDRA requires more than merely similar use or a similar mark. However, like other multifactor tests in trademark law, the six TDRA factors for dilution by blurring are discretionary and nonexclusive.[2108] In 2008, a District of Nevada court found dilution by blurring in *Visa Int'l v. JSL Corp.* even though the plaintiff did not satisfy all of the factors required under the TDRA.[2109] Visa did not submit any evidence to support the extent to which it was engaging in substantially exclusive use of the mark (factor three).[2110] Additionally, Visa provided no evidence of JSL's intent to create an association with its mark (EVISA) and

2103. *Id.*, at 433.
2104. 15 U.S.C. § 1125(c)(1) (Lanham Act § 43(c)(1)).
2105. *Victoria's Secret in V Secret Catalogue, Inc. v. Moseley*, 605 F.3d 382 (6th Cir. 2010).
2106. 15 U.S.C. § 1125(c)(2)(B) (Lanham Act § 43(c)(2)(B)).
2107. *Id.*
2108. *Visa Int'l Serv. Assoc. v. JSL Corp.*, 590 F. Supp. 2d 1306, 1320 (D. Nev. 2008).
2109. *Id.* (finding that defendant JSL Corporation's use of EVISA mark was likely to cause dilution by blurring of plaintiff's VISA mark).
2110. *Id.*, at 1318, 1320.

Visa's mark (VISA) (factor five).[2111] Although Visa provided no evidence for two out of the six factors, the court found that Visa had made "an exceptionally strong showing on the four other factors" showing dilution by blurring.[2112]

IV Dilution by Tarnishment

The second of the two types of dilution recognized by federal statute is dilution by tarnishment. Section 43 defines dilution by tarnishment as "association arising from the similarity between a mark or trade name and a famous mark that harms the reputation of the famous mark."[2113] Unlike blurring, no factor test is provided by statute. Under state laws, courts have generally found three broad categories of tarnishment: association of the senior mark with unwholesome activity; association of the senior mark with goods or services of poor quality; and subjecting the senior mark, or the mark's owner, to ridicule.

Unwholesome associations can range from use of a mark in pornography,[2114] to "safes" made to appear like bottles,[2115] to satirical movies.[2116] Any association which is likely to cause members of the consuming public to turn away from the mark, for any reason, is at least theoretically fair game. Interestingly, courts often treat marks associated with legal unwholesome activity as "tarnish-proof."[2117]

Association with goods or services of inferior quality is another category that covers a wide range of possible cases. In *Dan-Foam A/S v. Brand Named Beds, LLC,*[2118] the court upheld a dilution claim in which an unauthorized reseller of Tempur-Pedic products shipped those products in containers so small that the contents had to be folded, rolled, or held together with straps, thus producing a negative association in the minds of buyers who received the poorly packaged goods. In *Gideon's International, Inc. v. Gideon 300 Ministries, Inc.*,[2119] the court found tarnishment because defendant, a Christian ministry, solicited donations, something that plaintiff, also a Christian ministry, never did.

Tarnishment by ridicule or criticism is, however, a very narrow category. The TDRA creates exemptions, discussed below, for parodies and for noncommercial use. To sustain a tarnishment by ridicule claim, the defendant would have to appropriate

2111. *Id.*
2112. *Visa Int'l Serv. Assoc. v. JSL Corp.*, 590 F. Supp. 2d 1306, 1320 (D. Nev. 2008).
2113. 15 U.S.C. § 1125(c)(2)(C) (Lanham Act § 43(c)(2)(C)).
2114. For example, *Victoria's Cyber Secret, Ltd. Partnership v. V Secret Catalogue, Inc.*, 161 F. Supp. 2d 1339, 1355 (S.D. Fla. 2001) (domain names similar to Victoria's Secret for pornographic websites).
2115. *PepsiCo Inc. v. #1 Wholesale LLC*, 84 U.S.P.Q.2d 1040 (N.D. Ga. 2007) (Pepsi mark on good "commonly associated with the concealment of illicit narcotics").
2116. *American Dairy Queen Corp. v. New Line Productions, Inc.*, 35 F. Supp. 2d 727 (D. Minn. 1998) (a movie titled *Dairy Queens* would have portrayed dairy country in an unflattering and satirical way, thus tarnishing the Dairy Queen mark).
2117. *See Playboy Enterprises, Inc. v. Webbworld, Inc.*, 991 F. Supp. 543 (N.D. Tex. 1997) (Playboy's mark not tarnishable because it is used to promote sexually oriented materials).
2118. 500 F. Supp. 2d 296 (S.D.N.Y. 2007).
2119. 94 F. Supp. 2d 566 (E.D. Pa. 1999).

the mark and use it for commercial gain. For instance, in *Deere & Co. v. MTD Products, Inc.*,[2120] defendants used the John Deere deer logo in a commercial showing the deer running away in fear from defendants' lawn mower. In the post-TDRA world, these cases usually occur when the defendant registers an Internet domain name substantially similar to the famous mark.[2121] In *Jews for Jesus v. Brodsky*,[2122] for instance, the court found blurring and tarnishment when defendant registered the domain name jewsforjesus.org to post website hostile to the plaintiff.

V Specific Defenses to a Dilution Claim

The FTDA provides for three specific defenses against a dilution claim: fair use in comparative advertising, parody, criticism, or commentary; "any" noncommercial use; and "all forms" of news reporting and commentary.[2123] These large exceptions balance out the First Amendment concerns by limiting dilution claims to purely commercial disputes.

VI Preemption of State Laws

In general, the FTDA and TDRA do not preempt state laws, allowing states with dilution statutes to protect their locally famous marks. However, state laws are preempted in that state dilution claims against a mark on the Principal Register are barred.[2124]

VII Note on Dilution

Perhaps because of the newness of the doctrine and perhaps because the concept of dilution does not fit within the conceptual justifications of trademark protection in the US, its application by courts has been confused and unpredictable at best. Therefore, all practitioners in the US should beware of the problems inherent in this system.

The Dilution Act did not by its terms add dilution as one of the grounds for opposition to trademark registration under section 13 of the Lanham Act. The Trademark Amendments Act amended section 43(c) of the Lanham Act to include dilution as a ground for opposition under section 13(a).[2125] In discussing the Trademark Amendments Act, the House Judiciary Committee specifically referred to *Babson*

2120. 41 F.3d 39 (2d Cir. 1994).
2121. These cases will likely soon stop appearing as actions under the Lanham Act because they can now be brought more easily under the ACPA.
2122. 993 F. Supp. 282 (D. N.J. 1998).
2123. 15 U.S.C. § 1125(c)(3) (Lanham Act § 43(c)(3)).
2124. 15 U.S.C. § 1125(c)(6) (Lanham Act § 43(c)(6)). Marks on the Supplemental Register are not barred.
2125. The new statute amended the Lanham Act's provision on "Opposition to registration" to provide that "[a]ny person who believes that he would be damaged by the registration of a mark upon the Principal Register, including as a result of dilution under Section 1125(c) of this title, may ... file an opposition." 15 U.S.C. § 1063(a).

Bros. Co. v. Surge Power Corp.,[2126] a case where the TTAB held that dilution is not a ground for cancelation or opposition to registrations, as "illuminat[ing] the need for further legislation."[2127] In determining that the USPTO should have the ability to refuse to register marks based on dilution, Congress explained:

> [The Amendments to the Dilution Act are] necessary for several reasons. Resolution of the dilution issue before the Board, as opposed to Federal District Court, would result in more timely, economical, and expeditious decisions. Resolving the issue at the Board would provide certainty to competing trademark interests, before the applicant has invested significant resources in its proposed mark, and before dilution-type damage has been suffered in the marketplace by the owner of the famous mark. Also, the Board would give guidance to litigants and the Trademark Bar, through precedent, with respect to such issues as what qualifies as a "famous" mark, and what constitutes dilution, whether by blurring or tarnishment.[2128]

If the holder of a famous mark may oppose the registration of any subsequent marks, then the bestowal of fame upon the "famous" mark becomes the essential matter of proof for those opposing subsequent marks with a history of use.[2129] From the junior user's perspective, its rights to a concurrent use registration pursuant to section 2[2130] are cut off upon the senior user's acquisition of fame. In other words, the bestowal of fame upon the senior user does not give the junior user a right to register with the USPTO to protect the area of the market that the junior user has penetrated.[2131]

The Dilution Act creates great uncertainty for the junior user, so much that one may advise a junior user fearful of diluting another's mark to take a defensive posture in state court first, allowing it to carve out local territory without the threat of cancelation. Likewise, the plaintiff in a dilution claim will likely rush to the federal courts to oppose registrations, to take advantage of the Dilution Act's opposition provisions. However, a plaintiff may prefer to file in state courts to establish a dilution cause of action in an under-a-likelihood of-dilution burden rather than face the much more difficult (and puzzling) Moseley actual confusion burden.

2126. *Babson Bros. v. Surge Power Corp.*, 39 U.S.P.Q. 1953 (T.T.A.B. 1996).

2127. Trademark Amendments Act of 1999, H.R. REP. NO. 106-250, at 5 (1999), 1999 WL 528534, at *5.

2128. Trademark Amendments Act of 1999, H.R. REP. NO. 106-250, at 5–6 (1999), 1999 WL 528534, at *5–6.

2129. *See Enterprise Rent-A-Car Co. v. Advantage Rent-A-Car, Inc.*, 330 F.3d 1333, 1343 (Fed. Cir. 2003) ("Because there can be no dilution under the [Dilution Act] where the allegedly famous mark did not achieve fame prior to any use by the accused infringer, there can be no opposition").

2130. 15 U.S.C. § 1052.

2131. *See Enterprise Rent-A-Car, Co. v. Advantage Rent-A-Car, Inc.*, 330 F.3d 1333, 1343 (Fed. Cir. 2003) ("There is not a provision in the Lanham Act to allow for concurrent use registrations in the dilution context. In fact, when Congress amended … the Lanham Act in 1999 to add dilution under [the Dilution Act] as a ground for opposition, it also amended Section 1052, the section that grants the Board the power to issue concurrent use registrations, to make clear that dilution could not be considered in proceedings brought under that section").

§6 CYBERSQUATTING

Because domain names are registered on a "first-come, first-served" basis, a party may register a domain name containing its competitor's or another's mark.[2132] Such conduct clearly causes consumer confusion and would amount to trademark infringement.[2133] This predatory registration is the kind of harm the Lanham Act protects against. If this were the only harm, Article 43(d) of the Lanham Act would not be necessary.[2134]

Parties may abuse the domain name registration process in other ways that do not fit so neatly into typical Lanham Act analysis. While this practice first arose in humorous anecdote,[2135] the harm has become more common, more organized, and more severe.

The legislative history of the Act gives various examples: a party may register a domain name that is identical or confusingly similar to another's mark with the intent to extort money from the holder of the mark and prevent the holder of the mark from reflecting its mark on the Internet; to create confusion, to divert the mark holder's customers to the cybersquatter's own (often pornographic) site for commercial gain; or to defraud the public.[2136] All of these domain name registrations are actionable under section 43(d) of the Lanham Act if the mark holder can demonstrate that its trademark predates the registration of the domain name, and the holder of the domain name registree had a bad faith intent to profit from the registration of a domain name that is identical or confusingly similar to the trademark holder's mark.

Section 43(d)(1) provides as follows:

a. A person shall be liable in a civil action by the owner of a mark, including a personal name which is protected as a mark under this section, if, without regard to the goods or services of the parties, that person
   - has a bad faith intent to profit from that mark, including a personal name which is protected as a mark under this section; and
   - registers, traffics in, or uses a domain name that—
     - in the case of a mark that is distinctive at the time of registration of the domain name, is identical or confusingly similar to that mark;
     - in the case of a famous mark that is famous at the time of registration of the domain name, is identical or confusingly similar to or dilutive of that mark; or
     - is a trademark, work, or name protected by reason of Section 706 of title 18, United States Code, or Section 220506 of title 36, United States Code.[2137]

2132. *See supra*, Ch. 2, §2.VI.
2133. J. Thomas McCarthy, 5 McCarthy on Trademarks and Unfair Competition § 25A.41 (5th ed. 2021) (explaining how the use of a domain name may be a form of infringement).
2134. *Id.*
2135. *See* Dan L. Burk, *Trademarks along the Infobahn: A First Look at the Emerging Law of Cybermarks*, 1 Rich. J.L. & Tech. 1 (1995) (Princeton Review offers to transfer the kaplan.com domain name to the Kaplan Review in exchange for a case of beer).
2136. The Anticybersquatting Consumer Protection Act, S. Rep. No. 106-140, at 6–7 (1999), 1999 WL 594571.
2137. 15 U.S.C. § 1125(d)(1)(A).

I Bad Faith Requirement

Section 43(d)(1)(B)(i) provides a nonexclusive list of nine factors that courts may consider when determining whether a person has the requisite bad faith intent under section 43(d)(1)(A):

> (i) In determining whether a person has a bad faith intent described under subparagraph (A), a court must consider factors such as, but not limited to
> - the trademark or other intellectual property rights of the person, if any, in the domain name;
> - the extent to which the domain name consists of the legal name of the person or a name that is otherwise commonly used to identify that person;
> - the person's prior use, if any, of the domain name in connection with the bona fide offering of any goods or services;
> - the person's bona fide noncommercial or fair use of the mark in a site accessible under the domain name;
> - the person's intent to divert consumers from the mark owner's online location to a site accessible under the domain name that could harm the goodwill represented by the mark, either for commercial gain or with the intent to tarnish or disparage the mark, by creating a likelihood of confusion as to the source, sponsorship, affiliation, or endorsement of the site;
> - the person's offer to transfer, sell, or otherwise assign the domain name to the mark owner or any third party for financial gain without having used, or having an intent to use the domain name in the bona fide offering of any goods or services, or the person's prior conduct indicating a pattern of such conduct;
> - the person's provision of material and misleading false contact information when applying for the registration of the domain name, the person's intentional failure to maintain accurate contact information, or the person's prior conduct indicating a pattern of such conduct;
> - the person's registration or acquisition of multiple domain names which the person knows are identical or confusingly similar to marks of others that are distinctive at the time of registration of such domain names, or dilutive of famous marks of others that are famous at the time of registration of such domain names, without regard to the goods or services of the parties; and
> - the extent to which the mark incorporated in the person's domain name registration is or is not distinctive and famous within the meaning of subsection (c)(1) of Section 43.[2138]

In practice, the first four factors indicate a lack of bad faith and the last five factors indicate the presence of bad faith.[2139] The legislative history recognizes that presence or absence of any of these factors may not be determinative.[2140] For example, a periodic use does not preclude bad faith, and the provision of erroneous registration information does not necessarily show bad faith.[2141] Instead, the legislative history regards

2138. 15 U.S.C. § 1125(d)(1)(B)(i).
2139. Anticybersquatting Consumer Protection Act, S. Rep. No. 106-140, at 9 (1999), 1999 WL 594571.
2140. *Id.*
2141. *Id.*

these as "balancing factors," recognizing that caveats could exist not only for (B)(i)(IV) and (B)(i)(VIII) but also for all of the balancing factors.[2142]

The list of bad faith balancing factors is "nonexclusive and nonexhaustive."[2143] In addition to factor (IV) in section 43(d)(1)(B)(i), section 43(d)(2)(B)(ii) provides that bad faith shall not be found "in any case in which the court determines that the person believed and had reasonable grounds to believe that the use of the domain name was a fair use or was otherwise lawful."[2144]

A *Reverse Domain Name Hijacking under the UDRP*

The legislative history indicates that Congress was concerned that trademark holders may employ the ACPA in bad faith.[2145] In the instance where a bona fide domain name registration existed first, an interloper could register a trademark that was identical or confusingly similar to the domain name and then assert the provisions of section 43(d). In this instance, the domain name would have priority over the trademark. However, an unsuspecting domain name holder could find itself under attack from a second-comer with a trademark registration in hand. To attempt to cure this concern, section 43(d)(1)(A)(ii)(I) indicates that the mark needs to be distinctive at the time of the domain name registration.

II In Rem Jurisdiction over Domain Names

Due to the ease of registering domain names beyond territorial boundaries, Congress was concerned that domain name registrees may not be subject to personal jurisdiction in this country.[2146] Another concern was that registrees would intentionally provide false information to avoid service of process and evade personal jurisdiction. The ACPA creates an in rem cause of action by adding section 43(d)(2) to the Lanham Act:

> The owner of a mark may file an in rem civil action against a domain name in the judicial district in which the domain name registrar, domain name registry, or

---

2142. Anticybersquatting Consumer Protection Act, S. Rep. No. 106-140, at 9–10 (1999), 1999 WL 594571.

2143. *Id.*, at 10.

2144. 15 U.S.C. § 1125(d)(1)(B)(ii) (Lanham Act § 43(d)(1)(B)(ii)).

2145. "This section … protects against the rights of domain name registrants against overreaching trademark owners. Under a new section subparagraph (D)(iv) in Section 32(2), a trademark[]owner who knowingly and materially misrepresents to the domain name registrar or registry that a domain name is infringing shall be liable to the domain name registrant for damages resulting from the suspension, cancellation, or transfer of the domain name."

2146. "Additionally, some have suggested that dissidents and others who are online incognito for legitimate reasons might give false information to protect themselves and have suggested the need to preserve a degree of anonymity on the Internet particularly for this reason. Allowing a trademark owner to proceed against the domain names themselves, provided they are, in fact, infringing or diluting under the Trademark Act, decreases the need for trademark owners to join the hunt to chase down and root out these dissidents or others seeking anonymity on the Net." Anticybersquatting Consumer Protection Act, S. Rep. No. 106-140, at 11 (1999), 1999 WL 594571.

other domain name authority that registered or assigned the domain name is located if—

- the domain name violates any right of the owner of a mark registered in the Patent and Trademark Office, or protected under subsection (a) or (c); and
- the court finds that the owner—
  - is not able to obtain in personam jurisdiction over a person who would have been a defendant in a civil action under paragraph (1); or would have been a defendant in a civil action under paragraph (1); or
  - through due diligence was not able to find a person who would have been a defendant in a civil action under paragraph (1) by—
    a. sending a notice of the alleged violation and intent to proceed under this paragraph to the registrant of the domain name at the postal and e-mail address provided by the registrant to the registrar; and
    b. publishing notice of the action as the court may direct promptly after filing the action.[2147]

In an in rem action, a domain name is deemed to have its situs in the judicial district where the domain name registrar that registered or assigned the domain name is located, or where documents sufficient to establish control and authority regarding the disposition and use of the domain name are deposited with the court.[2148] In an in rem proceeding, a court that does not have jurisdiction over the situs will not have jurisdiction in the ACPA proceeding.[2149]

III Domain Name Registrars

In *Lockheed-Martin v. Network Solutions, Inc.*,[2150] Lockheed sued NSI for contributory infringement because of its registration of the skunkworks.com domain name. Lockheed held the trademark registration for Skunkworks for an aircraft design and construction laboratory, which gave it nationwide priority for the mark. Lockheed also argued that its USPTO registration of the Skunkworks mark gave NSI constructive notice of Lockheed's rights in the Skunkworks mark. Therefore, by registering the skunkworks.com domain name, NSI contributed to the domain name registree's infringement. The court specifically held that domain name registrars could not be held liable for domain name registrations.[2151]

Because registrars are not liable for contributory trademark infringement,[2152] a registrar need not inquire into whether a party is registering a domain name that contains another's mark, or even if that party has any rights in the domain name.

2147. 15 U.S.C. § 1125(d)(2).
2148. 15 U.S.C. §§ 1125(d)(2)(C)(i), 1125(d)(2)(C)(ii) (Lanham Act §§ 43(d)(2)(C)(i), 43(d)(2)(C)(ii)).
2149. 5 McCarthy, Trademarks and Unfair Competition § 25A:71 (5th ed.).
2150. 194 F.3d 980 (9th Cir. 1999).
2151. *Id.*, at 985.
2152. *See* 15 U.S.C. § 1114(2)(D) (Lanham Act § 32(2)(D)).

IV Domain Name Dispute Resolution

While the US created federal law to resolve disputes involving the Internet, the Internet Corporation for Assigned Names and Numbers (ICANN) created a dispute resolution protocol as part of its mandate to facilitate the coordination and management of specific technical, managerial, and policy development tasks that require central coordination.[2153]

Because the US government had been involved in the early development of the Internet, many parts of the domain name system were either performed by US government agencies or pursuant to contracts by US governmental agencies:[2154]

> On 1 July 1997, as part of the Administration's Framework for Global Electronic Commerce, ... President [Clinton] directed the Secretary of Commerce to privative the management of the domain name system in a manner that increased competition and facilitated international participation in its management.[2155]

In its "White Paper"[2156] addressing the management of Internet names and addresses, the US Chamber of Commerce encouraged the US government to end involvement. One of the suggestions on how to remove the administration of the Internet from the US was to form a private corporation with oversight capabilities. In 1998, ICANN was formed.[2157]

ICANN is a nonprofit, private California corporation created expressly to assume responsibility for the IP address space allocation, protocol parameter assignment, domain name system management, and root server system management functions previously performed under US government contracts.[2158]

As a part of its domain name system management responsibilities, ICANN created a dispute resolution policy in October 1999 called the UDRP or "Policy."[2159] The UDRP applies to all generic top-level domains (gTLDs). In other words, to receive accreditation from ICANN, registrars (that register these gTLDs) must agree to administer and abide by the UDRP. "Under the UDRP, accredited registrars are bound to refrain from taking any action regarding complaints received from trademark holders on the impact of registered domains until instructed to do so by the domain registrant or by an appropriate court or independent arbitrator."[2160] Where holders of trademarks allege that a registrant has committed an abusive registration of a domain name, and the mark holder chooses to arbitrate the dispute, the registration agreement obliges the

2153. *See* A QUICK LOOK AT ICANN, available at https://www.icann.org/resources/pages/factsheets-2012-02-25-en.
2154. *Image Online Design, Inc. v. Core Assoc.*, 120 F. Supp. 2d 870 (C.D. Cal. 2000).
2155. Memorandum of Understanding Between the U.S. Department of Commerce and Internet Corporation for Assigned Names and Numbers, available at https://www.icann.org/resources/unthemed-pages/icann-mou-1998-11-25-en.
2156. *See* Management of Internet Names and Addresses, 63 Fed. Reg. 31741 (1998), available at www.icann.org/general/white-paper-05jun98.htm (last updated July 22, 2000).
2157. *Image Online Design, Inc. v. Core Assoc.*, 120 F. Supp. 2d 870 (D.C.D. Cal. 2000).
2158. *Id.*
2159. *See generally* Domain Name Dispute Resolution Policies www.icann.org/udrp/#udrp.
2160. *See* John Magee, *Domain Name Disputes: An Assessment of the UDRP as Against Traditional Litigation*, 203 U. ILL. J.L. TECH. & POLY. 205 (2003).

registrant to submit to arbitration. This mandatory administrative agreement requires the proceeding to be conducted before one of the approved administrative-dispute-resolution service providers.[2161] There are currently six approved providers.[2162] The complainant in UDRP proceedings has the opportunity to select the service provider.[2163]

A *Resolving Disputes under the UDRP*

The UDRP prohibits the abusive registration of domain names.[2164] Paralleling the ACPA, the UDRP protects trademark holders from those who, in bad faith, register domain names that are identical or confusingly similar to the holder's mark.[2165] In the case where a party alleges that a domain name registrant has abused the domain name registration process, the registration agreement obliges the registrant to submit to the jurisdiction of the UDRP as well.

To file a claim under the UDRP, the holder of the mark files a complaint with one of the approved administrative-dispute-resolution service providers.[2166] The provider commences the action by notifying the holder of the disputed domain name[2167] that an administrative action is pending concerning the disputed domain name. In addition, the provider notifies the registrar of the domain name, and the registrar puts an administrative lock on the domain name—preventing transfer of the domain name.

The scope of the UDRP is narrow; it is only to resolve abusive registrations of domain names. To succeed on a UDRP claim, a complainant must demonstrate that: (1) it has rights in a trademark or service mark and the disputed domain name is identical or confusingly similar to complainant's mark; (2) the respondent has no rights or legitimate interests in the domain name; and (3) the respondent has registered and used the disputed domain name in bad faith.[2168]

2161. Uniform Domain Name Dispute Resolution Policy (UDRP), available at www.icann.org/dndr/udrp/policy.htm.

2162. Approved Providers for Uniform Domain-Name Dispute-Resolution Policy, available at www.icann.org/dndr/udrp/approved-providers.htm.

2163. John Magee, *Domain Name Disputes: An Assessment of the UDRP as Against Traditional Litigation*, 203 U. ILL. J.L. TECH. & POLY. 205 (2003).

2164. WIPO, Final Report of the WIPO Internet Domain Name Process, The Management of Internet Names and Addresses: Intellectual Property Issues, paras. 170–71 (Apr. 30, 1999), available at http://arbiter.wipo.int/processes/process1/report/finalreport.html ("Because of the elastic meaning of cybersquatting in popular terminology, we have therefore chosen to use a different term—abusive registration of a domain name—in order to attribute to it a more precise meaning").

2165. Cf. 15 U.S.C. § 1125(d) (Lanham Act § 43(d)) *with* Uniform Domain Name Dispute Resolution Policy, available at www.icann.org/dndr/udrp/policy.htm.

2166. *See supra*, Ch. 6, §5.IV. In referring to the parties in a UDRP proceeding, the author will refer to the holder of the mark as "complainant" and the holder of the domain name registration as "respondent."

2167. As determined by the domain name's *Whois* registration information. *See*, e.g., Network Solutions Enhanced WHOIS Directory, available at www.networksolutions.com/en_US/whois/index.jhtml.

2168. *See* UDRP para. 4(a).

B *Complainant's Rights in a Mark and Similarity under the UDRP*

Paragraph 4(a)(i) requires a complainant to establish that it has rights in a mark that are identical or confusingly similar to the disputed domain name to bring an action under the UDRP.[2169] A complainant may establish rights in a domain name by providing evidence of a USPTO registration.[2170] Most panels read paragraph 4(a)(i) to mean that the complainant's rights in the mark allow it to use the UDRP to resolve a dispute; some call this a "standing requirement."[2171] The other important element under paragraph 4(a)(i) is that the complainant's rights must predate the respondent's domain name registration.[2172]

Absent a USPTO registration, panels have permitted complainants to establish common law rights in a mark.[2173] To establish common law rights, a complainant must demonstrate that the mark has established secondary meaning.[2174]

To establish that the disputed domain name is identical or confusingly similar, a complainant needs only to make a facile comparison of the two. In fact, the burden for similarity under the UDRP is less than the burden for similarity under federal trademark law: all the complainant need to demonstrate is that the domain name includes the trademark.[2175]

It is under paragraph 4(a)(i) that panels consider whether appending "sucks" to a trademark constitutes a resultant domain name that is confusingly similar to the mark.[2176] Some do this to gripe about the trademark holder; this is appropriately called

2169. UDRP para. 4(a)(i).

2170. *See Nike v. Azumano Travel*, WIPO Case No. D2000-1598 (Feb. 17, 2001) (finding that Nike's registration with the USPTO gave it rights under para. 4(a)(i) of the UDRP).

2171. *See Spacy v. Alberta Hot Rods*, NAF Case No. FA 114437 (Aug. 1, 2002).

2172. *See Intermark Media, Inc. v. Wang Logic Corp.*, NAF Case No. FA 139660 (Feb. 19, 2003).

2173. *See British Broad. Corp. v. Renteria*, WIPO Case No. D2000-0050 (Mar. 23, 2000) (holding that its history indicates that the UDRP "does not distinguish between registered and unregistered trademarks and service marks").

2174. *See Galatasaray Spor Kulubu Dernegi v. Maksimum Iletisim A.S.*, WIPO Case No. D2002-0726 (Oct. 15, 2002).

2175. *See Kirkbi AG v. Dinoia*, WIPO Case No. D2003-0038 (Mar. 9, 2003).
("The test of confusing similarity under the Policy is confined to a comparison of the disputed domain name and the trademark alone, independent of the other marketing and use factors usually considered in trademark infringement or unfair competition cases").

2176. In *Full Sail, Inc. v. Spevack*, WIPO Case No. D2003-0502 (Oct. 3, 2003), the panel summarized five different rationales for finding that "sucks" appended to a mark creates a confusingly similar domain name. First, a domain name is confusingly similar to a trademark "when the domain name includes the trademark, or a confusingly similar approximation, regardless of the other terms of the domain name." *See Wal-Mart Stores, Inc. v. MacLeod*, WIPO Case No. 2000-0662 (Sept. 21, 2000); *Kendall/Hunt Publ. Co. v. Headhunterbob*, NAF Case No. FA 102247 (Jan. 14, 2002). Second, appending "sucks" to a domain name will lead to a diversion of customers because it will be pulled up by search engine queries for the trademark. *See WalMart Stores, Inc. v. Walsucks*, WIPO Case No. D2000-0477 (July 25, 2000). Third, the consumer may mistake the resultant websites at the "-sucks.com" domain name for the trademark holder's official complaint site. "Given the apparent mushrooming of complaint sites identified by reference to the target's name, can it be said that the regulation would be recognized as an address plainly dissociated from the complainant's?," *Direct Line Group Ltd. v. Purge I.T. Ltd.*, WIPO Case No. D2000-0583 (Aug. 16, 2000). Fourth, non-English speakers may not be familiar with the pejorative nature of the word "sucks," and, therefore, will be "cybergriping." In "sucks" cases, various panels have warned against excessive rigidity when regarding assessing similarity in reference to "sucks" sites and emphasize that emerging technologies require a different approach.[2177] However, panels often find that cybergriping cites are confusingly similar to the trademarks that they criticize.[2178]

C Rights and Legitimate Interests under the UDRP

To establish that a respondent has abused the domain name registration process, a complainant must make a prima facie showing that the holder of the domain name does not have legitimate rights or interests in the domain name.[2179] After this, the burden shifts to the respondent to demonstrate that it has rights and legitimate interests.[2180] Paragraph 4(c) of the UDRP establishes three ways in which a respondent can establish rights or legitimate interests in the domain name pursuant to paragraph 4(a)(ii):

- before any notice to you of the dispute, your use of, or demonstrable preparations to use, the domain name or a name corresponding to the domain name in connection with a bona fide offering of goods or services; or
- you (as an individual, business, or other organization) have been commonly known by the domain name, even if you have acquired no trademark or service mark rights; or
- you are making a legitimate noncommercial or fair use of the domain name, without intent for commercial gain to misleadingly divert consumers or to tarnish the trademark or service mark at issue.[2181]

---

confused about the source of origin of the "-sucks.com" domain name. *See ADT Servs. v. ADTSucks.com*, WIPO Case No. D2001-0213 (Apr. 26, 2001). Fifth, some panels have noted that in certain situations the disputed domain name may not be employing the word "sucks" in the pejorative sense, i.e., "Nothing sucks like Electrolux." *Vivendi Universal v. Scallen*, WIPO Case No. D2001-1121 (Nov. 7, 2001).

But, as *Full Sail* also notes, some panels have held that both "common sense and a reading of the plain language of the [UDRP] supports the view that a domain name combining the trademark with the word 'sucks' or other language clearly indicating that the domain name is not affiliated with the trademark owner cannot be confusingly similar to the trademark." *Lockheed Martin Corp. v. Parisi*, WIPO Case No. D2000-1015 (Jan. 31, 2001).

2177. *See Nat'l Alliance for the Mentally Ill Contra Costa v. Fouts*, NAF Case No. FA 204074 (Dec. 6, 2003) (citing *Brookfield Communications, Inc. v. W. Coast Enter. Corp.*, 174 F.3d 1036, 1054 (9th Cir. 1999)).

2178. *See*, e.g., *InfoSpace, Inc. v. Sunwave Communications*, NAF Case No. FA 198015 (Nov. 10, 2003).

2179. *See Intocast AG v. Lee Daeyoon*, WIPO Case No. D2000-1467 (Jan. 17, 2001).

2180. *See Do The Hustle, LLC v. Tropic Web*, WIPO Case No. D2000-0624 (Aug. 21, 2000) (finding that once complainant asserts that respondent has no rights or legitimate interests with respect to the domain, the burden shifts to respondent to provide "concrete evidence that it has rights to or legitimate interests in the domain name at issue").

2181. *See* IDRP para. 4(c).

The history of the UDRP indicates that paragraph 4(c) holds "safe harbor" provisions.[2182] Basically, the respondent may demonstrate that its use of the domain name does not harm the complainant's goodwill.

Panels consider paragraph 4(c)(i) and 4(c)(iii) together; the operative question is whether the respondent is attempting to usurp the complainant's goodwill. Claims may fail under paragraph 4(c)(i) if the respondent can demonstrate that its use is bona fide (i.e., absent bad faith),[2183] it has concurrent rights in the mark,[2184] or it was doing business as the domain name[2185] (a subset of this is that it is a generic domain name reseller).[2186] Under paragraph 4(c)(iii), parody,[2187] complaint,[2188] and hobby sites may prevail,[2189] as long as there is no evidence of commerce.[2190]

Paragraph 4(c)(ii) allows for a respondent who has built up a reputation around a domain name to keep it if it can demonstrate that it is commonly known by that domain name.[2191]

2182. ICANN, Second Staff Report on Implementation Documents for the Uniform Dispute Resolution Policy, Submitted for Board meeting of Oct. 24, 1999, para. 4.6 (Oct. 25, 1999), available at https://archive.icann.org/en/udrp/udrp-second-staff-report-24oct99.htm.

2183. *See Scholastic Inc. v. Master Games Int'l, Inc.*, WIPO Case No. D2001-1208 (Jan. 3, 2002) (finding that the respondent's use of the disputed domain name for a website regarding chess tournaments, particularly because the domain name appropriately described both the target users of respondent's services and the nature of respondent's services, was a bona fide use of the domain name).

2184. *See Kelly v. Qsoft Consulting Ltd.*, WIPO Case No. D2003-0221 (Apr. 30, 2003) (finding that the respondent had concurrent rights and legitimate interests in the mygaydar.com domain name where, at the time that the administrative proceeding was commenced, both parties had "homonymous trademark rights to the *Gaydar* mark" through their respective use of the mark in the U.S. and the U.K.).

2185. *See K2r Produkte AG v. Trigano*, WIPO Case No. D2000-0622 (Aug. 23, 2000) (finding that the respondent had rights and legitimate interests in the domain name k2rr.com where he registered the domain name for a website in connection with his mother's store, "Kirk et Rosie Rich").

2186. *See Fifty Plus Media Corp. v. Digital Income, Inc.*, NAF Case No. FA 94924 (July 17, 2000) (finding that the complainant failed to prove that the respondent had no rights in the domain name and had registered and used the domain name in bad faith where the respondent is an Internet business which deals in the selling or leasing of descriptive/generic domain names).

2187. *See Robo Enters., Inc. v. Tobiason*, NAF Case No. FA 95857 (Dec. 24, 2000) (holding that in order to qualify as a protected "parody," which would confer rights or a legitimate interest, the domain name itself must signify critical purposes, as opposed to imitation of the service mark).

2188. *See New York Press v. New York Press*, NAF Case No. FA 94428 (May 18, 2000) (finding that the respondent's use of its website for review and criticism of the New York press and its pending USPTO registration for the *New York Press* mark for use with his online publication is evidence that he began to use the domain name for a legitimate noncommercial use).

2189. *See Mattel v. Knox*, NAF Case No. 245916 (Apr. 21, 2004) (finding that the respondent's use of the ukbarbie.com domain name was to share its *Barbie* doll collection with the UK doll-collecting community was noncommercial and, therefore, fair use).

2190. *See Lockheed Martin Corp. v. Etheridge*, WIPO Case No. D2000-0906 (Sept. 24, 2000) (finding that the respondent has rights in the missionsuccess.net domain name where it was using the domain name in connection with a noncommercial purpose).

2191. *See Puky GmbH v. Agnello*, WIPO Case No. D2001-1345 (Jan. 3, 2002) (holding that the respondent's invoice, which demonstrated that it had been planning to trade under the name *Purkhon Ki Yaden*, was evidence that the respondent had rights or legitimate interests in the disputed domain name).

D Bad Faith under the UDRP

Paragraph 4(b) of the UDRP lists four nonexclusive factors to determine if a respondent's registration or use of a domain name is in bad faith pursuant to Policy paragraph 4(a)(iii):

- circumstances indicating that you have registered or you have acquired the domain name primarily for the purpose of selling, renting, or otherwise transferring the domain name registration to the complainant who is the owner of the trademark or service mark or to a competitor of that complainant, for valuable consideration in excess of your documented out-of-pocket costs directly related to the domain name; or
- you have registered the domain name in order to prevent the owner of the trademark or service mark from reflecting the mark in a corresponding domain name, provided that you have engaged in a pattern of such conduct; or
- you have registered the domain name primarily for the purpose of disrupting the business or a competitor; or
- by using the domain name, you have intentionally attempted to attract, for commercial gain, Internet users to your web site or other online location, by creating a likelihood of confusion with the complainant's mark as to the source, sponsorship, affiliation, or endorsement of your web site or location or of a product or service on your web site or location.[2192]

Panels have generally regarded paragraph 4(b) to require evidence of bad faith registration and use.[2193]

Paragraph 4(b)(i) protects against what the history of the ACPA referred to as "piracy," and the history of the UDRP refers to as the predatory and parasitical practices of exploitation.[2194] In its inception, ICANN intended for paragraph 4(b)(i) to protect against domain name registrants who intended to profit from the holder of the identical or confusingly similar mark.[2195] Panels have expanded paragraph 4(b)(i) to

---

2192. UDRP para. 4(b).

2193. *See* ICANN, Second Staff Report on Implementation Documents for the Uniform Dispute Resolution Policy, Submitted for Board meeting of Oct. 24, 1999, para. 4.6 (Oct. 25, 1999), available at https://archive.icann.org/en/udrp/udrp-second-staff-report-24oct99.htm; *see also Dow Jones & Co. v. Hephzibah Intro-Net Project Ltd.*, WIPO Case No. D2000-0704 (Sept. 4, 2000):

> (It may be that the Policy needs to be reviewed, particularly in relation to the requirement for showing use and registration in bad faith. It may seem inappropriate that a person with no legitimate right or interest in a name should be able to register it as a domain name adversely to one who has demonstrated such rights and interests[;] but the panel is bound to apply the Policy as it is).

2194. Cf. The Anticybersquatting Consumer Protection Act, S. Rep. No. 106-140, at 6–7 (1999), 1999 WL 594571 *with* WIPO, Final Report of the WIPO Internet Domain Name Process, The Management of Internet Names and Addresses: Intellectual Property Issues, para. 23 (Apr. 30, 1999), available at http://arbiter.wipo.int/processes/process1/report/finalreport.html.

2195. WIPO, Final Report of the WIPO Internet Domain Name Process, The Management of Internet Names and Addresses: Intellectual Property Issues, para. 170 (Apr. 30, 1999), available at http://arbiter.wipo.int/processes/process1/report/finalreport.html.

construe any attempted sale of a disputed domain name as evidence of bad faith.[2196] In addition, panels have even held a respondent's attempts to sell a disputed domain name in bad faith when the complainant initiated the offer.[2197] However, some panels have found that those who are in the business of selling domain names, and conduct bulk domain name registrations, do not evidence bad faith under paragraph 4(b)(i) by selling those domain names.[2198]

Complainants find paragraph 4(b)(ii) difficult to assert. Panels are split on whether "prevention ... from reflecting the mark in a corresponding domain name" limits claims under paragraph 4(b)(ii) to instances of whether respondent's activity prevents the mark holder from registering a domain name that is identical to its mark.[2199] Others construe "corresponding" to not require that the "preventing" domain name be identical to the mark. Additionally, complainants rarely establish the requisite pattern required by the "prevention ... and pattern" requirement of paragraph 4(b)(ii). Evidence that respondent holds multiple domain name registrations is not persuasive under paragraph 4(b)(ii);[2200] however, evidence that previous panels have ruled against respondent is very persuasive evidence that respondent has engaged in such a pattern.[2201] In an instance where the requisite bad faith exists under paragraph 4(b)(ii), a complainant will almost always be able to establish either paragraph 4(b)(iii) or 4(b)(iv).[2202]

Panels have interpreted paragraph 4(b)(iii) to protect the complainant's mark. A bad faith claim under paragraph 4(b)(iii) pivots on evidence of competition.[2203] The

2196. *See Am. Anti-Vivisection Soc'y v. "Infa dot Net" Web Serv.*, NAF Case No. FA 95685 (Nov. 6, 2000) ("[G]eneral offers to sell the domain name, even if no certain price is demanded, are evidence of bad faith").
2197. *See Marrow v. IceT.com*, WIPO Case No. D2000-1234 (Nov. 22, 2000) (stating that a panel should not "put much weight on the fact that it was the complainant who contacted respondent to see if it was interested in selling the domain name").
2198. *See Lumena s-ka zo.o. v. Express Ventures LTD*, NAF Case No. FA 94375 (May 11, 2000) (finding no bad faith where the domain name involves a generic term, and there is no direct evidence that the respondent registered the domain name with the intent of capitalizing on the complainant's trademark interest).
2199. *See Sanrio Co. v. Lau*, WIPO Case No. D2000-0172 (Apr. 20, 2000) (finding that the respondent's registration of sanriosurprises.com precluded complainant from registering its registered *Sanrio Surprises* mark as a domain name).
2200. *See Ingersoll-Rand Co. v. Gully*, WIPO Case No. D2000-0021 (Mar. 9, 2000).
2201. *Sony Corp. v. Zuccarini*, NAF Case No. 109041 (May 23, 2002) ("Complainant has provided evidence that respondent has a history of registering infringing domain names that incorporate the trademarks and service marks of others").
2202. *See Ingersoll-Rand Co. v. Gully*, WIPO Case No. D2000-0021 (Mar. 9, 2000) (finding that although the respondent's act of registering multiple domain names did not constitute bad faith registration and use pursuant to Policy para. 4(b)(ii), its practice of appropriating a complainant's mark to redirect Internet traffic to pornography constituted bad faith registration and use pursuant to Policy para. 4(b)(iv)).
2203. *See Mission KwaSizabantu v. Rost*, WIPO Case No. D2000-0279 (June 7, 2000) (interpreting "competitor" in the Policy to mean "one who acts in opposition to another and the context does not imply or demand any restricted meaning such as commercial or business competitor"). *But see Tribeca Film Ctr., Inc. v. Brusasco-Mackenzie*, WIPO Case No. D2000-1772 (Apr. 10, 2001) (rejecting the *Mission KwaSizabantu* approach and holding that "a respondent can 'disrupt the business of a competitor' only if it offers goods or services that can compete with or rival the goods or services offered by the trademark owner").

panels' definition of competition is a lot broader than under US trademark law, and panelists rarely regard the domain name holder's proximity to the mark holder as to be indicative of whether the parties are in competition.[2204] Panels have even found the existence of competition where the disputed domain results in a directory service that offers links to complainant's competitors.[2205] In addition, panelists rarely consider proximity or any other of the other infringement factors; quite simply, paragraph 4(b)(iii) does not require that a complainant establishes a likelihood of confusion, just only competition.

Panels have interpreted paragraph 4(b)(iv) to protect the consumers. Unlike a paragraph 4(a)(iii) claim, a paragraph 4(a)(iv) claim pivots on the existence of confusion, as well as commercial gain. However, unlike under US trademark law, proving confusion under paragraph 4(b)(iv) only requires a showing of similarity (proven out under paragraph 4(a)(i)). In other words, the mark's scope of use is of little importance.[2206] Paragraph 4(b)(iv) looks partially like a dilution claim, finding, for instance, because of the fame of the complainant's Britannica mark, the respondent's use of the britannica.com domain name to promote gambling is evidence of bad faith registration and use.[2207] Panelists commonly justify findings under Policy paragraph 4(b)(iv) by asserting that respondents could easily sell whatever products without appropriating the complainant's mark, rather than that the respondent's actions erode the distinctiveness of the complainant's mark.[2208]

In determining "commercial gain" under paragraph 4(b)(iv), panelists often infer pecuniary benefit even if there is no evidence of sales at the resultant website.[2209] Panels find this benefit from inferred revenues from advertising, links, and directory services at the resultant website as well as redirection from the disputed domain note to other domain names.[2210]

2204. *See, e.g., S. Exposure v. S. Exposure, Inc.*, NAF Case No. FA 94864 (July 18, 2000) (finding that the respondent acted in bad faith by attracting Internet users to a website that competes with complainant's business).

2205. *See Six Continents Hotels, Inc. v. Asia Ventures*, WIPO Case No. D2003-0659 (Oct. 14, 2003) (finding that redirecting Internet users seeking the complainant's mark to a website that lists competing services is evidence of bad faith registration and use pursuant to Policy para. 4(a)(iii)).

2206. *See supra*, Ch. 6, §5.IV.A.; *see also Goto.com, Inc. v. Walt Disney Co.*, 200 F.3d 1199, 1206 (9th Cir. 2000) ("With respect to Internet services, even services that are not identical are capable of confusing the public").

2207. *See Encyclopaedia Britannica Inc. v. Shedon.com*, WIPO Case No. D2000-0753 (Sept. 6, 2000) (finding that the respondent violated Policy para. 4(b)(iv) by using the domain name britannica.com to hyperlink to a gambling site).

2208. *See State Farm Mut. Auto.Ins.Co. v. Northway*, NAF Case No. FA 95464 (Oct. 11, 2000) (finding that the respondent can accomplish his stated purpose of providing news and information about State Farm without the use of State Farm's trademark in a name).

2209. *See Bank of Am. Corp. v. Out Island Props., Inc.*, NAF Case No. FA 154531 (June 3, 2003) (because that the disputed domain names resolved to search engines, and the panel inferred that the respondent received payment for pop-up advertisements, and that the domain names were registered and used in bad faith pursuant to Policy para. 4(b)(iv)).

2210. Types of legitimate benefits that typosquatters abuse include "click-through fees," which pay the referring website for customer's visits and "affiliate programs," which allow websites to act as promoters, usually through banner advertising, of another merchant's goods and services.

The factors under paragraph 4(b) are nonexclusive.[2211] A panel may consider the general intent of paragraph 4(a)(iii) to determine bad faith. Typosquatting (preying on consumers mistyping typographical errors) falls under the general application of Policy paragraph 4(a)(iii).[2212] "Passive holding" (domain name inactivity that amounts to bad faith) also arises under this application of paragraph 4(a)(iii).[2213]

§7 KEYWORD ADVERTISING

Whether or not the use or sale of trademarks in internet advertising constitutes trademark infringement has generated a new debate within the circuits. The primary dispute has been if trademark use in keyword advertising constitutes "use in commerce" under 15 U.S.C. § 1127 and therefore gives rise to an actionable trademark infringement claim.[2214]

Most circuits have found that keyword advertising sales of trademarks are "use in commerce" and a valid trademark infringement claim.[2215] However, in 2005 the

2211. *See Do the Hustle, LLC v. Tropic Web*, WIPO Case No. D2000-0624 (Aug. 21, 2000) ("[T]he examples [of bad faith] in Paragraph 4(b) are intended to be illustrative, rather than exclusive").

2212. *See Nat'l Ass'n of Prof'l Baseball League, Inc. v. Zuccarini*, WIPO Case No. D2000-1011 (Jan. 21, 2003).

("Typosquatting ... is the intentional misspelling of words with [the] intent to intercept and siphon off traffic from its intended destination, by preying on Internauts who make common typing errors. Typosquatting is inherently parasitic and of itself evidence of bad faith").

2213. *See Telstra Corp. v. Nuclear Marshmallows*, WIPO Case No. D2000-0003 (Feb. 18, 2000) ("[I]t is possible, in certain circumstances, for inactivity by the respondent to amount to the domain name being used in bad faith").

2214. The term "use in commerce" means the bona fide use of a mark in the ordinary course of trade, and not made merely to reserve a right in a mark. For the purposes of this chapter, a mark shall be deemed to be in use in commerce:

(1) on goods when:
   (a) it is placed in any manner on the goods or their containers or the displays associated therewith or on the tags or labels affixed thereto, or if the nature of the goods makes such placement impracticable, then on documents associated with the goods or their sale, and
   (b) the goods are sold or transported in commerce, and
(2) on services when it is used or displayed in the sale or advertising of services and the services are rendered in commerce, or the services are rendered in more than one State or in the US and a foreign country and the person rendering the services is engaged in commerce in connection with the services.

15 U.S.C. § 1127.

See, also, *Couture v. Playdom, Inc.*, 778 F.3d 1379 (Fed. Cir. 2015) (canceling the trademark PLAYDOM as the mark only appeared on a website marked "under construction" and no goods or serves were actually transacted).

2215. For example, *Boston Duck Tours, LP v. Super Duck Tours, LLC*, 527 F. Supp. 2d 205 (D. Mass. 2007); *Hearts on Fire Co., LLC v. Blue Nile, Inc.*, 603 F. Supp. 2d 274 (D. Mass. 2009); *800-JR Cigar, Inc., v. GoTo.com, Inc.*, 437 F. Supp. 2d 273 (D. N.J. 2006); Buying For *The Home, LLC v. Humble Abode, LLC*, 459 F. Supp. 2d 310 (D. N.J. 2006); *GEICO v. Google, Inc.*, 330 F. Supp. 2d 700 (E.D. Va. 2004); *Soilworks, LLC v. Midwest Indus. Supply, Inc.*, 575 F. Supp. 2d 1118 (D. Ariz. 2008).

Second Circuit's decision in *1-800 Contacts v. WhenU.com*[2216] deviated from other circuits when it held that trademark use in an unpublished directory of terms triggering pop-up advertising did not constitute use of the mark in commerce and therefore was not an actionable trademark infringement claim.[2217]

In 2009, the debate between the circuits over whether or not keyword advertising constitutes "use in commerce" came to a close when the Second Circuit reversed its position from its 1-800 Contacts holding. In *Rescuecom Corp. v. Google*, Inc.,[2218] the Second Circuit held that Google's sale of Rescuecom's mark as a search term in Google's Adwords and Keywords Suggestion Tool was "use in commerce."[2219]

2216. 414 F.3d 400 (2d Cir. 2005).
2217. *Id.*, at 403. WhenU.com delivered pop-up advertisements for 1-800 Contacts' competitors when computer users directly accessed 1-800 Contacts' website by using 1-800 Contacts' marks in an unpublished directory of terms. 1-800 Contacts' trademarks never appeared on the computer users' screen in the pop-up ads. *Id.*, at 405.
2218. 562 F.3d 123 (2d Cir. 2009).
2219. *Id.*, at 129–30. The Second Circuit included an appendix in the opinion "On the Meaning of 'Use in Commerce' in Sections 32 and 43 of the Lanham Act." *Id.*, at 131–41.

CHAPTER 7
Rights in Unregistered Marks

§1 LANHAM ACT SECTION 43(A)

I Generally

Apart from available state law claims, the owner of an unregistered mark may seek federal enforcement of rights under section 43(a) of the Lanham Act against one who uses that mark in a manner which may cause confusion as to the origin or sponsorship of goods or services. Moreover, section 43(a) also provides remedies where conduct by another misrepresents the nature, characteristics, qualities, or geographic origin of that person's or another's goods or services.

II Endorsement and Sponsorship Confusion: Section 43(a)

Section 43(a) is most prevalently used today to prevent use of trade dress by a third party. Trade dress is the overall business impression with which a consumer is confronted or the shape of the goods themselves or their packaging. Section 43(a) states that any person who, or on or in connection with any goods or services, or any container for goods, uses any word, term, name, symbol, or device which is likely to cause confusion, mistake or deception as to the affiliation, connection or association of such a person with another or the origin of the goods or services will be subject to the remedies outlined in the Lanham Act.[2220]

Section 43(a) has been applied to a wide variety of identifiers of source, including the inside of a Mexican restaurant,[2221] color alone,[2222] product configuration,[2223] and a

2220. 15 U.S.C. § 1125(a)(1) (Lanham Act § 43(a)(1)).
2221. *Two Pesos, Inc. v. Taco Cabana, Inc.*, 505 U.S. 763 (1992) (trade dress applicable to "Mexican theme" of restaurant).
2222. *Qualitex Co. v. Jacobson Products Co.*, 514 U.S. 159 (1995) (green-gold press pads were held sufficiently identifying source to warrant trademark protection).

host of other unregistered trade dress to prevent consumers from being misled about the origin or sponsorship of goods or services. In reality, the fact is that competitors are clearly using the broad provisions of section 43(a) to raise the cost of market entry and/or competition for market share. The two limitations on section 43(a) claims are that the plaintiff's trade dress must actually operate as a trademark to identify source and that the trade dress must not be functional. The Supreme Court in 1992 stated that trade dress cases brought under section 43(a) should be analyzed exactly like any other trademark case.[2224] In addition, section 43(a) may be applied to protect any registered or unregistered, distinctive mark (not only trade dress) from the likelihood of confusion as to origin, source, or sponsorship.[2225]

§2 FALSE ADVERTISING

Section 43(a) also makes actionable the use of any commercial representation which, in commercial advertising or promotion, misrepresents the nature, characteristics, qualities, or geographic origin of his or her or another person's goods, services, or commercial activities.[2226] This section makes actionable false advertising about your own or another's goods or services.

The Federal Trade Commission regulates the prosecution of false advertisements,[2227] and the FDA Administration prosecutes food producers that misbrand food, in a way, that is misleading.[2228] In addition, Article 43(c) provides private parties a cause of action when the misleading representation is likely to cause confusion, or exist in commercial advertising.[2229] Both competitors and noncompetitors can bring a Lanham act claim so long as the plaintiff:

(1) alleges an injury to a commercial interest in reputation or sales;
(2) shows economic or reputational injury flowing directly from the deceptive advertising.[2230]

A Lanham act claim can survive even if governmental agencies do not label the advertisement as false or misbranding.[2231]

Comparative advertising alone is not actionable under the Lanham Act. Truthful comparative advertising is perfectly acceptable as it assists consumers in making

---

2223. *Pagliero v. Wallace China Co.*, 198 F.2d 339 (9th Cir. 1962) (designs which are not functional or an aesthetic change in response to commercial desires is protected).
2224. *Two Pesos, Inc. v. Taco Cabana, Inc.*, 505 U.S. 763 (1992) (trade dress and trademark are protected under the same statute and there is no textual basis for analyzing them differently).
2225. *Allen v. Nat'l Video, Inc.*, 610 F. Supp. 612 (S.D.N.Y. 1985).
2226. 15 U.S.C. § 1125(a)(1)(B) (Lanham Act § 43(a)(1)(B)).
2227. Federal Trade Commission Act, 15 U.S.C. §§ 45(a), 52, 53.
2228. Federal Food, Drug, and Cosmetic Act, Pub. L. 113-108, 52 Stat. 1040, 21 U.S.C.§ 343(a).
2229. 15 U.S.C. § 1125(a)(1)(B) (Lanham Act § 43(a)(1)(B)).
2230. *Lexmark Int'l v. Static Control Components, Inc.*, 134 S. Ct. 1377 (2014).
2231. *POM Wonderful LLC v. Coca-Cola Co.*, 134 S. Ct. 2228 (2014) (holding that Food, Drug, and Cosmetic Act (FDCA) does not preclude a private party from bringing a Lanham Act claim challenging as misleading a food label that is regulated by the FDCA).

rational choices in the marketplace. However, misleading consumers by stating untrue claims regarding a competitor's product should be actionable because the competitor may not know of the advertisement or may incur the costs of other advertising to overcome the false association planted in the minds of the consumers by the untrue advertising. Section 43(a) concurrently recognizes how important a producer reputation is and also how fragile that reputation is in the minds of the consumers.

CHAPTER 8

Infringement and Remedies

The owner of a trademark has the exclusive right to use the mark in commerce.[2232] This right includes the right to use the mark itself on or in connection with identified goods or services as well as the right to license this right to third parties. Any attempt to use the mark by others not licensed by the owner of the mark, or adoption of a similar mark on similar goods or services, may give rise to an infringement claim by the registrant or first user. Section 32 of Lanham Act provides as follows:

1. Any person who shall, without the consent of the registrant—
   a. use in commerce any reproduction, counterfeit, copy, or colorable imitation of a registered mark in connection with the sale, offering for sale, distribution, or advertising of any goods or services on or in connection with such use is likely to cause confusion, or to cause mistake, or to deceive; or
   b. reproduce, counterfeit, copy or colorably imitate a registered mark and apply such reproduction, counterfeit, copy or colorable imitation to labels, signs, prints, packages, wrappers, receptacles or advertisements intended to be used in advertising of goods or services on or in connection with such use is likely to cause confusion, or to cause mistake, or to deceive.

The infringer of the mark shall be liable in a civil action by the registrant for the remedies hereinafter provided.[2233]

§1 LIKELIHOOD OF CONFUSION

I The Analytical Factors

In order to prevail under section 32 of the Lanham Act, and, for unregistered marks under section 43(a), the plaintiff must show that there is a likelihood that the consumer

2232. *See supra*, Ch. 6, §2.IV. Concurrent Lanham Act Registration.
2233. 15 U.S.C. § 1114(1) (Lanham Act § 32(1)).

will be confused, mislead, or deceived regarding the source or origin of the goods or services. That is, the plaintiff must show only a likelihood of confusion and need not establish actual confusion. Likelihood of confusion is the central requirement in actions both at common law and under the federal trademark statute.[2234] While each circuit has adopted its own list of elements and tests for determining likelihood of confusion, they are remarkably similar. The Second Circuit's version, set out in 1961 in *Polaroid Corp. v. Polarad Electronics Corp.*,[2235] is perhaps the most comprehensive and the most popular. It established eight factors to be considered in determining if there is a likelihood of confusion, and therefore a finding of infringement:

(1) Strength of plaintiff's mark.
(2) The degree of similarity of the marks.
(3) The proximity of the products or services in the marketplace.
(4) The likelihood that the plaintiff will bridge the gap (narrowing significant market differences).
(5) Evidence of actual confusion.
(6) Defendant's good faith in adopting the mark.
(7) The quality of the defendant's product or service.
(8) The sophistication of the buyers.[2236]

These criteria are not intended to be exhaustive nor is any one of the criterion intended to be dispositive.[2237] Furthermore, no specific combination of these criteria will guarantee a specific outcome. Rather, each case will be determined on the peculiar facts presented to the court. The relevant test for likelihood of confusion is only intended as a guide for courts to follow when considering all of the circumstances in a particular case. Courts are not to make their decision based on one fact.

For example, in *Polaroid v. Polarad*,[2238] the plaintiff claimed that Polarad infringed its trademark. Polaroid, of course, makes and sells photographic cameras and films. Polarad's primary line of business included microwave apparatus and television studio equipment. The Polaroid court held that regarding given the elements of strength of Polaroid's mark and the similarity of the two marks, Polaroid prevailed. However, analysis of the other factors either was inconclusive or dictated a finding of no confusion. That is, a particular finding on one or two elements will not be sufficient to support a finding of confusion.[2239]

2234. *Polaroid Corp. v. Polarad Electronics Corp.*, 287 F.2d 492 (2d Cir. 1961).
2235. *Id.*
2236. *Polaroid Corp. v. Polarad Electronics Corp.*, 287 F.2d 492, 495 (2d Cir. 1961).
2237. *Id.*, at 494. It should be said that all of the circuits note this same caveat. It is rare to see a court incorporate factors beyond those stated in *Polaroid* although the courts have provided the latitude to do so.
2238. 287 F.2d 492 (2d Cir. 1961).
2239. *Id.*, at 494.

A Circuit Variations

Each federal circuit has adopted its own list of factors to be taken into consideration when determining the likelihood of confusion.

The First Circuit considers the following:

(1) Similarity of the marks.
(2) Similarity of the goods.
(3) The relationship between the parties' channels of trade.
(4) The relationship between the parties' advertising.
(5) The classes of prospective purchasers.
(6) Evidence of actual confusion.
(7) The defendants' intent in adopting the mark.
(8) The strength of the plaintiff's mark.[2240]

The Third Circuit will consider the following:

(1) The degree of similarity between the marks.
(2) The strength of the plaintiff's mark.
(3) The price of the relevant goods.
(4) The duration during which the defendant used the mark without any actual confusion arising.
(5) The intent of the defendant.
(6) Evidence of actual confusion.
(7) Channels of trade.
(8) Extent of overlap in targeted markets.
(9) Similarity of functions of the marks.
(10) Other factors that might make the consumer believe or expect the defendant's goods emanate from the plaintiff.[2241]

The Fourth Circuit will consider the following:

(1) Strength or distinctiveness of the mark.
(2) Similarity of the two marks.
(3) Similarity of the goods or services on which the mark is used.
(4) Similarity of the two businesses.
(5) Similarity in advertising.
(6) Intent of the defendant.
(7) Actual confusion.[2242]

2240. *Keds Corp. v. Renee International Trading Corp.*, 888 F.2d 215 (1st Cir. 1989).
2241. *Interpalce Corp. v. Lapp, Inc.*, 721 F.2d 460 (3d Cir. 1983).
2242. *Pizzeria Uno Corp. v. Templeriple*, 747 F.2d 1522 (4th Cir. 1984). However, the Fourth Circuit is open to evaluating other factors. *See, e.g.*, *Perini Corp. v. Perini Constr., Inc.*, 915 F.2d 121

The Fifth Circuit will consider the following elements:

(1) Strength of the mark.
(2) Similarity of design between the marks.
(3) Similarity of the products.
(4) Identity of retail outlets and purchasers.
(5) Similarity of advertising channels.
(6) The defendant's intent.
(7) Actual confusion.
(8) Degree of purchaser care.[2243]

The Sixth Circuit will consider the following factors:

(1) Strength of the plaintiff's mark.
(2) Relatedness of the goods.
(3) Similarity of the marks.
(4) Actual confusion.
(5) Marketing channels.
(6) Likely degree of purchaser care.
(7) The defendant's intent in selecting the mark.
(8) Likelihood of expansion of the product lines.[2244]

The Seventh Circuit will consider the following elements:

(1) Similarity of mark.
(2) Similarity of products.
(3) Area and manner of concurrent use.
(4) The degree of care likely to be exercised by consumers.
(5) The strength of the plaintiff's mark.
(6) Actual confusion.
(7) Intent of the alleged infringer.[2245]

The Eighth Circuit applies the following test:

(1) The strength of the plaintiff's mark.
(2) Similarity of the marks.
(3) The degree to which the products compete.
(4) The defendant's intent.

(4th Cir. 1990); *Sara Lee Corp. v. Kayser-Roth Corp.*, 81 F.3d 455 (4th Cir. 1996); and *Rosetta Stone Ltd. v. Google, Inc.*, 676 F.3d 144 (4th Cir. 2012).

2243. *Streamline Production Systems, Inc. v. Streamline Manufacturing, Inc.*, 851 F.3d 440, 453 (5th Cir. 2017).

2244. *Frisch's Restaurant, Inc., v. Shoney's, Inc.*, 759 F.2d 1261 (6th Cir. 1985).

2245. *Helene Curtis Industries, Inc. v. Church & Dwight Co., Inc.*, 560 F.2d 1325 (7th Cir. 1977).

(5) Actual confusion.
(6) Degree of purchaser care.[2246]

The Ninth Circuit panels have been inconsistent in their application of the test. The broadest test lists the following considerations:

(1) Strength of the mark.
(2) Proximity of the goods.
(3) Similarity of the marks.
(4) Actual confusion.
(5) Marketing channels.
(6) Degree of care exercised by purchasers.
(7) The defendant's intent.
(8) Likelihood of expansion of the product lines.[2247]

The Tenth Circuit applies the following factors:

(1) Similarity of the marks.
(2) The defendant's intent.
(3) Actual confusion.
(4) Marketing channels.
(5) Purchaser care.
(6) Strength or weakness of the marks.[2248]

Finally, the Eleventh Circuit applies the following factors:

(1) The nature of the plaintiff's mark.
(2) Similarity of the marks.
(3) Similarity of the products.
(4) Similarity of the parties' retail outlets and customers.
(5) Nature of the parties' advertising.
(6) The defendant's intent.
(7) Extent of actual confusion.[2249]

Virtually all of the courts above list at least the following common denominators in their analysis of a likelihood of confusion.

2246. *Squirtco. v. Seven Up Co.*, 628 F.2d 1086 (8th Cir. 1980).
2247. *AMF, Inc., v. Sleekcraft Boats*, 599 F.2d 341 (9th Cir. 1979).
2248. 1-800 *Contacts, Inc. v. Lens.com, Inc.*, 722 F.3d 1229, 1239 (10th Cir. 2013).
2249. *Wesco Mfg., Inc. v. Tropical Attractions of Palm Beach, Inc.*, 833 F.2d 1484 (11th Cir. 1987).

B *Mark Similarity*

When considering whether two marks are similar, courts look at the similarity in sound, meaning, and appearance, in addition to the relative closeness in the sound, sight, and meaning of the marks.[2250] Any one or any combination of these can be influential in determining the similarity of a mark. It is not necessary for a mark to be exactly like another in order to be infringing. The Supreme Court has stated that if there is enough similarity to create confusion as to the source of the goods or services, the mark is infringing.[2251] The similarity test should focus on the basis of the total effect of the mark, rather than on a comparison of the individual features of the mark.[2252] Similarity in sound is examined by verbalizing the mark. Even in the absence of any spelling similarity, if the two marks are close in sound as spoken, the marks may be considered similar.[2253]

Similarity in appearance involves a visual analysis of the marks. Analyzing a mark by sight is especially appropriate for picture and graphic marks[2254] but also naturally deals with whether two word marks are spelled the same, have the same dominant features, or use the same type of script.

Similarity in meaning is examined through definition, context, and association. If two marks create the same association, they can be found similar in meaning.[2255] A mark may not be similar in sound or appearance, but if it means the same as the plaintiff's mark, it may be adjudicated as similar.[2256]

Foreign word marks are translated into English and assigned their meaning in English. In addition, word marks may infringe picture marks if the meaning is the same or closely related.[2257]

C *Mark Strength*

It is axiomatic in American trademark law that strong marks deserve more protection than weak marks. In determining whether a trademark is strong, most courts consider whether the mark is arbitrary, fanciful, suggestive, or descriptive. The more arbitrary or fanciful the mark is, the stronger it will be. In determining if a mark is strong, some

2250. Restatement (Third) Unfair Competition § 21(a) (1995).
2251. *Saxlehner v. Eisner & Mendelson Co.*, 179 U.S. 19 (1900) (general resemblance of the marks likely to mislead).
2252. *Mutual of Omaha Insurance Co. v. Novak*, 836 F.2d 397, 399 (8th Cir. 1987) (Mutant of Omaha found to be similar in overall appearance to Mutual of Omaha).
2253. *Standard Oil Co. v. Humble Oil & Refining Co., Esso, Inc. v. Standard Oil Refining Co.*, 363 F.2d 945 (5th Cir. 1966) ("Esso" and "S.O." are verbally similar); *G.D. Searle & Co. v. Chas. Pfizer & Co.*, 265 F.2d 385 (7th Cir. 1959) ("Bonamine" and "Draminine" are verbally similar).
2254. In examining picture and graphic marks, the T.T.A.B. looks at the overall visual impression of the mark. *Lacoste Alligator S.A. v. Everlast World's Boxing Headquarters*, 204 U.S.P.Q. 945 (T.T.A.B. 1979) (noting that a flying dragon was not similar to an alligator).
2255. *Hancock v. American Steel & Wire Co.*, 203 F.2d 737 (C.C.P.A. 1953) (CYCLONE and TORNADO for wire fencing are confusing as to similarity).
2256. *Standard Oil Co. v. Standard Oil Co.*, 252 F.2d 65 (10th Cir. 1958).
2257. *Mobil Oil Corp. v. Pegasus Petroleum Corp.*, 818 F.2d 254 (2d Cir. 1987) (PEGASUS was found to infringe Mobil's logo which constitutes a flying horse).

courts will also consider whether the mark is registered and whether that registration has become incontestable. The objective of analyzing a mark's strength is to determine the extent to which a mark has come to identify the source or origin of goods or services in the minds of the relevant consuming public. If a mark has a high degree of consumer recognition, it will be considered a strong mark. If there is a low degree of consumer recognition, it will be considered a weak mark.

D *Similarity of the Goods or Services*

When considering the similarity of the goods or services, US courts will be most concerned with the amount of direct competition between goods. If the goods are in direct competition, the amount of similarity of the actual products necessary to support an injunction and/or damages will be lower.[2258] That is, courts will conduct a detailed, side-by-side analysis of the goods or services at stake. However, the most important concern will usually be whether the relevant goods or services are in competition. If they are in competition, the showing necessary to support a finding of a likelihood of confusion will be lessened.

E *Channels of Trade and Advertising (Proximity)*

Courts will also consider whether or not the relevant goods or services are confronted by the same or similar consumer in the same or similar time, place, or manner. This is known as proximity of the products or services. This is largely a structural economic analysis of the relevant goods and services and how they find their way to the consumer. Proximity of the goods or services could address the physical location of a product in a store,[2259] whether the plaintiff's goods are sold only at wholesale and the defendant's goods or services are sold at retail,[2260] or whether the goods or advertising flows through commerce in a similar chain of control. Similarity of the products themselves is also part of this analysis.

F *Consumer Sophistication and Care*

When courts consider the consumer level of sophistication, they are primarily concerned with the comparative nature of the consumers who purchase the relevant goods

2258. *HRL Associates, Inc. v. Weiss Associates, Inc.*, 12 U.S.P.Q. 1819 (T.T.A.B. 1989), *aff'd*, 902 F.2d 1546 (Fed. Cir. 1990); *Borden Ice Cream v. Borden's Condensed Milk Co.*, 201 Fed. 510 (7th Cir. 1912) (stating that the likelihood of confusion between ice cream and milk is low due to the fact that the products do not directly compete).
2259. For example, snack foods such as potato and corn chips are placed in the same general area, often in the same aisle in grocery stores, whereas a soda product is not likely to be placed next to a powdered beverage. *See, e.g., Vitarroz Corp. v. Borden, Inc.*, 644 F.2d 960 (2d Cir. 1981). The greater the "space" between the two products, the less likely the confusion.
2260. *Dawn Doughnut Company, Inc. v. Hart's Foods Stores, Inc.*, 267 F.2d 358 (2d Cir. 1959) (retail and wholesale markets are distinguished in determining likelihood of confusion).

or services. If both parties' consumers are impulse buyers making purchasing decisions with little or no care or concern, it will be significantly easier to establish confusion than if the purchasers make buying decisions only after in-depth study or analysis implementing training or experience in the process.[2261]

G *Actual Confusion: Survey Evidence*

Evidence of actual confusion is only one element of the analysis of whether there is a likelihood of confusion. That is, it is possible (and in actual practice happens quite frequently) for there to be actual evidence of actual confusion and yet no likelihood of confusion. Although evidence of actual confusion is not a requirement in proving infringement, it weighs heavily in favor of the plaintiff.[2262] Proof of actual confusion is required, however, when damages are claimed.[2263] The premise behind this distinction is that if a party seeks to collect damages, he, she or it must show that damage occurred via a loss of sales due to consumers being confused.[2264]

Courts have recognized that it is difficult to find incidences of actual confusion,[2265] and it is a reversible error for a judge to ignore evidence of actual confusion in decision-making.[2266] Evidence of actual confusion must show that the confusion was somehow caused by the defendant and not merely the product of consumer error. For example, if a customer misreads a phone book and thereby inadvertently places a call to a junior user, it is considered consumer error and not actual confusion.[2267]

Evidence of actual confusion will not guarantee a finding of infringement. Instances of actual confusion must constitute a sufficient basis upon which to determine infringement has occurred. Actual confusion which is minimal will be weighted accordingly by the court.[2268]

Surveys are commonly utilized to determine if there is existence of actual confusion in the marketplace. To be admissible as evidence, surveys must be performed objectively without leading or misleading questions, they must be independently drafted and conducted, and they must not cause prejudice. Even when surveys

2261. *E. & J. Gallo Winery v. Consorzio Del Gallo Nero*, 782 F. Supp. 457 (N.D. Cal. 1991) (citing *Taylor Wine Co. v. Bully Hill Vineyards, Inc.*, 569 F.2d 731, 196 U.S.P.Q. 593 (2d Cir. 1978) (stating that purchasers of inexpensive wine are not connoisseurs who have any knowledge of wine selection).

2262. *Maternally Yours, Inc. v. Your Maternity Shop, Inc.*, 234 F.2d 538 (2d Cir. 1956) (confusion of directory assistance operators and misdirected mail evidence of actual confusion).

2263. *See infra* Ch. 8, §3.II. Damages.

2264. *Brunswick Corp. v. Spinit Reel Co.*, 832 F.2d 513 (10th Cir. 1987) (in order to recover damages a plaintiff must show loss of sales due to actual confusion). *But see Taco Cabana Int'l, Inc. v. Two Pesos, Inc.*, 932 F.2d 1113 (5th Cir. 1991) (volatility of the restaurant business and application of the "headstart" theory negate need to provide evidence of actual lost sales), *aff'd*, 505 U.S. 763 (1992).

2265. *AMF, Inc. v. Sleekcraft Boats*, 599 F.2d 341 (9th Cir. 1979).

2266. *Frostig v. Saga Enterprises, Inc.*, 272 Ore. 565, 539 P.2d 154 (1975) (actual confusion cannot be ignored by a judge in cases where similarity is slight).

2267. *Lang v. Retirement Living Publications Co.*, 949 F.2d 576 (2d Cir. 1991).

2268. *Id.* (actual confusion which does not create an injury is insufficient to show likelihood of confusion).

are conducted with the utmost care, there will still be objections by the party not submitting the survey. However, surveys are exceptionally important in infringement litigation. Some courts presume that the result of a survey would have been against a party who refused to commission a survey in support of that party's position.[2269]

H Intent

Courts have given inconsistent weight to the element of intent. Historically, intent was required in order to find confusion under common law.[2270] According to Judge Learned Hand, the intent to misdirect consumers from the plaintiff to the defendant was "the Law and Prophet" of the subject.[2271] However, this strict reading of unfair competition law is clearly far too rigid.[2272] Today, courts define the trademark right far more broadly than requiring actual predatory intent and focus on the effect on the marketplace. The intent of the defendant like "actual confusion" is only one element of the analysis.

Although a showing of actual predatory intent is not necessary to prevail in an infringement case in the US, a lack of predatory intent is not an absolute defense.[2273] Again, the point of infringement analysis is to determine the "likely" effect on the marketplace. If actual predatory intent was an absolute requirement or if the lack of predatory intent was an absolute defense, the focus would be shifted to the conduct of the defendant and away from the effect the defendant's conduct had on the marketplace. The effect on the marketplace is the primary consideration of US trademark law.

Historically, none of the prior federal trademark statutes required actual predatory intent to prove infringement.[2274] A distinction has been made between the occurrence of confusion and the intent of one producer to trade off of the goodwill of another.[2275] Finally, the Lanham Act itself does not require that actual predatory intent be established before a finding of infringement would be appropriate.[2276]

2269. *Pebble Beach Co. v. Tour 18, Ltd.*, 942 F. Supp. 1513, 1560 (S.D. Tex. 1996), *aff'd*, 155 F.3d 526 (5th Cir. 1998); *Gillette Co. v. Norelco Consumer Prods. Co.*, 946 F. Supp. 115, 130 (D. Mass. 1996).

2270. *McLean v. Fleming*, 96 U.S. 245 (1878) (intent not required where infringement is clear).

2271. *Yale Electric Corp. v. Robertson*, 26 F.2d 972 (2d Cir. 1928).

2272. *See* Kenneth L. Port, *Learned Hand's Trademark Jurisprudence: Legal Positivism and Myth of the Prophet*, 27 Pac. L. J. 221 (1996) (criticizing Learned Hand's rigid adherence to the old common law notion that predatory intent was necessary for a finding of infringement).

2273. *President & Trustees of Colby College v. Colby College-New Hampshire*, 508 F.2d 804 (1st Cir. 1975) (when likelihood of confusion is found, expression of "good faith" is not a defense).

2274. *Elgin Nat'l Watch Co. v. Illinois Watch Case Co.*, 179 U.S. 665 (1901) (1881 Act in effect); *Thaddeus Davids Co. v. Davids Mfg. Co.*, 233 U.S. 461 (1914) (1905 Act in effect); *Fleischmann Distilling Corp. v. Maier Brewing Co.*, 314 F.2d 149 (9th Cir.), *cert. denied*, 374 U.S. 830 (1963) (1946 Trademark Act in effect).

2275. *Lois Sportswear, U.S.A., Inc. v. Levi Strauss & Co.*, 799 F.2d 867 (2d Cir. 1986).

2276. 15 U.S.C. §§ 1114(1)(a) (Lanham Act § 32(1)(a)) and 1117 (Lanham Act § 35). Under the Lanham Act intent is required to obtain certain damages resulting from a finding of infringement. Lanham Act § 32(1)(b) and 32(2) (innocence in infringement activity directed by another party limits action to injunction on future printing of infringed mark).

I Likelihood of Bridging the Gap

When the goods or services of the parties to an infringement case are not in competition, most courts will also consider the likelihood that the plaintiff will bridge the gap between its goods or services and the defendant's goods or services. Such likelihood of bridging the gap can be established in two ways. The easiest way is arguing that although the plaintiff is not currently selling the defendant's products, the defendant's goods amount to a natural expansion of the plaintiff's line of business. The second method of establishing the likelihood that the plaintiff will or would bridge the gap is showing actual evidence of an actual intent by the plaintiff. Although they actually intended to bridge the gap, the presence of the defendant in that market makes such expansion difficult, or would thereby cause confusion in the minds of the consumer.[2277]

II Second-Comer Doctrine

Trademark protection is based upon first use. Any producer who enters the market with a mark which is similar to that of a producer who is already established in the marketplace runs the risk of being charged with infringement. Therefore, a new entrant must take time to investigate the availability of its intended mark or whether its intended mark will be too similar to an existing mark. Failure to investigate does not remove liability from the new user.[2278]

In fact, evidence that shows a junior user had knowledge of a senior user prior to his or her own adoption weighs more heavily against the junior user in an infringement action. This is particularly true when the senior user has established a strong presence in the market.[2279]

III Question of Law or Fact: Standard of Review

In the US, the standard by which an appellate court will review what the lower courts have done is sometimes as important as the merits of the case itself. Courts fundamentally consider all questions of law or questions of fact raised to it on appeal. Questions of law are reviewed de novo (meaning the court need not give deference to the lower court opinion because, presumably, the appellate court knows at least as well, if not

2277. *AMF Inc. v. Sleekcraft Boats*, 599 F.2d 341 (9th Cir. 1979) (both parties being engaged in diversification of product lines leads to the strong possibility that each will enter the other's market).

2278. *San Fernando Electric Mfg. Co. v. JFD Electronics Components Corp.*, 565 F.2d 683 (C.C.P.A. 1977) (it is well established in trademark law that junior users are subject to the rights of senior users and failure to search prior to adopting a mark does not relieve a junior user of liability). *See also Big O Tire Dealers, Inc. v. Goodyear Tire & Rubber Co.*, 561 F.2d 1365 (10th Cir. 1977).

2279. *J & J Snack Foods Corp. v. McDonald's Corp.*, 932 F.2d 1460 (Fed. Cir. 1991) (it is reasonable to expect that a newcomer will take sufficient care in adopting a mark when a well-known senior user exists).

better, what the law of any given subject is). Questions of fact are reviewed under the clearly erroneous standard (meaning unless the lower court made some clear error in its finding of facts, the appellate court will not disturb that finding because the lower court judge is present during the presentation of all evidence and can assess its credibility on a firsthand basis).

Likelihood of confusion is usually considered a question of fact and therefore reviewed under the clearly erroneous standard.[2280] In fact, the Restatement (Third) of Unfair Competition (1993) also classifies infringement as a question of fact. However, a number of courts now consider infringement to be a question of law and therefore reviewable under the de novo standard.[2281] Still others consider it a mixed question of law and fact where the analysis and evidence of each of the elements leading to the conclusion of infringement are questions of fact, but the actual finding of confusion itself in the end is a question of law.[2282]

Because the standard of review is such an important issue, one would prefer to have one consistent rule in the US. However, no such rule appears forthcoming. Each circuit's rule on this issue must be analyzed each time a case is appealed. The benefit of not having a nationwide, rigid rule on the appropriate standard of review is that in each case a good faith argument can be made by counsel that one or the other standard should prevail.

IV Reverse Confusion

By definition, trademark confusion results when consumers come to believe that products emanating from a second-comer are actually those of the entity with prior rights. When trade is diverted in this manner, consumers are confused, the market is upset and this is, therein lies, what is supposed to be the underlying justification of an injunction and/or damages.

However, if the second-comer devotes substantial resources in advertising and marketing the line of goods associated with the mark, consumers can be led to the belief that the first comer is the entity causing this confusion and believe that the first comer's products emanate from the second-comer.[2283]

This type of confusion is called reverse confusion. A specific example works best to illustrate this issue. In *Sands, Taylor & Wood Co. v. Quaker Oats Co.*,[2284] Quaker Oats was originally ordered to pay over USD 43 million in a reverse confusion case. In that case, Quaker Oats adopted the trademark "Gatorade is Thirst Aid" for use on its isotonic beverages. However, the plaintiff had already used and registered THIRST-AID for a variety of products including beverages. When Gatorade flooded the market with

2280. *See, e.g., Dieter v. B&H Industries, Inc.*, 880 F.2d 322 (11th Cir. 1989); *Smith Fiberglass Products, Inc. v. Ameron, Inc.*, 7 F.3d 1327 (7th Cir. 1993).
2281. *See, e.g., Giant Food, Inc. v. Nation's Foodservice, Inc.*, 710 F.2d 1565 (Fed. Cir. 1983).
2282. *See Bristol-Meyers Squibb Co. v. McNeil-P.P.C., Inc.*, 973 F.2d 1033 (2d Cir. 1992).
2283. *Sands, Taylor & Wood Co. v. Quaker Oats Co.*, 978 F.2d 947 (7th Cir. 1992).
2284. *Id.*

its "thirst-aid" commercials, purchasers of the plaintiff's goods came to the incorrect conclusion that the plaintiff's goods came from or were sponsored by Gatorade.

This is a classic case of reverse confusion. Quaker Oats was enjoined and initially (although reduced on appeal) ordered to pay USD 43 million in damages, prejudgment interest, and attorneys' fees.[2285]

However, the doctrine of reverse confusion will not allow mark holders to assert trademark law to protect expired copyrights.[2286] In *Dastar Corp. v. Twentieth Century Fox Film Corp.*,[2287] Dastar repackaged and sold a war movie, originally produced by Twentieth Century Fox, with an expired copyright. Part of Dastar's repackaging was to remove Twentieth Century Fox's mark and affix the Dastar mark to the movie. The Court held that the false origin of goods language in Lanham Act section 43(a)(1)(A) does not cover false designations of the producer or creator of a creative or communicative work, such as a movie. Specifically, the Court refused to allow section 43(a)(1)(A) to limit the right of the public to copy and use works on which the copyright had expired.[2288]

V Initial Interest Confusion

Although highly controversial and not predictable, some courts recognize the concept of initial interest confusion.[2289] Although the term "initial interest confusion" was coined to deal with cybersquatters, the idea of presale confusion is much older.[2290] Initial interest confusion occurs when a party makes a mark similar enough to encourage a purchaser to have interest in a product, even if the consumer realizes at some point prior to purchase that the product is not the one sought.[2291] In this way, the competitor captures the consumer's interest without committing actual confusion. Initial interest confusion has been used successfully in prohibiting some metatag or keyword searching[2292] and sometimes not.[2293] To be sure, initial interest confusion is more likely to be found when the products are similar or there is competition between the parties.

2285. *Sands, Taylor & Wood v. The Quaker Oats Co.*, 18 U.S.P.Q.2d 1457 (N.D. Ill. 1990) (award includes 10% profits on sales of the defendant's product along with prejudgment interest, attorney fees and costs).
2286. Thereby melding trademark law into copyright law to extend a concept of moral rights, a concept not protected in U.S. Copyright law.
2287. 539 U.S. 23, 123 (2003).
2288. *Id.*
2289. *Brookfield Commc'n, Inc. v. West Coast Entm't Corp.*, 174 F.3d 1036 (9th Cir. 1999).
2290. *Electronic Design & Sales, Inc. v. Electronic Data Sys. Corp.*, 954 F.2d 713 (Fed. Cir. 1992).
2291. *See generally* J. Thomas McCarthy, 4 McCarthy on Trademarks and Unfair Competition § 23:6 (5th ed. 2021).
2292. *Victoria's Secret Stores v. Artco Equip. Co., Inc.*, 194 F. Supp. 2d 704 (S.D. Ohio 2002).
2293. *Playboy Enter., Inc. v. Terri Welles, Inc.*, 78 F. Supp. 2d 1066 (S.D. Cal. 1999) *affirmed in part and reversed in part by Playboy Enter., Inc. v. Terri Welles, Inc.*, 279 F.3d 796 (9th Cir. 2002).

§2 DEFENSES

There are multiple defenses available in an infringement case. Any affirmative defense not raised in the answer is considered waived,[2294] so it is important to consider all available defenses at the outset of any infringement claim.

I Invalidity of Plaintiff's Mark

The first and usually the best defense is claiming that the plaintiff's mark is invalid. If the plaintiff's trademark is not valid, a defendant cannot be liable for infringement. The plaintiff may use federal registration as prima facie evidence of validity;[2295] if the mark has become incontestable, as conclusive evidence of validity;[2296] or claim that an unregistered mark is inherently distinctive. The defendant then has the burden of proof (a preponderance of the evidence) to show that the mark is not valid.[2297]

The most common ground for invalidity is that the plaintiff's mark is or has become generic. A mark is generic if the primary significance of the mark is to identify the product and not the producer.

In addition to these two popular defenses, section 33(b) of the Lanham Act lists several other defenses. These include fraudulently obtained marks, abandonment, deceptive use, marks used in violation of antitrust laws, and defenses such as laches and estoppel.[2298] Abandonment,[2299] descriptiveness,[2300] and functionality[2301] are also legitimate defenses.

II Fraud

Fraud in obtaining a federal registration is grounds for cancelation of a trademark registration at any point of time, including after incontestability has been established. However, some courts have found that common law rights asserted under section 43(a) of the Lanham Act are not affected even by a finding that a mark was fraudulently registered.[2302]

The elements of fraud are as follows:

2294. *U.S. Olympic Comm. v. Bata Shoe Co.*, 225 U.S.P.Q. 340 (T.T.A.B. 1984).
2295. 15 U.S.C. § 1115(a) (Lanham Act § 33(a)).
2296. 15 U.S.C. § 1115(b) (Lanham Act § 33(b)).
2297. *GTE Corp. v. Williams*, 904 F.2d 536 (10th Cir. 1990) (registration by the USPTO without requiring any showing of secondary meaning raises the presumption that a mark is arbitrary, fanciful, or suggestive).
2298. *Id.*
2299. *See supra*, Ch. 4, §3.II.
2300. *See supra*, Ch. 6, §2.II.
2301. *See supra*, Ch. 2, §3.III.
2302. *Orient Express Trading Co. v. Federated Dep't. Stores, Inc.*, 842 F.2d 650 (2d Cir. 1988) (assertion of common law rights is not precluded by fraudulent federal registration).

(1) A false representation regarding a material fact.[2303]
(2) Knowledge or belief that the representation is false.
(3) Intent to induce action or prevent action in reliance of the misrepresentation.[2304]
(4) Reasonable reliance on the misrepresentation.
(5) Damage resulting from the reliance on the misrepresentation.[2305] For a misrepresentation to be fraudulent, the misrepresentation must be made with the knowledge that it is false. Inaccuracies are not enough to substantiate a fraud claim.[2306] However, an innocent mistake made during prosecution can rescue a registration if corrected.[2307]

III Antitrust Violations

In order to claim antitrust violations as a defense to infringement, the trademark use must be more than incidental; it must be directly involved in the antitrust violation.[2308] The only party who is able to assert an antitrust claim is the party who is directly affected by such behavior.[2309]

IV Fair Use

There are two different types of defenses encompassed under the umbrella term of fair use. The first is the classic fair use defense that arises when the plaintiff's mark is descriptive in nature (not a fanciful or coined term)[2310] and the defendant uses it in a

2303. Material misrepresentations are those that would have prevented registration had they been disclosed at the time of registration. *Sentry Chemical Co. v. Pennwalt Corp. v. Sentry Chemical Co.*, 219 U.S.P.Q. 542 (T.T.A.B. 1983).
2304. However, in *Chutter, Inc. v. Great Management Group, LLC* and *Chutter, Inc. v. Great Concepts, LLC*, 2021 U.S.P.Q.2d 1001 (TTAB 2021), the TTAB expressed a willingness to allow "reckless disregard" for the truth of the assertion to satisfy this intent requirement.
2305. *See* 5 McCarthy, Trademarks § 31:61 (4th ed. 2004), *construed in San Juan Prod., Inc. v. San Juan Pools of Kansas., Inc.*, 849 F.2d 468 (10th Cir. 1988).
2306. *King-Size, Inc. v. Frank's King Size Clothes, Inc.*, 547 F. Supp. 1138 (S.D. Tex. 1982) (good faith belief of use sufficient for registration statement; use of honest but inaccurate statements does not prove fraud).
2307. *Universal Overall Co. v. Stonecutter Mills Corp.*, 379 F.2d 983 (C.C.P.A. 1967) (original application based upon fraudulent information will not defeat registration when amendment was made prior to publication).
2308. *Carl Zeiss Stiftuing v. V.E.B. Carl Zeiss, Jena*, 298 F. Supp. 1309 (S.D.N.Y. 1969), *modified*, 433 F.2d 686 (2d Cir. 1970).
2309. *Central Ben. Mut. Ins. Co. v. Blue Cross & Blue Shield Assoc.*, 711 F. Supp. 1423 (S.D. Ohio 1989).
2310. *Zatarains, Inc. v. Oak Grove Smokehouse, Inc.*, 698 F.2d 786 (5th Cir. 1983) ("Fish-fri" is descriptive and necessary for others to use in describing their products); *But* cf. *Car-Freshener Corp. v. S.C. Johnson & Son, Inc.*, 70 F.3d 267 (2d Cir. 1995) (whether the plaintiff's mark is descriptive is less important; focus should be on whether the defendant used the mark in a descriptive and nontrademark manner).

way to describe its goods or services and not to identify source.[2311] If the classic fair use defense is employed, then the defendant must prove that it is using the plaintiff's mark descriptively, fairly, and in good faith.[2312] There is a possibility of consumer confusion with descriptive fair use.[2313] However, the policy behind fair use seeks to deter undesirable monopolies over descriptive terms.[2314]

The second type of fair use is nominative fair use, which arises when the defendant uses the plaintiff's mark, not descriptively but rather in a traditional trademark sense to identify the plaintiff's goods or services.[2315] With nominative (i.e., naming the plaintiff) fair use the defendant uses the plaintiff's mark because there is no better way to identify the defendant's goods or services. There are two tests used in the federal circuits to determine whether or not a defendant's use of the plaintiff's mark qualifies as nominative fair use. The Ninth Circuit uses a three-prong test that requires the following elements:

(1) The product or service is not readily identifiable without use of the trademark.
(2) Only so much of the mark may be used as is reasonably necessary to identify the product or service.
(3) The user must not do anything that would, in conjunction with the mark, suggest sponsorship or endorsement by the trademark holder.[2316]

The Third Circuit constructed the following three-prong test for nominative fair use based on the Ninth Circuit's test:

(1) The use of the plaintiff's mark is necessary to describe both the plaintiff's product or service and the defendant's product or service.
(2) The defendant uses only so much of the plaintiff's mark as is necessary to describe the plaintiff's product.
(3) The defendant's conduct or language reflects the true and accurate relationship between the plaintiff and the defendant's products or services.[2317]

Therefore, it appears safe to say that the fair use defense is developing as a more effective response to a claim of trademark infringement.

2311. *Munters Corp. v. Matsui America, Inc.*, 909 F.2d 250 (7th Cir. 1990) (use determined to be fair and in good faith to describe their own product).
2312. 15 U.S.C. § 1115(b)(4).
2313. *KP Permanent Make-Up, Inc. v. Lasting Impression I, Inc.*, 543 U.S. 111, 122 (2004).
2314. *Id.*
2315. *Cairns v. Franklin Mint Co.*, 292 F.3d 1139, 1151 (9th Cir. 2002).
2316. *New Kids on the Block v. News Am. Publ'n Inc.*, 971 F.2d 302, 308 (9th Cir. 1992); *see also Brother Records, Inc. v. Jardine*, 318 F.3d 900, 908 (9th Cir. 2003).
2317. *Century 21 Real Estate Corp. v. Lendingtree, Inc.*, 425 F.3d 211, 222 (3d Cir. 2005).

V Laches, Acquiescence, and Estoppel

Failure or unreasonable delay in acting against a junior user or an infringer can be viewed as acquiescence in allowing another to use the same or a confusingly similar mark. The court is not obliged to enforce trademark rights under these circumstances.[2318] Use of an acquiescence defense is premised upon the senior party's knowledge and acceptance of a junior user's use of a mark.

Equitable estoppel is available to a defendant when a plaintiff has led the defendant to believe the plaintiff will not assert its rights, and the defendant has relied upon this assertion. The defendant must show that reliance creates a material prejudice against it.[2319]

The principle of laches is based upon the plaintiff's unreasonable delay in bringing an action of infringement against a defendant. Laches is closely related to acquiescence in that both assert that the plaintiff has failed to enforce their rights in a timely manner. Factors which may be considered in determining whether laches should apply include: harm to plaintiff; good faith of the defendant's assertion that they were ignorant of the plaintiff's rights; competition between the parties; and harm to the defendant.[2320] Since there is no statute of limitations with respect to the Lanham Act, laches have been utilized to effectuate a reasonable limitation upon which claims may be effectively barred.[2321] It should be noted that laches will not necessarily cure deliberate infringement.[2322]

VI A General First Amendment Defense

The Supreme Court is increasingly tasked with evaluating the intersection of the First Amendment and trademark law.[2323] In *Jack Daniel's Properties, Inc. v. VIP Products LLC*, the Supreme Court upheld a trial court's determination that the defendant infringed the distinctive and nonfunctional trade dress possessed by a liquor company in its packaging when it produced and sold parody, look-a-like dog toys.[2324] In doing so, it rejected the defendant's argument that its humorous intent required application of the Roger's Test to allow for freedom of speech under the First Amendment. According to the Ninth Circuit's application of that test, when a defendant's work is expressive (which it defined as "communicating ideas or expressing points of view"), the plaintiff

2318. *Conan Prop., Inc. v. Conano Pizza, Inc.*, 225 U.S.P.Q. 379 (5th Cir. 1985) (delay in asserting a right does not automatically defeat rights if the delay does not operate to evaporate the right).
2319. *Menendezx v. Holt*, 128 U.S. 514 (1888); *Flowers Indus., Inc. v. Interstate Brands Corp.*, 5 U.S.P.Q.2d 1580 (T.T.A.B. 1987) (consideration of the factors does not indicate sufficient evidence to find laches; there is no reasonable finding that the delay caused harm).
2320. 6 McCarthy § 31:1 (5th ed.). *Clamp Mfg. Co. v. Enco Mfg. Co.*, 870 F.2d 512 (9th Cir. 1989).
2321. *Clamp Mfg. Co. v. Enco Mfg. Co.*, 870 F.2d 512 (9th Cir. 1989) (laches used to determine damage limitations on infringement claim).
2322. *My-T Fine Corp. v. Samuels*, 69 F.2d 76 (2d Cir. 1934) (intentional copying overrides the two-year delay in filing suit).
2323. *See, e.g.*, *Matal v. Tam*, 137 S. Ct. 1744 (2017); *Iancu v. Brunetti*, 139 S. Ct. 2294 (2019); *Jack Daniel's Properties, Inc. v. VIP Products LLC*, 599 U.S. _ (2023).
2324. *Jack Daniel's Properties, Inc. v. VIP Products LLC*, 599 U.S. _ (2023).

must show that the "defendant's use of the mark is either (1) 'not artistically relevant to the underlying work' or (2) 'explicitly misleads consumers as to the source or content of the work'."[2325] While the Supreme Court did not explicitly overrule the Rogers Test in its holding, it did limit its possible application: the test should not be applied when the allegedly infringing use of the mark is as a designation of source for the alleged infringer's own goods.[2326] When the accused use is "trademark use," then the standard likelihood of confusion test, and not the Rogers Test, should be applied.[2327]

§3 REMEDIES

Available remedies for trademark infringement include injunctive relief, damages, and, in exceptional cases, the award of costs and counsel fees.

I Injunctive Relief

Injunctions are a form of equitable relief, which have been codified in the Lanham Act.[2328] Injunctions are issued in order to prevent continued wrongful actions. One of the requirements for injunctive relief is the unavailability or inadequacy of existing remedies. Inadequacy usually refers to the notion that money damages will not be an adequate remedy for the infringement activity. As such, injunctions serve a critical purpose in trademark infringement actions. Additionally, the TMA of 2020 restored the presumption of irreparable harm to this injunction analysis, which strengthens a plaintiff's argument that an injunction should be granted.[2329]

Trademark damages are somewhat unique in that they normally involve loss of business or business reputation due to the infringing use. This type of loss is not adequately addressed by the payment of damages.[2330]

Injunctive relief must be applied with careful consideration to the circumstances and facts at issue in a particular case.[2331] Upon a finding of infringement, a court may order a defendant to make disclaimers,[2332] discontinue use,[2333] or take steps to

2325. *VIP Products LLC v. Jack Daniel's Properties, Inc.*, 953 F.3d 1170, 1174 (2020) (citing to *Gordon v. Drape Creative, Inc.*, 909 F.3d 257, 265 (9th Cir. 2018) and referring to this as the *Rogers Test* from *Rogers v. Grimaldi*, 875 F.2d 994 (2d Cir. 1989)).
2326. *Jack Daniel's Properties, Inc. v. VIP Products LLC*, 599 U.S. _ (2023).
2327. *Id.*
2328. 15 U.S.C. 1116(a) (Lanham Act § 34(a)).
2329. *See infra* Part III, Ch. 1, §3.XIV.
2330. *Int'l Kennel Club, Inc. v. Mighty Star, Inc.*, 846 F.2d 1079 (7th Cir. 1988).
2331. *ALPO Petfoods v. Ralston Purina Co.*, 913 F.2d 958 (D.C. Cir. 1990) (injunction narrowed to provide definition of advertising to that which complies with Lanham Act § 43(a) definitions).
2332. *Ky. Fried Chicken Corp. v. Famous Recipe Fried Chicken, Inc.*, 157 U.S.P.Q. 697 (N.D. Ohio 1968) (the defendant required to disclaim any association with "Kentucky Fried Chicken").
2333. *S.S. Kresge Co. v. Tabacco*, 173 U.S.P.Q. 222 (E.D. Mich. 1972).

distinguish its goods or services from the plaintiff's goods or services.[2334] Destruction of packaging and any related tagging materials may also be ordered.[2335]

Injunctive relief may be ordered prior to actual infringement. Preliminary injunctions seek to prevent imminent damage which would result without the injunction.[2336] Conversely, injunctions may be ordered after a formal finding of infringement. Permanent injunctions can be modified when the facts and circumstances warrant such changes.[2337]

A *Injunctive Relief Against Domain Name Registrars*

The Lanham Act encourages domain name registrars to cooperate with the courts and establishes the court's authority regarding abusive registrations of domain names. Subsection 32(D)(i)(II) makes registrars subject to injunctive relief if they have: (1) not expeditiously deposited documents with the court "to establish the courts control and authority regarding the disposition of the registration and use of the domain name"; (2) transferred, suspended, or modified the domain name in the pendency of the action, except upon order of the court; or (3) willfully failed to comply with any such court order in regard to the domain name.[2338] The ACPA provides protections for registrars that create policies and procedures to allow cooperation with the courts.[2339] If a registrar takes the action of refusing to register, removing from registration, transferring, temporarily disabling, or permanently canceling a domain name, the Act provides immunity from most forms of relief, provided that the registrar acted in compliance with a court order under section 43(d) or implemented a reasonable policy to prohibit the registration of domain name that is identical to, confusingly similar to or dilutive of another's mark.[2340] "Thus, the Act protects a registrar when it complies with a court order under section 43(d) and disables, transfers, cancels, or removes from registration, a domain name as part of a 'reasonable policy' prohibiting the registration of domain names that are identical to, confusingly similar to, or cause dilution of another's mark."[2341] This immunity extends to the registrar (except if the registrar does not cooperate with the court as determined in section 32(2)(D)(i)(II))[2342] regardless of

2334. *Kellogg Co. v. National Biscuit Co.*, 305 U.S. 111 (1938), *reh'g denied*, 305 U.S. 674 (1938) (Kellogg may use "Shredded Wheat" and the pillow shaped biscuit if they distinguish themselves from other producers).
2335. 15 U.S.C. § 1118 (Lanham Act § 36).
2336. *Standard Oil Co. v. Standard Oil Co.*, 56 F.2d 973 (10th Cir. 1932) (long-standing recognition of Standard Oil would be disrupted without an injunction preventing use of a similar name).
2337. *United States v. Swift & Co.*, 286 U.S. 106 (1932) (removal of threat of monopoly sufficient to modify injunction).
2338. 15 U.S.C. § 1114(2)(D)(i)(II) (Lanham Act § 32(2)(D)(i)(II)).
2339. *See supra*, Ch. 8 §3[I][A].
2340. 15 U.S.C. § 1114(2)(D)(ii) (Lanham Act § 32(2)(D)(ii)).
2341. Steven R. Borgman, *The New Federal Cybersquatting Laws*, 8 TEX. INTELL. PROP. L.J. 265, 272 (2000).
2342. *See supra*, Ch. 8, §3.I.A.

whether the domain name is finally ultimately determined to infringe or dilute the mark in question.[2343]

In addition, section 32(2)(D) exempts domain name registrars from liability stemming from actions taken in connection with the registration process. Thus, registrars of domain names are not liable for the registration or maintenance of a domain name of another absent a showing of bad faith intent to profit from such registration or maintenance of the domain name.[2344] If a party makes a "knowing and material misrepresentation" to a registrar, and the registrar refuses to register or removes, transfers, disables, or cancels a domain name, then the party shall be liable,[2345] and the court may also grant injunctive relief to the domain name registrant.[2346] In the context of these actions by the registrar, the registrant of the domain name may file a civil action to establish that its registration or use of the domain name is not unlawful, and the court may grant injunctive relief to the domain name registrant.[2347]

II Damages

Damages refer to the various forms of monetary recovery available upon a finding of infringement. Damages can include lost profits, business losses, punitive damages, costs, and attorney's fees. Damages have also been held to include the cost of corrective advertising; in other words, the amount that would be necessary to correct the consumer misperception that had been created by the infringement.[2348] In actions based on section 43(c) of the Lanham Act, damages are not available unless the plaintiff can show, essentially, that the defendant willfully intended to trade on the plaintiff's reputation. In such cases, these monetary damages may be increased to three times the actual damages as the court deems just.[2349]

A *Profits*

Profits are awarded based upon the premise that infringing profits rightfully belong to the senior user. An award of profits is an equitable form of relief. Damages to the plaintiff may include all profits realized by the defendants stemming from the sales of the infringing goods,[2350] but profits are not awarded automatically. It is up to the court to determine if and how much should be awarded based upon lost profits.

2343. 15 U.S.C. § 1114(2)(D)(i)(I) (Lanham Act § 32(2)(D)(i)(I)).
2344. 15 U.S.C. § 1114(2)(D)(iii) (Lanham Act § 32(2)(D)(iii)).
2345. 15 U.S.C. § 1114(2)(D)(iv) (Lanham Act § 32(2)(D)(iv)).
2346. *Id.*; *see supra*, Ch. 8, §3.I.A.
2347. 15 U.S.C. § 1114(2)(D)(iv) (Lanham Act § 32(2)(D)(iv)).
2348. *Big O Tire Dealers, Inc. v. Goodyear Tire & Rubber Co.*, 408 F. Supp. 1219 (D. Colo. 1976) (1978) (USD 2.8 million awarded to plaintiff in damages).
2349. 15 U.S.C. § 1117 (Lanham Act § 35).
2350. *Polo Fashions, Inc. v. Craftex, Inc.*, 816 F.2d 145 (4th Cir. 1987) (award of profits from sales of infringing use properly trebled).

While the Lanham Act makes a defendant's willfulness a prerequisite for the awarding of profits under section 43(c), the Supreme Court clarified in 2020 that willfulness is not required for a court to award profits for a violation of 43(a).[2351] This holding settled confusion among the circuit courts as to whether there was a specific intent requirement for 43(a) violations[2352] and clarified that, while "a defendant's mental state is a highly important consideration in determining whether an award of profits is appropriate," the statute does not require any specific intent as a precondition to recovery of profits.[2353]

B *Damages for Counterfeiting*

Damages can be awarded for the counterfeiting of trademarks as well as for infringement. Lanham Act section 34(d) provides:

> - In a case involving the use of a counterfeit mark (as defined in section 34(d)) in connection with the sale, offering for sale, or distribution of goods or services, the plaintiff may elect, at any time before final judgment is rendered by the trial court, to recover, instead of actual damages and profits under subsection (a), an award of statutory damages for any such use in connection with the sale, offering for sale, or distribution of goods or services in the amount of—
> 1. not less than $500 or more than $100,000 per counterfeit mark per type of goods or services sold, offered for sale, or distributed, as the court considers just; or
> 2. if the court finds that the use of the counterfeit mark was willful, not more than $1,000,000 per counterfeit mark per type of goods or services sold, offered for sale, or distributed, as the court considers just.[2354]

C *Damages for Cybersquatting*

Sections 34(a) and 35(a) of the Lanham Act expressly allow courts to grant the same injunctive and monetary relief for cybersquatting that is currently allowed for trademark infringement, trademark dilution, and false advertising under the Lanham Act.[2355] In addition, the Act adds section 35(d),[2356] which allows the plaintiff to collect statutory damages:

> In a case involving a violation of Section 43(d)(1) of this title, the plaintiff may elect, at any time before final judgment is rendered by the trial court, to recover, instead of actual damages and profits, an award of statutory damages in the

2351. *Romag Fasteners, Inc. v. Fossil, Inc.*, 140 S. Ct. 1492 (2020).
2352. *See*, e.g., *Lindy Pen Co. v. Bic Pen Corp.*, 982 F.2d 1400 (9th Cir. 1993) (no willfulness in exploiting the trademark precludes award of profits).
2353. *Romag Fasteners, Inc. v. Fossil, Inc.*, 140 S. Ct. 1492 (2020).
2354. 15 U.S.C. § 1117(c) (Lanham Act § 35(c)).
2355. *See supra*, Ch. 8, §3.II.
2356. 15 U.S.C. § 1117(d) (Lanham Act § 35(d)).

> amount of not less than $1,000 and not more than $100,000 per domain name, as the court considers just.[2357]

In addition to these remedies, section 43(d)(1)(C) of the Lanham Act provides that "a court may order the forfeiture or cancellation of the domain name or the transfer of the domain name to the owner of the mark."[2358]

The remedies available in an in rem action are limited to an order for forfeiture or cancelation of the domain name, or its transfer to the owner of the mark.[2359]

III Other Forms of Relief

Additionally, the Lanham Act allows for a recovery of costs and attorney fees in exceptional cases.[2360]

2357. *Id.*
2358. 15 U.S.C. § 1125(d)(1)(C) (Lanham Act § 43(d)(1)(C)).
2359. 15 U.S.C. § 1114(2)(D)(i) (Lanham Act § 32(2)(D)(i)).
2360. 15 U.S.C. § 1117 (Lanham Act § 35).

PART IV Chip Protection

CHAPTER 1
Sources of US Chip Protection

§1 THE SEMICONDUCTOR CHIP PROTECTION ACT OF 1984

The nature of semiconductor chips is such that, in the normal course, they would not meet the stringent requirements for patent protection, nor, as inherently "useful articles," could they qualify for copyright protection.[2361] The circuit designs or technical drawings from which the chip is produced could possibly be protected as pictorial works, but neither the "mask" used to produce the embedded patterns in the chip, nor the chip itself, would receive protection.[2362] While initial development of a particular semiconductor chip can be the product of significant expenditure of effort and resources, once manufactured, a chip may be analyzed and reproduced, through reproduction of the mask, at comparatively low cost. In response to industry concerns over copying, Congress enacted the Semiconductor Chip Protection Act of 1984,[2363] as Chapter 9 of the Copyright Act, "Protection of Semiconductor Chip Products."[2364]

§2 SUI GENERIS LEGISLATION

This legislation creates sui generis protection for "mask works" embodied in semiconductor chips. Congress was quite clear in stating that this legislation, although technically incorporated into the Copyright Act, is not "a part of the Copyright Act's general provisions," but is "a sui generis form of intellectual property right, similar in many respects to existing copyright law but differing from copyright law in many

2361. For a more detailed discussion of this material *see* RICHARD H. STERN, SEMICONDUCTOR CHIP PROTECTION (1986); PAUL GOLDSTEIN, COPYRIGHT §§15.26 et seq. (1989).
2362. 17 U.S.C. § 113; *see* Part I, Copyright, Ch. 1, §2.IV.D.
2363. Pub. L. No. 98-620, 98 Stat. 3335, 3347-56 (1984).
2364. 17 U.S.C. §§ 901 et seq.

ways."[2365] Avoiding the somewhat murky issue of whether semiconductor chip protection is a proper exercise of Congress' power with respect to "writings" under Article I, section 8 of the Constitution,[2366] as opposed to the general congressional power with respect to interstate commerce, protection is limited to remedies for acts of infringement "by conduct in or affecting commerce."[2367]

§3 PREEMPTION

The legislation is designed to provide the exclusive source for protection of mask works, as its provisions expressly "preempt the laws of any State to the extent those laws provide any rights or remedies with respect to a mask work which are equivalent to those rights or remedies provided by [Chapter Nine]."[2368] On the other hand, it expressly does not preempt any federal copyright or patent claims which might be applicable to a semiconductor chip[2369]—for example, copyright claims with respect to computer programs embedded in a chip, or patent claims if a chip design can pass the stringent tests of patentability.

2365. H.R. Rep. No. 781, 98th Cong., 2d Sess. (1984). Implementing that idea, § 912(b) specifically states that, with a minor exception, the other provisions of the Copyright Act are not applicable to Ch. 9.
2366. Cf. Part I, Copyright, Ch. 1, §1.
2367. 17 U.S.C. § 910(a).
2368. 17 U.S.C. § 912(c).
2369. 17 U.S.C. § 912(a).

CHAPTER 2

Subject Matter of Protection

§1 LIMITATION TO MASK WORKS FIXED IN SEMICONDUCTOR CHIP PRODUCTS

Protection under the Chip Protection Act extends only to "a mask work fixed in a semiconductor chip product, by or under the authority of the owner of the mask work."[2370] It is the "mask work" used as the template for etching the circuitry into the chip, not the chip itself, that is protected, and then only if the mask work is fixed in a "semiconductor chip product." Since protection is limited to mask works fixed in semiconductor chips, other technologies, accomplishing similar results but without the use of semiconductors or masks in the manufacturing process, would not come within the ambit of protection.

§2 DEFINITIONS

I "Semiconductor Chip Product"

A "semiconductor chip product" is the final or intermediate form of any product:

(a) having two or more layers of metallic, insulating, or semiconductor material, deposited or otherwise placed on, or etched away or otherwise removed from, a piece of semiconductor material in accordance with a predetermined pattern; and
(b) intended to perform electronic circuitry functions.[2371]

2370. 17 U.S.C. § 902(a)(1).
2371. 17 U.S.C. § 901(a)(1).

Note that while fixation in a semiconductor chip product is a condition to protection, so that protection would not extend to works not involving the use of "semiconductor" products, the Act is not limited to any particular kind of semiconductor material.

II Mask Work

A "mask work" is a series of related images—however fixed or encoded:

(a) having or representing the predetermined, three-dimensional pattern of metallic, insulating, or semiconductor material present or removed from the layers of a semiconductor chip product; and
(b) in which series the relation of the images to one another is that each image has the pattern of the surface of one form of the semiconductor chip product.[2372]

The House Report with respect to the Semiconductor Chip Protection Act describes the mask work as "the layout determination and the sum total of the individual masks, set upon each other, used to fabricate the entire chip."[2373]

III Fixation

"A mask work is 'fixed' in a semiconductor chip product when its embodiment in the product is sufficiently permanent or stable to permit the mask work to be perceived or reproduced from the product for a period of more than transitory duration."[2374] This definition essentially mirrors the definition of "fixation" generally for copyrightability of original works of authorship.[2375]

§3 GOVERNMENTAL WORKS

Mirroring the Copyright Act,[2376] the Chip Protection Act excludes from protection mask works "prepared by an officer or employee of the United States Government as part of that person's official duties," while recognizing the right of the US Government to hold and enforce rights it receives as a transferee from one not an officer or employee.[2377]

2372. 17 U.S.C. § 901(a)(2).
2373. H.R. Rep. No. 781, 98th Cong., 2d Sess. (1984).
2374. 17 U.S.C. § 901(3).
2375. *See* Part I, Copyright, Ch. 1, §3.I.A.
2376. *See* Part I, Copyright, Ch. 1, §2.III.B.
2377. 17 U.S.C. § 903(d).

CHAPTER 3
Substantive Conditions of Protection

§1 ORIGINAL EXPRESSION

> Protection … shall not be available for a mask work that:
> 1. is not original; or
> 2. consists of designs that are staple, commonplace, or familiar in the semiconductor industry, or variations of such designs, combined in a way that, considered as a whole, is not original.[2378]

The Chip Protection Act thus adopts the copyright standard of originality, which requires both independent origin and some minimal degree of creativity, and it may be presumed that this standard will be applied to mask work protection in a manner similar to that in which it is generally applied.[2379] Indeed, it is even more explicit than the overall copyright standard in denying protection to staple, commonplace, or familiar articles.

Further, the Chip Protection Act follows the Copyright Act verbatim in limiting protection to "expression" rather than "idea."

The statute makes clear that in no case does protection for a mask work "extend to any idea, procedure, process, system, method of operation, concept, principle, or discovery, regardless of the form in which it is described, explained, illustrated, or embodied in such work."[2380]

Although there is a rich body of law attempting to grapple with the problem of separating "idea" from "expression,"[2381] given the nature of the work involved, it is not likely that the same degree of complexity will attach to this analysis with respect to mask works.

2378. 17 U.S.C. § 902(b).
2379. *See* Part I, Copyright, Ch. 1, §§ 2.III.C. and 3.II.B.
2380. 17 U.S.C. § 902(c).
2381. *See generally*, Part I, Copyright, Ch. 1, §3.II.B.

§2 NATIONAL ORIGIN

Protection is limited to mask works: whose owners are nationals or domiciliaries of the US at the time the work is registered or is first commercially exploited anywhere in the world, whichever occurs first (or whose owners are nationals or domiciliaries of foreign nations that are parties to a treaty, to which the US is also party, protecting mask works, or whose owners are stateless persons); or that are first commercially exploited in the US; or are the subject of a special Presidential proclamation.[2382]

2382. 17 U.S.C. § 902(a)(1). The President may extend protection to mask works whose owners are nationals or domiciliaries of a foreign nation, who would not otherwise come within the provisions of this section, upon finding that that nation extends equivalent protection to mask works of owners who are nationals or domiciliaries of the US. 17 U.S.C. § 902(a)(2).

Chapter 4
Formal Conditions of Protection

§1 FIXATION

The Chip Protection Act again follows the Copyright Act in conditioning protection for a mask work on "fixation." However, fixation here must be in a particular medium, and not simply any tangible medium of expression, as the Chip Protection Act limits protection to "a mask work fixed in a semiconductor chip product, by or under the authority of the owner of the mask work."[2383] As noted above, a mask work is "fixed" in a semiconductor chip product when its embodiment in the product is sufficiently permanent or stable to permit the mask work to be "perceived or reproduced from the product for a period of more than transitory duration."[2384]

§2 EXPLOITATION AND REGISTRATION

The Chip Protection Act protects mask works fixed in a semiconductor chip product upon registration or upon the date, if earlier, on which the work is first "commercially exploited" anywhere in the world.[2385]

I Exploitation

To "commercially exploit" a mask work "is to distribute to the public for commercial purposes a semiconductor chip product embodying the mask work."[2386] The term also

2383. 17 U.S.C. § 902(a)(1).
2384. 17 U.S.C. § 901(3).
2385. 17 U.S.C. §§ 902(a), 904(a).
2386. 17 U.S.C. § 901(a)(5).

includes an offer to sell or transfer a semiconductor chip product "when the offer is in writing and occurs after the mask work is fixed in the semiconductor chip product."[2387]

While protection is framed in the disjunctive (registration or commercial exploitation) in fact as discussed below, registration is essential to continuing protection.

II Registration

A *Requirement*

The Chip Protection Act appears to speak permissibly about registration:

> "the owner of a mask work *may* apply to the Register of Copyrights for registration of a claim of protection in the mask work."[2388] However, it also provides that any protection for a mask work will terminate "if application for registration ... is not made ... within two years after the date on which the mask work is first commercially exploited anywhere in the world."[2389] Since registration or exploitation is essential for the commencement of protection, the effect of this provision is to make registration mandatory for continuing protection.[2390]

B *Procedure*

Registration is accomplished by the filing of appropriate forms, as prescribed by the Register of Copyrights, accompanied by the necessary fees and deposit of specified identifying material.[2391] The application is examined, much the same way as examination of copyright applications; if in order, a certificate of registration is issued, effective as of the date on which the application, together with appropriate fees and identifying material, is received in the Copyright Office.[2392] If registration is refused, the applicant may bring an action for judicial review in the US District Court within sixty days of the date of refusal.[2393]

C *Effect of Registration*

Registration entitles the registrant to bring actions for infringement with respect to the protected mask work.[2394] If registration has been refused and the applicant has not directly appealed the refusal, the applicant may nevertheless institute a civil action for

2387. *Id.*
2388. 17 U.S.C. § 908(a) (emphasis added).
2389. *Id.*
2390. *See Anokiwave, Inc. v. Rebeiz*, No. 18-CV-629 JLS (MDD), 2018 WL 4407591, at *9 (S.D. Cal. Sept. 17, 2018) (emphasizing that under § 908(g) a "failure of Register of Copyrights to issue a certificate within four months after an application for registration is filed shall be deemed to be a refusal to issue a certificate").
2391. 17 U.S.C. § 908(c), (d).
2392. 17 U.S.C. § 908(e).
2393. 17 U.S.C. § 908(g).
2394. 17 U.S.C. § 910(b)(1).

infringement if notice thereof, together with a copy of the complaint, is served on the Register of Copyrights, who may then choose to become a party to the action.[2395]

In much the same way as with copyrighted works,[2396] the Chip Protection Act makes the certificate of registration prima facie evidence of the facts stated therein and of compliance with the registration requirements (although it does not mirror the Copyright Act's further presumption of validity).[2397]

§3 NOTICE

Notice—in the form of the words "mask work," the symbol "*M*," or the symbol Ⓜ [2398] together with the name of the owner or owners of the work—may be placed upon protected mask works and semiconductor chip products embodying protected mask works so as "to give reasonable notice of such protection." While notice is not a condition to protection, it does constitute prima facie evidence of notice of protection,[2399] and therefore where it is present, it would essentially preclude the availability of the limitations on liability accorded innocent infringers. The Register of Copyrights, pursuant to statutory direction, has prescribed, by regulation, exemplary methods of fixation of notice.

2395. 17 U.S.C. § 910(b)(2) ("the failure of the Register to become a party to the action shall not deprive the court of jurisdiction to determine [eligibility for registration]").
2396. *See* Part I, Copyright, Ch. 1, §3.I.D.3.
2397. 17 U.S.C. § 908(f).
2398. 17 U.S.C. § 909.
2399. *Id.*

CHAPTER 5
Ownership and Transfer

§1 OWNERSHIP

The "owner" of a mask work is defined as:

> the person who created the mask work, the legal representative of that person if that person is deceased or under a legal incapacity, or a party to whom all the rights ... of such person or representative are transferred.[2400]

Where a mask work has been made within the scope of a person's employment, "the owner is the employer for whom the person created the mask work or a party to whom all the rights ... of the employer are transferred."[2401] Presumably, in determining whether a work has been made within the scope of a person's employment, the "work for hire" standards developed by the courts under the Copyright Act would be applicable.[2402] Unlike the Copyright Act's definitions, the Chip Protection Act does not contemplate an alternative employer for hire status for specially commissioned work not within an employee's scope of employment. Presumably, a mask work might be developed jointly and the Copyright Act's standards with respect to determining joint authorship should be helpful.[2403]

As opposed to "ownership" of copyrighted works, which may involve multiple owners of exclusive rights relating to the infinitely divisible bundle of rights constituting copyright,[2404] ownership of mask works is essentially unitary. For the purposes of "ownership" and the concomitant ability to enforce rights, there is but the most limited divisibility, as the interest in the protected "mask work" is enforceable only by the

2400. 17 U.S.C. § 901(a)(6).
2401. *Id.*
2402. *See* Part I, Copyright, Ch. 1, §4.VI.A.
2403. *See* Part I, Copyright, Ch. 1, §4.IV.
2404. *See* Part I, Copyright, Ch. 1, §4.II.

"owner" of the work and "the exclusive licensee of all rights" with respect to the work.[2405]

§2 TRANSFER

The Chip Protection Act expressly recognizes the right of the owner of "the exclusive rights" in a mask work to "transfer all of those rights, or license all or less than all of those rights."[2406] Such transfer or license, however, even for a nonexclusive license, may be made only by a written instrument signed by the "owner" or the owner's authorized agent.[2407] Transfer or license may also be effected by operation of law, by will, and by the applicable state laws of interstate succession.[2408]

§3 RECORD OF TRANSFER: PRIORITY

If properly executed, transfers and any other document "pertaining to a mask work" may be recorded in the Copyright Office; recording a transfer or license "gives all persons constructive notice of the facts stated in the recorded document concerning the transfer or license."[2409] Recording, and the concomitant constructive notice, will determine the resolution of conflicting transfers:

> In any case in which conflicting transfers of the exclusive rights in a mask work are made, the transfer first executed shall be void as against a subsequent transfer which is made for a valuable consideration and without notice of the first transfer, unless the first transfer is recorded … within three months after the date on which it is executed, but in no case later than the day before the date of such subsequent transfer.[2410]

2405. 17 U.S.C. § 910(b)(1).
2406. 17 U.S.C. § 903(b).
2407. *Id.*
2408. *Id.*
2409. 17 U.S.C. § 903(c)(1).
2410. 17 U.S.C. § 903(c)(2).

CHAPTER 6

Scope of Exclusive Rights

The exclusive rights of the owner of a mask work are limited to the rights to:

(1) reproduce the mask work by optical, electronic, or any other means;
(2) import or distribute a semiconductor chip product in which the mask work is embodied; and
(3) induce or knowingly to cause another person to do any of the acts described in paragraphs (1) and (2).[2411]

The Act, thus, grants a broad reproduction right with respect to the mask work, covering any means of reproduction, and an exclusive distribution and importation right. In connection with the distribution and importation right, "the distribution or importation of a product incorporating a semiconductor chip product as a part thereof is a distribution or importation of that semiconductor chip product."[2412]

Finally, paragraph (3) appears specifically to create a right against contributory infringement.

2411. 17 U.S.C. § 905.
2412. 17 U.S.C. § 901(b).

CHAPTER 7

Limitations on the Scope of Protection

Rather than providing for a general "fair use" defense to infringement claims, the Chip Protection Act limits the exclusive reproduction right by providing an exception for "reverse engineering" and limits the distribution/importation right with a "first sale" exemption.

§1 REVERSE ENGINEERING

The Copyright Act generally does not deal with reverse engineering, so that the courts have applied fair use principles to reverse engineering of computer programs.[2413] The Chip Protection Act, however, expressly exempts certain forms of reverse engineering from liability for infringement of the exclusive reproduction right. Specifically, it is not an infringement of the exclusive rights of the owner of a mask work for:

(1) a person to reproduce the mask work solely for the purpose of teaching, analyzing, or evaluating the concepts or techniques embodied in the mask work or circuitry, logic flow, or organization of components used in the mask work; or
(2) a person who performs the analysis or evaluation described in paragraph (1) to incorporate the results of such conduct in an original mask work which is made to be distributed.[2414]

This latter provision would allow a competitor to use the results of a reverse engineering analysis to create a competing product that does not simply incorporate the protected mask work.[2415]

2413. *See* Part I, Copyright, Ch. 1, §7.IV.
2414. 17 U.S.C. § 906.
2415. *See Brooktree Corp v. Advanced Micro Devices, Inc.*, 705 F. Supp. 491 (S.D. Cal. 1988).

§2 FIRST SALE

As a limitation upon the exclusive rights to import or distribute a semiconductor chip product in which the mask work is embodied, the Chip Protection Act follows the Copyright Act[2416] in creating a "first sale" exemption:

> The owner of a particular semiconductor chip product made by the owner of the mask work, or by any person authorized by the owner of the mask work, may import, distribute, or otherwise dispose of or use, but not reproduce, that particular semiconductor chip product without the authority of the owner of the mask work.[2417]

§3 IMPORTATION OR DISTRIBUTION BY INNOCENT PURCHASER

The importation/distribution right (but not the reproduction right) is further limited by provisions completely immunizing from liability an innocent purchaser of an infringing semiconductor chip product who imports or distributes units of that infringing product before such innocent purchaser has notice of protection of the mask work embodied therein.[2418] Moreover, such an innocent purchaser of an infringing product who, subsequent to the purchase, receives notice of protection and thereafter imports or distributes the product will be liable "only for a reasonable royalty on each unit of the infringing semiconductor chip product" so imported or distributed;[2419] absent voluntary resolution, the amount of such a royalty is to be determined by the court in an action for infringement.[2420] The innocent purchaser immunity and damages limitation provisions will apply to "any person who directly or indirectly purchases an infringing semiconductor chip product from an innocent purchaser."[2421]

An "innocent purchaser" is defined as "a person who purchases a semiconductor chip product in good faith and without having notice of protection with respect to the semiconductor chip product."[2422] For these purposes, "having notice of protection" is defined as "having actual knowledge that, or reasonable grounds to believe that, a mask work is protected ...."[2423]

2416. *See* Part I, Copyright, Ch. 1, §6.III.B.
2417. 17 U.S.C. § 906(b).
2418. 17 U.S.C. § 907(a)(1).
2419. 17 U.S.C. § 907(a)(2) & (d).
2420. 17 U.S.C. § 907(b).
2421. 17 U.S.C. § 907(c).
2422. 17 U.S.C. § 901(a)(7).
2423. 17 U.S.C. § 901(a)(8).

CHAPTER 8

Duration of Protection

Protection for a qualifying mask work commences on the earlier of the date on which the work is registered or the date on which the work is first commercially exploited anywhere in the world, and endures for a period of ten years thereafter.[2424]

However, if protection commences by virtue of commercial exploitation, the protection will terminate (prospectively) if application for registration is not made within two years after such commencement date.[2425]

2424. 17 U.S.C. § 904. For these purposes, terms of protection run to the end of the calendar year in which they would otherwise expire.

2425. 17 U.S.C. § 908(a).

CHAPTER 9
Infringement and Remedies

Except to the extent specifically exempted, "any person who violates any of the exclusive rights of the owner of a mask work ... by conduct in or affecting commerce, shall be liable as an infringer of such rights."[2426]

§1 PROCEDURAL ISSUES IN INFRINGEMENT ACTIONS

I Registration

Just as with respect to copyright infringement claims, registration is a condition to the institution of actions for infringement with respect to the protected mask work.[2427] Similarly, if registration has been refused, the applicant may institute a civil action for infringement if notice thereof, together with a copy of the complaint, is served on the Register of Copyrights.[2428]

II Standing

As opposed to actions for infringement of copyright, it is only the "owner" of a protected mask work, or "the exclusive licensee of all rights" to a protected mask work, who may institute a civil action for infringement with respect to the mask work.[2429]

2426. 17 U.S.C. § 910(a).
2427. 17 U.S.C. § 910(b)(1).
2428. 17 U.S.C. § 910(b)(2) ("the failure of the Register to become a party to the action shall not deprive the court of jurisdiction to determine [eligibility for registration]").
2429. 17 U.S.C. § 910(b)(1).

III Statute of Limitations

An action for infringement must be commenced within three years after the claim accrues.[2430]

IV Actions Against State Instrumentalities

The Chip Protection Act specifically makes the states and state instrumentalities subject to its provisions and expressly abrogates any immunity which a state or state instrumentalities might claim under the Eleventh Amendment of the Constitution.[2431] As discussed above in connection with copyright,[2432] there are serious open questions as to the constitutionality of such abrogation of immunity.

§2 SUBSTANTIVE ISSUES IN INFRINGEMENT ACTIONS

In an infringement action, the plaintiff has the burden of proving that the defendant has infringed the plaintiff's exclusive right to reproduce the mask work or to distribute or import it. In connection with infringement of the exclusive right to reproduce the work, as with reproduction of copyrighted works, infringement may exist in the absence of exact copying; the House Report makes it clear that the fundamental issue is whether the allegedly infringing mask work is "substantially similar" to the registered mask work.[2433] Presumably, issues of "striking similarity" and access are to be treated much as they are in the case of copyright infringement.[2434]

In general, "the line of cases regarding infringement of fact-based works, compilations, and directories provides precedents more applicable [than those concerning fictional or imaginative works] to semiconductor chips."[2435]

§3 "INNOCENT" INFRINGEMENT

Immunity from liability for unauthorized importation or distribution is provided for an innocent purchaser of an infringing semiconductor chip product and liability is limited for such a purchaser who receives notice of protection with respect to the mask work after purchase but prior to importation or distribution.

There is no comparable immunity, limitation, or defense for "innocent" reproduction of a protected mask work.

2430. 17 U.S.C. § 910(d)(1).
2431. 17 U.S.C. §§ 910(a), 911(g).
2432. *See* Part I, Copyright, Ch. 1, §9.I.F.
2433. H.R. Rep. No. 781, 98th Cong., 2d Sess. 20 (1984).
2434. *See* Part I, Copyright, Ch. 1, §9.III.B.
2435. H.R. Rep. No. 781, 98th Cong., 2d Sess. 26 (1984).

§4 CRIMINAL INFRINGEMENT

Unlike the Copyright Act,[2436] the Chip Protection Act contains no provisions criminalizing infringement.

§5 REMEDIES

I Injunctive Relief

The Chip Protection Act expressly empowers the court in an infringement action to "grant temporary restraining orders, preliminary injunctions, and permanent injunctions on such terms as the court may deem reasonable to prevent or restrain infringement of the exclusive rights in a mask work ...."[2437] The language is identical to that in the Copyright Act and presumably will be interpreted in much the same way.[2438]

II Damages

A Actual Damages

Essentially tracking the language of the Copyright Act,[2439] the Chip Protection Act awards to the successful plaintiff in an infringement action the "actual damages suffered ... as a result of the infringement" as well as "the infringer's profits that are attributable to the infringement and are not taken into account in computing the award of actual damages."[2440] Again, as with the Copyright Act, the infringer has the burden of proving appropriate deductions from gross revenues and allocating profits to noninfringing activities: "In establishing the infringer's profits, [the plaintiff] is required to present proof only of the infringer's gross revenue, and the infringer is required to prove his or her deductible expenses and the elements of profit attributable to factors other than the mask work."[2441]

B Statutory Damages

The plaintiff in an infringement action under the Chip Protection Act may elect, at any time before final judgment is rendered, to recover statutory damages in lieu of actual damages and profits, "for all infringements involved in the action, with respect to any

2436. *See* Part I, Copyright, Ch. 1, §9.IV.
2437. 17 U.S.C. § 911(a).
2438. *See* Part I, Copyright, Ch. 1, §10.I.
2439. *See* Part I, Copyright, Ch. 1, §10.II.A.
2440. 17 U.S.C. § 911(b).
2441. *Id.*

one mask work for which anyone infringer is liable individually, or for which any two or more infringers are liable jointly and severally ...."[2442]

Statutory damages may be awarded in an amount up to USD 250,000 "as the court considers Just."[2443] Unlike the Copyright Act, registration is not a condition to the award of statutory damages. However, since registration is required within two years of the first commercial exploitation of the mask work for continued protection, statutory damages with respect to infringement of unregistered works would be applicable only to actions based upon acts of infringement occurring during that initial two-year period.

Given the similarity of statutory language, the US Supreme Court holding of a constitutional right to jury determination in claims involving statutory damages for copyright infringement[2444] presumably is applicable to statutory damages claims under the Chip Protection Act.

III Costs and Counsel Fees

Again tracking the Copyright Act, except with respect to the necessity for registration, the Chip Protection Act authorizes the court, in its discretion, to award to the prevailing party full costs, including reasonable legal fees.[2445] The US Supreme Court's determination that prevailing plaintiffs and prevailing defendants are to be treated alike in the exercise of the court's discretion in awarding legal fees[2446] would appear to be applicable here.

IV Impoundment, Disposition, and Seizure

While an action is pending, the court may order the impounding, on such terms as it may deem reasonable, "of all semiconductor chip products, and any drawings, tapes, masks, or other products by means of which such products may be reproduced, that are claimed to have been made, imported, or used in violation of [the exclusive rights in a mask work]."[2447] So too, upon conclusion of the action, as part of its final judgment, the court may "order the destruction or other disposition of any infringing semiconductor chip products, and any masks, tapes, or other articles by means of which such products may be reproduced."[2448] These provisions mirror the corresponding provisions of the Copyright Act.[2449]

Infringing imported articles are subject to seizure and forfeiture at the port of entry and are to be destroyed except where it is demonstrated that the importer had no

2442. 17 U.S.C. § 911(c).
2443. *Id.*
2444. *See* Part I, Copyright, Ch. 1, §10.II.B.3.
2445. 17 U.S.C. § 911(f).
2446. *See* Part I, Copyright, Ch. 1, §10.III.
2447. 17 U.S.C. § 911(e)(1).
2448. 17 U.S.C. § 911(e)(2).
2449. *See* Part I, Copyright, Ch. 1, §10.IV.

reasonable grounds for believing that the importation was infringing, in which case the infringing articles are to be returned to the country of export.[2450]

2450. 17 U.S.C. § 910(c)(2).

Bibliography

The following is a list of the major treatises and similar works relating to the material herein. In addition, there is a large number of important articles, primarily in law reviews, and monographs that are quite useful for specific subject areas, many of which have been cited in the text; they are far too numerous to include in a general bibliography.

Abrams, Howard B. & Tyler T. Ochoa, *Law of Copyright* (Thomson Reuters 2020).

Altman, Louis & Malla Pollack, *Callmann on Unfair Competition, Trademarks and Monopolies* (Thomson Reuters 2021).

Chisum, Donald S., *Chisum on Patents: A Treatise on the Law of Patentability, Validity, and Infringement* (Matthew Bender 2021).

LaLonde, Anne Gilson & Jerome Gilson, *Gilson on Trademarks* (Matthew Bender 2021).

Goldstein, Paul, *Goldstein on Copyright* (Wolters Kluwer 3rd ed. 2020).

Kirkpatrick, Richard L., *Likelihood of Confusion in Trademark Law* (PLI 2d ed. 2021).

McCarthy, J. Thomas, *McCarthy on Trademarks and Unfair Competition* (Clark Boardman Callaghan 5th ed. 2021).

Merges, Robert Patrick & John Fitzgerald Duffy, *Patent Law and Policy: Cases and Materials* (Lexis 6th ed. 2017).

Nimmer, Melville B. & David Nimmer, *Nimmer on Copyright* (Matthew Bender rev. ed. 2021).

Patry, William F., *Patry on Copyright* (Thomson Reuters 2021).

Patry, William F., *Patry on Fair Use* (Thomson West 2021).

Stern, Richard H. *Semiconductor Chip Protection* (Law & Business, Inc. 1986).

Index

G

H

I

R

S

U

V

W

www.ingramcontent.com/pod-product-compliance
Lightning Source LLC
LaVergne TN
LVHW020646300926
849161LV00004B/839